Doomsday Men

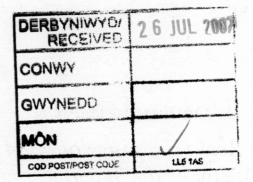

P. D. SMITH

Doomsday Men

The Real Dr Strangelove and the Dream of the Superweapon

ALLEN LANE
an imprint of
PENGUIN BOOKS

GW 29601738

ALLEN LANE

Published by the Penguin Group
Penguin Books Ltd, 80 Strand, London WC2R ORL, England
Penguin Group (USA) Inc., 375 Hudson Street, New York, New York 10014, USA
Penguin Group (Canada), 90 Eglinton Avenue East, Suite 700, Toronto, Ontario, Canada M4P 2Y3
(a division of Pearson Penguin Canada Inc.)
Penguin Ireland, 25 St Stephen's Green, Dublin 2, Ireland
(a division of Penguin Books Ltd)
Penguin Group (Australia), 250 Camberwell Road, Camberwell, Victoria 3124, Australia
(a division of Pearson Australia Group Pty Ltd)
Penguin Books India Pvt Ltd, 11 Community Centre, Panchsheel Park, New Delhi – 110 017, India
Penguin Group (NZ), 67 Apollo Drive, Rosedale, North Shore 0632, New Zealand
(a division of Pearson New Zealand Ltd)
Penguin Books (South Africa) (Pty) Ltd, 24 Sturdee Avenue, Rosebank, Johannesburg 2196, South Africa

Penguin Books Ltd, Registered Offices: 80 Strand, London WC2R ORL, England

www.penguin.com

First published 2007
1

Set in 10.5/14 pt PostScript Linotype Sabon
Typeset by Rowland Phototypesetting Ltd, Bury St Edmunds, Suffolk
Printed in Great Britain by Clays Ltd, St Ives plc

A CIP catalogue record for this book is available from the British Library

ISBN: 978-0-713-99815-3

www.greenpenguin.co.uk

Penguin Books is committed to a sustainable future
for our business, our readers and our planet.
The book in your hands is made from paper
certified by the Forest Stewardship Council.

For Bernard Smith (1925–2005)

I call on all scientists in all countries to cease and desist from work creating, developing, improving and manufacturing further nuclear weapons – and, for that matter, other weapons of potential mass destruction such as chemical and biological weapons.   Hans Bethe, 1995

Peace is the only battle worth waging.
                    Albert Camus, 8 August 1945

Contents

CONTENTS

IV

The Battle of the Laboratories

V

The End of Dreams

List of Illustrations

Acknowledgements

This book has grown out of more than ten years of research and writing on the relationship between science and literature. The so-called two cultures are actually more closely connected than is commonly believed, and, as I hope *Doomsday Men* shows, tracing those points where they meet and cross-fertilize can reveal fascinating insights into our shared history.

I am immensely grateful to the Department of Science and Technology Studies at University College London for asking me to teach an occasional course on science and literature and for making me an Honorary Research Fellow. I was also pleased to have the opportunity to present work-in-progress on *Doomsday Men* to a research seminar in the department in 2005 organised by Jane Gregory. The feedback from this and from students on my courses in the previous two years helped to shape my thinking as the project developed. Many thanks also to Martin Swales, Emeritus Professor of German at UCL, for sharing over the years his insights into literature and for inviting me to speak to the English Goethe Society on '*Faust*, Physicists and the Atomic Bomb' in 2006.

Being affiliated to an academic department has also allowed me to make full use of the excellent libraries at UCL, Imperial College and the University of London's Senate House. Librarians are the unsung heroes of non-fiction writing, and the staff at all these libraries were unfailingly helpful beyond the call of duty. Senate House overlooks Russell Square, where Leo Szilard stayed in 1933 and near where he had his *Eureka!* moment. I often thought of Szilard's association with this area as I walked through the square to the library in the morning.

Special thanks go to Jon Turney for commissioning *Doomsday Men* and for believing in the book throughout its period of gestation. Not only were our working lunches immensely enjoyable, but his judicious editing of the initial typescript has contributed greatly to the finished work. Many thanks also to Will Goodlad, who inherited the book at Penguin, for his enthusiasm and commitment as well as for his admirably flexible interpretation of deadlines. Thanks are due as well to John Woodruff, whose knowledge of both science and science fiction made him the ideal copy-editor for the book. Any errors that remain are, of course, entirely my own responsibility. I am also grateful to my literary agents – James Gill and Zoe Pagnamenta – for placing *Doomsday Men* with such excellent publishers in the UK and abroad.

Writing a study as broad in its scope as this inevitably makes one indebted to the work of many scholars. I have tried to acknowledge their contributions in both the endnotes and the bibliography, but thanks in particular to Professor Paul Brians, Professor H. Bruce Franklin, Roslynn D. Haynes, William Lanouette and Richard Rhodes, whose books I have referred to while writing *Doomsday Men*. Many people have offered help and advice during the three years of research and writing. In particular, I would like to thank Joanne Atkinson, Brian Balmer, Professor Paul Bishop, Rebecca Hurst, Manjit Kumar, Julian Loose and Peter Tallack. For help locating images used in the book I would also like to thank Andrey Bobrov (ITAR-TASS), Heather Lindsay (Emilio Segrè Visual Archives) and Felicity Pors (Niels Bohr Archive).

My father died while I was writing this book. I will never forget our conversations about books, writers and the life of the mind. The best of these typically began while we were walking across the South Downs and ended in a Sussex pub. This book is dedicated to him, although he never lived to see it finished. In the course of writing *Doomsday Men* I became aware of how the story of superweapons had touched previous generations of my own family. I am grateful to Major (Ret'd) R. G. Woodfield, MBE, Regimental Archivist of the Grenadier Guards, for providing information about my grandfather's military service.

Last but by no means least, I want to thank my partner, Susan, for reading the manuscript with a forensic eye for detail and for stoically putting up with my obsession with science, superweapons and other strangeloves during the last few years.

> All other things, to their destruction draw,
> Only our love hath no decay.
> John Donne, 'The Anniversary'

P. D. Smith
Hampshire, January 2007
http://www.peterdsmith.com

NOTE ON UNITS

For much of the period with which this book is concerned, many of the scientists and writers in my narrative were content to think in terms of inches, feet and miles, and pounds and tons. To retain this historical dimension, I have therefore chosen not to convert measurements to metric units.

Prologue

The Beginning or The End?

And he gathered them together into a place called in the Hebrew tongue Armageddon.

And the seventh angel poured out his vial into the air; and there came a great voice out of the temple of heaven, from the throne, saying, It is done. Revelation 16:16–17

Homo sapiens is the only species that knows it will die. The thought obsesses us. From the earliest marks made on cave walls to our most sublime works of art, the fear of death haunts our every creation. And in the middle of the twentieth century, human beings became the first species to reach that pinnacle of evolution – the point at which it could engineer its own extinction.

In February 1950, as the temperature of the cold war approached absolute zero, an atomic scientist conceived the ultimate nuclear weapon: a vast explosive device that would cast a deadly pall of fallout over the planet. Carried on the wind, the lethal radioactive dust would eventually reach all four corners of the world. It would mean the end of life on earth.

The world first heard about the doomsday device on America's most popular radio discussion programme, the *University of Chicago Round Table*. Four scientists who had been involved in building the atomic bomb discussed the next generation of nuclear weapons: the hydrogen bomb.

During the programme, one of the founding fathers of the atomic age, Leo Szilard, stated that it would be 'very easy to rig an H-bomb' to produce 'very dangerous radioactivity'. All you had to do, said

Szilard, was surround the bomb with a chemical element such as cobalt that absorbs radiation. When it exploded, the bomb would spew radioactive dust into the air like an artificial volcano. Slowly and silently, this invisible killer would fall to the surface. 'Everyone would be killed,' he said.[1] The fallout from his chilling suggestion spread fear around the world. For many it seemed as though the biblical story of Armageddon was about to be realized; the seventh angel would empty his vial into the atmosphere, and it would contain radioactive cobalt-60.

Those fears intensified when, in 1954, the United States detonated its biggest ever hydrogen bomb, scattering fallout over thousands of square miles of the Pacific. Such a bomb had been at the core of Leo Szilard's idea. Newspaper headlines around the world proclaimed the imminent construction of the cobalt bomb. In fiction and films, Szilard's deadly brainchild soon became the ultimate symbol of the threat humankind now posed to the very existence of our living, breathing planet.

The story of the cobalt bomb is an unwritten chapter of the cold war. For Szilard it was a dramatic way of warning people about weapons of mass destruction and the escalating arms race. Scientists had been praised by many for curtailing World War II with the atomic bomb. But in the cold war the creators of these apocalyptic superweapons were seen as holding the fate of the world in their hands. They had transformed the laws of nature into instruments of mass destruction and, as far as the public was concerned, there would soon be little to distinguish real scientists from that fictional master of megadeath, Dr Strangelove.

But scientists have not always been mad, and superweapons not always bad. When you look at the history of superweapons through the lenses of science and popular culture, a very different story emerges. Our feelings towards weapons of mass destruction and their inventors have been characterized by a deep ambivalence. Attitudes have swung like a pendulum from utopian hopes to doomsday fears. At the turn of the last century, scientists were seen as saviours, and it was confidently predicted that science was going to transform the world into what chemist Frederick Soddy memorably called 'one smiling Garden of Eden'.[2] It was the atom that would allow us to enter this mythical paradise. Finding the key that would unlock the energy in the dark heart of matter obsessed both scientists and fiction writers.

The dream of the superweapon also emerged at this time in popular culture, springing up alongside the visions of scientific utopia. For the superweapon was going to achieve what empires and religions had been unable to do since civilization began – to bring peace to the world. A scientific wizard would emerge from his mysterious laboratory bearing a weapon so terrible, so devastating, that no force on earth would be able to stand against it. This scientist would then compel the armies of the world to disarm. Thus the saviour scientist with his superweapon would set the world free from centuries of conflict and found a new scientific Jerusalem. It would be the beginning of a brave new world.

The reality turned out to be somewhat different. The chemist Fritz Haber thought he could save Germany with his superweapon – poison gas. But he was wrong. The suffocating yellow clouds of chlorine billowing across the fields of Ypres in 1915 marked the first use of a scientific weapon of mass destruction. Scientists said that it was a new, humane form of warfare, but ordinary people were appalled. Haber's wife committed suicide just days after the first use of poison gas. After World War I, Haber was branded a war criminal. But war had evolved, and the doomsday clock could not be turned back. The military on all sides quickly embraced Haber's new scientific weapon, and soldiers everywhere had to prepare themselves for a new and frightening way to die.

In the 1930s, a Japanese scientist, Shiro Ishii, tried to discover a superweapon that would allow his nation to conquer its enemies. He decided that viruses and bacteria were better weapons than the bullet and the bomb, and pioneered the search for a biological superweapon, committing the most appalling crimes against humanity as he did so. But once again, like some deadly pathogen, warfare had evolved, and in the cold war Ishii's research was acquired by the American military to help it develop ever more lethal weapons of mass destruction.

Chemistry and biology both did their worst in the twentieth century, as scientists struggled to realize the dream of the superweapon. But it was physics that eventually achieved what the other disciplines could not – a single bomb that could annihilate a whole city in a split second.

For Leo Szilard, it is the 'tragedy of mankind' that the story of the atomic bomb began with laudable hopes for a better future.[3] At the beginning of the twentieth century, people marvelled at the hidden worlds revealed by X-rays and were awestruck by the mysterious glow of the new miracle element, radium. Such discoveries offered tangible hopes that a new age was dawning.

The scientists who would lead the world into the atomic era emerged from Berlin's golden age of physics in the 1920s. Among them was Szilard himself, a brilliant yet eccentric Hungarian émigré, known to his friends as the 'inventor of all things'.[4] His vision of an atomic utopia was inspired in part by the fiction of H. G. Wells. The story of Szilard's mission to save the world takes us through the first, explosive years of the atomic age and into the cold war. It is a story that features three of his fellow countrymen: Eugene Wigner, John von Neumann and Edward Teller. Together they were the 'Hungarian quartet', a group of remarkable scientists who all played leading roles in the Manhattan Project to build the atomic bomb and later became key figures in cold-war America.[5] All were inspired by the dream of the superweapon.

The lives and attitudes of these extraordinary individuals reveal the true complexity of being a scientist in the most brutal century the world has known. Like his close friend Albert Einstein, Leo Szilard was a humanist who wanted to save the world with science, but his fellow members of the Quartet were less idealistic. In the cold war, angered by the Soviet Union's treatment of Hungary, they became fiercely anti-Communist. 'I don't think any weapon can be too large,' said mathematician von Neumann.[6] Teller, known to the public as 'Mr H-Bomb', agreed.[7] He became obsessed with the dream of building a bomb thousands of times bigger than the one that destroyed Hiroshima. His deadly vision came true in 1954, when a hydrogen bomb exploded with the force of millions of tons of conventional explosives, vaporizing a Pacific island. Unsurprisingly, both men helped inspire that maddest of mad scientists – Dr Strangelove.

The 1950s became the doomsday decade. It was the era, to quote one writer for the science fiction magazines, of the 'alphabet bombs'.[8] First the A-bomb incinerated two Japanese cities. Then Edward

Teller's H-bomb blasted its way into people's lives and minds. And finally there was the ultimate weapon that Leo Szilard warned the world about in 1950 – the C-bomb. In the 1960s, the world teetered on the brink of a global nuclear holocaust. In 1962, when America discovered that the Soviet Union was secretly shipping nuclear missiles to Cuba, everyone thought the doomsday clock was about to strike midnight. Like two scorpions in a bottle, the superpowers seemed hell-bent on mutual destruction. It was easy to believe that one of them was already building a doomsday machine, the cobalt super-weapon that destroys the world in Stanley Kubrick's cold-war classic, *Dr Strangelove or: How I Learned to Stop Worrying and Love the Bomb*. In the story of superweapons, it is often difficult to decide which is stranger – truth or fiction.

In the twentieth century, scientists were raised up to be gods only to be cast down as devils. Films and fiction first turned them into saviours who free the world from war. But as fears grew about super-weapons, those saviour scientists became mad scientists. In 1932, physicists attending a conference performed a play in which one of their own was cast as Dr Faust, the alchemist who sold his soul to the Devil for ultimate knowledge. This scientific performance came at a crucial moment in the history of science and the world. Soon Szilard would grasp how to release the energy of the atom, and the race for the atomic bomb would begin. As actors on the world's stage, scientists would eventually be forced to drop the saviour's mask. After Hiroshima they would increasingly play the role of the Strangelovean scientist. This was the price of their Faustian bargain.

The history of weapons of mass destruction in the twentieth century is not just about soldiers and scientists. They are not the only dooms-day men. Humankind's most terrible yet ingenious inventions were inspired by a desperate dream, one that was shared by a whole culture. For this reason, history, biography, science and fiction all have an equal part to play in this book.

I came to this subject through Leo Szilard's extraordinary life story. He was a brilliant man, bursting with original ideas on everything from science to politics and even fiction. He was, said one colleague, the greatest scientist never to have won a Nobel prize. Szilard was inspired by a vision of how science could transform the world, but he was also haunted by a fear of how people might misuse this power. His life epitomizes the glories and follies of twentieth-century science and history.

However, I soon realized that to fully explore the questions raised by Szilard's life, I would have to undertake something more wide-ranging than a biography. For Szilard's hopes and fears were deeply rooted in the popular culture of his day, as of course were those of all the doomsday men. To explain why some of the most gifted and idealistic men of the twentieth century spent so much effort trying to destroy the planet, I needed to pursue the origins of these hopes and fears, not only in the lives of the scientists but also in films, fiction and other popular media. Then I might be able to understand why not only the doomsday men, but ordinary men and women were so beguiled by the dream of the superweapon – a dream that may yet turn into a nightmare for us all.

I

The Dream

I would address one general admonition to all – that they consider what are the true ends of knowledge, and that they seek it not either for pleasure of the mind, or for contention, or for superiority to others, or for profit, or fame, or power, or any of these inferior things, but for the benefit and use of life . . . [that] there may spring helps to man, and a line and race of inventions that may in some degree subdue and overcome the necessities and miseries of humanity.

Francis Bacon, *Instauratio magna* (1620)

I

A Black Day

If sunbeams were weapons of war, we would have had solar energy long ago.
                                            George Porter

The football stadium at the University of Chicago had not been used for three years. In 1939 the university's president, Robert Hutchins, had made the controversial decision that football was a distraction in the academic life of a proud institution whose coat of arms displayed a phoenix rising triumphantly from the ashes, together with the motto *Crescat scientia, vita excolatur* – 'Let knowledge increase so that life may be enriched'. So the football team hung up its boots, and gradually the weeds took over the stadium.

Like the rest of the campus, the stadium had been built during the late nineteenth century in an English Gothic style. Even a progressive, New World university found it hard to shrug off the ghosts of the old world completely. With its gargoyles and crenellated walls, Stagg Field looked more like a medieval castle than a football stadium. It was certainly an unlikely setting for the most important scientific experiment of the twentieth century.

On a crisp December morning, a group of students were making their way through the fresh snow to the first lecture of the day. Their breath rose like smoke in the pale sunlight. A short, comfortably overweight man passed them, walking hurriedly towards the disused stadium. His stride was purposeful and his bearing dignified, an impression only slightly spoiled by his roly-poly gait. Near the west stands the snow was stained black as if ash had been scattered there. For the past few weeks military guards had been stationed outside the imposing stone portal that led beneath the stands. It was still an unusual sight on the campus, even in wartime, but no one would say what they were there to protect.

'Good morning, Dr Szilard,' said one of the guards. He pronounced it with a drawl, *See-lard*.

Leo Szilard smiled briefly at the soldier, whose nose had turned red in the subzero temperatures. Just the other day, he had taken pity on the man and had recommended a drink from his Budapest student days to combat the bitter cold: rum tea. But this morning there was no time for idle chat, and Szilard passed swiftly through the door and made his way down the gloomy corridor.

The previous night, restlessness had driven him out of his small and sparsely furnished room on campus. Szilard had called on a colleague and convinced him to brave the freezing night air and go for a late meal. Not that he was hungry; he had already eaten. But he had to talk to someone to ease the burden that was weighing on his mind. Over his second dinner that evening, Szilard confessed his fears about the next day's experiment. The precise nature of their work had to remain a secret, he told his biologist friend mysteriously, but if the experiment 'works too well' there might be an explosion. A big explosion.[1]

The corridor took Szilard underneath the west stands of Stagg Field to a slate-walled room. It was a doubles squash court, about sixty feet by thirty and thirty feet high. Incongruously, spotlights on tripods had been set up as if on a movie set. Szilard stepped gingerly over the cables. He trod carefully because the surface was as slippery as a dancefloor. A fine layer of grey powder lay on every surface – graphite dust, the purest graphite on earth. He could even taste it in the cold, still air. Szilard hurried up a staircase to the small spectators' balcony, about ten feet above the court and overlooking its north end. There were plenty of spectators already there, over thirty of them, and they were all scientists. But today there was no college final – today they would witness the beginning of a new age in science and warfare.

Szilard was breathing heavily. Despite the penetrating cold, he loosened his tie and unbuttoned his thick overcoat. The front of the balcony was packed with scientific monitoring equipment. Leona Woods, a shy 23-year-old graduate student and the only woman

The world's first nuclear reactor, CP-1, goes critical on 2 December 1942. No photographers were present, but Chicago Tribune *artist Gary Sheahan imagined the scene in 1957. Leo Szilard stands in the middle of the group at the left, holding a briefcase. Enrico Fermi is standing next to Walter Zinn, who is leaning with his elbow on the rail.*

present, was making last-minute adjustments together with a short, dark-haired man. That was Enrico Fermi. He was wearing a grey lab coat smeared with the same graphite dust that coated everything, even the snow outside the stadium. Just three years earlier, the Nobel prizewinning physicist had been forced to flee his native Italy with his Jewish wife because of Mussolini's anti-Semitic laws.

The squash court was eerily silent, and the scientists were speaking in whispers. Szilard nodded a greeting to his friend Eugene Wigner, who was deep in conversation with Crawford H. Greenwalt, who would later become president of the Du Pont Chemical Company. Wigner and Szilard had been close friends since the 1920s. Both men had left their homes in Budapest to study science in Berlin, but as the tide of fascism engulfed Europe they had made their way to America, as had many of their scientific colleagues gathered on the balcony that cold December morning.

Szilard looked down at the squash court. In its place loomed a large wooden scaffolding draped with grey rubberized sheeting. Inside this frame squatted a huge structure built of black bricks. This was Chicago Pile Number One, or CP-1 for short.

The world's first atomic pile, what we would now call a nuclear reactor, was as big as a house – about twenty feet high and twenty-five feet wide. It consisted of fifty-seven layers of pure graphite blocks, the layers alternating between solid blocks and ones which were hollowed out to hold slugs of uranium. The blocks containing the uranium formed a cube-like lattice within the pile. In all they had used 250 tons of graphite and six tons of uranium.

Each block had been cut by hand. That was the unenviable task of a young Canadian physicist, Walter Zinn. Today he stood with Fermi on the balcony, his fingernails still blackened by the graphite. Together with half a dozen colleagues and about thirty local Chicago lads, Zinn and another physicist, Herbert Anderson, had worked and cursed non-stop in twelve-hour shifts for six solid weeks – until last night, the evening of 1 December 1942, when their labour was finally complete. Now all that remained was to see whether theory could be turned into reality and the energy of the atom released.

The spark that ignites an atomic chain reaction is a neutral particle – one with no electric charge – called, reasonably enough, a neutron. The nucleus of an atom of uranium-235 can be split in half when struck by a neutron. This is fission, the reaction at the heart of a nuclear reactor – and of an atomic bomb. Changing the mass of an atomic nucleus, either by splitting it (fission) or combining it with another nucleus (fusion), creates energy. Albert Einstein showed just how much energy was locked up inside every atom. His equation $E = mc^2$ states that the amount of energy liberated when matter is annihilated equals the mass of the matter multiplied by the speed of light squared. The speed of light is 186,000 miles per second, so there is a vast reservoir of potential energy in matter. On 6 August 1945, when the first atomic bomb exploded above Hiroshima, just 1 per cent of the bomb's uranium was transformed into the energy that devastated the Japanese city.

Every time a uranium nucleus splits, two or three spare neutrons are expelled, and each of these freed neutrons can split another nucleus. The neutrons this frees can in turn split between four and nine more nuclei, and so on in a succession of reactions involving an exponentially increasing number of atomic nuclei. This is what physicists call a supercritical chain reaction – a potentially explosive atomic wildfire spreading through the fabric of matter, turning it into pure seething energy.

That morning on the squash court, however, Fermi and Szilard did not want an explosive reaction, but a controlled one – a critical reaction in which just enough neutrons are produced to keep the chain reaction self-sustaining. They were also trying to make this reaction work using natural uranium, of which only 0.7 per cent was the highly fissile variety, uranium-235. To do this they needed to slow down the lightning-fast neutrons. This was the crucial task performed by the bricks of pure, black graphite: they acted as the moderator.

As an extra means of keeping the nuclear reaction under control, they had inserted cadmium rods into the pile. Cadmium is one of the most powerful absorbers of neutrons, and if there are no neutrons flying around in the pile, then there's no chain reaction. Today, as an insurance policy, three young physicists stood on an elevator platform above the pile, ready to flood it with a cadmium-salt solution, just in case something went wrong and the rods didn't work. These three were known, only half-jokingly, as the 'suicide squad'.

Walter Zinn had designed the final cadmium rod to drop back automatically into the pile should the neutrons rise above a certain level. They christened this rod 'ZIP' in honour of its creator. If ZIP failed, then another rod could be released from the balcony by cutting a rope. A rather sheepish-looking physicist stood ready with an axe. If that failed to close down the pile, then there was the suicide squad, and after that ... well, in 1942 no one had heard of the words 'meltdown' and 'Chernobyl'.

At 9.45 a.m. Enrico Fermi and his team began the painfully slow process of withdrawing the cadmium rods from the pile, thus increasing the flux of neutrons. As they did so, final checks were made on the measuring equipment and the safety mechanisms. Once this was completed, everyone's eyes turned to the man from Rome. He glanced down at his watch; it was 11.30. Fermi looked round at the expectant faces and smiled.

'I'm hungry,' he said. 'Let's go to lunch.'

Enrico Fermi was the captain of the team of forty-two scientists who had worked on the project. Unlike the Italian, Leo Szilard wasn't a hands-on kind of scientist. Fermi had been annoyed when Szilard declined the opportunity of helping to build the graphite pile. Some said he didn't like getting his hands dirty, but Szilard knew his strengths, and sawing through graphite blocks was not one of them. He was an ideas man, someone who could see solutions before most people had even grasped the problem. A friend once memorably described the portly physicist as an 'intellectual bumblebee', a foot-loose fertilizer of ideas.[2]

When Leo Szilard had first suggested in 1939 that atomic bombs were a real possibility, Fermi's incredulous response had been 'Nuts!'[3] Since then, he had learned to treat the unconventional Hungarian's insights with greater respect, although Fermi was never completely comfortable with his mercurial colleague. 'He is extremely brilliant', admitted Fermi in 1954, 'and . . . he seems to enjoy startling people.'[4]

Although he was no graphite cutter, Szilard had provided many of the key theoretical insights during the building of the atomic pile. He suggested the pile's lattice structure, the geometrical arrangement of uranium spheres within the hollow graphite blocks designed to maxi-mize the effect of the neutrons. He also realized that it was essential to use *pure* graphite as a neutron moderator. Impurities simply absorbed neutrons, working against a chain reaction. (This was a subtlety which Hitler's best atomic physicists – including quantum theorist Werner Heisenberg – failed to grasp. As a result, their bomb project remained largely wishful thinking.)

Most importantly it was Leo Szilard who, in 1933, had first seen how to unlock the fearsome forces in the heart of every atom. It came to him in a flash of insight while he was crossing a road near Russell Square, in London's Bloomsbury. The key was a neutron chain reac-tion, a domino effect rippling through matter and releasing an ever-greater flood of neutrons. Uncontrolled, it would cause an explosion more powerful than any yet created by humankind; controlled, it could supply the world with an unlimited supply of cheap energy. Since this scientific epiphany nine years earlier, the prospect of atomic energy had dominated Szilard's every dream and nightmare. And now his bold idea was about to be put to the test.

After an uneasy lunch, during which they discussed everything apart from the day's experiment, the physicists returned to the squash court.

At 2.20 p.m. they again began withdrawing the thirteen cadmium rods, little by little. Enrico Fermi kept a sharp eye on the dials of the neutron counters. At 3.25, he was ready to remove the final rod.

'Pull it out another foot,' he called to George Weil, who was down on the squash court operating the control rod.[5] Everyone's eyes were fixed on that rod. It was marked in feet and inches, showing how much of the cadmium remained inside the pile absorbing neutrons.

'This is going to do it,' said Fermi to Arthur Compton, the physicist in overall charge of the Chicago project. 'Now it will become self-sustaining. The trace will climb and continue to climb. It will not level off.'[6]

The forty-two scientists scarcely breathed as they faced the implacable black mass of graphite and radioactive uranium. According to Herbert Anderson, 'At first you could hear the sound of the neutron counter, clickety-clack, clickety-clack. Then the clicks came more and more rapidly, and after a while they began to merge into a roar.'

The number of neutrons was so high that the counters could no longer cope. Fermi, his voice steady, asked for the chart recorder to be switched on. Now there was just the faint scratching of the pen as it moved across the paper. The graph showed a steadily increasing level of neutrons. 'It was an awesome silence,' recalled Anderson with real emotion.[7]

'I couldn't see the instruments,' said George Weil. 'I had to watch Fermi every second, waiting for orders. His face was motionless. His eyes darted from one dial to another. His expression was so calm it was hard.'[8]

Fermi studied the rising graph, glancing away only to make calculations with his slide rule. 'His gray eyes betrayed his intense thinking, and his hands moved along with his thoughts,' his wife Laura wrote later, imagining the scene.[9]

Suddenly, the Italian's face broke into a broad smile and he closed his slide rule. 'The reaction is self-sustaining,' he said quietly, looking round at his colleagues on the balcony. 'The curve is exponential.'[10]

It was what everyone had hoped for, but no one had dared believe would happen: the pile had gone critical. But instead of ordering Zinn to drop the emergency rod, Fermi waited. For what to his fellow scientists seemed a lifetime, he stared at the inexorably rising line of the graph. It was as if the sceptical physicist could scarcely believe the evidence of his own scientific instruments.

Then Fermi gave the order they had all been waiting for: 'ZIP in!' It was 3.53 p.m. For 28 minutes they had watched the world's first nuclear reactor in operation. The atomic age had begun.

There were no cheers that day, but the excitement and relief were felt by everyone. Fermi smiled across at Leo Szilard and then shook Compton by the hand. Eugene Wigner produced a bottle of straw-bound Chianti from a brown paper bag and presented it to the Italian physicist. It had been no mean feat tracking one down during wartime. They toasted their success and the new age of science with Chianti in paper cups. Wigner recalled that as they drank the bitter-sweet wine, 'we sent up silent prayers that what we had done was the right thing'.[11] Afterwards they all solemnly signed their names on the Chianti bottle for posterity.

That evening, Compton telephoned James B. Conant, who was leading the US Government project to turn atomic energy into a superweapon. Compton's message was in code, but its meaning was crystal clear:

'The Italian navigator has landed in the New World'.

'How were the natives?' asked Conant.

'Very friendly.'[12]

Enrico Fermi and Leo Szilard stood alone on the balcony overlooking the now dormant atomic pile after the others had left. Both of them knew what their success meant. The world was at war. That very day the US State Department revealed that two million Jews had already been killed by Hitler and a further five million were now at risk. Perhaps Hitler's physicists had already built an atomic pile like theirs and were even now creating an atomic bomb.

More than anyone, Leo Szilard had seen this moment coming. For almost a decade he had been warning of its consequences. Before the war, few would listen to his fears. Now, as Szilard had told his colleagues just two months earlier, they were entering a new and terrible age. 'One has to visualize a world', he said, 'in which a lone airplane could appear over a big city like Chicago, drop his bomb, and thereby destroy the city in a single flash. Not one house may be left standing and the radioactive substances scattered by the bomb may make the area uninhabitable for some time to come.'[13]

No wonder that as Szilard turned to Fermi and shook his hand, he told him: 'This day will go down as a black day in the history of mankind.'[14]

2

The Gift of Destruction

He had in his hands the black complement to all those other gifts science was urging upon unregenerate mankind, the gift of destruction . . . H. G. Wells, *The World Set Free* (1914)

On 2 December 1952, the University of Chicago held a celebration. On the squash court beneath the Stagg Field stadium, twenty-four of the original forty-two scientists, including Enrico Fermi and Leo Szilard, came together with leading politicians and businessmen to 'mark the end of the first decade of the atomic age and the beginning of the second'.[1] The straw-covered Chianti bottle they had all signed ten years earlier was displayed as the first sacred relic of the atomic age. The newspapers reported that its proud owner had insured the empty bottle for $1,000.

The *New York Times* devoted a series of articles to the anniversary. William L. Laurence, the only journalist to have been given access to the atomic bomb project, compared the scientists to the mythic heroes of antiquity. 'That afternoon ten years ago', wrote Laurence, 'witnessed the lighting on earth of a new type of fire, the first of its kind since the legendary Prometheus taught man the use of fire and started him on the slow march to civilization.'

Laurence went on to say that their achievement 'brought civilized mankind one of the greatest threats to its existence'.[2] Within three years of the Chicago chain reaction, two Japanese cities had been destroyed by atomic weapons. Eugene Wigner wondered whether they had unlocked 'a giant' whom they could not control.[3] It was a fear shared that December by people around the world, for the previous

12

month America had exploded the world's first hydrogen bomb – the ultimate weapon of mass destruction.

On 1 November 1952, the darkness of the tropical night was rent by an artificial sun whose heat burnt the skin of sailors watching from thirty miles away. In an instant a small Pacific island called Elugelab was vaporized, leaving a crater more than a mile across. The fireball created by the hydrogen bomb was three miles wide, and a cloud of lethal radioactive by-products soared high into the stratosphere. Its awesome energy came from the same processes that fuel the sun – the fusing together of hydrogen atoms.

But the scientists had got their sums wrong. The thermonuclear explosion was more than twice as powerful as they had expected. The 'Mike' H-bomb test was the largest non-natural explosion the world had yet seen, equivalent to more than ten million tons of conventional high explosive. The Hiroshima bomb had the explosive power of a mere 12,500 tons of explosive. Even though it was a thousand times less powerful, it was enough to incinerate more than a hundred thousand Japanese, and fatally injure tens of thousands more.

Nobody has discovered a more powerful explosive than the hydrogen bomb – at least not yet. A year and a half after the Mike test, America exploded a bomb equivalent to 15 million tons of TNT (15 megatons in nukespeak). This test, at Bikini Atoll, remains the largest bomb ever detonated by the United States. But in the deadly game of one-upmanship that was the cold war, the Soviets had to go one step further. In 1961 they detonated a thermonuclear monster of about 60 megatons. It could have been bigger. The bomb's yield had been limited for the test; the device was capable of 100 megatons.

The decision to develop the next generation of nuclear weapons in America had been made by President Truman in 1950. Even before his decision was announced, on 1 February, the *New Statesman* had declared that 'the whole future of civilisation' was at stake. The British journal argued that these 'new weapons of mass destruction' would make a Third World War 'inevitable'. It would be a war fought by 'methods of mass murder which would outstrip the wildest dreams of the SS and Himmler'.[4]

President Truman turned a deaf ear to such warnings and to the misgivings voiced by many leading scientists. Men such as James Conant and Robert Oppenheimer, who had played key roles in the Manhattan Project, as the atomic bomb project was code-named, left him in no doubt what they thought. In their official advice to the President they said the new bomb 'represents a threat to the future of the human race which is intolerable': it was a 'weapon of genocide'. They also declared themselves 'alarmed' at the 'possible global effects of the radioactivity' from H-bomb explosions.

Enrico Fermi and his Nobel prizewinning colleague Isidor Rabi were also appalled by the prospect of working on the new bomb. They told the President: 'The fact that no limits exist to the destructiveness of this weapon makes its very existence and the knowledge of its construction a danger to humanity as a whole. It is necessarily an evil thing considered in any light.'[5]

But when Truman convened the fateful meeting in the Oval Office of the White House on 31 January, their voices were not heard. The only one at the table who argued against the bomb (known as the 'Super') was David E. Lilienthal, the former head of the Atomic Energy Commission and a man with a mission to promote the brave new world of atomic energy. It was like saying 'no to a steamroller,' he said later.[6]

The sign on Harry S Truman's desk read THE BUCK STOPS HERE. The no-nonsense President had made up his mind some days before the meeting. Four months earlier, the Soviets had shocked the world by testing their first atomic device. America was no longer the only atomic power in the world. In the words of one reporter, whether America liked it or not she was now a competitor in an 'atomic rat race'.[7] Time magazine, which regularly carried full-page advertisements for Boeing bombers ('Potent weapons for world peace'[8]), spoke for the President in its editorial of 30 January: 'The simple fact, unpleasant though it might be, was that if the Russians are likely to build an H-bomb, the US will have to build it, too.'[9]

For 42-year-old Edward Teller, the so-called father of the H-bomb, it was a personal triumph. Like Leo Szilard, the fiercely anti-Communist Teller was a Hungarian émigré. Even while Szilard and Enrico Fermi were designing and building the first atomic pile in 1942, Teller had been working on the calculations that would make the hydrogen bomb a reality. After the Soviet atomic bomb test, he campaigned tirelessly for the green light from the politicians. When Szilard heard that Truman had approved the H-bomb, he told a friend that 'now Teller will know what it is to feel guilty'.[10] As the man who had first urged President Roosevelt to build the atomic bomb, Leo Szilard was no stranger to guilt.

Television was the must-have consumer product in 1950. The year before there had been a million seven-inch black and white sets in America. Now there were ten times that number. Two weeks after what the press called President Truman's 'cosmic' decision, the most famous scientist in the world made an appearance on television.[11]

A film crew descended on 112 Mercer Street, the picturesque weatherboarded house in the sleepy university town of Princeton that had been Albert Einstein's home for the last fifteen years. It was the premiere of a new weekly discussion programme hosted by Eleanor Roosevelt. Seated at his desk dressed in what the *New York Times* described as 'a sweater jacket and tieless, open-collared shirt', Einstein declared that the world now stood on the brink of 'annihilation'.[12]

With his famously unkempt hair and deeply furrowed brow, Einstein gave the impression of having grown weary of the world's folly. In truth his health was failing. 'I look like a spectre', he told quantum physicist Erwin Schrödinger.[13] But Einstein still cared passionately about promoting world peace. Now he genuinely feared that in its search for 'the means to mass destruction', science might endanger the world. If the project to build the hydrogen bomb was successful, he warned, then 'radioactive poisoning of the atmosphere and hence annihilation of any life on earth has been brought within the range of technical possibilities'.[14]

In the studio discussion after Einstein's filmed statement, David Lilienthal, Robert Oppenheimer and physicist Hans Bethe added their voices to the growing chorus of concern about the atomic arms race. But Lilienthal also tried to give atomic energy a positive gloss. He held up a two-pound chunk of uranium to the TV cameras and, as he had done many times before, boasted that it contained 'the energy equivalent of thousands of tons of coal'. It was, he said, a 'whole new source of energy to do man's work'.[15]

Lilienthal declared that the future was atomic. But people had heard promises of unlimited energy before, and many were starting to wonder if they had a future at all in a thermonuclear world. When novelist William Faulkner had first met Einstein, he was so overawed by the great physicist that the wordsmith couldn't speak. But in his Nobel acceptance speech in 1950, Faulkner captured the mood of atomic anxiety perfectly: 'there are no longer problems of the spirit. There is only the question: When will I be blown up?'[16]

In the week before his appearance on Eleanor Roosevelt's programme, Hans Bethe had tried to make the world a safer place. Together with eleven other leading scientists, Bethe, who had been a key figure in the Manhattan Project, made front-page news when he asked the United States Government to pledge that it would never be the first to use the hydrogen bomb. In 1938, the German-born Bethe had explained how the fusion of hydrogen into helium gave the sun its immense energy. Now he was being asked to build a bomb that would unleash that same energy on men, women and children. As the press pointed out even before the Mike test, when the H-bomb explodes 'a little bit of the searing sun will have hit the earth'.[17] Such a bomb, said Hans Bethe, was 'no longer a weapon of war, but a means of extermination of whole populations. Its use would be a betrayal of all standards of morality and of Christian civilization itself.'[18]

But the fear of Soviet aggression was a powerful argument in favour of developing the hydrogen bomb, even for Bethe and his colleagues, who declared themselves willing to work on the project while condemning it as immoral. Harold C. Urey, the man who won a Nobel prize in 1934 for discovering the H-bomb's fuel, heavy hydrogen, spoke for many people when he said, 'I value my liberties more than I do my life.'[19]

In Europe, where the after-effects of the last world war still scarred cities and people alike, the absurd logic of such statements (can you have liberty without life?) caused widespread alarm. Einstein's apocalyptic warning was splashed across nearly every front page. In France the paper *Aurore* printed a startling headline across three columns: WHEREVER IT FALLS THE H-BOMB WILL OBLITERATE ALL HUMAN LIFE FOR A THOUSAND YEARS.[20] You didn't need Einstein's brain to work out that Europe would be the battlefield of World War III. As the *New Statesman* put it, 'the British people know perfectly well that, even if America and Russia might survive an atomic war, Britain and Western Europe would not.'[21]

These concerns were also being expressed in popular culture. The classic Boulting brothers film *Seven Days to Noon*, released in the year of the H-bomb decision, reveals both the growing anxieties about atomic war and a feeling that scientists had betrayed the ideals of their discipline. Professor Willingdon, a British scientist who worked on the Manhattan Project, disappears from his government research establishment together with an atomic bomb. Conveniently, the device fits neatly into the professor's Gladstone bag – the first briefcase nuke. Willingdon threatens that, unless the British prime minister agrees to stop building atomic weapons, he will destroy twelve square miles of central London.

The professor, played by Barry Jones, is tormented by the thought that atomic war will mean the 'total destruction of mankind'. People, he says, are 'moving like sleepwalkers to annihilation'. Willingdon speaks for many real-life scientists at this time when he admits that he has 'lost faith in the value of his work'. He had accepted the necessity of building an atomic bomb before the Nazis, but now he has been told to design an even more terrible weapon: 'When I was a young man I saw in science a way of serving God and my fellow men. Now I see my life's work used only for destruction. My dream has become a nightmare.'[22] Leo Szilard was about to bring that nightmare one step closer to reality.

In homes right across America, people tuned in to the NBC radio network each Sunday afternoon to listen to the country's most popular discussion programme – the *University of Chicago Round Table*. Broadcast since the 1930s, it had become a national institution. Even today the University of Chicago still proudly displays the actual table around which such opinion-formers as John F. Kennedy, Jawaharlal Nehru and Adlai Stevenson discussed the issues of the day. At a time when most programmes were scripted and predictable, the *Chicago Round Table* had a reputation for lively debates. Listeners who tuned in on 26 February 1950 were not disappointed.

Around the table that day were four scientists who had contributed to the Manhattan Project. Leading the debate was a dynamic, youthful-looking geochemist, Harrison Brown. One of his guests – Frederick Seitz – would later become a much respected president of the US National Academy of Sciences. Another – Hans Bethe – would win a Nobel for stealing the secret of the sun's energy. The other participant

The University of Chicago Round Table, *26 February 1950. Around the table are (from the left), Harrison Brown, Frederick Seitz, Hans Bethe and Leo Szilard.*

that day was Leo Szilard, about whom a colleague once quipped that he was the greatest scientist never to have won a Nobel prize. Einstein was tieless for his appearance on national television. By contrast, the four scientists who faced each other on 26 February across the famous round table opted for dark suit and tie, even though it was a radio broadcast.

On the table stood a world globe, the kind that children love to spin. In front of each participant was an angled lectern for their notes. All four men knew each other well. Szilard, Brown and Seitz met every month or so at Einstein's Princeton home, together with chemist Linus Pauling and biologist Hermann Muller, to discuss the political and social implications of atomic energy. This informal gathering of concerned scientists was known as the Einstein Committee.

It was Professor Bethe of Cornell University who initially took the lead in the Round Table discussion. He was an insider on the H-bomb project and a close friend of Edward Teller, the driving force behind the new bomb. Bethe pointed out that for now the H-bomb – or 'Hell Bomb' as it was known in the press[23] – existed only in the minds of its would-be creators. But, he added cautiously, 'it is possible that we can make this bomb'.[24] It would use the energy of an atomic bomb to trigger a fusion reaction, which would be fuelled by heavy hydrogen. When it exploded, for a fleeting instant it would be as though a fragment of the sun itself blazed upon the surface of the earth.

Hans Bethe was 'the living picture of the thinker', the descendant of a long line of German university professors, recalled Laura Fermi.[25] No one knew more about fusion than this dignified academic mandarin. In a soft but precise voice, Bethe explained that if it were built, the H-bomb would 'certainly be very large,' perhaps a thousand times as powerful as the Hiroshima bomb. In the future, he predicted, even the biggest cities, such as New York, could be destroyed with a single bomb.

Frederick Seitz, aged 39, had just become professor of physics at Illinois University. In the 1930s he'd been Eugene Wigner's first graduate student at Princeton. This balding and rather grave-looking man was one of the eleven physicists who had supported Bethe's call for America to rule out first use of the H-bomb. This afternoon he contributed a frightening figure to the debate.

The 'flash effect' of a hydrogen bomb would, he said, cover at least twenty miles. In other words, even that far from the explosion you would receive severe, life-threatening burns. At Hiroshima, where so many thousands of people were horrifically burned, the flash effect extended for less than a mile. The casualties from an H-bomb would be numbered in the millions, but no one around the table appeared visibly shocked. The figures they dealt with in their daily work were faceless.

Harrison Brown glanced down at his notes, and then turned to Hans Bethe, saying, 'One sees in the press, from time to time, statements concerning destruction by another source – namely, radioactivity.' This was the new possibility Einstein had raised on Eleanor Roosevelt's programme. Today, Bethe confirmed Einstein's worst fears about the invisible killer, radioactivity. He explained how the neutrons produced by the exploding hydrogen bomb would create radioactive carbon-14 in the atmosphere: 'This isotope of carbon has a life of 5,000 years. So if H-bombs are exploded in some number, then the air will be poisoned . . . for 5,000 years.' Almost as an afterthought, he added: 'It may well be that the number of H-bombs will be so large that this will make life impossible.'

Leo Szilard was listening intently to Bethe, who was seated to his right. The German physicist was eight years younger than Szilard, who had just turned 52. The two scientists had very different characters. Bethe was a brilliant theorist as well as a good team player, an increasingly vital skill in the post-war era of so-called big science. Szilard thought teams belonged on football pitches. Science, for Szilard, was a personal battle of wits between him and nature. Einstein, who had been his friend for thirty years, shared this view. For both men, nature was a mysterious and sublime realm, a source of unending challenge and inspiration. Neither man liked the new corporate science that had grown out of the Manhattan Project, with its big budgets and bureaucratic procedures.

As Bethe finished speaking, Szilard's eyes sparked with a sudden intensity. He had been waiting for this moment. He began by disagreeing with Bethe's view of the threat from radioactivity. 'It would take a very large number of bombs', said Szilard, 'before life would be in danger from ordinary H-bombs.' But, he continued, 'it is very easy to rig an H-bomb, on purpose, so that it should produce very dangerous radioactivity.' He then proceeded to give his listeners, both around the table and in their homes across America, a lesson on how to construct a doomsday bomb.

First he explained how an atomic explosion creates dangerous radioactive elements. 'Most of the naturally occurring elements become radioactive when they absorb neutrons,' he said. 'All that you have to do is to pick a suitable element and arrange it so that the element captures all the neutrons. Then you have a very dangerous situation. I have made a calculation in this connection. Let us assume that we make a radioactive element which will live for five years and that we just let it go into the air. During the following years it will gradually settle out and cover the whole earth with dust. I have asked myself: How many neutrons or how much heavy hydrogen do we have to detonate to kill everybody on earth by this particular method?'

Szilard paused and looked around the table as if expecting a reply. 'I come up with about 50 tons of neutrons as being plenty to kill everybody, which means about 500 tons of heavy hydrogen.'

Harrison Brown watched Szilard intently, trying to absorb the implications of what he was saying. His head was large, almost imposing, but with chubby, boyish features. Swept back from a high forehead was a mane of thick dark hair through which ran a flash of grey. After his death, a friend would memorably describe Szilard's boyish face as being like that of a 'sad, gentle, mischievous cherub'.[26]

'You mean, Szilard,' said Brown, 'that if you exploded 500 tons of heavy hydrogen and then permitted those neutrons to be absorbed by another element to produce a radioactive substance, all people on earth could be killed . . . ?'

Szilard replied, 'If this is a long-lived element which gradually settles out, as it will in a few years, forming a dust layer on the surface of the earth, everyone would be killed.'

Brown's specialism was the chemistry of rocks, particularly extra-terrestrial ones. *Time* magazine had recently pictured him holding up a meteorite. Now he chose a geological analogy that he was familiar with: 'You would visualize this, then, something like the Krakatoa explosion, where you would carry out, let us say, one large explosion or a series of smaller ones. The dust goes up into the air and, as was the case in that particular explosion, it circled the earth for many, many months, and even years, and gradually settled down upon the surface of the earth itself?'

Szilard leant back in his chair and spread his hands emphatically: 'I agree with you . . .' The analogy with a volcano was good. Szilard liked it. He had clearly made his point. The doomsday weapon had been born.

Hans Bethe had been listening to Szilard with growing irritation. Although his face still bore the mild-mannered smile that habitually played around his lips, a frown now creased his forehead. It was not that he disagreed scientifically with what Szilard was saying, rather that he was irritated by this typically Szilardian flight of fancy. There was no need to exaggerate the current situation. The H-bomb was going to be quite bad enough – why frighten people with what might come next?

'You may ask', said Szilard, anticipating his critics, 'who would want to kill everybody on earth?' Any country that wanted to be unbeatable in the field of war, was his dramatic answer. That would be the advantage conferred on any nation that owned the doomsday device – a hydrogen bomb rigged in the way he had outlined, using zinc or, as he later suggested, cobalt.

'Let us suppose,' he explained, 'that we have a war and let us suppose that we are on the point of winning the war against Russia, after a struggle which perhaps lasts ten years. The Russians can say: "You come no farther. You do not invade Europe, and you do not drop ordinary atom bombs on us, or else we will detonate our H-bombs and kill everybody." Faced with such a threat, I do not think that we could go forward. I think that Russia would be invincible.'

Harrison Brown was clearly struggling with the implications of what Szilard was saying. Would a nation really kill everyone, he asked, rather than suffer defeat? Szilard frankly admitted that he didn't know the answer to this. But he added this chilling coda: 'I think that we may threaten to do it, and I think that the Russians might threaten to do it. And who will take the risk then not to take that threat seriously?'

In a public lecture the following month, Brown told his audience that he was now convinced that there were men who would be prepared to destroy all life on earth if they could not have their own way. 'Can we doubt for a moment,' he asked, 'that Hitler in the desperation of defeat would have killed everything, had he had it in his power to do so?'[27]

That February afternoon, the Round Table panel moved on to

consider the possibility of vast hydrogen bombs carried in ships. If exploded in the Pacific, the radioactivity from such monstrous devices would drift across America on the prevailing westerly winds, poisoning the land and its people. It was a new and frightening danger for America. The fear of ship bombs would create headlines for the rest of the decade as America and Russia vied with each other to build the biggest H-bombs. But, as Szilard pointed out, such radioactivity is impossible to control. The awful irony facing them, added Harrison Brown, was that it was 'easier to kill all the people in the world than just a part of them.' 'This is definitely so,' agreed Szilard.

Before the discussion drew to a close, Hans Bethe talked about his statement calling upon the United States to rule out first use of the hydrogen bomb. Bethe explained that he was willing to work on the bomb in order 'to keep our bargaining position and not to be confronted, one day, with an ultimatum from Russia that they have the H-bomb and can destroy us.'

Unlike Frederick Seitz, Szilard had not been one of the signatories to Bethe's plea. He did not hide his disapproval now. 'I read the statement,' said Szilard, 'and I was really more impressed by the sentiment in it than by its logic.'

Neither Bethe nor Seitz were particularly surprised by his blunt words, but Szilard widened his critique to make a point that was central to the whole debate about the hydrogen bomb and weapons of mass destruction generally. Bethe's statement, according to Szilard, was just the tip of the iceberg. In 1939, he said, the American people were of one mind that it was 'morally wrong and reprehensible to bomb cities and kill women and children'. But gradually this firm conviction had been eroded: 'during the war, almost imperceptibly, we started to use jellied gasoline bombs against Japan, killing millions of women and children; finally we used the A-bomb'.

The level of terror imposed in warfare had been rising steadily throughout the twentieth century. Now there was a 'general uneasiness among the scientists' about how their science would be used in the future. 'It is easy for the scientists to agree that we cannot trust Russia,' said Szilard, 'but they also ask themselves: To what extent can we trust ourselves?' It was a chilling thought for a country that had just authorized the construction of what would become the most terrible explosive device the world had ever seen. And after the H-bomb, what next? The doomsday bomb, perhaps?

The next day, the *New York Times* splashed Leo Szilard's comments about a doomsday bomb across its front page. Its breathless headline read: ENDING OF ALL LIFE BY HYDROGEN BOMB HELD A POSSI-BILITY – RADIOACTIVITY THE KILLER. William Laurence told how the 'four leading atomic scientists' had warned that 'the hydrogen bomb, if developed, could be rigged in such a way as to exterminate the entire world's population or most of it'. The scientists had re-vealed 'hitherto unknown information' about the 'potential horrors' of a war fought with hydrogen bombs. A photograph showed Szilard discussing the issues with his fellow scientists.

Laurence also described to his readers how a hydrogen bomb could 'transmute' an element such as cobalt into a 'radioactive element about 320 times as powerful . . . as radium'. He continued: 'This deadly radioactive cobalt would be scattered into the atmosphere and carried by the westerly winds all over the surface of the earth. Any living thing inhaling it, or even touched by it, would be doomed to certain death.'[28] For the first time, the cobalt doomsday bomb had hit the headlines. In the coming years it would often return to remind people that humankind now had ultimate power over life and death on earth.

The *New York Times* was not alone in picking up on these fears of atomic apocalypse. The counter-attack on what *Time* magazine called 'hydrogen hysteria' was led by David Lilienthal.[29] Speaking at New York's Town Hall a few days after the broadcast, Lilienthal criticized what he called the 'prophets of hydrogen Doomsday', accusing these 'Oracles of Annihilation' of sensationalism. But his criticisms were blatantly political. 'Hopelessness and helplessness are the very oppos-ite of what we need', said the former head of the AEC. 'These are the emotions that play right into the hands of destructive Communist forces.'[30]

Those were strong words in the year that Senator Joe McCarthy began his anti-Communist witch-hunts in America. The nation that had invested so much in its atomic future could not afford to lose the support of its people. Lilienthal's targets were clearly Szilard and

Einstein, and for most people around the world Einstein was 'an oracle not to be questioned'.[31]

But in the autumn of 1950, Szilard's fears of a cobalt bomb were given independent scientific backing. Dr James R. Arnold of the Institute for Nuclear Studies, Chicago, looked at whether such a weapon was technically feasible. According to *Newsweek*, the 'brilliant, boyish (aged 27) physicist' had 'started out, slide rule in hand, to demolish Szilard's arguments. But he finished by agreeing on many points.'

Arnold's calculations showed that the doomsday device described by Leo Szilard would have to be an enormous weapon, 'perhaps two and a half times as heavy as the battleship *Missouri*'.[32] The heavy hydrogen (deuterium) that fuelled the H-bomb would cost as much as the Manhattan Project, $2 billion. In addition, at least 10,000 tons of cobalt would be needed to create the lethal radioactive isotope, cobalt-60, when the bomb exploded. Most of Szilard's assumptions about the cobalt bomb were confirmed by the Chicago scientist. Virtually the only area of uncertainty was whether the radioactive dust from such a doomsday bomb would be evenly distributed around the world.

Although Arnold concluded that 'the human race is in no *immediate* danger', because such a weapon would require 'a full-scale effort by a major country over many years', he was convinced that 'the vast majority of the race can be killed off in this way'.[33] The only ray of hope that *Newsweek* could find was that 'those who would use the weapon for murder must be willing to accept suicide in the bargain'.[34]

As well as being the birthplace of the atomic age and the cobalt bomb, the University of Chicago was home to the world's most important journal on atomic affairs – the *Bulletin of the Atomic Scientists*. It was the *Bulletin* that commissioned James Arnold to assess Leo Szilard's frightening prediction about a doomsday weapon. The *Bulletin* was conceived in the Stineway Drug Store on 57th Street, east of the University, where Russian-born biophysicist Eugene Rabinowitch met his colleagues Hyman Goldsmith and sociologist Edward Shils for coffee every day.

The first issue appeared on 10 December 1945, a few months after the Hiroshima and Nagasaki bombs. In June 1947 the *Bulletin*'s cover gained its iconic image of the doomsday clock, designed by Martyl Langsdorf, the wife of a Manhattan Project physicist. Initially this graphic representation of how close we were to a nuclear holocaust was set at seven minutes to midnight. But after the first Soviet atomic test in 1949, the clock was reset to just three minutes before doomsday, in order to reflect the magazine's growing concern at the world situation. The countdown to atomic Armageddon had begun.

The *Bulletin*'s co-founder Edward Shils knew Leo Szilard well. The journal provided a platform for the campaigning scientist, publishing his peace plans and his short fiction, which he started writing after 1947. When his friend died in 1964, Shils wrote a perceptive memoir. Szilard hated being tied down, said Shils, to a person, a job, or a home: 'He was a restless, homeless spirit. He owned no property, very few books ... Hotel lobbies, cafés, Jewish delicatessens, poor restaurants, and city pavements were the setting for the discussions which were his main form of communication – he said the age of books had passed.'[35] His favourite deli was a regular haunt of Central European refugees on upper Broadway in New York. There he could rediscover the food and the old-world atmosphere of his youth – the coffee houses of Budapest and Berlin where he spent many hours debating politics and science with some of the brightest brains of the age.

Szilard once told Shils that he saw himself as a 'knight errant' in the scientific world, someone who needed 'to be free to go wherever important ideas in science or in the effort to protect the human race would take him'.[36] Apart from a letter to the *New York Herald Tribune* in March 1950 rebutting Lilienthal's criticisms, Leo Szilard made no further public comments on the cobalt bomb. This was wholly in character. Like a neutron in a chain reaction, Szilard liked to think of himself as the vital spark that ignites an explosion of ideas. He had set the ball rolling with the *Chicago Round Table* broadcast. Now there were new horizons to explore – such as his biological research into phage (viruses which infect bacteria) with Aaron Novick – as well as the small matter of saving the world from atomic doomsday.

According to Edward Shils, Szilard was a one-man peace movement, tirelessly pressing his case with the politicians and opinion-formers in

Washington. Once when Shils visited him at a hotel, he found Szilard holding two long-distance telephone calls simultaneously. The phones were in different rooms, and he was 'going back and forth, putting down the receiver in one room while he went to take up the conversation in the other'. In each room were groups of 'actual and potential collaborators', none of whom seemed to know quite what was happening. But Szilard liked it that way; he was always surrounded by an air of intrigue and expectation. Leo Szilard was, said his friend memorably, 'an extraordinarily sweet and calmly desperate genius'.[37]

James Arnold had been shocked to discover that the science of destruction had progressed to such a degree that 'a practicable method for self-destruction' could be built with current technology. In the coming years, as Arnold had predicted, the science of destruction made rapid progress and the arms race gathered momentum. In 1953, the doomsday clock moved forward to just two minutes before midnight as the United States and the Soviet Union tested H-bombs within nine months of each other. That year the young Sylvia Plath gave voice to the atomic angst of her generation in the poem 'Doomsday':

> The streets crack through in havoc-split ravines,
> The doomstruck city crumbles block by block;
> The hour is crowed in lunatic thirteens.[38]

Throughout the 1950s and into the 1960s, the cobalt doomsday bomb became a familiar spectre. In best-sellers such as Nevil Shute's *On the Beach* (1957) and Hollywood films such as the *Planet of the Apes* series, it was a symbol of man's Promethean hubris. The British film *Seven Days to Noon* came out in the year in which Leo Szilard described the cobalt bomb. In the film, as in real life, people began to blame the scientific creators of these weapons for giving humankind such godlike power over the future of life on earth.

People's anxieties about the scientists they had once hailed as saviours, as paragons of progress, found expression in the figure of one fictional scientist. Stanley Kubrick's 1964 black comedy *Dr Strangelove* brilliantly captured the insane logic of the arms race and the science of destruction. Kubrick's film also features Szilard's doomsday device – the cobalt bomb.

Dr Strangelove, an ex-Nazi scientist working for the United States, came to personify the alliance between cold-war science and power politics. Memorably played by Peter Sellers as a psychotic rationalist, Dr Strangelove has been identified with many real scientists of the time. The father of the H-bomb Edward Teller, the German rocket designer Wernher von Braun, computer pioneer John von Neumann, physicist and nuclear strategist Herman Kahn, even Henry Kissinger – all have been suggested as possible models for this unforgettable character created by Kubrick and British author Peter George.

Leo Szilard thought it was simplistic to blame scientists alone for the technologies of destruction. In his view, the roots of the problem ran far deeper. The dream of the superweapon was not limited to scientists such as Dr Strangelove. Scientists and engineers may have built the Bomb, but the dream was there many years before. Fiction writers, journalists, film-makers, ordinary men and women had all known this dream. Szilard was once asked whether he agreed that it was the tragedy of the scientist to make great advances in knowledge which are then used for purposes of destruction. He replied without hesitation: 'My answer is that this is not the tragedy of the scientist; it is the tragedy of mankind.'[39]

3

The Plutonium Collector

The process of decay was forestalled by the powers of the light-ray, the flesh in which he walked disintegrated, annihilated, dissolved in vacant mist, and there within it was the finely turned skeleton of his own hand . . . and for the first time in his life he understood that he would die.

Thomas Mann, *The Magic Mountain* (1924)

A few months after Leo Szilard unveiled his vision of the doomsday bomb, the FBI raided a house in the suburbs of Denver and arrested a 28-year-old research scientist. The astonished neighbours watched as the quiet, bespectacled man was led in handcuffs across the toy-littered lawn of the house where he lived with his wife and three children. Next day the G-men announced to the press that Sanford Lawrence Simons had been charged with the theft of plutonium.

Sanford Simons was working at the University of Denver on top-secret studies of the upper atmosphere for the United States Air Force. During the war he had been employed on the Manhattan Project at Los Alamos, New Mexico, where the atomic bombs were built. In 1946 he had removed from the weapons laboratory a glass vial containing plutonium, the new artificial radioactive element that was at the heart of the Nagasaki atomic bomb. After a brief search, the FBI found the plutonium, still in its original glass vial, hidden beneath his rented home. FBI agent Russell Kramer refused to say how much Simons had taken or what it was worth, but when pressed by journalists, he said that he'd heard figures ranging from $500 to $200,000.

In the drawer of a dresser in the Simons' house, the G-men also found several pieces of uranium.

He admitted straight out that he'd taken the radioactive material. But Simons, who had trained as a metallurgical engineer, claimed it was just a 'souvenir' of his time at Los Alamos, which he left in July 1946. Flanked by two impassive US Marshals sporting Humphrey Bogart fedoras, Simons talked freely with the journalists after he had been committed for trial. Unshaven and handcuffed, though still clutching his pipe, Simons seemed remarkably unfazed by his predicament. Under the Atomic Energy Act he faced a possible maximum sentence of five years in prison and a $10,000 fine. Just a few weeks earlier, the FBI had arrested Ethel and Julius Rosenberg in New York on suspicion of atomic espionage. They were both convicted the following year. Despite pleas for clemency from around the world, including from Einstein, the couple were subsequently executed in the electric chair.

'Why did I take it?' said Simons sheepishly, in answer to reporters' questions. 'Well, it seems pretty silly now, but I've always collected mineral samples. I realized almost instantly that I didn't want it, but it was like having a bull by the tail. I couldn't let go!'

One of the newspapermen asked how he managed to smuggle the plutonium out of the top-secret military research laboratory.

Simons grinned: 'I just walked out with it.' He explained that the plutonium sample had been lying around on his desk for some time. No one had asked for it back, and eventually he simply couldn't resist it. 'There was no real check-up on what was taken out of the place at that time,' he added with a shrug.

You wouldn't have guessed it from what Simons said, but in the 1940s fissile elements such as plutonium and uranium-235 were more precious than gold to the atomic bomb project. They were the result of a vast expenditure of money and effort. Whole cities of workers laboured to produce these lethal elements in vast industrial complexes built specifically for the Manhattan Project. Each gram was the product of thousands of working hours. It was not unusual to see scientists down on their hands and knees, sweeping the floor with Geiger counters, hunting for any stray pieces of metal that might have been dropped. Sometimes the Geiger counter would crackle furiously as it passed over a tiny orange or black speck on someone's lab coat,

Research scientist Sanford Lawrence Simons – the 'plutonium collector' – in the custody of two US Marshals in Denver, August 1950.

revealing the telltale signs of radioactivity. Even the smallest particle of fissionable matter was extremely valuable, and lab coats were routinely treated with chemicals to reclaim these elements.

Sanford Simons hid the stolen plutonium under his house. He had good reason to. Plutonium has been called the most dangerous element on earth. The glass vial and its deadly contents remained in its hiding place for four years. The FBI became aware of its presence there only after they were tipped off. Simons had let slip in conversation with a friend that he had some plutonium. In the year that Joe McCarthy stoked fears about a Communist fifth column infiltrating American society, to admit that you had a key ingredient for the atomic bomb stashed in your home was simply asking for trouble.

Outside the courtroom, a reporter put it to Agent Kramer that taking plutonium as a 'souvenir' was a rather corny excuse. The FBI man nodded in agreement and said, without a trace of humour, 'He's a pretty corny guy.'

During his trial the defence pointed out that Simons had never been in trouble with the police. More importantly, he was not a 'Red' and had no 'Communist connections'. The defence attorney based his case on the popular image of the scientist. He argued, somewhat unconvincingly, that scientists are 'all darned fools' when it came to experiments. He claimed that scientific curiosity alone had prompted Sanford Simons to take the samples of plutonium and uranium in 1946. It was a case of the irresistible allure of forbidden knowledge, Your Honour, and, as everyone knew, no scientist worth his slide-rule could resist that. But Judge Lee Knous was not particularly impressed by this argument. For taking a pinch of plutonium, the disgraced scientist was sentenced to eighteen months in a Federal prison.[1]

The 'plutonium collector', as the press dubbed the unfortunate Simons, was driven by a dangerous fascination for the deadly element. Its discovery at the beginning of 1941 marked the point where science could claim to have exceeded the dreams of the alchemists. Plutonium was first identified by chemist Glenn Seaborg, who bombarded uranium with deuterons (the nuclei of heavy hydrogen atoms) and painstakingly separated out the resulting transmuted elements. He recalled that the critical chemical identification took place on the 'stormy night' of 23 February 1941, in Room 307, Gilman Hall at the University of California, Berkeley. Twenty-five years later the room was dedicated as a National Historic Landmark. The 28-year-old son of Swedish immigrants to the United States was a dynamic and ambitious scientist, the only person to have an element named after him during his lifetime – element 106, seaborgium.

An alchemist would probably have felt quite at home in Seaborg's laboratory. It was usually dense with fumes and steam from the processes used to isolate the microscopic amounts of this new matter. By March, he and his co-worker Joseph W. Kennedy had managed to isolate half a microgram of the new artificial element. Talking about this and his subsequent work identifying other new elements heavier than uranium, Seaborg commented:

When you are working with invisible amounts of a new substance, the task of identification is immensely difficult. In one instance, we had only five atoms and a few hours to make a positive identification through chemical analysis. The difficulty can be understood when one realizes that the ink in the dot of an 'i' on this page you are reading contains something on the order of a billion atoms.[2]

From 1942, Glenn Seaborg worked for the Manhattan Project at the University of Chicago. This part of the programme to build the world's first atomic superweapon was code-named by the military 'Met Lab'. Here too, Leo Szilard worked with Enrico Fermi to develop CP-1, the first nuclear reactor. In the storm of neutrons unleashed within this graphite and uranium pile, the new element, plutonium, would be born. Seaborg was put in charge of developing the chemical process to extract plutonium after it had been created in the reactor.

Until August 1942, Seaborg had just millionths of a gram of plutonium to work with. The day when he was able to display the first sample of a visible amount of a plutonium compound to his fellow scientists was 'the most exciting and thrilling' he had experienced at Chicago: 'It is the first time that element 94 – or any other synthetic element, for that matter – had been exposed for the eye of man to behold . . . my feelings are akin to a new father engrossed in the development of his offspring since conception.'[3]

Showing off the newborn element to his colleagues set a precedent, and afterwards visitors to the Met Lab insisted on being shown it. Seaborg later confessed, with a mischievous twinkle in his eye, that due to plutonium's value and toxicity, most people only ever saw a solution of green ink in a test tube. The man who beat the alchemists at their own game was awarded the 1951 Nobel Prize in Chemistry, while arguably his most diehard fan, Sanford Simons, was still locked up in jail.

Glenn Seaborg shared the prize with his University of California colleague Edwin McMillan, whose discovery of element 93, the short-lived neptunium, had led Seaborg to his lethal chemical child. Neptunium has 93 protons in its nucleus, which is why it is number 93 in the periodic table of the elements. An atomic nucleus consists of protons and neutrons. Many elements, uranium among them, can exist in several different forms, depending on how many neutrons the atom's nucleus has. These different forms of the element are known as isotopes. Plutonium, element 94, has fifteen isotopes. They range from the lightest, plutonium-232 with 138 neutrons, to the heaviest, plutonium-246 with 152 neutrons. In his career, Seaborg helped to identify over a hundred different isotopes.

When uranium-238 captures a neutron it becomes the unstable isotope uranium-239. Within minutes this transmutes into neptunium-239, which just over two days later becomes plutonium-239. This is the reaction that took place inside Szilard and Fermi's prototype reactor, CP-1. It is now known that minute traces of plutonium do occur naturally in uranium ore, created by the release of neutrons.

In its solid form, plutonium is a silvery metal which quickly turns yellow when exposed to air. It is warm to the touch – it feels alive, and in a sense it is, constantly emitting a stream of alpha particles (helium nuclei, consisting of two protons and two neutrons). A large piece of plutonium placed in water, would radiate enough heat to bring the water rapidly to the boil. Indeed, this heat has been utilized to produce electricity to power everything from cardiac pacemakers to spacecraft. But bring together too much plutonium in one place and it will go critical, creating a potentially explosive chain reaction. The Nagasaki bomb contained just 13 lb of plutonium and produced the explosive power of 20,000 tons of chemical high explosive. A mere 1 lb can yield 10 million kilowatt-hours of energy. As Seaborg quickly realized, 'element 94 is almost twice as fissionable as uranium-235', a finding of huge importance for the atomic bomb project.[4] Uranium-235, the rare isotope of natural uranium used in the Hiroshima bomb, was difficult to separate. Seaborg's discovery meant that bombs could be built with less fissionable material.

Just after the 'Fat Man' plutonium bomb was dropped on Nagasaki, a Los Alamos scientist, Harry Daghlian, was fatally injured while assembling pieces of plutonium for an experiment to determine plutonium's critical mass. A chunk of the warm, silvery metal slipped from his fingers into the assembly, causing it to go prematurely critical. In the fraction of a second before he could scatter the blocks to stop it exploding, he saw the air around the assembly glow with an eerie blue light as it was ionized by lethal radiation. The nuclear scientist died twenty-five days later. Each stage of Daghlian's radiation sickness was documented by his fellow scientists, eager for knowledge about the lethal new element. The official record states that they obtained 'most spectacular pictures'.[5]

Plutonium is aptly named after the god of the underworld and death. According to Seaborg, plutonium is 'one of the most deadly substances known, it has unusual – and unreal – properties'.[6] It is highly toxic. At Los Alamos the chemists had a policy of 'immediate high amputation' if plutonium entered a cut.[7] Once inside the body it accumulates at bone surfaces, from where it irradiates surrounding tissues and fatally destroys bone-marrow cells. There is nothing that can be done once it is absorbed into the body: plutonium-239 has a half-life of over 24,000 years. Plutonium remains in your bones long after you are dead and buried.

Plutonium from the Nevada Desert nuclear tests in 1952 and 1953 drifted out of America and settled invisibly on Great Britain within days. Tests on soil samples gathered in Hertfordshire have only recently revealed this chilling fact. It is estimated that our biosphere contains several tons of plutonium, a legacy of atmospheric weapons testing in the 1950s and 1960s.[8] Leo Szilard's vision of global dooms-day through nuclear poisoning was happening sooner, but more gradually, than anyone realized. It would not be until the mid-1950s that concerns were voiced about the health effects of the fallout from nuclear tests.

It was this deadly element that so intrigued the 24-year-old Sanford Simons that he was prepared to risk his liberty to possess it. Otto Frisch, whose calculations of critical mass were crucial in the early stages of the bomb project, understood this dangerous fascination with these deadly new elements. When the silvery blocks of highly fissionable uranium-235 were first delivered to Los Alamos in April 1945, he felt an overwhelming 'urge to take one'.[9] They were the first pieces ever made of uranium-235 metal, the element that would blast the heart out of Hiroshima. Somewhat incongruously, Frisch thought that the heavy metal would make a nice paperweight.

Precious elements such as gold have long exerted an almost mystical power over human minds. Gold, the sun-like metal that never rusts or corrodes, promised its owner earthly riches but also eternal life. Alchemists have walked a weary path down through the centuries in their fruitless quest for the secret of this metal. They believed the discoverer of the philosopher's stone would be able to speed up the natural processes by which, according to alchemistic lore, metals evolve beneath the earth's surface from base lead to noble gold. Their search was in vain, but there was a nugget of truth in their belief: elements can be transmuted, both in the laboratory and in the earth's interior, where it has been happening since our planet was first formed. Tragically, however, once we gained this elemental knowledge of the secrets of matter it gave us the key not to eternal life, but to mass destruction on an almost unimaginable scale.

In a lecture delivered one year after the atomic bombing of Japan, Leo Szilard told a Chicago audience that the 'first and only successful alchemist' had been God. But when plutonium was created, fulfilling the dream of the ancient alchemists, the first use that humankind found for the new element was to create a bomb to destroy a city. 'I sometimes wonder,' said Szilard, 'whether the second successful alchemist may not have been the Devil himself'.[10]

The foundations of the Atomic Age were laid at the beginning of the twentieth century, creating both a new science and popular dreams of a utopia in which humankind had access to unlimited power. Szilard and his fellow atomic scientists grew up in this age of the atom. The hopes and fears provoked by this revolutionary science, expressed in fiction, newspaper articles and films, tell us as much about ourselves as they do about our understanding of the physical world. At times in this fantastic story, in which the dreams of the alchemists are realized and Strangelovean fantasies give birth to the 'Hell Bomb', science and fiction seem almost indistinguishable. To trace the roots of what Leo Szilard termed 'the tragedy of mankind' we need to follow the dream of the superweapon back to its origins in both scientific discovery and popular culture.[11]

The story of atoms begins in the fifth century BC. The Greek philosophers Leucippus and Democritus believed that matter was made up of unchanging, indestructible atoms. These were the smallest things in the physical world. Our word 'atom' comes from the Greek word *atomos*, meaning 'indivisible'. In 1803 John Dalton, a Manchester Quaker, revived atomism. In his hands it became a powerful tool in the dominant science of the nineteenth century – chemistry.

Dalton proposed a theory in which elements could be distinguished from one another by the relative weights of their atoms. The atoms of each element were unique, he said, and had the same weight. They could not be created nor destroyed, merely rearranged to form new compounds. It was impossible, said Dalton, for lead to change into another element, such as gold. To believe otherwise meant following in the footsteps of the alchemists.

Although there were lingering doubts as to whether atoms really existed, by the mid-nineteenth century Dalton's theory had been widely accepted. But exactly 100 years after Dalton's influential 1803 lecture, a new scientific era dawned. His axiom that no man would ever split an atom was about to be challenged.

Ernest Rutherford followed his wife, Mary, out into the night air. He was relieved to feel a slight breeze on his face. It was a sultry June evening and everyone was feeling uncomfortably warm – the women laced into constricting corsets, their husbands buttoned into starched collars and dinner jackets. It was a blessed relief to step out of the dining room and into the garden.

Earlier that day, Rutherford, who was visiting Paris, had called unannounced at Marie Curie's laboratory in the rue Cuvier. He had been surprised to find that for once she was not working at her bench. Instead, she was defending her doctoral thesis in the students' hall of the Sorbonne. Her four-year quest for new elements had been successful, and today, 25 June 1903, the examiners had given their scientific seal of approval to her arduous research.

Rutherford also called on his old friend Paul Langevin, whom he had known as a research student at Cambridge eight years earlier. Langevin immediately invited the Rutherfords to a celebratory dinner with the Curies at his villa opposite the Parc Montsouris, together with Sorbonne physicist Jean Perrin and his wife. Now, as they stood in Langevin's garden, Marie's husband, Pierre, suddenly drew a small glass vial from his waistcoat pocket. As he held it up against the night sky between his thumb and forefinger, a bright new star suddenly shone from the heavens. A soft, blue-green light illuminated their upturned faces. It was the new, luminous element that had made headline news around the world – radium.

Ernest and Mary would remember the moment for the rest of their lives. The vial was partly coated with zinc sulphide and contained a relatively large quantity of priceless radium in solution. 'The luminosity was brilliant in the darkness and it was a splendid finale to an unforgettable day,' wrote Ernest.[12] The dinner guests were transfixed by the ethereal radiation. It was as if they were seeing a light from another world, a strange realm that nobody yet fully understood.

The light of transmutation shone brightly in the Paris night. Rutherford and his co-worker Frederick Soddy had explained the previous year that in watching the glow they were seeing atoms of radium disintegrate, as the element transmuted down through Dmitri Mendeleev's periodic table towards dull, inactive lead. It was something everyone had thought was impossible. In the eerie light of the radium, Ernest could see that Pierre's hands, like those of his wife, were painfully swollen and scarred from constant exposure to the penetrating rays emitted by the radioactive element. He even seemed to have difficulty holding the tiny vial steady between his fingers.

The Curies had led the world in isolating the new radiant element and identifying its properties. Ernest Rutherford's work on the causes of radioactivity was similarly groundbreaking, but as yet his ideas, though published, were just hypotheses. So when Mary Rutherford asked over dinner where radium's energy came from, Pierre's reply was frank: 'We just don't know.' Had it absorbed the rays of the sun? Or did its energy come from some force within the element itself? No one could say for certain. 'We have made a discovery of forces and power beyond present knowledge, quite beyond imagination,' said

Marie and Pierre Curie pictured in a chromolithograph by 'Imp' from Vanity Fair *(1904).*

Pierre solemnly. 'It is a revolution ... we are walking into strange territory, a no man's land of scientific mystery.'

At 44, Pierre Curie was twelve years older than Ernest Rutherford. A tall and dignified man with a dark, neatly trimmed beard, he looked genuinely worried as they discussed the future uses to which their discovery might be put. Would the human race benefit from knowing these 'secrets of nature'? Looking round at the faces of his fellow diners that June evening, he asked a question that has since tormented many scientists: 'What if such a dangerous force falls into the hands of warring men?'[13]

Within a mere forty years, the power of the atom, revealed in the Curies' glowing vial of radium, would be released by a group of scientific refugees from Europe working in – of all places – a squash court on the campus of Chicago University. When the first plutonium bomb was detonated in the Nevada desert just before dawn on 16 July 1945, the flash of atomic light was so bright that it could have been seen from the moon. It was as if a second sun had risen in the sky, a new and terrible morning star, lighting the way to an uncertain future.

The last decade of the nineteenth century saw a series of astonishing discoveries about the nature of matter, culminating in the moment when Pierre Curie held aloft that beguiling vial of luminous radium. But the first hints of the new physics came from a small German university in 1895. It was a discovery that quite literally transformed our way of looking at ourselves and the world.

On a late November afternoon, a physicist at the University of Würzburg was setting up an experiment with a Crookes tube, a glass vacuum tube with wires sealed into each end which allowed an electric current to build up inside. It was named after the famous English chemist Sir William Crookes, who had pioneered the investigation of electrical discharges in vacuum tubes, principally what were called cathode rays. When the current to the tube was switched on, a violet or green glow could be seen starting at the positive (anode) end of the tube and gradually fading before it reached the negative (cathode) end.

The experimenter, Professor Wilhelm Conrad Röntgen, had constructed a box of black, light-proof card around the glass tube. He was fascinated by the tube's ability to create rays. Today he wanted to see if any could penetrate beyond its glass walls. But, as the electric current built up inside the tube, he became aware of a strange green glow coming from a bench a metre away. He switched the current off, and the glow faded.

When Röntgen switched the current back on again, his eyes were fixed on the adjacent bench. Again a green light shone out, as if something in the gloomy room had been 'smitten with a ray of bright sunshine'.[14] He struck a match and went over to investigate. On the bench he found a small cardboard screen coated with barium platino-cyanide, a chemical whose atoms emit light, or fluoresce, when struck by rays. Röntgen found that whenever the Crookes tube was charged with electricity, the screen glowed with its distinctive green light.

The 50-year-old physicist knew that he had made the discovery of his life. A mysterious ray was being generated in the Crookes tube and passing right through its lightproof covering. This was something quite new and unexpected. The rather staid professor became so absorbed in his astonishing discovery that he completely lost track of time. The clock ticking on the wall above his bench was forgotten. When he failed to return home for dinner, his puzzled wife dispatched a servant to find him. But as soon as he'd eaten, the distracted Röntgen grabbed his hat and coat and hurried back to the laboratory. There he continued exploring the mysterious rays late into the night. Indeed, so mysterious were these rays that Röntgen christened them 'X' for unknown – X-rays.

Over the course of the following days and nights he saw what no person had ever seen before. When he held his hand between the tube and the fluorescent screen, he could see a shadow of his hand cast by the invisible X-rays. But inside the shadow, Röntgen suddenly realized he could also see the bones of his own hand. It must have been a heart-stopping moment. He could see through his own flesh and blood! But what kind of rays could pass through human flesh? Soon Röntgen, a keen photographer, found that he could capture images with these unearthly rays, which travelled effortlessly through a thick book, a plank of wood and even a thin sheet of metal.

Wilhelm Röntgen was working such long hours that his wife began to fear for his health. So he finally plucked up the courage to tell her what he had discovered. When her husband said that he had found a way to see through solid objects, she must have thought he had taken leave of his senses. To prove that he was not mad, he placed her hand on a photographic plate and powered up the Crookes tube. When the plate was developed, his wife saw an image of the bones in her hand surrounded by a ghostly veil of insubstantial flesh. On one skeletal finger was the dark band of her wedding ring. It was an astonishing image, verging on the miraculous.

Another person at this time who saw his own hand X-rayed, described the experience: 'Every bone is perfect, even the cartilaginous spaces between being discernible. It is impossible to describe the feeling of awe that one experiences on actually seeing the image of his own skeleton within the enshrouding flesh.'[15] For Röntgen's wife, as for many people, the sight of her own bones was a chilling reminder of her own mortality.

Röntgen finally announced his discovery in a scientific journal at the end of December 1895. The news travelled fast and within days, the world's press was hailing his new rays as a 'marvellous triumph of science'.[16] Some readers simply didn't believe the newspaper reports, refusing 'to be hoodwinked by sensation-mongering journalists', as one writer put it.[17] But it was hard to ignore the evidence of your eyes. Soon X-ray photographs, like ghostly glimpses of a hidden world, were appearing in all the newspapers and journals of the day.

At a public lecture where Professor Röntgen demonstrated X-ray photography, the final images, or 'shadowgrams', were greeted with the kind of cheering and loud applause that was usually reserved for great theatrical performances. This was science for the common man. But emperors too were impressed. Kaiser Wilhelm II personally awarded Röntgen an important Prussian decoration after attending one of his lecture. The world was awestruck by the Röntgen rays, as they were soon being called, although never by their extremely modest discoverer.

According to one journal, 'civilized man found himself the astonished owner of a new and mysterious power'. The writer continued:

Never has a scientific discovery so completely and irresistibly taken the world by storm. Its results were of a kind sure to acquire prompt notoriety. The performances of 'Röntgen's rays' are obvious to the man in the street; they are repeated in every lecture-room; they are caricatured in comic prints; hits are manufactured out of them at the theatres; nay, they are personally interesting to every one afflicted with a gouty finger or a misshapen joint, and were turned to account, at the last Nottingham Assizes, to secure damages for an injury to a lady's ankle.[18]

In laboratories and law courts alike, Röntgen's discovery was the subject on everyone's lips. Visitors to the Crystal Palace Exhibition in London queued impatiently to see 'the Wondrous X Rays, the Greatest Scientific Discovery of the Age'. Posters promised that visitors would be able to 'Count the coins within your purse', although at a charge of threepence – a considerable sum for working people – those purses would be rather less full when they left than when they arrived.[19]

In 1896, newspapers were full of haunting, ethereal 'shadow pictures'. Among the many images were skeletal hands, a 'living but chloroformed mouse' whose diaphanous shoulder blades looked like 'the wings of a bee', a two-day-old puppy, a chicken with a broken leg laid out like a bony marionette, even an ancient Egyptian mummified bird stripped of its wrappings for the first time in thousands of years by the mysterious rays.[20] To the popular mind, Professor Röntgen was a scientific wizard, drawing back the veil of appearances so that people could gaze for the first time upon nature's hidden secrets.

The popular American magazine *McClure's* sent a reporter to interview the wizard of Würzburg in his laboratory. The room where the miraculous had been revealed was 'bare and unassuming to a degree'. Professor Röntgen entered his laboratory 'like an amiable gust of wind'. His 'whole appearance bespeaks enthusiasm and energy', claimed the man from *McClure's*, adding that 'his long, dark hair stood straight up from his forehead, as if he were permanently electrified by his own enthusiasm'. From Röntgen to Einstein, unruly hair has always been seized upon by journalists as a sign of eccentric genius if not incipient madness. Clearly, the figure of the scientist-inventor was as instantly recognizable in 1896 as he is today in characters such as Dr Emmett Brown from the *Back to the Future* films.

The reporter described the Professor as a Sherlock Holmes of science, 'a man who, once upon the track of a mystery which appealed to him, would pursue it with unremitting vigour'. Nevertheless, this scientific sleuth remained baffled by X-rays, as Röntgen frankly admitted to the awe-struck interviewer.

'Is it light?' asked the reporter.

'No,' replied the Professor.

'Is it electricity?'

'Not in any known form.'

'What is it?' asked the man, his voice hushed.

'I don't know.'[21]

America was engulfed by a wave of 'Röntgen mania'. The Professor himself was so appalled by the unscientific media frenzy that his first interview was also his last, and he withdrew forthwith from the limelight. But the damage had been done. Within two months of Röntgen's discovery hitting the headlines, Philadelphia and Chicago had sold out of Crookes tubes. A worried assemblyman in Somerset County, New Jersey, brought forward a bill in the State Legislature banning the use of X-ray opera glasses in the theatre. A similar concern for public decency led an English firm to market X-ray-proof underwear for ladies.

A contributor to *Photography* magazine put the salacious possibilities of Röntgen's discovery into verse:

> The Roentgen Rays, the Roentgen Rays,
> What is this craze:
> The town's ablaze
> With the new phase
> Of x-ray's ways.
> I'm full of daze,
> Shock and amaze,
> For now-a-days
> I hear they'll gaze
> Thro' cloak and gown – and even stays,
> These naughty, naughty Roentgen Rays.[22]

In February 1896, media mogul William Randolph Hearst telegraphed America's most famous scientist and inventor, Thomas Edison, asking for a 'cathodograph' of the living human brain.[23] Never one to turn down a good publicity opportunity, Edison agreed.

Expectant reporters staked out Edison's laboratory at West Orange, New Jersey, eager for news of this latest scientific marvel. Inside his 'invention factory', America's own Wizard worked day and night to capture the matter of the mind on a photographic plate.[24] Of course, it was impossible, and after three weeks of waiting in the cold the newshounds ran out of patience and departed.

Edison did, however, produce one of the first fluoroscopes, a device which enabled live, instantaneous X-ray images to be seen on a fluorescent screen. It must have been an extraordinary, almost revelatory experience for people at this time to see such images from within their own bodies. Ordinary moving pictures were scarcely a year old. Louis Lumière had patented his cinematograph in 1895. The technological innocence of people at this time is difficult to imagine in our own age of virtual reality. An audience at one of the first films by the Lumière brothers, *L'Arrivée d'un train en gare de La Ciotat* (1895), ran from their chairs at the sight of a train hurtling towards them from the screen.

Georges Méliès, the pioneer of the trick film, made one of the first movies about X-rays in 1897, although like others of its day it was just a minute long. In the film, *Les Rayons Roentgen*, a man steps behind a screen, where – lo and behold – the X-ray of his skeleton appears. But then, with masterly cinematic sleight of hand, the skeleton steps out from behind the screen and the man's empty skin drops to the floor. It's a superb visual joke, and the film ends with a slapstick explosion as the X-ray equipment blows up, killing the scientist.

When the American Wizard's fluoroscope went on public display, hundreds waited in line to see 'Edison's Beneficient [sic] X-ray Exhibit'.[25] The savvy inventor was soon marketing the 'Thomas A. Edison X-ray Kit' and even produced a hand-held X-ray device. As the craze gripped the nation, an Iowa farmer claimed to have transmuted a piece of metal worth 13 cents into $153 worth of gold by using X-rays. It was even suggested by a New York newspaper that the College of Physicians and Surgeons were using X-rays 'to reflect anatomic improvement on the ordinary methods of learning'.[26] Such was the public hunger for miraculous science that, within a year of their discovery, over a thousand articles and fifty books had been published on X-rays.

The medical potential of Röntgen's new technique for seeing inside bodies was immediately realized. The veil of flesh could now be withdrawn at will, with obvious diagnostic applications. One of the first medical X-rays shows a needle in the foot of a Manchester dancing girl, taken just weeks after Röntgen's announcement. Such was the eagerness of medics to find people to X-ray that one wit commented that 'suitable patients are at a premium. A woman who has absorbed a needle, a man harbouring a projectile, is a *persona grata* at every Surgical Institute in the Old and New Worlds.'[27]

On the battlefield, bicycle-powered X-ray machines, which looked as though they had been designed by Heath Robinson, effortlessly located bullets in bodies. Surgeons no longer needed their often inadequately sterilized probe: 'Modern science has provided the surgeons with a probe which is painless, which is exact, and, most important of all, which is aseptic'.[28]

Thomas Mann's classic novel *The Magic Mountain* (1924) explores the attitudes of a generation doomed to die in the trenches of World War I. This pathology of an age sleepwalking towards the abyss of war is set in a sanatorium in the Swiss mountain resort of Davos. Here the main character, Hans Castorp, has his first X-ray. The gloomy X-ray laboratory smells of 'stale ozone' and reminds him of a 'technological witches' kitchen'. The radiologist proclaims X-rays as a 'triumph of the age' and, like a conjuror, announces the start of the process: 'The magicking is about to begin!' With these words his assistant pulls a lever and releases an electrical display worthy of any mad scientist's laboratory:

Now, for the space of two seconds, fearful powers were in play – streams of thousands, of a hundred thousand of volts, Hans Castorp seemed to recall – which were necessary to pierce through solid matter. They could hardly be confined to their office, they tried to escape through other outlets: there were explosions like pistol-shots, blue sparks on the measuring apparatus; long lightnings crackled along the walls.[29]

Hans Castorp's cousin is the first to be examined with the fluoroscope. Castorp watches, fascinated by 'a bag, a strange, animal shape' which 'expanded and contracted regularly, a little after the fashion of a swimming jelly-fish'. Suddenly, he realizes what it is. Castorp is shocked: 'Good God, it was the heart . . .' This glimpse into the living body of his cousin is a profoundly moving experience for Castorp. He is overwhelmed by conflicting emotions. Although he is unable to take his eyes away from the image of 'this lean *memento mori*', he feels that it is forbidden knowledge, something no one should see. As he looks at his own hand rendered translucent on the fluoroscope's screen, he realizes why he feels so ambivalent:

And Hans Castorp saw, precisely what he must have expected, but what it is hardly permitted man to see: he looked into his own grave. The process of decay was forestalled by the powers of the light-ray, the flesh in which he walked disintegrated, annihilated, dissolved in vacant mist, and there within it was the finely turned skeleton of his own hand, the seal ring he had inherited from his grandfather – a hard, material object, with which man adorns the body that is fated to melt away beneath it, when it passes on to another flesh that can wear it yet a little while . . . He gazed at this familiar part of his own body, and for the first time in his life he understood that he would die.[30]

At Davos, the X-ray machine is invaluable in diagnosing tuberculosis. Elsewhere the therapeutic uses of the rays were also rapidly exploited, often with dubious results. In December 1896, a Viennese doctor used X-rays to treat a five-year-old girl with hirsutism, a condition in which too much hair grows on the body. Her back was exposed to X-rays for two hours a day for sixteen days. The unwanted hair did indeed fall out, but at a high cost to the patient: the poor child's back became acutely inflamed, as if she had been badly scalded. 'This accident was full of instruction,' observed her doctor dryly, before reducing the X-ray treatment to ten minutes a day.[31] Elsewhere, doctors began prescribing what were known as 'X-ray séances' to cure everything from cancer to painful inflammations.[32]

Scientists had little understanding of what X-rays were or what effects they had on the body. Their use posed grave risks to both patient and radiologist. Long exposures were needed for photographs: forty minutes was not uncommon. By the end of 1896, twenty-three incidents of burns had been reported. In March that year, the great Wizard himself, Edison, noted that his eyes were sore after experimenting with X-rays. His assistant, Clarence Dally, suffered rather more serious injury. He was fated to become the first of many 'martyrs to science through the Roentgen rays', to quote the title of a book by a radiologist who himself died of cancer.[33]

High-energy electromagnetic radiation, such as X-rays, can punch electrons out of atoms. This results in atoms becoming electrically charged, a process known as ionization. Such ionized atoms can be highly unstable. In living tissue they can cause changes leading to serious genetic damage, illness and ultimately death. But X-ray injuries often take time to appear, and for many years the full dangers went unrecognized.

Dally worked with X-rays for several years with little or no protection. Initially he was helping Edison develop an X-ray light bulb for mass production. But when Dally's hair fell out and he developed painful ulcers that refused to heal, Edison wisely decided that 'it would not be a very popular kind of light', and dropped the idea.[34] However, Dally continued to work with X-rays, and it was not long before his radiation burns developed into cancer. Eventually, his left arm was amputated up to the elbow and his right removed up to the shoulder, but even these drastic measures failed to save him. He died in 1904 at the age of 39. In 1936 a monument was erected in Hamburg to the X-ray and radium martyrs. Initially only 169 names were remembered, but by 1959 that death toll had risen to 360. Although Röntgen's name is not one of them, Marie Curie's is.

While X-rays were celebrated by journalists, fiction writers highlighted the potential dangers of this new knowledge. Just weeks after the discovery of X-rays, a wonderfully grotesque short story called 'Röntgen's Curse' was published in the popular *Longman's Magazine*. Written by C. H. T. Crosthwaite, it tells how a scientist named Herbert Newton is determined to make a great discovery and be 'hailed as the greatest benefactor of the human race in modern times'. Inspired by the possibilities of Röntgen's 'photography of the invisible', Newton feels there's 'no limit to the power which might be acquired by one who could make the X-rays his servants, and compel them to obey him'.[35]

Newton's dream is to go far beyond what Röntgen achieved: 'I would not rest until the physician should be able to see and examine any part of the human organism ... as if he had the eye of the Creator.' Like Mary Shelley's Dr Frankenstein, Newton has Promethean ambitions: he dreams of 'snatching from Nature the secret of life itself'. Newton becomes obsessed with this quest, shutting himself away from his family night and day in his laboratory, until finally the ultimate prize is within his grasp.[36]

H. G. Wells's classic 'scientific romance' *The Invisible Man* was published the following year. Griffin, the archetypal mad scientist, denies that his discovery depends on 'these Röntgen vibrations'. Nevertheless, in order to make objects transparent by lowering their 'refractive index', he exposes them to 'two radiating centres of a sort of ethereal vibration'. In a period obsessed with mysterious rays, some form of radiation had to be involved in Wells's fantastic scientific experiment. The chilling description of Griffin watching his body gradually disappear is imaginable only in an age of X-ray photography. Griffin briefly becomes a living X-ray photograph, before vanishing altogether.[37]

In 'Röntgen's Curse', Newton exploits X-rays in an altogether different way. His great discovery is to invent a chemical that when dropped into the eye makes X-rays visible: 'I was satisfied that I had made one of the most wonderful discoveries of modern times ... I had in my grasp a talisman that would unlock for me the secrets of the universe. The fruit of the tree of knowledge hung within my reach. Ambition, desire, curiosity, tempted me. I must eat of it, even if the penalty were death, or worse.'[38]

But the moment Newton gazes on the world with X-ray vision he realizes that to see everything as if 'with the Divine eye' is truly terrible. Whatever he looks at, except metal, is now transparent to his gaze: 'It was a ghastly and sickening sight to look down at my legs and body and see the bare bones of my own skeleton ...' But there is worse to come. As he sits down with his family for breakfast, the sight of them stripped of flesh threatens to drive him insane:

I was not ill, I was not mad. It was childish and foolish to be thus upset by the sight of the human frame. I reasoned with myself, and tried to conquer and overcome my disgust, but it was impossible. It was not merely that I saw my family in the form of skeletons sitting around me. The horror lay in the life of the skeletons. They were not like the dry bones in a museum of anatomy or in the valley of death. They looked fresh and clammy, and the skulls wagged and mouthed at me in a manner that made my skin creep with disgust to see them eating or pretending to eat, lifting the bony fingers to the gumless jaws, which they moved in the act of chewing.[39]

This delightfully farcical moment brings the reality and horror of modern science into the genteel Victorian dining room. The chilling *memento mori* of the X-ray intrudes into the heart of that most sacred nineteenth-century institution, the family. Having made the discovery of the century, Newton realizes that he cannot even tell his wife what he has achieved lest she feels 'outraged and offended that I should see her thus'. The advance of science is nothing compared to the sense of propriety of a Victorian lady.[40]

Unable to reveal his triumph, Newton creeps dejectedly to his bed where gradually the effects of the chemical wear off. The scientist is forced to confront the result of his hubris. He has succeeded in making a real scientific discovery, but, unlike his illustrious namesake, Newton finds that he is not made of the 'stuff of which the pioneers and heroes of science are made'. When, after several days, he recovers enough to leave his bed, Newton is almost relieved to find that his wife has cleared out his laboratory and converted it into a billiard room.[41]

At the end of the nineteenth century, writers and scientists alike dreamed of the godlike power that nature's secrets would give them. But X-rays reminded people of their own mortality: they were not gods after all, but mere flesh and bone. 'Röntgen's Curse' exposes the flip side of science. Newton is appalled by the remarkable power he discovers; he even gives his secret discovery away. Wells's invisible man also finds his discovery has unexpected and tragic consequences: Griffin is corrupted by the desire for scientific power and dreams of a rule of terror over his fellow man. Ultimately, invisibility brings him nothing but an early and violent death.

Stories of scientists obsessed by the desire for knowledge, heedless of house and home, were not new. They begin with tales of medieval alchemists, the first searchers for forbidden natural knowledge. Chaucer's *Canon's Yeoman's Tale* (1387) is one of the earliest. Chaucer's alchemist is, we learn, 'to wys, in feith, as I bileeve . . . For whan a man hath over-greet a wit, / Ful oft hym happeth to mys-usen it.' This moral has travelled down the centuries, being found in the many versions of the story of Dr Faustus, a real sixteenth-century necromancer and all-round rogue, as well as in Mary Shelley's classic study of scientific arrogance, *Frankenstein* (1818). Knowledge reveals many wonders, but, as Herbert Newton and Wells's Invisible Man found to their cost, it is a fickle genie, one who can turn on his master without warning.

Like 'Röntgen's Curse', Honoré de Balzac's novel of extreme chemistry, *Quest for the Absolute* (1834), cautioned its bourgeois readers that the secrets of nature can be gained only at a high cost to the individual scientist. By the end of the century, H. G. Wells's *Island of Dr Moreau* suggested that the price of such knowledge might be the scientist's very humanity. As we shall see, from Dr Moreau to Dr Strangelove is but a small step.

The readers of popular magazines at the beginning of the twentieth century were enthralled by scientific stories such as 'Röntgen's Curse'. This appetite for scientific romances was encouraged first by the immensely popular adventures of Jules Verne and then by Wells's short stories and novels, fictions which broadened the childhood horizons of Edward Teller, Leo Szilard and many others. In the pages of these journals, fact and fiction rubbed shoulders. Stories by Wells about fictional scientists might be printed in the same issue as a factual article about the miracle of X-ray photography or the next great scientific wonder. A public which had little scientific education was thrilled by tales of Promethean struggles in the laboratory, whether they were imagined or true. Science was hot news, and Röntgen and other scientists were heroes, modern-day wizards who held their audiences spellbound with the wonders of nature and who promised to conjure them a brave new technological future. Science was going to change the world.

4

Nature's Secrets

The All-Master sealed a symbol of His might
Within a stone, and to a woman's eye
Revealed the wonder. Lo, infinity
Wrapped in an atom – molecules of light
Outshining centuries! No mortal sight
May fathom in this grain the galaxy
Of suns, moons, planets, hurled unceasingly
Out of their glowing system into the night.
John Hall Ingham, 'Radium' (1904)

As the new century dawned, forecasters confidently predicted that an age of 'universal progress' was about to begin, with science and technology in the vanguard.[1] The illustrated monthly magazines, which had revolutionized the reading habits of millions of ordinary people in Britain and America, were the heralds of this new age. The nineteenth century had been, to quote the populist *Strand Magazine*, 'the century of Science writ largest'. Science had fathered inventions which had utterly transformed society: 'railways and steamships, telegraphs and telephones, electric lighting and traction, the phonograph and the motor-car, Röntgen's rays and Marconi's messages'. No one could doubt that the twentieth century would more than match this 'record of the marvellous'.[2]

Of course, not everyone was happy with this brave new world. In 1907 one American commentator complained bitterly that 'the scientific spirit seems now to dominate everything. The world in future is to be governed from the laboratory.'[3] But this was a minority view.

W. J. Wintle, writing in the *Harmsworth Magazine*, asked: 'Will the world be better and happier in the new century?' His answer was 'unquestionably in the affirmative' because '[s]cientific progress tends to moral advancement'.[4] The mechanized slaughter of World War I would show just how little progress had been made in the field of morality. But thirteen years before this war to end wars broke out, the *Harmsworth* could still beguile its readers with the technological wonders of tomorrow's world.

Mr Wintle thought that by 'the end of the twentieth century the man in the street' would look back on 1901 and 'wonder how his ancestors could have existed with such a lack of the conveniences to which he himself is accustomed'. Wintle confidently predicted that wireless pocket telegraphy would mean that businessmen were never out of touch with the office, even when in the restaurant. The 'electro-scope' would enable people 'to watch a scene at a distance of hundreds of miles'. It scarcely needed to be said that this invention would be must-have technology for 'busy men, who cannot attend the races'. In the field of war, Wintle anticipated that electric machine guns firing bullets at a rate of 3,000 a minute and mines detonated remotely by 'Hertzian waves' would revolutionize combat.[5] Mobile phones, television, and radio-controlled bombs – Wintle's predictions were not so far off the mark.

Whereas steam had driven the industrialized nineteenth century, it was clear by 1901 that electricity would be the energy of the twentieth. As Wintle put it, 'electricity is the secret of progress'.[6] Electric light was still something of a novelty. Albert Einstein was born in 1879, the year the incandescent light bulb was independently invented by Edison and Joseph Swan. In 1901, when a reporter visited Swan, he observed enviously that 'electricity was much in evidence in Mr Swan's own house; everywhere electric lights and bells'.[7]

The Einstein family business, run by the young physicist's father and uncle, was in the vanguard of the energy revolution, designing electricity supply systems and other electro-technologies. Based as they were in Munich, their firm had the honour of supplying the first electric lighting to that great Bavarian cultural event, the *Oktober-fest*, though Einstein himself took a dim view of beer-drinking. The Einsteins were not alone in trying to exploit the potential of this new power. More than five hundred inventions a week were registered at the British Patent Office in the first year of the new century.

H. G. Wells's story 'Lord of the Dynamos' (1895) depicts electricity as the power behind the modern mechanized metropolis. The electric

Illustration for W. J. Wintle's 1901 article 'Life in Our New Century'. The caption read: 'The coming of the airship will necessitate roof stations. This is our artist's suggestion for one at the Mansion House Corner, London.'

dynamos in the story were futuristic gods whose power could be used for good or evil, like all scientific advances. In 1900 the historian Henry Adams toured the Exposition Universelle in Paris. For Adams, born in 1838, the dynamo was as mysterious as religion, an 'occult mechanism' beyond his comprehension. The connection between 'steam and the electric current' was no more graspable to him than that between the 'Cross and the cathedral'. The forty-foot-high dynamos on show at this world fair in the French capital were the embodiment of 'silent and infinite force': 'Among the thousand symbols of ultimate energy, the dynamo was not so human as some, but it was the most expressive.'[8]

The English aristocrat and novelist Edward Bulwer-Lytton was equally enthralled by electricity. In his 1871 Darwinist fantasy, *The Coming Race*, an American engineer stumbles across a subterranean civilization while exploring a deep mine. The beautiful yet ruthless people he discovers have created an aristocratic utopia using the power of an inexhaustible energy called vril. This energy flows through all matter and combines the properties of electricity and magnetism as well as mental energy. The people are called Vril-ya after their miraculous energy. It even gives them the ability to read minds and control inanimate matter at will.

The Vril-ya use this energy to give life to humanoid machines – robots. With their mechanical, vril-powered wings, these tall, sphinx-like beings are unmistakably angelic. This utopian society has abolished war, crime and envy. Yet, true to evolutionary principles, the Vril-ya are merciless towards neighbouring, less advanced peoples. They regard our surface-dwelling species as uncivilized and believe it is their destiny to eliminate us and take control of the earth.

Vril is a truly awe-inspiring energy source, and humans would have stood no chance on the battlefield, at least in the 1870s. The narrator describes 'tubes' of vril that could be fired at any object up to six hundred miles away. These missiles could, says the narrator, 'reduce to ashes within a space of time too short for me to venture to specify it, a capital twice as vast as London'. The 'terrible force of vril' can also be directed using a 'Vril Staff' in the form of an energy beam. Its power reduces bodies to 'a blackened, charred, smouldering mass . . . rapidly crumbling into dust and ashes'.[9]

The overwhelming power of vril brings 'the art of destruction to such perfection' that no army can stand against it and win. For this reason, the 'age of war' has ended for the Vril-ya, who realized that a war between two armies equipped with this force could result only in mutual annihilation. The force of the Vril Staff could also be modified, 'so that by one process it destroys, by another it heals'. The 'life-giving' force of vril has enabled these people to live well beyond a human lifespan and to banish disease.[10]

Bulwer-Lytton's popular novel raised an immensely influential idea that was to take hold in the following century: that the discovery of an inexhaustible energy source would transform society into a utopia. The super-energy would produce superweapons so destructive that war would be redundant. Economic prosperity, social harmony, long life, good health and peace – all would flow from the new energy source. For Bulwer-Lytton, writing in the shadow of Darwin, it was an evolutionary step that would lead to the emergence of a super-race.

Edward Bulwer-Lytton was inspired by electricity to dream up vril. Its miraculous properties would be attributed first to radium and later to atomic energy. From its medical benefits to its destructive power, radium was soon heralded as the energy source that would transform society. Indeed, some even claimed that Bulwer-Lytton had predicted its discovery.[11] Today the name vril still lives on, although not in quite the way Bulwer-Lytton might have wanted. It was hijacked by John Lawson Johnston, from Scotland, who wanted a catchy name for his new invention, 'fluid beef', which he decided to call Bovril.

These days, scarcely a week passes without a news story about a new application of genetics that promises to save lives. Similarly, at the turn of the century, reports about scientific advances that would lead to cheap and limitless energy beguiled readers many of whose homes were still lit by gaslight. One report told how the 'world-renowned' French chemist Marcelin Berthelot had pinned his hopes for 'limitless energy' on exploiting the heat at the centre of the earth: 'We shall find in this heat the support of all life and all industry.'[12] In 1899, one of the strangest of such schemes, based on the novel qualities of 'liquid air', was hailed by the press as a revolution. New York inventor Charles E. Tripler astounded a reporter from McClure's by reducing 'the air of his laboratory to a clear, sparkling liquid that boils on ice, freezes pure alcohol, and burns steel like tissue paper'.

Air forms a liquid at −196°C, and its constituent gases begin to boil at temperatures just above this. With his patented machine for producing large quantities of liquid air, Tripler claimed to be able to run an engine on nothing but thin air. The initially sceptical reporter watched as Tripler poured his liquid air into the engine. His eyes widened as within seconds the piston began to pump vigorously, driving the flywheel: 'the little engine stood there in the middle of the room running apparently without motive power, making no noise and giving out no heat or smoke, and producing no ashes'.[13]

It was indeed an 'almost inconceivable marvel', and Tripler confidently predicted that coal and wood would soon be redundant as fuels. As he reasonably pointed out, 'air is the cheapest material in the world'. Still more revolutionary was his claim to be able to create more liquid air with his machine than it took to power the engine. That meant he had discovered the holy grail of energy: a way of generating free power.

Charles Tripler's vision of boilerless ocean liners and locomotives running on nothing but air had investors and eternal optimists flocking to his door. A stock company valued at $20 million was soon formed to put the discovery to commercial use. Utopia was just around the corner, or so they thought. Of course, Tripler never managed to create free energy, and his idea joined all the other perpetual motion machines on the scrapheap of science.[14]

At the same time as Tripler was beguiling American investors with an energy source that defied the laws of thermodynamics, another, rather more promising discovery was being made in Paris: the mysteriously glowing element radium. Sir William Crookes, inventor of the tube that led to the discovery of X-rays, was not one to be taken in by outlandish tales of perpetual motion. But even he was willing to admit in 1901 that radium was a whole new ballgame. The dapper Sir William, sporting an immaculately trimmed white goatee and finely twirled mustachios, told a journalist that 'as an example of seemingly continuous energy – something of which we had previously no conception – who can tell of what fresh achievement it may be the forerunner?'[15]

*

Umberto Eco's *The Name of the Rose* is a dark novel about zealotry and forbidden knowledge. The Franciscan monk Brother William of Baskerville, whose name hints knowingly at the scientific detective Sherlock Holmes, is investigating a series of monastic murders. He has a keen eye for 'the evidence through which the world speaks to us like a great book'.[16] The solution to this medieval mystery seems to lie in a profane manuscript which was read by all the victims. In this godly community, someone wants to teach the monks a lethal lesson about the dangers of forbidden knowledge.

This fatal manuscript has its deadly equivalent in the atomic age. For there is a real text whose pages are literally lethal to its readers. The three black notebooks used by Marie Curie in her experiments from December 1897 are still so radioactive that they have to be kept in a lead safe in the Bibliothèque Nationale in Paris. Anyone wishing to consult them must sign a form acknowledging that they are aware of the risks. They are among the most haunting documents of the atomic age.

The Curies' makeshift laboratory, its furniture and Marie's notebooks became radioactive by contact with the chemicals processed by the first two atomic scientists. Visitors at the time reported that the walls of the laboratory 'glow visibly at night'.[17] Marie Curie died in 1934 of leukaemia contracted through her exposure to radioactivity.

It was Henri Becquerel's discovery of natural radioactivity, a few months after Röntgen's X-rays were revealed, that propelled Marie Curie into her dangerous quest for radioactive elements. Unlike Röntgen's X-rays, the discovery of the so-called Becquerel rays provoked little public interest. But the fact that uranium emitted rays apparently similar to X-rays had a greater impact on the course of the next century than any other scientific discovery.

Henri Becquerel came from a thoroughly scientific family. His father and grandfather had both been eminent scientists. Becquerel's own son would also follow in his father's footsteps. In the 1840s, Becquerel's grandfather told his son: 'I will never be satisfied with explanations they give why some chemicals and minerals shine in the dark. Fluorescence is a deep mystery and nature will not give up the secret easily.'[18] Father and son dedicated their lives to the study of this strange phenomenon, which most people thought was caused by the slow release of absorbed sunlight.

When Becquerel heard that Röntgen had discovered rays that could affect photographic plates, he began investigating whether visible fluorescence was accompanied by invisible X-rays. He assumed that sunlight was needed to make the fluorescent chemicals active, and so his experiment consisted of leaving sealed photographic plates, on which some uranium sulphate had been placed, out in the sun. But a spell of cloudy weather intervened, and Becquerel put his experimental apparatus away, locking the uranium sulphate and the photographic plate in a dark drawer. It was lucky that he did, and even more fortunate that he later decided to develop the plate. For when he did so, he was amazed to see an image. By the end of February 1896 he could tell the French Academy of Sciences that 'there is an emission of rays without apparent cause. The sun has been excluded.'[19] It was an astonishing discovery: matter produced rays which came not from the sun but from some unknown energy source deep within itself.

By the end of 1897, Marie Curie had just given birth to her first child, Irène. The 30-year-old chemist was now on the lookout for a suitable subject for her doctoral thesis. She was intrigued by the idea of Becquerel rays, and set about investigating them by testing as many metals and minerals as she could. Both Becquerel rays and X-rays had the unusual effect of enabling air to conduct electricity, and Curie began looking for elements with this property. She soon found that the dark, lustrous mineral pitchblende, which contains uranium, made air more conductive than pure uranium. This suggested the presence of some other element that was a more powerful emitter of Becquerel rays than even uranium. Curie had found a subject for a doctorate: isolating whatever substance was responsible, and explaining the phenomenon that Becquerel had discovered. She set to work using pitchblende from the mines of St Joachimsthal in Bohemia (Jáchymov in today's Czech Republic).

Ernest Merritt, Professor of Physics at Cornell University, introduced Marie Curie's discoveries to the readers of a contemporary popular magazine. He came up with an apt analogy to describe the difficulty of the task Curie faced in separating radium from pitchblende. Her job, he said, was like that of a 'detective who starts out to find a suspected criminal in a crowded street'. Pitchblende, a heavy brown-black uranium ore, is 'one of the most complex of minerals, containing twenty or thirty different elements, combined in a great variety of ways'.[20] There is a single gram of radium in seven tons of pitchblende. But Marie Curie was a remarkable and tenacious chemical detective.

Merritt's article was accompanied by two striking illustrations. One was a photograph of a chunk of pitchblende in normal light. The other was rather more dramatic. It was taken by placing the rock directly onto a photographic plate. No camera was used: the Becquerel rays themselves made the exposure. In this photograph, said Merritt, 'every crack and seam where radium is present has made its impression, while the ordinary rock in which the ore is embedded has left no trace'.[21] This rock looks like a volcano at night, with glowing lava streaming down its fissures. The photograph creates an eerie impression, and powerfully evokes the hidden forces within matter. Many of the first fictional descriptions of atomic explosions would liken them to erupting volcanoes.

Formed billions of years ago in the hearts of stars which exploded as supernovae, blasting their contents through our Galaxy, uranium provides the main source of heat within our planet. The heat from its radioactive decay also drives the tectonic shifting of the continents. Ironically, given the future importance of uranium in the development of nuclear weapons, Merritt comments: 'If uranium had proved to be the only radioactive substance, I doubt whether the subject would have aroused very general interest.' It seems scarcely believable, but in 1904, uranium seemed a rather unexciting element. In contrast, the properties of radium were dramatic and, most importantly for the media, photogenic. For as Professor Merritt commented dryly, 'the scientific investigator is by no means devoid of the taste for something sensational'.[22]

By the end of 1898, Marie Curie had returned from what Merritt called her 'journey into an unexplored land' with truly sensational news – not one but two new elements.[23] It had taken her a year. The first one she named polonium, in honour of her Polish homeland. The other she called radium, from the Latin for ray, *radius*. In her scientific papers announcing the new elements, she also coined the term 'radio-activity'.

Polonium is more radioactive than radium or uranium. A milligram of polonium-210 emits as many alpha particles as 5 grams of radium. A capsule containing half a gram of polonium-210 can reach a temperature of 500°C and provide a lightweight heat source to power thermoelectric cells in artificial satellites. But polonium is also more difficult to isolate. There are about 100 micrograms in a ton of uranium ore. Isolating it is like finding a grain of salt in a sack of sugar.

Like polonium, radium is luminescent, and has a blue glow. 'The light given out is sometimes so bright that it is possible to read by it,' Merritt told his readers.[24] Marie Curie once talked about the joy she felt on entering her laboratory at night and seeing the rows of faintly glowing tubes. They were like fairy lights, she said. She even used to keep some radium salts by her bed so she could see it glowing in the dark – an atomic nightlight. Radium metal is pure white but blackens in air. It emits alpha, beta and gamma rays. Radium-226 loses just 1 per cent of its radioactivity in 25 years, decomposing ultimately into lead. Its rays cause diamonds to shine 'with a clear phosphorescent light'.[25] Imitation stones do not, as more than one shocked lady attending a lecture on radium discovered to her cost. But radium rays are also dangerous. Marie and Pierre Curie soon found that exposure for just five minutes was enough to produce nasty sores, although strangely these did not appear for several days.

From 1899, Marie Curie worked her way through tons of pitch-blende, delivered to her from the St Joachimsthal mine. Mixed in with the sackfuls of reddish-brown dust were pine needles from the Bohemian forest where the pitchblende had been dumped after the uranium had been extracted. Marie did the chemical work of separation while Pierre concentrated on the theoretical physics. The Ecole de Physique et de Chimie Industrielles in Paris, where Pierre taught, gave the Curies a disused medical dissection room to work in. Marie described it as 'a wooden shed with a bituminous floor and a glass roof which did not keep the rain out'.[26] The Chemist Wilhelm Ostwald called it a cross between a stable and a potato shed. Boiling hot in summer and freezing in winter, it was totally inadequate as a laboratory. But Marie Curie was not one to complain.

Although she appeared shy and reserved to those who met her for the first time, Curie was in fact a determined and single-minded woman. By all accounts she relished what was a formidable challenge of separating out the new elements: 'I had to work with as much as 20 kilograms of material at a time, so that the hangar was filled with great vessels full of precipitates and of liquids. It was exhausting work to move the containers about, to transfer the liquids, and to stir for hours at a time, with an iron bar, the boiling material in the cast-iron basin.'[27]

It took Marie Curie almost four years of back-breaking work to isolate one-tenth of a gram of radium chloride. By July 1902, she had enough to convince even the sceptical world of science 'that radium is truly a new element'.[28] The result of her dangerous labours was a rather ordinary-looking substance: white crystals, like coarse-grained salt. But as Merritt told his readers in 1904, 'a pinch of this innocent-looking salt costs more than a thousand dollars'.[29] Radium was at least a hundred times more valuable than gold.[30] This was far more than even the alchemists could have dreamed of. But more important than its monetary value was the wealth of knowledge it promised. As one contemporary put it, locked up in this 'strange substance' were all 'the riddles of matter and energy'.[31]

The twentieth century has been called the century of the electron, the subatomic particle that makes possible our electronic computer age. In the year that Marie Curie began her search for new radioactive elements, on the other side of the English Channel a Cambridge physicist, J. J. Thomson, made the first discovery of a particle smaller than an atom – the negatively charged electron. It enabled Thomson to construct a theory of atomic structure that would later become known by the rather wonderful name of the plum pudding model (or, as Thomson himself put it rather less memorably, 'a number of negatively electrified corpuscles enclosed in a sphere of uniform positive electrification.'[32])

According to Thomson, electrons were unimaginably small, a mere fraction of the size of the smallest atom, hydrogen, which was itself so tiny that a crowd of them 'equal in number to the population of the whole world would be too small to have been detected by any means then known to science'.[33] In fact, there is no consensus on its size, or even on what 'size' really means when applied to the electron. Estimates vary from 20,000 times smaller than an atom, right down to it being a dimensionless point. The electron possesses charge, and is responsible for creating electric fields and thus magnetic fields. These in turn give rise to electromagnetic waves: radiation across a huge spectrum of wavelength and frequency, from radio waves, through visible light, to X-rays and gamma rays. The existence of this subatomic particle was the first evidence that atoms were not solid and might even be divisible. John Dalton's atomic theory, which had ruled unchallenged for a century, suddenly looked distinctly shaky. Was it possible that atoms could be split after all?

In 1898, J. J. Thomson's brilliant 27-year-old assistant, Ernest Rutherford, deepened the understanding of atomic structure still further by identifying and naming alpha, beta and gamma rays as forms of radiation. All radiation is dangerous to humans but some forms are more harmful than others. Alpha radiation consists of relatively heavy particles (the positively charged nuclei of helium atoms) which can be easily stopped, even by a sheet of paper. Beta radiation is more penetrating and can cause skin injury. It consists of lighter particles, which were later realized to be electrons. Like light and X-rays, gamma rays are forms of electromagnetic radiation. They can travel several metres through air and are extremely dangerous, potentially lethal. Cobalt-60, the radioactive product of the deadly cobalt bomb discussed at the Round Table in 1950, is a powerful source of gamma radiation.

Ernest Rutherford was born in New Zealand, to where his grandfather, a wheelwright from Dundee, Scotland, had emigrated in 1843. After graduating with a double first in mathematics and physical science from Canterbury College, Christchurch, he won a scholarship to Cambridge in 1894. According to those who knew him, Rutherford never quite lost the gruff manner of a pipe-smoking colonial farmer. He was, said Paul Langevin, a 'force of nature'.[34] Another colleague compared him to a battleship ploughing through a stormy sea. A brilliant experimentalist who famously commented that all science was either physics or stamp collecting, Rutherford was notoriously sceptical about new theories. A visitor to Cambridge's Cavendish

THE DREAM

Laboratory, which he directed in typically no-nonsense style from 1919, once asked about the significance of Einstein's theories. 'That stuff!' harrumphed Rutherford. 'We never bother with that in our work.'[35]

Following his researches with Thomson at the Cavendish, Rutherford was offered the Macdonald Chair of Physics at McGill University, Montreal, in 1898. Once there, Rutherford focused all his energies on understanding radioactivity. He had noticed that, like radium, the naturally radioactive element thorium produced a gas, or 'emanation' as it was then called. In October 1901 he asked the 24-year-old chemist Frederick Soddy to find out what it was. Soddy, born at Eastbourne in Sussex, had spent a couple of years researching at Oxford before taking a post as chemistry demonstrator at McGill. He recalled that at this time Rutherford was an 'exuberant, natural young man with a moustache and breezy manner, full of the *joie de vivre* of the indefatigable investigator . . . There was a spirit of adventure about him coupled with a dogged determination to reach his quest.'[36]

The two men became acquainted at a meeting where Soddy had presented a paper on the indivisibility of the atom. He engaged in a characteristically robust debate with the physicists – including Rutherford – arguing against the existence of subatomic particles, and concluded with the comment: 'I feel sure chemists will retain a belief in, and a reverence for, atoms as concrete and permanent entities, if not immutable, certainly not yet transmuted.'[37] But when Soddy investigated the problem Rutherford had set him, he found that the thorium emanation or 'thoron' was an inert gas, possibly argon (it was subsequently identified as an isotope of radon). If true, this was a shocking discovery. How was it possible that the element thorium, a solid, was turning into another element, a gas? According to Dalton and everything that Soddy had ever been taught, elements could not change. Transmuting one element into another was the preserve of alchemists.

It was true that some people, even at the dawn of the twentieth century, still clung doggedly to the dreams of alchemy. The Swedish playwright August Strindberg became obsessed with transmuting lead oxide into gold in the 1890s. He even published a text on chemistry, *Antibarbarus*, in 1894 and claimed to have successfully created gold.

Despite his hopes of winning the Nobel Prize in Chemistry, few believed him, due in part to his unconventional views on science. Strindberg had once been spotted by the owner of an open-air restaurant injecting an apple hanging from a tree with a syringe full of morphia. When the worried owner asked what he was doing, Strindberg replied that he wanted to observe the apple's reaction. 'I am a botanist,' he explained. The *patron* decided he was probably from the nearby asylum.[38]

Such eccentric behaviour might be expected of a man who claimed to be walking in the footsteps of the alchemists. But Frederick Soddy was a trained chemist, and the most eccentric thing Rutherford ever did was to stride around his laboratory singing 'Onward Christian Soldiers'. Nevertheless, Soddy could see that there was no alternative explanation: 'if a chemist were to separate, say, silver from lead and found that as fast as he separated it the silver reformed in the lead, the only possible conclusion would be that lead was changing spontaneously into silver'.[39] He recalled turning to his colleague and saying, 'Rutherford, this is transmutation: the thorium is disintegrating and transmuting itself into argon gas.'[40]

Rutherford was equally shocked: 'They'll call us alchemists, charlatans, and try to cut off our heads!'[41]

In 1902, Rutherford and Soddy announced their astonishing findings to the world. Atoms did indeed spontaneously disintegrate, creating energy in the process. Their so-called 'disintegration hypothesis' showed that radioactive substances such as thorium and radium were in a state of constant but gradual disintegration. Their atoms were perpetually firing off streams of energetic, bullet-like particles. The process was likened at the time to a 'series of explosions'.[42] Transmutation and radioactivity were the same process. As Soddy put it, the 'expulsion of rays is the break-up of the atom'.[43]

If they had been proved wrong, it could have been fatal for the careers of these two young scientists. But they were right, and both men would go on to win Nobel prizes. Rutherford and Soddy also established the principle of radioactive decay. We talk now of the half-life of, for example, thoron, as being one minute, so that, in Soddy's words, '60 seconds from any time of starting, the quantity of thoron is only half what it was to begin with'.[44] Soddy recalled these days as being among the most exciting of his life, filled with 'intense mental exaltation'. Through their work on the theory of atomic disintegration, the pieces of the radioactivity 'jig-saw puzzle' were gradually being fitted into a coherent whole.[45]

In the autumn of 1902, Rutherford and Soddy used what was at the time the latest in laboratory technology: a liquid-air machine. But they were not interested in repeating Charles Tripler's spurious experiments to create free energy. Instead, they used liquid air to cool the gases produced by thorium and radium to pure liquids, thus helping to demonstrate to a sceptical scientific establishment that one element could indeed give birth to a new one. The disintegration of the radium atom to yield an atom of radon gas and an alpha particle was described by Frederick Soddy as 'surely the strangest transformation of matter in the whole history of chemical discovery!'[46] It heralded a revolution in the way people thought about matter, one that would yield an energy source more awesome than even Tripler could have imagined.

On 16 March 1903, a few months before Rutherford's visit to Paris, the true 'mystery of radium', as the London *Times* called it, suddenly dawned on the world. Pierre Curie informed the French Academy of Sciences that pure radium chloride was always 1.5°C warmer than its surroundings. This happened 'without combustion, without chemical change of any kind, and without any change in its molecular structure'.[47] Radium could melt more than its own weight of ice every hour. It was astounding news. According to Marie Curie, it 'defied all contemporary scientific experience'.[48] And, for the first time, atomic energy had been described in terms of heat to a non-scientific audience.

People had heard about radium's extraordinary rays. Indeed three days later, Sir William Crookes gave what *The Times* said was a 'beautiful demonstration' of radium rays to the Royal Society. Using a screen of zinc sulphide, he revealed the brilliant phosphorescence that occurs when it is placed near radium: 'Viewed through a magnifying glass, the sensitive screen is seen to be the object of a veritable bombardment by particles of infinite minuteness, which, themselves invisible, make known their arrival on the screen by flashes of light, just as a shell coming from the blue announces itself by an explosion.'[49]

But Pierre Curie's announcement revealed 'forces of a totally different order of magnitude'. *The Times* told its readers: 'Apparently we have in radium a substance having the power to gather up and convert into heat some form of ambient energy with which we are not yet acquainted.'[50] Although dreams of perpetual motion (like Tripler's) were ruled out by the newspaper, the mysterious source of the energy seemed to be challenging the laws of thermodynamics, those fundamental principles of nineteenth-century physics that were carved in stone on the tablets of science. The world stood on the brink of a 'new wonderland' of science. As the respected *Edinburgh Review* put it:

A Crookes tube does not produce X-rays unless we pass a current through it; a lamp gives no light unless we keep it supplied with oil: but uranium and radium continue to give out Becquerel rays day after day and year after year, with no outside stimulus of any kind, and with an intensity that shows no measurable diminution . . . What is the source of the energy of their rays?[51]

A few weeks after Pierre Curie's announcement, Soddy wrote an article summarizing recent advances in radioactivity. Significantly, he said that people now had to think of matter 'not only as mass, but also as a store of energy'. Soddy was writing two years before Albert Einstein began to consider the equivalence of matter and energy. The amounts of energy in matter were 'colossal', said Soddy. Together with Rutherford, he had made a rough estimate: 'The energy of radioactive change must therefore be at least twenty-thousand times, and may be a million times, as great as the energy of any molecular change.'[52]

The potential energy locked up within matter and slowly released in the radioactive glow of radium was indeed colossal. To illustrate this idea of matter as energy, Soddy then used an extraordinary image. From now on people should, he said, 'regard the planet on which we live rather as a storehouse stuffed with explosives, inconceivably more powerful than any we know of, and possibly only awaiting a suitable detonator to cause the earth to revert to chaos'.[53]

In February that year, Sir William Crookes had vividly depicted the amount of potential energy in radium by saying just one gram could raise the entire fleet of the British Navy several thousand feet into the sky. Newspapers duly provided graphic illustrations showing the pride of the Admiralty hoisted unceremoniously into mid-air. Soddy was in Boston at the time this story broke in the American press. He mentioned it in a letter to Rutherford, saying that Sir William had been misunderstood as saying a gram of radium could 'blow the British Navy sky high'.[54] Sir William had been merely trying to depict the potential energy, not conjure up a superweapon. But as nuclear historian Spencer Weart has said, 'scientist, press, and public had together crafted a new thought'.[55] It wasn't that far short of the truth.

In France, Gustave Le Bon, a science writer who knew the publicity value of dramatic predictions, told a newspaper that it would not be long before a scientist invented a radioactive device to 'blow up the whole earth'.[56] Even the innately cautious Rutherford echoed Soddy's notion, 'playfully' suggesting to a friend that with the 'proper detonator . . . an explosive wave of atomic disintegration might be started through all matter which would transmute the whole mass of the globe into helium or similar gases, and, in very truth, leave not one stone upon another'. It might have been a casual remark between friends, but it was too good not to print, and it duly appeared in January 1904.[57]

In the same month as this frightening prospect was reported, Frederick Soddy gave a lecture to a military audience on the latest advances in radioactivity. Unlike Rutherford, Soddy was not afraid of looking into the future and speculating publicly about the applications of pure science. Today he would tempt fate. Whoever cracked the secret of atomic energy, he said, 'would possess a weapon by which he could destroy the earth if he chose'.[58] The idea of the atomic chain reaction had been born and with it a scenario that would have quickened the heartbeat of Dr Strangelove himself: an atomic doomsday bomb.

At the end of 1903, Marie and Pierre Curie learned that they, together with Henri Becquerel, had won the Nobel Prize in Physics. Pierre was a man who could not be flattered by honours. He did not visit Stockholm to collect the award for two years. Both Marie and Pierre were feeling the effects of radiation poisoning: his legs shook and he suffered unexplained pains. Both of them struggled against fatigue.

In his Nobel lecture, which he finally delivered in 1905, a year before his tragic death in a street accident, Pierre returned to the subject he had raised at the dinner party with Rutherford and his wife. He spoke of his fears 'that radium could become very dangerous in criminal hands'. Pierre implicitly compared himself to Alfred Nobel who, as well as establishing the Nobel awards just four years previously, had also invented dynamite and hoped thereby to end war. Powerful explosives may have 'enabled man to do wonderful work', said Pierre, but they are also 'a terrible means of destruction in the hands of great criminals who are leading the peoples towards war'.

Pierre's words were dignified and far from sensational, but his concerns were clear. He acknowledged that more good than harm came from scientific discovery. But he left his distinguished audience – gathered together to celebrate the achievements of science – with a distinct sense of unease about the future. As they set out on a journey of discovery that could yield unimaginable power, it was right, he said, that they should ask 'whether mankind benefits from knowing the secrets of Nature'.[59] It was a question that would echo down through the twentieth century.

At the beginning of 1904, a reporter from the *Strand Magazine* arrived in Paris to interview the discoverers of radium. Cleveland Moffett, a writer of mystery stories including a minor classic, 'The Mysterious Card',[60] met Pierre Curie in 'one of the rambling sheds' at the Ecole de Physique et de Chimie Industrielles where he and Marie had isolated radium and polonium.[61]

When he first saw Pierre, the 'tall, pale man, slightly bent' was intently watching 'a small porcelain dish, where a colourless liquid was simmering'. This was the painstaking chemistry of refining radium by crystallization. The pure metal had still not been isolated, Pierre Curie told the reporter. What they were now trying to obtain was radium chloride: 'small white crystals, which may be crushed into a white powder, and which look like ordinary salt'.[62]

Pierre showed Moffett a sealed glass tube 'not much larger than a thick match' which was partly covered by lead and contained a white powder. He explained that the radium in the tube was very radioactive: 'Lead stops the harmful rays, that would otherwise make trouble.' He pulled up his sleeve to reveal a 'forearm scarred and reddened from fresh-healed sores', caused by the radioactive element. Pierre explained how Henri Becquerel had travelled to London carrying in his waistcoat pocket a small tube of radium for a lecture. About a fortnight later 'the professor observed that the skin under his pocket was beginning to redden and fall away, and finally a deep and painful sore formed there and remained for weeks before healing'.[63]

Would Monsieur Curie say therefore that radium was 'an element of destruction', asked the reporter.

'Undoubtedly it has a power of destruction,' replied Pierre, 'but that power may be tempered or controlled.'[64]

Cleveland Moffett noted that the physicist's hands 'were much peeled, and very sore from too much contact with radium'. Pierre told him that for several days he had been unable to dress himself.[65]

'Was it true,' asked Moffett, adding with a dramatic emphasis, '*could* it be true, that this strange substance gives forth heat and light ceaselessly and is really an inexhaustible source of energy?'

Pierre repeated the extraordinary details of radium's innate heat. He added: 'a given quantity of radium will melt its own weight of ice every hour'.

'For ever?' asked the journalist.

The cautious scientist hesitated. 'So far as we know – for ever.'[66]

Then the dignified physicist led Moffett into a darkened room where the reporter from the *Strand* saw with his own eyes – just as Rutherford had a few months before – the 'clear glow' of radium in the tube. The light it gave off was, noted the amazed writer, bright enough to read a page by.

'Then radium may be the light of the future?' he asked.[67]

Pierre shook his head. Patiently he explained, as he had done many times before to journalists, that 'we should pay rather dearly for such a light'. People exposed to large quantities of radium would suffer paralysis, blindness and various nervous disorders. And then there was the cost. 'Radium is worth about three thousand times its weight in pure gold,' said Pierre. In 1904 a kilogram cost £400,000. There were perhaps just four grams in the whole world: 'you could heap it all in a tablespoon', he said.[68]

Cleveland Moffett listened as Pierre told him about his recent journey to London, where he had delivered a lecture on radium. There he had met Crookes, who had shown him a 'curious little instrument' he had just invented. The English chemist called it a spinthariscope, from the Greek word for scintillation, or bright spark.[69] Sir William explained that he had taken the word from Homer's *Hymn to Apollo*. There it describes the radiance of the ancient god Apollo, often associated with the sun:

> Here from the ship leaped the far-darting Apollo,
> Like a star at midday, while from him flitted scintillations of fire,
> And the brilliancy reached to heaven.[70]

In this way a 2,500-year-old description of a Greek god became the name of a device that revealed the wonders of radium to thousands of ordinary people in the twentieth century.

The spinthariscope consisted of a fluorescent screen, a shiny brass magnifying eyepiece and a minute fragment of radium – too small to be seen with the naked eye, but enough to last for 30,000 years according to some estimates.[71] Looking through the lens in a darkened room revealed a sparkling display, 'scintillations of fire' as the classically trained Sir William would have said. Soon advertisements for these simple devices appeared in all the newspapers.

Neurologist Oliver Sacks, author of *Awakenings*, recalls that the spinthariscope was a fashionable scientific toy in the Edwardian period, selling for a few shillings. When he was a boy, his Uncle Abe showed him one. Sacks 'found the spectacle enchanting, magical, like looking at an endless display of meteors or shooting stars'.[72] For Pierre Curie, the 'vision' he saw through the spinthariscope was 'one of the most beautiful and impressive he had ever witnessed; it was as if he had been allowed to assist at the birth of a universe – or at the death of a molecule'.[73]

While in Paris, Moffett also met Dr Jean Danysz, a biologist from the Institut Pasteur who had been doing tests with radium on animals. 'I have no doubt that a kilogramme of radium would be sufficient to destroy the population of Paris,' Danysz said coolly:

Men and women would be killed just as easily as mice. They would feel nothing during their exposure to the radium, nor realize that they were in any danger. And weeks would pass after their exposure before anything would happen. Then gradually the skin would begin to peel off and their bodies would become one great sore. Then they would become blind. Then they would die from paralysis and congestion of the spinal cord.[74]

Danysz was speaking forty years before Hiroshima and Nagasaki. Combine this view of the lethal radioactivity of radium with the explosive tube of Bulwer-Lytton's fictional vril, which can be fired at cities hundreds of miles away, and you have a nuclear missile.

Dr Danysz added that, paradoxically, animals 'thrive' after a short exposure to radium. This real but temporary effect led to radium soon being marketed as a health tonic – 'liquid sunshine' as the labels claimed. But such radium tonics had lethal consequences for anyone who drank them regularly. The apparently beneficial effects are caused by the body over-producing red blood cells, a natural defence mechanism which makes the person feel briefly invigorated. One Pittsburgh industrialist drank a brand of radium water called 'Radithor' every day. He liked it so much he even sent crates of the tonic to his friends. But it slowly poisoned him, and he died painfully: the bones in his jaws were decaying and he was suffering from anaemia and a brain abscess.[75]

Danysz and his colleagues at the Institut Pasteur had also found that radium slowed the development of moth larvae by a factor of three. 'It was very much as if a young man of twenty-one should keep the appearance of twenty-one for 250 years!' Danysz boasted to the journalist, with rather unscientific exaggeration.[76] Not only was radium a potential energy source, but it might also be the elixir of eternal youth. There were precedents here too in alchemy. The mythical philosopher's stone was not just about making gold, it was also capable of curing all human ailments. The quest to discover the secret of this miraculous power – the source of both wealth and health – has enthralled people ever since.

The fantastic claims being made for radium echoed another of the alchemists' dreams. For radium promised humankind the ultimate power, the power of the gods: the Parisian biologists claimed to have used the 'strange stimulation' of radium *to create life* where there would have been no life'.[77] One of the most famous alchemists was Paracelsus (1494–1541), who left a remarkable body of texts and teachings. A true Renaissance man, he rejected book-learning as the route to knowledge and instead taught his students to trust the evidence of their own senses: 'He who wishes to explore Nature must tread her books with his feet.'[78] A firm believer in using chemistry to both diagnose and treat disease, Paracelsus has even been praised by the Prince of Wales in 1982 as an early practitioner of holistic medicine.[79] But among his more outlandish boasts was that with alchemy he could create life itself.

The writer and scientist Johann Wolfgang von Goethe satirized the hubris of scientists in his version of the *Faust* story by alluding to the recipes of Paracelsus. Mephistopheles has to lend a hand to breathe life into a homunculus, or 'little man', which Faust's overly ambitious assistant, Wagner, is seeking to create by alchemical means. A century later, in 1908, Somerset Maugham's novel *The Magician* described how a modern-day alchemist (based on the real occultist Aleister Crowley) attempts to create a living being, also by Paracelsian techniques. But in the age of radium it seemed that science might finally realize this ancient dream.

The Parisian scientists told Moffett how unfertilized sea-urchin eggs had been miraculously stimulated into growth. He informed his readers that 'we may in the future be able to produce new species of insects, moths, butterflies, perhaps birds and fishes, by simply treating the eggs with radium rays'. He suggested that, given greater quantities of radium, even mammals might be changed in this way, 'to produce new species among larger creatures, mice, rabbits, guinea-pigs, etc'. Moffett also told how French scientists were using radium to create 'monsters'. They had found that tadpoles exposed to radium developed differently, their tails began to disappear and they grew 'a new breathing apparatus'.[80] In the 1950s, fears about radioactivity and genetic mutation would spawn now classic monster movies, such as *Godzilla* and *Them!* The stirrings of Frankenstein's monster can be heard in these words of Moffett's, and perhaps for that reason he chose not to dwell on this frightening subject.

Cleveland Moffett ends his article on radium's miraculous potential with the triumphant claim that 'we are entering upon a domain of new, strange knowledge and drawing near to some of Nature's most hallowed secrets'.[81] It was a message of hope. But now, in an age that has become deeply ambivalent about science and scientists, it sounds more like a warning.

Following the discoveries made by the Curies, matter soon came to be seen as a 'reservoir of atomic energy'.[82] Sir William Crookes had suggested in a speech to physicists in Berlin in 1903 that if natural radioactivity was caused by the disintegration of atoms, then all matter was in a state of inevitable decay: 'This fatal quality of atomic dissociation appears to be universal and operates whenever we brush a piece of glass with silk; it works in the sunshine and raindrops, and in the lightnings and flame; it prevails in the waterfall and the stormy sea.'[83] As someone commented, matter – the basic substance of the universe – was 'doomed to destruction'.[84]

In the previous century, the laws of thermodynamics had raised the frightening prospect of what was called 'the heat death of the universe'. The second of these laws asserts the irreversibility of natural processes, whereby heat cannot be transferred from a cold body to a hot one. Related to this is the concept of entropy, which is a measure of the unavailability of a system's energy to do work. As the physicist Rudolph Clausius said in 1850, entropy is always increasing. The implication of these laws is that in the distant future, when entropy ultimately reaches a maximum, the universe's heat will have dissipated to such an extent that life will become unsustainable.

In *The Time Machine*, H. G. Wells's Time Traveller, 'drawn on by the mystery of the earth's fate', journeys forward 30 million years to a time when 'the red-hot dome of the sun had come to obscure nearly a tenth part of the darkling heavens'. The earth has fallen silent and is gripped by freezing winds. 'All the sounds of man, the bleating of sheep, the cries of birds, the hum of insects, the stir that makes the background of our lives – all that was over.'[85] For all our insight into the universe and its workings, humankind is ultimately powerless before the laws of thermodynamics. As the philosopher of science Alfred North Whitehead said, in the ancient world it was gods who determined the fates of mortals. But in the modern world, the laws of physics have become the 'decrees of fate'.[86]

Wells's novel appeared in the year that Röntgen chanced upon the astonishing rays that could render solid matter transparent. The discovery of radioactivity and the disintegration of matter added a new scientific doomsday to the eventual heat death of the solar system. A writer for the *Edinburgh Review* was shocked by the apocalyptic implications: Sir William's idea conjured up 'an appalling scene of desolation – of quasi-annihilation'.[87]

In his 1909 novel *Tono-Bungay*, H. G. Wells rendered yet another memorable scene of desolation. The book is an attack on the values of capitalism and the new consumer society. Tono-Bungay is a health tonic which has much in common with the radium tonics widely available at the time. The narrator, George Ponderevo, describes his uncle's invention and marketing of this successful (though totally useless) medicine. According to its inventor, it's 'the secret of vigour', but for George, who like Wells had studied the sciences, it's nothing but 'a quack medicine'.[88]

In this ambitious novel, Wells uses a powerful scientific metaphor for the terminal decay of society: radioactivity. To save his uncle's business, George makes a foolhardy trip to Africa to smuggle back a quantity of radioactive ore. It contains 'canadium', which they hope to use to make the 'perfect filament'. 'We'd make the lamp trade sit on its tail and howl,' predicts George's greedy uncle. 'We'd put Ediswan and all of 'em into a parcel with our last trousers and a hat, and swap 'em off for a pot of geraniums.'[89]

The pitchblende-like radioactive ore is called 'quap' in the novel: it is 'the most radioactive stuff in the world . . . a festering mass of earths and heavy metals, polonium, radium, ythorium, thorium, carium, and new things too.'[90] But quap is far more radioactive than even radium and polonium: 'those are just little molecular centres of disintegration, of that mysterious decay and rotting of those elements, elements once regarded as the most stable things in nature'.[91]

In comparison, quap is 'cancerous', says George. It is 'something that creeps and lives as a disease lives by destroying; an elemental stirring and disarrangement, incalculably maleficent and strange'. Perhaps influenced by Sir William Crookes's doomsday vision, George offers a remarkable one of his own, inspired by the creeping contagion of radioactivity:

To my mind radioactivity is a real disease of matter. Moreover it is a contagious disease. It spreads. You bring those debased and crumbling atoms near others and those too presently catch the trick of swinging themselves out of coherent existence ... When I think of these inexplicable dissolvent centres that have come into being in our globe ... I am haunted by a grotesque fancy of the ultimate eating away and dry-rotting and dispersal of all our world. So that while man still struggles and dreams his very substance will change and crumble from beneath him ... Suppose indeed that is to be the end of our planet; no splendid climax and finale, no towering accumulation of achievements but just – atomic decay! I add that to the ideas of the suffocating comet, the dark body out of space, the burning out of the sun, the distorted orbit, as a new and far more possible end – as science can see ends – to this strange by-play of matter that we call human life.[92]

The African landscape where the seam of quap breaks to the surface has been devastated by radioactivity. The coast is a 'lifeless beach' littered with rotting fish. Stretching as far as the eye can see is an atomic wasteland which is 'blasted and scorched and dead'.[93] People who stay there too long sicken and die. This powerful passage, written decades before anyone grasped the full dangers of radioactive contamination, now brings to mind the poisoned landscape around Chernobyl. For Wells, his Dantean vision of ultimate decay is a metaphor for a society that had nowhere to go but down. Today it also offers a haunting vision of the dark side to our dreams of atomic utopia.

George Ponderevo's bleak view of an atomic apocalypse that comes not with a bang but a whimper was also an accurate reflection of the science of the day. The unchanging atom of Newton and Dalton was replaced by a chaotic atom that one writer described in 1903 as 'the scene of indescribable activities, a complex piece of mechanism composed of thousands of parts, a star-cluster in miniature, subject to all kinds of dynamical vicissitudes, to perturbations, accelerations, internal friction, total or partial disruption.'[94]

With this dynamic view of matter came the equally strange idea that instead of being solid, the atom consisted mostly of echoing space: 'the ratio of an atom to an electron ... is the ratio of St Paul's Cathedral to a full stop'. The British writer Dr Caleb Williams Saleeby developed the now standard analogy as early as 1904: 'Just as the planets are revolving around a centre, so the electrons in each of the atoms that go to make up those planets are also revolving round an atomic centre – revolving at a speed hundreds of times faster than the speed of the planets which they compose.'[95]

This dramatic image of atoms as miniature solar systems was published seven years before Ernest Rutherford showed that atoms do indeed have a tiny, compact nucleus surrounded by electrons. Such ideas often gain popular currency before they are given the seal of scientific authority. Indeed, the history of scientific superweapons shows that the imaginations of writers like H. G. Wells have been way ahead of the scientists and the generals.

As we shall see, fiction and the popular imagination often work together to give an idea critical momentum, eventually allowing it to cross from fantasy to reality. The foresight of fiction writers was acknowledged after the terrorist attacks on the World Trade Center and the Pentagon on September the 11th, 2001. After this audacious strike, the FBI paid a visit to Hollywood to find out what possible terrorist scenarios the scriptwriters thought might be in store for America in the new era of 'asymmetric warfare'. It emerged in 2002 that al-Qaeda terrorists had themselves been inspired by Hollywood. Prisoners revealed that they watched Roland Emmerich's 1998 remake of the cold-war classic *Godzilla* and hoped to emulate the monster's destruction of landmark buildings in New York, such as the Brooklyn Bridge. Similarly, science and fiction came together in the dream of the superweapon to produce some of the world's most terrible weapons of mass destruction.

The world, it seemed, was built not on solid rock but on shifting sands. Matter was dynamic and unstable. To X-rays and radio waves, apparently impenetrable 'solid' matter was transparent. People began to look at the world around them with new eyes. When the artist Wassily Kandinsky first read about Rutherford's new theory of atomic structure, it hit him with a 'frightful force, as if the end of the world had come. All things became transparent, without strength or certainty.'[96] But there were still stranger revelations to come.

In 1895, the inventor of Wells's time machine had explained that

'Time is really only a fourth dimension of Space'. Two years later, Wells's Invisible Man used a 'geometrical expression involving four dimensions' to make his great yet tragic discovery. Joseph Conrad was so taken by the idea of time as an extra dimension that he attempted a scientific romance of his own on the subject. He had seen an X-ray machine in operation in 1898 and had been moved to comment that 'there is no space, time, matter, mind as vulgarly understood, there is only the eternal something that waves and the eternal force that causes the waves . . .'[97]

Conrad's novel *The Inheritors: An Extravagant Story* (1901), which he co-wrote with Ford Madox Ford (who used his family name, Hueffer), is a strange work about a conspiracy masterminded by people from the 'Fourth Dimension' – the future. The 'Dimensionists' hoped to begin their 'reign of terror' imperceptibly: 'They were to come like snow in the night: in the morning one would look out and find the world white.'[98] This paranoid idea of a secret coup taking place beneath a surface of apparent normality anticipates the alien invasion themes of 1950s America, in films such as *Invasion of the Body Snatchers*. Conrad's inspiration was not fear of invasion, but the revelation of X-rays and the new dimensions of mathematics and physics: the disturbing realization that the world was full of forces and radiations that no one had thought possible.

Ten years after Wells's Time Traveller entered the fourth dimension and glimpsed the end of the world, Albert Einstein, an unknown patent officer from Berne in Switzerland, would transform the scientific understanding of time and space, overthrowing the absolutes of Newtonian physics and laying the foundations of a 'new physics' that would be as strange as the wildest dreams of science fiction writers. In that same year, this physicist who grew up surrounded by the latest electrical inventions would also set out the mathematics that proved something scientists and their public were just beginning to grasp: the equivalence of matter and energy. An atom of matter was indeed a vast and terrible reservoir of energy, as Frederick Soddy had predicted. The revolution had truly begun.

It would be many years, however, before the new physics could reveal to the world the full power of the atom. It was not physics but the science of the previous century, chemistry, that first attempted to create a means of destruction so awesome that – as in Bulwer-Lytton's novel – war would be unthinkable. The dream of the superweapon was about to become reality.

II

The Chemist's War

One must understand that the greatest evil that can oppress civilized peoples derives from wars, not, indeed, so much from actual present or past wars, as from the never-ending and constantly increasing arming *for future war. To this all of the nation's powers are devoted, as are all those fruits of its culture that could be used to build a still greater culture.*

Immanuel Kant,
Speculative Beginning of Human History (1786)

5

The Prospero of Poisons

I have to confess that I felt rather proud
of the simple device of my suffocating cloud.
The Prospero of poisons, the Faustus of the front
bringing mental magic to modern armament.
           Tony Harrison, *Square Rounds* (1992)

In spring 1915, a gunshot shattered the night-time silence of Dahlem, a leafy suburb of Berlin. It was closely followed by the sound of another shot, this time more muffled. Clara Haber was still alive when her son found her, lying on the lawn outside their house. At first, thirteen-year-old Hermann couldn't work out what had happened. Was it a bungled burglary, or had his mother disturbed enemy agents trying to sabotage his father's top-secret war work?

Beside Clara's crumpled body lay his father's army pistol. A few weeks ago he had held it in his young hands. He had been surprised how heavy it was – a dead weight of cold steel. In the grey light of the early dawn, Hermann could see a bloody stain on his mother's dress. She had been shot point blank in the chest. He ran from Clara's side to rouse his father, but Fritz Haber was still in a deep chemical sleep, heavily sedated with sleeping pills, and had not heard his wife shoot herself through the heart.

A few hours earlier, at their home in the grounds of the recently founded Kaiser Wilhelm Institute for Physical Chemistry and Electro-chemistry, they had all been celebrating Fritz Haber's return from the Western Front. Professor Haber, the Institute's director, cut a striking figure that evening. With his new military uniform, his shaven

83

Fritz Haber in military uniform, 1916.

bullet-head and duelling scar, he looked every inch the Prussian officer. The Kaiser had just promoted him to the rank of captain, a meteoric rise in a society which honoured military virtues above all others. Soon he would be awarded the ultimate military accolade in the Kaiser's gift: the Iron Cross.

Haber was a proud Prussian and an ambitious scientist. A few days earlier, at Ypres in Belgium, Haber had directed the first battlefield use of poison gas in World War I. His deadly brainchild was the first of a new generation of scientific superweapons, a weapon it was hoped would decisively alter the course of the war. At Ypres, the scientist had been blooded on the field of battle.

Just before Fritz Haber returned home from Ypres, Clara had visited the wife of her second cousin, Dr Zinaide Krassa. Clara admitted that she was disturbed by her husband's obsessional commitment to his war work. She took with her the private letters he had written from the Belgian front line. Clara confided in her friend that she had seen secret experiments being conducted on animals, both in the laboratory and outside in the leafy grounds of the Institute, in which they were exposed to varying concentrations of poison gas and then dissected to observe the effects on their lungs. It was clear to Dr Krassa that Clara was distressed by what she had seen. But no one suspected that she might take her own life.

An accident a few months earlier had also affected her deeply. One morning a few days before Christmas 1914, an explosion had rocked her husband's Institute. Clara rushed out of the house and across the lawn. Inside the Institute, the machine hall on the ground floor was unusually silent. She was relieved to see Fritz leaning against a bench. But although unharmed, he was obviously in shock. He stared fixedly at the floor and muttered something over and over to himself.

Clara pushed her way through a huddle of scientists and technicians. Lying on the floor was Otto Sackur, a gifted young scientist from Breslau, her home town. As doctoral students, he and Clara had studied at the university together. Otto had taken an active part in Clara's public defence of her doctoral thesis in 1900. The local newspaper reported how he had asked probing questions, but she had answered them 'valiantly and bravely, like a man'.[1] She had been the first woman to be awarded a doctorate in chemistry at Breslau and one of the first in the whole of Germany. As a scientist, she understood full well what her husband was doing in the war. As a human being, she hated it.

It was Clara who had helped Sackur to find a position at the Institute just a couple of years ago. Now that same man lay sprawled in front of her with his face blown off. His eyes, nose and mouth had disappeared, reduced to a bloody pulp. His brain was visible through his shattered forehead. Clara knelt down beside him and asked one of the engineers to cut open his collar. As they removed the starched collar, Otto raised his head. He was still alive.

Fritz Haber was uninjured. But he'd had a lucky escape. An engineer told Clara that her husband had been just about to enter the gas room when he was asked to look at a problem with the high-pressure compressor. As he did so, an explosion shook the whole building. Professor Gerhardt Just ran out of the laboratory cradling his right arm. His hand had been blown off. The other scientists had to carry Otto Sackur out of the gas room, which was now dense with smoke. Haber did nothing to help. He could only stand there saying over and over again, 'Poor Just, poor Just.'

The two scientists had been developing a new chemical compound, for use in howitzer shells, which brought together the power of high explosive with the irritant effect of tear gas. They had just combined dichloromethylamine with cacodyl chloride. Otto had raised the beaker up to eye level so as to observe it better. It was then that the highly unstable compound exploded in his face.[2] It had been the Institute's first foray into the development of chemical weapons. This experiment was never tried again, but it was the beginning of an intensive programme of weapons research at the Institute that would last for the duration of the war and beyond.

Sackur did not survive for long. 'He died as a soldier on the battle-field,' said Haber later. He managed to win a war pension for the man's widow and daughter, and recommended Professor Just for an Iron Cross. It was awarded a month before Haber's top-secret chemical weapon was used on the Western Front. Thanks to Haber, scientists were now soldiers, and a new front line had been opened up that reached right into the chemist's laboratory.

When Clara visited Zinaide Krassa with her husband's letters from the front, she was 'in despair' at the 'terrible effects of gas war', as her second cousin later recalled.[3] Physicist James Franck was among the scientists hand-picked by Haber to oversee the use of poison gas on the battlefield. According to Franck, the sensitive and idealistic Clara 'wanted to reform the world'.[4] By contrast, her husband was interested only in helping Germany to win the war. A converted Jew, Fritz Haber wanted to prove beyond question his loyalty to Kaiser and country. '*Im Frieden der Menschheit, im Kriege dem Vaterland,*' was Haber's motto as a scientist: in peacetime he worked for humanity, but in wartime for the Fatherland.[5] Haber was convinced that science and scientists would win the war for his country.

Clara committed suicide early on the morning of 2 May 1915, just over a week after her husband's scientific weapon was released on unsuspecting French Algerian troops near Ypres. In the silence of that night, Clara had written several farewell letters. Then she took her husband's pistol from its holster, went out into the garden and, after first firing into the air, she shot herself. She lived for a few hours after Hermann found her. Fritz had refused to listen to her protests about his misuse of science. Thanks to the sleeping pills, he didn't hear her pistol shots either.

According to some, Clara had warned her husband that if he did not stop working on the new weapons, she would kill herself. Her biographer has argued that she saw chemical weapons as a perversion of science, corrupting a discipline that should be offering insights into life, not inventing ever more terrible means of destroying it.[6] Many years later, after both Fritz and Hermann were dead, the Institute's engineer, Hermann Lütge, offered another motive for her suicide. He claimed that during the reception that evening, Clara had surprised her husband kissing Charlotte Nathan, the young woman who would become Haber's second wife in 1917.[7] No one could corroborate this claim, but it is clear that the Habers were by no means happily married. Charlotte Nathan archly described Clara and Fritz's difficult relationship as a 'Strindberg marriage'.[8] Clara's final letters could have revealed her true motive. Unfortunately, none have survived, and neither her family nor Haber's ever discussed the matter. Her protest against the misuse of science – if that is what she intended – went unnoticed.

On the same day as his wife's suicide, Fritz Haber departed for the Eastern Front. He had been ordered to supervise a gas attack on Russian forces. His young son must have been distraught at being left in these circumstances, without either of his parents. Six weeks later, on 12 June 1915, Haber wrote to a friend that it was good to be at the front line where the bullets were flying. 'There,' he wrote, 'only the moment counts and what one can do within the confines of the trench is one's only duty.'[9]

In the same letter he wrote passionately about how the experience of war awoke in him romantic notions of heroism inspired by patriotic poetry. He also admitted that when the din of battle finally abated, he could still hear the voice of his dead wife. But he remained fixated on his task of perfecting his chemical weapon, and he pursued this terrible grail with a religious fervour. For Haber, his success or failure would determine the outcome of the war: 'The responsibility is the most terrible of all,' he wrote, 'the awareness that a wasted day or a delayed order costs blood that I could have spared with more hard work and energy. That is the whip that I always feel hanging over me.'[10]

'Perhaps chemistry is the final weapon, the superior weapon, which will give the people who use it properly – who master it! – world wide supremacy. Perhaps even the Empire of the World!'[11] These are not Haber's words, but those of a fictional scientist, Professor Hoffman, in André Malraux's haunting study of warfare, *The Walnut Trees of Altenburg*, written during World War II. Hoffman is an unmistakable portrait of Haber. Malraux's novel is based on an eyewitness account of a real gas attack that took place on 12 June 1915, the day that Fritz Haber was writing to his friend about his memory of Clara.[12]

After leaving Berlin and his traumatized son, Haber travelled east to the Carpathian front. However, he soon realized that the terrain there was unsuited to an attack using poison gas, and proceeded to the sector of the front line nearly forty miles west of Warsaw, near Bolimów on the River Bzura. This is where the gas attack in Malraux's novel takes place. In reality the first attack was a failure, causing fifty-six casualties among the German troops. In Malraux's novel, as the professor arrives at the front to supervise the second attack he is 'beaming with joy' at the favourable conditions: 'The wind's still perfect, still perfect!'[13]

On the evening of the attack, Professor Hoffman praises chemistry as the 'superior weapon'. The other German officers are not convinced, and the professor seizes the opportunity to enthuse about poison gas, reciting a litany of noxious war gases and their effects. Chlorine: 'easy to liquefy, disastrous to the human organism, very cheap, mind you!' Phosgene: 'ten times as strong as chlorine'. Mustard gas: 'the best fighting gas of all'.[14]

Malraux's German narrator, Vincent Berger, says that Hoffman has 'the infectious power of those extreme neurotics who impose the atmosphere of their own genius or madness'.[15] Like Griffin, H. G. Wells's mad scientist in *The Invisible Man*, Professor Hoffman has become addicted to the drug of his own scientific power. The professor tries to sway the sceptical officers with an argument that became

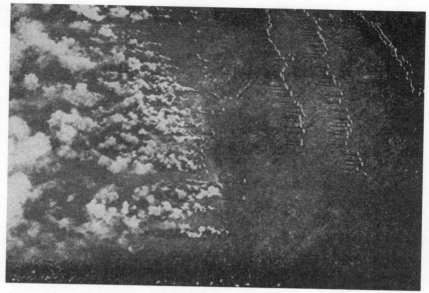

An aerial view of a German gas attack on the Eastern Front in World War I.

familiar in the interwar years: poison gas is 'the most humane method of warfare', he argues.[16] Fritz Haber himself infamously claimed that chemical warfare was 'a higher form of killing'.[17] But despite the Professor's coldly rational arguments, a question from one of the German officers is left hanging unanswered in the air: 'why are we despised?'[18]

The next morning, Berger and the other soldiers watch the cloud of gas as it drifts silently across the River Bzura and over the Russian trenches:

A long cloud of dust was floating in the sunshine. Not feathering out like the dust in the wake of a car, but uniformly thick and tall, like a wall . . . The sheet of gas went on growing, swamping the parallel trunks of the apple-trees to the same height, then their branches. Soon the bottom of the valley was only a yellow fog . . . [19]

This scientific fog has the 'look of a war machine' as it rolls towards the Russian lines. A riderless horse charges wildly at the yellow cloud and is 'swallowed up in the vast silence'.[20] Then the order comes to advance. What the German soldiers discover is unlike any wartime

89

experience they have had. The Professor has described the human effects of the noxious mix of phosgene and chlorine: 'The opaque cornea first goes blue, the breath starts to come in hisses, the pupil – it's really very odd! – goes almost black.'[21] But this clinical description falls far short of the full horror of the actual gas attack.

The chemical superweapon leaves in its wake a scene worthy of Dante's *Inferno*. It is a scientific apocalypse, a hell created by humankind, revealing (as Malraux puts it) that the depths of the earth 'teemed with monsters and buried gods'.[22] The Russian trenches now lie in a 'valley of death'[23] where everything – from the plants to the birds and the bees – appears to be dead and already rotting:

The path began to slant more steeply . . . In the middle of it a man was leaping on all fours, with such spasmodic jerks that it seemed he was being bounced along. Naked. Two yards off, the apparition lifted its grey face and whiteless eyes, opened its epileptic mouth as though to scream...Mad with pain, moving like any madman, as though its body was now only possessed by torment, with a few frog-like leaps it plunged into the putrescence.

Then, in the prehistoric silence, there was a scream, a scream of utter agony which ended up in a mew . . .

Above the path there were some Russian greatcoats scattered all over the place, shirts hanging, as though carbonized, on the fantastic branches; but not a sign of an explosion. And close by, in a tiny clearing concealed behind a row of sunflowers, some thirty men lay crumbling in a T-shaped trench: an enemy advanced post.

All dead, more or less naked, scattered across a pile of tattered clothes, clutching each other in convulsive groups . . . Feet were sticking out of this petrified swarm of dead bodies, big toes curled like fists.[24]

But what particularly appals Berger, more than their 'lead-coloured eyes, more than those hands twisting in the empty air', is 'the absence of any wound. The absence of blood.'[25] Death had come without warning and without mercy, a silent, creeping chemical killer.

Malraux's novel gives voice to the widespread feeling after World War I that humankind had stepped beyond the pale in developing such scientifically efficient weapons of mass destruction. Poison gas seemed to be an expression of our darkest and most deadly desires. 'The Spirit of Evil was stronger here than death', says Berger.[26] He feels that a 'human apocalypse . . . had just seized him by the throat'.[27]

When they see the human effect of the new weapon, the German soldiers throw down their guns and carry to the ambulances those among their former enemies who are not yet dead, seeking through individual acts of kindness to overcome the 'inhumanity' of what had been done that day. The military advance becomes what Malraux memorably describes as an 'assault of pity'.[28] But tragically, compassion comes at a price: as they help the Russians, the German soldiers unwittingly expose themselves to potentially lethal doses of the gases that are still hanging invisibly in the air. In the actual attack there were 350 German gas casualties. No one counted the number of Russians killed or injured. Exact figures were not kept, but there could have been as many as half a million Russian military gas casualties in the course of the war.[29]

Professor Hoffman is unperturbed by the human suffering. He only has eyes for the effectiveness of his weapon: 'You see! You see! Absolutely decisive!'[30] Malraux's description of Hoffman/Haber is haunting. The chain-smoking professor is obsessed with his quest for what he calls the 'superior weapon'. He has a chilling gleam in his eye as he enthuses about the science of destruction, driven by his eagerness to please his political masters and his superweapon fantasies.

André Malraux wrote his novel in the first half of 1942, the year in which Leo Szilard and Enrico Fermi successfully unleashed the atom's energy in Chicago. This was also the time when the Third Reich was planning the Final Solution, at the Wannsee Conference. And it was another gas developed at Haber's Institute that would permit this scientifically efficient genocide to take place – hydrogen cyanide. It was developed as a fumigant for pest control between 1919 and 1923 in the form known as Zyklon B. One of the chief researchers was Ferdinand Flury, whom Haber had placed in charge of chemical weapons research during World War I. The gas acts on the nervous system and causes instant death. The Germans rejected hydrogen cyanide as a battlefield weapon in World War I, although the French did use it in shells.[31]

Malraux's Professor Hoffman describes hydrogen cyanide as a 'perfect poison' in an enclosed space: 'the victim is seized with convulsions and falls dead in a tetanic rigor'.[32] The SS first used Zyklon B to gas some six hundred Soviet prisoners of war at Birkenau. This gas, which was invented to kill vermin, was used with appalling efficiency as a means of mass murder. Among its many thousands of victims at Auschwitz were Fritz Haber's own relatives.

Another scientist who worked with Haber on the Eastern Front judged the June attack 'a complete success'. Otto Hahn described how initially a change in wind direction caused panic among the German troops. Unarmed, but wearing his gas mask (at this stage only members of Haber's gas warfare unit had respirators), Hahn rallied the German soldiers and led the attack. 'Not a single shot was fired,' he recalled. Thanks to the gas they advanced nearly four miles. Like Vincent Berger, he saw 'a considerable number of Russians poisoned by the gas'. According to Hahn, they 'lay or crouched in a pitiable condition . . . I felt profoundly ashamed and perturbed. After all, I shared the guilt for this tragedy.'[33]

Before joining Haber's chemical warfare unit, Hahn had fought on the Western Front. The chemist had been awarded the Iron Cross (2nd Class) for forming an impromptu machine gun unit with captured Belgian weapons. Called up at the start of the war, he had experienced the extraordinary Christmas of 1914, when English, French and German troops called a spontaneous truce and left their trenches to celebrate Christmas in no man's land. Hahn later recalled how 'The English gave us their good cigarettes, and those among us who had candied fruit gave them some. We sang songs together, and for the night of 24/25 December the war stopped.'[34] But by Boxing Day the unofficial truce had ended, and it was back to legalized murder.

As early as the 1880s, Friedrich Engels had predicted that Germany would wage a world war 'of an extension and violence hitherto un-dreamt of'. It was the logical outcome of the 'mutual outbidding in armaments' in which nations were involved. He warned that the future would bring a massacre on an unprecedented scale. Tomorrow's con-flicts would be total wars.[35] All the benefits of the modern industrial society – railways, telephones, aircraft – meant that war could now be waged faster and with ever more destructive weapons. Some thought that new technology would usher in an era of lightning wars. But they were wrong. Instead, new inventions such as machine guns and barbed wire favoured defenders, and in World War I, Engels's prediction came true. Faced with the new technologies of war, Alfred von Schlieffen's master plan for a rapid conquest of France quickly fell apart, and in its place a network of defensive trenches spread from Belgium to Switzerland. Within weeks Europe was transformed into a 'mausoleum of mud'.[36]

While recuperating behind the lines, Hahn was told to report to Fritz Haber at a Brussels hotel. The two chemists already knew each other. The 34-year-old Hahn worked at the Kaiser Wilhelm Institute for Chemistry, next door to Haber's Institute in Dahlem, conducting research into radium and radioactivity. Hahn knocked on Haber's hotel door at noon, and was surprised to find the eminent professor still lying in bed. 'From his bed he gave me a lecture', Hahn recalled, 'about how the war had now become frozen in place and that the fronts were immobile.'[37] Haber told him that what was needed to break the stalemate was the introduction of 'new weapons'. He intended to use chlorine gas clouds to force the enemy out of their trenches. Hahn pointed out that this would be in breach of the Hague Peace Conferences of 1899 and 1907, which banned 'poison or poisoned weapons'.[38] Such an attack would be universally condemned, he predicted. Haber did not disagree, but he argued, somewhat disingenuously, that as the French had already used tear-gas grenades, Germany would not be the first to use gas weapons. More importantly, he said, it was an opportunity to bring the war to a speedy conclusion: 'countless lives' could be saved.[39]

Hahn was convinced, and joined Haber's gas warfare unit, initially code-named the 'decontamination unit', but known later as the Pioneer Regiment. Other scientists who were recruited included James Franck and Gustav Hertz, both of whom later won Nobel prizes, as did Hahn. Hans Geiger, who invented the radiation counter that bears his name, also worked on chemical weapons during World War I. Hahn's colleague Lise Meitner supported his decision to work on chemical weapons, telling him in March 1915 that lives would be saved if a winning weapon could be invented. And in any case, she said, 'if you don't do it someone else will'.[40] Such reasoning would lead eventually to the alliance of scientists and generals that became a feature of the cold-war arms race.

Some scientists did resist, however. The physicist Max Born 'hated the idea of chemical warfare and . . . refused to take any part in it.' He even 'broke off all personal relations with Haber' and chose to work instead on aircraft radios.[41] A former colleague of Haber, the chemist Hermann Staudinger, asked the Red Cross to condemn the use of chemical weapons. Haber angrily attacked him as unpatriotic.[42] But such principled scientists were in the minority. As Haber's biographer, Margit Szöllösi-Janze, says, there is no doubt that, like Haber, most scientists were 'fascinated' by the possibility of applying science to war. They were eager to take part.[43]

At just after 5 p.m. on Thursday 22 April 1915, another German artillery barrage began. High-explosive shells rained down on the French Algerian troops dug in around Langemarck near the ancient Belgian market town of Ypres. Those brave enough to poke their heads above their trenches, saw a strange cloud drifting slowly towards them across the shell-pocked no man's land. At first the cloud looked white, but as it approached it became thicker and turned a sulphurous yellow-green colour. Carried on the light north-easterly breeze, it moved at about a foot a second, never rising much above the height of a man.

Some soldiers had stripped to the waist in the warm weather. Now they watched curiously as the cloud drew nearer. They were not especially alarmed, having no idea what it was. The cloud crept towards them like an eerie sea mist. The opposing front-line trenches were close here, just fifty yards apart at some points, and the cloud soon reached the first French soldiers. Chlorine gas is twice as dense as air. When it reached the parapets of the French trenches, it rolled down on top of the men like a slow waterfall. It was then the soldiers realized that they were being attacked by a new and deadly weapon.

Samuel Auld, a British chemistry professor, saw the attack. He described the reaction of the soldiers: 'First wonder, then fear; then, as the first fringes of the cloud enveloped them and left them choking and agonized in the fight for breath – panic. Those who could move broke and ran, trying, generally in vain, to outstrip the cloud which followed inexorably after them.'[44]

Initially they felt 'an intense pricking in the nasal passages and also in the throat'.[45] But then, as they inhaled more, it felt as though their eyes, nose and throat were on fire. Uncontrollable spasms of coughing racked their bodies. Chlorine kills by destroying the lining of the lungs. As the lungs become inflamed, fluid builds up, frothing out of the victim's mouth. According to one man who was gassed by chlorine, it felt as though his chest was filling up with soap bubbles.[46] There follows a slow, terrible death, in which the victim drowns in his own liquefied lungs. The poet Wilfred Owen, who was killed in action in 1918, describes the horror of a gas attack:

> As under a green sea, I saw him drowning.
> In all my dreams, before my helpless sight,
> He plunges at me, guttering, choking, drowning.[47]

Disoriented and terrified, soldiers threw away their guns and struggled desperately to climb into fresh air. Any thought of the war vanished from their minds as they fought for breath and for dear life. Many never made it out of their trenches. Afterwards, the shiny brass buttons of all the soldiers caught in the gas had turned green.

The German infantry advanced cautiously behind the cloud of gas. At the last minute they had been issued with improvised cotton mouth-pads. Only the troops of the Pioneer Regiment had been issued with respirators. They were in charge of releasing the gas from the six thousand or so cylinders that had been dug in along a four-mile sector of the line. Fritz Haber had personally supervised the installation of the heavy steel cylinders. They were, said the men, as unwieldy as a corpse.

The go-ahead for the experimental attack had been given in January. It was Haber's show from beginning to end. He had come up with the idea of releasing chlorine from thousands of cylinders and had even organized their supply. He personally tested the effectiveness of the poison gas clouds. Once he almost died when the wind changed and he was caught in the chlorine without a mask. The Pioneer troops began digging holes for the cylinders on 5 April. Ten cylinders were connected to one lead outlet pipe, which pointed towards French lines. On 22 April about 150 tons of chlorine was released.[48] For the first time, scientists were at the front line, leading an attack.

The terrain around Ypres was not ideal for a gas attack. The advancing German soldiers had to pause at patches of low-lying land where the heavy gas still lingered, wraith-like, in the air. But they encountered no resistance; the enemy had either run from the gas or had been overwhelmed by it. A rifleman from Cologne recalled that they walked with their guns tucked under their arms, as if on a casual hunt for wild game.[49] Arthur Conan Doyle, creator of the scientific detective Sherlock Holmes, wrote angrily that the German soldiers 'took possession of . . . trenches tenanted only by the dead garrisons whose blackened faces, contorted figures and lips fringed with blood and foam showed the agonies in which they had died'.[50] The Germans took two thousand prisoners. British soldiers reported that Germans bayoneted many of those they found overcome by fumes.[51]

The number of casualties remains disputed. The Allies claimed five thousand dead and twice as many injured in the attack, but those figures were almost certainly exaggerated.[52] Depending on how long they were exposed to the gas, some men recovered quite quickly. Others spent their last desperate hours coughing and retching as they gasped for breath. The strain on their hearts, as their lungs gradually filled with fluid, was usually fatal. Many of those who survived faced a future of illness. The threat of chronic bronchitis and lung cancer would plague gas victims for the rest of their lives.[53]

The individual fear and suffering of the victims cannot be doubted. The outrage felt by Lieutenant Colonel G. W. G. Hughes of the medical corps was typical:

I shall never forget the sights I saw by Ypres after the gas attacks. Men lying all along the side of the road between Poperinghe and Ypres, exhausted, gasping, frothing yellow mucus from their mouths, their faces blue and distressed. It was dreadful, and so little could be done for them. I have seen no description in any book or paper that exaggerated or even approached in realization of the horror, the awfulness of those gassed cases. One came away from seeing or treating them longing to be able to go straight away at the Germans and to throttle them, to pay them out in some sort of way for their devilishness. Better for a sudden death than this awful agony.[54]

Like the British public, *The Times* was furious at Germany's flouting of the Hague conventions. It was, said the newspaper, a method of war 'up to now never employed by nations sufficiently civilized to consider themselves bound by international agreements'.[55] British researchers had been exploring the possibilities of tear gas since the end of 1914 and had developed a 'stink bomb' codenamed 'SK' after South Kensington, where the Imperial College scientists who invented it were based.[56] But soldiers on all sides hated the idea of such weapons. As the cold-war military strategist Bernard Brodie put it, rather unsympathetically, it was the 'traditional reluctance of the military professions to be killed by anything but traditional weapons'.[57] Most German commanders refused to take part in Haber's 'experiment' in gas warfare. One general admitted that 'the commission for poisoning the enemy just as one poisons rats struck me as it must any straightforward soldier; it was repulsive to me'.[58]

Many thought that gas warfare was unchivalrous. But the gentlemanly values displayed in no man's land at Christmas 1914 were outmoded in a war fought with artillery and machine guns. Many writers, such as Malraux, saw chemical warfare as symbolic of the inhuman nature of war in the twentieth century. But the horrors of what we would now call 'conventional' weapons are often overlooked. A French soldier described the appalling fate of his friend:

The death of Jégoud was atrocious. He was on the first steps of the dugout when a shell (probably an Austrian 130) burst. His face was burned; one splinter entered his skull behind the ear; another slit open his stomach, broke his spine, and in the bloody mess one saw his spinal cord gliding about. His right leg was completely crushed above the knee. The most hideous part of it all was that he continued to live for four or five minutes.[59]

Such individual tragedies were part of the daily experience of soldiers at the front line. In 1916 at the Battle of the Somme, 20,000 British soldiers were killed by machine gun fire in the first bloody minutes of the assault. For those, such as the German writer Ernst Jünger, who lived through that unimaginable carnage, it was obvious that chivalry was a thing of the past: 'Like all noble and personal feelings it had to give way to the new tempo of battle and to the rule of the machine.'[60] A new age of warfare had dawned in which scientists and engineers joined forces with the military to find the most efficient means of destruction for the least expenditure of men and materiel.[61] It was the age of the superweapon.

6

The Man Who Ended War

'Peace upon earth!' was said. We sing it,
And pay a million priests to bring it.
After two thousand years of mass
We've got as far as poison-gas.

Thomas Hardy, *Christmas: 1924*

Francis Bacon, one of the founders of what we now call the scientific method, argued that knowledge is power. Nowhere has this been more powerfully demonstrated than on the battlefield. People have always exploited nature's secrets to gain the upper hand in war. Gunpowder is said to have been discovered in ancient China by Taoist monks searching for the alchemical elixir of eternal life. If that is true, no discovery could ever have so profoundly disappointed its creator. Humankind, it seems, is fated to fall victim to its own ingenuity.

The Catholic Church once tried to put a stop to the science of destruction. A twelfth-century pope banned the cutting-edge battlefield technology of the day – the crossbow. Such a mechanical killing machine was unchivalrous, he said. However, he saw nothing wrong with using it against 'heathens', such as Muslims.[1]

At the end of the nineteenth century, Alfred Nobel set scientists a bad example when he invented an explosive which he called dynamite, from the Greek word for power, *dunamis*. 'I would like', he told a friend in 1876, 'to produce a substance or a machine of such frightful, enormous, devastating effect, that wars would become altogether impossible.' The man whose name became synonymous with scientific achievement made his fortune from the science of destruction. He justified his profits with the hope that 'on the day that two army corps can mutually annihilate each other in a second, all civilised nations will surely recoil with horror and disband their troops'.[2]

Nobel was not alone in this hope. In 1890, an article on 'War in the Future' predicted that in coming conflicts whole regiments would be 'annihilated' at a stroke. The new sciences of destruction meant, said the writer of the article, that 'none but the best troops will endure the prolonged and severe trial to their nerves'.[3] Within a generation these predictions had begun to be realized.

According to historian John Bourne, World War I was the first modern war, the result of 'a century of economic, social and political change'.[4] Advances in technology, such as the electric telegraph, telephones, typewriters, railways and the internal combustion engine, meant that armies could be mobilized quicker than ever before. Military inventions such as machine guns and quick-firing rifled cannon allowed armies to deploy fearsome firepower. As one writer correctly anticipated in 1891, attackers could be 'mown down as corn falls, not before the sickle, but the scythe'.[5] Machine guns and improved artillery forced soldiers to take shelter in trenches. Then poison gas and high explosive shells were invented to drive them back out again.

Even the appearance and role of the infantry changed in the course of the war:

In 1914 the British soldier went to war dressed like a gamekeeper in a soft cap, armed only with rifle and bayonet. In 1918 he went into battle dressed like an industrial worker in a steel helmet, protected by a respirator against poison gas, armed with automatic weapons and mortars, supported by tanks and ground-attack aircraft, and preceded by a creeping artillery barrage of crushing intensity.[6]

The military required devastating force to guarantee victory, and the key to ever greater firepower lay in the hands of the scientist.

If physics – especially atomic physics – was the science of World War II, then chemistry was the science of World War I. The German public in particular was fully aware of the key role played by their chemists, such as Fritz Haber. In 1915 *The Times* reported one German civilian as saying: 'The health and physical welfare not merely of the troops in the field but of the nation at large, and the security of the Empire, rest upon our chemists' shoulders.'[7]

Before the war, Haber's process for synthesizing ammonia, which allowed nitrogen to be harvested from the air, was rightly hailed as a great breakthrough. As populations rapidly increased across Europe, there arose an urgent need for artificial, nitrogen-based fertilizers. In 1898, Sir William Crookes had conjured up a Malthusian demon: unless chemists could find a way to utilize the nitrogen in the air around us, 'the great Caucasian race will cease to be foremost in the world, and will be squeezed out of existence by races to whom wheaten bread is not the staff of life'.[8]

It was Haber who saved Europe from hunger. His revolutionary method for capturing atmospheric nitrogen, discovered in 1911 and quickly developed on an industrial scale by Carl Bosch at the Badische Anilin- und Soda-Fabrik (better known today as BASF – the 'Chemical Company', as their advertising puts it), gave the world for the first time cheap and plentiful artificial fertilizer. But as well as being necessary for healthy plants, nitrogen is an essential ingredient of explosives, an irony Tony Harrison explores in his witty yet powerful play about Fritz Haber, *Square Rounds*: 'The nitrogen you brought from way up high / now blows the men you saved into the sky.'[9] (Haber would have been delighted that Harrison wrote his play in verse, for the cultured chemist loved versifying, even in his laboratory.)

It has been estimated that without Haber's process for manufacturing ammonia, Germany would have exhausted its supplies of explosives within a year. Rather than bringing war to a speedy end, science prolonged the slaughter. In Harrison's play, Haber washes his hands of responsibility for this: 'I'm only the inventor how can I guarantee / no one will turn my nitrates into TNT?'[10]

Harrison memorably describes Fritz Haber as 'the Prospero of poisons, the Faustus of the front'.[11] Every German soldier marched off to the mechanized slaughter of World War I with a copy of Goethe's *Faust* in his knapsack. In Goethe's classic play based on the life of the sixteenth-century alchemist, Faust's insatiable lust for knowledge raises awkward questions about the modern quest for scientific understanding. Haber was just as passionate as Faust about uncovering nature's secrets, and like him Haber also failed to grasp the human cost of his search. Scientific knowledge is worthless – even dangerous – without self-knowledge, suggests Goethe. That is an important but often overlooked moral for the technoscientific age in which we now live.

In October 1914, when Frederick Soddy gave his inaugural lecture at Aberdeen University, he used Haber's process for taking nitrogen from the air as an example of how science could be 'used for evil as well as good'. There was, he said, no better evidence of this than the use of 'scientific weapons of destruction' in the war that had just begun.[12] Soddy's real, but premature, fear was that the secret of atomic power was just around the corner. As early as 1904 he had predicted that whoever discovered how to release the energy of the atom would have 'a weapon by which he could destroy the earth if he chose'.[13] But before atomic bombs became a threat, chemistry had yet to do its worst.

For the Hampshire poet Edward Thomas, Easter 1915 was not a time of celebration as it should be, but of mourning:

> The flowers left thick at nightfall in the wood
> This Eastertide call into mind the men,
> Now far from home, who, with their sweethearts, should
> Have gathered them and will do never again.[14]

For those men far from home – like Thomas himself, who was killed at Arras in 1917 – the war was about to become still more terrible. When Fritz Haber's new weapon was first used a couple of weeks after Easter, the Allies didn't know what had hit them. First carbon monoxide gas was suggested. Then, due to the yellow colour of the cloud, sulphur dioxide. Ironically, this gas – which produces spasms of coughing – had first been proposed as a weapon a century before by a British naval officer.

In 1812, Thomas Cochrane, tenth Earl of Dundonald, suggested using fireships laden with sulphur as a way of flushing Napoleon's troops out of French coastal fortifications. Although a governmental committee rejected the plan as inhumane, the idea did have enough military potential to merit keeping it top secret. Cochrane doggedly resurrected his plan in subsequent campaigns up to the 1850s, and it was also considered for use in the Crimean War. By then the British even had a defence against chemical weapons. In 1854, the industrial chemist John Stenhouse proudly showed off his charcoal respirator to the Royal Scottish Society of Arts. It was, he said, a defence against infectious 'miasmas' and the 'suffocating bombshell', invented as a result of 'the longing for a short and decisive war'.[15]

But Thomas Cochrane was not the first chemical warrior. The Byzantine navy had used a chemical weapon against Arab ships in AD 673. It was an incendiary whose secret composition remains unknown to this day, but was probably a fiery mix of naphtha or sulphur and quicklime.[16] The multi-talented Leonardo da Vinci, who was a gifted military engineer as well as a great artist, invented a 'deadly smoke' (in effect a tear gas) consisting of a shell containing sulphur and arsenic dust.[17] And much later, in the American Civil War, there were many plans for chemical weapons, including chlorine gas shells.

But if the idea of chemical warfare was not new, the scale of the attack at Ypres in 1915 certainly was. According to Samuel Auld, the British officer and chemist who saw the first gas attack, it 'left a battlefield such as had never been seen before in warfare, ancient or modern, and one that has had no compeer in the whole war except on the Russian front.' A deserter had warned the Allies that mysterious steel cylinders were being readied for an attack with a terrible new weapon. 'No one believed him at all, and no notice was taken of it,' said Auld bitterly.[18] Soldiers were not issued with gas masks, even though the technology had existed for sixty years. After the attack, the *Daily Mail* had to appeal to the women of Britain to make home-made face masks for their men at the front. The upmarket department store Harrods encouraged its wealthy customers to make 'Respirators for the Troops', advertising products 'as per official requirements', such as 'absorbent cotton wool covered gauze, with wide elastic band, 3/9 per doz'.[19] The appeal was successful and millions of masks were made. As a defence against poison gas they were worse than useless.

It was surprise that made the gas attack so effective, both at Ypres and on the Eastern Front. In André Malraux's novel *The Walnut Trees of Altenburg*, Vincent does not understand whether the gas works 'chemically, or by means of bacilli, or simply by restricting the air supply of whoever it encircled'.[20] He is an educated man, an academic, yet even he doesn't understand what kind of threat the gas poses. Before the attack, Vincent listens to the ordinary soldiers around him as they wait to advance behind the gas cloud. For them the gas is a total 'mystery', with almost magical powers. They have heard that it kills without any outward signs. One soldier speculates that the victims will be left rigid, frozen 'like dead men in a shop window'. Another wonders whether the river too will be stopped dead in its tracks, as if frozen in time.[21]

The geneticist J. B. S. Haldane, whose father identified the gas used at Ypres, claimed after the war that science offered 'the humanization of warfare' with gas weapons. He even wrote a book to argue his case, called *Callinicus* after the man who invented Greek fire. (It means 'he who conquers in a noble or beautiful manner'.) Haldane, who fought in World War I, tells how soldiers at the front 'removed their respirators from their faces and tied them round their chests, as it was there that they felt the effects of the gas'.[22] For the ordinary soldier, poison gas was a strange and frightening weapon. In the 1950s the public fear of fallout was also made more terrifying by the strangeness of the new threat created by scientists.

When, on 29 April 1915, *The Times* printed the scientific report in which Haldane's father concluded that chlorine was the gas used at Ypres, such was the revulsion at this new form of killing that the paper compared the effects with biological warfare:

Men have died in the hospitals who had struggled out of the gas zone thirty or even forty hours before. The entire system is poisoned. The bodies turn purple, a form of galloping pneumonia follows, respiration runs up to as high as fifty per minute. To all intents and purposes the man dies of pneumonia. The Germans might as well shoot diphtheria, enteric [typhoid], or Asiatic cholera germs as this disease-producing gas.[23]

But biological weapons – which, as we shall see, had already been explored in fiction – remained the one superweapon not deployed in war during the twentieth century, in Europe at least.

*

I'll prove Chemistry is humanity's best friend
and by using its potential bring war to an end.[24]

These words are spoken by Fritz Haber in the play *Square Rounds*. The claim that science could save the world from war, which was only ever achieved in fictional utopias, was made as early as 1864. A British popular science journal argued that 'if science were to be allowed her full swing, if society would really allow that "all is fair in war", war might be banished at once from the earth as a game which neither subject nor king dare play at'. The writer used the example of Greek fire to imagine a chemical superweapon that could defeat any army: 'Globes that could distribute liquid fire could distribute also lethal agents, within the breath of which no man, however puissant, could stand and live. From the summit of Primrose Hill, a few hundred engineers, properly prepared, could render Regent's Park, in an incredibly short space of time, utterly uninhabitable . . .' Science 'would be blessed' for abolishing conventional warfare.[25] Even soldiers would prefer these new weapons. How could it be more humane to 'gouge out their entrails with three-cornered pikes' and leave them to die in agony, he asked. The argument that chemical warfare was more humane would be used by Haber and other of its advocates, such as Haldane, throughout the twentieth century. Those on the receiving end of these weapons in World War I were notably less enthusiastic.

Fritz Haber was always an ambitious man. But once the war began, friends and relatives noted that he appeared to have become obsessed with searching for a decisive weapon that would win the war for Germany. Whenever he talked about chemical warfare and his mission to create the ultimate weapon, Haber, like Malraux's Professor Hoffman, had an evangelistic gleam in his eye. In 1913/14 the staff at Haber's Institute consisted of just five scientists, ten assistants, and thirteen volunteers and students. By 1916 his chemists were working solely on military projects. In Dahlem and at other sites across Berlin, Haber coordinated the efforts of nearly 1,500 scientists and technicians. The war created more work for chemists.

Even after the war, when Haber was branded a war criminal by the Allies, he showed no remorse. What is more, he flouted the Versailles Treaty by secretly working with the German military to improve its expertise in chemical warfare, and even helped other countries, including Russia and Spain, to develop chemical capabilities. In 1920 he told a meeting of German military chiefs that 'gas weapons are definitely no more inhumane than flying bits of metal'.[26]

Haber worked tirelessly in his quest for a scientific solution to the war. But his obsession has to be seen in the light of the almost millennial faith in scientific progress at the start of the twentieth century. In the popular mind there were no limits to what scientists would achieve in the new century. Frederick Soddy had predicted in 1909 that atomic power would enable science to 'make the whole world one smiling Garden of Eden'.[27]

Fritz Haber himself had shown that the science of the previous century, chemistry, could provide the world with enough nitrogen fertilizer to bring that verdant new Eden within reach. If science could make the stony ground fertile and abolish hunger, then perhaps it could also resolve that most intractable of human problems – war. Ironically, as Alfred Nobel believed, to do that scientists had to create a truly terrible superweapon. Thanks to Haber, poison gas became the first weapon of mass destruction.

Up to 1915, poison gas was a weapon that had existed mainly in the minds of writers. According to Haber's younger son, Ludwig, 'gas can trace a direct descent from science fiction'.[28] In novels and stories written before World War I, authors fantasized about scientific weapons of awesome destructive power. They dreamt up weapons so fearsome that war itself became unthinkable. Science achieved what even religion had failed to do – to bring peace on earth. In these fictions, scientists themselves are transformed into saviours.

A new literary genre arose in Europe in the wake of the Franco-Prussian War of 1870–71: future war stories, which fanned the invasion fears of the magazine-reading public. Beginning with G. T. Chesney's 'The Battle of Dorking' (1871), these stories typically described Teutonic invaders reducing 'the quiet squares of Bloomsbury ... to great yawning ruins', to quote a 1906 bestseller.[29] It was a speculative (though non-fictional) study of future wars in this vein that shocked Tsar Nicholas II into taking the unprecedented step of calling an international conference at The Hague in 1899, in order to limit the weapons that could be used in war. High on his list of undesirable weapons was one that did not even exist yet – poison gas.[30]

In the pages of fiction, however, wars had already been fought and won, not just with chemical weapons, but also with biological and nerve agents. The French illustrator and writer Albert Robida's *La Guerre au vingtième siècle*, published in 1887, described and depicted a war fought in 1945 that was eerily prescient in its scientific weaponry. In Robida's war, between France and Germany, airships bombard armoured vehicles on the ground and civilians in a town are killed by chemical shells exploding 'in a greenish cloud'. Robida describes how, thanks to 'recent advances in science', both armies are able to use mines laden with 'malignant fever bacilli' and other germs, as well as 'paralysing gas bombs'.[31] By the end of the nineteenth century, scientific romances were conjuring up images of invincible invaders and scientific superweapons. H. G. Wells's classic 1898 novel *The War of the Worlds* featured Martians armed with a fearsome 'heat-ray' as well as chemical weapons: rockets containing 'Black Smoke', a heavy gas that hugs the ground like chlorine.

For real soldiers fighting on the Western Front in cratered, moon-like landscapes, having to face clouds of suffocating gas, flame-throwers (first used in 1914) and attacks from above by aircraft, it must have seemed as if they had entered an alien world, dreamt up by the crazed imagination of a fiction writer. The futuristic aspects of modern warfare were not lost on one American professor of chemistry at the time. Chas Baskerville described how battle-hardened soldiers ran in terror from the 'weird waves' of gas and how later, when respirators were issued, the masked soldiers looked like strange 'anteaters' rather than human beings. He too saw the parallels in fiction, adding that when one day the history of gas warfare was written, 'it will prove to be a document that would have caused Jules Verne to turn green with envy'.[32] But it was not just poison gas that was born in the minds of fiction writers.

The British military was deeply sceptical about the value of superweapons, believing that old-fashioned soldiering would win the day. So when British inventors came up with a new weapon, the top brass failed to grasp its full potential. The weapons were transported to the front in conditions of utmost secrecy. Their crates were marked simply

TANK, and indeed they did look more like a water cistern than a deadly superweapon. But surprising the enemy with a fiendish new invention offended the British sense of fair play. As a result, when the tank was first used, in 1916 at the Somme, too few were sent into battle and their effect was indecisive.

Before it appeared on the battlefield, the tank had already rumbled its way across the pages of fiction. Albert Robida predicted tanks as early as 1883. Then, thirteen years before the metal monsters saw the light of day, H. G. Wells described their use in battle in his story 'The Land Ironclads' (1903). This was closely followed by Captain C. E. Vickers' story 'The Trenches' (1908). The tank's inventor, engineer Ernest Swinton, had read these stories. Indeed, Swinton was himself a writer whose stories had appeared in *Strand Magazine*.[33]

The idea of scientific superweapons, from heat rays to gas bombs, became firmly rooted in the public consciousness in the years before World War I. Most novels and stories about them accepted without question that social progress was an automatic result of scientific advance. This optimistic vision of the future would last long into the twentieth century, despite the technological horrors of World War I. Indeed, it would make a deep impression on Leo Szilard, who in the last year of the war was a young and very green recruit in the Austro-Hungarian army. The man who in 1950 came up with the doomsday bomb was, appropriately enough, an ordnance cadet learning how to use explosives.

As we have seen, Edward Bulwer-Lytton's *The Coming Race* – inspired by the sciences of evolution and electricity – was one of the first novels to link the discovery of new energy sources with superweapons. Vril gave its owners godlike power, and as a result warfare had become an act of suicide. In a world where both sides are armed with superweapons, the fear of mutually assured destruction (subsequently abbreviated to 'MAD') acts as a deterrent. The message from Bulwer-Lytton and many later writers was that peace could be won in the laboratory.

Frank Stockton's *The Great War Syndicate*, published in America in 1889, is typical of many subsequent novels to examine the role of science and scientists in war. Stockton predicts the alliance between science and industry that would become a distinctive feature of total war in the twentieth century. His matter-of-fact account of a war between the United States and the global superpower of the day, Great Britain, tells how the unprepared US Government accepts an offer from a syndicate of industrialists to fight the war. Motivated by the desire to avoid the harmful economic effects of a 'dragging war', the Syndicate is formed from 'men of great ability, prominent positions, and vast resources, whose vast enterprises had already made them known all over the globe'.[34]

From the outset, these global capitalists know they need a winning weapon. They employ eminent scientists to advise on buying up patents in 'certain recently perfected engines of war, novel in nature'. These include revolutionary armour plating for their ships and a devastating missile, the 'instantaneous motor-bomb', launched not by gunpowder but by the new energy source of the day – electricity. How these missiles work is a 'jealousy guarded secret'.[35] Their use is supervised by a team of 'scientific men'. Indeed, in Stockton's novel, the military has little role in the war; the ship from which the instantaneous motor-bomb is fired is crewed by merchant seamen, and the missile is launched by scientists. This is 'experimental' warfare, writes Stockton, conducted at the touch of a button.[36] Twenty-six years later, the first use of poison gas would be described by Fritz Haber as a *Versuch*, an 'experiment'.[37]

Frank Stockton's novel dramatically anticipates the age of total war that would begin in World War I and lead to the vast scientific and industrial endeavour of the Manhattan Project. The Syndicate mobilizes the 'manpower' (a word coined in 1915)[38] of the entire nation in its efforts to defeat the British: 'In the whole country there was scarcely a man whose ability could not be made available in their work, who was not engaged in their service; and everywhere, in foundries, workshops, and ship-yards, the construction of their engines of war was being carried on by day and by night.'[39]

The instantaneous motor-bomb is so devastating that the Syndicate decides to make a public demonstration of its power on a disused fortress. This reluctance to spring a surprise attack on an enemy with a new weapon shows that the belief in fair play was equally strong in both Great Britain and America. However, Fritz Haber felt no such constraints and, by 1945 this change in attitude had been accepted on both sides of the Atlantic. Leo Szilard's pleas for the power of the atomic bomb to be demonstrated on an uninhabited island rather than on an unsuspecting city fell on deaf ears.

BRITISH OFFICERS WATCHING THE EFFECT OF THE MOTOR-BOMBS.

British officers are filled with 'amazement and awe' as they watch the devastation caused by the instantaneous motor-bombs. From Frank Stockton's The Great War Syndicate *of 1889.*

Like modern nuclear weapons, the motor-bomb could be set to explode either above or below the surface of the ground. To destroy the fortress, a ground-penetrating missile is used. In an instant the fort is vaporized, producing an ominous mushroom cloud: 'a vast brown cloud . . . nearly spherical in form, with an apparent diameter of about a thousand yards'. Like atomic fallout, the 'vast dust-clouds' are carried across the land by the breeze, 'depositing on land, water, ships, houses, domes, and trees an almost impalpable powder'.[40] For the British military, as for the Japanese in 1945, the new weapon is utterly beyond their comprehension. 'This was not war,' said the British. 'It was something supernatural, awful!' Shock and awe began in the minds of writers such as Frank Stockton.[41]

With its two-dimensional characters and deadpan style, *The Great War Syndicate* did not deserve to win any literary awards. But such books had a powerful effect. They changed attitudes to war, creating an expectation that, thanks to science and technology, future conflicts would be quick and low in casualties. As Stockton says at the end of his novel:

The desire to evolve that power which should render opposition useless had long led men from one warlike invention to another. Every one who had constructed a new kind of gun, a new kind of armor, or a new explosive, thought that he had solved the problem, or was on his way to do so. The inventor of the instantaneous motor had done it.[42]

In this fictional war between Britain and America, just one man died: a coal loader on one of the Syndicate's ships who was killed by a falling derrick.

At the end of Stockton's story, the Great War Syndicate is rewarded with a vast sum of money for preventing a drawn-out and costly war. Faced with the Syndicate's superweapon, Britain enters an alliance with the United States to dominate the world. But Stockton leaves his reader with an ominous afterthought: with such a devastating weapon, future wars would be 'battles of annihilation'.[43]

The science of biology provided M. P. Shiel with his superweapon in *The Yellow Danger* (1898), in which an invading army from the Far East is defeated by a new virus. Shiel dehumanizes the Chinese and Japanese by describing them as locusts and rodents. This common propaganda tactic, employed both by the Nazis against Jews and by America against the Japanese in World War II, opens the door to a war of total extermination, a final solution.[44]

The oriental army is led by Dr Yen How. In a confrontation with the British hero, John Hardy, the key role to be played by science in the carnage becomes clear. When Yen How taunts Hardy that a vast army of more than 20 million men is waiting to invade Britain on the other side of the English Channel, Hardy replies:

'Ten good men against a hundred million rats – I bet on the men.'
  'Poh! I bet on the rats.'
  'On the side of the men – science.'
  'Science. What sort of science?'
  'The science of the gunmaker, of the tactician, of the —.'
  'Well?'

'Need I say it?'

'Yes, say it.'

'Of the – chemist.'[45]

Faced with insurmountable odds, only weapons of mass destruction can save the day for Britain. Supplied with vials of a new virus from 'Dr Fletcher of Harley Street', Hardy injects prisoners with the disease and releases them in mainland Europe, which has been completely overwhelmed by the invaders. A needle-prick marks the right forearm of each prisoner, and 'as they went walking toward the town, an ink-black spot appeared on their cheek, and a black froth ridged their lips'.[46] The 'new Black Death' turns Europe into 'a rotting charnel house'.[47] In three weeks, 150 million Chinese and Japanese invaders are dead. Infected people are also transported back to Asia in the hope that the entire population of 400 million will be wiped out.

Shiel's novel appeared in the same year as Wells's classic *The War of the Worlds*, which compares the Martians' genocidal campaign against humans to the 'ruthless and utter destruction our own species has wrought' upon animals and 'inferior races', such as the Tasmanians.[48] In both books, microscopic germs rescue Britain from certain annihilation.

These genocidal fantasies were by no means unique. A whole genre of 'Yellow Peril' fiction followed in the wake of Shiel's book, in which superweapons were often deployed to defeat the invading Oriental 'hordes'. President Harry S Truman, who authorized the dropping of the atomic bomb on cities in Japan, was a keen reader of *McClure's* and other popular magazines which published many stories such as these before World War I. Like Leo Szilard, Truman grew up in the culture of the superweapon, a culture that nurtured fantasies about wiping out whole cities, and indeed races, at the press of a button.

Missiles which could take out any target, microscopic viruses which could annihilate vast armies without a shot being fired – these were the imaginary scientific weapons at the dawn of the new century that inspired the real sciences of destruction. Fritz Haber was obsessed with the search for a scientific weapon which would wipe out Germany's enemies, and poison gas was the result. But it was not the overwhelmingly devastating weapon its inventor had hoped for. Not until 1945 would science give humankind a weapon to match the imaginations of the writers of popular fiction – the atomic bomb. But to read European and American fiction from the years before 1914 is to enter the dark dreams of the young Dr Strangelove. Such dreams would become terrible reality in the cold war and make possible the cobalt doomsday bomb.

The United States of America entered World War I under the slogan of 'the war to end wars'. Never has idealism been so badly used. From Hollis Godfrey's *The Man Who Ended War* (1908) to H. G. Wells's *The World Set Free* (1914), the idea of fighting a final battle to win universal peace had gripped readers in Europe and America. Wells's novel even introduced the phrase the 'war that will end war'.[49]

Once again, science played a vital role in these stories. A new figure emerged in pre-war fiction – the saviour scientist, a Promethean genius who uses his scientific knowledge to save his country and banish war for ever. It is the ultimate victory for Science and Progress. In *His Wisdom The Defender* (1900), Simon Newcomb, one of the most famous astronomers of his day, tells how a scientific genius with 'the responsibility of a god' decides to 'put an end to war now and for-ever'.[50] The inventiveness of such super-scientists know no bounds. The figure of the saviour-scientist appears repeatedly in the science fiction magazines of the inter-war years (known as 'pulps' because they were printed on cheap paper), culminating in comic-strip super-heroes such as The Flash, aka mild-mannered chemist Jay Garrick.[51]

In Roy Norton's *The Vanishing Fleets*, published in 1907, a scientist discovers 'the most powerful force the world has ever known'.[52] Using radium, he and his assistant-daughter have found a way of defeating gravity. The President of the United States tells them: 'In our hands has been given by a miracle the most deadly engine ever conceived, and we should be delinquent in our duty if we failed to use it as a means for controlling and thereby ending wars for all time.'[53]

The President orders the construction of anti-gravity aircraft at the American naval base of Guantanamo Bay. They are built in secret in a government programme to exploit radioactivity. Faced with the anti-gravity planes, the most sophisticated weapon systems of the day – battleships – become redundant overnight: they can be lifted straight out of the water and dropped where they can do no harm. *The Vanishing Fleets* showed its readers how 'science was bringing an end to brute force'.[54]

Published in the same year as Norton's novel, Hollis Godfrey's *The Man Who Ended War* is a gripping scientific thriller. Both writers were probably inspired by sensationalist 1903 press reports that radium had the power to blow the British navy out of the sea. Godfrey, a lecturer in engineering at the Massachusetts Institute of Technology, tells how a German scientist's discovery of a new radium-like element becomes 'one of the greatest things in modern science . . . a force greater than anything yet obtained'. John King, a science journalist with pacifist tendencies, uses its 'radio-active energy' to create a superweapon.[55]

In the year before Godfrey's novel appeared, the British Royal Navy had launched what was thought to be the ultimate war machine – the battleship HMS *Dreadnought*. Its steel armour made it impervious to most shells, and its guns could bombard targets eight miles away. Such ships were the most fearsome fighting machines on the planet. Britain and Germany were locked in a costly arms race to build the biggest and the best ships. A country's battleships, writes Godfrey, 'seemed to personify the might of the nation'. But not for long. John King's new radioactive element emits rays which 'decompose' metal and paralyse people. Battleships exposed to the rays simply 'vanished like a bursting soap-bubble', the sailors falling senseless into the waves.[56]

Armed with this weapon, the pacifist John King issues an ultimatum to all the nations of the world, ordering them to disarm or lose their fleets. He travels round the world in a submarine armed with his superweapon, sinking a ship from each navy until they agree to his demands. After the loss of many ships, even the world's most notorious 'war lord', the German Kaiser, finally agrees to disarm. Having won his prize, John King makes the ultimate sacrifice for the good of humanity: he destroys both himself and his device. 'The world and the man who stopped all war were both at peace,' writes Godfrey. John King had saved the world with science.[57]

Godfrey's novel was one of many promoting the idea that through revolutionary science and the actions of an idealistic scientist, war could be made a thing of the past. It's unsettling today to find the

The narrator of Hollis Godfrey's The Man Who Ended War *(1908) watches as the 'radio-active energy' of John King's superweapon makes battleships vanish like a 'bursting soap-bubble'.*

rhetoric of the cold war (and even of post-9/11 America) in fiction written before World War I. As historian H. Bruce Franklin commented, American popular fiction from this time gave birth to 'a cult of made-in-America superweapons and ecstatic visions of America defeating evil empires, waging wars to end all wars, and making the world eternally safe for all democracy'.[58]

The fascination with super-scientists and superweapons in the years before World War I also gave us the name of the weapon that would overshadow the second half of the twentieth century – the atomic bomb. It is not surprising that it was H. G. Wells who came up with the phrase. He was, after all, the writer who made the scientific romance his own. As we shall see, when his novel *The World Set Free* was read by Leo Szilard in 1932, it filled the young scientist's imagination with both fears of the atomic bomb and hopes for a world liberated by atomic energy. In Wells's novel, world peace comes about only after a global atomic holocaust. As in all these fictional views of science and war, it is the superweapon that brings peace and, ultimately, utopia.

In the Allied nations, the public was outraged by the use of chemical weapons, an attitude encouraged by anti-German propaganda. The shock at their use is comparable to the reaction to the dropping of the atomic bomb in 1945. Both weapons represented a step change in the conduct of war and in particular its implications for civilians. Poison gas and atomic bombs were both indiscriminate weapons, designed to kill and maim over large areas of territory. Mustard gas (first used by the Germans in July 1917) could even be used to render tracts of ground uninhabitable for months. The Chief of Staff of the American army, Peyton C. March, was appalled to see almost two hundred 'small children brought in from about 10 miles from the rear of the trenches who were suffering from gas in their lungs, innocent little children who had nothing to do with this game at all'.[59]

After the use of the new gas weapon at Ypres, rumours spread among civilians about further secret weapons. An article published in *The Times* within a few weeks of the Ypres attack purported to be a news report by 'a neutral' in Germany. But in style and content it is indistinguishable from the scientific romances from the pages of

Strand Magazine or *McClure's*. Titled 'Fog Bombs for London', it tells the reader all of Germany is 'talking of the coming invasion of London by a fleet of Zeppelins'. While drinking in a Munich bar, the reporter learns that the Germans were keen to exploit 'the power of the latest creations of Count Zeppelin, aided by a highly trained staff of scientists'. The reporter notes that Germany's use of 'death-dealing gases' proves that she is 'fully alive to the part which chemical research can play in twentieth-century warfare'. Now, thanks to that expertise, her 'highly skilled scientists' have produced *Nebelbomben*, 'fog bombs', which hide the Zeppelins from the ground, making them invisible to searchlights at night or even the human eye in daylight.

Then, during a train journey, the reporter meets a conveniently loquacious young German. He is surprisingly keen to spill the beans about this new wonder weapon which explodes in the air to cloak the approach of Zeppelins from guns and aeroplanes. 'I saw it myself,' the young German tells the undercover journalist, who in reality probably had not left the shores of England to get his story. 'It was grand. The fog spread for many kilometres nearly instantaneously. With several bombs 20 kilometres square could be covered.' The talkative young man ends with a threat that must have had Londoners glancing nervously up at the sky which, thanks to the English weather, was of course cloudy, even without *Nebelbomben*. 'You will soon hear more of it,' he warns, no doubt with a Prussian click of the heels. Within a fortnight of this article appearing in *The Times*, London was hit by its first Zeppelin air raid.[60]

In 1906, 12-year-old amateur photographer Jacques Henri Lartigue snapped images of balloons at the start of the inaugural Gordon Bennett balloon race in the Jardin des Tuileries, Paris. It was a memorable sight for the boy. In his diary entry for 30 September 1906, he reported the common view that balloons and airships would soon become 'one of the most powerful weapons of war'.[61] Two years later, H. G. Wells depicted just such a scenario in *The War in the Air*. In 1915 such machines – no doubt already familiar to young Lartigue from Jules Verne's stories – brought a new terror to the streets of London, dropping ninety bombs.[62] Some historians have argued that these bombs should also be classed as a form of chemical weapon, one which would become in World War II the most lethal weapon of all: the incendiary bomb.[63]

In World War I, chemical warfare did not prove to be the decisive weapon that Fritz Haber had dreamed of. At Ypres it only temporarily broke the stalemate of trench warfare. Once the element of surprise was lost and defensive measures introduced, the only effect of poison gas was to increase the suffering of soldiers, adding one more terrible way in which to kill and be killed. Advocates of chemical warfare claimed that it was a more humane weapon than high-explosive shells. They quoted death rates showing that there was a relatively low proportion of fatalities among gas casualties; you were less likely to kill your enemy using chlorine than high explosive, they said. It didn't take the military analysts long to decide that this was in fact an advantage: 'the wound-producing weapon has a greater strategic value than the one which kills outright'.[64] But this had nothing to do with humanitarian concerns. The dead were promptly buried, but the wounded had to be cared for. This placed demands on fellow soldiers, thus preventing them from fighting and slowing down an advancing army.

Five months after Fritz Haber's first gas cloud was released at Ypres, the German secret weapon was turned on its inventors by the British army at the Battle of Loos, albeit with mixed success: there were over two thousand British casualties from their own poison gas. But an arms race had begun in which the scientists and soldiers joined forces. As soon as effective gas masks were available for the troops, scientists found chemicals that attacked the skin, or they added sneezing powders into gas shells. These entered the mask and forced the wearer to remove it, thus exposing himself to other lethal gases. When the Germans first used mustard gas, they combined the relatively slow-acting agent with chloropicrin, a strong lachrymator (tear gas). As one American chemist said angrily, 'Soldiers were thus intended to weep at their own funerals.'[65]

Germany led the world in chemistry at the start of the twentieth century and so had a head-start in the search for new chemical weapons. After chlorine, the more lethal phosgene gas was used on the battlefield. This smelled deceptively of new-mown hay, but killed every creature exposed to it by corroding the lung tissue and causing asphyxia. Mustard gas (which is really an atomized liquid) smells of garlic and attacks the skin, causing terrible blisters, as well as fatally damaging the throat and lungs. It is so toxic that during post-mortems, medics were often affected by gas remaining in the lungs of victims. Mustard gas was used by Saddam Hussein's army during Iraq's war against Iran. Most notoriously, Iraq's military used it against its own people in the Kurdish town of Halabja in 1988. Aircraft dropped a mixture of bombs filled with chemical and nerve agents on the town, killing an estimated five thousand civilians.

Germany was the first to use both phosgene and mustard gas. The battlefield around Ypres became a testing ground. Mustard gas was first used there in July 1917. American artist John Singer Sargent's painting *Gassed* records his experience of visiting a medical post after an attack in July 1918 and depicts a line of blinded men shuffling along, helplessly holding on to the man in front. Within days of the first use of mustard gas, British scientists had determined that the chemical was a dichloroethyl sulphide. The race was then on to find a way of weaponizing it for the Allies. In America, one of the key chemists in this race was James B. Conant, a man who would later play a pivotal role in the development of the next generation of weapons of mass destruction – the atomic bomb.

By November 1918, the French alone had produced nearly three million shells filled with mustard gas. In the event that the war should last into 1919, the Allies had prepared for a massive assault using gas cylinders mounted on tanks which would have advanced during an artillery barrage, saturating the ground and air with poison. Haber's superweapon had been turned against his own soldiers with devastating effect. One German corporal, gassed in the final year of the war, would never forget his experience. His name was Adolf Hitler.

By the end of the war a total of 75,000 people – scientists and service personnel – were engaged in chemical weapons development. (The Manhattan Project would employ the efforts of twice that number.) Both Britain and America had set up specialist facilities dedicated to the new form of scientific warfare, at Porton Down and Edgewood Arsenal respectively. In the last year of the war almost a third of all German shells contained chemical warfare agents. But it is a sign of how far the Allies had progressed in chemical warfare that it wasn't Haber who discovered the ultimate chemical weapon. That distinction went to W. Lee Lewis, who before the war had been employed monitoring water quality in public swimming pools in America. Although it was discovered too late to be used in World War I, 'Lewisite', as the gas came to be known, marked America's rise to world dominance in the field of scientific superweapons.

Lewisite was actually a relatively simple compound containing chlorine and arsenic, made from three easily available and cheap chemicals. Like mustard gas, it destroyed skin tissues and was fatal if inhaled. But it was also a systemic poison and could kill merely by being deposited on a person's skin. Excruciating pain in the eyes and skin was followed by vomiting. It could kill a man in a minute, after exposure to a concentration of just 50 parts per million. Although it was not deployed in Europe, the Japanese used it against the Chinese in 1934, and the Soviets developed it in various forms during the cold war. For Lewis, his terrifying gas represented 'the most efficient, most economical, and most humane, single weapon known to military service'.[66] But once the war was won, the public on both sides of the Atlantic began to worry that in the next war ordinary civilians would be on the receiving end of these indiscriminate weapons.

No major airborne gas attacks had been launched during World War I. Fritz Haber and Count Zeppelin had both been keen from the beginning to experiment with dropping gas bombs from the air, but the commander of Germany's military, Erich von Falkenhayn, had ruled this out.[67] In 1917, the British War Cabinet thought it likely that a Zeppelin gas raid would happen, but they didn't want to alarm Londoners by issuing gas masks. 'It would be impossible to train the London population to put on their masks even if they had them,' said Lord Derby, Secretary of State for War.[68] As the war reached its conclusion, the American commander of Edgewood Arsenal, William Walker, was itching to drop his one-ton mustard gas bombs on German cities: 'not one living thing, not even a rat, would live through it', he boasted.[69]

The American journalist Will Irwin had reported on the 1915 Ypres gas attacks for the *New York Tribune*. Appalled by what he had seen, after the war Irwin warned the American public what the effects of Lewisite would be in a future conflict:

it was invisible; it was a sinking gas, which could search out the refugees of dugouts and cellars; if breathed, it killed at once ... Wherever it settled on the skin, it produced a poison which penetrated the system and brought almost certain death. It was inimical to all life, animal or vegetable. Masks alone were of no use against it ... An expert said that a dozen Lewisite bombs ... might with a favorable wind have eliminated the population of Berlin.[70]

Lewis angrily protested that his weapon didn't kill vegetation. But for many people, after World War I it was easy to imagine themselves in a future war living in constant fear of the sound of aircraft engines overhead and the invisible poisons that might be carried on the wind.

In the early days of the war, scientists such as Rutherford's colleague Henry Moseley were sent to the front line as ordinary soldiers. The death of the gifted physicist at Gallipoli, aged just 28, convinced Frederick Soddy that political and social progress was even more urgent than scientific advances. He turned increasingly away from scientific research and towards economic and political theory.

The introduction of U-boat warfare and the first German gas attack in early 1915 led the editor of *Nature* to demand that the British military exploit the expert knowledge of 'the men of science'.[71] The authorities soon agreed that scientists were more useful in a laboratory than in a trench. 'Man invents: monkeys imitate. The war is going to be won by inventions,' said Admiral Lord Fisher, the first chairman of the British Board of Invention and Research, in his 1916 letter accepting the post.[72]

Like Haber in Germany, most scientists were keen to contribute to the war effort and to raise the profile of their disciplines. Only one scientist in America refused to take part in chemical warfare research.[73] Most believed that warfare actually accelerated scientific discovery and that this in turn would lead to benefits for society. It was a classic Faustian bargain: you sold your scientific soul to the military for the promise of a better society in the future.

In an article on 'The Man of Science after the War', a scientist at Dalhousie University posed the question that was in many of his colleagues' minds: 'If it was in the power of science to make war so frightful, is it not within her essentially beneficent capabilities to make the coming day of peace fuller, richer and more glorious than ever day in the past has been?'[74] Science was, after all, the engine of social progress. Hadn't it given us anaesthetics to ease pain, and electricity to bring light into the darkness?

Many scientists also believed that applying science to warfare would lead inevitably to more humane weapons. But ordinary people, especially soldiers returning from the front line, often saw new weapons as merely increasing the suffering of war. An article in the American weekly *The Nation* condemned science for becoming obsessed with 'the will to destroy'. Science had become a 'mad dog' that needed to be muzzled. In the future it should restrict itself to the 'work of peace', not war.[75]

A writer for the Boston *Sunday Herald* felt similarly betrayed:

For half a century we have liberally endowed, supported, and encouraged the scientists. Community funds paid for the institutions in which they were educated and underwrote their experiments. And all the while, we believed that these endeavors were promotions in the interest of civilization . . . Today we stand horror-stricken before the evidence of inhumanities only made possible through scientific advancement . . . Chemistry, you stand indicted and shamed before the Bar of History! You have prostituted your genius to fell and ogrish devices . . . You have turned killer and run with the wolf-pack.[76]

The message forcefully expressed here was that science was no longer progressive, but was taking society down the road to a new barbarism. Such sentiments found a receptive audience among a public shocked and disillusioned by the carnage of World War I. The scientist had once been the man who ended war and heralded an era of wealth and good health. But after World War I, the scientist's halo slipped. The scientific saviour was becoming Dr Strangelove.

7

Einstein's Open Sesame

When all the poison gases are exhausted, a man, made like all other men of flesh and blood, will in the quiet of his room invent an explosive of such potency that all the explosives in existence will seem like harmless toys beside it.

Italo Svevo, *Confessions of Zeno* (1923)

'Modern war is essentially a struggle of gear and invention,' wrote H. G. Wells in an angry letter to *The Times* in June 1915, demanding that scientists be at the heart of the British war effort. 'Each side must be perpetually producing new devices, surprising and outwitting its opponent,' he argued.[1] World War I did indeed stimulate an outpouring of invention from scientists and engineers, as well as from writers and ordinary citizens. In the year that the first soldiers were gassed in their trenches at Ypres, there were Zeppelin bombing raids on London and Paris, and the liner *Lusitania* was sunk by a German submarine. It was clear to everyone that wars could now be won or lost in the laboratory.

Even before Fritz Haber had unleashed his superweapon, America's scientific wizard, Thomas Edison, told the press: 'The present war has taught the world that killing men is a scientific proposition.'[2] He promised the American military a lethal armoury of superweapons and predicted that 'the soldier of the future will not be a sabre-bearing, blood-thirsty savage but a machinist; he will not shed his blood, but will perspire in the factory of death at the front line.'[3]

Despite his claims, by the end of the war Edison had failed to come up with a single usable idea. However, the public on both sides of the

Atlantic were eager to come forward with suggestions for the new factory of death. The British Board of Inventions and Research (BIR) was set up in response to the demands of people like Wells and was manned by such esteemed scientists as J. J. Thomson and Sir William Crookes. By the end of the war it had considered over a hundred thousand suggestions sent in by the public, and a similar number were submitted in America. Only thirty were found to be useful.

One of the British suggestions was to train cormorants to peck out the mortar between bricks. They were to be released over the Ruhr in Germany, where their pecking would, it was claimed, bring down the chimneys of the Krupp steel and armament factories, responsible for making the supergun known as the Paris Gun, capable of firing a shell some eighty miles. Another proposed that sea lions be used to locate submarines by sound. This idea at least was followed up by the BIR. Indeed, Ernest Rutherford conducted pioneering research during World War I into the use of underwater sound detection systems – what later became known as sonar, or ASDIC.[4]

For armchair designers of superweapons, heat rays were the weapon of choice. Archimedes – who had the original *Eureka!* moment – is said to have defended Syracuse against Roman invaders using mirrors to focus the sun's rays. After the discovery of X-rays and then radioactivity, death rays became indispensable for writers of futuristic fiction. From the 'sword of heat' wielded by Wells's Martians to the light sabres in *Star Wars*, heat rays have proved perennial science fiction favourites.

The short story 'When the Earth Melted', written by A. Wilkinson in 1918, describes how a heat ray is invented by a mad scientist – his 'ugly, twisted smile' is a dead giveaway. However, he starts off as a classic saviour scientist, using his 'ultra-conductor ray' to destroy a Chinese invasion fleet that is threatening the United States: 'only a huge mass of smoking, steaming wreckage' was left. But, unable to win the woman of his dreams, he turns the ray on his fellow men in a fit of suicidal rage, ending all life on earth. Future visitors from Mars are left to ponder the results of man's scientific hubris: 'From this catastrophe let us learn the lesson that the attempted usurpation of the power of the Supreme Being means death.'[5]

Martin Swayne's story 'The Sleep-Beam', which appeared in the same year, is rather more imaginative if equally fantastic. Dr Van Hook's scientific superweapon is a ray that prevents people from sleeping. This very English superweapon looks suspiciously like a wind-up gramophone player: 'a square metal box, with a black funnel projecting from it'. Initially sceptical, the military are soon convinced by a demonstration. 'It's the crowning horror – it's hell,' exclaim the awestruck top brass. 'It's the devils of the deepest night let loose. High explosives and liquid flame are nothing to it.' The message to the war-weary reader was clear, even in the fourth year of a war that science had failed to win for either side. As the general says to the inventor, 'you've found the way to end the war in a week or two'. Where science is concerned, hope springs eternal.[6]

In 1921, rumours of a German 'death ray' so alarmed the British Government that the Department of Scientific and Industrial Research (which succeeded the BIR), asked Rutherford and Sir William Bragg to find out whether such a weapon was feasible. Experiments were conducted to see whether rays could be used to detonate explosives. The idea of a death ray was eventually dismissed by the scientists, but such reports continued to crop up regularly. In 1924 Winston Churchill was asked to write an article about future warfare. After consulting a friend, the scientist Frederick Lindemann, he predicted that a deadly ray was indeed a likely weapon. In fact rays did prove vital in World War II, but in the form of radar, an idea tested as early as 1904 by a young German engineer.[7]

One man who needed no convincing about the decisive role science would play in future wars was Hugo Gernsback. In 1926 he began publishing *Amazing Stories*, the first magazine devoted to the kind of scientific fiction popularized by Jules Verne and H. G. Wells. At first Gernsback christened the genre he claimed to have discovered 'scientifiction'. Three years later he wisely dropped this ungainly name and called it 'science fiction' instead. The chief annual awards for outstanding science fiction writing are named 'Hugos' in his honour.

Gernsback was born in 1884 in Luxembourg. From an early age he was fascinated by electricity, and after emigrating to the United States in 1904, he set up a dry-cell battery business. Shocked by Americans' ignorance of science, Gernsback soon switched to writing, publishing his first article – on building radios – in 1905. Three years later he founded his first magazine, 'to teach the young generation science, radio and what was ahead for them'.[8]

By 1911, the indefatigable Gernsback had turned his hand to fiction, publishing the futuristic serial 'Ralph 124C 41+' in his magazine *Modern Electrics*. For Gernsback, as well as many subsequent writers in the genre, science fiction offered the ideal vehicle for technological blue-sky thinking. There is little or no attempt to create believable characters, but the gadgetry of the future is explained in loving detail. Fantastic inventions, saviour scientists, damsels in distress, super-weapons, space travel and the obligatory bug-eyed monsters – these were the ingredients that fuelled the boom in futuristic fiction that the pulp magazines created after 1926.

Hugo Gernsback's technology magazine *The Electrical Experimenter*, begun in 1914, combined science fiction (including death-ray stories, such as engineer George F. Stratton's 'The Poniatowski Ray' in January 1916) with enough articles on gadgets and do-it-yourself inventions to satisfy even the most demanding technophile. The issue of November 1915 had articles on 'How to Build a Dictaphone Desk Set', as well as instructions for assembling a 'Simple Electric Egg Beater – fits any bowl'. In an article entitled 'What the Housewife Should Know About Electricity', L. Shaw Jr tried to convert the magazine's male readers into missionaries for science: 'get busy Mr Man and tell the women folks something about electricity'.[9]

With war raging in Europe and Fritz Haber's scientific superweapon barely six months old, new weapons were topical. *The Electrical Experimenter* contained a long article with a full-page illustration on 'The Electro-magnetic Gun and Its Possibilities', as well as an unsigned piece, probably by Gernsback himself, on 'Warfare of the Future: The Radium Destroyer'. In this, Gernsback points out that 'the European War has clearly demonstrated what a tremendous part modern science plays in the offense as well as in the defense of the contending armies'. It was, he said, 'not a war so much of men as of machines'.[10]

In common with other scientific idealists, Gernsback believed that war could be abolished by the invention of a scientific superweapon. Only when 'some scientific genius (or shall we call him devil?) invents a machine which at one stroke is capable of annihilating one or several army corps' will soldiers think long and hard before offering themselves 'to be slaughtered by the hundred thousand'. Present warfare is bad enough, writes Gernsback, 'with its poison shells, its deadly chlorine gas, its bomb-throwing aeroplanes, its fire-spraying guns, its murderous machine guns'. But what does the future of warfare have in store for us, he asked, 'when the scientists of a hundred years hence begin making war on each other?'

In fact, the professional futurologist was bang on target with his prediction. According to Gernsback, the future's most terrible weapons would come once scientists had discovered how to 'unlock atomic forces'. But in 1915, he thought it would take an entire century to solve 'the puzzle of the atom'. The colour cover of *The Electrical Experimenter*'s November 1915 issue features an eye-catching artist's impression of what Gernsback imagined an atomic superweapon would look like. The 'Radium Destroyer' is in fact a radio-controlled tank – a year before tanks appeared on the Western Front – with an 'atomic gun'. Its lethal combination of armour plating and death rays is reminiscent of H. G. Wells's mechanized Martians in *The War of the Worlds*. Indeed, in Byron Haskins' 1953 film of the book, the invaders use both a Wellsian heat ray and a more futuristic green atomic disintegrator ray that seems to pay homage to the Radium Destroyer's death ray.

Gernsback explains how the 'solid green "Radium-K" emanation . . . has the property of setting off spontaneously the dormant energy of the Atom of any element it encounters except lead'. Everything hit by the atomic gun disappears into a 'dense cloud of vapor'. The lethal power of the Radium Destroyer is demonstrated on a city of 300,000 people, leaving just a 'vast crater in the ground' and a 'titanic Vapor cloud'. The inhabitants were, of course, evacuated well before the city was vaporized. It would take another world war to convince the public that a whole city of people could be destroyed without warning.

In the same year that Hugo Gernsback was speculating about the horrors of future atomic warfare, a novel appeared which echoed his hopes that, in the right hands, the power of the atom might abolish war altogether. *The Man Who Rocked the Earth*, by Arthur Train and Robert Williams Wood, is set in 1916 in the middle of a world war that has reached a bloody stalemate, both on the battlefield and in the laboratory: 'the inventive genius of mankind . . . had produced a multitude of death-dealing mechanisms, most of which had in turn been rendered ineffective by some counter-invention of another nation'.[11]

Suddenly, a mysterious scientific inventor, symbolically named Pax, sends a radio message to the world demanding the cessation of hostilities and the abolition of war. Pax uses uranium to power a futuristic aircraft that is identical to the flying saucers that would fascinate America during the cold war. The 'Flying Ring' is doughnut-shaped, with portholes in the side and a ray of bright light projecting downwards. His aircraft and his superweapon are powered by atomic energy. Like Gernsback's Radium Destroyer, the disintegrating ray invented by Pax sets off an explosive chain reaction in matter. The ray is lavender blue in colour, evoking the glow of radium.

Pax provides a demonstration of his fearful weapon by destroying the Atlas Mountains near the Mediterranean. Eyewitnesses describe the apocalyptic effect: 'Instantly the earth blew up like a cannon – up into the air, a thousand miles up. It was as light as noonday . . . The ocean heaved spasmodically and the air shook with a rending, ripping noise, as if Nature were bent upon destroying her own handiwork. The glare was so dazzling that sight was impossible.'[12] The flash of an atomic explosion is so bright that it blinds anyone who dares to look at it. Observers of the first atomic bomb test in July 1945 were provided with welder's goggles to avoid damaging their eyes. It was, said Robert Oppenheimer, quoting the Bhagavad Gita, like 'the radiance of a thousand suns'.[13]

The Man Who Rocked the Earth contains other striking parallels with real nuclear weapons. An Arab mussel-gatherer and his two brothers were out in their boat when they were caught in the 'Lavender Ray'. At first they noticed no ill-effects. However, five days later 'all three began to suffer excruciating torment from internal burns, the skin upon their heads and bodies began to peel off, and they died in agony within the week'.[14]

Exactly forty years after this was written, a Japanese fishing boat in the Pacific, the *Lucky Dragon*, had the misfortune to be caught in the fallout from an American hydrogen bomb test at Bikini Atoll. Nearby islanders and the Japanese fishermen experienced radiation

In The Man Who Rocked the Earth *(1915), Pax's 'Flying Ring' uses its atomic disintegrating ray to destroy the Atlas Mountains near the Mediterranean. The crew of a nearby fishing boat later die after being exposed to the radiation.*

sickness – vomiting, diarrhoea, skin burns and hair loss. By the end of the year one of the fishermen was dead, and the other twenty-two were still in hospital, receiving blood transfusions. As early as 1904, Jean Danysz, the biologist who worked with the Curies, had described such effects as skin loss as a result of radiation exposure and predicted that two pounds of radium could wipe out the population of Paris. Now, just months after the first weapon of mass destruction was used at Ypres, a popular novel anticipated the horrors of future super-weapons.

In *The Man Who Rocked the Earth*, Pax loses patience with the warring Europeans and threatens to use the unparalleled power of atomic energy to shift the earth on its axis so that Strasbourg becomes the new North Pole. He tells the world that Europe will become a wasteland: 'The habitable zone of the earth will be hereafter in South Africa, South and Central America, and regions now unfrequented by man. The nations must migrate and a new life in which war is unknown must begin upon the globe.'[15]

This idea also recurs in the atomic age. In the era of ever-larger H-bomb tests, headlines and even a film – *The Day the Earth Caught Fire* – envisioned the earth's orbit being disastrously disturbed. Such themes in popular culture carried an important and far-reaching message. The forces contained in the atom offered humankind truly god-like power over not just their own fate but that of the entire planet. Superweapons – of which Szilard's cobalt bomb was the most terrible – fundamentally changed our relationship to the earth.

Pax achieves his dream of a world without war: 'The nations ceased to build dreadnoughts, and instead used the money to send great troops of children with [their] teachers travelling over the world.'[16] Ironically, Pax doesn't live to see the utopia he has created as he is accidentally killed by his own invention. But once again, a scientist and his superweapon have saved the world from the scourge of war. It is easy now to dismiss the novel as a scientific fairy tale, one in which sometimes dubious science provides a fantastic solution to the problem of war. But such fictions do provide powerful evidence of how people identified atomic energy and atomic weapons as the key to a utopian future. The saviour scientists of the future would be physicists.

Benjamin Hooker is a Harvard physicist in *The Man Who Rocked the Earth* who manages to track down the maverick scientist, Pax, to his secret laboratory before he dies. Hooker is full of fantastic dreams of how atomic energy might be used to abolish war and disease. He has read Frederick Soddy's *The Interpretation of Radium* and believes that he can use 'the quantum theory' to improve on Pax's application of atomic energy. 'A single ounce of uranium', he says excitedly,

contains about the same amount of energy that could be produced by the combustion of ten tons of coal – but it won't let the energy go. Instead it holds on to it, and the energy leaks slowly, almost imperceptibly, away, like water from a big reservoir tapped only by a tiny pipe . . . If, instead of that energy just oozing away and the uranium disintegrating infinitesimally each year, it could be exploded at a given moment you could drive an ocean liner with a handful of it.[17]

Hooker demonstrates to a colleague how to induce an atomic reaction in a piece of uranium. He describes how the atoms 'disintegrate, their products being driven off by the atomic explosions with a velocity about equal to that of light . . . The amount of uranium decomposed in this experiment couldn't be detected by the most delicate balance – small mass, but enormous velocity.'

His friend comments that this is 'momentum equals mass times velocity'. It's tempting to replace momentum with energy and to see in this explanation an allusion to the most famous equation of all, $E = mc^2$. For Einstein's equation explains what Hooker is trying to describe – the vast amount of energy in the invisibly small atomic reaction: energy equals mass times the velocity of light squared. Is that to read too much into this passage? Perhaps. But, as we have seen, Frederick Soddy had already discussed matter as energy in 1903.

Clearly, the knowledge that a small quantity of matter contains a vast amount of energy enters popular fiction long before the atomic nucleus was split. Atomic energy was beguiling readers and writers with the dream of unlimited power before most scientists would even consider the idea. 'If we could control this force and handle it on a large scale,' says Hooker, bursting with excitement, 'we could do anything with it – destroy the world, drive a car against gravity off into space, shift the axis of the earth perhaps!'[18]

Like the Roman god Janus, science has two faces. In 1915, while Fritz Haber and his team of chemists at the Institute for Physical Chemistry and Electrochemistry in Dahlem were developing the poison gases that they hoped would win the war for Germany, in the same building a 36-year-old theoretical physicist was trying to glimpse the mind of God.

Albert Einstein's office was temporary. He had been lured from Zurich to Berlin in 1914 by Germany's leading physicist, Max Planck, and the chemist Walther Nernst. They had offered him membership of the prestigious Prussian Academy of Sciences and a research professorship at the University of Berlin. The salary was extremely generous, and he was not even expected to teach. In addition they promised him his own institute of physics. But the war had delayed its construction and now it would not open until 1917. In the same month that Haber watched chlorine gas drift over the French trenches at Ypres, Einstein told a friend that wartime Berlin felt like a 'madhouse'.[19] The war had driven Germany insane. Technological progress, said a gloomy Einstein, was 'like an axe in the hand of a pathological criminal'.[20]

In October that year he blamed 'the aggressive characteristics of the male creature' for war.[21] He had a point. Five months earlier, Clara Haber had committed suicide in the Institute's grounds, some said as a protest at her husband's war work. Rather than turn their skills to inventing weapons, the atomic scientists Marie Curie and Lise Meitner trained as radiologists in order to be able to X-ray wounded soldiers. Later, Meitner was part of the Dahlem team that first split the uranium atom. Although she had been forced into exile from Germany in 1938, she refused to help build the atomic bomb.

Einstein wasn't alone in feeling that Berlin had become a madhouse. The Dadaists agreed with the revolutionary physicist. Richard Huelsenbeck and Hugo Ball were starting to give their anarchic performances in the nightclubs of Berlin, before fleeing to Zurich to publicly found the movement.[22] In November, an inmate of the asylum that was Berlin presented four scientific papers to the Prussian Academy of Sciences. The theory Einstein set out over four winter evenings was so revolutionary that his opponents branded him a scientific Dadaist.

The general theory of relativity was the culmination of a scientific journey that had begun when Einstein was 17 with a thought experiment about riding on a wave of light. That was in 1896, the year Röntgen's X-rays made headline news. He didn't put his ideas on paper until 1905, Einstein's *annus mirabilis*. In this single year, he wrote five astonishingly original scientific papers. The first was, he told a friend, 'very revolutionary'.[23] It proposed an alternative theory of light: that it consists of a stream of particles, now called photons, each of which carried a tiny amount, or quantum, of energy. From this interpretation of the nature of light would flow astonishing discoveries about the subatomic realm. They formed the basis of quantum theory, which proved to be a particularly troublesome child for its father.

In another of his 1905 papers, Einstein proposed a novel way of determining the size of atoms, at a time when some leading scientific figures still doubted their very existence. His third paper was a study of the erratic movement of molecules, known as Brownian motion. But it was the paper that he completed in June 1905, 'On the Electrodynamics of Moving Bodies', that would transform the way we look at the cosmos. It is better known today as the theory of special relativity. In it Einstein rewrote the rules governing how we perceive the universe around us and overturned many of our common-sense notions about time and space. In particular, he established that the speed of light always remains constant at 186,000 miles per second. All electromagnetic radiation, from X-rays to radio waves, travels at this speed. Nothing can go faster.

One of the implications of this revolutionary idea is that our understanding of time has changed. Einstein realized that if he were able to travel at the speed of light, as he had imagined in his thought experiment, time itself would cease for him. In the relativistic universe there is no single clock keeping time throughout the vast reaches of space. Furthermore, because light takes time to travel, there is always a time lag in communicating information. 'Time cannot be absolutely defined,' Einstein told a friend in 1905. When you look up at the stars in the night sky, you see starlight that has taken many years to travel through space at the fastest speed in the universe – the speed of light.

According to Einstein, there is no longer any universal 'now', no simultaneity of experience between observers in different parts of the galaxy. The universal time of Newton, in which events happened at the same moment throughout space, has been shattered into fragments of local time.

Einstein's theory changed space, too. If you did manage to travel at near light speed, you would see clocks in the world you left behind running more slowly, and space contracting – any ruler you happened to pass would shrink in length. But as your speed increased, so too would your mass. That's something particle physicists at CERN (the European Organization for Nuclear Research) see every day – the more energy they pump into a particle to make it go faster, the more massive it gets. This shows that energy and mass are part of the same equation. In fact, space, time and mass are all relative properties: they are not fixed, but change with velocity. Although he was no Dadaist, Einstein's universe was certainly bizarre.

Having completed his paper on relativity, Einstein kvetched to a friend that 'the value of my time does not weigh heavily these days; there aren't always subjects that are ripe for rumination. At least none that are really exciting.'[24] It was an astonishing comment, given the originality of the four papers he had written in the last few months. But one thought did emerge to lighten the tedium of Einstein's days in 1905:

Namely, the relativity principle, in association with Maxwell's fundamental equations, requires that the mass be a direct measure of the energy contained in a body; light carries mass with it. A noticeable reduction of mass would have to take place in the case of radium. The consideration is amusing and seductive; but for all I know, God Almighty might be laughing at the whole matter and might have been leading me around by the nose.[25]

God was not teasing. Einstein wrote up his insight in a three-page paper called 'Does the Inertia of a Body Depend on Its Energy Content?' In it Einstein tentatively suggested that 'if a body emits the energy L in the form of radiation, its mass decreases by L/V^2'. As in his paper on relativity, L denoted energy (*lebendige Kraft* or 'vital energy') and V was the speed (velocity) of light. His far-reaching conclusion was that 'the mass of a body is a measure of its energy content'.[26] In 1907 he would express this relationship in the form we know it today: energy (E) released in the form of light (c) results in a reduction in mass (m) by an amount E/c^2. The equation was $E = mc^2$.

The light emitted by the vial of radium held up by Pierre Curie that evening in Paris in 1903 revealed a very gradual decrease in mass. As Benjamin Hooker in *The Man Who Rocked the Earth* pointed out, the amounts involved were minute. But when these tiny amounts of matter are multiplied by the speed of light squared, the release of energy is enormous – almost enough to rock the earth. On 6 August 1945, only a small amount of the uranium-235 in the atomic bomb dropped on Hiroshima, less than two pounds, fissioned and was transformed into pure energy. Its explosive power was equivalent to more than 12,000 tons of high explosive. As Einstein realized in 1905, matter was frozen energy. Or as Frederick Soddy had said two years earlier, the earth was a storehouse stuffed with explosive.[27]

In 1907, Einstein was still working in the medieval Swiss town of Berne as a relatively unimportant patent officer, or as Einstein himself put it in his inimitable style, as a 'respectable Federal ink pisser'.[28] He worked a forty-eight-hour week at the patent office. But just occasionally he pushed his work aside, opened a special drawer in his desk and took out his own research. With characteristic irony, the scientist who was having trouble finding an academic position named the drawer the 'Department of Theoretical Physics'.

It was at just such a moment in 1907 that Einstein had what he later called 'the happiest thought of my life'. Gazing out of the large window in his third-floor office while thinking about relativity, Einstein saw a builder on the red-tiled roof of the building opposite. He was struck by an extraordinary idea: if the man were to fall, he wouldn't feel his own weight. For a brief moment he would be weight-less, free of gravity – at least until he hit the ground. This 'happy' thought (the weightlessness, not the builder hitting the ground) led Einstein to the equivalence of gravity and acceleration. From there he was able to extend his special theory of relativity to a general theory, in which gravity was no longer a mysterious force, as Newton had supposed, but an intrinsic part of the structure of spacetime.

It was this revolutionary vision of a new, relativistic universe that Einstein laid before the Prussian Academy of Sciences in the winter of

1915. According to his startling theory, starlight would bend as it passed near massive bodies such as the sun. Einstein explained that matter – planets and stars – causes space itself to curve, producing the effect we call gravity. Just as a person standing in the middle of a trampoline produces a marked dip in the fabric, so mass stretches the fabric of space, pulling everything towards it, even light itself.

Einstein challenged astronomers to test his theory by observing the positions of stars that lay near the sun in the sky, which without special apparatus is possible only during an eclipse. According to Einstein, 'at such times, these stars ought to appear to be displaced outwards from the sun'.[29] He even predicted the degree of displacement. His theory was, said fellow German physicist Max Born, 'a great work of art'.[30] Once he had completed it, Einstein didn't exactly cry *Eureka!*, but he did confess to being 'beside myself with joy and excitement for days'.[31]

The first British scientist to hear about Einstein's general theory of relativity was the young physicist James Chadwick. He was spending the war interned at a former racecourse just outside Berlin, despite the best efforts of Einstein's colleagues to have him released. Even under lock and key, Chadwick managed to continue his research into the atom by obtaining a brand of German toothpaste that contained radioactive thorium. Seventeen years later, in 1932, it would be Chadwick who discovered the particle that would unlock the energy inside matter predicted by Einstein's equation $E = mc^2$. The mysterious glow of radium had illuminated the pathway to the heart of the atom.

Fritz Haber and Albert Einstein didn't quite see eye to eye. Although he respected Haber as a scientist, Einstein once admitted to Max Born that he considered the Nobel prizewinning chemist to be a 'raving barbarian'.[32] For one thing, Haber couldn't stomach Swabian food. The discoverer of relativity loved the simple country cooking of his home town, Ulm, in the southern German region of Swabia. Einstein's second wife, Elsa, his cousin whom he married in 1919, came from the same region and encouraged his taste for their local dishes such as *Spätzli*, the soft egg noodle that is a staple ingredient in Swabian cooking. Haber was known to refer to *Spätzli* as 'mush'.[33]

Apart from food, the war was another bone of contention between

Albert Einstein with Fritz Haber at the Kaiser Wilhelm Institute for Physical Chemistry and Electrochemistry, 1914.

the two men. Einstein was elated when the war ended, despite the fact that his homeland had been defeated.[34] On 9 November 1918, the man who had pinned a medal to Röntgen's chest for discovering

X-rays was suddenly out of a job – Kaiser Wilhelm II was forced to abdicate and a republic was proclaimed. That same day, Einstein's lecture on relativity was cancelled – 'due to revolution', as he wrote in his course notes.[35] Whereas the physicist Arnold Sommerfeld expressed his dismay at 'everything unspeakably miserable and stupid' at this time,[36] Einstein was overjoyed. He was optimistic that his country now had a democratic future: 'Germans who love culture will soon again be able to be as proud of their fatherland as ever – and with more justification than *before 1914*'.[37]

In contrast, the inventor of chemical weapons wept at the defeat of Germany. Fritz Haber's daughter recalls how, after the Kaiser's abdication, she and her father attended a performance of Friedrich von Schiller's play about France's tragic saviour, Joan of Arc, *Die Jungfrau von Orleans*. She was shocked to see tears streaming down his face.[38] Haber took defeat personally: his superweapon had failed to win the war and save the Fatherland. It wasn't just Germany that had lost, but science too.

Haber was not alone in his bitterness. After the war, the groundless rumour spread that the German military had been stabbed in the back by spineless politicians. It was a dangerous myth, and it fuelled nationalist resentment in the coming years. When the German republic was proclaimed and the armistice signed in November 1918, a 29-year-old German corporal was recovering in hospital fifty miles north of Berlin after being half-blinded by mustard gas. Adolf Hitler was appalled when he heard news of the armistice:

Everything went black before my eyes. I tottered and groped my way back to the dormitory, threw myself on my bunk and dug my burning head into my blanket and pillow . . . So it had all been in vain. In vain all the sacrifices . . . in vain the death of two millions . . . There followed terrible days and even worse nights . . . In these nights hatred grew in me, hatred for those respon-sible for this deed. In the days that followed, my own fate became known to me . . . I, for my part, decided to go into politics.[39]

For his invention of poison gas, Fritz Haber was placed on an Allied list of war criminals. He grew a beard to avoid being recognized on the street and even went to Switzerland to evade arrest. But after a few months the threat was removed, and by 1919 he was back in charge of his Institute. That year he was awarded the Nobel Prize in Chemistry. The press on both sides of the Atlantic was outraged. But in his desire to use science to end the war, Haber could claim to be a scientist who walked in the footsteps of Alfred Nobel.

Military men on all sides now accepted that scientific weapons of mass destruction, such as poison gas, were a part of modern warfare. In Britain, the official Holland Report on chemical warfare concluded without hesitation in 1919 that gas was a 'legitimate weapon in war'. The Committee that drew up the report assumed that it was a 'foregone conclusion' that gas would be used in the future, 'for history shows that in no case has a weapon which has proved successful in war ever been abandoned by Nations fighting for existence'.[40]

At the war's end, Germany was on its knees. It had lost 1,773,000 soldiers killed and more than four million were wounded. The streets of Berlin teemed with returning soldiers, angered and embittered after futile years of bloodshed. At the same time, refugees from the east flocked into the city. All were hungry. Berliners had been forced to endure what physicist Max Born called 'turnip winters' during the war.[41] Food shortages meant that turnips became the key ersatz ingredient in everything from jam to flour and even beer. But by the end of the war people were dying of starvation. The pinched faces of malnourished children in Käthe Kollwitz's unforgettable etchings speak powerfully of the suffering of Berliners in these years. To hunger was added a new scourge, disease. As the war ended, an epidemic of Spanish flu swept across Europe, killing three hundred people a day in Berlin.

The city and the land were ripe for revolution. In the final days of the war, sailors waving red flags had mutinied, taking control of the city of Kiel, an act that sparked revolution throughout Germany. The Russian Bolsheviks had led the way in the previous year. Now workers with red armbands and rifles roamed the streets of Berlin, looting and beating up officials associated with the old regime. At one point, Einstein was summoned to save the rector and several university professors from an uncertain fate, when they were taken hostage by radical students. He and Max Born passed through streets 'full of wild looking and shouting youths with red badges' on his way to the Reichstag.[42] There, Einstein negotiated first with the Students' Council and finally with the new Chancellor, Friedrich Ebert himself. Einstein's colleagues regarded him as a 'high-placed Red', he told his mother proudly.[43] That was why the students trusted him. While the would-be saviour scientist, Fritz Haber, was hiding behind his freshly grown beard, Einstein was being hailed as a man of the people – a popular hero.

This could not be said for most scientists after the war. In contrast to the general pre-war optimism about science and technology, there was now a pervasive doubt about what the future held. Some people argued that it was unfair to criticize scientists for their lethal inventions. As someone wittily observed during World War I, 'to blame chemistry for the horrors of war is a little like blaming astronomy for nocturnal crime'.[44] But German expressionist writer Georg Kaiser had experienced gas warfare at first hand. His play cycle, *Gas I* and *Gas II*, written during and after the war, shows how the desire of industry and science for the ultimate energy source could all too easily degenerate into a quest for the ultimate weapon.

One of the great novelists of the Weimar Republic, the Berliner Alfred Döblin, echoed Kaiser's fears in his futuristic fable *Mountains, Oceans and Giants* (1924). Set in the twenty-third century, his novel chronicles humankind's disastrous attempts to control and exploit the forces of nature across five hundred years, from the replacement of natural food with scientific substitutes to the catastrophe brought about when Greenland's glaciers are melted by harnessing the energy of volcanoes. This Faustian exploit leads to the discovery of a force of nature that gives science ultimate control over matter. But it is a power that this technologically advanced civilization cannot control.

By the end of Döblin's novel, people have turned their backs on cities and science to re-establish agricultural communities: humankind returns to nature. The message of the book is clear: 'We were not mature enough for these things.'[45] Döblin, who was trained in the medical sciences, depicts a civilization which has not grown wise in proportion to its power. His warning is clear and parallels that in Goethe's *Faust*: greater knowledge does not necessarily lead to wisdom and self-understanding. The fears expressed in Döblin's novel echoed across the decades. Many of his themes would return in the fiction of the 1950s, when writers imagined the atomic mushroom cloud billowing above their cities.

The German playwright Bertolt Brecht had been a medical orderly during the war. In 1918 he caused uproar when he recited his poem 'The Legend of the Dead Soldier' in public. The poem tells how a dead soldier was dug up by medical men, revived with a 'fiery schnapps' and sent back to the trenches to fight for the fatherland. In the previous year, a short play published in the British *Strand Magazine* had described a similarly grotesque scenario.

'Blood and Iron' appeared in *Strand* in 1917. Perley Poore Sheehan and Robert H. Davis's dramatic sketch expresses the anger and resentment now felt by many people towards scientists. A German scientist has created a half-man, half-machine: a 'supersoldier'.[46] This World War I RoboSoldier has a telescopic eye with night vision, a metal leg and hands, and metal teeth which can 'bite barbed wire in twain'. Before the war, even superweapons had served the best interests of humanity. But now the scientist places his lethal creation at the service of the unmistakably Teutonic Emperor. As Fritz Haber had said, at times of war a scientist's loyalty was not to humanity, but to his ruler.

The scientist in 'Blood and Iron' treats the Emperor with 'an air of fawning enthusiasm'. He is 'a small, thin man' with 'bulging eyes, horn spectacles' and – rather predictably for a scientist – a 'heavy head of grey hair'. No matter how badly wounded the soldier is, boasts the scientist, science can now return him to the trenches as a 'supersoldier – no longer a bungling, mortal man – but a beautiful, efficient machine!' He promises the Emperor 'a million cripples transformed into a million fighting units'.

For turning shattered men into superweapons, the scientist is immediately awarded the highest honour the Emperor can bestow: the Order of Merit. 'You have brought the greatest advance in the history of civilization,' proclaims the Emperor. As in Brecht's poem, the man of science is no longer the saviour of the people but the servant of the despised regime. It would be a theme Brecht himself would return to many years later in his great cold-war play on the misuse of science, *The Life of Galileo*.

But despite his mechanized body, the supersoldier – who is known only as Number 241 – still has a mind of his own. In halting, robotic tones he tells the Emperor that the advance of science means that he will now be brought twice to the slaughter. Now that science can resurrect men, even death cannot guarantee a release from the suffering of war: 'By – doubling – the – strength – of – your – army – you – have – multiplied – human – grief.' The powerful implication of 'Blood and Iron' is that progress has been perverted. Science no longer sets people free, but enslaves them. The drama ends with the scientific supersoldier killing the Emperor with his bare, metallic hands.

Just as it seemed as though people were becoming disillusioned with scientists, a new scientific hero hit the headlines in 1919, one whose fame would soon exceed even Röntgen's or Marie Curie's. On 6 November, almost exactly a year after the Kaiser had abdicated, Albert Einstein's theory of general relativity was spectacularly confirmed. Earlier that year, two scientific expeditions had set out to observe an eclipse of the sun from West Africa and Brazil. The results of the British expeditions were announced in Burlington House, in London's Piccadilly, at a joint meeting of the Royal Society and the Royal Astronomical Society.

The atmosphere in the room was tense as the assembled scientists waited for the announcement. It felt like a scene from a Greek tragedy, recalled Alfred North Whitehead, who was in the audience. The only difference was that in the modern era the laws of physics had become the decrees of fate. Standing beneath a portrait of the most famous physicist of them all, Sir Isaac Newton, the president of the Royal Society stressed the significance of the occasion: 'This is the most important result obtained in connection with the theory of gravitation since Newton's day.'[47] The photographs of stars visible near the eclipsed sun bore out Einstein's prediction that the sun's mass would warp the geometry of space, causing starlight to be bent. A new understanding of gravity had been born.

The next day, even the usually cautious London *Times* could hardly conceal its excitement. REVOLUTION IN SCIENCE, shouted its headline, NEW THEORY OF THE UNIVERSE – NEWTONIAN IDEAS OVERTHROWN.[48] Einstein could only sigh at such bold claims. On the wall of his spartan study in Haberlandstrasse was a picture of his scientific hero, Sir Isaac Newton. Later he even felt moved to apologize in print to the great English physicist. 'Newton, forgive me; you found just about the only way possible in your age for a man of highest reasoning and creative power.'[49] Although in politics and even in his science Einstein was described as a Bolshevist, he was in reality a reluctant revolutionary.[50]

Arthur Eddington, the Cambridge professor of astronomy who had led the West African expedition to observe and photograph the eclipse, wrote to Einstein the following month to tell him that 'all England is talking about your theory'.[51] A Quaker and a pacifist, Eddington had refused to fight in the war. 'I cannot believe that God is calling me to go out to slaughter men,' he had bravely told the draft board.[52]

That December in Germany, the popular Berlin *Illustrirte Zeitung* depicted a brooding Einstein on its cover. The caption read 'A new celebrity in world history: Albert Einstein. His research signifies a complete revolution in our concepts of nature and is on a par with the insights of Copernicus, Kepler, and Newton.'[53] This solemn photograph of Einstein, with his head resting on his hand and his eyes cast downwards showed a man who has stared deeply into the nature of things. He appears as a modern seer or even a wizard, a nickname regularly applied to Edison in America. In the atomic age, the scientific wizard would even have a magic formula that mystified and terrified the public in equal measure. Following the dropping of the atomic bombs on Hiroshima and Nagasaki, Einstein was depicted on the cover of *Time* against a mushroom cloud on which was written his equation $E = mc^2$.

Einstein was unimpressed by his new-found fame. He told a friend that 'the newspaper drivel about me is pathetic'.[54] To his former wife, Mileva Marić, he wrote: 'I feel now something like a whore. Everybody wants to know what I am doing all the time.'[55] Einstein never sought the limelight, but once it had found him he was happy to use it to highlight what he felt were deserving causes, such as pacifism and Zionism. Fame had its downside, though. Although he liked nothing better than to puff away at a cigar, Einstein was shocked when a man from a tobacco company visited him one day and asked if he would allow his now famous face to be printed on a box of their latest product, 'Relativity Cigars'. Without a word, Einstein showed him the door. Despite all the media frenzy, fame never went to his head – although, as he said to a Swiss friend in 1919, 'with fame I become more and more stupid, which of course is a very common phenomenon'.[56]

In 1919 and 1920, Einstein gave his first series of candid interviews to journalist Alexander Moszkowski. Their conversation covered a wide range of subjects from atomic energy to the education of women. His views turned out to be surprisingly conservative on both these issues. Women were not natural scholars, he said, and he refused to agree that the latent energy in matter, revealed by his equation $E = mc^2$, would 'be the panacea of all human woe'. Moszkowski was disappointed on this last point: 'I drew an enthusiastic picture of a dazzling Utopia, an orgy of hopeful dreams, but immediately noticed that I received no support from Einstein for these visionary aspirations.'

'At present,' Einstein replied,

there is not the slightest indication of when this energy will be obtainable, or whether it will be obtainable at all. For it would presuppose a disintegration of the atom effected at will – a shattering of the atom. And up to the present there is scarcely a sign that this will be possible. We observe atomic disintegration only where Nature herself presents it, as in the case of radium, the activity of which depends upon the continual explosive decomposition of its atom. Nevertheless, we can only establish the presence of this process, but cannot produce it; Science in its present state makes it appear almost impossible that we shall ever succeed in so doing.[57]

But a few months later, Ernest Rutherford announced that he had done just that. In the final year of the war, he had failed to attend government meetings to report on his research into submarine detection. Explaining his absence, he told the committee quite bluntly that his experiments were more important – he had disintegrated the atom. Rutherford had found that when he fired alpha particles into a container of nitrogen gas, atoms of oxygen and nuclei of hydrogen were created. He deduced that the alpha particles were punching the hydrogen nuclei – which he later christened protons – out of the nitrogen atoms.

Rutherford published his results in 1919. 'We must conclude', he wrote, that the nitrogen atom is disintegrated under the intense forces developed in a close collision with a swift alpha particle, and that the hydrogen atom which is liberated formed a constituent part of the nitrogen nucleus . . . The results as a whole suggest that if alpha particles – or similar projectiles – of still greater energy were available for experiment, we might expect to break down the nuclear structure of many of the lighter atoms.[58]

This was the realization of the alchemists' dream of transmutation: of transforming one element into another. The newspapers claimed that he had split the atom, but the curmudgeonly Rutherford insisted on calling it 'artificial disintegration'.[59] In 1920 he suggested that protons and electrons might join together in the atomic nucleus to form 'neutral doublets'.[60] This is the first mention of the particle that would one day revolutionize atomic physics. The neutron, discovered in 1932 by his colleague James Chadwick, would fulfil Rutherford's dream of an electrically neutral particle that could be fired into the heart of an atom and blow it clean apart.

When Moszkowski raised the subject of atomic energy again with Einstein, after Rutherford's results had been published, Einstein 'declared with his usual frankness, one of the treasures of his character, that he had now occasion to modify somewhat the opinion he had shortly before expressed', the journalist wrote. Nevertheless, Einstein was still sceptical about exploiting atomic energy: 'in Rutherford's operations the atom is treated as if he were dealing with a fortress: he subjects it to a bombardment and seeks to fire into the breach. The fortress is still certainly far from capitulating, but signs of disruption have become observable. A hail of bullets caused holes, tears, and splinterings.'[61]

Clearly Einstein still believed that the dream of unlimited supplies of energy was a long way off. However, when he was asked by a newspaper later that year, he responded more positively. On 25 July 1920, the *Berliner Tageblatt* newspaper ran a feature article under the headline I GRAM OF MATTER = 3,000 TONNES OF COAL. As French demands for German coal (part of the huge burden of reparations imposed by the Versailles Treaty) became ever more difficult to meet, scientists were being questioned about possible alternative energy sources. Haber, Nernst, Planck and Einstein all contributed to the feature. In the light of Rutherford's transmutation of nitrogen, Einstein comments that 'it is not improbable, that from this will come new energy sources of enormous power'.[62]

Alexander Moszkowski was already convinced that the popular dream of unlimited atomic energy was within reach, now that Rutherford had shown that 'it is possible to split up atoms of one's own free will'. Indeed, he felt there was another reason for optimism: 'It seems feasible that, under certain conditions, Nature would automatically continue the disruption of the atom, after a human being had intentionally started it, as in the analogous case of a conflagration which extends, although it may have started from a mere spark.'[63] Moszkowski had put his finger on the key to atomic energy: a chain reaction.

Fiction too explored this possibility. A couple of years later, the English chemist and popular novelist Alfred Walter Stewart, under his pen name of J. J. Connington, described how Rutherford had shattered the atom. In his scientific thriller *Nordenholt's Million* (1923), mutated bacteria destroy the nitrogen in the soil, threatening humanity with starvation. It is a dynamic technocrat, Nordenholt, and atomic energy that eventually save the human race from extinction. The atom's energy is released by an explosive chain reaction. The physicist, who is working with uranium, describes how:

if we could trap that store of energy which evidently lies within the atom we should have Nature at our feet. She would be done for, beaten, out of the struggle: and we should simply have to walk over the remains and take what we wanted.

To achieve his goal, Connington's physicist is trying to create an explosive chain reaction in matter. He graphically depicts this using a row of matchboxes:

it requires a certain force in a blow from my finger to knock down one of these boxes; and if I take ten boxes separately, it would need ten times that force to throw them all flat. But if I arrange them so that as each one falls it strikes its neighbour, then I can knock the whole lot down with a single touch. The first one collides with the second, and the second in falling upsets the third, and so on to the end of the line. Well, that is what I have been following out amongst the atoms.[64]

Ten years later, when James Chadwick announced the discovery of the neutron – the particle that could penetrate the atomic nucleus – Leo Szilard was the first to see that this was Moszkowski's 'spark' that would ignite the atomic fire. Neutrons would create an atomic domino effect. Alexander Moszkowski was nearer the truth than he suspected when he concluded his interview with the discoverer of relativity in 1919: 'Einstein's wonderful "Open Sesame", mass times the square of the velocity of light, is thundering at the portals.'[65]

III

The Dark Heart of Matter

The creative scientist has much in common with the artist and the poet. Logical thinking and an analytical ability are necessary attributes of a scientist but they are far from suf-ficient for creative work. Those insights in science which have led to a breakthrough operate on the level of the subconscious. Science would run dry if all scientists were crank turners and if none of them were dreamers.   Leo Szilard

8

The Capital of Physics

*The deeper we search the more we find there is to know, and
as long as human life exists, I believe it will always be so.*

Albert Einstein (1933)

On 6 January 1920, a young Hungarian stepped off the train in Berlin
after a long and tiring journey. The 21-year-old Leo Szilard had left
his home in Budapest on Christmas Day. The photograph in his
passport showed a serious but fresh-faced man with large and wistful
eyes, reminiscent of the young Einstein.

When this portrait was taken just a few weeks earlier, Szilard had
been staring into an unknown and possibly dangerous future. He
knew one thing for certain: he urgently needed to leave his homeland.
Since the collapse of the Austro-Hungarian Empire at the end of
World War I, Hungary had been swinging between political extremes
of the left and the right. Béla Kun's Communist government lasted
just a few months before it was kicked out in autumn 1919 by a
right-wing regime led by the former commander of the Austro-
Hungarian navy, Miklós Horthy de Nagybánya.

It soon became clear to Szilard that he was not wanted in Horthy's
Hungary. When he and his younger brother, Bela, tried to resume
their engineering studies at Budapest's Technical University in September, they were confronted at the entrance by a group of right-wing
students.

'You can't study here! You're Jews!' they shouted. When the
brothers tried to argue, they were beaten up.[1] Traumatized by this
treatment, Szilard immediately applied for an exit visa. At first he was

turned down. According to Horthy's secret police, he and his brother were among the top five 'most aggressive and dangerous' Communist students at the university.[2] They were being followed by plain-clothes police.

Leo and Bela were certainly not dangerous revolutionaries. In spring 1919, the brothers had founded the Hungarian Association of Socialist Students, an amateurish attempt at political organization. At its one and only meeting, Leo handed out copies of his plans for socialist tax reform. He had also attended meetings of the Galilei Circle, an influential discussion group of radical students and intellectuals. But more importantly for the anti-Semitic Horthy regime, the Szilards were Jewish.

Eventually, after an anxious wait and the payment of a number of bribes, Leo received his exit visa. Bela would follow in his brother's footsteps a few months later. The visa was valid only for travel from 25 December to 5 January. When Christmas Day finally arrived, Leo was so terrified of being stopped by Horthy's secret police at the train station that he bought a one-way ticket to Vienna on a Danube steamship. He lugged on board a large suitcase crammed with books and clothing. Tucked beneath the inner sole of a shoe in his luggage was a bundle of banknotes his father had given him. It was most of the family's savings.

Szilard sat on the steamer to Vienna, watching his homeland pass slowly by and anxiously wondering what the future had in store for him. A man on the bench opposite noticed his long face and asked why he was looking so sad.

'I am leaving my country, perhaps for good,' confessed Szilard. He assumed that the man was local, possibly a farmer. It turned out that he was a Hungarian émigré who had spent the last forty years in Canada and was on a return trip to the land of his birth.

The man smiled at Szilard. 'Be glad! As long as you live you'll remember this as the happiest day of your life!'[3]

The winter train journey from Vienna to Berlin should have taken a day. But Germany was a shadow of its former, imperial self, riven by civil disorder and strikes. The shortage of coal halted the train for days at a time, marooning it in a silent, snowy landscape. The journey lasted a whole week.

The flight from home was a recurrent theme in the restless life of Leo Szilard. From now on, 'home' would always be provisional. There was never time to grow attached to a locale. The nervous glance over a shoulder while clutching all his earthly possessions in a suitcase – these became defining experiences for Szilard.

The year he arrived in Berlin, a failed Austrian artist and war veteran formed the National Socialist party in Munich. During the early 1930s, fearing an imminent Nazi seizure of power, he kept his bags packed by the front door of his rented room. Soon after Hitler became chancellor, Szilard caught the first Vienna-bound train out of Berlin, retracing the journey he had made in 1919. He had lived in Berlin for thirteen years. Now a refugee in a Europe poisoned by anti-Semitism, he travelled first from Vienna to London, and then eventually to America.

But even in the land of the free, Szilard still lived out of a suitcase. How else could you live in a world where at any moment a lone bomber might appear high in the sky and drop a single devastating bomb? Edward Shils recalls that when he visited Szilard in his room in Chicago, his bookshelves were bare. 'He had no physical property other than his clothing.'[4] Even when he eventually married in 1951, he kept what he called his 'Big Bomb suitcase' packed and ready to go. 'If you want to succeed in this world,' said Szilard, 'you don't have to be much cleverer than other people, you just have to be one day earlier than most people.'[5]

He only used his Big Bomb suitcase once. During the Cuban Missile Crisis, he and his wife caught the first flight to Geneva. At the offices of CERN he called on a friend he had first met in 1920s Berlin, the physicist Victor Weisskopf. Never one to underplay the drama of the moment, Szilard announced: 'I'm the first refugee from America.'[6]

Berlin in the twenties was not just another European city; it was a state of mind. After the bloody revolutions and street fighting in the first years of the Weimar Republic came the hyperinflation of 1922 and 1923. Newspaper presses were used to print banknotes which were scarcely worth the paper they were printed on by the time they hit the streets. Then, with the currency reform of 1924 and American loans, came a period of prosperity and growth which lasted until the

Wall Street Crash and the worldwide Depression that followed. In this decade the population of Berlin doubled to nearly four million; only London and New York were bigger. The city turned its back on its imperial past and embraced modernity. These were the Golden Twenties, a time of unparalleled sexual freedom, of easy living and easy money – for some at least. But despite the new prosperity, Berlin still felt like a 'doomed city', a modern Pompeii living on the edge of a volcano.[7] The eruption came in 1933, throwing Hitler into power and casting a dark pall across Europe and the world.

Through the bloodshed and the boom years, Berlin remained a cauldron of creativity. According to the historian of Berlin Alexandra Richie, 'for a few brief sparkling years the city attracted a sheer concentration of talent which has not yet been equalled in Europe'.[8] The sometimes harsh reality of life for ordinary Berliners was captured in remarkable works including Alfred Döblin's novel *Berlin Alexanderplatz* (1929) and *The Threepenny Opera* by Bertolt Brecht and Kurt Weill, whose opening in 1928 was a night people remembered all their lives.[9] The savage drawings and paintings of George Grosz portrayed Berlin street life, while the tortured symbolic images of Max Beckmann laid bare the inner torments of a people journeying into the abyss.

Ordinary Berliners began a love affair with the moving image in the 1920s. In 1913 there had been just 28 cinemas, but by 1919 there were 245. The month after Leo Szilard arrived in Berlin, the expressionist film *The Cabinet of Dr Caligari* opened in the city. This chilling film about a murderous scientist who controls the mind of his zombie-like assistant, Cesare, echoes the story of the supersoldier in Sheehan and Davis's play 'Blood and Iron'. But Dr Caligari's hypnotic power over Cesare is also a parable of political control. Thomas Mann's 1929 story 'Mario and the Magician' picked up this theme, exploring the mesmeric control that demagogues like Hitler could exert over entire nations.

Berlin became the intellectual centre of Europe, a cultural magnet which attracted, among others, English writer Christopher Isherwood, and later the poets Stephen Spender and W. H. Auden. Isherwood's *Berlin Stories*, which became the film *Cabaret*, immortalized the myth of the Golden Twenties. This is the Berlin of smoke-filled jazz clubs and seedy cabarets, of the Charleston and Josephine Baker – the black singer and actress whose dances wearing nothing but a girdle of bananas caused a sensation in a city that became, as Stefan Zweig put it, the orgiastic 'Babylon of the world'.[10]

In the late 1920s, the physicist Victor Weisskopf was studying for his PhD at Göttingen, not far from Berlin. He often travelled to the city to see his friend Eugene Wigner and recalls being 'just a little shocked' by the 'sexual revolution' going on in Berlin at this time. Weisskopf admits that he was 'young, somewhat prudish, and certainly a bit provincial'.[11] For his city friend, Leo Szilard, Berlin in the 1920s must have seemed a world away from the stately elegance of the Hungarian capital, where he had grown up.

Mark Twain called the brash, edgy city the 'German Chicago'.[12] Berliners have a character all of their own: 'They are the New Yorkers of Central Europe,' says Otto Friedrich, in his study of Berlin in the 1920s.[13] Einstein arrived in the city in 1914, having been lured there with an exceptionally generous deal that freed him from the need even to lecture. 'I now comprehend the Berliners' smugness,' he said in 1914, 'for there is so much happening around them that their inner emptiness does not pain them as it would in a quieter place.'[14]

While Berlin's nightclub and cabaret culture boomed, the Nazis and the Communists fought for dominance on the streets. Exactly a year before Leo Szilard set foot in Berlin, the bloody Spartacus uprising had filled Berlin's wide avenues with gunfire. It ended with the Communist leaders, Karl Liebknecht and Rosa Luxembourg, being murdered in cold blood by the authorities. Many hundreds died on the streets in the vicious fighting that flared up repeatedly throughout 1919. In the spring of 1920 it was the turn of the Right to make their bid for power. On 24 February, Adolf Hitler set out the Nazi programme in Munich. In Berlin the following month, when the right-wing militia, the Freikorps, were ordered to disband, they staged a coup.

During what became known as the Kapp Putsch, Otto Hahn and other scientists formed a *Technische Nothilfe*, a Technical Flying-Squad, to keep essential services running. Hahn and James Franck travelled every evening from leafy Dahlem to the district of Schöneberg to stoke the furnaces of the power station that had been deserted by striking workers, working from 10 p.m. until first light. During the day, back in their Dahlem laboratory, Hahn and his colleague Lise Meitner pushed at the frontiers of nuclear knowledge, exploring the decay products of uranium.[15] Einstein's friend Max Born, now in Frankfurt, was an 'ardent supporter of socialist government' and opposed to the right-wing counter revolution.[16] Again, politics had spilled onto the streets of Berlin, as it would again and again in the years before Hitler took power.

Despite 'unfriendly' officials whose job it was to enforce the limits that were placed on foreigners studying in Berlin, Szilard eventually enrolled at the Königliche Technische Hochschule (Institute of Technology) at the start of 1920. Here he continued the electrical engineering studies he had begun in Budapest in September 1916. First war then revolution had interrupted his studies. Now another revolution intervened – a revolution in physics.

Although he completed the spring term at the Institute of Technology, a new horizon beckoned: 'physics attracted me more and more'.[17] Before the year was out, Szilard had switched to the Friedrich-Wilhelm University, where he could take courses in physics. This university was a world leader in physics, boasting scientists of the calibre of Max Planck, who began the quantum revolution with his 1900 investigation into black-body radiation, and Max von Laue, who had pioneered the use of X-rays to obtain diffraction images of crystals, which made it possible to calculate how the atoms were arranged in the crystal lattice.

Max Planck, a rather austere and gaunt man, was the most respected physicist in Germany at this time. In November 1920, Szilard applied to Planck to take one of his courses. 'I only want to know the facts of physics,' he told the Nobel laureate. 'I will make up the theories myself.' Fortunately Professor Planck was amused by the young student's chutzpah and mentioned his comment to James Franck. He in turn told Hungarian chemist Michael Polanyi, also in Berlin, that a 'curious young man called Szilard' had appeared at the university.[18] For the first time, Leo Szilard had made an impression on the physics community.

It was, said Szilard, 'the heyday of physics', and Berlin was the place to be if you were a physicist.[19] One of the highlights of studying in the capital of physics was the Wednesday afternoon colloquium of the Deutsche Physikalische Gesellschaft, the German Physical Society, held at the old university building in the heart of the city beside the River Spree. At this forum all the latest advances in physics from around the world were summarized and debated – from Rutherford's artificial transmutation of the atom just the year before, to the fluorescence of uranyl salts, and how to reconcile light interference with the photoelectric effect.

Through war, strikes and revolutions, the colloquium continued. When bullets were flying in the streets outside, participants were simply asked to keep away from the windows. In the winter, when fuel was short, participants sat in their overcoats; Berlin's bitter cold was soon forgotten in the heat of the debate. According to no lesser authority than Einstein, the Berlin colloquium was the most extraordinary gathering of physicists anywhere in the world.[20]

The meetings were held in a large classroom containing three rows of seats. At the front sat past and future Nobel prizewinners: Albert Einstein, Max Planck and Max von Laue, as well as the chemists Walther Nernst and Fritz Haber. In the second row were James Franck, Hans Geiger, Gustav Hertz and Lise Meitner, whom Einstein called 'our Madame Curie'.[21] The quantum physicists Werner Heisenberg, Wolfgang Pauli and Erwin Schrödinger also attended when they were visiting Berlin. In April 1920 the Danish physicist Niels Bohr came to the colloquium and met Einstein for the first time. At about the same time, Leo Szilard started attending the weekly meetings.

From 1921, Eugene Wigner was also a regular participant. Like Leo Szilard, he had fled Budapest after becoming the victim of anti-Semitic abuse and was now studying chemistry at the nearby Institute of Technology.[22] At first Wigner was bewildered by the technical language used at the colloquium – phrases such as 'ionization energy'. But so enthralling was the level of debate that he kept coming back.

During each colloquium, the organizer, Max von Laue, would announce the titles of four or five new scientific papers that had just been published and choose someone to read each paper and prepare a spoken review of it for the following week. Unclear reviews would provoke probing questions from the intimidating front row. When

Eugene Wigner (1902–95) left Budapest in 1921 to study chemical engineering in Berlin and became a lifelong friend of Leo Szilard. This photograph was taken in about 1948.

Wigner's first turn came, he was apprehensive; as he later recalled, Einstein in particular was 'always ready to comment, to argue, or to question any paper that was not impressively clear'. Einstein's favourite comment was, 'Oh no. Things are not so simple.'[23] Einstein himself had perfected the art of asking deceptively naive questions. 'Einstein's questions,' recalled physicist Philipp Franck, 'which very often threw doubt upon a principle that appeared self-evident, gave the seminar a special attraction.'[24] But despite the presence in the audience of these stellar figures from physics, Wigner never felt nervous about speaking: 'Albert Einstein made me feel I was needed.'[25]

After each colloquium, discussions continued in the coffee house late into the evening. For both Szilard and Wigner, Berlin's cafés were a home from home. Wigner recalled that in Budapest 'you were not only allowed to linger over coffee, you were supposed to linger, making intelligent conversation about science, art and literature'.[26] Szilard's favourite haunt was the neo-Gothic Romanisches Café. It was 'the centre of everything', recalled one regular some fifty years later, 'a big, ugly place, across from the Kaiser Wilhelm Memorial Church, but everybody went there, the writers, the actors, everybody'.[27]

Like many who met him, Eugene Wigner was immensely impressed by Einstein's 'simplicity and innate modesty'. He 'inspired real affection' in people and had 'a great many lovable traits'.[28] When Wigner first met him, Einstein was already a celebrity. On his visit to America in 1921, thousands had flocked to his public lectures. Wigner was clearly awed by meeting the great physicist: 'His personality was almost magical,' he recalled seventy years later.[29] Einstein himself confessed at this time that in Berlin 'every child knows me from photographs'.[30] Even so, he remained approachable. 'He could have made a great show of his own importance,' said Wigner. 'He never thought to do so.'[31]

According to a physicist who worked with Einstein, 'there were two kinds of physicists in Berlin: on the one hand was Einstein, and on the other all the rest'.[32] Philipp Frank, who took over the chair of physics at the German University in Prague after Einstein left, was told by his students that Einstein had said, 'I shall always be able to receive you. If you have a problem, come to me with it. You will never disturb me, since I can interrupt my own work at any moment and resume it immediately as soon as the interruption is past.'[33] Frank noticed that Einstein remained an outsider in the Berlin academic community, with its Prussian emphasis on formality and rank.[34]

The young Leo Szilard soon became a close friend of Einstein.

According to Wigner, who got to know Szilard at the weekly colloquia, his fellow Hungarian was never intimidated by great men: 'If Szilard had seen the President of the United States at a meeting or the President of Soviet Russia, he would have promptly introduced himself and begun asking pointed questions. That was Szilard's way.'[35]

Szilard had introduced himself to Einstein after one of the colloquia and soon he was accompanying Einstein on his way home each Wednesday, a journey which took them first past the Reichstag, then the Brandenburg Gate and the Tiergarten, until they reached Einstein's apartment in the well-to-do Schöneberg district. Szilard also became a regular at the afternoon tea parties Einstein and his wife held for young researchers. At the time, Szilard was surviving on the modest amounts he earned by tutoring fellow students in mathematics. The Russian émigré Eugene Rabinowitch, who was studying chemistry at Berlin, recalls being invited back to Szilard's room after one of Einstein's seminars. The room was so frugal that they all had to sit on the floor to drink tea.[36] There's no doubt that Szilard would have relished the opportunity to indulge his boyish sweet tooth on Einstein's free tea and cakes. Edward Shils recalled how, even in the 1950s, lunch for Leo Szilard 'was a glass of buttermilk into which he poured the entire contents of the sugar bowl, followed by sherbet'.[37]

Both the student and the professor saw themselves as outsiders in the conservative world of German physics. They shared many other things too: a contempt for bourgeois values, a boyish sense of humour, strong socialist convictions, a healthy lack of respect for all forms of authority and (both men having grown up in liberal Jewish families) a dislike of organized religion. For Leo Szilard, Einstein became an intellectual father figure.

Although he respected Einstein immensely, Szilard did not hesitate to challenge his mentor. Once, at the Kaiser Wilhelm Institute in Dahlem, as Albert Einstein was slowly but methodically explaining to colleagues how to conduct an experiment with X-rays, a voice interrupted him.

'But, Herr Professor, what you have just said is simply nonsense!'

There was a barely audible gasp from the those present, and many turned to see who had the audacity to contradict the world-famous physicist. Even Einstein looked surprised at first, although as a student in Zurich he had been notorious for his casual if not rude attitude towards his own professors. Einstein thought for a moment about what he had said, and then smiled. His Hungarian friend was right.[38]

Within a year of meeting Einstein, Leo Szilard felt that he knew the great physicist well enough to ask him a favour. Would he take a special seminar on statistical mechanics? Einstein agreed, and in the winter term of 1921 Szilard invited a select group of friends to take part in the seminar on this area of physics that seeks to explain the properties of a system by applying statistical methods to its atomic or molecular constituents. The course was a great success, and it gave Szilard the inspiration he needed for his doctoral thesis. According to Wigner, it was a 'splendid seminar . . . Einstein beautifully projected the spirit of the theory and showed us its inner workings'.[39]

As well as Eugene Wigner, Szilard invited three other Hungarian friends studying in Berlin to Einstein's course: John von Neumann, who would play a key role in the development of the computer in the cold war, Dennis Gabor, who later invented holography, and Albert Kornfeld, an engineering student who was staying in the same apartment block as Leo and his brother Bela. Wigner and von Neumann later worked on the Manhattan Project with Szilard, as did another of his Hungarian friends, Edward Teller, who came to Germany in 1926. Not only were they from the same country, but all four men (as well as Gabor) came from the same quarter of Budapest. They were christened the Hungarian Quartet by Wigner.[40] These four brilliant minds helped to create the most terrible weapons the world has seen – the atomic bomb and the hydrogen bomb. They also opened the door to the ultimate weapon – the cobalt doomsday bomb. For this, and for their hawkish stance in the cold war, Edward Teller and John von Neumann (who came to Berlin to study with Haber) would later become models for the fictional Dr Strangelove.

In the same year as Einstein's seminar on statistical mechanics, another person who would play a key role in the history of the atomic bomb was also in Germany. During the summer of 1921, Robert Oppenheimer, then aged 17, visited the country his father had left in 1898. His grandfather, who lived in Hanau, had given him a collection of minerals. To add to it, Robert visited the St Joachimsthal mine, the source of Marie Curie's uranium ore and of the uranium eventually used in the atomic bomb. It was this trip that sparked his lifelong passion for science.

True to his impatient nature, Leo Szilard started his doctorate 'rather early' in his studies at the University.[41] Max von Laue had suggested to him a problem on the theory of relativity, and Szilard spent the end of 1921 grappling with the theory's subtleties. Von Laue had been one of the first physicists to appreciate the revolutionary nature of Einstein's thinking. In the year that Einstein first wrote down the equation $E = mc^2$, von Laue had visited the 28-year-old patent officer in Berne and together they spent a day walking round the city's medieval streets. As the two men journeyed to the frontiers of physics and back again, they paused on the high bridge over the River Aare, and von Laue surreptitiously dropped the cheap cigar Einstein had given him into the swirling alpine waters below. Einstein's taste in cigars was appalling, decided von Laue, but his judgement in science was impeccable.

After six months of sustained thought, Szilard decided he couldn't 'make any headway' with the problem on relativity. According to Wigner, Einstein's seminars on statistical mechanics gave Szilard 'sour feelings toward higher mathematics'. He began to suspect (wrongly, in Wigner's view) that 'he was not bright enough to change theoretical physics'.[42] In typically combative style, he made an asset of a weakness. 'There is no need to study mathematics,' Szilard would say. 'One can always ask a mathematician!'[43] Einstein had the same attitude, and while working on his general theory of relativity, he did just that – he asked a mathematician, his old friend Marcel Grossmann, for help.

By Christmas 1921, Szilard knew that relativity was not going to provide him with the basis for an original thesis. He needed a new idea, and settled down to some serious thinking. 'Christmastime is not a time to work,' he decided, 'it is a time to loaf, so I thought I would just think whatever comes to my mind.'[44] He turned up the collar of his overcoat against the bitter winter winds and paced Berlin's streets, deep in thought:

I went for long walks and I saw something in the middle of the walk; when I came home I wrote it down; next morning I woke up with a new idea and

I went for another walk; this crystallized in my mind and in the evening I wrote it down. There was an onrush of ideas, all more or less connected, which just kept on going until I had the whole theory fully developed. It was a very creative period, in a sense the most creative period in my life, where there was a sustained production of ideas. Within three weeks I had produced a manuscript of something which was really quite original.[45]

Szilard had his thesis. But as he had dropped Max von Laue's topic, he didn't dare take it to him. Instead, he turned to the world's most famous physicist. At the end of one of Einstein's seminars, Szilard asked him if he would listen to his idea.

'Well, what have you been doing?' asked Einstein.

Szilard told him about the idea that had come to him while walking through the icy streets of Berlin. When he had finished, Einstein was astonished.

'That's impossible. This is something that cannot be done!'

'Well, yes, but I did it,' replied Szilard.

Einstein looked incredulous. 'How did you do it?'[46]

For the next ten minutes Szilard explained, and at the end Einstein smiled. Not for the last time in his life, Leo Szilard had done the impossible.

His thesis was on the second law of thermodynamics. He had made good use of Einstein's seminars, for he drew on statistical mechanics rather than experimental evidence to demonstrate the validity of this fundamental principle of physics. With uncharacteristic modesty, Szilard described it as 'not really a beginning, it was not the cornerstone of a new theory, it was rather the proof of an old theory'.[47] Reassured by Einstein's reaction, Szilard plucked up the courage to visit Max von Laue. The following morning he received a telephone call from von Laue accepting the thesis.

Six months later, Szilard extended his thinking on thermodynamics and wrote a paper which explored the 'relationship between information and entropy'. In the 1950s, at the start of the computer age, this paper was hailed as 'a cornerstone of modern information theory'.[48]

There was no doubting the originality of Szilard's insights into these problems. But Einstein was clearly concerned that his young friend's

THE DARK HEART OF MATTER

personality might make it difficult for him to settle into academic life. After all, Einstein's informal manner and approachability was the exception not the rule in German academia. Once Leo Szilard was awarded his PhD, Einstein suggested that he consider following in his own footsteps, and apply to work in a patent office. 'They were the happiest years of my life,' said Einstein. 'Nobody expected me to lay golden eggs.'[49]

Einstein was a shrewd judge of character: he could see that Leo Szilard was a maverick. This would be both Szilard's great strength and his weakness. It allowed him to think outside the box and see atomic bombs where others saw only disintegrating atoms. The downside was that because his ideas were so far ahead of current thinking, less perceptive scientists were often exasperated by what they saw as his flights of fancy. In his article on future war, Hugo Gernsback had said 'modern science knows not the word Impossible'.[50] That could have been Leo Szilard's motto.

162

9

The Inventor of All Things

Our conscience is clear . . . and that is the essential thing. Our
intentions were pure. Our ideal was to create.

Pierre Boulle, '$E = mc^2$' (1965)

Albert Einstein was once asked where his laboratory was. He grinned like a schoolboy and held up his pen. Leo Szilard was also – as Eugene Rabinowitch said – 'an idea man par excellence'.[1] Experimentalists such as Enrico Fermi were often annoyed by Szilard's reluctance to get his hands dirty in the laboratory. Szilard didn't help matters by appearing unexpectedly in laboratories and offering unasked-for advice to other scientists about how best to conduct their experiments. The physicist Isidor Rabi once pleaded with Szilard to leave him in peace. 'You are reinventing the field. You have too many ideas. Please, go away!'[2] However, Szilard's advice often turned out to be right. This habit earned him the nickname 'Director General' at the Kaiser Wilhelm Institute where Eugene Wigner worked in the mid-1920s. Leo Szilard could be a difficult, even infuriating character, but those who saw beyond this came to value his insights.

Another Hungarian friend of Szilard's in Berlin, Dennis Gabor, remembered that he

hardly ever went to the lab – he sat out in the garden in a deck chair and thought. His chief activity was talking to friends: he rang them up, he talked with them in cafés. He knew everyone and gladly gave advice to all physicists and biologists. Szilard wanted to discuss everything, and to pass on his ideas by word rather than by writing.[3]

According to Gabor, 'he used to discuss all his inventions with me. I was so full of admiration that I felt quite stupid in his presence. Of all the many great men I have met in my life, he was by far the most brilliant.'[4] Gabor recalls a conversation in a Berlin cafe – probably Szilard's favourite, the Romanisches Café – during which Szilard explained how to design an electron microscope. In 1931 he even patented this idea, but the Nobel prize for inventing an electron microscope went to another scientist, Ernst Ruska, in 1986.

Leo Szilard also patented a design for a particle accelerator, in 1929 – several years before Ernest O. Lawrence, who received a Nobel in 1939 for his cyclotron. Szilard was always ahead of the game, whether it was physics or food: in the 1950s the now portly physicist even invented a means of producing low-fat cheeses for epicures worried about their waistlines. 'Had he pushed through to success all his new inventions,' said Dennis Gabor, 'we would now talk of him as the Edison of the twentieth century.'[5]

Szilard often played the role of catalyst, inspiring others with his original ideas. 'He loves to seize a problem in its early, exciting stage, and to work on it furiously until he begins to glimpse the answer,' said journalist Alice Kimball Smith. 'Then he is likely to move on to something else, leaving the tedious labor – and the laurels – to others.'[6] His friend, editor and peace campaigner Norman Cousins, considered him to be one of the most significant scientists of his generation: 'The restless inventiveness of his mind knows few modern counterparts.'[7] A colleague in the 1950s described Szilard simply as 'the inventor of all things'.[8]

Eugene Wigner shared this respect for Szilard's achievements: 'Throughout my long life I had the chance to meet very talented people, but I never met anybody more imaginative than Leo Szilard. No one had more independence of thought and opinion.' After a moment's reflection, he added: 'You may value this statement better if you recall that I knew Albert Einstein as well.'[9]

It was Szilard, after all, who realized that in the early 1930s atomic energy was within reach. He was at least seven years ahead of Einstein in this area. It would be the maverick Hungarian scientist who eventually broke the news to the great physicist in 1939 that the uranium atom had been split. From boyhood, Szilard had enjoyed reading H. G.

Wells and futuristic fiction. After the atomic bombs were dropped on Japan, he even began writing Wellsian stories himself to express his fears for the future. By contrast, Einstein had no time for science fiction, preferring detective fiction. Scientific fiction seemed to give Leo Szilard the creative edge over his mentor and indeed other scientists, such as Rutherford and Fermi, who in the 1930s would dismiss his ideas for releasing atomic energy. Science fiction allowed him to glimpse the future.

Eugene Wigner was Szilard's most loyal friend, and their friendship would last a lifetime. Wigner recalled that when they first met, at the Berlin physics colloquia in 1921, his 'first impression was of a vivid man about 5 feet 6 inches tall, a bit shorter even than I was. His face was a good, broad Hungarian face. His eyes were brown. His hair, like my own, was brown, poorly combed, and already receding from his forehead.' He added, drily, 'A full head of hair is quite nice, but we survive without it.' Szilard spoke fluent German, 'with a striking clarity and vigor'. Like some unpredictable quantum phenomenon, he also had the unnerving ability to appear and disappear when you least expected it: 'You might see him for a moment at the colloquium, but then he was gone. Several days later, he appeared at your front door with several bold ideas and not quite enough patience. Leo Szilard was always in a hurry.'[10]

According to Wigner, Szilard realized during Einstein's seminars that he would not be able to make a significant contribution to quantum mechanics. 'Complex abstractions rarely appealed much to Szilard.'[11] Instead, from 1922, despite Wigner's efforts to draw him into his own research into quantum mechanics, Leo Szilard struck off in a new direction, collaborating with Herman Mark in his research on X-rays at Dahlem.

In the space of two years, Leo Szilard had established a reputation for himself in one of the foremost physics research institutes in the world. The hopeful student of electrical engineering who stepped off the train from Vienna in January 1920 had come a long way in a very short time. His brother Bela recalls how in those first months 'Leo spent most of his time just sitting and thinking, seldom reading course books, and rarely attempting the practical exercises'. His logical attitude to life sometimes bemused his brother. One evening Bela said,

'Close the window; it's cold outside.' Leo replied: 'I will close the window, but that will not make it less cold outside.'[12]

In their spare time, the two students of electrical engineering amused themselves by dreaming up fantastic, Heath-Robinson solutions to imaginary problems. One idea was to speed up haircuts by applying a slight electric current to barbers' chairs, so that customers' hair would stand on end. Another was prompted by the sight of Berlin women repeatedly pulling up their stockings: Leo proposed to prevent slippage by equipping stocking tops with flexible iron threads and placing magnets in women's jacket pockets.[13] Such scientific flights of fancy had amused the brothers since childhood.

Eugene Wigner described Szilard as a child prodigy, like their mutual friend and mathematical genius John von Neumann.[14] Leo Szilard himself recalls that he was 'a very sensitive child and somewhat high-strung'.[15] Like Einstein, Szilard had a family background in engineering. His father was a civil engineer and his uncle was an architect who designed the family home, a lavish villa still standing at 33 Fasor, Budapest. This became home to three generations of his mother's family, and Szilard grew up in a house which echoed to the games and songs of seven children. His cousins and siblings soon recognized that Szilard was 'the brainiest among us'. His liking for logic also showed up early. His cousins, the Scheibers, decided he was 'number headed'.[16]

As a child, Szilard was a keen reader. Like many other boys of his generation he loved the adventure stories of the best-selling German writer Karl May. Encouraged by his father's own tales of his work as an engineer, from an early age he also read books about engineers, such as Van Eyck's accounts of the history of engineering. Throughout the first half of the twentieth century, engineers were portrayed as dynamic heroes in German popular fiction. An example is Bernhard Kellermann's futuristic *Der Tunnel* (1913), about an engineer's epic struggle to build the first transatlantic tunnel. After World War I, the *Zukunftsroman*, or future novel, became an immensely popular genre in Germany. The technological adventures of Hans Dominik were spectacularly successful, selling in their millions. The Faustian exploits of the engineers now turned towards the final frontier – the conquest of space. In the late 1920s, the dream of interplanetary travel would also inspire Leo Szilard.

Thanks to Szilard's childhood idolizing of heroic engineers, he became an avid reader of *Der gute Kamerad* ('The Good Friend'), a monthly boys' magazine. It was a German version of Hugo Gernsback's *The Electrical Experimenter*, a mixture of scientific romances and articles about how to build electrical gadgets. Szilard himself was never much good with his hands, so Bela was put in charge of the practical construction work. They loved building things, and the brothers were over the moon when an uncle returned from a trip to England with a Meccano set. Again, it was Bela who did the construction and Leo who supplied the designs. Typically, his ideas were impossibly bold for the meagre number of Meccano parts in their set. But as a child and an adult, Leo never let his dreams be limited by practicalities.

For the young Leo Szilard, the stories and engineering projects in *Der gute Kamarad* provided a springboard into the magical world of the imagination. It was a world he never quite left behind. His unique creativity remained deeply rooted in this culture of technological invention. During his formative years, popular adventure fiction in Europe and America idealized the figure of the lone inventor, a character familiar from the pages of Jules Verne and H. G. Wells. In 1915, Hugo Gernsback, whose pulp magazine *Amazing Stories* would soon herald a new scientific genre of fiction, pointed to people like Edison, Bell and Marconi as the heroes of the modern age: 'Always it is a dreamy pioneer, an intrepid free-lance, aflame with enthusiasm, who enriches his country with a radically new labor-saving device or way of utilizing energy.'[17] In superweapon fiction, such as *The Man Who Rocked the Earth*, the scientist is typically a solitary genius, rational, honest and 'aflame with enthusiasm' for his latest ideas. His only flaw is arrogance, a permissible trait in one so obviously brilliant and destined to save the world. Leo Szilard, the 'lonely pioneer', fitted this description perfectly.[18]

At a time when electricity was replacing gas lighting in the more affluent homes of Budapest, the young Szilard's imagination was gripped by the new invisible power source. As a boy, Einstein had been

'The War of the Future': a 1928 cover illustration for the children's magazine
Le Petit Inventeur (No. 23). Let us hope, says the caption, that neither we
nor our descendants will ever have to experience those terrible wars in which
the sciences are applied in the dreadful cause of destruction.

similarly intrigued. His father and uncle ran an electrical engineering business in Munich. Born in 1879, the year in which the electric light bulb was invented, Einstein grew up listening to his uncle's excited descriptions of his latest electrical invention. This experience was a major influence on his future scientific interests.

Szilard soon progressed from *Der gute Kamarad* to Győző Zemplén's *Theory and Practical Applications of Electricity*, quickly absorbing the dry textbook's explanations and experiments. Szilard, the budding director general, supervised his brother's construction of a two-way crystal radio telegraph. Their grand idea was to send messages from one end of the family's large apartment to the other. But because Szilard could not be bothered to learn Morse code, the project failed. Their next electrical endeavour was potentially more dangerous. The brothers placed electrodes in a glass jar of water and watched as hydrogen and oxygen bubbled up. But as they couldn't work out how to capture the gases separately, they soon lost interest. 'That's just as well,' Bela told his brother's biographer, 'because Leo's next step was to explode the gases with a match to enjoy a "big bang".'[19]

One of the stories published in the first issue of Gernsback's *Amazing Stories* was 'The Man Who Saved the Earth' by Austin Hall. In this apocalyptic story of heat rays and saviour scientists, a character argues that 'an inventor is merely a poet with tools' and that 'the really great scientist should be a visionary'.[20] In the 1950s Leo Szilard often described himself as being on a mission to 'save the world'. Throughout his life he saw himself as a scientist in the mould of these early science fiction heroes, as both a visionary and an inventor. He said as much in the year before his death:

The creative scientist has much in common with the artist and the poet. Logical thinking and an analytical ability are necessary attributes of a scientist but they are far from sufficient for creative work. Those insights in science which have led to a breakthrough operate on the level of the subconscious. Science would run dry if all scientists were crank turners and if none of them were dreamers.[21]

Leo Szilard was certainly no 'crank turner'. But practical invention formed an essential part of his scientific life and his self-image. His first German patent, filed in 1923, was for an X-ray sensitive cell, followed by patents for mercury vapour lamps. The sale of these patents to Siemens gave Leo Szilard a very necessary source of income. By 1924 he had become Max von Laue's assistant – a great honour, but one with very little financial reward. Szilard may have ignored Einstein's advice to find a job at a patent office, but he used Einstein's experience of patents to become financially independent.

Many of Szilard's inventions were never developed and ended up gathering dust on the patent office shelf. Often the intellectual stimulus of coming up with an idea was the only reward he wanted. Unlike other scientists, he showed little interest in the mundane business of conducting experiments and publishing results in academic journals. The thrill of invention was like a drug. Possessed by a compulsive intellectual wanderlust, he was always impatient to move on to the next brilliant idea – and he was never short of ideas. But as Szilard researcher Gene Dannen has said, 'when you are as far ahead of your time as Szilard often was, the obstacles to the acceptance of your ideas can be almost insurmountable'.[22] The life of a visionary scientist was not going to be easy.

One of Leo Szilard's ideas did make the long journey from patent to fully functional machine. It was not a revolutionary new cyclotron, but a household refrigerator. In the winter of 1925/26, Einstein read a shocking story in the newspaper. A Berlin family, including several children, had died in their beds one night when poisonous fumes leaked from the coolant system of their refrigerator. The former patent officer was deeply shocked. But this human tragedy was by no means a rare occurrence. From the 1870s until 1929, the toxic gases methyl chloride, ammonia and sulphur dioxide were commonly used as refrigerants. As the ownership of refrigerators increased, so too did the number of poisonings. Some people even started keeping their refrigerator outside the house.

'There must be a better way,' said Einstein as he showed Leo Szilard the newspaper report. Szilard agreed, and the two physicists set out to design a safe refrigerator. They decided from the outset that owner-ship and profits on any inventions would be shared jointly. However, Szilard was just about to climb the next rung on the academic ladder and become a *Privatdozent*, a lecturer. In Germany this was a position not funded by the university; instead, lecturers received the fees paid by the students for attending a course. So Einstein generously suggested that if the young lecturer's income ever dropped below what he had earned as von Laue's assistant, then the Professor would waive his right to the refrigerator royalties. Although Einstein always enjoyed the appliance of science, especially if it meant saving lives, he clearly saw this project as a way of helping his young friend's career.

Their collaboration was a great success. The two physicists worked together on this now forgotten project for seven years. From 1926, Einstein and Szilard filed more than forty-five patent applications for refrigerators in various countries. In the autumn of 1926, Szilard began supervising the construction of prototypes at Berlin's Institute of Technology where he had been a student just a few years earlier. They came up with three highly innovative designs. As Szilard explained in a letter to his brother, 'all three machines work without moving parts and are hermetically sealed'.[23] Clearly, the desire to avoid fumes leaking from the refrigerator remained uppermost in their minds. Several companies expressed interest in their ideas, including AB Electrolux and the Allgemeine Elektrizitäts Gesellschaft (the German General Electric Company, or AEG).

Their most original attempt to tackle the problem of refrigeration, one that has found a far wider use today than either scientist could ever have imagined, was a revolutionary pump in which liquid metal was circulated by an electromagnetic field. It was an invention that could have come straight out of the pages of one of the electrical gadget magazines that Szilard loved as a boy.[24] Einstein's uncle, who invented dynamos and lighting systems, would also have been delighted by this example of electrotechnical ingenuity. He always said his nephew would go far.

The Einstein–Szilard pump had no moving parts because it used an electromagnetic field to push a liquid metal, such as potassium, through a cylinder. This acted as a piston to compress a refrigerant gas. As in conventional refrigerators, the gas then discharged its heat into the environment as it liquefied. When it was allowed to expand again, the refrigerant cooled and so absorbed heat from the cabinet of the refrigerator. Development work began on this ingenious refrigerator in autumn 1928 at the research institute of AEG. Szilard hired his Hungarian friend Albert Kornfeld (who later changed his name to Korodi) to work on the electrical engineering problems. He was assisted by another of Szilard's fellow countrymen, Lazislas Bihaly. Szilard himself was employed by AEG as consultant on the project. At last, he could officially call himself 'Director General'.

Together with royalties from other patents, his consultancy for AEG on the electromagnetic pump brought his annual earnings to $3,000 (about £30,000 today). It is not known whether Einstein ever took his share of the earnings from their joint bank account, but according to Korodi he took a close interest in the four-year project to develop the Einstein–Szilard pump, inspecting each prototype. Gene Dannen, who talked to Korodi in Hungary before he died in 1995, says that Korodi remembered visiting Einstein's Berlin home with Leo Szilard at least a dozen times to discuss this and Szilard's other inventions. 'I didn't talk to Einstein about physics,' said Korodi with a laugh.[25] He left that side of things to the Director General.

Unfortunately, when the two physicists started their search for a new and safer type of refrigerator, unknown to them an American chemist was also working on the same problem, but from a completely different angle. Thomas Midgley was a scientist at General Motors who also invented leaded petrol to prevent 'knocking' (pre-ignition) and later died from its side effects. He had been given the task of searching for a non-toxic and non-flammable refrigerant. In 1928, just as AEG began developing the Einstein–Szilard electromagnetic pump, Midgley discovered a 'miracle compound' which was later patented under the brand name of Freon.

Freon was the first of the chlorofluorocarbons, or CFCs, a group of organic compounds containing the elements carbon, fluorine (as well as other halogens such as chlorine) and hydrogen. They are colourless gases or liquids and have no smell. Most importantly from the point of view of refrigerators, they are non-flammable and toxic only in large quantities. Thomas Midgley chose a dramatic way to demonstrate this when he revealed his new compound to the public. At a meeting of the American Chemical Society in April 1930, Midgley inhaled Freon deep into his lungs and then used it to blow out a candle. No one would be poisoned in their beds by this gas – it was perfectly safe. Or so people thought. In the 1990s, a build-up of CFCs in the earth's atmosphere was blamed for the depletion of the ozone layer. This artificial chemical had threatened to irrevocably damage the biosphere of the whole planet.

When it was invented, Freon was thought to be a major step forward in producing safe refrigerators. In 1923, only 20,000 American households owned a refrigerator. By 1935, Frigidaire and its competitors had sold eight million new Freon refrigerators in the United States alone.[26] The ingeniously engineered refrigerators dreamed up by Leo Szilard and Albert Einstein at the end of the 1920s stood no chance in the marketplace. Nevertheless, AEG continued to back development work on the Einstein–Szilard electromagnetic pump until 1932, when the Depression began to bite and the company was forced to slash its research projects by half. The pump was one of the casualties.

And so, unfortunately, no one ever used an Einstein–Szilard refrigerator to keep their groceries cool. The two men's work wasn't wasted, though. In 1942, as scientists at Chicago were planning how to build the first atomic pile and drawing up plans for the reactors that would produce the explosive new element, plutonium, it occurred to Leo Szilard that the electromagnetic pump would be ideal for cooling nuclear reactors. Exactly ten years after AEG shelved the commercial development of the Einstein–Szilard refrigerator, Szilard submitted a paper to his fellow Manhattan Project scientists on 'A magnetic pump for liquid bismuth'.[27]

In November 1942, just a few weeks before the historic pile beneath the Stagg Field football stadium went critical, Szilard wrote: 'The main purpose of operating a bismuth cooled power unit during the war is the production of about 1 ton of 94. This amount might be needed in order to win the war by means of atomic bombs, though one may hope that a smaller quantity will be sufficient.'[28]

Szilard assumed that a quarter of the uranium-235 in 150 tons of uranium would be transmuted into plutonium, or '94' as he called it. He estimated this would produce 600 lb of plutonium in about 200 days. Ever on the lookout for ingenious inventions, he also predicted that because bismuth absorbed neutrons to form polonium, his reactor would also produce 250,000 luminous torches for the armed forces. The fact that the electromagnetic pump had no moving parts and thus required no servicing made the idea attractive for nuclear reactors as well as refrigeration.

At this time John Marshall became Szilard's 'hands', the person who did all the Director General's experimental work. Marshall was married to the physicist Leona Woods, the best known of the women scientists working on the Manhattan Project and the only woman present when the Chicago pile went critical. She thought Szilard was 'a really amazing man'. But according to her husband, 'Szilard was one of these guys who is a little bit too bright. He had the right conclusion as to what should be done but it would turn out in practice to be something that couldn't be done for twenty years.'[29]

In the end, Szilard's friend Eugene Wigner, who was in charge of reactor design, decided on a simpler solution than the electromagnetic pump: water-cooled reactors. Once again, Szilard had been too far ahead of his time. But he wasn't daunted by this setback. By 1944 he was already looking forward to the coming age of nuclear power generation. In April he suggested using liquid metal cooling in a fast neutron reactor which was designed to produce as much plutonium as it burned. He called this revolutionary type of reactor a 'breeder', because it bred fuel. Enrico Fermi was immediately sceptical of this idea, just as he had been when Szilard first suggested, in 1939, that atomic bombs were possible. But Szilard was nothing if not tenacious. He brought up the idea again in 1945, claiming that he was 'fairly confident' that breeder reactors could be built which 'double the investment of plutonium within about a year'.[30]

In a breeder reactor, the fuel consists of 90 per cent uranium-238 together with 10 per cent plutonium. There is no graphite to moderate the reaction by slowing neutrons. The fast neutrons are absorbed by the uranium, which is then transmuted into fissionable plutonium. The great advantage of this type of reactor is that, rather than merely burning uranium to create energy, the naturally abundant uranium-238 isotope is used in a cyclical process that simultaneously generates both fission energy and more nuclear fuel than there was in the first place.

As John Marshall said, in 1945 this was blue-sky thinking. But seven years later the Atomic Energy Commission revealed that it had built an experimental breeder reactor at Arco, Idaho. It worked by burning fissionable uranium-235 and using the neutrons released to transmute a 'blanket' of uranium-238 surrounding the reactor core into plutonium. This plutonium could then be used in other reactors or in atomic bombs. Walter H. Zinn was its designer, and, like his cadmium safety rod in the 1942 pile, it was nicknamed ZIP, which this time was short for 'Zinn's Infernal Pile'. Zinn revealed the details of the new reactor to the American public. One feature was its 'unique' electromagnetic pump.[31]

Progress on transforming Leo Szilard's idea into reality has been slow. America has built just one commercial breeder reactor, which started operating in Michigan in 1969. Ironically, given his scepticism about the initial idea, it was called Fermi I. It is France that pioneered the subsequent commercial development of breeder reactors, beginning in the 1970s during the oil crisis. The French operated a fast neutron reactor power plant successfully from 1973 to 1990. It was named, appropriately enough, Phénix, after the mythical bird that is reborn in fire. For out of the nuclear fire of this reactor, new fuel was created.

After Phénix came Superphénix, built in 1985 thirty miles east of Lyon at Creys-Malville, on the Rhône. Like all fast neutron reactors it uses the Einstein–Szilard pump as part of a liquid metal cooling system. The French used liquid sodium. In 1998, the Russians revealed that they had been using lead–bismuth cooled reactors for forty years in their nuclear submarines. Both these liquid metals were proposed by Leo Szilard in his Manhattan Project research paper of April 1944. Indeed, future developments in reactor design lie in the direction of fast breeder reactors, probably using liquid metal coolants. Liquid metal cooling has also been used in reactors on satellites. Most recently, in 2005, liquid metal pumps have been miniaturized for use in computers, providing a revolutionary new approach to cooling for CPUs and even fuel cells.[32]

From Szilard's theoretical work on thermodynamics (inspired by Einstein's seminars on statistical mechanics) and the creative brainstorming of these two visionary physicists came an idea for a practical solution to an urgent problem that has subsequently been used in ways unimaginable at the time. In fiction too, their revolutionary pump has made its mark. In Tom Clancy's cold-war thriller *The*

Hunt for Red October (1984), the Soviets develop a silent, and thus undetectable, submarine thanks to an electromagnetic seawater propulsion system based on the Einstein–Szilard principle. American scientists did actually explore this idea in the 1950s but found it unfeasible, given the available technology.[33]

With their safer refrigerator, Einstein and Szilard had wanted to use science to save lives. But in an ironic twist to the story of the Einstein–Szilard pump, Szilard revived the idea in the atomic age as a way of creating the new fissile element plutonium for bombs. The invention that both of these humanistic scientists hoped would prevent deaths became part of the atomic arms race. Szilard's work on the electromagnetic pump helped to provide him with an income during the turbulent years to come. The patents he applied for during the 1920s allowed him to concentrate all his creative energies on the subject that came to dominate his life – atomic energy. The cold war began, appropriately enough, in a refrigerator.

Einstein and Leo Szilard began designing refrigerators in 1926. This was also the year in which the final member of the Hungarian Quartet arrived in Germany. Edward Teller, born in 1908, was the youngest of the four Hungarian émigrés. Szilard was the oldest. John von Neumann was born in 1903, and Wigner a year later.

Teller began his scientific career by studying chemistry at Karlsruhe, where Fritz Haber had once taught. Like Szilard, he soon realized that physics was the more promising field and in 1928 moved first to Munich, where he studied under Arnold Sommerfeld, and then to Leipzig, where he became a postdoctoral student in the department of the brilliant quantum theorist, Werner Heisenberg. It was an extraordinary period to be working in physics. According to Szilard's Berlin friend Victor Weisskopf, there had never been a time in science 'in which so much has been clarified by so few in so short a period'.[34]

The quantum revolution, which Einstein had helped to spark in 1905, had now been taken over by a new, younger generation of physicists which included Heisenberg and the Austrians Wolfgang Pauli and Erwin Schrödinger. Under their leadership, the physical world became stranger than the worst nightmares of the classical physicists. The new physics was founded on the counter-intuitive, even disturbing, principles of probability and uncertainty – notions which undermined the previously accepted view of the physical universe. Even causality and objective reality were challenged in this new era of subatomic physics. For Einstein, who had always been a reluctant revolutionary, such ideas were anathema. To his dying breath he refused to believe that the subatomic realm departed fundamentally from the laws that governed the macroscopic universe. Throughout the 1920s, the atomic nucleus remained shrouded in mystery, concealing the secrets of its composition from the curious eyes of the nuclear physicists. The great breakthrough in understanding would come in 1932. By then the golden age of physics was drawing to a close, and for Berlin, the city that had become the capital of physics, the party was almost over.

On 7 November 1926, Joseph Goebbels stepped off the train at the Anhalter Bahnhof in Berlin where, six years earlier, Leo Szilard had arrived. Adolf Hitler had just appointed the 29-year-old *Gauführer*, or area commander, of Berlin. Goebbels had fallen under the spell of this political Caligari. In April, Goebbels wrote in his diary: 'Adolf Hitler, I love you, because you are both great and simple. A genius.'[35] His task was to build Hitler's power base.

Einstein had long suffered from anti-Semitic attacks in Germany. Hitler had ranted about what he saw as the malign influence of 'Hebrew' science on the German 'soul'. Within the physics community, anti-Semites such as Nobel prizewinning physicist Philipp Lenard began opposing what they called 'Jewish physics' and promoting their own 'Aryan physics'. Soon, nationalists gathered outside Einstein's Berlin home to shout insults against him and relativity. At one point a reward was offered to anyone who killed Einstein. When the Jewish foreign minister Walther Rathenau was assassinated near Dahlem in 1922 by a reactionary gang, Einstein was thought to be next in line. Rathenau, whose father had founded AEG, was a close friend of Einstein's. After his murder the physicist seriously considered leaving Germany. Fritz Haber managed to convince him to remain.

When Hitler came to power in 1933, many of Germany's greatest physicists would be expelled from their positions under new racial laws. By then the Hungarian Quartet had all fled their new country.

America would be their final destination. With them they took the knowledge that could have given the Third Reich the key to absolute power – the superweapon.

10

Faust and the Physicists

You see things; and you say, 'Why?'
But I dream things that never were; and I say, 'Why not?'
The Serpent in George Bernard Shaw's
Back to Methuselah (1921)

On Christmas Day 1931, the passengers of the SS *Leviathan* crowded on deck to watch as their ship approached Manhattan Island, the gateway to the New World. Six months earlier, the world's tallest building had been officially opened here – the Empire State Building, a towering monument to the technological age and an anticipation of tomorrow's cities. In the future, as Fritz Lang's 1926 film *Metropolis* had shown, architecture would touch the skies.

But in 1931 most people still had their feet firmly on the ground. In the aftermath of the Depression that had followed the Wall Street Crash, the immediate future was a long way from utopia. Little of the new skyscraper's two million square feet of office space had been rented, and New Yorkers quickly renamed it the Empty State Building.

The *Leviathan* had left England on 19 December with Leo Szilard on board. He was supposed to be giving lecture courses in Berlin – one on atomic physics with Lise Meitner and the other on new work in theoretical physics with Erwin Schrödinger. But the chance to spend a year working on mathematical physics at Princeton University had been too good to miss. The offer had come from Eugene Wigner, who along with John von Neumann had accepted a post at Princeton the year before. A personal letter from Albert Einstein had secured Szilard a visa, and as the cancer of fascism spread across Europe he was seriously considering whether he should move permanently to the land of the free.

No one who approaches New York from the sea can fail to be moved by the city's breathtaking skyline. It is a sight that seems quintessentially modern – *the* city of the twentieth century. Typically, though, Leo Szilard also sensed the vulnerability of the great metropolis:

As the boat approached the harbour, I stood on deck watching the skyline of New York. It seemed unreal, and I asked myself, 'Is this here to stay? Is it likely that it will still be here a hundred years from now?' Somehow I had the strong conviction that it wouldn't be there. 'What could possibly make it disappear?' I asked myself . . . and found no answer. And yet the feeling persisted that it was not here to stay.[1]

When he wrote these words, two decades later at the height of the cold war, with America and the Soviet Union preparing to test their new hydrogen superbombs, every schoolchild knew what could make New York or any other city disappear. But at the end of 1931, Szilard seemed to have few grounds for his doomsday fears. Perhaps it was his sixth sense for the 'tragedy of mankind' that warned Szilard that an extraordinary year was about to dawn in atomic physics, comparable in its impact to 1895, when Wilhelm Röntgen saw the bones in his hand revealed by mysterious rays.[2] For, as Hans Bethe has said, 1932 was the year in which atomic physics was born.

All roads led to Blegdamsvej 15 if you were a physicist in the 1920s and 30s. This was Niels Bohr's Institute for Theoretical Physics in Copenhagen. The brilliant Ukrainian physicist George Gamow recalled that 'the Institute buzzed with young theoretical physicists and new ideas about atoms, atomic nuclei, and the quantum theory in general'.[3]

Niels Bohr was a superb footballer and as a young man had played for a top Danish club. But in physics, the tall, softly spoken Bohr was in a league of his own. He was the 'deepest thinker I ever met', said Paul Dirac, the English physicist who in 1928 correctly predicted the existence of antimatter.[4] 'I have seen a physicist for the first time,' said the German physicist Carl Friedrich von Weizsäcker after meeting

Bohr. 'He suffers as he thinks.'[5] Together with Ernest Rutherford, Bohr had mapped the basic structure of the atom, and later, in the 1920s, he helped to shape the quantum revolution – despite strong resistance from its founder, the former patent officer from Berne. Indeed, he had as profound an influence on the course of twentieth-century physics as did Einstein himself. After they met for the first time in Berlin, Einstein wrote to Bohr that 'not often in life has a person, by his mere presence, given me such joy as you'.[6]

Einstein's debates in the late 1920s with Bohr on quantum theory were like a scientific clash of the Titans. Einstein could never accept the indeterministic quantum mechanics of the 1920s that grew out of his own 1905 paper on the photoelectric effect. In it he used Max Planck's notion of quantized energy and argued that light was not a wave but a stream of particles – photons. Einstein was right to describe his own paper as 'very revolutionary'.[7] In fact it was this rather than his more famous paper on relativity that won him his Nobel prize in 1921. But as a new generation of physicists carried the red banner of quantum revolution into ever stranger territory, Einstein clung doggedly to what he called 'objective reality'. As he told his friend Max Born in 1926, God does not play dice.[8] If an electron could choose its direction 'of its own free will', he said, 'I would rather be a cobbler, or even an employee in a gaming house, than a physicist'.[9]

From the mid-1920s, while he was collaborating with Leo Szilard on refrigerator designs, Einstein began to plough a long and lonely intellectual furrow in theoretical physics. His goal was what he called a unified field theory. He believed until his dying day that this would bring relativity and the quantum realm together in one theory describing the movement of planets as well as subatomic particles. His quest isolated Einstein from the new generation of nuclear physicists, who with their increasingly counter-intuitive ideas about the subatomic realm challenged the very foundations of classical physics and provided the conceptual tools to build the atomic bomb. These new, revolutionary physicists – people such as Walther Bothe, James Chadwick and Frédéric Joliot-Curie (Marie Curie's son-in-law) – were Einstein's intellectual children. When he disowned them, the former footballer Niels Bohr became their father figure.

Bohr's annual conference, to which he invited about thirty physicists, was the highlight of the physics year. In 1932, from 3 to 13 April the brightest minds in physics gathered together in Copenhagen. In a few years' time, many of them would be working on the atomic bomb. But for now they still had time for a little light-hearted play-acting. Each year the conference ended with what George Gamow called a 'stunt pertaining to recent developments in physics'.[10] The year before, Gamow had rounded up proceedings with a cartoon history of quantum mechanics, starring Mickey Mouse in the lead role.[11] This year marked the centenary of Goethe's death, so they decided to stage a version of the German writer's greatest play, *Faust*.

Scientists attending the 1932 conference at Niels Bohr's Institute for Theoretical Physics in Copenhagen. Among those pictured are Werner Heisenberg, Max Delbrück, Lise Meitner, Paul Ehrenfest, Carl Friedrich von Weizsäcker and Paul Dirac.

Written when the industrial revolution was transforming Europe, *Faust* draws on the story of a sixteenth-century alchemist to ask what is the purpose of knowledge and how we can have progress without increasing human suffering. It is a remarkable work, one that acknowledges the indebtedness of science to its earlier, hermetic roots in alchemy while looking forward to the scientific world of the future. By chance, the final part of *Faust* was published in the year the word 'scientist' was coined. Goethe's Faust is a proto-scientist whose desire to know nature's deepest secrets leads him to strike a fateful bargain with Mephistopheles, the fallen angel who is the Devil's representative on earth. By usurping the authority of God, Faust becomes an iconic figure of human hubris, like Dr Frankenstein.

In the sixteenth century, the story of Faust – a disreputable dabbler in alchemy and the occult, who came to a sticky end in an explosive experiment – was used by the Church to frighten people about the dangers of non-Christian knowledge. Goethe's play reworks the classic theme for the modern age. His Faust is not a mad scientist, as the Church had once tried to portray him. Instead, Goethe celebrates the spirit of inquiry while highlighting the dangers of misapplied knowledge. True scientific understanding is life-affirming and creative, not destructive and exploitative, Goethe suggests.

At the beginning of the play, Faust longs to know 'the inmost force / That bonds the very universe'.[12] It is a scientific and philosophical goal he pursues tirelessly throughout his life, regardless of the cost to himself or others around him. True to the scientific spirit of the age in which it was written, Goethe's *Faust* does not question the value of such knowledge.

Goethe's portrait of the unsatisfied searcher for knowledge is tragic not because Faust loses his eternal soul, as happens in the original sixteenth-century tale. Instead, the quest of the modern Faust is tragic because, until the final moments of his life, this brilliant man does not truly understand himself. What is the point of knowing nature's deep-est secrets, Goethe asks, if humankind never attains self-knowledge? The Faustian scientist might control the forces of nature but he does not understand, let alone control, himself. The implications were not lost on the atomic physicists gathered at Bohr's Institute in spring 1932.

The physicists' *Faust* was written by the younger scientists present, their literary skills no doubt boosted by the products of Copenhagen's other claim to fame – the Carlsberg Brewery, which also happened to be one of Danish science's most generous benefactors. Max Delbrück, a friend of Szilard's from Dahlem who would later be a central figure in the post-war revolution in molecular biology, did most of the writing. Goethe's characters were replaced with the great physicists of the day, their younger colleagues donning masks to play them. Mephistopheles became the irascible Austrian Wolfgang Pauli, while Faust became Paul Ehrenfest, a close friend of Einstein. The role of God was reserved, appropriately enough, for their gentlemanly host, Niels Bohr.

The play parodied Goethe's masterpiece and allowed the next generation of physicists to poke fun at their esteemed elders, who were sitting in the audience. Wolfgang Pauli's rudeness was legendary. In the play he bluntly tells the painfully polite Niels Bohr (God) that his latest theory is 'crap'.[13] But Bohr is also gently mocked. His almost

Cover of the script for the 1932 Copenhagen performance of Faust, *designed by the Danish scientist and poet Piet Hein.*

pathological fear of being too critical becomes the motto of the play, emblazoned on the text's cover: *Nicht um zu kritisieren* (Not to criticize).[14] Even Einstein doesn't escape unscathed. His flawed unified field theory, which created a media storm when it was published in 1929, is lampooned as the son of a flea.

At times the play is anarchic, even Dadaist, in its celebration of the bizarre world of quantum theory. But the new physics was full of weird and wonderful notions. Niels Bohr once greeted one of Pauli's theories with the comment: 'We are all agreed that your theory is crazy. The question, which divides us, is whether it is crazy *enough* to have a chance of being correct. My own feeling is that it is not crazy enough.'[15]

The audience of the physicists' *Faust* were not surprised, therefore, when 'The Group Dragon' and 'Donkey-Electrons' appeared on stage in the Quantum Mechanical Walpurgis Night scene. As Dirac says in the play, 'our theories, gentlemen, have run amuck'.[16] The physicists transformed Faust's death scene at the end of the play into a moment of supreme bathos. Paul Ehrenfest utters Faust's famous dying words just as he is about to be immortalized by a throng of press photographers: 'To this moment I want to say: / Do stay, you are so beautiful!'[17]

In the physicists' *Faust* this becomes a wonderfully witty moment, although humour was the last thing in Goethe's mind as he penned this poignant scene. The physicists are making fun of their colleagues' vanity and self-importance. By highlighting the theme of fame, they were making an important point. In the coming years, nuclear physicists would indeed feature ever more frequently in the media. A new age of science was dawning. As actors on the world's stage, scientists would be increasingly forced to drop the mask of the saviour. Instead, as they were drawn ever closer to government and the military, they began to be feared by the public and viewed as Strangelovean mad scientists. This would be the price of their Faustian bargain.

Griffin, the megalomaniac scientist in the film of *The Invisible Man* (1933), knows the temptation of such power and pays the ultimate price for hubris: 'I wanted to do something tremendous, to achieve what men of science have dreamt of since the world began, to gain wealth and fame and honour, to write my name above the greatest scientists of all time.'[18] Indeed, one physicist featured in the play would, after Hiroshima and Nagasaki, rival even Einstein's fame: Robert Oppenheimer.

Another physicist who would enter the media spotlight this year made a brief appearance at the end of the play as Faust's over-ambitious assistant, Wagner. James Chadwick is portrayed by his fellow physicists as 'the personification of the ideal experimentalist'. In the play's manuscript there is a sketch of him looking very serious and wearing the scientist's trademark white lab coat. He walks on stage after Faust's death scene, balancing a black ball on one finger. 'The neutron has come to be,' declares Chadwick's character. 'Loaded with Mass is he, / Of Charge, forever free.'[19] This rather sinister figure at the end of the play was announcing an extraordinary discovery, one of which Faust himself would have been proud. James Chadwick had found one of the basic constituents of matter – the third elementary particle.

Ernest Rutherford and Niels Bohr's planetary model of the atom – a nucleus orbited by electrons – was widely accepted. But the structure of the nucleus remained unknown. In 1919, Rutherford had found that nitrogen atoms under bombardment disintegrated to produce hydrogen nuclei. He coined the term 'proton' for these particles, after British chemist William Prout's term for elementary hydrogen atoms, 'protyle'. Rutherford then suggested that the core of the atom consisted of alpha particles together with protons and electrons. Significantly, in 1920 he speculated that protons and electrons might join together, forming what he called 'neutral doublets'.[20] The search had begun for the neutron.

James Chadwick had spent World War I interned in Germany, where his scientific activities were limited to experiments with radio-active toothpaste. A tall and rather aloof man, Chadwick became assistant director of Rutherford's Cavendish Laboratory at Cambridge in 1923. Chadwick set himself the task of tracking down the hypo-thetical neutron. The first major clue came in 1930. Two German scientists, Walther Bothe and Herbert Becker, found that a light, silvery metal called beryllium could be made to emit radiation when bombarded with alpha particles from polonium. But this was no ordinary radiation – it was more powerful than anything so far detected from natural radioactivity or artificial transmutations, such as Rutherford's. It could penetrate eight inches of lead.[21]

Marie Curie's daughter, Irène, and her husband Frédéric Joliot, working at the Radium Institute in Paris, claimed that this was gamma radiation. What's more, they said they had used this strong radiation to punch protons out of hydrogen-containing materials, such as paraffin wax. This was an extraordinary claim. Gamma radiation is essentially a highly energetic form of light, and although photons – particles of light – had been known to knock electrons out of the way, the idea that they could dislodge a particle two thousand times as massive, such as a proton, seemed fantastic. So Chadwick thought, when he read the Curies' paper in January 1932.

Primed by Rutherford's theory that the atomic nucleus is made up of protons and neutral particles, Chadwick realized that this was the chance he had been waiting for. After three weeks of intense work using equipment which resembled 'a piece of discarded plumbing', Chadwick announced that Bothe and Becker's powerful radiation was not gamma rays, but neutrons.[22]

The mysterious radiation detected by the two German physicists was now explained. Beryllium was emitting a particle as solid as a proton, but with one vital difference. The neutron, as its name suggests, has mass but no electrical charge. And because it is electrically neutral, the neutron can penetrate right into the heart of the atomic nucleus – unlike the positive protons and alpha particles, which are repelled. The neutron was what the atomic scientists had been waiting for: an ideal tool to probe the dark heart of matter.

James Chadwick mailed a hurried announcement of his discovery to a scientific journal on 17 February 1932. A few evenings later, he told a rapt group of his Cambridge colleagues, including novelist and physicist C. P. Snow, how he had made his remarkable discovery. At the end of his talk he sat down and (as Snow recalled) said, 'now I want to be chloroformed and put to bed for a fortnight'.[23]

The discovery of the neutron earned Chadwick the honour of being portrayed in the physicists' *Faust* in Copenhagen a couple of weeks later. But even as the physicists were performing their skit, two other scientists at the Cavendish Laboratory were homing in on the centre of the atom without the benefit of the neutron. John Cockcroft and

Ernest Walton succeeded in accelerating protons to a sufficiently high speed to shatter an atom. To do this they had effectively built a gun that fired subatomic particles.

With its spark-gap spheres and glass vacuum tubes held together with plasticine, their apparatus would not have seemed out of place in the laboratory of Rotwang, the mad scientist in Fritz Lang's *Metropolis*, or Henry Frankenstein in James Whale's 1931 film of Shelley's classic. The operator of this early particle accelerator had to sit in a lead-lined tea chest. Uncomfortable and primitive it might have been, but it worked, and it became the ancestor of such engineering triumphs as the Large Hadron Collider at CERN in Geneva. On 14 April, the day after the Copenhagen Conference finished, Cockcroft and Walton fired protons at lithium atoms. Each lithium atom struck by a proton split into two alpha particles, essentially helium nuclei. It was the first time that a machine had shattered an atomic nucleus.

The press pounced on the story, eager to herald the dawn of the Atomic Age and a revolutionary new energy source. But Cockcroft and Walton's boss, Rutherford, rebuked the journalists. Although the energy released was relatively large, he told them, only one proton in ten million penetrated a target nucleus. Atomic engines were not just around the corner. Warming to his subject, and always pleased to confound the fourth estate, Rutherford denied that the search for new sources of power interested any of his scientists at the Cavendish. 'The urge and the fascination of a search into one of the deepest secrets of nature,' was their only motive, he boasted.[24]

It was a noble claim. But however pure their motives, the secrets of nature that Rutherford and his physicists were revealing would have profound implications for everyone on the planet. The physicist Paul Langevin was no friend of the press that had once revealed his secret love affair with Marie Curie. But he knew that physics was about a lot more than a few men in tweed jackets tinkering with atoms. Physics was going to change the world. 'You're taking it all much too seriously,' he told a young historian who had just fled Hitler's Germany:

Hitler? It won't be long before he breaks his neck like all other tyrants. I'm much more worried about something else. It is something which, if it gets into the wrong hands, can do the world a good deal more damage than that fool who will sooner or later go to the dogs. It is something which – unlike him – we shall never be able to get rid of: I mean the neutron.[25]

The discovery of a new particle and a machine to smash an atom were astonishing enough, but there was more to come. On the day after Chadwick submitted his note on the discovery of the neutron to *Nature*, an American scientific journal received a paper from Harold C. Urey announcing a new isotope of hydrogen known as deuterium, or heavy hydrogen. It would later become the fuel of the hydrogen bomb.

As scientists gradually assembled the knowledge that would later allow them to construct nuclear weapons, the German military began funding research into the missiles that would deliver them. In the spring of 1932 a black sedan car pulled up at an abandoned arsenal in a northern suburb of Berlin. Inside was an officer from the Army Ordnance Department. Walter Dornberger had come to see a group of young, starry-eyed scientists and engineers who had called themselves the Society for Space Travel (Verein für Raumschifffahrt). Somewhat optimistically, they had renamed the 120-hectare piece of scrubland they were using for their experiments, Berlin's Rocketport. That day Dornberger met a dynamic fair-haired student who wanted to be the Columbus of space. His name was Wernher von Braun.

Dornberger took an immediate liking to the 20-year-old Prussian *Junker* and hired him to design rocket motors for the German army. Once Hitler was in power, Dornberger became head of the Third Reich's missile programme. At one meeting, as Dornberger was explaining to the Führer the potential of Wernher von Braun's missiles, a 'strange, fanatical light' came into Hitler's eyes. 'What I want is annihilation!' exclaimed the Führer.[26] After the war, Dornberger and von Braun found a new paymaster. Dornberger took his engineering and organizational expertise to the New World, first working for the US Department of Defense and later becoming vice president of the Bell Aircraft Corporation. Von Braun also found a warm welcome in America, initially designing rockets for the US military and later for the space race. He later recalled that first meeting with Dornberger:

That was the beginning. The Versailles Treaty hadn't placed any restrictions on rockets, and the army was desperate to get back on its feet. We didn't care much about that, one way or the other, but we needed money, and the army seemed willing to help us. In 1932, the idea of war seemed to us an absurdity. The Nazis weren't yet in power. We felt no moral scruples about the possible future abuse of our brainchild. We were interested solely in exploring outer space. It was simply a question with us of how the golden cow would be milked most successfully.[27]

Outer space may well have been Wernher von Braun's goal, but his first rockets were designed for earthbound targets. In September 1944 the first of his ballistic missiles, the V-2 (V for *Vergeltungswaffe*, 'vengeance weapon'), hurtled down on London at supersonic speed. Its one-ton warheads killed 2,700 Londoners during the war. When the first V-2 hit London, von Braun is said to have commented drily to his colleagues, 'The rocket worked perfectly except for landing on the wrong planet.'[28] He and his colleagues even had plans for a rocket that could hit New York. From intercontinental ballistic missiles to atomic and hydrogen bombs, the seeds of the cold-war technologies of mass destruction were already being sown in 1932, the year before Hitler came to power.

Leo Szilard claimed to have read Goethe's *Faust* at the age of six. Four years later he read *The Tragedy of Man*, a dramatic poem inspired by *Faust*. Written in the 1860s, this work by Imre Madách (now a classic of the Hungarian theatre) also explores the human quest for understanding and power over nature. It retells for the scientific age the Biblical story of Adam and Eve's expulsion from the Garden of Eden for daring to eat from the tree of the knowledge of good and evil.

The Tragedy of Man made a deep impression on Leo Szilard. There was one scene in particular that he often recalled in later life. In it, Lucifer shows Adam the future of life on earth. The dying sun has become 'a dull, red sphere', and a new ice age has descended on the planet. Adam despairs that earth has become 'a gigantic grave' and all human achievements, whether scientific or artistic, have been lost. In contrast, Lucifer gloats at man's helplessness: 'Science could not avert earth's destiny,' he says.[29]

These apocalyptic scenes anticipate the icy wastelands seen by H. G.

Wells's Time Traveller as he journeys forward to the earth's dying days. The second law of thermodynamics shocked the nineteenth century with its notion of a heat death for the universe, the result of entropy. The idea that the arrow of time decreed the unavoidable end of everything suggested to writers that all human endeavour would ultimately prove futile. For Madách, our tragedy was that we have the wit to grasp the laws of nature, but not the power to change them.

Leo Szilard never forgot his countryman's poem. As he told a journalist in 1945, *The Tragedy of Man* influenced his whole life and taught him that human survival often depended on a 'narrow margin of hope'.[30] This thought would sustain him through the bleak and frightening years that followed the dropping of the atomic bomb, when nuclear war seemed imminent. The poem also filled him with a passionate desire to prove Lucifer wrong. It became his lifelong purpose to show that – as he said to Niels Bohr in 1950 – science really could 'save the world'.[31]

Szilard returned from his trip to America in May 1932. The collaboration with the mathematicians at Princeton had not been a great success. Instead, he had spent most of his time getting to know the physicists at New York University, where he became great friends with the head of physics, Professor Richard T. Cox. Before he left, Szilard organized a petition among his fellow scientists protesting against Japan's attack on the Chinese port of Shanghai in February of that year. It was the first of Szilard's many attempts to involve scientists in politics. Clearly, the world very much needed to be saved.

In Berlin at the beginning of the 1930s, even scientists couldn't ignore politics. Eva Striker (now Eva Zeisel), the niece of the Hungarian chemist Michael Polanyi, moved to Berlin at this time. A gifted designer of ceramics, she recalls there was a pervasive feeling of 'hopelessness and disgust with Western civilization' at the time.[32] Brutal street fights between Nazis and Communist gangs were common. According to Stephen Spender, there was 'a sensation of doom to be felt in the Berlin streets'.[33]

But despite this, for Eva Striker and many others, Berlin remained 'the center of the world'.[34] Striker's parties, held in her central Berlin studio with its high windows, drew together artists, scientists and intellectuals from across the city. The expressionist painter Emil

Nolde, who lived in the same building, and Hungarian writer Arthur Koestler, for a while Eva's lover, were often seen there. 'My studio became an annex of the Romanisches Café,' she said, 'the Forum Romanum for the exchange of ideas on how best to save the world.'[35] Among those at Eva Striker's parties ever keen to discuss plans for saving the world was Leo Szilard.

In the elections of September 1930, the Nazis had received almost 20 per cent of the vote. Szilard wrote to Einstein: 'From week to week I detect new symptoms, if my nose doesn't deceive me, that peaceful [political] development in Europe in the next ten years is not to be counted on.' Never one to overlook practicalities, he added: 'Indeed, I don't know if it will be possible to build our refrigerator in Europe.'[36] Szilard did in fact have an excellent nose for impending disaster. From the mid-1920s he had begun to doubt that democracy would survive in Germany. 'I thought that it might survive one or two generations', he later recalled.[37] Early on, he decided that the future of Germany lay in the hands of its young people, and for this reason he hatched one of his earliest schemes for saving the world: his plan for 'Der Bund' – The League.

Leo Szilard's League would be for 'boys and girls who have the scientific mind and a religious spirit'.[38] He envisaged that the brightest young people would be identified at an early age and brought together to form what he called a 'spiritual leadership class with inner cohesion'.[39] After all, as *New York Times* science editor Waldemar Kaempffert put it in 1945, 'religion may preach the brotherhood of man; science practices it'.[40] Szilard wanted the League to set an example of purpose and community to society as a whole. It would offer a 'life of sacrifice and service': 'The sacrifice shall be so severe that this path will only be followed by those who are imbued with the desired spirit.'[41]

Szilard's elite group would influence public opinion and politics, either by directing government or advising it. The League will, he wrote, 'represent some form of structure in public life, which would leave an imprint on the whole spiritual life of the community'.[42] His idea of a secular sect that guides and inspires society anticipates the 'Order' described in Hermann Hesse's great novel *The Glass Bead Game* (1943).

In 1928 Szilard read H. G. Wells's *The Open Conspiracy*. Wells called for an 'intellectual rebirth' in society and warned of 'such war as man has never known before'.[43] He concluded with a rousing vision of the future:

The Open Conspiracy is the awaking of mankind from a nightmare, an infantile nightmare, of the struggle for existence and the inevitability of war. The light of day thrusts between our eyelids, and the multitudinous sounds of morning clamour in our ears. A time will come when men will sit with history before them or with some old newspaper before them and ask incredulously, 'Was there ever such a world?'[44]

Wells argued that to avoid war and improve society, what was needed was an 'Open Conspiracy' of society's elite – industrialists, scientists, technocrats. Wells had described this elite as early as 1905 in *A Modern Utopia*. Then he had named them the Samurai.

After World War I, during which nations mobilized their scientific, technological and industrial resources to an unprecedented degree, many people – including Hugo Gernsback – thought that the society of the future would be led by an elite of technocrats. J. J. Connington's novel *Nordenholt's Million* had described how a ruthlessly efficient industrialist steps in to save humankind when feckless politicians have failed. The subtext to this and other novels was beguiling but dangerous: government by committee is inefficient; in the scientific age, we need strong individuals who will take decisive action based on science and statistics.

Leo Szilard was hugely impressed by *The Open Conspiracy* in 1928. He told friends that in the opening pages Wells had summarized the urgent problems facing the world, including the need for a new social and political order. It was, after all, only what Leo Szilard had himself been saying. In February 1929 he wrote to Wells praising his book. 'Let me tell you,' he said, 'speaking for myself and many friends of mine, we are very glad and think it rather important you have written the *Open Conspiracy*.' Szilard requested a meeting with the famous English writer. Shrewdly, he asked his friend Einstein to add a greeting to the letter, praising Wells as 'one of the great pioneers in the struggle toward better socialistic structures'.[45]

Even H. G. Wells was not immune to praise from the most famous scientist of the age. Szilard's ploy worked, and the following month he travelled to London where he met and dined with Wells. The writer was at the peak of his fame. He was perhaps the most widely read author in the English language. Both Stalin and Roosevelt (who became President in November 1932) were fans. Szilard eagerly explained his idea for the League, or, as he told Einstein in a letter from England, 'our plan'.[46]

Unfortunately, this was not a good time for Wells: his wife had died a year or so earlier, and he was in the process of moving house. Although he was keen to encourage like-minded people, Wells never became too closely involved with them, however enthusiastic they were. Whether it was the stress of moving or because he couldn't make up his mind about the Hungarian scientist's 'plan', Szilard's requests for a further 'hour or two' of his time, either in England or during Wells's forthcoming French holiday, were unsuccessful.[47]

Although his visit did not secure the support of the English writer, while he was in London Szilard met someone whose influence would prove decisive. Otto Mandl was a successful Viennese businessman and H. G. Wells fan. He had organized the translation of Wells's works into German and had himself translated and edited many of Wells's books, including *The Open Conspiracy*. The two men soon found that they shared the same bold vision of the future, and Szilard became a close friend of Mandl and his wife, the Hungarian pianist Lili Kraus.

A year later, Leo Szilard made another trip to London to rally support for the League. This time he met the radical writer and journalist H. N. Brailsford. Afterwards, Brailsford wrote to their mutual friend, Albert Einstein, about the young scientist and his bold plans. Szilard clearly had 'the religious spirit' that he hoped to impart to other young members of his organization, Brailsford said, but frankly he doubted whether the scientist could organize such an ambitious movement.[48]

In his reply, Einstein said that Szilard had 'assembled a circle of excellent young people, mostly physicists, who are in sympathy with his ideas. But as yet there is no organization of any kind.' He complimented Szilard for being 'a fine, intelligent man, who is ordinarily not given to illusions'. However, although he was sympathetic to Szilard's aims, he also doubted that the League would ever exist. Einstein added: 'Perhaps, like many such people, he is inclined to overestimate the significance of reason in human affairs.'[49]

In 1932, Leo Szilard found himself at a turning point. Indeed, as his hopes for a lucrative refrigerator design rapidly faded, the 34-year-old entered a period of profound uncertainty and self-doubt that seriously worried his friends. At Princeton he had again decided that he did not want to pursue physics on a purely abstract and mathematical level. He even considered giving up science altogether. In October he wrote to his friend Eugene Wigner that there were 'more noble causes than to do science'. Clearly, Szilard was thinking of his utopian vision for society, the League. But he did admit that, 'of course, physics interests me still one full magnitude more than refrigerators'.[50]

Throughout his restless life, Szilard struggled to find an intellectual home: a position or institution where he could put down roots and be free to dream up bold and grand designs for science and humanity. Academia was too restricting for such an unconventional and foot-loose thinker. He had hoped that the revolutionary electromagnetic pump would guarantee his financial freedom by providing a flow of royalties. Now, as that project reached its end, Wigner and other friends became concerned about his 'depressed' state of mind and what he was going to do with his life.[51] Significantly, despite his personal lack of direction – he even considered starting again in an entirely new field, biology – Szilard picked nuclear physics as the most intriguing area of science. James Chadwick's discovery of the neutron and the splitting of the atom by two other members of Rutherford's team were momentous enough, but it was a novel that really fired his imagination.

When he returned from America in May 1932, Szilard found that Mandl and his wife were now living in Berlin. It was here that Szilard had what he later called a 'memorable conversation' with him. It centred on Szilard's favourite topic: the future of humankind and how to save us from our self-destructive instincts. Otto Mandl told Szilard that he now knew how 'to save mankind from a series of ever-recurring wars that could destroy it'. According to Mandl, there was a 'heroic streak' in humankind. 'Man is not satisfied with a happy idyllic life,' he said, 'he has the need to fight and to encounter danger.' In order to satisfy this desire for heroism, humanity needed to save itself by launching 'an enterprise aimed at leaving the earth'.

Szilard told Otto Mandl that his idea was 'somewhat new to me' and that he 'really didn't know whether I would agree with him'. However, he added,

if I came to the conclusion that this was what mankind needed, if I wanted to contribute something to save mankind, then I would probably go into nuclear physics, because only through the liberation of atomic energy could we obtain the means which would enable man not only to leave the earth but to leave the solar system.[52]

For the man who had tried for the last five or so years to promote a utopian order inspired by science, the grandeur of Mandl's idea must have impressed Leo Szilard, even if it seemed (to put it mildly) rather ahead of its time.

At about the same time as this futuristic conversation, and probably on Mandl's recommendation, Szilard began reading a scientific novel by H. G. Wells written almost twenty years earlier – *The World Set Free*. Later, Szilard admitted that 'the impression which this book made on me was deeper than I knew'.[53] In fact, its vision of the future bowled him over.

'At different times,' said Leo Szilard during the height of the cold war, 'different physicists have been given the dubious honor of being called the "father of the atomic bomb." But in truth, the father of the atomic bomb was no physicist – he was a dreamer and a writer.'[54] His name was H. G. Wells.

No one describes the end of the world quite like Wells. He is a master of the doomsday moment, when people stare into the abyss. That is quite an achievement for a writer who lived before the age of nuclear warfare. In his most famous apocalyptic novel, *The War of the Worlds*, doomsday came from Mars, a planet named appropriately enough after the god of war. But in the novel Leo Szilard read in 1932, *The World Set Free*, the means of annihilation were manufactured on the earth. In this as in so much else, Wells was a trendsetter. His novel was written in 1913. Before then, two out of three fictional apocalypses were caused by nature. But after 1914, it is humankind that causes the end of the world, and usually with weapons of mass destruction.[55]

In previous works, Wells had invented tanks, fantastic heat rays and gas-filled missiles. Now, in *The World Set Free*, he imagined a weapon that would transform warfare and the history of the world – the atomic bomb. Wells was the first to use the phrase. It was inspired by the fascination with radioactivity in the early years of the twentieth century. What one reviewer called Wells's 'fiendish "atomic bombs"' had at their heart a new, explosive radioactive element, like plutonium.[56] Wells called it Carolinum.

Writing before World War I, Wells describes how a solitary French aircraft, with a crew of just two, is all that is needed to deliver the new atomic superweapon onto the German capital. It was a glimpse of a new age of warfare – one that would not be fully realized until World War II – in which weapons of mass destruction were used on civilians:

He had in his hands the black complement to all those other gifts science was urging upon unregenerate mankind, the gift of destruction . . .

The sky below grew clearer as the Central European capital was approached . . . Away to the north-eastward, in a cloudless pool of gathering light and with all its nocturnal illuminations still blazing, was Berlin. The left finger of the steersman verified roads and open spaces below upon the mica-covered square of map that was fastened by his wheel. There, in a series of lake-like expansions, was the Havel away to the right, over by those forests must be Spandau; there the river split about the Potsdam island, and right ahead was Charlottenburg, cleft by a great thoroughfare that fell like an indicating beam of light straight to the imperial headquarters. There, plain enough, was the Thiergarten; beyond rose the imperial palace, and to the right those tall buildings, those clustering, be-flagged, be-masted roofs, must be the offices in which the Central European staff was housed. It was all coldly clear and colourless in the dawn . . .

'Ready!' said the steersman.

The gaunt face hardened to grimness, and with both hands the bomb-thrower lifted the big atomic bomb from the box and steadied it against the side . . .

The bomb flashed blinding scarlet in mid-air and fell, a descending column of blaze eddying spirally in the midst of a whirlwind . . . When he could look down again it was like looking down upon the crater of a small volcano. In the open garden before the Imperial castle a shuddering star of evil splendour spurted and poured up smoke and flame towards them like an accusation.[57]

Leo Szilard first read this in Berlin in 1932, the year the neutron was discovered and a machine was used to split the atom. Hitler was poised to seize power in Germany, and an uncertain future awaited Europe. They must have been chilling words indeed. There had already been one world war since Wells wrote his novel, a war in which science had proved its military value beyond doubt and in which for the first time aeroplanes had played a key role.

The German air raids on London that began in 1915 had shocked the government in London. From that moment, the British military decided that long-range strategic bombing would be a decisive weapon in any future war. Unlike the German Luftwaffe, the Royal Air Force was equipped and organized long before World War II with a view to bombing an enemy into submission. As Prime Minister Stanley Baldwin told Parliament in November 1932, aircraft had transformed warfare:

I think it is well for the man in the street to realise that there is no power on earth that can protect him from being bombed. Whatever people may tell him, the bomber will always get through . . . The only defence is in offence, which means that you have to kill more women and children more quickly than the enemy if you want to save yourselves.[58]

Thanks to General William ('Billy') Mitchell, America too had woken up to the new threat from the air. In 1921 Mitchell had organized military exercises to demonstrate to the American public the effectiveness of aerial bombing. On 29 July his bombers conducted a mock air raid on New York. The next day, the *New York Herald* described an apocalyptic scene for its readers:

The sun rose today on a city whose tallest tower lay scattered in crumbled bits of stone . . . Bridges did not exist . . . The sun saw, when its light penetrated the ruins, hordes of people on foot, working their way slowly and painfully up the island . . . Rich and poor alike, welded together in a real democracy of misery, headed northward ... Always they looked fearfully upward at the sky ... [59]

In 1932, as Leo Szilard was reading *The World Set Free*, Billy Mitchell hit the headlines again. He advocated the use of fire-bombing in any future war with Japan. As he put it, their towns were 'built largely of wood and paper', making them 'the greatest aerial targets the world has ever seen'.[60] His advice was heeded by the American military and, well before Pearl Harbor, plans for fire-bombing Japanese cities were drawn up. In World War II, hundreds of thousands of Japanese civilians would be incinerated in US air raids.

Written in 1913, Wells's novel about atomic warfare was indebted to the science of its day. His radioactive Carolinum is an unstable element. It can be provoked into a 'degenerative process' which produces a 'furious radiation of energy' – what Wells calls a 'continuing explosive'.[61] The energy from the exploding element melts everything it touches, spreading radioactivity and creating an artificial volcano in the ground that erupts for years. It creates a scene of utter devastation. As one reviewer noted, 'the new bomb pours out destruction, radium-born, for years and years'.[62] Today, Wells's account of an atomic explosion resembles a nuclear reactor in catastrophic meltdown – an out-of-control Chernobyl.

Wells's descriptions of the bomb sites are visions of hell. But this is a hell of human devising. Where the atomic bomb has exploded there is 'a zone of uproar, a zone of perpetual thunderings, lit by a strange purplish-red light, and quivering and swaying with the incessant explosion of the radio-active substance. ...' Clouds of 'luminous, radio-active vapour drift sometimes scores of miles from the bomb centre ... killing and scorching all they overtook.' The air has 'a peculiar dryness and a blistering quality' that scars the skin and lungs, which refuse to heal.[63]

The atomic war Wells describes takes place in 1956, in a decade he did not live to see, but one which did indeed face a real threat of atomic doomsday. The fictional war ravages the earth. In the end, over two hundred cities across the world, from Chicago to Tokyo, are reduced to radioactive wastelands, dead zones, even more hellish than the radioactive landscapes Wells first described in *Tono-Bungay*.

The earth has been devastated by a global atomic holocaust. It is, as Wells says, the Last War.

As one contemporary reviewer observed, *The World Set Free* showed H. G. Wells in his 'scientific, world-reforming mood'.[64] After the success of his scientific romances, Wells came to see himself not just as an artist, but as the 'prophet of an efficient future'.[65] Creating characters and stories was not enough, he decided. The writer had to change the world. *The World Set Free* does not, in fact, describe the end of life on earth. Rather, it is a true apocalypse, in the Biblical sense of the word, in that it describes a moment of revelation and an end that is also a beginning. For Wells's true purpose is to show us the origins of a utopia built on the power of the atom.

The invention of the atomic bomb, predicts Wells, would make war redundant. Previously, war had been viewed as the continuation of politics by other means, an idea first expounded in the nineteenth century by the Prussian general and war theorist Carl von Clausewitz. This notion had made war socially acceptable, even useful.[66] But the atomic bomb would change that. War in an age of superweapons – as Bulwer-Lytton and Frank Stockton had realized – became mutual suicide. Clearly, a war which ends in annihilation for all participants is very bad politics.

As well as this revolution in global politics, H. G. Wells anticipated today's threat of stateless groups and terrorists armed with weapons of mass destruction. He shows how proliferation leads to nuclear anarchy:

Destruction was becoming so facile that any little body of malcontents could use it; it was revolutionizing the problems of police and internal rule. Before the last war began it was a matter of common knowledge that a man could carry about in a handbag an amount of latent energy sufficient to wreck half a city.[67]

In another story, 'The Stolen Bacillus' (1895), Wells even describes how a suicidal terrorist infects himself with a deadly virus so that he can spread disease in a city, a possibility which today no longer seems like fiction.[68]

In *The World Set Free*, military and political leaders do not comprehend the lethal power that they hold in their hands. Instead, the world has to learn this lesson through bloody experience. Only then will it be 'set free', only then will humankind see the error of its ways and establish a system of world government committed to peace and human dignity. The story Wells tells is about humanity being reborn in the elemental fires of the atomic bombs. It is a story which is almost alchemistic in its symbolism of a journey through fire to wisdom. The spokesman of Wells's utopia is the character Marcus Karenin, who, as one reviewer commented rather archly, is 'an educationalist with the appearance of a member of the Labour Party'.[69] According to Karenin, before the atomic war the world was 'ailing': 'It was in sore need of release, and I suppose that nothing less than the violence of those bombs could have released it and made it a healthy world again. I suppose they were necessary.'[70] The world is set free by war, reborn like a phoenix emerging from the atomic fires into a new world.

The Russian writer and engineer Yevgeny Zamyatin was a great fan of Wells's utopian idealism and helped to popularize his works in the Soviet Union. Zamyatin's own remarkable futuristic novel, We (1924), describes how a utopia arises from the ashes of just such a war: 'True, only 0.2 of the population of the terrestrial globe survived; but then, cleansed of its millennial filth, how glowing the face of the earth became! Then, too, the surviving two tenths certainly came to know bliss in the many mansions of The One State.'[71] But all that glitters is not gold, and Zamyatin's utopia turns out to be an oppressive dictatorship, a scientific dystopia.

Karenin's belief that a global nuclear holocaust was necessary to prepare the way for utopia re-emerged in the cold war. It is caricatured in Dr Strangelove's excitement at the prospect of surviving a nuclear holocaust down a mineshaft ('ten women to each man').[72] American survivalist fiction gloried in the prospect of urban society being wiped out and returning to the frontier life. Even today, such attitudes seem to have a powerful, millennial attraction. Fictional eco-catastrophes, such as The Day After Tomorrow (2004), carry a moralistic subtext that welcomes the end of civilization as deserved punishment for humankind's environmental sins.

In 1932, the year the atom seemed to be revealing its secrets, H. G. Wells's vision of an atomic utopia struck a chord with Leo Szilard.

Wells, one of the first British novelists to have had a formal scientific education, describes science in the novel as 'the awakening mind of the race'.[73] This is typical of his later, almost mystical, view of science. *The World Set Free* is a paean to the Faustian spirit of scientific progress – from the prehistoric discovery of fire to the atomic age, and onwards to the stars. Like Szilard, Wells believed that a technoscientific elite should govern society. As one Wells scholar has said, he came to see in science 'the only hope for the survival of the human race which was otherwise doomed to destruction by its selfish individualistic strivings and vast, amoral technology'.[74] It was the atom and the faith in its limitless energy that inspired this beguiling dream of science as the saviour of humankind.

The down-to-earth Ernest Rutherford had no time for science fiction fantasies of atom-powered utopias. In the year that H. G. Wells's novel appeared, he admitted during a lecture given in America that the power in the atom was 'many million times greater than for an equal weight of the most powerful known explosive'. But, he added quickly, this power would become available only if we could 'cause a substance like uranium or thorium to give out its energy in the course of a few hours or days, instead of over a period of many thousands or millions of years'. Referring directly to Wells's novel, which was provoking a wave of press speculation about atomic energy, he said that this prospect was not 'at all promising'.[75]

Like Einstein, Rutherford was a killjoy when it came to the possibility of exploiting the energy of the atom. But ironically it was Rutherford's co-worker on radioactivity who inspired 'the Shakespeare of science fiction' with the atomic dream.[76] Unlike Rutherford, Frederick Soddy was a man of bold vision and keenly aware of science's potential to change the world. Indeed, he has been credited with originating the idea of the social responsibility of science.[77] It was Soddy's idealistic vision of the future of atomic energy in his best-selling work of popular science, *The Interpretation of Radium* (1909), that captured the imagination of first Wells and then, in 1932, Leo Szilard. Soddy sparked an extraordinary human chain reaction, from science to fiction and then back again to science, with his utopian promise of cheap, clean, limitless energy:

A race which could transmute matter would have little need to earn its bread by the sweat of its brow. If we can judge from what our engineers accomplish with their comparatively restricted supplies of energy, such a race could transform a desert continent, thaw the frozen poles, and make the whole world one smiling Garden of Eden. Possibly they could explore the outer realms of space, emigrating to more favourable worlds as the superfluous to-day emigrate to more favourable continents.[78]

Early on in Wells's novel, Professor Rufus at Edinburgh University gives an inspiring lecture. Rufus is a thinly disguised portrait of Soddy, whose *Interpretation of Radium* was based on his lectures at Glasgow University. In his book Soddy had compared the energy in uranium with the fuel that had powered the nineteenth century – coal:

This bottle contains about one pound of uranium oxide, and therefore about fourteen ounces of uranium. Its value is about £1. Is it not wonderful to reflect that in this little bottle there lies asleep and waiting to be evolved the energy of at least one hundred and sixty tons of coal? The energy in a ton of uranium would be sufficient to light London for a year. The store of energy in uranium would be worth a thousand times as much as the uranium itself, if only it were under our control and could be harnessed to do the world's work in the same way as the energy in coal has been harnessed and controlled.[79]

Parts of Rufus's lecture are lifted virtually word for word from Soddy's book:

[W]e know now that the atom, that once we thought hard and impenetrable, and indivisible and final and – lifeless – lifeless, is really a reservoir of immense energy ... This little bottle contains about a pint of uranium oxide; that is to say about fourteen ounces of the element uranium. It is worth about a pound. And in this bottle, ladies and gentlemen, in the atoms in this bottle there slumbers at least as much energy as we could get by burning a hundred and sixty tons of coal. If at a word in one instant I could suddenly release that energy here and now, it would blow us and everything about us to fragments; if I could turn it into the machinery that lights this city, it could keep Edinburgh brightly lit for a week.[80]

Like Frederick Soddy, Rufus sees in radioactivity 'the dawn of a new day in human living'. The atom represents not only a utopian future, but human destiny: 'I see the desert continents transformed, the poles no longer wildernesses of ice, the whole world once more Eden. I see the power of man reach out among the stars'.[81] According to Rufus – and H. G. Wells – the fruit of the tree of atomic knowledge will eventually take us back to the Eden from which humankind was once banished. This is the atom presented as the promised land, and its discovery as humankind's destiny. It was a powerful dream, more mythical than scientific, and it inspired Soddy, Wells and Szilard alike.

Marcus Karenin represents the fulfilment of Rufus's dream. After the Last War, Karenin also has his eyes fixed on the final frontier: 'This ball will be no longer enough for us; our spirit will reach out'.[82] This is the vision of man's heroic destiny that Otto Mandl described to Leo Szilard in 1932, a vision that Szilard thought could be realized only with nuclear physics. In William Cameron Menzies' utopian movie *Things to Come* (1936), for which Wells wrote the screenplay, Karenin becomes the Faustian leader Cabal. At the end of the film, with the stars of the universe as his backdrop, Cabal speaks directly to the audience, his eyes burning with a disturbing intensity:

For Man, no rest and no ending. He must go on, conquest beyond conquest. First this little planet and its winds and waves, and then all the laws of mind and matter that restrain it. Then the planets about it. And at last out across immensity to the stars. And when he has conquered all the deeps of space and all the mysteries of time, still he will be beginning.[83]

But, as *The World Set Free* showed, this beguiling dream of the atom could become a nightmare. The same gleaming metropolis that is powered by atomic energy might one day cower from the threat of atomic bombs. Perhaps it was just such a thought that crossed Leo Szilard's mind as his ship approached the skyline of New York for the first time in 1931.

Ominously, Frederick Soddy speculated that 'the legend of the Fall of Man' may have originated with an ancient and now forgotten civilization which discovered atomic energy 'before, for some unknown reason, the whole world was plunged back again under the undisputed sway of Nature, to begin once more its upward toilsome journey through the ages'.[84] Only the elemental force of the atom could – to use the infamous phrase of the general in charge of

America's cold-war nuclear weapons, Curtis E. LeMay – blast a civilization back to the stone age.

In the year Szilard first read *The World Set Free*, the American physicist and rocket pioneer Robert Goddard wrote a fan letter to Wells telling him that *The War of the Worlds* had made 'a deep impression' on him as a teenager. Indeed, Goddard's papers are full of references to Wells. Ironically, his letter came a few months before Wells predicted guided missiles in a BBC radio talk.[85] Wernher von Braun was also inspired by science fiction and was a keen fan of the German *War of the Worlds*, Kurd Lasswitz's *Auf zwei Planeten* ('On Two Planets', 1897).[86] 'I shall never forget how I devoured this novel with curiosity and excitement as a young man,' wrote von Braun. 'From this book the reader can obtain an inkling of the richness of ideas at the twilight of the nineteenth century upon which the technological and scientific progress of the twentieth is based.'[87] Both the dream of space travel and the dream of atomic energy first took shape in the pages of fiction. But alongside both these dreams, the nightmare of the superweapon – today's weapons of mass destruction – also took root.

When *The World Set Free* fell into Leo Szilard's hands in 1932, just as he was hesitating over whether to continue working in physics, his mind was uniquely primed to receive both the scientific and the social message of Wells's novel. It is perhaps the clearest example of fiction influencing science. Wells's novel supplied one of the sparks needed to make Szilard burst into creativity. As the fuse burnt in his mind, Europe descended into chaos. The countdown to war had begun.

It had been a dramatic year in physics. After the electron and the proton, the third elementary particle – the neutron – had been discovered. The veils were being stripped away from the atomic nucleus. Scientists were now using machines to smash atoms, transmuting matter into different chemical elements. It was an almost godlike power, beyond the dreams of any previous generation of scientists, and one for which the alchemist Faust would have sold his immortal soul. But still the goal of atomic energy remained elusive. The following year, his mind still buzzing with the possibilities opened up by H. G. Wells's novel, Leo Szilard would realize how to do this.

In 1932, Szilard approached Lise Meitner at the Kaiser Wilhelm

Institute for Chemistry in Dahlem about collaborating on nuclear experiments. Although they had taught together on courses, Meitner doubted that Szilard's background in probability theory and statistics would make him the ideal partner in her ongoing attempts to probe the structure of the atomic nucleus. It's tempting to speculate about what might have happened if they had indeed begun working together in 1932. Within months, Szilard had discovered how to use the neutron to release the power of the atom. But by then fascism had intervened and Szilard had left Germany for England. Had he stayed, it is possible that Germany and not the Allies would have discovered the secret of the atomic bomb.

11

Eureka!

And if some physicist were to realize the brightest dream of his kind and teach us to unlock the energy within the atom, the whole race of man would live under the threat of sudden destruction.

William McDougall,
World Chaos: The Responsibility of Science (1931)

At noon on 30 January 1933, millions of Germans were listening to the radio as Adolf Hitler was sworn in as the new German Chancellor. Leo Szilard was living at Dahlem in the faculty club of the Kaiser Wilhelm Institute, Harnack House. He had a small room on the third floor under the eaves, usually reserved for visiting scholars. It was a temporary measure while he decided what to do next. Perhaps for the first time, Szilard felt truly alone and without a clear sense of where his life was going. His closest scientific friends – Einstein, Wigner and von Neumann – were all working in the United States now. He knew it was only a matter of time before he too would have to leave Germany. But where should he go? And what should he do? There was the possibility of teaching physics in India, but the New World also beckoned. The only thing he knew for certain was that remaining in Berlin was no longer an option.

Although the Nazis were the largest single party in the German Parliament, the Reichstag, they didn't yet have a majority. New elections were scheduled for 5 March 1933. Szilard could see that Germany was headed for disaster under Hitler, but his fellow Hungarian, Michael Polanyi, who worked at the KWI for Fibre Chemistry in Dahlem, was less concerned. Polanyi believed that 'civilized Germans would not stand for anything really rough happening', Szilard recalled.[1] Like many others, he placed his faith in the Germany of Goethe, Beethoven, Hermann von Helmholtz and Max Planck – a land with rich traditions of culture, scholarship and science. But Leo Szilard had a more realistic approach:

Germans always took a utilitarian point of view. They asked, 'Well, suppose I would oppose this thinking, what good would I do? I wouldn't do very much good, I would just lose my influence. Then why should I oppose it?' You see, the moral point of view was completely absent, or very weak . . . [2]

On 3 February, Szilard travelled home to Budapest. He warned his family that it was time to leave. 'Hitler and his Nazis are going to take over Europe,' he told them. 'Get out now. Leave Europe – before it's too late!'[3] Having delivered this blunt warning to his bemused relatives, he returned to Berlin in time to see the Reichstag go up in flames at the end of the month. When Szilard voiced his suspicions to Polanyi that the Nazis were behind the fire, his friend was shocked. 'Do you really mean to say you think that the Secretary of the Interior had anything to do with this?' Polanyi asked, incredulously. Szilard could only shake his head in despair at his friend's naivety and told him to accept a lectureship in chemistry he had been offered at Manchester University in Britain. Polanyi demurred, for a while at least.[4]

The next day, Hitler declared a state of emergency and suspended the parts of the Weimar constitution that protected civil liberties. The playwright and poet Bertolt Brecht saw the writing on the wall and fled his homeland immediately. He was just the kind of radical intellectual whom Hitler hated. The black, gold and red flag of the Weimar Republic was lowered over Berlin. The Republic, which had filled Albert Einstein with such wonderful hope for the future of Germany after World War I, was now in its dying days. Einstein would soon be abused in German newspapers and his name banned from physics classes.

On 20 March, the first Nazi concentration camp, Dachau, began receiving inmates. Soon even Weimar, the former capital of the Republic and once home to Goethe, Schiller and Bach, would have its own concentration camp – Buchenwald. After 1943, forced labour from a sub-camp of Buchenwald known as Mittelbau-Dora would build Wernher von Braun's V-2 missiles in secret factories, buried deep beneath the Harz mountains. At least 20,000 of Mittelbau-Dora's prisoners died in the process, many times more than were killed by the missiles themselves.

The day after Dachau opened its gates, Lise Meitner wrote to Otto Hahn, who was lecturing in America, to tell him that the KWI had been ordered to fly the new Nazi national flag. 'It must have been very difficult for Haber to raise the swastika,' she wrote. But, like Michael Polanyi, she still trusted in the decency of ordinary Germans and hoped for the best. Hitler would moderate his views and govern in a 'conciliatory' way, she believed.[5]

Albert Einstein had spent the winter and spring teaching in America. On 28 March he arrived back in Europe and, appalled by events in his homeland, immediately renounced his German citizenship. It was the second time he had done so, having rejected the land of his birth as a teenager to escape military service. It was the last straw for Leo Szilard. He grabbed his two suitcases, which for some time now had been packed and ready to go, and took the first Vienna-bound train out of Berlin. He travelled first class, hoping that he would not be questioned too much by the secret police. 'The train was empty,' Szilard remembered. 'The same train on the next day was over-crowded, was stopped at the frontier, the people had to get out, and everybody was interrogated by the Nazis.'[6]

Within a week of Szilard's flight from Berlin, Hitler's regime had passed a law banning 'non-Aryans' from government positions. This included university lecturers. For now the *nichtarisch* Lise Meitner was safe, as she was an Austrian national. Her nephew, Otto Frisch, was less lucky and left for London. For most Jewish academics it was the end of their careers, in Germany at least. At German universities, 20 per cent of scientists were Jewish. In physics the proportion was even higher.[7] Students and lecturers failed to speak up as their Jewish colleagues were expelled in April and May. Max Born, Einstein's radical friend and sparring partner over quantum theory, was among those dismissed. He learnt from a newspaper article that he had been sacked as head of the Göttingen Institute for Theoretical Physics, where he had worked for twelve years. 'It seemed to me like the end of the world,' he wrote later. 'I went for a walk in the woods, in despair, brooding on how to save my family.'[8]

For now at least, Fritz Haber, a baptized Jew who had served at the Front in World War I, was safe. But he was ordered to get rid of his Jewish staff. Among them was Irene Sackur, daughter of Otto Sackur, the young chemist killed while experimenting on chemical weapons in 1915. This was a step too far, even for Haber. At the end of April he handed in his resignation. His letter to the Nazi minister of education spoke of the pride with which he had served his German homeland for his entire life. In America, Otto Hahn had defended Hitler's actions to the media, claiming that the ascetic German Führer 'lived almost like a saint'.[9] On his return he temporarily took over Haber's Institute. The Jewish members of staff were dismissed.

Haber was a broken man. He was suffering from chronic angina and had now been forced out of the research institute to which he had devoted his entire life. For a proud man, it was deeply humiliating. To friends, the 64-year-old admitted feeling profoundly bitter.[10] Einstein wrote him a pointed letter saying he was pleased to hear that 'your former love for the blond beast has cooled off a bit'.[11] Haber had only months to live. Forced into exile by the country he had tried to save with his chemical superweapon, he spent his last days wandering rootlessly through Europe. In July 1933 he visited London, staying at a hotel on Russell Square in Bloomsbury while he explored the possibility of working in England. He met Frederick G. Donnan, a tall and rather dashing professor of chemistry at nearby University College London, who sported a black eyepatch. During World War I, he had worked on the production of mustard gas. Now he was attempting to arrange a fellowship for Germany's leading chemical warfare expert.

In the summer of 1933, another scientist who had fled Hitler's Germany was living on Russell Square. Leo Szilard had brought his two suitcases to the Imperial Hotel, less costly than Haber's hotel but just down the road. There Szilard stayed until the autumn, when he moved to the Strand, where he found a room at an even better rate.

Before travelling to London, Leo Szilard had spent some days in Vienna. Here he had called on Gertrud (Trude) Weiss, a quiet 24-year-old woman with a striking full-moon face and dark, lustrous eyes. They had met in 1929 in Berlin, where she was studying biology and physics at the university. In her spare time she also worked on a film magazine, *Close Up*. Friends recall the two of them at Eva Striker's bohemian parties, deep in discussion about films such as Fritz Lang's latest movie, *Frau im Mond* (Woman in the Moon, 1929), the 'first serious space travel film'. It is rumoured that the young Wernher von Braun helped with the cutting-edge special effects.[12]

Szilard had formed close friendships with several women, but the opposite sex always remained something of an enigma to the peripatetic scientist. A childhood companion, Alice Eppinger, fell in love with him and even followed him to Berlin. But although their families hoped they might marry, Szilard felt unable to propose. He broke the news to Alice as gently as he knew how. He used an example from a popularization of science he was reading, Maurice Maeterlinck's *La Vie des abeilles* ('The Life of the Bee', 1901). 'In each family there are three kinds of bees,' Szilard told her. 'A queen, workers and drones. Imagine this is a family of bees and I am a worker.' Understandably, Alice looked puzzled, so he quickly added: 'Listen Alice, I am not the marrying kind. I do not want to have children. I am a worker, not a drone.'[13]

It was the truth, but it broke Alice's heart. In 1938, a friend who was concerned about his lack of a career, bluntly advised Szilard to marry at the first opportunity, 'preferably a woman who considers the realities somewhat more than you do'.[14] Szilard objected that this solution was far too 'drastic'. 'Anyway,' he replied, 'why should a woman who has sense of reality mary [*sic*] a man who has none.'[15] As usual, his logic (if not his English) was flawless. Despite this, Leo Szilard did eventually marry, although it took him until 1951 to propose to Trude Weiss.

As well as renewing his friendship with Trude in Vienna, Szilard applied his organizational skills to the plight of his fellow academics exiled from Germany. By chance, the Director of the London School of Economics, William Beveridge, was staying at his hotel. Szilard introduced himself and suggested that a committee should be formed to provide assistance. Beveridge was impressed: 'He suggested that I come to London and that I occasionally prod him on this, and if I prodded him long enough and frequently enough he thought he would do it,' said Szilard. He left promptly for London. 'In a comparatively

THE DARK HEART OF MATTER

short time,' Szilard added, 'practically everybody who came to England had a position, except me.'[16]

This was the beginning of the Academic Assistance Council (AAC). The Council, which changed its name in 1935 to the Society for the Protection of Science and Learning (SPSL), dedicated itself to helping academics fleeing from the Nazis. From 1933 until the beginning of World War II, the SPSL quietly rescued about 1,200 scholars and their families from Germany, Spain, Portugal, Austria, Czechoslovakia and Italy. The organization still exists and is now known as the Council for Assisting Refugee Academics.

Leo Szilard arrived in London in April. He checked into the Imperial Hotel, overlooking the elegant gardens of Russell Square designed in the previous century by Sir Humphry Repton. The British Museum and Library, University College (UCL) and the London School of Economics were all within a fifteen-minute walk. T. S. Eliot – known as the 'Pope of Russell Square' – worked in his garret office at number 24 for the publisher Faber & Faber, and in nearby Gordon Square was the fine Georgian townhouse where Virginia Woolf had once lived. In the previous century, a young Charles Darwin had lived nearby. As usual, Leo Szilard liked to be at the centre of things.

In summer 1933, two very different scientific refugees – Haber and Szilard – were staying in this part of London. That year there had been a price war between Russell Square's two main hotels. Both had advertised in *The Times*, the Hotel Russell offering 'Bedroom, bath and breakfast' at 10s. 6d. and 12s. 6d., the Imperial Hotel advertising the same at 9s. 6d. and 7s. 9d. Unlike most refugees, Fritz Haber didn't need to economize, and booked into the Hotel Russell. Leo Szilard, who was effectively running the AAC for no pay and living off his refrigerator patents, chose the cheaper one.[17] For the scientist who once declared that 'there is no place as good to think as a bathtub', what made the hotel irresistible were its famous Turkish baths.[18]

Politically, the nationalist Haber and the socialist Szilard had little in common. However, unlike the purist Ernest Rutherford, for whom knowledge was its own reward, both men were enthralled by the idea of science as power. Neither Szilard nor Haber had set out in their scientific careers intending to create new weapons, but both scientists were to play key roles in developing a new generation of scientific superweapons. Haber thought that chemical weapons would make him the saviour of his country. Szilard, an internationalist fired by an idealistic vision of how science should transform human life and society for the better, wanted to save the world by building the atomic bomb before Hitler. These two very different characters were both doomsday men.

What might these two refugee scientists have said to each other if they had met while walking through the neatly manicured gardens of Russell Square, just outside their hotels? The Nobel prizewinning chemist Fritz Haber was at the end of his career, had been disowned by his country and thrown out of the institute he founded, and now had just a few months to live. Every few steps, he had to pause and catch his breath. He was a shadow of the dynamic man he had once been. By contrast, Leo Szilard, the budding nuclear physicist, was 35 years old, his figure still slim and youthful. He would have been striding past the London plane trees in the square, perhaps on his way to see his and Haber's mutual friend, Professor Donnan at UCL. For Donnan – who was active on behalf of the AAC – had also offered Leo Szilard a job.

Szilard came with the best possible references from some of the greatest physicists of the age, including Einstein, Max von Laue and Schrödinger. Even Faust had recommended him. Paul Ehrenfest (aka Faust in the Copenhagen performance) had sent Donnan a warm personal testament: 'Szilard is a *very rare* example of a man, because of his combination of great *purely scientific* acumen, his ability to immerse himself in and solve technical problems, his fascination and fantasy for organizing, and his great sensitivity and compassion for people in need.'[19] Tragically, within weeks of writing this letter of recommendation, Ehrenfest committed suicide. According to the note he left, one of his reasons was that he was in despair at the incomprehensible quantum realm.

That summer, London was brimming with brilliant scientists and other intellectuals fleeing Hitler's Germany. Among them was another future doomsday man – Edward Teller. He also visited Frederick Donnan at University College to discuss the possibility of a job, and Donnan arranged for him to spend a year with the other budding

Fausts at Bohr's Institute. Typically, Leo Szilard couldn't make up his mind whether to accept Donnan's offer of a position at UCL. In any case, he was too busy saving Germany's other forsaken intellectuals.

At the beginning of November, Fritz Haber was back in London, staying in the same hotel on Russell Square. His visit in July had paid off. Haber's British friends in chemical warfare, Sir Harold Hartley and Sir William Pope, had secured a position for him at Cambridge University, where he would be free to continue his research. Ten years earlier, Ernest Rutherford had refused to shake Haber's hand when he visited Cambridge. Now the University welcomed their country's former enemy and asked him to stay as long as he wished.

At Cambridge, Haber was visited by fellow refugee scientists, including Max Born and Michael Polanyi, the latter having finally taken Szilard's advice and accepted the position at Manchester University. Born recalls that Haber appeared 'ill, depressed, lonely, a shadow of his former self'. When he tried to arrange a meeting between Haber and Rutherford, the physicist again refused, 'saying frankly that he did not want to shake hands with the inventor of poison gas warfare'.[20] After just two months in Cambridge, Haber's health worsened, partly because of the damp English weather. He moved to Switzerland to recuperate, but died in Basel at the end of January 1934.[21]

When Edward Teller returned from Copenhagen in the autumn of that year, a job was waiting for him in the chemistry department of UCL. Before formally offering Teller the position, Donnan insisted that he complete some essential background reading: Lewis Carroll's *Alice's Adventures in Wonderland* and *Through the Looking-Glass*. 'He did not want to import a barbarian into England,' recalled Teller.[22] But in the New Year, the 26-year-old physicist received two job offers from America. One was from Eugene Wigner, who wanted Teller to join him and the other member of the Hungarian Quartet, John von Neumann, at Princeton. The other was from George Washington University, where his friend George Gamow was chairman of the physics department. This last offer was too tempting to decline. But the father of the hydrogen bomb never forgot the generosity of the English. They were, he said, 'truly among the most hospitable and ethical people in the world'.[23]

Leo Szilard was also fond of England. The reserve of the natives suited his own essentially shy character, and he felt a deep sympathy with the country and its people. But, he added shrewdly, 'I am not yet sure about the sympathy being mutual.'[24]

Throughout 1933, Szilard worked tirelessly and selflessly on behalf of his fellow refugee academics. The money he had earned from his patents, including the refrigerator designs, allowed him to live without financial worries, for the time being at least. His daily routine at the Imperial Hotel began with breakfast in the plush restaurant, followed by a leisurely and extended soak in a bath – the only luxury the decidedly non-materialistic Szilard permitted himself. It was not uncommon for him to spend three hours in a tub, awaiting Archimedean inspiration. However, it was not in the bath that Leo Szilard had his *Eureka!* moment in 1933, but on a Bloomsbury street.

'The passage of the invisible neutron into the nucleus of the atom is like an invisible man passing through Piccadilly Circus: His path can be traced only by the people he has pushed aside.'[25] This was the wonderful image Lord Rutherford used in 1932 to describe the effect of the neutron on the atom. The following year, he surveyed the astonishing progress that had been made in 'breaking down the atom'. Speaking to colleagues at the British Association's conference in Leicester, he outlined how James Chadwick's 'most remarkable' neutron could be used as a tool of transmutation, for instance changing oxygen into carbon.[26] The subatomic invisible man could pass freely through atoms, thanks to its lack of an electrical charge. It could even enter the dark heart of matter, the nucleus.

As a purist, Ernest Rutherford had little interest in the potential applications of science. He wanted to understand how 'the nuclei of atoms were made', not how to release the energy of the atom. According to David Wilson, Rutherford's biographer, 'his lack of imagination in translating the results of his work from the laboratory to the outside world of technology, profit and commerce' was a serious failing.[27] So when Rutherford allowed himself the luxury of anticipating what advances might lie twenty or thirty years ahead, he was scathing about the chances of releasing atomic energy. Certainly, he told his audience at the British Association conference in 1933, scientists would use increasingly powerful particle accelerators – such as his colleagues

Cockcroft and Watson had built – to smash apart the stuff of matter. But, ever keen to nip sensationalist press stories in the bud, Rutherford rejected the idea that proton accelerators could be used to generate power:

We might in these processes obtain very much more energy than the proton supplied, but on the average we could not expect to obtain energy in this way. It was a very poor and inefficient way of producing energy, and anyone who looked for a source of power in the transformation of the atoms was talking moonshine.[28]

Moonshine!

Leo Szilard frowned as he read the word, late on the morning of Tuesday 12 September 1933, and glanced around the lobby of the Imperial Hotel, as if he expected the concierge to share his consternation. *Moonshine* . . . He muttered the word under his breath. If there was one thing in science that really made Szilard angry, it was experts who said that something was impossible. He looked back at the long article on page 7 of that day's *Times*. The paper had devoted two of its lead columns to the British Association conference, and Rutherford's speech on transmuting the atom was reported almost word for word.

Leo Szilard was anything but a purist when it came to science. In the right hands, science could transform the world. In the wrong hands, it just might destroy it. Szilard folded his paper and looked out through the lobby window to Russell Square, where the leaves of the plane trees were just beginning to turn gold in anticipation of autumn. He needed to think. So, as he had done in Berlin a decade ago, when he was trying to conjure up an original idea for his thesis, Szilard took to his feet. He left the hotel lobby and set off into the grey light of an overcast September day.

Many years later in America, Szilard would recall this moment, as he walked the streets of London, pondering subatomic physics and Rutherford's comments to the great and the good of British science. 'I remember that I stopped for a red light at the intersection of Southampton Row.'[29] The London traffic streamed by, but he scarcely noticed the vehicles. Instead, in his mind he saw streams of subatomic particles bombarding atoms.

As the traffic lights changed and the cars stopped, the physicist stepped out in front of the impatient traffic. A keen-eyed London cabby, watching Szilard cross the road, might have noticed him pause for a moment in the middle. Szilard may even have briefly raised his hand to his forehead, as if to catch hold of the beautiful but terrible thought that had just crossed his mind. But that taxi driver could have no inkling of the gravity of the moment, even though it would affect the course of both his life and the lives of his children. For that was when Leo Szilard saw precisely how to release the energy locked up in the heart of every atom, a self-sustaining chain reaction created by neutrons:

As I was waiting for the light to change and as the light changed to green and I crossed the street, it suddenly occurred to me that if we could find an element which is split by neutrons and which would emit two neutrons when it absorbed *one* neutron, such an element, if assembled in sufficiently large mass, could sustain a nuclear chain reaction. I didn't see at the moment just how one would go about finding such an element, or what experiments would be needed, but the idea never left me. In certain circumstances it might become possible to set up a nuclear chain reaction, liberate energy on an industrial scale, and construct atomic bombs. The thought that this might be in fact possible became a sort of obsession with me.[30]

In his lecture, Rutherford had described how the neutron 'could go freely through atoms, and had a good chance of entering the nucleus and of either disturbing or being captured by the nucleus'.[31] But what Szilard had just realized, before anyone else, was that the reaction might not terminate in a single nucleus – it could spread, explosively. As if anticipating this dangerous idea, the sceptical Rutherford promptly poured cold water over it in a BBC radio lecture one month later. Indeed, Szilard may have listened to it at the Imperial Hotel. If he didn't, then he certainly saw the reports on it in the following day's *Times*.

'It has sometimes been suggested,' said Rutherford in the lecture, 'from analogy with ordinary explosives, that the transmutation of one atom might cause the transmutation of a neighbouring nucleus, so that the explosion would spread throughout all the material. If that were true, we should long ago have had a gigantic explosion in our laboratories with no one remaining to tell the tale.'[32] The 'explosion' in a single atom, he emphasized, does not 'spread to the neighbouring nuclei'. But this is precisely what Leo Szilard had decided could happen. Hearing Britain's leading Nobel prizewinning physicist declare it was impossible only made him more convinced that he was on the right track. After all, what did these experts know?

Szilard would spend the next decade of his life trying to convince others that he was right. He even tried to convince Lord Rutherford, an act of unforgivable chutzpah which earned Szilard the distinction of being the only person to be thrown out of the physicist's Cambridge office. It was clearly going to be an uphill struggle.

The scientist and writer Jacob Bronowski said that there was only one part of his friend's story of the *Eureka!* moment near Russell Square that he found improbable: 'I never knew Szilard to stop for a red light.'[33] Did the idea of a nuclear chain reaction come to him in one dazzling epiphany? This is what Szilard said almost thirty years later. But memories are not always reliable, and he liked a good story. Perhaps the idea of the chain reaction grew gradually over countless walks around Bloomsbury that autumn, as he pondered the provocative statements of the undisputed master of the nucleus, Ernest Rutherford.

One thing we do know, however, is that as he hatched his explosive idea about how to release atomic energy, Szilard was also thinking about *The World Set Free*. A few days after he put the finishing touches to his first scientific account of the chain reaction, in March 1934, Leo Szilard wrote to Sir Hugo Hirst, founder of the British General Electric Co. 'As you are on holiday you might find pleasure in reading a few pages out of a book by H. G. Wells which I am sending you,' wrote Szilard confidently to Sir Hugo, who was staying at Cannes on the French Riviera. 'I am certain you will find the first three paragraphs of Chapter The First (The New Source of Energy, page 42) interesting and amusing . . .'

The pages Szilard posted to the South of France are some of the most evocative in Wells's novel. They concern a scientist, Holsten, and his discovery of how to release the energy of the atom. Leo Szilard believed that he had actually worked out how to do this and now he wanted Sir Hugo – a potential financial backer for the essential experiments that would now have to be conducted – to share his excitement. Strangely enough, Wells's scientist makes his discovery in 1933 while working in London's Bloomsbury. The significance of this coincidence in time and space was not lost on Leo Szilard. 'Of course, all this is moonshine,' he told Sir Hugo, echoing Rutherford,

but I have reason to believe that in so far as the industrial applications of the present discoveries in physics are concerned, the forecast of the writers may prove to be more accurate than the forecast of the scientists. The physicists have conclusive arguments as to why we cannot create at present new sources of energy for industrial purposes; I am not so sure whether they do not miss the point.[34]

When it came to the future of atomic energy, Szilard sided with the novelists rather than the physicists.

H. G. Wells's scientist, Holsten, was born in 1895, just three years before Leo Szilard. Like many children of his generation, Holsten's interest in the realm of the atom was sparked by Sir William Crookes's spinthariscope. The stellar scintillations of the disintegrating radium atom viewed through this toy opened up new worlds of possibility. Holsten was 38 when he solved 'the problem of inducing radio-activity in the heavier elements and so tapping the internal energy of atoms'.[35] The year was 1933, twenty years into the future when Wells was writing, but the very year in which Szilard grasped the significance of a neutron chain reaction.

Holsten is a Faustian scientist, 'possessed by a savage appetite to understand'.[36] Faust searched for the 'the inmost force / That bonds the very universe'.[37] Holsten discovered that secret by setting up 'atomic disintegration in a minute particle of bismuth'. This explosive reaction, in which the scientist is slightly injured, produces radioactive gas and gold as a by-product. The quest of the alchemists is over – gold can now be created on demand. But Holsten has also discovered something far more valuable than even gold: 'from the moment when the invisible speck of bismuth flashed into riving and rending energy, Holsten knew that he had opened a way for mankind, however narrow and dark it might still be, to worlds of limitless power'.[38]

When Holsten realizes the implications of what he has found, his

Caricature of H. G. Wells from 1913.

mind is thrown into turmoil. Like Szilard, he goes for a walk to think things through. But the knowledge of what he can now do sets him apart from everyone he passes on the street. It makes him feel 'inhuman', like an outsider in his own country:

All the people about him looked fairly prosperous, fairly happy, fairly well adapted to the lives they had to lead – a week of work and a Sunday of best clothes and mild promenading – and he had launched something that would disorganise the entire fabric that held their contentments and ambitions and satisfactions together.

A startling, even shocking, thought now occurs to him. Suddenly he 'felt like an imbecile who has presented a box of loaded revolvers to a Crêche [*sic*]'.[39] Holsten has realized that his discovery will lead to a superweapon.

In what is one of the most powerful moments in the book, Holsten then meets an old school friend who is out walking his dog, and they stop to talk. Holsten tries hard to tell his friend 'the wonder of the thing' he has discovered. But the gulf in understanding between the scientist and the ordinary man in the street is unbridgeable.[40]

Before he strikes his fateful bargain with Mephistopheles, Goethe's Faust longs for ultimate understanding of the universe and its laws. In a poignant scene, Outside the City Gate, he walks with his assistant among his fellow citizens. It is a holiday, and there is dancing and singing. Suddenly it is painfully clear to Faust that he will never be like these ordinary people. He will always be an outsider. His intense, almost physical desire for knowledge and understanding isolates him from the trials and joys of everyday life.

'Two souls, alas, are dwelling in my breast,' cries the tormented Faust. One part of him knows 'joyous earthy lust', or physical experience. But 'the other soars impassioned from the dust', a hauntingly beautiful expression of intellectual yearning – the desire for knowledge, for science.[41] Faust, the archetypal scientist, has tasted the forbidden fruit. Now he cannot rest, but must engage in a lifelong quest for knowledge, even if the price be self-destruction and the loss of his immortal soul.

On his walk, Holsten, like Faust, passes the carefree Sunday strollers, a fallen man mingling with the innocent. In his head is the knowledge that will quite literally bring the world they know to an end. He sees himself 'a loose wanderer from the flock returning with evil gifts from his sustained unnatural excursions amidst the darknesses and phosphorescences beneath the fair surfaces of life'.[42] Holsten is Doomsday Man personified.

The moral crisis Holsten experiences is Faust's, but it is also the dilemma facing all scientists in the modern age. As if in recognition of the universal resonance of such a moment, Glenn Seaborg, who discovered the explosive element used in the Nagasaki bomb, described how when he heard in 1939 that the uranium atom had been split, he walked 'the streets of Berkeley for hours', his mind alive with the beauty and the terror of the moment.[43]

Leo Szilard too was overwhelmed by the historic nature of just such a moment. Like Holsten, he wandered through the streets of Bloomsbury with the knowledge of life and death, of good and evil, seething in his brain:

He was oppressed, he was indeed scared, by his sense of the immense consequences of his discovery. He had a vague idea that night that he ought not to publish his results, that they were premature, that some secret association of wise men should take care of his work and hand it on from generation to generation until the world was riper for its practical application. He felt that nobody in all the thousands of people he passed had really awakened to the fact of change; they trusted the world for what it was, not to alter too rapidly, to respect their trusts, their assurances, their habits, their little accustomed traffics and hard-won positions.[44]

These are Holsten's thoughts, but this could as well be Szilard walking round Russell Square, twenty years after Wells was writing. Like Holsten, Szilard now faced a terrible decision: whether to make public his discovery and risk his ideas being exploited to create atomic weapons, or to keep his fatal knowledge secret.

The similarities between the two scientists are indeed striking. Both the fictional and the real scientist were born at the beginning of the atomic age, Holsten in the year X-rays were discovered, 1895, and Szilard in the year radium was discovered, 1898. Szilard had read Wells's novel just the previous year. It is clear that he saw the novel as prophetic, and frequently referred to it in relation to key moments in both his life and the discovery of atomic energy. He shared Holsten's dreams and his nightmares. To Leo Szilard in 1933, he *was* Holsten. It is a remarkable fusion of the scientific and the fictional.

Holsten tries to predict the effect of his discovery on humanity as he walks around London. But in the end he decides that 'it is not for me to reach out to consequences I cannot foresee ... I am a little instrument in the armoury of Change. If I were to burn all these papers, before a score of years had passed some other man would be doing all this ...'[45] Such self-justification has now become familiar. Science (so the argument goes) is not the product of one mind alone, as is art or literature: it is a Leviathan whose steady progress is the result of many minds. Suppressing the findings of one scientist is futile. It is only a matter of time before another will make that same discovery.

But Leo Szilard decided to try to stop the scientific Leviathan. Unlike Holsten, he would eventually opt for secrecy, a decision which offended the beliefs of most scientists. Rather than write up his idea in a scientific paper for publication, Leo Szilard worked out the details of critical mass and a self-sustaining chain reaction with neutrons, and then patented it. In 1935, after several failed attempts to convince the military of its value, he gave the patent to the British Admiralty on conditions of absolute secrecy.

Not until 1939 would Szilard see the experimental proof of his idea, late one February evening in a Columbia University laboratory in New York. In the meantime he spent six years desperately trying to prevent Hitler's physicists from discovering his secret and making an atomic bomb.

12

Wings over Europe

Out of the libraries come the killers.
Mothers stand despondently waiting,
Hugging their children and searching the sky,
Looking for the latest inventions of the professors.

Bertolt Brecht, *1940*

War was in the air in 1933. Leo Szilard foresaw a Europe divided into two armed camps, and he believed that an accidental war, triggered by a misunderstanding, was now a real possibility. 'Suppose if you have a large German and a large French air force,' he said in August, and 'the false alarm is spread in Paris that the German air force has left the German airports, [then] no French government, even the most pacifist one, could take the responsibility for holding back their air force to wait for confirmation of that rumour.' Szilard would be 'astonished' if such an accidental war did not happen 'within the next 5 or 10 years'.[1]

Surveying scientific and world events from his chair in the lobby of the Imperial Hotel, Leo Szilard might well have read the *Times* review of Wells's latest book, *The Shape of Things to Come*, at the beginning of September 1933. Once again, Wells had donned his prophet's robes. This time he predicted that the next war would start in 1940 and would be fought with weapons of mass destruction. But their use would not be restricted to the battlefield, as in the last war. This time air raids with gas bombs would wipe out whole cities. He imagined the appalling effects of such a raid on the city Szilard had just left, Berlin:

We went down Unter den Linden and along the Sieges Allee, and the bodies of people were lying everywhere, men, women and children, not scattered evenly, but bunched together very curiously in heaps, as though their last effort had been to climb on to each other for help. This attempt to get close up to someone seems to be characteristic of death by this particular gas. Something must happen in the mind. Everyone was crumpled up in the same fashion and nearly all had vomited blood. The stench was dreadful, although all this multitude had been alive twenty-four hours ago. The body corrupts at once. The archway into the park was almost impassable . . . [2]

H. G. Wells had been one of the first to realize the potential of aircraft in warfare. To the 1941 edition of *The War in the Air*, written way back in 1907, Wells added a bitter epitaph: 'I told you so. You *damned* fools.' But Wells was not the only Cassandra in town. In 1933, E. M. Forster observed that 'war has moved from chivalry to chemicals'.[3] Another novel that year described gas bombs being dropped on London: 'Oxford Street, Piccadilly, the Mall, Trafalgar Square, the Strand, Fleet Street, Ludgate Hill, were carpeted with the dead. The entrance to every tube station was piled high with the bodies of those who had made one last mad effort to escape from the poison gas.'[4]

In the 1930s, the prospect of gas warfare led to anxiety in the press and popular fiction alike. The idea of whole cities being annihilated within minutes was widely accepted. It was reported that a mere 42 tons of Lewisite could wipe out the entire population of London. In 1932, a German novel speculated – with more than a little *Schadenfreude* – about a devastatingly effective pre-emptive air strike on France by Britain. In the novel, a lethal mix of high-explosive bombs, incendiaries and mustard gas is dropped on all of France's major industrial towns and communication centres.[5] Ironically, it would be German cities that would, within ten years, experience the appalling force of air power.

A popular British novel from the previous year, *The Gas War of 1940* by Miles (aka Stephen Southwold), describes a world war breaking out on 3 September 1940 with a German blitzkrieg on Poland. Gas air raids are central to the story:

In a dozen parts of London that night people died in their homes with the familiar walls crashing about them in flames; thousands rushed into the streets to be met by blasts of flame and explosion and were blown to rags; they came pouring out of suddenly darkened theatres, picture-houses, concert and dance halls, into the dark and congested streets to be crushed or trodden to death.[6]

End-of-the-world stories like these became so popular with Germans in the interwar period that they even coined a word for them – *Weltuntergangsromane*. Once Hitler came to power, British newspapers began to carry ominous stories about Germany's preparations for war. On 6 September 1933, *The Times* ran an article on a new German study of military science. It was a handbook for total war, which even promoted the use of biological weapons. Modern warfare was a 'bloody battle' and 'a contest of material', the author argued. War is about 'gas and plague, it is tank and aircraft horror'. As well as advising German schools to teach military science to children as young as six, the book promoted the idea that war was not merely destructive, but 'the eternal renewer; it creates as it destroys'.[7] Although much less common as a fictional theme at this time, biological warfare did appear in British civil servant Bernard Newman's 1931 novel *Armoured Doves*.

The possibility of an atomic war also featured in public fears. In the same year that Leo Szilard read Wells's novel about atomic bombs, the former diplomat Sir Harold Nicolson, husband of Vita Sackville-West, revisited the subject. His novel *Public Faces*, a stylish satire on British politics, raised the possibility that atomic bombs would be the weapons that won the next war.

While he was with the Foreign Office, Nicolson had been sent on a mission to Béla Kun's Soviet-style government at Budapest in 1919. His novel certainly made an impression on one young Hungarian scientist. Edward Teller, then in Göttingen, recalled how he was told to read the novel by the other physicists in the department. They had all been fascinated by Nicolson's account of how politicians might deal with the responsibility of possessing the most powerful weapon ever invented – a superweapon handed to them by physicists. It is clear that in Nicolson's view, politicians could not be trusted with such weapons of mass destruction.

H. G. Wells had been warning for years that the lack of understanding of science at the highest levels of society meant that opportunities for social progress were lost and increased the likelihood of an abuse of power – atomic power. In Nicolson's *Public Faces* the world is taken to the brink of war when rogue elements in the British Government try to intimidate other nations with atomic weapons developed in secret using a plutonium-like element. An atomic bomb is, as the British Cabinet swiftly realizes, a 'weapon of world dominion'.[8]

In a show of force, an atomic bomb is dropped into the Atlantic from a rocket-plane. With a hundred rockets like these armed with atomic bombs, 'we could rule the world', boasts the Air Minister.[9] But the demonstration goes catastrophically wrong. The huge atomic explosion sets off a devastating tidal wave which kills tens of thousands of people in America. Britain's political leaders are shocked by what has been done in their name and, after calling on the world to disarm, they dispose of their atomic weapons.

Public Faces appeared in 1932, the same year as Aldous Huxley's satire on a planned scientific society, *Brave New World*. Huxley's novel describes how, after a devastating Nine Years' War fought with biological and chemical weapons, 'there was a choice between World Control and destruction'. It was a choice that Wells and many scientists believed would soon face the world. But Huxley was deeply sceptical about a society ruled by technocrats. In the new utopia, even science has to be censored to preserve the status quo. As one of its leaders says, 'what's the point of truth or beauty or knowledge when the anthrax bombs are popping all around you?'[10] However, in 1946, Huxley noted that his omission of nuclear energy from his biological dystopia was a 'vast and obvious failure of insight'.[11]

Biological, chemical and atomic weapons were already the cause of widespread anxiety, as can be seen from the fiction of the period, although the phrase 'weapons of mass destruction' did not become common until 1937. That year the Archbishop of Canterbury used the phrase for what is thought to be the first time in his Christmas sermon. 'Who can think without horror of what another widespread war would mean,' he told his congregation, 'waged as it would be with all the new weapons of mass destruction?'[12]

The winning combination of aeroplanes and weapons of mass

destruction had been tried and tested in the years immediately after World War I. In 1919 Winston Churchill advocated the use of the newly formed RAF to drop gas bombs – in this instance tear gas – to quell 'uncivilised tribes' in Iraq and elsewhere, who were rebelling against the British Empire. 'I do not understand this squeamishness about the use of gas,' said Churchill. Such weapons would, he hoped, 'spread a lively terror' among the victims.[13] The next year, a rebellion of a hundred thousand tribesmen in Iraq was crushed from the air. Nine thousand Iraqis were killed for the loss of just nine RAF men.

Aircraft had initially been welcomed as an unambiguous sign of human progress. For writers such as Rudyard Kipling ('As Easy as ABC', 1912), the figure of the aviator had embodied hopes for a new scientific future that would soar up and away, leaving behind the petty constraints of the past. Now, in a time of international tension, the sight of strange aircraft above a city brought a frisson of fear to the people on the ground.

Robert Nichols and Maurice Browne's play *Wings over Europe*, first performed in New York in 1928, explores the relationship between science, politics and the superweapon in an age of aerial warfare. It depicts the explosive encounter between an idealistic scientist and the obdurate conservatism of the British Government. The action takes place around the Cabinet Table in Number 10 Downing Street, a setting which anticipates the memorable scenes across the War Room table in *Dr Strangelove*. As in Nicolson's *Public Faces*, the spotlight is on the politicians and how they respond to the dawn of the atomic age.

The scientist, Francis Lightfoot, announces to the British Prime Minister that he has just made the discovery of the century – atomic energy. 'Yesterday, Man was a slave; to-day he's free. Matter obeys him,' proclaims the elated Lightfoot.[14] Breathlessly, he outlines to the Cabinet how atomic energy will utterly transform life and society: limitless energy; the power to transmute elements, creating gold on demand (thus upsetting the monetary system which was based on the gold standard); and weapons of unimaginable power which – once the knowledge spreads – will be available to any nation, indeed to any individual.

'One man can easily release enough force to destroy civilization,' says Lightfoot with irrepressible enthusiasm, trying to explain the potential of atomic weapons. 'He touches a spring; the atoms about the piece of mechanism begin to redistribute themselves at an undreamt-of-speed – at such a speed that not only he, but his house, his street, his borough, London itself, disappears, if he so wishes . . . is blown up . . .'[15]

The politicians do not share the scientist's enthusiasm. In fact, they are horrified by this vision of atomic anarchy and by the idea that their traditional view of the world is about to be turned upside down. Scientific revolutions are fine, but social revolutions are a step too far. Perhaps in this new atomic age – horror of horrors! – politicians will lose their grip on power.

'Physics and politics are not quite the same,' says the Prime Minister, gently trying to prepare Lightfoot for disappointment. 'Yours is a perfect world of form and number.'[16] By contrast, the world of politics is anything but perfect. Lightfoot, bursting with Wellsian visions of how society should be reformed in the atomic age, is bitterly disillusioned when the politicians ask him to suppress his revolutionary discovery.

As his dream of the future collapses before his eyes, Lightfoot is transformed from a saviour scientist into a mad scientist. He tries to blackmail the British Government, threatening to annihilate the whole of Britain with an atomic explosion unless they allow the revolution to occur. Doomsday is averted only when Lightfoot is killed in a freak accident. But just as the politicians think that it's safe to return to their outmoded way of life, they receive an ultimatum from a group of scientists who have also developed atomic weapons. Their aeroplanes, laden with atomic bombs, are already in the air above London and 'the capitals of every civilized country' in the world. Clearly, nothing can stand in the way of scientific progress – but is social progress similarly inevitable? At the end of the play, the politicians can no longer avoid facing the reality of the atomic age: 'Gentlemen, those wings even now sound over Europe. Are we with them or against them?'[17]

*

By the beginning of 1934, Leo Szilard had moved out of genteel Russell Square. He was now living a twenty-minute walk away at the Strand Palace Hotel, where the rooms were cheaper. His savings were dwindling, but he still needed time to think. January had brought remarkable news: Irène and Frédéric Joliot-Curie announced that they had created radioactivity artificially. The actual discovery had taken place at the end of 1933, just as Wells had predicted in *The World Set Free*. After bombarding aluminium foil with alpha particles, they found that it continued to be radioactive even after the alpha source was removed.

In 1935 they received the Nobel Prize in Chemistry for what was widely regarded as one of the great discoveries of the century. In his acceptance speech, Frédéric echoed the warning given by his father-in-law, Pierre Curie. Before long, he said, scientists would be able to create 'transmutations of an explosive type'. He even suggested that a catastrophic chain reaction might be possible, an atomic 'cataclysm' which could spread through all matter, transforming the planet into a fiery supernova.[18] His warning preyed on the minds of the Manhattan Project scientists right up to the final hours before the Trinity atomic test in 1945. The possibility of a doomsday bomb began to seem more like fact than fiction.

For Leo Szilard, artificial radioactivity was further evidence that he was on the right track: if alpha particles could do this, what might neutrons do? Physics had become 'too exciting for me to leave it', Szilard later recalled.[19] He settled into his room at the Strand Palace Hotel and dedicated his life to dreaming up experiments with artificial radioactivity and neutrons. But for a serious scientist like Szilard, even dreaming required a rigorous routine:

I remember that I went into my bath – I didn't have a private bath, but there was a bath in the corridor in the Strand Palace Hotel – around 9 o'clock in the morning. There is no place as good to think as a bathtub. I would just soak there and think, and around 12 o'clock the maid would knock and say, 'Are you all right, sir?' Then I usually got out and made a few notes, dictated a few memoranda. I played around this way, doing nothing, until summer came around.[20]

The result of this aquatic brainstorming was Szilard's patent, which detailed for the first time the concept of critical mass and a self-sustaining chain reaction with neutrons. This formed the scientific basis of the 1942 atomic pile constructed at Chicago University, as well as the atomic bomb. His patent, filed on 12 March 1934, is one of the founding documents of the atomic age. But for now, only Leo Szilard knew its significance, 'and I knew it because I had read H. G. Wells'.[21]

Szilard's fifteen-page patent named beryllium as the element he thought would most likely sustain a neutron chain reaction. It was the element that had led James Chadwick to the discovery of the neutron in 1932. To Szilard, lying in his bath, it was the obvious candidate. His faith in beryllium was also bolstered by incorrect data about its atomic weight; it was not for another three years that a more accurate value was found. Significantly, Szilard also identified uranium as a potential element for a chain reaction.[22]

Fiction writers were also fascinated by the nuclear potential of the silvery metal beryllium. In a remarkable science fiction story written in the year that Leo Szilard applied for a patent detailing an atomic chain reaction in beryllium, Isaac R. Nathanson described how a scientist achieved precisely this, using the same element. 'The World Aflame', published in the science fiction pulp magazine *Amazing Stories*, contains echoes both of Goethe's *Faust* and of Wells's *The World Set Free*.

It begins with a passionate lecture on atomic energy by a scientist, Professor Samuel Mendoza. The parallels with Professor Rufus (aka Frederick Soddy) and his lecture at the start of Wells's novel are clear. He paints a utopian picture of how, when the atom's energy has been unlocked, 'a truly new age of man will be ushered in' and life revolutionized. But he also issues an apocalyptic and, as it turns out, prophetic warning: 'with the coming of this all-powerful jinni of science, comes also unequalled responsibility . . . Man will either rise to the heights of the gods, or, if he does not take care, he may just as easily destroy himself!'[23]

With this ominous thought in mind, Professor Mendoza begins his experiment to release the atom's energy: 'When the beryllium atoms begin to kick out neutrons heavily, we'll turn on full force and see

Cover illustration for Isaac R. Nathanson's 'The World Aflame', published in Amazing Stories: *'The brilliantly incandescent beryllium suddenly turned to a strange bluish-white radiation of such dazzling intensity as to all but overpower the senses.'*

what happens.'[24] But as he raises the voltage to unprecedented levels and the temperature of the beryllium increases to two million degrees, 'something let go with an awful, explosive roaring . . . The brilliantly incandescent beryllium suddenly turned to a strange bluish-white radiation of such dazzling intensity as to all but overpower the senses.'[25]

Professor Mendoza has created the self-sustaining chain reaction with neutrons that Szilard was dreaming about in his bathtub at the Strand Palace Hotel. But Mendoza's chain reaction spirals out of control. The 'disintegrating beryllium' radiates such vast quantities of energy that the laboratory and the entire physics building are blown apart. Frédéric Joliot-Curie's nightmare has come true.

As the beryllium disintegrates, the flood of neutrons sets off reactions in other elements. J. J. Connington's scientist in *Nordenholt's Million* had described the chain reaction as a domino effect spreading through matter – an explosive self-sustaining chain reaction. Even Rutherford, in the early days of radioactivity before World War I, had confided to a colleague that he thought 'some fool in a laboratory might blow up the universe unawares' by unleashing a 'wave of atomic disintegration through matter'.[26]

Professor Mendoza almost becomes that fool. He only just succeeds in halting the rapidly spreading chain reaction. But although it is not the end of the earth, it is the end of Mendoza's career. Brilliant though he is at physics, the professor's 'entirely too open and critical views on such public matters as religion, politics, industry and society in general' have won him powerful enemies at the university.[27] The explosion and the destruction of university buildings provides an excuse to sack the troublesome scientist. But the 'all-powerful jinni of science' is out of the bottle. Soon it falls into the hands of America's enemies – in this case Japan – and, despite his idealism and hopes for 'a new age of man', Professor Mendoza's discovery becomes a doomsday weapon.[28]

An 'atomic bomb' explodes in the American countryside, triggering a chain reaction in soil and rocks. It becomes a 'fiery cancer . . . slowly consuming the earth's substance'.[29] The description of the bomb site is straight out of H. G. Wells's novel – a volcano of disintegrating, molten matter. But it was an idea that can be traced back to the photograph of glowing radioactive ore in Ernest Merritt's article on Marie Curie. This time the chain reaction is uncontrollable. The earth is doomed. But even though the 'awful Jinni of atomic energy' will cause the death of the planet, such is Nathanson's belief in science and the atom that he still describes it as 'the saviour of mankind'.[30] For it is through the power of the atom that space travel is finally achieved. Before the earth is transformed into a 'world aflame', humankind fulfils its Wellsian destiny, leaving the earth for new worlds and new futures.

Leo Szilard could only dream of the kind of funding Professor Mendoza had secured in order to create his chain reaction using beryllium. Many people believe that if Szilard had received adequate funding, he might have split the atom before 1938. Instead, Szilard spent the years 1934 to 1939 in a scientific wilderness, banging on doors trying to convince people that his dream could come true. Sir Hugo Hirst's company, General Electric, remained unconvinced by Szilard's (and Wells's) predictions of limitless energy, as were the financiers he approached. No one wanted to listen to the exiled Hungarian scientist with a big idea and a grand vision of the future. Atomic energy was strictly 'for the science fiction fans', Leo Szilard was told.[31]

In spring 1934, Eugene Wigner visited London to check up on his friend. Leo Szilard showed him equations describing an atomic chain reaction using beryllium that he hoped would produce enormous amounts of heat or even a violent explosion. Wigner was astonished. Together they visited Rutherford at Cambridge to discuss the idea. As Szilard's biographer says, it was a meeting that 'might have changed the course of nuclear research and with it modern history'.[32] Rutherford had the facilities and the scientists who could have tested Szilard's idea. But the meeting went disastrously from the outset.

The gruff, curmudgeonly Rutherford was an intimidating figure, both physically and intellectually. He had made his view abundantly clear on many occasions: atomic energy was moonshine. Understandably, Leo Szilard was very nervous. Perhaps for this reason, he didn't explain his idea properly, telling Rutherford that the chain reaction could be made to work with alpha particles. He didn't even mention neutrons. It was a fatal mistake. No one on the planet knew more about what alpha particles could or could not do than Ernest Rutherford.

The noble lord's mood darkened still further when Szilard said he had already patented his idea. Pure scientists didn't take out patents – they published their ideas in scholarly journals so that the whole scientific community could assess their worth. At the turn of the century, when J. J. Thomson had discovered the electron, they had a toast in the Cavendish: 'To the electron: may it never be of any use to anybody.'[33] When Szilard asked if he could test his ideas – which he had just patented – using the Cavendish's world-class facilities, Rutherford exploded. 'I was thrown out of Rutherford's office,' a horrified Szilard explained to Edward Teller later that year.[34] Indeed, when Teller attended a lecture by Rutherford at Cambridge in the autumn, the veteran atomic physicist publicly poured scorn on certain 'crazy people' who were promoting the idea of atomic energy.[35] It was clear whom Rutherford had in mind.

For the next four years in England, Szilard committed himself full-time to the search for his neutron chain reaction. But unlike Lise Meitner and Enrico Fermi, who were also exploring the potential of the neutron, Szilard had no laboratory, no fellow researchers and, most importantly, no funding. An outsider in the British scientific community, he had to beg for laboratory time at London's St Bartholomew's Hospital. Here, during the summer of 1934, he was able to make use of the radium samples used to treat cancer to conduct a few inconclusive experiments with beryllium. However, working together with Thomas A. Chalmers, a hospital staff member, Szilard did discover a new and extremely useful method for separating isotopes. As he said, 'these experiments established me as a nuclear physicist, not in the eyes of Cambridge, but in the eyes of Oxford'.[36]

Eventually a meeting with Frederick Lindemann, the director of Oxford's Clarendon Laboratory and later scientific advisor to Winston Churchill, landed Szilard a fellowship, funded by ICI, at Oxford in 1935. There Szilard was at last able to conduct original research into how neutrons are absorbed by the atomic nucleus. Niels Bohr described it as 'beautiful' research.[37] Even Rutherford was forced to acknowledge grudgingly it was an advance in understanding. By 1936, Leo Szilard had switched his interest from beryllium to indium.

In March he wrote to Bohr, suggesting that the rare isotope uranium-235 might be the ideal candidate for a neutron chain reaction. This time his hunch was right, but he would not see the proof for three years.

As well as continuing his experiments to find an element with which he could create a self-sustaining chain reaction, Szilard tried repeatedly but unsuccessfully to convince colleagues, such as Fermi, to keep their atomic research secret. His own patent was kept under lock and key at the British Admiralty. But other physicists were deeply sceptical about this obsessive desire for secrecy. In James Whale's 1933 film of *The Invisible Man*, one of Griffin's colleagues voices his suspicions about the mad scientist: 'straightforward scientists have no need for barred doors and drawn blinds'.[38] Secrecy offended the spirit of science, at least before the cold war.

Uranium had been one of the four elements Szilard had identified early on as potential candidates for a chain reaction. If he had received adequate research funding from the start, he might well have discovered that uranium emitted the neutrons needed to sustain a chain reaction before 1939.[39] Much later, Szilard admitted that he was actually pleased that he hadn't discovered this earlier. If he had, Nazi scientists might have been the first to create the atomic bomb. Szilard even joked that he should be awarded a Nobel Peace Prize for *not* discovering uranium fission in the 1930s.[40]

In April 1934, Szilard wrote a declaration which he hoped would be signed by Nobel laureates, condemning the Japanese invasion of China. His draft statement began: 'The discoveries of scientists have given weapons to mankind which may destroy our present civilization if we do not succeed in avoiding further wars.'[41] By then, he knew how such doomsday weapons might be made. It was, he thought, just a matter of time before H. G. Wells's atomic bomb was ready to be dropped from a lone aircraft on a real city.

IV

The Battle of the Laboratories

A weapon has been developed that is potentially destructive beyond the wildest nightmares of the imagination; a weapon so ideally suited to sudden unannounced attack that a country's major cities might be destroyed overnight by an ostensibly friendly power. This weapon has been created not by the devilish inspiration of some warped genius but by the arduous labor of thousands of normal men and women working for the safety of their country.

Henry DeWolf Smyth,
Atomic Energy for Military Purposes (1945)

13

'Power Beyond the Dream of a Madman'

It is by devising new weapons, and above all by scientific leadership, that we shall best cope with the enemy's superior strength.   Winston Churchill, 3 September 1940

[O]n May 1, 1976, had the reader been in the imperial city of Peking, with its then population of eleven millions, he would have witnessed a curious sight. He would have seen the streets filled with the chattering yellow populace, every queued head tilted back, every slant eye turned skyward. And high up in the blue he would have beheld a tiny dot of black, which, because of its orderly evolutions, he would have identified as an airship. From this airship, as it curved its flight back and forth over the city, fell missiles – strange, harmless missiles, tubes of fragile glass that shattered into thousands of fragments on the streets and house-tops. But there was nothing deadly about these tubes of glass. Nothing happened. There were no explosions ... One tube struck perpendicularly in a fish pond in a garden and was not broken. It was dragged ashore by the master of the house. He did not dare to open it, but, accompanied by his friends, and surrounded by an ever-increasing crowd, he carried the mysterious tube to the magistrate of the district. The latter was a brave man. With all eyes upon him, he shattered the tube with a blow from his brass-bowled pipe. Nothing happened. Of those who were very near, one or two thought they saw some mosquitos fly out. That was all. The crowd set up a great laugh and dispersed ...

Had the reader again been in Peking, six weeks later, he would have looked in vain for the eleven million inhabitants. Some few of them he would have found, a few hundred thousand, perhaps, their carcasses festering in the houses and in the deserted streets, and piled high on the abandoned death wagons.[1]

This is 'the unparalleled invasion of China', as described by American writer Jack London in 1906. Having just reported on the war between Russia and Japan as a journalist, London was surprised – not to say disturbed – at how advanced the Japanese were in their mastery of modern weapons. In his news articles he voiced xenophobic fears about the 'Yellow Peril'. The fear had begun to grow in some parts of Europe and America that the sleeping giant of China might learn from Japan and embrace industrialization to become an economic superpower.[2] In his short story 'The Unparalleled Invasion', London returned to these themes, creating a disturbing narrative about scientific superweapons and genocide.

The story shows how the Russo-Japanese war heralds 'the awakening of China'. With her 'four hundred millions and the scientific advance of the world', China soon becomes 'the colossus of the nations'. London sees China's strength as lying in her vast and increasing population. Soon 'there were two Chinese for every white-skinned human in the world'. The world is 'terrified' by this fact and by the growing power of China: 'there was no way to dam up the over-spilling monstrous flood of life'. France tries to halt the tide of Chinese immigrants into French Indo-China, but – in a prefiguring of the start of the Vietnam War – 'the French force was brushed aside like a fly'.[3]

Jacobus Laningdale is the saviour scientist who finds the brutal answer to the threat from the East. (Either by chance or design, he shares his initials with Jack London.) Laningdale is 'a very obscure scientist', a professor working in the laboratories of the Health Office of New York City. He comes up with an ingenious idea which, in a very unscientific way, he keeps secret. Rather than publishing it, he asks for a holiday. 'On September 19, 1975, he arrived in Washington,' writes London. 'It was evening, but he proceeded straight to the White House, for he had arranged an audience with the President. He was closeted with President Moyer for three hours. What passed between them was not learned by the rest of the world until long after.'[4] Science and the state had joined arms against a common threat.

It was to be a mutually rewarding alliance in the coming years. From pure science, lethal technologies would flow.

Initially, troops from American, European and other nations mass along China's borders. Then solitary airships appear above Chinese towns and cities, dropping their fragile cargo of glass test tubes. Inside each tube is a mosquito carrying a lethal pathogen. In this way, 'a score of plagues' are unleashed on China. This is biological warfare:

Every virulent form of infectious death stalked through the land . . . The man who escaped smallpox went down before scarlet fever. The man who was immune to yellow fever was carried away by cholera; and if he were immune to that, too, the Black Death, which was the bubonic plague, swept him away. For it was these bacteria, and germs, and microbes, and bacilli, cultured in the laboratories of the West, that had come down upon China in the rain of glass.[5]

What Jack London describes is not just a limited attack on a nation's army, but total warfare against a whole people – genocide, designed in the laboratory. With its borders sealed by foreign armies, China is isolated from the world, its people quarantined until the country is turned into a 'charnel house'. As well as the familiar diseases, 'a new and frightfully virulent germ' has been created. No one is immune to it. An entire nation is annihilated by science, the Janus-headed god of the modern world, offering miracle cures in one hand and super-weapons in the other: 'it was ultra-modern war, twentieth century war, the war of the scientist and the laboratory, the war of Jacobus Laningdale. Hundred-ton guns were toys compared with the micro-organic projectiles hurled from the laboratories, the messengers of death, the destroying angels that stalked through the empire of a billion souls.'

'And so perished China,' writes Jack London at the end of his genocidal fantasy. After the victorious nations divide up the land among themselves, they agree to ban these 'laboratory methods of warfare'.[6] Clearly, such total wars could be waged only against the 'yellow peril', not against white people.

Or could they? In 1953, at the height of the cold war, American military scientists began experimenting with insects as carriers of biological agents. In laboratories at Fort Detrick, Maryland, *Aedes aegypti* mosquitoes were bred by the million on a rich diet of blood and syrup. The aim was to produce 130 million a month and infect them with yellow fever – a particularly nasty disease with a 33 per cent fatality rate. Cluster bombs dropped from aircraft would be used to deliver the disease-carrying mosquitoes onto the enemy's population. Tests were conducted (although not with infected mosquitoes) in a residential part of Savannah, Georgia. They showed that 'within a day the mosquitoes had spread a distance of between one and two miles, and bitten many people'.[7] By the end of the decade, malaria and dengue (or breakbone fever) had also been weaponized for use in this way. Experiments were conducted using fleas and flies infected with other fatal diseases. Indeed, in the summer of 1999, when New Yorkers suddenly started coming down with West Nile encephalitis – another virus spread by mosquitoes – scientists immediately suspected a terrorist attack.[8]

Jack London's story first appeared in *McClure's* magazine in 1910. Three years later, H. G. Wells's *The World Set Free* would also fantasize about a time in the near future when a scientific weapon dropped from a lone aircraft would destroy a city. Such stories were regularly serialized in the popular magazines of the day. One avid young American reader was Harry S Truman, who would himself one day order the use of an atomic superweapon.

In 1910, Truman was a farmer, working his grandmother's land near Grandview, Missouri. Magazines such as *Everybody's* and *Adventure*, packed with illustrated short stories, would arrive regularly for him at Grandview's post office. He admitted to his childhood sweetheart Bess Wallace that his reading was 'confined to *Everybody's* and one or two other fifteen-cent or muckrake magazines and numerous farm publications'.[9] He was also a subscriber to *McClure's*. On 26 May 1913 he wrote to Bess: 'I read the Mary Roberts Rinehart in *McClure's*. It is a grand story, really good enough to appear in *Adventure*. Could I possibly compliment it more highly? I suppose I'll have to renew my subscription to *McClure's* now so I won't miss a number. There are several good stories in this number.'[10]

In 1911 he had admitted to Bess how he wished that *Everybody's* came every day.[11] When it did arrive he was overjoyed: '*Everybody's* came at last and there was plenty of action, wasn't there?' In the same letter, written in June, the man who would order the attacks on Hiroshima and Nagasaki wrote: 'Uncle Will says that the Lord made a white man from dust, a nigger from mud, then threw up what was left and it came down a Chinaman. He does hate Chinese and Japs. So do I. It is a race prejudice, I guess.'[12]

In 1910, the young Missouri farmer had read a poem that so impressed him that he wrote out part of it on a piece of paper and kept it in his wallet for the next fifty years. As the paper became worn and tattered, Truman recopied these lines. He did this thirty or forty times. On his way to the Potsdam conference in 1945 he took out this piece of paper and read the poem again. In its words he found reassurance that the terrible weapon that would soon be dropped on an unsuspecting Japanese city would ultimately lead to a new world order. These were the lines that President Truman treasured so dearly:

> For I dipt into the future, far as human eye could see,
> Saw the Vision of the world, and all the wonder that would be;
> Saw the heavens fill with commerce, argosies of magic sails,
> Pilots of the purple twilight dropping down with costly bales;
> Heard the heavens fill with shouting, and there rain'd a ghastly dew
> From the nations' airy navies grappling in the central blue;
> Far along the world-wide whisper of the south-wind rushing warm,
> With the standards of the peoples plunging thro' the thunder-storm;
> Till the war-drum throbb'd no longer, and the battle-flags were furl'd
> In the Parliament of man, the Federation of the world.
> There the common sense of most shall hold a fretful realm in awe,
> And the kindly earth shall slumber, lapt in universal law.[13]

These lines are from *Locksley Hall*, written over a hundred years earlier by the English poet Alfred, Lord Tennyson after he had experienced the most advanced technology of the day – a journey on the first steam train from Liverpool to Manchester in 1830. The poem looks beyond present disappointments to a bright future when the secret of flight has been discovered. After a war fought in the air, during which 'there rain'd a ghastly dew', armed conflict is banished once and for all. The war-drums are silenced and world government is achieved, a 'Federation of the world'.

It is a vision of utopia which has been achieved at the price of a final war fought with a superweapon dropped from the air, a vision which could easily have been penned by Jack London or H. G. Wells. Indeed, one of their contemporaries, Simon Newcomb, quoted Tennyson's poem in his novel about a saviour scientist, *His Wisdom The Defender* (1900).

In Newcomb's novel, Professor Campbell (a 'twentieth-century Faust') discovers a revolutionary antigravity force and secretly builds airships which he uses to compel nations to abandon war. On the scientist's banner are emblazoned the words 'When the war-drum throbs no longer and the battle flag is furled, / In the Parliament of Man, the Federation of the world.'[14] In 1900, this was to be the utopian rallying cry of the new century.

Stories such as Newcomb's and London's show how the dream of a superweapon that could destroy an enemy at a single stroke enthralled the twentieth century from its earliest years. At Hiroshima in August 1945, it was physics rather than biology and chemistry that provided the know-how. Japan was itself engaged in research aimed at building an atomic bomb, but its scientists lagged far behind America's. However, in the search for a biological superweapon, Japan led the world both before and during World War II.

When Japan occupied Manchuria in 1932, it transformed the whole region into 'one gigantic biological and chemical warfare laboratory'.[15] This was the work of one scientist, a young Japanese Army doctor, Shiro Ishii. He was a brilliant microbiologist and, like Fritz Haber, fiercely nationalistic. Described by one colleague as having a 'sharp voice and a hypnotic appearance',[16] the tall and rather scholarly Ishii quickly gained a reputation as the 'army's crazed surgeon'.[17] In 1932 he set up a laboratory in Manchuria to test biological warfare in the field. His laboratory was near Harbin, now China's eighth-largest city and the capital of Heilongjiang province.

At the Harbin laboratory, experiments were conducted on live prisoners using both biological and chemical agents. None of the prisoners who were brought to the laboratory left alive. If Ishii needed a human brain for experiments, his guards would go straight to the cells, select a prisoner and split his or her head open with an axe. Like the Nazis, the Japanese in such establishments were convinced of their racial superiority. They believed Chinese and Korean people to be subhuman, and that experimenting on them was therefore little different from using guinea pigs or monkeys. Indeed, in official reports of experiments, humans were referred to as monkeys and differentiated solely by nationality.

Shiro Ishii's military masters were greatly impressed with the results of his work at Harbin. As a reward he received generous funding to develop a major, top-secret biological weapons complex at Ping Fan, on the outskirts of Harbin. Construction began in 1936. When it was completed, in 1939, what became known as Unit 731 'rivaled Auschwitz-Birkenau in size'.[18] Covering over two square miles and containing over seventy buildings, it was capable of developing, testing and mass-producing bioweapons. Back in 1915, Thomas Edison had predicted that warfare would become a mechanized 'factory of death'.[19] Here, and later in the vast scientific, military and industrial endeavour of the Manhattan Project, that prediction came true.

Unit 731 contained cutting-edge laboratories and a prison that could hold 200 human guinea pigs. The needs of the three thousand staff (including three to five hundred scientists) were catered for with a thousand-seater auditorium, bars, restaurants, library, swimming pools, schools for the children, a Shinto temple and a brothel. While the workers enjoyed themselves, at least three thousand human beings perished in the experiments that Ishii and his scientists conducted. They developed a hellish arsenal of pathogens, including plague, cholera, typhoid, dysentery, anthrax, tetanus, gas gangrene and small-pox. The atrocities committed here and at Harbin in the search for biological weapons equalled the excesses of the most infamous of Nazi scientists, such as Joseph Mengele.

In 1936, Shiro Ishii delivered a speech to his colleagues in the new conference room at Ping Fan. He welcomed his fellow scientists and officially inaugurated their research programme. He admitted that they might feel 'some anguish as doctors' who were used to curing people, rather than using their biological skills to kill. But he told them to ignore these qualms. 'I beseech you to pursue this research', he said with genuine conviction. He reassured his colleagues that they were merely engaged in the traditional, indeed Faustian, quest to find 'the truth in natural science' and to discover 'the unknown world'.

And he called upon them as members of the Japanese armed forces 'to successfully build a powerful military weapon against the enemy'.[20] Intellectual curiosity and patriotism: from Haber's laboratory in Dahlem to Oppenheimer's at Los Alamos, scientists would find the same justifications.

Ishii was utterly convinced of the importance of his research, both to science and to Japan. His enthusiasm spread among his fellow scientists like one of his lethal viruses. Ishii thus demonstrated to his superiors not only that he was a brilliant scientist, but that he could plan, organize and efficiently run a major facility such as Unit 731. People like Shiro Ishii, who could weld science and war together to produce deadly new weapons, would be increasingly valued by governments and regimes around the world in the coming years.

The poisonous fruits of Ishii's research were used against the Chinese and the Soviets. In July 1942, Ishii personally led a campaign of bio-warfare against the Chinese population in Nanjing. As well as coordinating the contamination of wells with typhoid, he handed out chocolates laced with anthrax to local children. Among the weaponry developed by Ishii and his team were bacteria-filled artillery shells and bombs filled with plague-infested fleas to be dropped from the air. All the weapons they developed were tested on prisoners. Field tests were conducted using people who were tied to stakes near Unit 731 while munitions were exploded near them. The facility even had its own airfield from which aircraft laden with experimental bombs could take off.

Although General Ishii never achieved his goal of developing a biological superweapon, tens of thousands of people were killed by his bioweapons. After the war, neither Ishii nor his colleagues were prosecuted in the Japanese War Crimes Trial that began in May 1946. His biological research on human beings became his passport to freedom. A decision was made at the highest level in Washington to grant immunity in return for access to Ishii's valuable data on the effectiveness of biological pathogens. Although America was further ahead than Japan when it came to developing effective munitions, it was unable to conduct the extensive programme of human experimentation that Ishii had pursued. It became a key part of the American cold-war weapons programme.

The historian Sheldon Harris claimed that no writer of fiction, from Dante to Mary Shelley, 'could possibly rival the real-life misdeeds of Ishii and his fellow researchers'.[21] But in fact fiction had anticipated such horrors – in novels such as M. P. Shiel's *Yellow Danger* and the genocidal bioweapons in Jack London's story – showing that the dream of scientific mass murder lies deep in the collective consciousness.

On the evening of 30 October 1938, a radio programme of music by a New York City dance band was interrupted for a news bulletin. It brought shocking news for Americans: New York was being invaded. A reporter standing on a Manhattan rooftop described the ruthless armoured invaders to his listeners, who could hear behind his terrified voice the sound of car horns as traffic jammed the streets of the city.

'The enemy's now in sight above the Pallisades,' cried the reporter. 'Five – five great machines. The first one is crossing the river. I can see it from here, wading, wading the Hudson like a man wading through a brook.' Then, as the reporter watched helplessly, the armoured machines began pumping out a lethal black smoke. Americans were being attacked with chemical weapons. The New Yorkers thronging the streets began falling 'like rats' into the East River.

Worried listeners tuning in to the radio broadcast that evening heard disturbing reports of bomb-like cylinders 'falling all over the country'.[22] It certainly sounded as though America was being invaded. For a nation that had heard the news of Japanese attacks in China using chemical and biological weapons, and had watched as Hitler's power in Europe grew ever greater, it seemed as though the war everyone had been fearing had finally begun with a surprise attack on America. For the last twenty years the experts had been warning that the next war would be different from the last. This one would be fought with weapons of mass destruction, and not just soldiers but civilians would be the targets. This time it would be a war of terror.

On that Sunday evening in October 1938, New York experienced that terror. 'Everybody was terribly frightened,' recalled a nurse who was holding a party. 'Some of the women almost went crazy.'[23] The radio station and the police were inundated with phone calls from terrified Americans. 'Residents of New Jersey covered their faces with wet cloths as a protection against poisonous gases and fled from their homes carrying with them their most valuable possessions,' reported the *Manchester Guardian*.[24] Doctors and nurses rushed to hospitals to treat the thousands of expected gas casualties. Roads were quickly jammed with cars trying to leave the city.

At Orange, New Jersey, a man ran into a cinema shouting warnings about the invasion. The building emptied within minutes. 'Panic evacuations' were reported elsewhere, and people told the police that they had witnessed 'the invasion' with their own eyes. A man burst into an Indianapolis church screaming, 'New York is destroyed. It's the end of the world. We might as well go home to die. I've just heard it on the radio.' The service ended abruptly and the frightened congregation rushed home.[25]

Those who had listened to the broadcast from the very beginning knew that this was no terrestrial invasion force. The invaders were from Mars. This dramatic news bulletin was not reality, but fiction – a radio adaptation of H. G. Wells's *The War of the Worlds* by Orson Welles and the Mercury Theatre. The impact of the radio programme shocked its makers and indeed Wells himself. It was an extraordinary moment in broadcasting history, a moment when people's deep anxieties about the threat from weapons of mass destruction were revealed.

A third of all listeners had been convinced that the broadcast described a real invasion. Among those who tuned in halfway through, the proportion rose to 63 per cent.[26] Many thought that a foreign power was behind the attack. 'I never believed it was anyone from Mars,' said one person. 'I thought it was some kind of a new airship and a new method of attack.'[27] Most people thought that Hitler was the culprit. In their genocidal brutality and advanced weaponry, Wells's Martians did indeed offer a foretaste of what was to come in Europe.

Thirty years earlier, a writer for the *Contemporary Review* had asked whether science could abolish war. 'Each fresh invention', he wrote, 'has been heralded by prophecies that its appalling deadliness must make war so terrible that no ruler would dare to unleash its horrors.'[28] The following year, in 1909, one of Harry Truman's favourite magazines greeted the Zeppelin with the question 'Does this new machine mean the end of war?'[29] Similarly, one of the inventors of the aeroplane, Orville Wright, said after the 1918 Armistice that his creation 'has made war so terrible that I do not believe that any country will again care to start a war'.[30] From Zeppelins and death rays to the plans of Edward Teller and other scientists in the 1980s for a space-based weapons system (labelled 'Star Wars' after the science fiction blockbuster), the dream of the superweapon has exerted a powerful grip on the collective imagination, promising both a terrible death and world peace. For much of the twentieth century, humankind walked a dangerous tightrope between these two possibilities.

In 1938, a confusion of fiction with reality revealed the true power of this dream. Poison gas was the superweapon that struck fear into the heart of America. Just after World War I, an American writer described it as 'the final consummate weapon of mass murder'. The next war, he said, 'will no longer be an heroic contest of mind, courage, and prowess, but a mad mingling in mutual annihilation'.[31] Gas was held to be the ultimate scientific superweapon, a force of apocalyptic potential, what American journalist Will Irwin described as 'a power beyond the dream of a madman'.[32] But the Strangelovean dreams of future madmen would not be about poison gas. In the next war, science would produce a more terrible weapon – the atomic bomb.

In the same year that Orson Welles terrified America with a fictional invasion, the English writer J. B. Priestley published a popular novel about 'three insane brothers who . . . tried to destroy the world at one stroke'.[33] *The Doomsday Men* conjures up a deadly combination of religious fanaticism and physics that would not be paralleled in the real world until the Japanese apocalyptic cult Aum Shinrikyo infiltrated the Kurchatov Institute during the 1990s, almost certainly in an attempt to recruit Russian nuclear scientists and obtain atomic weapons.[34] Priestley's readable yarn tells how an atomic device is created at a secret laboratory in the Mojave Desert. Strangely, the location – Death Valley ('the sullen hot floor of the world'[35]) – anticipates the area where the real atomic bomb was built and tested seven years later. Indeed, the first atomic bomb was exploded in a desert called the Jornada del Muerto – the Journey of the Dead.

At the beginning of *The Doomsday Men*, American physicist

George Glenway Hooker is in England, visiting 'that Mecca of good physicists', the Cavendish Laboratory at Cambridge. Hooker is 'an awkward young man with a shy manner, disgraceful trousers, and an ability, almost amounting to genius, for landing himself in uncomfortable hotels'. Like Leo Szilard in 1933, he has ended up at a hotel in London's Bloomsbury. Hooker is 'the only genuine magician in the neighbourhood', for this atomic physicist can 'transform what we call matter . . . into light'.[36]

But for the moment, Hooker's mind is not on physics. He is trying to track down his brilliant colleague, Professor Paul Engelfield, formerly of the University of Chicago where he had conducted pioneering research bombarding 'heavy nuclei'. Having located the enigmatic Engelfield in London, Hooker follows him back to America and his secret desert laboratory. There he has used a cyclotron to create 'an artificial element, very difficult to produce', which has 'a very high atomic number'. As Hooker says, Engelfield is clearly a 'madman' – and like all mad scientists he is hopelessly vain. He names this new element after himself – 'paulium'. Mad he may be, but his science is sound and he intends to use this unstable, plutonium-like heavy element to create a vast atomic explosion that he hopes will destroy the surface of the earth.[37]

Together with his two brothers, Engelfield has founded a doomsday cult, the Ark of the Brotherhood, which has an unhealthy obsession with the Book of Revelation. 'I have a chance of performing the last and greatest experiment known to science,' Engelfield tells Hooker. 'To release the earth's energy to destroy – I hope in a flash – the life on it.' This mad scientist believes that life is an accident: matter 'has no business thinking and feeling. That's the mistake.' For this reason, man is 'doomed from the start. He can't possibly find a lasting place for himself in this universe.' As rational beings, our greatest achievement, says the coldly logical Engelfield, is to understand our 'own noble despair' and to grasp the ultimate pointlessness of life. Our 'one last triumphant stroke' is to choose the time of our death, like Socrates committing suicide, 'leaving the mindless cosmos to its own damned dance of blind energies, for ever'.[38]

Engelfield's scientific nihilism is strikingly similar to Satan's stance in Imre Mádach's *The Tragedy of Man*, the Faustian work that so impressed the young Leo Szilard. Humankind might be smart enough to understand the laws of nature, but we can't do anything to change them. Ultimately, gloats Satan, man is powerless. That was the kind of pessimism that really infuriated Szilard.

At first, George Hooker is sceptical about Professor Engelfield's claim that atomic energy could destroy the world: 'We've been splitting atoms for years,' he says. 'You don't even get a Nobel prize for it any more.'[39] But although he thwarts the physicist's doomsday plans, Hooker was wrong on this last point. For in the same year that *The Doomsday Men* appeared, scientists split the uranium atom clean in two. Not only did it win them a Nobel prize, but it meant that Szilard's idea of a chain reaction was no longer a pipe dream.

It was not just Leo Szilard who was intrigued by the discoveries of the neutron and artificial radioactivity. Scientists around the world had also grasped the revolutionary possibilities. Foremost among them was Enrico Fermi. Together with his team in Rome, Fermi began systematically bombarding all the known elements with neutrons. Leo Szilard described this as an essential but 'rather boring task' which, if he had the money, he would have hired somebody else to do.[40] But the brilliant experimentalist Fermi – whom Wolfgang Pauli labelled the 'quantum engineer' – was the perfect man for this exacting empirical task.[41] He and his team spent 1934 and 1935 patiently bombarding the elements (including uranium) with neutrons. Unfortunately, Fermi misunderstood the nature of the results. He was not the only one: the whole of the physics community was mistaken about what happened when heavy elements were bombarded with neutrons.

The conventional wisdom at the time was that uranium absorbed neutrons to form bigger, artificial elements, which Fermi called transuranic (or transuranium) elements. A German chemist, Ida Noddack, had the temerity to point out in September 1934 that Fermi and the physicists had got it all wrong. She suggested that the uranium atom had split in two, forming elements lower down the periodic table. But Fermi dismissed this idea, and chemists, including Noddack's friend Otto Hahn, advised her not to pursue this line of argument as the physicists found it frankly absurd. This mistaken advice was in fact a blessing in disguise. If physicists had understood in the 1930s what was really happening to the bombarded nuclei, Germany might have been in a position to develop atomic weapons during World War II. As Emilio Segrè, Fermi's colleague, said later, 'God, for His own inscrutable reasons, made everyone blind at that time to the phenomenon of nuclear fission.'[42]

In Berlin, Lise Meitner and Otto Hahn had spent the three years before 1938 bombarding uranium with neutrons and analysing the resulting products. In March that year, German troops occupied Meitner's homeland, Austria. Because she was Jewish she was finally forced to flee the country in which she had worked for three decades. Before she left for Stockholm, where she had been invited to work, Meitner and Hahn held one last meeting to discuss the puzzling results of their research. In particular, Meitner advised her chemist colleague not to publish his latest findings on the bombardment of uranium. These seemed to suggest that radium – a lighter element than uranium – had been formed. But it was simply unthinkable that light elements could be created from heavier ones. It had to be a mistake. Further experiments were needed.

Lise Meitner spent Christmas 1938 in the small Swedish town of Kungälv, near Gothenburg. She invited her nephew, Otto Frisch, who was working at Niels Bohr's Copenhagen Institute, to stay with her. It was, he later said, 'the most momentous visit of my whole life'.[43]

When he arrived, Frisch found his aunt poring over a letter from Hahn. The content was 'startling'.[44] Hahn had written the letter late at night on 19 December. Working with his colleague Fritz Strassmann, he had now found that not radium but barium seemed to be produced when uranium was bombarded by neutrons. Barium, element 56 in the periodic table, is just over half the weight of uranium (number 92). Neither Hahn nor Strassmann could explain how this might come about. Hahn wrote in desperation to his exiled physicist colleague in the hope that she could come up with a suitably 'fantastic explanation'.[45] Lise Meitner did not disappoint them.

Otto Frisch simply couldn't believe what Hahn had written.

'Is it just a mistake?' he asked.

'No,' replied his aunt without hesitation. 'Hahn is too good a chemist for that.'[46]

The result of the experiment was so extraordinary that aunt and nephew decided to go for a brisk walk in the Swedish snow to see if they could work out exactly what had happened. Was it possible, they speculated, that the atomic nucleus was not a hard solid, like a rock, but had a soft, elastic structure, rather like a drop of liquid? Both George Gamow and Niels Bohr had already argued as much. Was this the evidence to support their hypothesis?

After Meitner and Frisch had been walking for some time, they sat down on a fallen tree trunk in the snowy landscape and began calculating whether the known electrical forces within an atom were consistent with such a structure. They concluded that the 'uranium nucleus might indeed resemble a very wobbly, unstable drop, ready to divide itself at the slightest provocation, such as the impact of a single neutron'.[47] And if the uranium nucleus had divided, as Frisch and Meitner were beginning to suspect, then as well as barium Hahn could also expect to discover krypton.[48]

But this was not all. Meitner calculated that the two nuclei created by the division of the uranium atom would possess a huge amount of energy, about 200 million electronvolts (MeV). The energy change in a chemical reaction is typically just a few electronvolts. At first the two physicists were puzzled about the source of this energy. Then they realized that a small amount of mass would be lost in the process of division, which Frisch later termed fission, after the process whereby two biological cells divide. About one-fifth the mass of a proton would be lost. Suddenly – thanks to Albert Einstein and relativity – all was clear. As Frisch explained, 'whenever mass disappears energy is created, according to Einstein's formula $E = mc^2$, and one-fifth of a proton mass was just equivalent to 200 MeV . . . it all fitted!'[49]

On 3 January 1939 Frisch returned to Copenhagen, barely able to contain his excitement. When he broke the news to Niels Bohr, the Danish physicist struck his head with his hand in astonishment. 'Oh what idiots we all have been!' said Bohr. It was 'wonderful' news.[50] Immediately Frisch and Meitner began writing up their explanation of this momentous discovery. As Meitner had now returned to Stockholm, they worked long-distance over the telephone. In the meantime, Bohr left on a prearranged visit to the United States and promised not to discuss the matter until Frisch and Meitner's paper appeared.

Meitner immediately wrote to Otto Hahn telling him the remarkable news that she was 'fairly certain' that the uranium atom had split in two. 'You now have a beautiful, wide field of work ahead of you,' she promised. Poignantly, the exiled Meitner added that 'even though I stand here with very empty hands, I am nevertheless happy for these wondrous findings'.[51]

On 21 December 1938, the same day that Meitner received Otto Hahn's extraordinary letter, Leo Szilard finally admitted defeat. He was now living in New York, at the King's Crown Hotel, near Columbia University. His brother Bela and Trude Weiss had finally heeded his warnings about Hitler and had also moved to New York. But no one would listen to Szilard when it came to atomic energy.

After five years of research, even Szilard had to reluctantly admit that his dream seemed to be little more than what Lord Rutherford had always said it was – moonshine. Even Einstein laughed at the idea. He had recently told the *New York Times* science journalist, William Laurence, that no one would find the secret of atomic energy by bombarding the nucleus. 'We are poor marksmen,' said Einstein with a wry smile, 'shooting at birds in the dark in a country where there are very few birds'.[52] The day that Frisch and Meitner were learning of the discovery that would make his dream of a chain reaction reality, Szilard sat down and wrote a terse note to the British Admiralty asking them to withdraw his patent. It must have been a desperately hard thing to do.

On 16 January 1939, Niels Bohr arrived in New York on board the SS *Drottningholm*. On the pier to greet him were Enrico Fermi and his wife Laura. They had themselves arrived just the previous month, having emigrated from fascist Italy and its newly passed anti-Semitic laws, stopping off in Stockholm to pick up Enrico's Nobel Prize in Physics. Laura Fermi thought that Bohr had aged: 'He stooped like a man carrying a heavy burden. His gaze, troubled and insecure, shifted from the one to the other of us, but stopped on none.'[53] Perhaps he had aged under the weight of the news he was carrying to the New World.

At first Bohr refused to discuss the discovery publicly, to allow Frisch and Meitner time to publish their paper and to claim priority.

Hahn and Strassmann's paper describing their experiment had appeared in Germany on 7 January but would not arrive in the United States until almost two weeks later. In the meantime, Leo Szilard remained in the dark.

During the transatlantic voyage, Bohr had discussed this revolution in the understanding of the atom with the Belgian physicist Léon Rosenfeld. Once in America, Rosenfeld went to Princeton where, knowing nothing of Bohr's promise to Frisch, he began to spread the extraordinary news. A few days later, Leo Szilard happened to be in Princeton visiting Eugene Wigner, who was in hospital suffering from jaundice. Szilard was staying in his friend's apartment and visiting each day to, as Wigner recalled, 'raise my spirits with gentle Hungarian conversation'.[54]

It was at Princeton that Szilard heard about fission. It must have been an extraordinary revelation. Like Fermi and the rest of the physics community, he had believed that the heavy uranium nucleus was absorbing neutrons to create new, larger elements, or trans-uranics. Indeed, the Italian experimentalist had won his Nobel prize for 'discovering' these elements. Now that explanation had been overturned. Suddenly, Leo Szilard realized that the vision of a self-sustaining neutron chain reaction was within reach: 'I saw immediately that these fragments, being heavier than corresponds to their charge, must emit neutrons, and if enough neutrons are emitted in this fission process, then it should be, of course, possible to sustain a chain reaction. All the things which H. G. Wells predicted appeared suddenly real to me.'[55]

In the course of their excited discussions in the Princeton infirmary, Wigner recalled that he and Szilard 'developed all of the essential points of fission theory'. In the coming weeks, as physicists such as Bohr and John Wheeler began publishing papers on fission, Wigner was 'pleased to see that . . . Szilard and I had seen farther . . . at several points'.[56]

Within days of learning about the fission of uranium, Szilard was writing to the financier Lewis L. Strauss (who would later chair the AEC), telling him about the 'very sensational new development in nuclear physics'. Szilard still had no official position at a university and he was always on the look-out for a potential source of funding.

It was 'exciting news for the average physicist', he told Strauss. 'The Dept of Physics at Princeton, where I spent the last few days, was like a stirred-up ant heap'. As ever, Szilard had his eye on future applications: fission might, he said, 'lead to a large-scale production of energy and radioactive elements, unfortunately also perhaps to atomic bombs'.

One can share Szilard's elation as he tells Strauss that the discovery has revived his high hopes of 1934, 'which I have as good as abandoned in the course of the last two years'.[57] The next day, despite developing a high temperature and a severe cold, Szilard made his way to the Broadway office of Western Union and cabled the British Admiralty:

REFERRING TO CP10 PATENTS 8142/36 KINDLY DISREGARD MY RECENT LETTER STOP WRITING LEO SZILARD.[58]

As Leo Szilard was cabling London, Bohr and Fermi were discussing fission publicly for the first time, at a conference at George Washington University organized by George Gamow. Across America, researchers hurried to their laboratories to duplicate Hahn and Strassmann's experiment. The media were quick to spot a good science story. POWER OF NEW ATOMIC BLAST GREATEST ACHIEVED ON EARTH, shouted the *Washington Evening Star*'s headlines; VAST ENERGY FREED BY URANIUM ATOM cried the *New York Times* at the end of January.[59] Science Service, a leading news agency, sent a journalist to interview Bohr. His report tried to calm public fears of a new superweapon with apocalyptic potential:

First of all, the physicists are anxious that there be no public alarm over the possibility of the world being blown to bits by their experiments. Writers and dramatists (H. G. Wells's scientific fantasies, the play *Wings over Europe* and J. B. Priestley's current novel, *Doomsday Men*) have over-emphasized this idea. While they are proceeding with their experiments with proper caution, they feel that there is no real danger except perhaps in their own laboratories.

Science Service also played down the idea of 'atom-motors', and that 'atomic energy may be used as some super-explosive, or as a military weapon'.[60] Indeed, until 1943 Bohr remained sceptical about exploiting the power of the atom. That was the year in which he escaped from Nazi Europe and finally saw with his own eyes the astonishing scientific and industrial achievement of the Manhattan Project. Only then did he acknowledge that the atomic bomb was not just science fiction. In contrast, Szilard never needed convincing. 'You know what fission means,' he told Edward Teller in Washington that month. 'It means bombs.'[61]

The American physicist Luis Alvarez was having his hair cut when he read the headlines about fission. With his hair only half-cut, he leapt from the barber's chair and rushed to tell his colleagues at the University of California, Berkeley. One of them, Glenn Seaborg, said that the discovery of fission 'seemed beautifully obvious'.[62] Around the world, other physicists reacted similarly. In Warsaw the young Polish physicist and future winner of a Nobel Peace Prize, Joseph Rotblat, repeated Hahn and Strassmann's experiment as soon as he heard about it. In April he travelled to England to work with neutron-discoverer James Chadwick. Within six months he was conducting feasibility studies on an atomic bomb.

Rotblat had 'always believed that science should be used in the service of mankind. The notion of utilizing my knowledge to produce an awesome weapon of destruction was abhorrent to me.' But an article by German scientist Siegfried Flügge on atomic explosives, published that summer in the renowned science journal *Die Naturwissenschaften*, raised the appalling possibility that Hitler's scientists might build the bomb first. 'The only way to stop the Germans from using it against us', reasoned Rotblat, 'would be if we too had the bomb and threatened to retaliate.' It was the logic of deterrence, the rationale that would push the world to the brink of nuclear Armageddon during the second half of the twentieth century. But Rotblat later rejected deterrence because 'a psychopath' like Hitler would use atomic weapons even when faced with the threat of annihilation.[63] As Szilard said in 1950, such a leader might even press the button of a doomsday machine.

Around the world, atomic physicists were quick to realize both the promise and the threat of the new discovery. In Paris, Frédéric Joliot-Curie and his team immediately began exploring the possibility of a neutron chain reaction. But on 2 February 1939 they received a letter from Leo Szilard with a request that astonished them. He asked them to refrain from publishing anything on fission. Szilard had not made this extraordinary request lightly. A discussion with Enrico Fermi had left him deeply troubled. Isidor Rabi, at New York's Columbia University, had told him that when he had raised the possibility that fission could lead to a bomb, Fermi's response was 'Nuts!' Unfortunately, neither Rabi's nor Szilard's grasp of American slang was advanced enough to translate this expression. So they paid Fermi a visit.

When they tackled the Italian physicist about the chances of building an atomic bomb, Fermi reluctantly admitted, 'well there is a remote possibility that neutrons may be emitted in the fission of uranium and then of course a chain reaction can be made'.

Rabi pressed him. 'What do you mean by "remote possibility"?'

'Well, ten per cent,' said Fermi, grudgingly.

'Ten per cent is not a remote possibility if it means that we may die of it,' replied Rabi. 'If I have pneumonia and the doctor tells me that there is a remote possibility that I might die, and it's ten per cent, I get excited about it!'

After this conversation it was apparent to Leo Szilard that he and Fermi had very different attitudes to the implications of fission: 'We both wanted to be conservative, but Fermi thought that the conservative thing was to play down the possibility that this may happen, and I thought the conservative thing was to assume that it would happen and take all the necessary precautions.'[64]

Szilard now began to fight two battles to save the world. The first was scientific: to prove that atomic power was finally within reach. The second was political: he wanted to prevent German scientists from discovering the secret of atomic energy first. His letter to Joliot-Curie was part of this battle. But scientists always abhor secrecy, and the French scientists failed to recognize the threat from German science. When Joliot-Curie discussed it with his colleagues, Hans von Halban's view was that 'we would be mad not to publish'. Lew Kowarski – a fan of H. G. Wells – agreed: 'someone will be first; why not us?'[65]

They therefore rejected Szilard's proposal and instead began working flat out to prove that a chain reaction was possible. Their groundbreaking research papers, published in March and April 1939, would, as Kowarski later put it, 'set alarm bells ringing in the major capitals', including Berlin.[66] For the time being, Leo Szilard had to admit defeat on this front.

In his scientific battle, Szilard made better progress. Together with Walter Zinn, who later helped to build the Chicago atomic pile, he set up an experiment at Columbia University to see whether neutrons were produced when the uranium atom splits in two – if they were, then his idea of a self-sustaining chain reaction would finally have become reality. Since that day in London in 1933 when he first thought of how to release the energy of the atom, Szilard had been trying to convince other people. Just the year before, in 1938, General Electric sent Szilard packing with the insulting comment that nuclear energy was strictly 'for the science fiction fans'.[67] Now, in a deserted laboratory on a cold March evening in 1939, Szilard would finally discover whether he had been tilting at windmills for the last six years.

At first the screen of the oscilloscope remained blank. Then Walter Zinn realized that it wasn't plugged in. Both men laughed nervously at this silly mistake and peered again at the grey screen. They didn't have long to wait. 'We turned the switch and we saw the flashes,' recalled Szilard. Uranium fission did create additional neutrons. 'We watched them for a little while and then we switched everything off and went home. That night there was very little doubt in my mind that the world was headed for grief.'[68]

By early summer 1939, rapid progress had been made towards achieving a chain reaction. In February, Niels Bohr had revealed that it was the isotope of uranium known as uranium-235 that was most susceptible to fission. But it existed in very small quantities, at the level of 0.7 per cent in natural uranium, which is nearly all uranium-238. Anyone wanting to produce a bomb would first have to overcome the huge practical problem of separating uranium-235 from natural uranium. As far as Bohr was concerned, this meant that no one would be building atomic bombs in the near future.

In March, both Szilard and Joliot-Curie detected secondary neutrons during the fission of uranium. The following month, Joliot-Curie and his team published their view that a chain reaction using uranium was within reach. In Germany, the physical chemist Paul

Harteck – a friend of Szilard's who had once worked at Fritz Haber's institute in Berlin – promptly contacted the War Office. 'We take the liberty of calling your attention to the newest development in nuclear physics,' Harteck wrote, 'which in our opinion, will probably make it possible to produce an explosive many orders of magnitude more powerful than conventional ones . . . That country which first makes use of it has an unsurpassable advantage over the others.'[69]

In America, while the German War Office was considering Harteck's research proposal for a super-explosive, the *New York Times* reported that members of the American Physical Society had argued publicly 'over the probability of some scientist blowing up a sizeable portion of the earth with a tiny bit of uranium'. The physicists argued that if the difficulties surrounding the separation of uranium-235 could be surmounted, then the 'creation of a nuclear explosion which would wreck as large an area as New York City would be comparatively easy. A single neutron particle, striking the nucleus of a uranium atom . . . would be sufficient to set off a chain reaction of millions of other atoms.'[70]

Even before this dramatic claim was made, Eugene Wigner had written to Leo Szilard telling him that he now felt 'very strongly, that the US Government should be advised of the situation'.[71] Szilard agreed. In July, three members of the Hungarian Quartet met in New York to decide on a plan of action. Wigner travelled to the metropolis from Princeton. Edward Teller was teaching during the summer at Columbia University. Leo Szilard was busy designing what became in 1942 the world's first operational nuclear reactor.

All three (together with another colleague from Berlin, Victor Weisskopf) had been involved in the attempt to suppress news of advances in fission research. Now that the details were out in the open, they agreed that the situation was serious. The publication the previous month of Siegfried Flügge's paper 'Can Nuclear Energy Be Utilized for Practical Purposes?' had shocked them all. Flügge was a colleague of Otto Hahn's at the Kaiser Wilhelm Istitute for Chemistry. It was obvious that German scientists were hot on the trail of the atomic bomb. In England, Joseph Rotblat came to the same conclusion, and his thoughts turned to designing an atomic bomb, despite his hatred of war.

The Hungarians had already made initial approaches to the US military, but without success. 'It's just some crazy worrying by a few foreigners,' said Wigner, summing up the attitude of the American authorities.[72] What also concerned the Hungarians was the possibility that the Nazis might gain control of the rich uranium mines in the Congo, then a colony of Belgium. In an attempt to prevent this, Szilard and Wigner decided to enlist the help of the most famous scientist on the planet, Albert Einstein, who just happened to be close friends with the Queen of Belgium.

The BBC correspondent Alistair Cooke once marvelled that 'Szilard – a scientific brain beyond our comprehension – couldn't drive a car'. His driver on Wednesday 12 July was Wigner, who collected Szilard from his hotel in his Dodge coupé. Together they drove out to Peconic, Long Island, where the great physicist was on vacation, dividing his time between his two great passions – physics and sailing.

According to Wigner, they found the 60-year-old Einstein 'dressed in an old shirt and unpressed pants, apparently perfectly content to be thinking only of physics'.[73] They sat together on the porch of the white weatherboarded cottage, drinking iced tea and discussing the latest application of physics – atomic bombs. Einstein was still ploughing his lonely furrow in physics, searching for the elusive theory that would unify the quantum with the cosmic realm. He had not heard about fission. But when he realized that chain reactions might be possible, he said softly, '*Daran habe ich gar nicht gedacht*' – 'I hadn't thought of that.'[74]

Einstein was 'horrified' by the idea that the Nazis might build an atomic bomb.[75] With that in mind he was happy to sound the alarm, even though, as Szilard said later, 'it was quite possible that the alarm might prove to be a false alarm.'[76] Sitting on his Peconic porch, Einstein dictated a letter in German for the Belgian ambassador in Washington, warning that superbombs might be made using uranium from their mines in the Congo. It was also agreed to send a letter to the State Department informing them that they intended to warn Belgium. After this, the two Hungarian scientists returned to New York. Before they left, they watched as Einstein climbed into his dinghy and sailed off contentedly across the bay.

'This story shows that we were all green,' Szilard said later. 'We

Albert Einstein and Leo Szilard re-enact the writing of their letter to President Roosevelt, for the 1946 'March of Time' documentary Atomic Power.

did not know our way around in America, we did not know how to do business, and we certainly did not know how to deal with the government.'[77] Instead of posting the letters, Szilard turned to some insiders for advice. One of the men he talked to was Dr Alexander Sachs, the vice president of a Wall Street bank and a personal friend of President Roosevelt. Sachs told Szilard that they had it all wrong. This was a matter for Roosevelt himself.

So Szilard made another journey out to Peconic to see Einstein, this time chauffeured by Edward Teller. Einstein greeted them in his dressing gown and slippers and dictated a new letter. But it was no simple matter writing to the President of the United States of America. 'We did not know just how many words one could put in a letter which a President is supposed to read. How many pages does the fission of uranium rate?'[78] Einstein suggested a brief outline of a letter, and Szilard returned to New York in Teller's 1935 Plymouth to prepare two versions for Einstein's approval. The typist hired by

Szilard soon decided that he was a 'nut' when she heard that the letters were addressed to Roosevelt and concerned a new superbomb.[79]

In the end, Einstein preferred the longer of the two versions. This letter, dated 2 August 1939, is the one that Sachs eventually took to his friend, President Roosevelt. At auction in 1986, the shorter version (which was not even sent) sold for $220,000. Just as Jacobus Laningdale went to the President with his idea for a biological weapon in Jack London's story, so now the physicists presented their proposal for a superweapon to FDR himself. Einstein and Szilard's letter warned him that 'extremely powerful bombs' could be made using uranium. 'A single bomb of this type, carried by boat and exploded in a port, might very well destroy the whole port together with some of the surrounding territory,' they wrote. They warned the President that the Germans were already trying to build the bomb, employing the formidable scientific resources at Dahlem in Berlin where both Einstein and Szilard had once worked.

As well as drawing the President's attention to this dangerous situation, the letter also proposed that scientists should begin working closely with the government:

In view of this situation you may think it desirable to have some permanent contact maintained between the Administration and the group of physicists working on chain reactions in America. One possible way of achieving this might be for you to entrust with this task a person who has your confidence and who could perhaps serve in an inofficial [sic] capacity.[80]

It is clear that Leo Szilard saw himself as ideally suited to fulfilling this role. But although over the last six years he had spent more time than anyone else thinking about the chain reaction and its impact on society, this project would prove too big even for the 'Director General'.

14

Conceived in Fear

> *Black as vermin, crawling in echelon*
> *Beneath the cloud-floor, the bombers come:*
> *The heavy angels, carrying harm in*
> *Their wombs that ache to be rid of death.*
> *This is the seed that grows for ruin,*
> *The iron-embryo conceived in fear.*
> Cecil Day-Lewis, 'Bombers' (1938)

In the aftermath of World War I, Pierrepont B. Noyes, an American Rhineland Commissioner, wrote a thriller called *The Pallid Giant* about the causes of war. Noyes identified fear – the 'pallid giant' of the title – as the culprit. 'The ghastly development of war's destructiveness during the last fifty years', he wrote, has made nations 'think in terms of fear, and there is no more deadly poison in human counsels than fear.'[1]

The Pallid Giant was reissued after the destruction of Hiroshima and Nagasaki. The novel described how a previous, advanced civilization had wiped itself off the face of the earth in a 'holocaust of self-destruction'.[2] In 1909, Frederick Soddy had speculated about a mythical Eden, an ancient civilization created and destroyed by the power of the atom. Now, in the atomic age, this idea gained a new significance. 'Think for a moment,' says a character in *The Pallid Giant*,

what could happen to a race of men whose material inventions placed in their hands unlimited power for destruction before they had developed moral

inhibitions sufficient to prevent their using that power to destroy themselves
. . . Put it another way: what would happen to men possessed of a 100 percent
power to conquer others and only 25 percent power to conquer themselves?[3]

For many people in 1945, this seemed an accurate assessment of the
situation facing the world.

Noyes suggests that when a civilization discovers the greatest secret
of nature, atomic energy, it marks the final stage in the evolution of
human destructiveness. Then, as happens in *The Pallid Giant*, the way
is clear to create 'a force of universal death', the ultimate superweapon.
For Noyes in 1927, this was a scientific weapon about which there
had been much speculation – an atomic death ray.[4] After the invention
of this weapon there could be no talk about a war to end wars, as
Wells had suggested in *The World Set Free*. According to Noyes, in
a world where armies face each other with weapons of absolute
destructiveness 'war would end all war, by ending man'.[5]

Noyes was right. It was fear that led to the invention of the atomic
bomb. The émigré scientists who had already suffered at the hands of
the Nazis were understandably afraid of what Hitler would do if
armed with an atomic bomb. But paradoxically, these scientists were
also motivated by the hope that – as H. G. Wells had imagined
back in 1913 – atomic energy would herald a new dawn for human
civilization. The superweapon itself would, if terrible enough, force
the world to renounce war. But the utopian Wells was also enough of
a realist to know that much blood would be shed first. Utopia would
only be achieved after humankind had passed through the elemental
fires of the atomic bombs. For many physicists, including Leo Szilard,
Eugene Wigner and Edward Teller, even after the horrors of Hiroshima
and Nagasaki, still the dream lived on – the dream of unlimited energy
and absolute power.

Fear made the atomic bomb a reality in 1945. Fear of Hitler's
scientists galvanized America's unequalled military, industrial and –
thanks to the Third Reich's anti-Semitic policies – scientific resources
into making a supreme effort. As it turned out, this fear, although not
irrational, was unfounded. The German atomic bomb project, riven
from the start by internal rivalry, never came near to creating a usable
weapon. Despite possessing some of the world's greatest scientists –

albeit Aryan ones, such as Hahn and Heisenberg – their science was flawed from the outset. For instance, they remained unaware that pure graphite could be used in a reactor (something Szilard grasped at the start of the war) and were convinced that the critical mass needed for a bomb was measured in tons rather than a few pounds.

In its scale and speed, the Manhattan Project was an accomplishment beyond even the imaginings of most science fiction writers. William Laurence, the *New York Times* reporter who was the only journalist allowed access to the atomic bomb project during wartime, recalls chemist and Harvard president James B. Conant saying to him, 'they won't believe you when the time comes that this can be told. It is more fantastic than Jules Verne.' The pragmatic journalist replied bluntly: 'They'll believe it if it works!'[6]

By 1947, Laurence could boast that 'only three other men have seen as many of the bombs in action as I have'. Like many others, he was clearly awestruck by the terrible power of the superbomb. Standing in front of the Fat Man plutonium bomb before it was dropped on Nagasaki, Laurence felt that he was 'in the presence of the supernatural'.[7]

According to Laurence, one of the Manhattan Project's greatest achievements was 'bringing together into a smoothly functioning team the long-hairs and the short-hairs, who in normal peacetime used to growl at each other from a safe distance'.[8] It was not the first time that scientists had mobilized on behalf of their nation in wartime: Chemists in America and Europe had done so during World War I. But the scale of the Manhattan Project dwarfed all previous scientific collaborations with the military. Its success made it a model for weapons research in the cold war. The long-hairs and short-hairs were stuck with each other.

Leo Szilard once said that his favourite past-time was 'baiting brass hats'.[9] He was never happy taking orders from the military, or anyone else for that matter. Einstein's letter to President Roosevelt – partly drafted by Szilard – showed the key role the Hungarian physicist thought he himself should play in the development of the atomic bomb. Britain and Germany were already at war when Alexander Sachs finally saw Roosevelt in October 1939. The President didn't understand the physics, but he immediately grasped the potential significance of a new super-explosive and wasted no time in setting up a committee to investigate Szilard's claims.

The Advisory Committee on Uranium met for the first time on 21 October 1939. Wigner, Teller, Szilard and Sachs were present, along with Lyman J. Briggs, Director of the Bureau of Standards, America's national physics laboratory since 1901, as well as Lieutenant Colonel Keith F. Adamson and Commander Gilbert C. Hoover, ordnance experts from the army and navy respectively.

At the meeting, Szilard patiently explained his idea for a uranium–graphite pile and the possibility that one uranium bomb could have the power of 20,000 tons of chemical explosive. Colonel Adamson, from the Aberdeen Weapons Proving Ground, was distinctly unimpressed by this talk of an atomic bomb that could devastate an entire city. He told Szilard that he had been standing next to an ordnance depot when it exploded and the force had not even knocked him down. The colonel openly sneered at the science fiction idea of a superweapon. 'At Aberdeen,' he told the scientists, 'we're offering a $10,000 reward to anyone who can use a death ray to kill the goat we have tethered to a post. That goat is still perfectly healthy.'[10]

Adamson then proceeded to lecture the scientists. 'He told us that it was naive to believe that we could make a significant contribution to defense by creating a new explosive,' recalled Szilard. 'He said that if a new weapon is created, it usually takes two wars before one can know whether the weapon is any good or not.'[11] Eugene Wigner, a quiet and thoughtful man, had sat there impassively as the military man lectured them. But his next words made the mild-mannered Wigner hopping mad.

'Gentlemen,' said Colonel Adamson patronizingly, 'armaments are not what decides war and makes history. Wars are won through the morale of the civilian population.'[12]

Barely able to conceal his anger, and speaking in a 'high-pitched voice',[13] Wigner rounded on the colonel: 'If this is true then perhaps we should cut the army budget thirty percent and spread that wonderful money through the civilian population.'[14]

It's fair to say that this first official encounter between long-hairs and short-hairs did not produce a meeting of minds. However, it did result in the first government funding for the atomic bomb – a modest

$6,000, a figure plucked out of the air by Teller, to help buy graphite for Szilard's experimental reactor. 'After the meeting,' said Teller, 'Szilard nearly murdered me for the modesty of my request; and Wigner, in his gentler way, seemed ready to assist him.'[15] But the Hungarian conspiracy had made a big step forward in pushing the US Government towards a superbomb project, an enterprise that would eventually cost the American tax payers $2 billion, around $50 billion in today's money.

The difficulties the scientists encountered in the Advisory Committee on Uranium set the trend for the next two years. At every step of the way, Leo Szilard and his colleagues had to overcome scepticism and constantly nag the government to commit funding. But tenacity was one of Szilard's God-given gifts, and he kept at it until he got what he wanted. In the meantime, he and Enrico Fermi kept themselves busy designing a uranium–graphite pile at Columbia University. He also supplied Sachs with a steady stream of memos on potential applications of atomic energy. Armed with these science fictional speculations about vast ship-borne bombs, radiological weapons and atomic powerhouses, Sachs kept up the pressure on the government.

One of Szilard's most important scientific contributions to the bomb project was his discovery that it was essential to remove the boron usually present in graphite. Because boron absorbed neutrons, it seemed at first that graphite would be unsuitable as a moderator in an atomic pile. This was what stymied the German attempts to build a reactor.[16] Fortunately, unlike Joliot-Curie, Szilard decided to keep this important discovery secret from the scientific community. Despite heavy criticism from Fermi, he refused to publish his research because of its strategic importance. Szilard's insight into this problem, and his skill at negotiating with industrial suppliers to secure pure graphite, gave the American project a head start. According to Bethe, 'Szilard contributed in a very major way to the early success of perhaps the most important branch of the Manhattan Project.'[17] As early as 1940, even German scientists realized that reactors were the key to producing the new fissile element, plutonium. And Leo Szilard now knew how to build a reactor.

*

From 5 September 1940 until the middle of November, London endured nightly bombing attacks by the Luftwaffe. In the Blitz, 13,000 tons of high explosives and 12,000 incendiary bombs were dropped on the British capital. When Bela's wife expressed her sorrow at this outrage, Leo remarked gloomily that 'Before this war is over there will be bombs thousands of times more powerful than those in the Blitz.'[18]

In Britain, other scientists exiled from Germany and driven by a fear of what Hitler's physicists might be discovering were engaged in calculations that would make Szilard's predictions a reality. The British scientific community believed – in common with Niels Bohr – that the technical difficulty of separating the fissile isotope uranium-235 from natural uranium would rule out an atomic bomb for many years. Churchill (advised by Szilard's friend at Oxford, Frederick Lindemann) told his Cabinet this in August 1939. Rudolf Peierls, a German physicist now working in England, thought so too. He had calculated that a critical mass of natural uranium – the amount needed to create a self-sustaining and potentially explosive reaction – would be as much as several tons. He didn't even bother to work out a critical mass for uranium-235 as no one thought it was possible to separate sufficient quantities of this isotope from the far more abundant uranium-238.

But that was before Lise Meitner's nephew, Otto Frisch, began to consider the problem. Like Peierls, Frisch was now working in England, at Birmingham University. He decided that uranium-235 could be separated. But how much of it would be needed to create an explosion? For the answer to this he turned in 1940 to his friend Peierls. Together they calculated the critical mass of uranium-235. 'To my amazement,' said Frisch, 'it was very much smaller than I had expected; it was not a matter of tons, but something like a pound or two'[19] – in other words, about the size of a large egg (uranium is about as dense as gold). In a flash, both men saw that it was possible after all to build an atomic bomb, and not one that had to be carried to its target on a ship, as Einstein and Szilard had told Roosevelt, but a bomb small enough to be dropped from an aircraft.

Frisch and Peierls went to see Mark Oliphant, their Australian boss at Birmingham, with their discovery. He immediately realized its significance and told them to write up their findings in a report for the British Government. Their brief memorandum, 'On the Construction of a "Super-bomb", Based on a Nuclear Chain Reaction in Uranium', was finished in March 1940. Oliphant sent it with a covering note to Henry Tizard, chair of the government committee set up to explore ways of using science in the war against Germany. Tizard was impressed, and Oliphant was instructed to set up a small subcommittee to assess the feasibility of the atomic bomb. The members of the subcommittee included John Cockcroft and James Chadwick. They met at Burlington House, Piccadilly, where twenty years earlier – beneath the portrait of Sir Isaac Newton – the announcement had been made that eclipse observations had confirmed Einstein's general theory of relativity. Now another group of British scientists met to consider a more deadly implication of relativity: the vast reservoir of energy trapped in the heart of matter.

In their memo, Frisch and Peierls described in detail how a bomb could be built using a sphere of uranium 'made in two (or more) parts which are brought together first when the explosion is wanted'.[20] In the bomb dropped on Hiroshima, the uranium was brought to explosive criticality by firing a piece of uranium-235 into a subcritical mass of the isotope. Frisch also explained how uranium-235 could be separated by a thermal diffusion method using gaseous uranium hexafluoride, producing 1 gram a day.

They made plain the enormous explosive power of a uranium bomb, and also highlighted 'the effects of . . . radiation on human beings'. Describing for the first time in a scientific paper the effects of fallout, Frisch and Peierls noted that 'it is difficult to tell what will happen to the radioactive material after the explosion. Most of it will probably be blown into the air and carried away by the wind. This cloud of radioactive material will kill everybody within a strip estimated to be several miles long.' In a passage which anticipated the lethally radioactive black rain that fell after the Hiroshima bomb, they predicted that 'if it rained the danger would be even worse because active material would be carried down to the ground and stick to it, and persons entering the contaminated area would be subjected to dangerous radiation even after days'. The scientists also warned that, because its effects could not be contained or predicted, 'the bomb could probably not be used without killing large numbers of civilians, and this may make it unsuitable as a weapon for use by this country'.[21]

The atomic bomb, said Frisch and Peierls, would be 'practically irresistible'. They predicted that 'effective protection is hardly possible' against such 'super-explosions'. Only 'deep cellars or tunnels' might offer some protection, but only if air could be supplied from an uncontaminated area. As no shelter could offer protection against the bomb, and as 'Germany is, or will be, in the possession of this weapon', they argued that the only practical policy was 'counter-threat with a similar bomb'. For this reason they advised the speedy development of an atomic bomb. In the meantime they recommended that 'detection squads' be set up to monitor radioactivity levels in the event of surprise attacks.[22] The following year, Frisch saw James Chadwick armed with a Geiger counter checking bomb craters in Liverpool, afraid that German planes might already be dropping radiological, or 'dirty', bombs.

By late summer 1941, the scientists had convinced the British Government that an atomic bomb could be made. At the end of August, Winston Churchill approved the proposal to develop a bomb. 'Although personally I am quite content with the existing explosives,' he wrote, 'I feel we must not stand in the path of improvement'.[23]

As Churchill was giving the go-ahead to the British atomic bomb (innocuously code-named 'Tube Alloys'), Mark Oliphant was on his way to the United States to find out why his American colleagues had not yet responded to the British scientists' report. The bluff Australian was not impressed with what he found on the other side of the Atlantic. The attitude of Lyman Briggs, a former soil scientist now nearing retirement, typified for Oliphant the lack of urgency among his American allies. Briggs showed Oliphant the Frisch–Peierls memo, together with other British reports on the atomic bomb, locked away in a safe in his office. 'No one had read them,' said the exasperated Oliphant. 'I don't believe that mild-mannered old gentleman had read them! Not one of them knew what I was talking about.'[24]

'Amazed and distressed', Oliphant voiced his concerns in a typically robust manner to everyone he met.[25] He made a deep impression on cyclotron-builder Ernest O. Lawrence at Berkeley. 'The waste of time is criminal,' Lawrence agreed.[26] He immediately arranged for Oliphant to see Vannevar Bush and James Conant. Bush, an engineer by train-ing, headed up the newly created Office of Scientific Research and Development (OSRD), an organization which oversaw the mobil-ization of American science for military purposes. Conant was the Chairman of the National Defense Research Committee (NDRC), a subsidiary of the OSRD, which had absorbed Briggs's Uranium Committee the year before.

Unknown to Oliphant, a secret copy of the British report had reached Bush and Conant – despite appearances, the atomic bomb was quite definitely on the agenda. Gradually, Oliphant's brusque lobbying won the two men round. When Bush officially received the report, he took it personally to the President on 9 October 1941. Slowly but surely, the machinery of American bureaucracy was gearing up to build the most terrible weapon the world had yet seen.

On Saturday 6 December 1941, a cold and crisp Washington morn-ing, James Conant convened a meeting of the key players in the Uranium Committee. He had important news for his colleagues: FDR had authorized an 'all-out' project with the ultimate aim of building an atomic superbomb.[27] The newly reorganized project was to be known as S-1, Section 1 of the OSRD. Conant told them that Harold Urey was to continue his promising work on isotope separation by diffusion at Columbia, while Lawrence would work on electro-magnetic separation at Berkeley. In Chicago, Arthur Holly Compton would pursue theoretical studies and bomb design. He was also to investigate the new element plutonium and its possible use in a bomb. Two years after Einstein and Szilard wrote to Roosevelt, America was finally set on a course to build the atomic bomb. The next day, Pearl Harbor was attacked without warning by Japanese planes, killing 2,403 American soldiers and civilians. The United States of America was at war.

In November 1940, for the first time in a decade, Leo Szilard began receiving a salary. It was paid by James Conant's NDRC. Together with Enrico Fermi, Szilard was developing a graphite-moderated reac-tor at Columbia. As ever, he was reluctant to get his hands dirty handling the graphite. With his new income he hired two assistants for that – Bernard Feld and John Marshall, Jr. When he heard this,

Edward Teller couldn't resist nicknaming his Hungarian friend *Feld-marschall* – 'field marshal'. At least it was a step up from Director General.

Before the President finally gave the go-ahead for the atomic bomb project, Szilard had been growing increasingly impatient with the US Government. Like Frisch and Peierls in Britain, he was still classed as an enemy alien by the authorities. Ironically, the very scientists who knew most about the atomic bomb were deemed untrustworthy by the Allies. As a result, neither Szilard nor Fermi were told about the new low estimates for the critical mass of a bomb. Neither did they know that Harold Urey had made considerable progress by the end of 1941 in separating uranium-235. 'Urey's contract specified that he was not supposed to discuss his results with Fermi and me, who were not cleared,' said Szilard. 'Therefore we were not able to put two and two together and come out with the simple statement that bombs could be made out of reasonable quantities of uranium-235.'[28]

Leo Szilard credited Mark Oliphant with kick-starting the Manhattan Project. Oliphant disregarded 'international etiquette' and told 'all those who were willing to listen what he thought of us', wrote Szilard later:

Considerations other than those of military security prevent me from revealing the exact expressions he used. If Congress knew the true history of the atomic energy project, I have no doubt but that it would create a special medal to be given to meddling foreigners for distinguished services, and Dr Oliphant would be the first to receive one.[29]

As a result, by the start of 1942 there was a new sense of urgency about the atomic bomb. Szilard and the other 'meddling foreigners' were delighted. In January, Szilard moved to Chicago. Compton had insisted that Szilard and Fermi relocate to the city. Compton now had a clear plan of action. It was a tight schedule: they were aiming for a chain reaction by January 1943 and a functional bomb by January 1945.

Moving to Chicago annoyed Leo Szilard. He was happy in New York where he had established a network of scientific and business contacts. His brother Bela was there, as was Trude, who was now working at a New York hospital. It was the first sign that the physicists were losing control of the project. According to the historian of the atomic bomb Richard Rhodes, from the outset of the American atomic energy programme

scientists were summarily denied a voice in deciding the political and military uses of the weapons they were proposing to build . . . A scientist could choose to help or not to help build nuclear weapons. That was his only choice. The surrender of any further authority in the matter was the price of admission to what would grow to be a separate, secret state with separate sovereignty linked to the public state through the person and by the sole authority of the President.[30]

Despite his irritation at being forced to move to Chicago, Szilard soon felt at home living on the campus, with its late-nineteenth-century, grey-stone neo-Gothic buildings. It reminded him of Oxford, but it was not that different from leafy Dahlem either. Rather than living in a hotel, he rented a room with maid service in the comfortable Quadrangle Club, and settled down to work on his brainchild.

As far as the Manhattan Project was concerned, the University of Chicago was known by the code name of the Metallurgical Labora-tory, shortened to Met Lab. Szilard eventually became the Met Lab's chief physicist. The physicists worked first in the three-storey Eckhart Hall. Their objective was to achieve what Szilard had first visualized back in Russell Square in 1933 – a self-sustaining chain reaction with neutrons. Inside what was essentially a nuclear reactor, the storm of neutrons released from the fissioning uranium would transmute the uranium-238 into the new element, plutonium. With this element, the scientists hoped to be able to build atomic bombs without the need for the difficult process of separating uranium-235 from uranium-238. Although Szilard never worked on the design of bombs, Met Lab's work was crucial to the success of the whole bomb project. The military importance of Met Lab was apparent when armed guards were posted at Eckhart Hall to check passes.

Szilard never liked being surrounded by armed guards. He hated bureaucracy even more, and as the federal government became ever more involved in the project, so this steadily increased. During 1942, he subjected the leaders of the project to a stream of complaints about

Fourth-anniversary reunion of CP-1 scientists on the steps of Eckhart Hall, Chicago, 2 December 1946. Front row, from left to right: Enrico Fermi, Walter Zinn, Albert Wattenberg and Herbert Anderson. Leona Woods Marshall is in the middle row, and next to her in the raincoat is Leo Szilard.

slow progress and the growing threat from Germany. On 26 May 1942 he wrote to Vannevar Bush: 'Nobody can tell now whether we shall be ready before German bombs wipe out American cities.'[31]

The implication behind all these complaints was of poor management. Szilard always believed he should have been in charge of the atomic bomb project. After all, no one had invested more time, energy and brainpower in atomic energy – its science, engineering and political implications – than Leo Szilard. Now he could only stand by and watch as his brainchild was gradually taken over by other people. 'If the project could have been built on ideas alone,' said Wigner later, 'Szilard alone could have done it.'[32] Although he bore the brunt of Szilard's incessant kvetching, Compton respected the troublesome Hungarian. He reassured his irate boss, Bush, by saying that Szilard was 'one of the most valuable members of our organization'.[33] But he couldn't halt the complaints.

As Teller ruefully acknowledged, Szilard's name means 'doggedly determined, or to put it less politely, rather stubborn'.[34] In September 1942, Szilard prepared a memo for the project with the provocative title 'What Is Wrong With Us?' In it he admitted that 'I am, as a rule, rather outspoken, and if I do not call a spade a spade I find it rather difficult to find a suitable name for it.'[35] Again he complained about delays, as well as an increasing tendency to force scientists to concentrate on a very specific area of research. This 'compartmentalization' of knowledge was a security measure imposed by Washington to prevent the spread of classified information. Soon every aspect of the project was on a need-to-know basis. But, as Szilard later put it, 'compartmentalization of information poisons the discussion'.[36] Scientific progress depends on the free flow of information, and that, in Szilard's view, was not happening. It was ironic that this complaint came from the man who had done more than anyone to introduce secrecy into the science of atomic energy.

But in this 1942 memo, Szilard did a great deal more than just kvetch. He also demonstrated once again the depth of his thinking on the implications of atomic energy. Writing weeks before the world's first atomic pile went critical in Chicago, he called for all the scientists on the project to devote 'more thought to the ultimate political necessities which will arise out of our present work'.[37] With a dig at the johnny-come-latelys in Washington, many of whom had once dismissed his idea of atomic energy as science fiction, Szilard began by saying that 'these lines are primarily addressed to those with whom I have shared for years the knowledge that it is within our power to construct atomic bombs'. Ominously, he predicted that such bombs 'will bring disaster upon the world'. 'We cannot have peace', Szilard told his colleagues,

in a world in which various sovereign nations have atomic bombs in the possession of their armies and any of these armies could win a war within twenty-four hours after it starts one. One has to visualize a world in which a lone airplane could appear over a big city like Chicago, drop his bomb, and thereby destroy the city in a single flash. Not one house may be left standing and the radioactive substances scattered by the bomb may make the area uninhabitable for some time to come.[38]

Szilard looked into the future and saw that the fears of science fiction writers would soon be realized. In that future lay the nightmare of a single aircraft appearing far above a city, carrying a weapon that could annihilate the whole metropolis. Both H. G. Wells and Jack London had fantasized about this prospect at the beginning of the century. In Arthur Train and Robert Williams Wood's *The Man Who Rocked the Earth*, their saviour scientist, Pax, also used airpower to force the world to acknowledge that 'either war or the human race must pass away forever'.[39] That moment was fast approaching. Szilard saw clearly the dangers that faced a world armed with superweapons yet divided by fear and mutual distrust. More than any other scientist at this time, he believed that he and his colleagues had a special responsibility to show the politicians that there was a more important prize to be won than being the first nation to own a superbomb. Soon every physicist around the world would be able to master the science of the atomic bomb. Then the real prize – peace – would be lost.

'Those who have originated the work on this terrible weapon,' wrote Szilard, 'and those who have materially contributed to its development, have, before God and the World, the duty to see to it that it should be ready to be used at the proper time and in the proper way.'[40] It was a powerful reminder to the scientists of their responsibilities as human beings. But, once again, no one was listening to Szilard's warnings. Far from having a greater say in how the bomb was to be used, the scientists would become ever more distanced from the results of their labour. Despite inventing the world's most powerful weapon, the saviour scientist would soon be powerless. He or she would become a mere cog in a military machine.

A few days before Szilard wrote those words, on 17 September 1942, the army had taken control of the S-1 project. On 23 September, the 46-year-old military engineer Leslie R. Groves was promoted to brigadier general and officially took command of the secret project known to the army as the Manhattan Engineer District. According to a colleague, he was 'the biggest sonovabitch I've ever met in my life, but also one of the most capable individuals'.[41] The man who had just overseen the construction of the Pentagon was ruthless, arrogant and rude. But he was also efficient and indefatigable. If anyone could build the bomb and keep the long-hairs in line, General Groves could.

Groves visited the Met Lab on 5 October. As far as Szilard was concerned, it was hostility at first sight. 'How can you work with people like that?' he asked after meeting Groves.[42] There would be open warfare between the two men until the Manhattan Project had achieved its goal. Then Groves finally succeeded in doing what he had wanted to do from day one: he had Szilard excluded from official research on atomic energy.

Groves never trusted Szilard, the one scientist who did most to push America into building the atomic bomb. 'Groves thought Szilard was the perfect spy', said fellow Met Lab scientist Samuel K. Allison.[43] Szilard had a 'German' accent, erratic movement patterns, and he never missed an opportunity to challenge authority. On one occasion Groves even drafted an order for Szilard's immediate arrest and internment as an enemy alien. Fortunately, Secretary of War Henry L. Stimson refused to sign it. Later, in 1963, Groves remarked bitterly that 'few enemies were causing us as much trouble' as Leo Szilard.[44]

Groves had Szilard placed under round-the-clock surveillance. An Army Counterintelligence report from 24 June 1943 provides a wonderful snapshot of the eccentric and, to the military, suspiciously foreign scientist:

Subject is of Jewish extraction, has a fondness for delicacies and frequently makes purchases in delicatessen stores, usually eats his breakfast in drug stores and other meals in restaurants, walks a great deal when he cannot secure a taxi, usually is shaved in a barber shop, speaks occasionally in a foreign tongue, and associates mostly with people of Jewish extraction. He is inclined to be rather absent minded and eccentric, and will start out a door, turn around and come back, go out on the street without his coat or hat and frequently looks up and down the street as if he were watching for someone or did not know for sure where he wanted to go.[45]

Leo Szilard had experienced the secret police in Hungary and Germany. Now, in the land of the free, he encountered them again. For scientists it was the dawn of a new era of collaboration with the military. From now on they would have to become accustomed to working beneath the dark veil of secrecy. Once hailed as saviours, scientists were now – as Princeton physicist Henry DeWolf Smyth said in 1951 – reduced to being little more than 'tools of war'.[46]

15

Devil's Work

It's devil's work. But suppose other devils make it first?
Pearl S. Buck, *Command the Morning* (1959)

1942 was the year in which atomic energy became a reality. On a cold squash court at the University of Chicago on 2 December, Leo Szilard's dream of releasing the power locked inside the atom came true. As the pen of the chart recorder showing neutron production in the heart of the atomic pile rose sharply off the measurable scale, Szilard turned to Enrico Fermi and said that it was a 'black day' in human history. Even the sceptical Fermi now knew that they had taken the first step on the road to the atomic bomb. It was the crucial experiment that demonstrated to the last remaining sceptics that the chain reaction was not just theory, and that atomic energy was not mere moonshine.

The names of both Fermi and Szilard appeared in the 1955 US Government patent as the inventors of the nuclear reactor. The two men had a rather stormy relationship. More than once Fermi refused to speak to his unorthodox Hungarian colleague. Fermi, the great experimentalist, quickly lost patience with Szilard's off-the-wall insights and ingenious inventions. Like Rutherford, Fermi saw himself as a pure scientist who did not need to worry about politics or how his ideas might be used or abused. For him, knowledge was its own reward; for Szilard it was merely the beginning.

In July 1942, Hans Bethe called on Edward Teller at the Met Lab. Both men had been invited to attend a gathering of top physicists in Berkeley. Before they left Chicago, Teller took Bethe to see the atomic pile being constructed on the squash court beneath Stagg Field Sta-

dium. When he saw the 'tremendous stacks of graphite', Bethe finally
'became convinced that the atomic-bomb project was real, and that it
would probably work'.[1] Until then, Bethe had distanced himself from
work on the atomic bomb. Instead, he had agreed to start work at
MIT on radar, believing that this would have a more immediate
impact on the course of the war.

On the train to California, Bethe and Teller discussed the plans to
build a plutonium fission bomb. Bethe recalls that Teller regarded its
success as a certainty, so much so that he had already moved on to
the next generation of nuclear weapons – the hydrogen bomb. Talking
in German, they brainstormed about ways of using the unimaginable
temperatures generated by a fission bomb to ignite Harold Urey's
1932 discovery, deuterium.

The Berkeley meeting had been organized by the 38-year-old J.
Robert Oppenheimer, a tall, chain-smoking theoretical physicist with
a love of Sanskrit and poetry. The elite group of physicists who met
that summer shared Teller's view that the fission bomb was a foregone
conclusion. All that remained was to hammer out the technicalities.
Instead, the theoreticians focused their combined brainpower on
fusion. They spent most of their time discussing how to build what
they termed the 'Super' – a hydrogen bomb.

Some frightening theoretical possibilities emerged during the
Berkeley brainstorming sessions. On paper, the Super seemed attractive as a weapon. Obtaining deuterium was far more straightforward
and less costly than either separating uranium-235 or manufacturing
plutonium. Fission is when a heavy nucleus splits into two smaller
nuclei, sometimes liberating enough neutrons to propagate a fission
chain reaction. Fusion, by contrast, takes place between elements
towards the top of the periodic table: two light nuclei are forced
together to form a new nucleus, plus a free neutron. As with fission,
loss of mass releases energy. Theoretically, the size of a thermonuclear
fusion bomb is unlimited, as the fuel for the bomb (deuterium or heavy
hydrogen) can be increased to any quantity. In 1942, the physicists
calculated that every pound of deuterium was the equivalent of nearly
40,000 tons of chemical explosive. As its name suggested, the Super
would be vastly more devastating than even the fission bomb. It was
a true superweapon.

When he went to meet to Arthur Compton to report on the progress they had made, Oppenheimer also mentioned a theoretical risk that their freewheeling discussions had thrown up. 'I'll never forget that morning,' recalled Compton, who was on holiday in an idyllic lakeside cottage in northern Michigan. Oppenheimer explained that they had been working on the Super, but that during their discussions Teller had calmly revealed the possibility that a fission bomb might trigger a thermonuclear chain reaction, not just in deuterium, but in other naturally occurring elements.

Compton was appalled. 'Was there really any chance that an atomic bomb would trigger the explosion of the nitrogen in the atmosphere or of the hydrogen in the ocean?' he wrote, looking back on that day. 'This would be the ultimate catastrophe. Better to accept the slavery of the Nazis than to run a chance of drawing the final curtain on mankind!' Compton sent Oppenheimer straight back to Berkeley with instructions to find 'a firm and reliable conclusion that our atomic bombs could not explode the air or the sea'.[2]

Despite the threat of an atomic doomsday, something both Rutherford and Pierre Curie had thought possible, the physicists at Berkeley all felt that the conference had gone well. For Teller, it was the first time he had worked with 'Oppie', as Oppenheimer was known to his colleagues. It was after this meeting that Teller learned that there was to be a separate laboratory where the bomb would be designed and built. The results of Oppenheimer's summer conference also greatly impressed both Vannevar Bush and James Conant. They knew now that the atomic bomb, and potentially the hydrogen bomb, could be decisive in this war and in future wars. The superweapon was no longer merely a dream.

In June, the month before Oppenheimer's conference, another crucial meeting took place – at Harnack House in Dahlem, Berlin, where Leo Szilard had lived during his final weeks in Germany. Hitler's military met with Germany's leading atomic scientists to discuss building an atomic bomb. Werner von Heisenberg gave a lecture on their research to Armaments Minister Albert Speer and his colleagues. The physicist Carl-Friedrich von Weizsäcker – identified in Einstein's letter to Roosevelt as a crucial figure in any Nazi bomb project – had suggested as early as 1940 that a reactor could be used to create a new fissionable element that would be ideal for an 'atomic explosive'.[3] Heisenberg told the Nazi top brass that, 'Given the positive results achieved up until now it does not appear impossible that, once a uranium burner [reactor] has been constructed, we will one day be able to follow the path revealed by von Weizsäcker to explosives that are more than a million times more effective than those currently available.'[4]

At the June meeting it was agreed that Heisenberg and his team would now focus their energies on building a reactor, both as a power source and to create plutonium for bombs. Unknown to the Germans, within six months Fermi and Szilard at Chicago would build such a reactor. The German scientists, their efforts divided between at least four competing research groups, never managed to design a reactor capable of going critical.

Adolf Hitler was deeply sceptical about the dream of atomic energy. When Albert Speer reported back on Heisenberg's research, the Führer remarked that 'the scientists in their unworldly urge to lay bare all the secrets under heaven might some day set the globe on fire'.[5] Ironically, at that very moment in California, physicists were indeed calculating the likelihood of just such an outcome. If he was unimpressed by the prospect of atomic bombs, Hitler was much more enthusiastic about Wernher von Braun's deadly brainchild. According to Hitler, the V-2 was 'revolutionary for the conduct of warfare in the whole world' and he demanded that the Army manufacture hundreds of thousands of the missiles.[6] It was an impossible goal, but hundreds of millions of Reichmarks were ploughed into the project.

The V-2, the world's first ballistic missile, was successful launched on 3 October 1942. It broke the sound barrier and reached an altitude of sixty miles. This was the first time that a rocket had reached the edge of space. In the words of one historian, the V-2 'must be considered the greatest technological achievement of the Third Reich'.[7] Two months later, as the Chicago scientists achieved the world's first atomic chain reaction, Speer prioritized mass production of the missile.

After the war, Wernher von Braun and his team of 126 scientists and engineers, having chosen to surrender to the Americans rather than the Russians, were whisked away to Fort Bliss, Texas. Here they would lay the foundations for the Apollo space project and the

A V-2 rocket being prepared for launch at Cuxhaven, Germany, 1945. This photograph was taken in the months after the fall of Nazi Germany during Operation Backfire, organized by the British to evaluate the V-2 rocket system. Eight complete rockets were assembled, three of which were launched, with the assistance of captured German firing troops and rocket scientists.

intercontinental ballistic missile, the technology that from the 1960s would threaten the world with apocalypse at the push of a button. For many, von Braun embodied the dark side of the scientific quest for new frontiers, regardless of the human cost. In the words of Tom Lehrer's song:

> 'Once the rockets are up,
> who cares where they come down?
> That's not my department,'
> says Wernher von Braun.[8]

In the 1930s and 40s, thousands of lives were sacrificed perfecting the lethal technologies of both Shiro Ishii, the Japanese microbiologist who tested bioweapons on Chinese prisoners, and Wernher von Braun, whose missiles were built by slave labourers. But in the cold war such unsavoury histories were ignored. For Carl Sagan, von Braun personified the 'dread ambiguity' of science and technology in the modern world. His rocket, said Sagan, 'will prove to be either the means of mass annihilation through a global thermonuclear war or the means that will carry us to the planets and the stars'.[9]

It was this ambiguity that also resulted in Einstein and Szilard's design for a safe refrigerator pump being used in breeder reactors to produce plutonium for nuclear bombs. Technology intended to save lives as well as so-called pure science could also be exploited. As Aldous Huxley argued, the much vaunted 'purity' of science is often short lived: 'Pure science does not remain pure indefinitely. Sooner or later it is apt to turn into applied science and finally into technology. Theory modulates into industrial practice, knowledge becomes power, formulas and laboratory experiments undergo a metamorphosis, and emerge as the H-bomb.'[10]

It was General Groves who personally appointed Robert Oppenheimer to head Site Y, as the secret atomic bomb laboratory was known. They met for the first time two days after the V-2 first took to the skies, on 5 October, when Groves introduced himself to the Met Lab scientists. Within a fortnight Groves had offered him the job. As physicist and biographer Jeremy Bernstein says, Oppenheimer was an unlikely choice for director of the lab: 'He was an aesthete who read poetry in several languages, and he had a ton of left-wing baggage.' But Groves took an instant liking to Oppenheimer. In particular, he liked the fact that Oppenheimer didn't (as he put it) 'tell me what to do'.[11]

Groves had not wanted the job of running the Manhattan Project. He was a no-nonsense army engineer who was sick of being a desk jockey. Managing a bunch of scientific 'prima donnas' was not how he had intended to spend the war.[12] The last thing he wanted was an awkward customer, like Szilard, heading up the bomb lab, challenging his every decision. Oppenheimer was ideal for the job, thought Groves, despite his dubious political views. 'He's a genius. A real genius,' said Groves later. 'Why, Oppenheimer knows about everything. He can talk to you about anything you bring up. Well, not exactly. I guess there are a few things he doesn't know about. He doesn't know anything about sports.'[13]

A month after being appointed director, Robert Oppenheimer had proposed a site for his new laboratory. He had spent time in New Mexico after returning from his trip to Europe in 1933, on which he visited the St Joachimsthal mines. Los Alamos was about thirty miles from Santa Fe. Oppenheimer loved the harsh landscape here, and with his brother owned a small ranch nearby, in the upper Pecos Valley. Sixteenth-century Spanish explorers had named the location Los Alamos after the poplar trees in the canyon. It was an ancient landscape of deep canyons and caves in which traces of the first inhabitants of the Americas could still be found. To the west of Los Alamos were the Jemez Mountains, while to the east lay the Sangre de Cristo range, whose Truchas Peaks rose to 13,800 feet. In the distance was the Valle Grande, the crater of what had once been the largest volcano on earth. It was a landscape that was familiar with awesome explosions.

Oppenheimer and Groves personally inspected the site in November. The mesa, the flat high ground overlooking the canyon, was home to the Los Alamos Ranch School for boys. The students, who included William S. Burroughs and Gore Vidal, could (as William Laurence said) 'do their algebra on horse-back' if they were so inclined.[14] The only access to the mesa was up a winding mountain road. Isolation was essential, said Groves, for reasons of safety (in case of unplanned explosions) and security. Eventually the top-secret research facility would be surrounded by armed guards, barbed-wire fences and dogs.

'Nobody could think straight in a place like that,' objected Szilard when the school was proposed as the home of the Manhattan Project. 'Everybody who goes there will go crazy.'[15] By 1945 there were 6,000 people living there. With just five bathtubs between them, Szilard would have hated it. Edward Teller arrived with the first of the scientists in late March 1943. The place was 'both peculiar and outlandish' he said, but it 'became dear to many who lived there'.[16]

In November 1942, two men appeared at the Los Alamos Ranch School. One of the former pupils, Stirling Colgate, recalled that 'we were required to say our yes sirs to a Mr Jones, who was wearing a fedora, and to a Mr Smith, who was wearing a porkpie hat. The names were obviously pseudonyms.'

Colgate was a keen student of physics and instantly recognized 'Mr Jones' as Ernest O. Lawrence, the inventor of the cyclotron. 'Mr Smith' was Robert Oppenheimer. The schoolboy had seen their photographs in his textbooks. 'The discovery of fission had been big news,' said Colgate:

In fact, we were even aware of the idea of a chain reaction. Clearly, the school was about to be converted to a laboratory to work on a very secret physics project. Why else would top physicists be visiting a place out at the end of nowhere with no water, no roads, no facilities? What was really going on was obvious! We were secretly amused by the pretense.[17]

Stirling Colgate later became a nuclear weapons physicist. His interest in physics may have been precocious, but the military applications of physics were widely discussed at the time. In 1939 the news of fission had provoked as much excitement around the world as had greeted the discoveries of X-rays and radium forty years before. In the year following Hahn and Strassmann's experiment demonstrating fission, at least a hundred scientific papers were published on the subject. Newspapers and magazines were quick to pick up on the news and herald the dawn of the atomic age.

In September 1939 the British popular science journal *Discovery* published a prophetic editorial by C. P. Snow, which began: 'Some physicists think that, within a few months, science will have produced for military use an explosive a million times more violent than dynamite.' Snow's article had the dramatic title 'A New Means of Destruction?' What Snow said confirmed Szilard's fears about the proliferation of atomic knowledge, fears that had haunted him for the last six years. 'It is no secret,' wrote Snow:

laboratories in the United States, Germany, France and England have been working on it feverishly since the Spring. It may not come off. The most competent opinion is divided upon whether the idea is practicable. If it is, science for the first time will at one bound have altered the scope of warfare. The power of most scientific weapons has been consistently exaggerated; but it would be difficult to exaggerate this.[18]

Snow warned that if 'the uranium bomb . . . is not made in America this year, it may be next year in Germany'. He was also pessimistic about the future, doubting that 'men can be trusted with a new weapon of gigantic power'. For him, the idealism that had accompanied the invention of flight showed that high hopes for a new discovery are often wrong: 'we cannot delude ourselves that this new invention will be better used'.[19]

Douglas Mayer, writing in the same journal, quoted Joliot-Curie's team in Paris as claiming that there was a 'considerable' danger of 'a system containing uranium in high concentration' exploding once the chain reaction had started. The world now faced a choice, concluded Mayer: 'Will it create a streamlined world where a pinch of salt is sufficient fuel for the *Queen Mary*, or shall we have a Wellsian chaos with each nation dropping bouquets of uranium bombs in a policy of encirclement?'[20]

In the month that Europe went to war, superweapons haunted people's fears of what was to come. At the end of September, Hitler bragged about the terrors of a new superweapon that he intended to unleash on Britain. An anonymous correspondent to *The Times* poured scorn on the idea: 'What, many of us ask, can it be this time: some new and fearful gas; a death ray; some super-atomic bomb; germs; pilotless aeroplanes; or something we cannot even imagine?' It was this same scepticism about new weapons that had caused British military commanders in 1915 to ignore reports at Ypres that gas cylinders were being deployed. The letter, signed 'Civilian', rejects the idea that new weapons win wars. 'Our belief that we are fighting to destroy evil will make us welcome sacrifice and bear these "new weapons" with fortitude in our struggle to destroy civilization's greatest menace.'[21] But civilians would need more than fortitude to survive a war fought with superweapons.

By 1940, the possibility of 'the development of an explosive a million times more powerful than dynamite' was common knowledge.[22] In February the previous year, at a meeting of the American Physical Society at Pupin Hall, Columbia University's physics laboratory, Bohr and Fermi had discussed the different responses of uranium-235 and uranium-238 under bombardment from neutrons. Bohr had just revealed that it was the rare isotope uranium-235 that had fissioned in Hahn and Strassmann's experiment. Listening intently in the audience was the *New York Times*' science correspondent.

'I watched them write strange hieroglyphics on the blackboard,' wrote William Laurence later, 'heard them speculate about the possibility of a chain reaction, about fantastic amounts of energy being liberated. And as I sat there listening and watching, the figures on the blackboard suddenly started a chain reaction in my brain.' Afterwards he rushed up to Bohr and Fermi.

'Does this add up to an atomic bomb?' he blurted out.

There could not have been two more cautious scientists on the planet, as far as atomic energy was concerned. Fermi had just described Szilard's idea of an atomic bomb as 'Nuts!' In response to Laurence's question, Fermi estimated that it might take twenty-five or fifty years to build a bomb. But Laurence was not reassured. He described himself as a 'frightened man' after this physics conference.[23] The journalist did, however, manage to restrain himself from speculating in print about any imminent threat from an atomic bomb.

A year later, in 1940 when the news broke that uranium-235 had been separated, Laurence decided to voice his fears about a superbomb. Apparently it was his wife who finally convinced him to go public. 'If the world is to come to an end,' she told him, 'let it know the worst as soon as possible.' Before he started writing, Laurence had to first convince his editor that he was not 'attempting to emulate Jules Verne and H. G. Wells as writers of scientific fiction'.[24] The result was a dramatic front-page story in the *New York Times*, headlined VAST POWER SOURCE IN ATOMIC ENERGY OPENED BY SCIENCE.

A subheading echoed the fears of Szilard and his Hungarian friends: 'Germany Is Seeking It'.

In his article, Laurence proclaimed that the separation of uranium-235 was 'regarded as ushering in the long dreamed of age of atomic power, and, therefore, as one of the greatest, if not the greatest, discovery in modern science'. However, because of 'the tremendous implications this discovery bears on the possible outcome of the European war', scientists were 'reluctant to talk about this development'. Ominously, he reported that the Nazi government had already 'ordered its greatest scientists to concentrate their energies on the solution of this problem'. He raised the frightening spectre of German scientists 'carrying on their tasks feverishly at the laboratories of the Kaiser Wilhelm Institute at Berlin.' Beneath the subheading 'Terrific Explosive Power', Laurence stated that 'one pound of U-235 contains as much energy as 15,000 tons (30,000,000 pounds) of TNT'.[25]

Laurence had hoped that his article in the highly respected *New York Times* would 'galvanize Washington into action'. America needed to build the bomb before the Germans did. Instead, all that happened was that a Congressman cited his article during a speech 'on the threat of atomic energy to the petroleum industry'.[26] So towards the end of the year, he wrote another article on the subject, which was duly published in September by the *Saturday Evening Post*.

Unknown to Laurence, behind the scenes the wheels of government were gradually moving. After the war, Laurence discovered that the FBI had contacted the *Post*'s editor and demanded that the September issue be taken out of circulation. They even contacted libraries across America, telling them to remove it from their shelves. Anyone specifically requesting it was to be reported to the FBI. After VE day, Army Intelligence showed Laurence both his articles, 'beautifully preserved in cellophane'. They had been found by intelligence officers among files compiled by the Nazis on atomic energy.[27]

During the war, the Office of Censorship in America prevented newspapers from writing about atomic fission or even speculating about Nazi progress towards atomic energy. However, one rather remarkable story somehow managed to slip through. On 27 November 1944, *Time* magazine published a science piece titled 'V-3?' on the Nazis' new secret weapon, the ballistic missile. 'The terrible novelty of V-2 had by no means worn off yet,' claimed *Time*, 'but London last week was already abuzz with speculation about V-3 – supposedly an atomic bomb.'[28] The article openly discussed German plans for a missile with an atomic warhead. Indeed, recent research suggests that Nazi scientists working independently of Heisenberg may have designed just such a weapon and possibly even tested a prototype. So seriously was the threat taken that in the previous year Allied planes bombed the factory at Rjukan, Norway, that produced heavy water, an alternative neutron moderator to graphite.

Time's science writer also discussed a dispatch from London claiming that German scientists might have found a way to use a 'Neuman' demolition charge to create an implosion. Such an imploding charge might be used to mimic the conditions in a dense star and 'develop pressures of tens of thousands of tons per square inch at the center, perhaps enough to disintegrate an unstable atom such as uranium and release its explosive atomic energy'. The explosion would be of 'unheard-of violence'.[29] Unknown to the writer of this article, implosion was precisely how the Los Alamos scientists intended to trigger the plutonium bomb that destroyed Nagasaki, thanks to the calculations of another member of the Hungarian Quartet, John von Neumann.

Apart from *Time*'s article on the nuclear missile, the subject of atomic bombs was taboo for journalists during the war. But there was one part of the media that the intelligence services ignored, at least initially: the science fiction pulp magazines. *Astounding Science Fiction*, under its editor John W. Campbell, Jr – author of one of the all-time classics of science fiction, 'Who Goes There?' (1938) – had long ago cornered the market in stories speculating about the applications of atomic energy. As well as having a large readership among technophile adolescents, *Astounding* was also read by scientists. According to Louis N. Ridenour, a scientist who worked on radar during the war and who was himself a writer of science fiction, *Astounding* was 'actually read by a certain number of highly educated people for its occasional thoughtful stories in which the impact of rapidly developing science on society is more or less intelligently examined'.[30]

Many of the stories in *Astounding* explored the implications of power generation from atomic energy. Robert A. Heinlein's 'Blowups Happen', written in 1939 and published in September 1940, included a detailed account of 'the most dangerous machine in the world – an atomic power plant'. In common with journalists and even some scientists at this time, Heinlein's story suggests – wrongly – that a reactor was the same thing as a 'uranium bomb'. The operators of Heinlein's reactor, known as 'the bomb', live in fear of making a mistake and causing 'an explosion which would dwarf the eruption of Krakatoa to popgun size'. Indeed, a 'blowup' at the reactor could 'destroy the entire human race'. Understandably, the plant's atomic engineers are placed under enormous stress, believing as they do that 'the lives of every human being on the planet' depend on their decisions.[31] To identify early signs of stress, psychiatrists are employed to observe the engineers. One of them is a 'Dr Silard'. This was the first of several appearances that Szilard would make in fiction and film in the coming years.[32]

Two years after 'Blowups Happen', Lester del Rey's 'Nerves' also described a reactor accident which threatens the future of the planet. It appeared just two months before Fermi and Szilard's top-secret atomic pile went critical. According to del Rey, the issue of *Astounding* containing his story was classified secret when it arrived at the Manhattan Project facilities. Technicians were unable to read it unless they had top security clearance, even though in the rest of America it was freely available on the news-stands.

The atom still fascinated fiction writers, as it had ever since the discovery of radium. Campbell himself, under the pen name of Don A. Stuart, had imagined a reactor that runs on water as early as 1934 in his story 'Atomic Power'. A. E. van Vogt's 'The Great Engine', from 1943, described a miraculous 'atomic engine' which enables humankind to achieve Otto Mandl's dream of interplanetary travel. Theodore Sturgeon's 'Artnan Process', from June 1941, finds a fantastic solution to a problem which the Manhattan Project scientists were very much concerned with at the time: how to separate fissile uranium-235 from natural uranium in large quantities. However, it is extremely unlikely that Sturgeon's idea of a mould that consumes uranium and then excretes the rare, fissionable isotope ever occurred to scientists in the real world.[33]

ATOMIC POWER PLANT

Within 50 years, cyclotron generators like these will provide unlimited atomic energy

The secret of atomic power has long been sought because it is the mightiest untapped source of energy science knows. The power locked in the atom is inconceivably great and its release, even in part, would instantly reduce all other forms of power plants to antiquated and obsolete equipment. Electricity would be grossly inefficient in comparison. The power plant shown is based on experiments being carried on in universities and by commercial power companies. For complete details, see page 14

ATOMIC POWER PLANT

An illustrator for Amazing Stories *in October 1939 tries to predict what an atomic power plant will look like fifty years in the future. According to the caption: 'The power locked in the atom is inconceivably great and its release, even in part, would instantly reduce all other forms of power plants to antiquated and obsolete equipment.'*

Clifford D. Simak's 'Lobby' (1944) is more realistic. This account of the development of an 'atomic power plant' suggested that the revolutionary new energy source would face opposition from the conventional 'power lobby' in America. Simak's atomic scientist, Butler, is a classic inventor-scientist motivated by utopian dreams:

You've seen his kind. Has one ruling passion. The only thing that counts with him is atomic power. Not atomic power as a theory or as something to play around with, but power that will turn wheels – cheap. Power that will free the world, that will help develop the world. Power so cheap and plentiful and safe to handle that no man is so poor he can't afford to use it.[34]

It was this vision, inherited from Soddy and Wells, that had inspired Szilard for the last decade.

Like Heinlein, Simak believed that a power plant could explode like a bomb. Butler therefore builds his prototype reactor in Montana, away from cities. When it is sabotaged by businessmen who own conventional power stations, Butler's business partner, Cobb, witnesses the explosion in his helicopter at night. Simak's remarkable description anticipates accounts of the top-secret Trinity test, conducted just a year later in the desert wasteland of New Mexico:

Suddenly the sky above the peak flashed.

That was the word that best described it – flashed. There was no consciousness of fire, no flame, no glow – just a sudden, blinding flash, like a photographer's bulb popping – a million bulbs popping. A flash that came and lasted for one split second, then was gone, leaving a blackness that for a moment blotted out the moon and the snowy peaks – a blackness that persisted until one's eyes could readjust themselves.

The ship plowed on, while Cobb, blinded, reached out for something to clutch, instinctively reacting to the bewilderment of blackness.

Sound came. A sudden clap of sound that was vicious and nerve-wrenching. Like one short gasp of a million thunders rolled together.

The 'copter bucked and plunged and Cobb reached out blind hands, hauled back on the wheel to send it rocketing skyward. Beneath him the ship jerked and trembled, wallowing in tortured air.[35]

In pulp fiction of this period, science or scientists are rarely criticized. Accidents happen because of political or commercial pressures that cause human errors. Cleve Cartmill's story 'Deadline', from March 1944, is an exception. It depicts an irresponsible scientist who has succeeded in building an atomic bomb. Its contents so shocked the American secret services that as soon as it was published in *Astounding*, Army Intelligence agents swooped on the editor, the author and even the illustrator. They were convinced that Cartmill must have had a source inside the Manhattan Project. As he explained, however, the only source he had was articles, such as William Laurence's, published in 1940. Eventually Army Intelligence reluctantly accepted his account, but still threatened to shut *Astounding* down. However, Campbell successfully argued that *Astounding* had such a reputation for publishing stories about atomic energy that if they suddenly stopped printing them it would be a dead give-away to the Nazis that America was building an atomic superweapon.

Cartmill's story is about a war between two imaginary world

powers, the Seilla and the Sixa. The Sixa have almost lost the war and have been forced to retreat to their heartlands in Ynamre. Although his story appears to be pure fantasy, the fact that 'Ynamre' spells 'ermany' backwards reveals Cartmill's true purpose. Read 'Seilla' backwards and you find the Allies; similarly, the 'Sixa' are the Axis powers. Cartmill's story is in fact a thinly disguised depiction of World War II.

The plot of 'Deadline' is familiar now from countless cold-war thrillers, such as the James Bond movies. A mad scientist working for the Sixa has developed an atomic bomb. It is made from sixteen pounds of uranium-235, and the Seilla scientists are afraid that the 'explosion of energy would be so incomparably violent, its sheer, minute concentration of unbearable energy so great, that surrounding matter would be set off'. This was the doomsday scenario that had terrified Arthur Compton during his Michigan holiday in 1942. The Seilla's secret agent infiltrates the enemy's lines to find and destroy the atomic bomb. 'They started out to conquer the world,' he says. 'But now they are about to lose it. We, the Seilla, would not dare to set off an experimental atomic bomb.' But the Sixa are so 'desperate' that they would risk destroying the world for a chance of victory.[36]

Dr Sitruc, the mad atomic scientist who has built the doomsday bomb, is a 'slender man with snapping dark eyes, an odd-shaped face, and a commanding air'. His love of power and his cavalier attitude to the survival of the human race mark him out as a forerunner of that other Germanic scientist of atomic megadeath, Dr Strangelove.

'You're like a god here,' says the agent to Dr Sitruc as they face each other over the 'most destructive weapon the world has ever known'.

'I have control of the greatest explosive force in world history and my whims are obeyed as iron commands,' sneers Dr Sitruc, pistol in hand and with a smirk on his thin lips.

He is prepared to take the chance 'that all animate life will be destroyed in the twinkling of an eye' by his bomb.[37] World dominion is worth that risk. Fortunately, the agent outwits Dr Sitruc and is able to defuse the bomb. The world is saved – this time not *by* a scientist, but *from* a scientist. From now on, scientists would be increasingly depicted in film and fiction as part of the problem, rather than the solution. That was the price they would pay for realizing the dream of the superweapon. The saviour scientist began to make way for the Strangelovean mad scientist.

The atomic bomb that Cartmill describes is not the Hiroshima bomb, but it's a good guess. The modest critical mass of uranium-235 (Cartmill's bomb is small enough to be carried) and the description of the 'fuse' (actually the initiator, a neutron-producing assembly of radium and beryllium) were close enough to the real thing to scare the pants off Military Intelligence. But although the critical mass of uranium in the actual atomic bomb was smaller than top German physicists like Heisenberg believed it needed to be, it was not quite light enough for someone to carry. The secret service failed to ban Cartmill's story, but they did later prevent the publication of one by Philip Wylie, 'The Paradise Crater', which described a Nazi attempt to gain revenge on America with atomic bombs secretly built in the Nevada Desert. As far as Military Intelligence were concerned, the science fiction writers were too far ahead of the game.

Robert A. Heinlein, who produced some of his greatest short stories for *Astounding* in the early years of World War II, wrote what is easily this period's most chilling account of war in the atomic age. It was a story widely read by those working on the Manhattan Project. 'Solution Unsatisfactory', published in May 1941 under his pen name Anson MacDonald, describes not an atomic bomb, but rather the use of radioactive isotopes as a radiological weapon. Heinlein called this a 'consciously Wellsian story', one in which he set himself the task of thinking through the implications of an 'Absolute Weapon'.[38] The title refers to the situation that results from the invention and use of the superweapon – a global American military dictatorship.

Colonel Clyde C. Manning 'was one of the army's No. 1 experts in chemical warfare'.[39] In Heinlein's story he is called out of retirement to head up the top-secret nuclear research laboratory in Maryland, 'War Department Special Defense Project No. 347'. With his scientific and military background, Manning combines the skills of both Oppenheimer and Groves. He is a fictional General Ishii in charge of developing not biological but atomic weapons of mass destruction. Heinlein clearly grasps the powerful position such administrator-scientists would hold in warfare and the Big Science of the future.

Manning's assistant, John deFries, who narrates the story, is in no doubt that the Colonel has the necessary skills:

[T]here was certainly no one else in the United States who could have done the job. It required a man who could direct and suggest research in a highly esoteric field, but who saw the problem from the standpoint of urgent military necessity. Left to themselves, the physicists would have reveled in the intellectual luxury of an unlimited research expense account, but, while they undoubtedly would have made major advances in human knowledge, they might never have developed anything of military usefulness, or the military possibilities of a discovery might be missed for years.[40]

Initially, Manning's task is to find 'a way to use U235 in a controlled explosion'. The objective is an atomic bomb, 'a one-ton bomb that would be a whole air raid in itself'. In the future his scientists hope to build a 'war rocket' that could deliver uranium bombs onto their enemies, 'then we would be in a position to make most anybody say "uncle" to Uncle Sam'. But in 1944, Dr Estelle Karst – a rare female scientist in a field dominated by men in both fact and fiction – makes a discovery. She is working on the medical uses of 'artificial radio-actives', isotopes, and has found that the ones she has produced are far more radioactive than required for medical purposes. Dr Karst is not herself developing weapons but, as Manning quickly realizes, these isotopes are 'lethal'.[41]

Manning postpones work on the atomic bomb, which has turned out to be more complex than expected. Thanks to his background in chemical warfare, he has spotted a new weapon: radioactive isotopes. Known as 'K-O dust' after its inventors, Karst and Obre, the lethal radioactive powder is tested on horses. 'After they had died,' says deFries, 'any part of their carcasses would register on a photographic plate'.[42] Once the powder was scattered over an area, the radioactivity could not be neutralized. Every living thing would die, and the area would be uninhabitable until the isotope's radioactivity naturally declined. Karst had stumbled upon a truly terrible weapon of mass destruction.

For Manning, the K-O dust 'is not just simply sufficient to safeguard the United States, it amounts to a loaded gun held at the head of every man, woman, and child on the globe!' Given enough uranium and a knowledge of physics, soon any nation would be able to produce the K-O dust in just a few months. The world would be like 'a whole room full of men, each armed with a loaded .45'. It was a truly Wellsian scenario. As the British writer had said back in 1913, discovering the atomic bomb was like giving a loaded revolver to a crèche. Manning admits he had even considered killing everyone who knew the secret, including himself, to protect the world. But he quickly saw that this idea was 'sheer funk'.[43] K-O dust would soon be discovered by some other scientist – the same argument of inevitability used by Wells's scientist, Holsten.

True to his military background, Manning decides that America must use the new superweapon first, 'to enforce a worldwide peace, ruthlessly and drastically'. A '*Pax Americana*' is the only way, he decides, to prevent another nation from getting the upper hand and to keep the secret in America, at least for now. It is agreed that the dust will be used by the British against Nazi Germany as a demonstration of the weapon's lethal power. (Heinlein's story was written before Pearl Harbor, so America was not yet at war with Japan.) While deFries accompanies the dust to Britain, the scientists who developed it have been confined to the laboratory to keep the weapon's secret on American soil. Warning leaflets are dropped on German cities telling people to leave immediately. 'We were morally obliged to try', says deFries, knowing that they will be ignored.[44] The real targets of the first atomic weapons, Hiroshima and Nagasaki, were never warned. In Heinlein's story the target is Berlin. All it takes is the flick of a switch in an aircraft, and the dust is spread over the city. Such is the simplicity of mass murder in the modern age.

When deFries returns to America he learns that Dr Karst committed suicide on hearing that her medical discovery had been used to slaughter civilians. The film footage taken from aircraft over Berlin some days later shows that the dust has been appallingly effective. The images in the film are shocking. 'You have not seen them,' says deFries, speaking directly to the reader. 'They were never made public, but they were of great use in convincing the other nations of the world that peace was a good idea.'[45] Similarly, the American forces of occupation in Japan confiscated all film and photographs of the effects of the Hiroshima and Nagasaki bombs. Images of the dead and injured were suppressed and often destroyed. Most of the surviving images were hidden by Japanese and by Americans who believed the world should, one day, see the effect of atomic bombs on people.[46]

'The last sequence,' says deFries, 'showed Berlin and the roads around it a week after the raid. The city was dead, there was not a man, a woman, a child – nor cats, nor dogs, not even a pigeon. Bodies were all around, but they were safe from rats. There were no rats.' After seeing the film, deFries (who later dies from the effects of radiation) comments, 'I left what soul I had in that projection room and I have not had one since.'[47]

In Washington, some disagree with Manning's policy of imposing a Pax Americana. 'The world has seen a lot of weapons which were going to make war an impossibility too horrible to contemplate,' says the Secretary of the Navy. 'Poison gas, and tanks, and airplanes – even firearms, if I remember my history.' But faced with the Strangelovean alternative of living 'in sealed underground cities', the President agrees. Ultimatums are issued to every head of state: 'we are outlawing war and are calling on every nation to disarm completely at once. In other words, "Throw down your guns, boys; we've got the drop on you!"' Nations must surrender their aircraft – the only means of dropping the dust – to the United States. Japan accepts only when it is threatened with attack: the American fleet was 'halfway from Pearl Harbor to Kobe, loaded with enough dust to sterilize their six biggest cities'.[48]

But apart from a 'Four-days War' during which New York and Moscow are dusted, the United States is victorious. The superweapon has won. Subsequently a supranational body, including a 'corps of world policemen', is set up to supervise 'the unbeatable weapon'. Its director is the soldier-scientist who developed the weapon. He has absolute power: 'Manning was the undisputed military dictator of the world.' It is an unsatisfactory solution to a problem, but it is the only solution, argues Heinlein's narrator. Neither deFries nor Manning are happy with it. But a doomsday war has been postponed, and for now at least, the world has not committed suicide.[49]

The dilemmas Heinlein raises about the uses of science and the control of superweapons would soon become very real. Not surprisingly, as John W. Campbell said, 'this story was read, and widely discussed, among the physicists and engineers working on the Manhattan Project'.[50] Indeed, Heinlein's idea of a radioactive super-weapon was under serious consideration in the very month that the story was published. Arthur Compton's National Academy of Sciences committee investigated the military applications of atomic fission for Vannevar Bush. Compton's committee declared that both 'violently explosive bombs' and a 'violently radioactive' dust were feasible as weapons. The latter would become possible after the chain reaction had been achieved, 'not earlier than 1943'.[51] One of the first uses of Szilard's atomic reactor might have been to create a real 'K-O dust'.

In July 1941, the popular magazine *PIC* correctly predicted that 'this war will be won or lost in the laboratory'. The magazine thought that uranium-235 would be used to power aircraft: 'A lump of this U-235 the size of an ordinary pack of cigarettes would supply power enough to run the greatest bomber in the world for three continuous years of unceasing flight.' It also speculated that a radioactive 'death dust' would be developed.[52] At the end of the year, Henry DeWolf Smyth and Szilard's friend Eugene Wigner investigated the idea of a death dust. They 'concluded that the fission products produced in one day's run of a 100,000 kw chain-reacting pile might be sufficient to make a large area uninhabitable'. But they stopped short of recommending the use in weapons of these 'particularly vicious' radioactive poisons.[53]

Death dust remained on the agenda, however. The subject was revisited at the start of 1943 by a Met Lab committee chaired by James Conant, who had worked on chemical weapons in World War I. Conant's committee looked at the possibility that Germany might use the poisonous radioactive fission products created in a reactor to make radiological bombs – what we would now call dirty bombs. Although they concluded that an attack on America using such bombs was unlikely, the possibility that Germany might use them remained real until the end of the war in Europe. Military personnel were even trained in the use of Geiger counters before the Normandy landings in order to investigate suspicious bomb sites.

Although Wigner and Smyth were not keen on the idea of death dust, the subject was revived by a rather unlikely Manhattan Project scientist – Enrico Fermi. A pure scientist in the Rutherford mould,

Fermi didn't like war work. 'After he had sat in on one of his first conferences here,' Oppenheimer recalled, 'he turned to me and said, "I believe your people actually *want* to make a bomb." I remember his voice sounded surprised.'[54]

Nevertheless, Fermi did make one shocking proposal about weapons. He privately suggested to Oppenheimer in April 1943 that radioactive isotopes might be used to contaminate Germany's food supply. Oppenheimer considered the idea 'promising', and discussed it with both General Groves and Edward Teller.[55] The Hungarian came up with strontium-90 as the most effective isotope for this purpose. Strontium is chemically similar to calcium, and strontium-90 would be absorbed by the body and deposited in bones and teeth, causing leukaemia and bone cancer. Fears about the presence of this isotope in the biosphere would later lead to a ban on the atmospheric testing of atomic weapons, despite Teller's heated opposition.

In a letter written on 25 May 1943, Oppenheimer explained to Fermi that it would not be difficult to produce the strontium. But he suggested not pursuing the idea unless an effective means of delivery could be developed. 'I think we should not attempt a plan unless we can poison food sufficient to kill half a million men.' Manhattan Project physicist Joseph Rotblat, who later won a Nobel Peace Prize, first read this letter forty years after it was written, having obtained it under the Freedom of Information Act. He was deeply shocked: 'I am sure that in peacetime these same scientists would have viewed such a plan as barbaric; they would not have contemplated it even for a moment. Yet during the war it was considered quite seriously.'[56]

The potential of radiological warfare continued to be explored throughout the cold war by all sides. A death dust was almost used during the Korean War. In 1954, General MacArthur confided to Jim Lucas of the Washington *Daily News* that he had asked permission to 'sow a 5 mile wide belt of radioactive cobalt – which he assured me "we had in abundance" – along the Yalu [River], thus permanently sealing Korea off from China'. The plan was vetoed by 'those fools in Washington' only after the British voiced their strong opposition.[57]

Robert A. Heinlein's fictional account of an 'Absolute Weapon' was not the only such story read by scientists on the Manhattan Project. Enrico Fermi's wife, Laura, enjoyed Harold Nicolson's *Public Faces* in 1941. Another physicist's wife had given it to her after she and her husband had read it. Alice K. Smith, also the wife of a physicist and later a historian of the bomb project, saw the play *Wings over Europe* with her husband. They 'were so impressed that they had bought a copy of the script'.[58] Los Alamos physicist Robert Wilson read Thomas Mann's pathology of the European mind, *The Magic Mountain*, with its evocative description of X-rays. In a letter from Los Alamos, Wilson referred to 'this magic mesa'.[59] On their hilltop, these modern-day magicians genuinely believed they were going to save America and rid the world of war with their scientific superweapon. It is not surprising, therefore, that someone – perhaps Leo Szilard – bought a copy of the most famous account of atomic bombs and the utopian future for the Met Lab library: H. G. Wells's *The World Set Free*.

It was no idle boast when, in 1949, science fiction writer Theodore

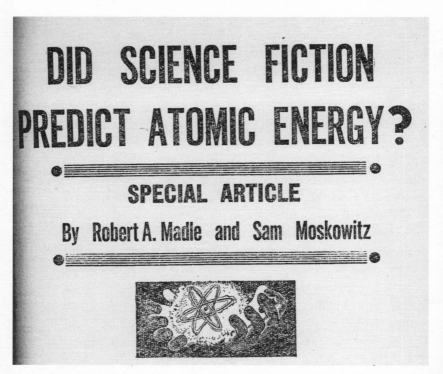

Science fiction seemed to have predicted many aspects of the cold-war world. This headline is from the November 1952 issue of Science Fiction Quarterly.

Sturgeon said: 'There is good reason to believe that, outside of the top men in the Manhattan District and in the Armed Forces, the only people in the world who fully understood what had happened on 6 August 1945 were the aficionados of science fiction.'[60] As John W. Campbell put it, the science fiction writers were no longer mere 'wild-eyed dreamers'.[61] The dream had become a terrible reality.

16

Destroyer of Worlds

This revelation of the secrets of nature, long mercifully with-held from man, should arouse the most solemn reflections in the mind and conscience of every human being capable of comprehension.   Winston Churchill (1945)

At the end of 1939, Otto Frisch was working at Birmingham University. He dreaded the coming hostilities. 'We all imagined scenes out of H. G. Wells's *The Shape of Things to Come*: a fleet of aeroplanes dropping thousands of bombs, buildings toppling, millions fleeing . . .'[1] Wells, the idealistic visionary of science, was appalled by the role that scientists were going to play in this destruction and by the idea that 'thousands of clear and active minds, each indisputably sane, could, in an atmosphere obsessed by plausible false assumptions about patriotic duty and honour, cooperate to produce a combined result fantastically futile and cruel.'

Readers of H. G. Wells's fiction were familiar with mad scientists – Griffin or Moreau, for example – as well as those who hoped to improve the world, men like Holsten and Karenin. But who, asked Wells in *The Shape of Things to Come*, were these faceless scientists working in secret laboratories to develop weapons of mass destruction?

The people engaged in this business were, on the whole, exceptionally grave, industrious and alert-minded. Could they revisit the world to-day individually we should probably find them all respectable, companionable, intelligible persons. Yet in the aggregate they amounted to an organization of dangerous lunatics. They inflicted dreadful deaths, hideous sufferings or tormented lives upon, it is estimated, about a million of their fellow creatures.[2]

Building the atomic bombs that devastated two Japanese cities in 1945 was the result of an enormous industrial, military and scientific effort. It could perhaps be argued that, like General Ishii's Unit 731, it was an 'organization of dangerous lunatics'. But the scale of the enterprise and the speed with which it was completed remains breath-taking, even today. Almost certainly America was the only country that could have achieved this while fighting a world war. Fear mar-shalled the talents of the greatest scientists and engineers in the world, and, overseen by the brusque and bullying General Groves, they translated pure science into military reality.

Niels Bohr had told colleagues that to separate uranium-235 from natural uranium on an industrial scale, a country would have to transform itself into a vast factory. When Bohr eventually arrived at Los Alamos at the end of 1943, Edward Teller anticipated a satisfying moment of *Schadenfreude*. 'I was prepared to say, "You see . . ." But before I could open my mouth, he said: "You see, I told you it couldn't be done without turning the whole country into a factory. You have done just that."'[3]

The Manhattan Project had four main sites. As well as the Met Lab at Chicago, there was Oak Ridge, near Clinton, east Tennessee, where uranium-235 was separated from uranium-238; and Hanford, near the town of Richland, Washington, the site of the reactors that created plutonium, and the facilities to separate this from the uranium fuel. The fourth, top-secret site in the superweapon project was Los Alamos, the laboratory where the bombs were designed and made.

The atomic bombs were known by the innocuous code name 'the gadget'. It was a name that could have come straight from the pages of a science fiction pulp, or one of Hugo Gernsback's technology magazines. Indeed, with an average age of 25, many of the scientists and technicians on the Manhattan Project had been weaned on a diet of sci-fi and gadget pulps. The atomic bomb owed its existence to this technophile culture, with its saviour scientists and superweapons, as much as it did to the individual genius of its scientists and engineers.

Indeed, the Manhattan Project scientists sometimes described their work as being straight out of a science fiction story. The Hungarian mathematician Peter Lax, the nephew of Szilard's friend Albert Korodi, had arrived in America in 1941, aged just 15. While studying at New York University in 1945, he received his call-up papers for the army. But the front line for Lax turned out to be the Neutron Department at Los Alamos, working on the development of the first plutonium bomb. 'It was like a piece of science fiction,' he said, 'working with an element which was not to be found in the Periodic Table.'[4]

The Manhattan Project employed up to 130,000 people at any one time. Many thousands more were involved indirectly, working for big corporations such as Union Carbide and Du Pont, a company which had also produced chemical weapons during World War I. By the end of the war there were 6,000 people working on the 'magic mesa' at Los Alamos. The majority of the scientists at Los Alamos, or the Hill as they called it, found the work stimulating and indeed great fun. Hans Bethe said that for many of the scientists, the 27 months they spent there building superweapons was the best time of their lives.

Laura Fermi arrived at Los Alamos in August 1944 with her two young children, Nella and Giulio. By this time, Los Alamos was a thriving community:

Into that city went scientists from all parts of the United States and England, to disappear from the world. For two and a half years the city was not marked on the maps, had no official status, was not part of New Mexico, its residents could not vote. It did not exist. That city was Los Alamos to those living there, Site Y to the few outsiders who knew about its existence, Post Office Box 1663 to correspondents and friends of the inhabitants.[5]

The Fermis were assigned Apartment D in building T-186. Below them, in Apartment B, lived Rudolf and Genia Peierls. As Teller said, everyone on the Hill became 'one big, happy family'.[6]

Enrico Fermi had worked first at Met Lab, then at Hanford, where Du Pont was constructing the huge reactors for plutonium production. In common with the other top atomic scientists, he had a personal bodyguard. But such was the secrecy surrounding the project that he was unable to tell Laura what he was working on. One scientist announced to his wife the news that they were going to New Mexico with the words: 'I can tell you nothing about it. We're going away that's all.'[7] Like most of the other spouses, Laura did not know the lethal nature of her husband's work until the news broke about the destruction of Hiroshima.

The Manhattan Project began and ended with two crucial scientific experiments: one in 1942 when the Chicago atomic pile went critical, and the second in 1945 when the first atomic bomb was detonated. The Trinity test, as Robert Oppenheimer rather cryptically named it, demonstrated beyond doubt the terrible explosive power of the new element, plutonium.

In April 1943 Oppenheimer convened an inaugural conference at Los Alamos for the key bomb scientists. Its purpose was to bring everyone up to speed on the current state of knowledge about the bomb and to establish what problems remained to be solved. For some of them, the opening lecture by Robert Serber was a revelation. The policy of compartmentalization – something Szilard constantly criticized – meant that their knowledge had been restricted to the specific area in which they were working. Now the true scale of the endeavour became clear. 'The object of the project,' said Serber, 'is to produce a practical military weapon in the form of a bomb in which the energy is released by a fast neutron chain reaction in one or more of the materials known to show nuclear fission.'[8]

Serber told them in 1943 that they now believed the critical mass for uranium-235 was 33 lb, in the form of a core about the size of a cantaloupe melon. For plutonium it was just 12 lb, or about the size of a tennis ball. Both would need to be enclosed in a heavy tamper, or shell, of uranium. The uranium would reflect the neutrons back into the heart of the bomb, increasing the number of potential fission reactions and thus the explosive yield of the bomb. According to Bethe, 'relatively little nuclear physics' was needed at Los Alamos.[9] They were there to engineer a military weapon. But problems remained. Devising a way of rapidly bringing together a critical mass so as to avoid a premature and thus inefficient detonation caused by stray neutrons was one major hurdle.

Eventually two different bomb designs were developed, one for uranium-235 and the other for plutonium. The former used a gun barrel to fire a plug consisting of tamper and core into the subcritical mass, thereby bringing it to explosive criticality. For plutonium this method would not work. The critical mass had to be brought together much more rapidly in order to avoid predetonation. As an alternative, Seth Neddermeyer came up with the ingenious yet technically difficult idea of using chemical explosives to create an implosion, instantly compressing a sphere of plutonium into a critical mass.

John von Neumann was called in to work on this promising solution, as well as the complex hydrodynamics of explosions. The brilliant Princeton mathematician was already working for the military designing the specially shaped charges used in the armour-piercing bazooka. In October 1943, together with Teller, he applied his knowledge on the dynamics of shock waves to the problem of how to use conventional explosives to implode the sphere of plutonium. The plan was for the explosives to squeeze the plutonium at pressures greater than those at the centre of the earth, instantly compressing the core into criticality and setting off the nuclear explosion. It was a revolutionary design, but because of its complexity a full-scale test was needed. No one wanted to drop an atomic bomb that did not explode, thus delivering years of research into the hands of an enemy. By contrast, the scientists were now so certain that the uranium bomb would explode, that it was never tested – at least not until it was dropped on the city of Hiroshima.

There had never been a physics experiment quite like Trinity. The bomb was winched up a hundred-foot wooden tower at the location that would become known as the original Ground Zero. A series of reinforced concrete bunkers had been built to house cameras and scientific instruments, from seismographs to ionization chambers, which would record every aspect of the explosion. The data would travel down some five hundred miles of heavy cabling. The gadget consisted of a five-foot sphere containing shaped charges of high explosives around a core of plutonium no bigger than a tennis ball. The plutonium had been created in reactors like the one Fermi and Szilard had built in Chicago in 1942. As the scientists gingerly inserted the plutonium into the bomb casing, the new element felt warm to the touch, as if it were alive.

The initial date of the test had been set for 4 July, but it was

Physicist Norris E. Bradbury sits next to 'the gadget', the code name for the atomic bomb exploded in the Trinity test, July 1945. Bradbury was in charge of assembling the high-explosive charges (known as lenses) which surrounded the plutonium core of the superweapon.

delayed until the 16th. Truman responded by postponing the Potsdam Conference with Churchill and Stalin. More than just scientific reputations depended on the outcome of this scientific experiment. The fate of nations was at stake.

The piece of arid land where the test was conducted had been named the Jornada del Muerto by the first Spanish explorers who passed through the area. The Journey of the Dead was a fitting name for a landscape that was to witness the detonation of the most destructive device yet constructed. In the early hours of 16 July, well before sunrise, staff were bussed in from Los Alamos. The sleepy audience gathered in the dark, twenty miles north of Ground Zero, on Compañia Hill. They included Hans Bethe, Edward Teller and the young physicist Richard Feynman. James Chadwick had come along in order to see just how powerful the neutron he had discovered thirteen years ago really was.

At Base Camp, about ten miles from Ground Zero, Enrico Fermi resurrected the nightmare scenario that had so frightened Compton three years earlier. He annoyed both his colleagues and General Groves by offering to take wagers on whether the bomb would ignite the atmosphere 'and, if so, whether it would merely destroy New Mexico or destroy the world'.[10] It was a theoretical possibility that haunted many people that morning. Meanwhile, Robert Oppenheimer waited nervously in the concrete control bunker nearly six miles south of Ground Zero, the closest observation point to the bomb.

At the last minute, the test had to be delayed again because of a violent thunderstorm. A new detonation time was set for 5.30 a.m. As lightning flickered in the sky, the scientists and the generals became increasingly edgy. Up on Compañia Hill was William Laurence, the only journalist allowed to witness 'the first fire ever made on earth that did not have its origin in the sun'.[11] He recalled how they were told to lie down, facing away from the blast with their faces turned to the ground. Dark welder's glass was handed out to protect their eyes from the blinding flash. Edward Teller advised him to rub suntan lotion on his exposed skin as protection against the dangerous UV radiation. 'It was an eerie sight,' said Laurence, 'to see a number of our highest-ranking scientists seriously rubbing sunburn lotion on their faces and hands in the pitch blackness of the night, 20 miles away from the expected flash.'[12]

At 5.25 a.m. a green flare was fired from Oppenheimer's control bunker and a siren wailed into the night. At Base Camp the scientists and soldiers lay down in shallow trenches that looked like graves. One minute before detonation, another warning flare was fired and again a siren sounded, echoing across the desert. These warnings were repeated at zero minus ten seconds. For Isidor Rabi, waiting anxiously at Base Camp, those final ten seconds lying in the darkness lasted an eternity. Then suddenly, said Rabi,

there was an enormous flash of light, the brightest light I have ever seen or that I think anyone has ever seen. It blasted; it pounced; it bored its way right through you. It was a vision which was seen with more than the eye. It was seen to last forever. You would wish it would stop; altogether it lasted about two seconds. Finally it was over, diminishing, and we looked toward the place where the bomb had been; there was an enormous ball of fire which grew and grew and it rolled as it grew; it went up into the air, in yellow flashes and into scarlet and green. It looked menacing. It seemed to come toward one.

As Rabi stared at the fireball, mesmerized, he realized that 'a new thing had just been born; a new control; a new understanding of man, which man had acquired over nature.'[13]

Alongside him at Base Camp was Fermi's colleague Emilio Segrè. When he saw the 'unbelievable brightness' burning through the dark glass, for a sickening moment he too feared 'the explosion might set fire to the atmosphere and thus finish the earth'.[14] Philip Morrison, also at Base Camp, was astonished by the heat of the explosion on that cold, dark desert morning: 'It was like opening a hot oven with the sun coming out like a sunrise.'[15]

Enrico Fermi felt the shock wave strike him forty seconds after the blast. True experimentalist that he was, Fermi had prepared a test to estimate the strength of the blast. He dropped small pieces of paper from a height of six feet. They travelled about eight feet in the blast wave. Using his trusty slide-rule, he calculated the yield at 10,000 tons of TNT. Later his wife joked that 'he was so profoundly and totally absorbed in his bits of paper that he was not aware of the tremendous noise'.[16]

On Compañia Hill, moments before the explosion, Laurence could see the 'first faint signs of dawn' in the east:

And just at that instant there rose from the bowels of the earth a light not of this world, the light of many suns in one. It was a sunrise such as the world had never seen, a great green super-sun climbing in a fraction of a second to a height of more than 8,000 feet, rising ever higher until it touched the clouds, lighting up earth and sky all around with a dazzling luminosity.

It was, Laurence thought, like 'an elemental force freed from its bonds after being chained for billions of years.' He also described the 'great cloud' that formed, 'a giant column, which soon took the shape of a supramundane mushroom'.[17]

For a 'very short but extremely long time', the landscape around Laurence and the others on the hill was completely and eerily silent as they gazed in awe at the expanding fireball. It was like 'a vibrant volcano spouting fire to the sky'. Thirty years before, Wells too had

The Trinity atomic test. At 5.30 a.m. on 16 July 1945, just before dawn, an artificial sun rises from the desert of the Jornada del Muerto, New Mexico.

imagined an atomic explosion as being like a volcano. Then, about a hundred seconds after the flash, came the 'first cry of a newborn world'. 'The thunder reverberated all through the desert, bounced back and forth from the Sierra Oscuro, echo upon echo. The ground trembled under our feet as in an earthquake.' Prometheus, as Laurence said, 'had broken his bonds and brought a new fire down to the earth'.[18]

The chemist George B. Kistiakowsky had fought with the White Russian Army before he came to America. The explosives expert had made the gadget's specially shaped charges ('lenses') which focused the force of the implosion onto the plutonium core. Unlike the physicists, he had a fairly low expectation of the power of the bomb. He left the safety of the concrete control bunker seconds before detonation to watch the explosion. Kistiakowsky was knocked off his feet by the blast at a distance of 10,000 yards. As he said afterwards, the explosion at Trinity was 'the nearest thing to doomsday that one could possibly imagine. I am sure that at the end of the world – in the last millisecond of the earth's existence – the last man will see what we have just seen!'[19]

Brigadier General Thomas F. Farrell, Groves's deputy, was also in the control bunker. In his official report to the War Department of what he saw that July morning, the experienced soldier struggled to find words to express the enormity of the moment:

The effects could well be called unprecedented, magnificent, beautiful, stupendous and terrifying. No man-made phenomenon of such tremendous power had ever occurred before. The lighting effects beggared description. The whole country was lighted by a searching light with the intensity many times that of the midday sun. It was golden, purple, violet, grey and blue. It lighted every peak, crevasse and ridge of the nearby mountain range with a clarity and beauty that cannot be described but must be seen to be imagined. It was that beauty the great poets dream about but describe most poorly and inadequately. Thirty seconds after the explosion, came, first, the air blast, pressing hard against the people and things; to be followed almost immediately by the strong, sustained, awesome roar which warned of doomsday and made us feel that we puny things were blasphemous to dare tamper with the forces heretofore reserved to the Almighty.[20]

At the moment of the explosion, Farrell voiced the deep anxiety that many felt, but few would admit. As night was turned to day and the desert melted in the heat of the superbomb, the battle-hardened soldier cried out: 'The long-hairs have let it get away from them!'[21]

Five miles away from Farrell, James Conant also feared that the atmosphere had been ignited: 'The whole world has gone up in flames,' he thought in a fleeting but terrible moment of utter panic.[22]

The violence and intensity of what they all witnessed that morning was unprecedented. Over a hundred miles away, the residents of Gallup, New Mexico reported that their windows rattled in their frames. People thought that a meteorite had impacted nearby. The flash of the Trinity blast was seen as far away as Amarillo, Texas, 450 miles to the east. It was bright enough to light up the face of the moon for an instant. The flash had such an unearthly brilliance that it was glimpsed a hundred miles away by Georgia Green, who was being driven to an early class at the University of New Mexico. When the bomb exploded she cried out, 'What was that?'[23] Georgia was blind.

Edwin McMillan, the nuclear physicist whose discovery of element 93 (neptunium) had led Glenn Seaborg to plutonium, was on the hill with Laurence. He recalled that:

The whole spectacle was so tremendous and one might almost say fantastic that the immediate reaction of the watchers was one of awe rather than excitement. After some minutes of silence, a few people made remarks like, "Well, it worked," and then conversation and discussion became general. I am sure that all who witnessed this test went away with a profound feeling that they had seen one of the great events of history.[24]

A few hours after the blast, the young physicist Herbert Anderson was driven in a lead-lined army tank to Ground Zero. He observed the bomb crater through the tank's periscope. 'The sand within a radius of 400 yards was transformed into a glasslike substance the colour of green jade. A steel rigging-tower weighing 32 tons, at a distance of 800 yards, was turned into a twisted mass of wreckage. The tower at Zero was completely vaporized.'[25] Analysis of the debris revealed that the explosion had been bigger than Fermi had calculated – the equivalent of 18,600 tons of TNT, or 18.6 kilotons in the language of the new nuclear age.

Szilard's friend from the Berlin years, Victor Weisskopf, watched the Trinity test from Base Camp. The initial flash of light was too bright to look at, even through welder's glass. Afterwards, Weisskopf recalled seeing a reddish glowing smoke ball rising with a thick stem of dark brown color. This smoke ball was surrounded by a blue glow which clearly indicated a strong radioactivity and was certainly due to the gamma rays emitted by the cloud into the surrounding air. At that moment the cloud had about 1,000 billions of curies of radioactivity whose radiation must have produced the blue glow.[26]

In his autobiography, Weisskopf describes this 'uncanny' glow around the initial cloud as 'a blue halo surrounding the yellow and orange sphere, an aureole of bluish light around the ball'. He was reminded of a painting by Matthias Grünewald, the Isenheim Altarpiece, which he had once seen in the Alsatian town of Colmar. One of the wings of this folding masterpiece, painted in about 1515, depicts the Resurrection. This striking image shows Jesus almost entirely enclosed in an ascending sphere of bright yellow and orange, surrounded by a bluish halo, against a night sky. To be reminded of the Resurrection of Christ by the explosion of an atomic bomb was, as Weisskopf acknowledged, 'a paradoxical and disturbing association'.[27]

As he watched the awesome explosion, Robert Oppenheimer, who had studied Sanskrit, recalled some ancient lines from the sacred Hindu text, the Bhagavad Gita: 'Now I am become Death, the destroyer of worlds.'[28] Later, Oppenheimer said that he knew that a new world had been born that morning in the desert. He also understood that the problems it raised were as old as humankind itself:

When it went off, in the New Mexico dawn, that first atomic bomb, we thought of Alfred Nobel, and his vain hope, that dynamite would put an end to wars. We thought of the legend of Prometheus, of that deep sense of guilt in man's new powers, that reflects his recognition of evil, and his long knowledge of it.[29]

In 1962, just days before the Cuban Missile Crisis and the threat of global nuclear war, General Groves asked Oppenheimer why he had named the first test of the atomic bomb Trinity. Oppenheimer replied that he wasn't entirely sure himself, 'but I know what thoughts were in my mind. There is a poem of John Donne, written just before his death, which I know and love.' In his reply to the general, he quoted a passage from Donne's 'Hymne to God My God, in My Sicknesse':

As West and East
In all flat Maps – and I am one – are one,
So death doth touch the Resurrection.

The theme of this poem, and of another by Donne which Oppenheimer recommended to Groves, 'Batter My Heart, Three Person'd God', is the paradox of what Richard Rhodes rightly calls 'destruction that might also redeem'.[30]

For both Oppenheimer and Weisskopf, as well as many other scientists including Leo Szilard, although the atomic bomb was a device of ultimate destruction it also held out the possibility of creating a lasting peace. They hoped that the atomic superweapon would prove so terrible that nations would forgo war and embrace peace. But was the atomic bomb big enough, Niels Bohr asked Oppenheimer when he first arrived at Los Alamos. The visionary scientist hoped that the weapon would be so destructive that war would be meaningless, other than as an act of mutual suicide. The fictional saviour scientists had also hoped that their superweapons would bring about lasting peace. Wells predicted that the world would have to pass through the fires of atomic war before it was transformed into what Frederick Soddy had memorably called 'one smiling Garden of Eden'.[31] Many scientists watching the Trinity test shared this dream of a new world arising like a phoenix from the atomic ashes. After death would come resurrection.

Such thoughts might even have been in President Truman's mind, less than a month after Trinity, when he heard that the atomic bomb had destroyed Hiroshima. On his way to the Potsdam Conference, at which three world leaders shaped the post-war world, Truman had re-read those lines from Tennyson's poem that he had copied out thirty-five years earlier, in the same year that Jack London had fantasized about a scientific superweapon wiping out the threat from the Far East. When Truman was interviewed in 1951 by journalist John Hersey, whose reports on Hiroshima for the *New Yorker* had shocked America, the President spoke of the significance that Tennyson's lines held for him: 'I guess that's what I've been really working for ever since I first put that poetry in my pocket.'[32] Tennyson had written of a final war in which 'there rain'd a ghastly dew' and of an ensuing age of peace in which 'the Parliament of man, the Federation of the world' is established.[33] Truman clearly saw an anticipation of both the United Nations and the atomic bomb in those lines penned a century earlier by an English poet. But Tennyson would have been utterly appalled by the hellish weapons that progress and science created in the twentieth century. In the future, the price of peace would be high indeed.

On a spring night in May 1942, Air Marshal Arthur Harris, Commander in Chief of British Bomber Command, conducted his first thousand-bomber raid against Germany. It was the start of a new and terrible tactic in the war against Hitler's Third Reich. Harris was convinced that the war could be won by strategic area bombing, or 'carpet bombing', as opposed to the precision bombing of specific targets.

The ancient Rhine city of Cologne was the target of the raid, code-named Millennium. Air Vice-Marshal Baldwin accompanied the mission in a Stirling bomber. He described how 'the sky was full of aircraft all heading for Cologne'. As they approached the city, he 'caught sight of the twin towers of Cologne cathedral, silhouetted against the light of three huge fires that looked as though they were streaming from open blast furnaces'. After Baldwin's bomber dropped its bombs and headed for home, he looked back and saw an unforgettable scene of devastation: 'the fires seemed like rising suns and this effect became more pronounced as we drew further away . . . it seemed that we were leaving behind us a huge representation of the Japanese banner. Within nine minutes of the coast, we circled to take a last look. The fires then resembled distant volcanoes.'[34]

In Cologne, 480 people were killed. That is not a huge death toll in a vicious and bloody war, but it was to be the beginning of a concerted campaign against what was referred to as enemy 'morale', a euphemism for civilians. In the year that poison gas first rolled across the Ypres fields, British mathematician Frederick W. Lanchester had argued that the objective of air warfare should be to overwhelm 'the fire-extinguishing appliances of the community', with the result that 'the city may be destroyed in toto'.[35]

On 24 July 1943, when the attack on Hamburg code-named Operation Gomorrah began, Lanchester's abstract prediction became brutal reality. For three nights and days the city was attacked from the air with high explosives and incendiaries. On the night of 27/28 July, a massive raid took place. It unleashed something never before seen in the history of warfare. The Hamburg Fire Department called it a *Feuersturm*, a 'firestorm'. As the inferno caused by the bombing forced hot air upwards, sucking in air from the surrounding districts, it created hurricane-force winds. Trees tumbled like matchsticks; civilians were blown screaming into the flames; window panes melted in the intense heat. People attempting to flee became stuck fast in the now-molten asphalt of the roads, unable to escape the raging fires. As many as 50,000 people died, more than the total killed in all the air raids on Britain in World War II.

Physicist and mathematician Freeman Dyson, who in the 1950s worked in America on designs for a nuclear spaceship, was at the time a civilian operations analyst for British Bomber Command. He was disturbed by the Hamburg raids. The operation made him question his daily role of 'carefully calculating how to murder most economically another hundred thousand people'. After the war he even compared himself to the Nazi analysts and bureaucrats doing similar work: 'They had sat in their offices, writing memoranda and calculating how to murder people efficiently, just like me. The main difference was that they were sent to jail or hanged as war criminals, while I went free.'[36]

Terrible though Operation Gomorrah was, the tactics of firebombing had yet to be perfected. This happened during 1945. Research conducted by British and American scientists using recreations of German and Japanese towns – accurate down to the correct make of soft furnishings – had revealed the optimum mix of high explosives and incendiaries. This knowledge was used in the raids on Dresden and Tokyo in the final year of hostilities. They are among the most horrific acts of war to be carried out in the whole of the twentieth century.

A sense of the awfulness managed to penetrate even the censored and jingoistic media of the day. *Newsweek* reported the bombing of Dresden beneath the headline NOW TERROR, TRULY. It quoted Associated Press: 'Allied air chiefs had decided to adopt deliberate terror bombing of German population centers as a military means of hastening the Reich's surrender by snarling up communications and sapping morale.'[37] British and American bombers incinerated and pulverized the elegant city of Dresden. At least 35,000 people were either burnt alive or blown apart – soldiers, women, children, even Allied prisoners of war. The precise death toll will never be known.

The novelist Kurt Vonnegut was a 22-year-old GI and, at the time of the raid, a prisoner of war in Dresden. 'They burnt the whole damn town down,' he recalled.[38] In his novel *Slaughterhouse 5* (1969), his character Billy Pilgrim describes the city afterwards as being 'like the moon'.[39] Vonnegut and his fellow prisoners had to collect corpses after the raid. They dug down through the rubble into basements where people had thought they would be safe. What the GIs found resembled 'a streetcar full of people who'd simultaneously had heart failure. Just people sitting there in their chairs, all dead. A firestorm is an amazing thing. It doesn't occur in nature. It's fed by the tornadoes that occur in the midst of it and there isn't a damn thing to breathe.'[40]

Before the raid, said Vonnegut, Dresden had been 'the most beautiful city in the world'. After the swarms of British and American bombers had left, Allied newsreels of the city boasted that Dresden had been 'bombed to atoms'. Vonnegut was profoundly shocked by the experience: 'We had no idea that our side was capable of such indiscriminate destruction.' It was, he said, a 'total calamity of civilization'.[41] Afterwards even Winston Churchill questioned the strategy of bombing German cities 'simply for the sake of increasing the terror ... The destruction of Dresden remains a serious query against the conduct of Allied bombing.'[42] By the end of the war, some 600,000 Germans, mostly civilians, had been killed by bombing. In Japan, the figure would rise even higher.

In 1945 the commander of the United States Army Air Forces, Major General Curtis E. LeMay, was tasked with taking the war to the Japanese mainland. For LeMay, killing civilians was not an ethical problem: 'We're at war with Japan. We were attacked by Japan. Do you want to kill Japanese, or would you rather have Americans killed?'[43] He ordered over three hundred of the latest B-29 bombers to attack Tokyo on the night of 10 March. Man and nature conspired that night to produce truly horrific results. The US Strategic Bombing Survey described how the prevailing 20 mph wind created not just a firestorm but a 'conflagration'. This 'wall of fire' swept across fifteen square miles in six hours, burning everything in its path. At least 100,000 people were killed and over 41,000 seriously injured.[44]

This was killing on an unimaginable scale. At the time, the justification for such carnage was that because the Japanese Government had mobilized the entire population in the war effort, civilians were deemed a legitimate military target. Newspaper headlines conditioned the public in America and Britain to view such bombing as part of the normal course of war. In pre-war fiction, it had always been the enemy – the 'baddies' – who targeted civilians. Now British and American planes were routinely bombing cities, indiscriminately killing men, women and children in their thousands. For Einstein's close friend Max Born, forced out of Germany by the Nazis, this was a step too far:

Britain was in the war precisely to fight this kind of barbarity. Can one rid the world of an evil by committing the same evil, planned and amplified? I think one cannot. The bombing war as practised by the allied air forces appeared to me, right from the beginning, as morally wrong. That it was also strategically wrong has now been proved without doubt.[45]

The moral objections of Born and others has subsequently been vindicated. Since 1980, the use of incendiary bombing on civilian targets has been prohibited under international law.[46]

The news reports of area bombing of cities in Germany and Japan in the final stages of the war served another important purpose. They mentally prepared Allied populations for the next generation of weapons of mass destruction: the atomic bomb. According to Rudolf Peierls, one of the scientists who helped to make this superweapon a reality, 'without this background the atomic bomb raids on Japan might not have taken place'.[47]

In 1953, Churchill recalled that there 'never was a moment's discussion as to whether the atomic bomb should be used or not'.[48] That was not Leo Szilard's view. Once it became clear that the Nazis did not have the bomb, Szilard was determined that it should not be used on a Japanese city without warning.

Joseph Rotblat shared this view. He had been shocked to hear General Groves admit at an informal dinner party held at Los Alamos in March 1944 that 'the real purpose in making the bomb was to subdue the Soviets'. At the time, Niels Bohr used to come to Rotblat's room every morning at 8 a.m. to listen to the BBC World Service news on his radio. Rotblat's conversations with Bohr convinced him that the Nazis were not the real target of the atomic bomb. 'When it became evident, toward the end of 1944, that the Germans had abandoned their bomb project,' recalled Rotblat, 'the whole purpose of my being in Los Alamos ceased to be, and I asked for permission to leave and return to Britain.'[49]

As soon as Rotblat expressed his desire to go, the military authorities at Los Alamos forbade him to tell anyone why he wanted to leave. His colleagues were informed that he was leaving for personal reasons. His decision to get out was an act of great moral courage. Why did other scientists not follow him? On the 'magic mesa' there was little if any debate among the scientists about the morality of what they were doing. As historian Richard Rhodes notes, 'Oppenheimer had sold it as work that would end the war to end all wars and his people believed him.'[50]

Later, Joseph Rotblat identified three different moral stances among his fellow Los Alamites. One group was motivated by 'scientific curiosity – the strong urge to find out whether the theoretical calculations and predictions would come true'. These scientists wanted to wait until the bomb had been tested before discussing its use as a weapon. Others argued that using the bomb to end the war with Japan would save American lives; only then would they 'take a hand in efforts to ensure that the bomb would not be used again'. Another group believed that the project should have been halted once it became clear that there was no Nazi bomb. However, they 'were not willing to take an individual stand because they feared it would adversely affect their future career'. But these three groups 'were a minority in the scientific community', those with a 'social conscience'. The vast majority of scientists on the Hill were not bothered by moral scruples: 'they were quite content to leave it to others to decide how their work would be used'.

When Rotblat asked to leave Los Alamos, military intelligence immediately accused him of being a Soviet spy. Their allegations were pieced together from hearsay and surveillance. He refuted all the charges. Before leaving America, Rotblat visited the Chadwicks, who were now living in Washington. He then boarded a train bound for New York, carrying a suitcase and a box containing his research notes and correspondence. 'When I arrived there a few hours later, the box was missing. Nor, despite valiant efforts, was it ever recovered.'[51] Rotblat sailed for Britain on Christmas Eve 1944, leaving behind his work on the atomic superweapon and determined to dedicate his life to peaceful uses of science.

Unknown to the scientists on the Manhattan Project, from an early stage both government and military planners shared General Groves's view that the real purpose of the atomic bomb was to target Japan so as to intimidate the Soviets. 'The target is and was always expected to be Japan,' wrote Groves in a memo to Secretary of War Stimson on 23 April 1945.[52] According to Rotblat, the Manhattan Project scientists never for one moment imagined that the bomb would be dropped on Japan: 'All our concentration was on Germany.'[53]

The evidence that Japan was always the real target emerged as early as 5 May 1943, just a few months after Fermi and Szilard's pile went critical. The high-level Military Policy Committee, of which Groves was a member, ruled out using an atomic bomb on Germany because of the risk of an unexploded bomb falling into the hands of Nazi scientists. They agreed that the 'best point of use would be on a Japanese fleet concentration'.[54] The idea that from such an early stage Germany was not considered to be the main target deeply shocked Hans Bethe and other scientists, who learned of these secret notes only in 1995.

For Leo Szilard and his fellow émigrés, the threat was unquestionably from Germany's formidable scientists and industrial expertise. They wanted an atomic bomb to deter Hitler from using one first. They never considered the possibility that such a weapon would be used against a non-nuclear nation.

*

One man who was determined that the atomic bomb should be used on Japan was James F. Byrnes, President Roosevelt's director of the Office of War Mobilization. Byrnes had told Roosevelt in spring 1945 that the atomic bomb could be politically dangerous: 'if the project proves a failure, it will then be subjected to relentless investigation and criticism'.[55] When Roosevelt died, his successor, President Truman, appointed Byrnes to the so-called Interim Committee, which discussed targeting. As his biographer has said, Byrnes believed that the bomb should be used as soon as possible in order to 'show results'.[56] He also ruled out any warning or a demonstration on an unpopulated area. He was equally opposed to sharing research on the atomic bomb with the Soviet Union.

The historian Ferenc Szasz has rightly pointed out that 'the scientists who opposed the combat use of the weapon before August, 1945, were a small, out-of-power minority'.[57] Foremost among that minority was Leo Szilard. In the spring of 1945 he had convinced Einstein to write another letter to the President, and this time Einstein asked if Szilard could meet Roosevelt to air his concerns about the use of the bomb. Roosevelt died before the meeting could take place, and the new President directed him to James Byrnes.

They met at Byrnes's home at Spartansburg, South Carolina, in May 1945. Szilard was accompanied by Harold Urey. Both scientists were deeply concerned about how the use of the atomic bomb would affect both America's reputation and the political climate of the post-war world. Szilard had written a document, originally for Roosevelt, which discussed these issues and the future of atomic energy. In it he predicted that the use of atomic bombs against Japan would lead not to peace, but to preparations for a new and more terrible war: 'the first bomb that is detonated over Japan will be spectacular enough to start a race in *atomic* armaments between us and other nations'.[58]

He also warned that America's enemies might one day 'smuggle' atomic bombs into the country and 'carry them by truck into our cities'. They would be 'virtually impossible' to detect and could be used to blackmail the government at times of tension. 'Such bombs,' he said, 'may remain hidden in cellars of private houses in our cities for any number of years or they may remain hidden below the ground buried in gardens within our cities or buried in fields on the outskirts of our cities.' In this nightmare future he had sketched for America's new leaders, Szilard described how suddenly and without warning 'all of our major cities might vanish within a few hours'.[59]

Szilard predicted that in the post-war world there would be a race between America and the Soviet Union to build bombs. In six years they would be able to threaten the United States with devastation: 'most of our major cities might be completely destroyed in one single sudden attack and their populations might perish'.[60] To counter this and the future threat from nuclear-armed missiles, Szilard proposed a number of ingenious methods for the international control of atomic energy and arms.

But his words fell on deaf ears. It soon became clear that instead of negotiation, Byrnes preferred an aggressive foreign policy, similar to that described in Heinlein's science fiction story 'Solution Unsatisfactory'. Armed with the superweapon, he hoped to dictate a Pax Americana. The threat from the Soviet Union was uppermost in Byrnes's mind. The war would be over in six months, he said, and Soviet troops were already in Szilard's homeland, Hungary: 'Russia might be more manageable if impressed by American military might', he recalls Byrnes saying. 'A demonstration of the bomb might impress Russia.'

Szilard was 'completely flabbergasted' by the idea that 'rattling the bomb might make Russia more manageable'. The United States intended to intimidate the USSR. All Szilard could do was to try to impress upon the politician his fears that by using the bomb 'we might start an atomic arms race between America and Russia which might end with the destruction of both countries'. Leo Szilard left the meeting more worried than when he arrived:

I was rarely as depressed as when we left Byrnes' house and walked toward the station. I thought to myself how much better off the world might be had I been born in America and become influential in American politics, and had Byrnes been born in Hungary and studied physics. In all probability there would then have been no atomic bomb and no danger of an arms race between America and Russia.[61]

On his way back to Chicago, Szilard stopped off in Washington and met Oppenheimer, who was about to attend a meeting of the Interim Committee, set up that month to consider the use of the bomb.

Szilard told him that he thought it would be a great mistake to drop the atomic bomb on Japan. Oppenheimer flatly disagreed.

'The atomic bomb is shit,' said the man who had built it.

Szilard was shocked. 'What do you mean by that?' he asked.

'Well, this is a weapon which has no military significance,' explained Oppenheimer, rather disingenuously. 'It will make a big bang – a very big bang – but it is not a weapon which is useful in war.'[62]

Szilard could only shake his head in disbelief at Oppenheimer's words. They served to further deepen his concerns. He did not place much hope in Oppenheimer and his three fellow scientists who had been appointed to advise the Interim Committee. Szilard was convinced that the committee itself had been carefully picked to include those in favour of using the bomb. The politicians wanted to frighten the Soviets, and the military wanted something to show for the $2 billion that had been spent on the atomic superweapon. And as far as Leo Szilard was concerned, the physicists advising the committee, including Fermi, were all 'men who could be expected to play ball on this occasion'.[63]

General Groves was furious when he found out that Szilard had been to see Byrnes without asking permission. But 'permission' and 'chain of command' were alien concepts to Szilard. Once again, Arthur Compton – a member of the scientific advisory panel to the Interim Committee – stepped in as peacemaker. He attempted to mollify both sides by asking Szilard and his fellow Chicago scientists to set up their own committee to consider what should be done with the bomb and report back to the advisory panel. It was chaired by Met Lab physicist James Franck, who had worked on chemical weapons with Fritz Haber and Otto Hahn during World War I. Szilard and Eugene Rabinowitch were members of what became known as the Franck Committee. Its report (largely written by Szilard) proposed a demonstration of the bomb to 'avoid mass slaughter but yet convince the Japanese of the destructive power of the bomb'. But, as Szilard later admitted, 'what we did not discuss enough, was that Japan was defeated; the war could be ended by political means and need not be ended by military means'.[64]

When a demonstration of the atomic bomb over an uninhabited area was rejected by the Interim Committee, Szilard finally realized he was powerless to prevent its use against Japan. But he remained utterly convinced that this was the wrong decision and became even more determined that the voices of the dissenting scientists should be heard. At the very least, history should know that not every scientist agreed with the course of action adopted by Groves and Oppenheimer.

Szilard drafted a petition to put the scientists' views on record. Fifty-three Chicago scientists signed the first version. All the leading physicists put their names to it, as did most of the biologists. But Szilard noticed that none of the chemists had. 'This was so striking that I went over to the chemistry department to discover what the trouble was,' he wrote later:

What I discovered was rather disturbing: the chemists argued that what we must determine was solely whether more lives would be saved by using the bomb or by continuing the war without using the bomb. This was a utilitarian argument with which I was very familiar through my previous experiences in Germany. That some other issue might be involved in dropping a bomb on an inhabited city and killing men, women, and children did not occur to any of the chemists with whom I spoke.[65]

Szilard also wrote to Edward Teller at Los Alamos asking him to circulate a petition, allowing those scientists who wished to register 'their opposition on moral grounds to the use of these bombs in the present phase of the war' to do so.[66] Teller turned to Oppenheimer for advice. He was shocked by Oppenheimer's 'impatience and vehemence' when it came to Szilard's views. Oppenheimer argued that the use of the bomb was a matter solely for politicians and the military, not for scientists. What he didn't reveal to Teller was that he – a scientist – was already advising the government on the use of the bomb. And his advice was to go ahead and drop it on a Japanese city.

Edward Teller's reply to Szilard, dated 2 July 1945, is a remarkably revealing statement by a scientist justifying his fascination with super-weapons and absolving himself of responsibility for their use. He told his friend that he had decided not to circulate the petition. 'I have no hope of clearing my conscience,' he said. 'The things we are working on are so terrible that no amount of protesting or fiddling with politics will save our souls.' Teller claimed to have worked on the bomb not from a sense of duty or pleasure, but 'because the problems interested me'. He also cast doubt on Szilard's stand against dropping the bomb. 'I do not feel that there is any chance to outlaw any one weapon.'

In a clear reflection of Oppenheimer's view, Teller says that 'The accident that we worked out this dreadful thing should not give us the responsibility of having a voice in how it is to be used.' He argued that secrecy must be lifted so that this responsibility can be 'shifted to the people as a whole'. Having absolved scientists of responsibility for the use of their lethal handiwork, Teller placed his hopes on the distant prospect of world peace: 'If we have a slim chance of survival, it lies in the possibility to get rid of wars.' People needed to be convinced 'that the next war would be fatal'. He concluded his letter thus: 'I feel that I should do the wrong thing if I tried to say how to tie the little toe of the ghost to the bottle from which we just helped it to escape.'[67]

Despite this setback, Szilard did send copies of the petition to Los Alamos. But he didn't hold out much hope that Teller's colleagues would sign. Indeed, unknown to Szilard, one of them had even proposed dropping a dozen atomic bombs simultaneously on Japan. 'Of course, you will find only a few people on your project who are willing to sign such a petition,' admitted Szilard in his covering letter, 'and I am sure you will find many boys confused as to what kind of a thing a moral issue is.'[68] But the atomic scientists on the Hill were never given the opportunity to find out what a moral issue really was. Oppenheimer refused to allow the petition to be circulated.

The final draft of Szilard's petition was written the day before the first atomic bomb was detonated in the New Mexico desert, creating for an instant a man-made sun on earth. The petition predicted that this 'new means of destruction' was just the first step on the road to an even more terrible weapon: 'there is almost no limit to the destructive power which will become available in the course of their future development'. It also warned that the 'nation which sets the precedent of using these newly liberated forces of nature for purposes of destruction may have to bear the responsibility of opening the door to an era of devastation on an unimaginable scale'.[69] Here was a clear anticipation of the hydrogen bomb.

Eventually, 68 scientists registered their moral objections by signing. On 24 July, Compton, in his letter to Groves forwarding the petition, mentioned that a poll he had conducted of 150 scientists found a majority in favour of a demonstration of the weapon and a new offer to the Japanese to surrender. The petition never reached the President. By the time Groves sent it to Stimson, Truman had already attended the Potsdam Conference with James Byrnes, and was awaiting news of the superweapon's use against the enemy.

Hiroshima, 6 August 1945 – the day on which the dreams of a scientific superweapon became reality. Jack London and H. G. Wells had imagined this day in fiction, and sown the seed in the collective consciousness. Humankind had been beguiled by terrible dreams of a weapon so awesome that a city filled with men, women and children could be destroyed by a single bomb dropped by a lone aircraft high up in the sky. Scientists such as Fritz Haber and Shiro Ishii had applied their specialist knowledge to realize this vision of a superweapon, but with only limited success. Leo Szilard knew that only physics could create such a weapon, but he had long dreaded the day when it became a reality. He feared that it might lead to war on an apocalyptic scale.

For the people of Hiroshima on the morning of 6 August, it was the beginning of just another humid, summer's day. Across the city, people were heading off to work on bicycles and trams. In the parade grounds around the sixteenth-century castle, soldiers were stripped to the waist, exercising in the pale morning sunlight. There was scarcely a cloud in the sky, and the temperature was already edging up towards a sultry 30°C.

Some eight thousand schoolchildren were busy in the centre of the city, clearing firebreaks. In March, tens of thousands had died in firestorms unleashed by an incendiary attack on the capital. Hiroshima was the headquarters of the Japanese 2nd Army, home to over 40,000 troops. Their city was a target. But for some reason unknown to its people, Hiroshima had been spared the firebombs that had devastated other towns and cities in the Land of the Rising Sun. Soon the inhabitants of Hiroshima would understand why.

An air-raid warning had sounded just after seven o'clock, followed twenty minutes later by the all-clear. At 8.15 the drone of three B-29 bombers caused some people to pause and look up anxiously. But what could a couple of planes do against a whole city? Thousands of feet above them in the blue sky, the big planes seemed like harmless, fragile silver insects. This time there would be no air-raid warning.

One minute later a new kind of bomb exploded 1,900 feet above the city of Hiroshima. The ferocity of the energies released – heat, light, nuclear radiation and pressure – was without parallel on the surface of the earth. A slug of the rare uranium isotope uranium-235 had been fired into a sphere of uranium-235 to create a critical mass. A little over 1 per cent of the uranium in the bomb (less than 2 lb) fissioned, instantly converting a tiny amount of mass into pure energy.[70] But it was enough to blast the heart out of the sprawling Japanese city.

When the atomic bomb exploded it created a fireball. Its initial temperature was several million degrees centigrade, and its pressure several hundred thousand bars. On the ground immediately beneath the fireball – the point known as the hypocentre – the pressure 'was estimated to be [between] 4.5 and 6.7 tons per square meter'.[71] For a split second, the temperature on the ground soared to around 3,000 to 4,000°C; no element, including carbon, remains solid at 4000°C.

The thermal energy of an atomic bomb, a searing flash of electromagnetic radiation, travels at the speed of light – 186,000 miles per second. People up to half a mile away were instantly burned to carbon, their internal organs evaporated, their charred and shrunken bodies locked in the precise position they were in at the moment of the explosion. Even a mile away, the temperature of exposed surfaces such as skin rose to a blistering 540°C.

As the fireball rapidly expanded, it created a destructive shock wave and a wall of air travelling at supersonic speed. Windows fragmented into a hail of lethal projectiles, driven by hurricane-force winds that tore clothing from bodies and lacerated flesh. Buildings were pulled apart like toys and set ablaze, casting a dense pall of dust and smoke over the city. A bright summer's morning instantly became night.

The definitive Japanese account of the bombing describes what happened in those terrible moments immediately following the explosion:

With a violent flash that ripped the sky apart and a thunderous sound that shook the earth to its foundation, Hiroshima was pounded to the ground in an instant. Then, from where a whole city once was, a huge column of fire bounded straight up toward heaven. A dense cloud of smoke rose and spread out, covering and darkening the whole sky. The earth below became shrouded in heavy darkness. The dead and wounded lay fallen, piled up, everywhere: the carnage was like a scene in hell. Then, fires broke out all over and soon merged into a huge conflagration, which grew in intensity moment by moment. As a fierce whirlwind blew, half-naked and stark naked bodies, darkly soiled and covered with blood, began moving; in clustered groups resembling departed spirits, they staggered away in bewildered flight from the inferno. One after another fell down and died. Countless others lay trapped under fallen debris and were burned alive; their pathetic voices calling for family members, and for help, could be heard within the wildly dancing flames . . .

When their hands hung down, the blood accumulated in the fingertips and caused throbbing pain, so they held their arms up and forward; burned so badly that the skin peeled and hung loosely, their raw hands and arms oozed and dripped blood. They looked just like ghosts. Barely managing not to fall over, they stumbled along in continuous lines to escape from fiery death.[72]

Seiko Ikeda was one of the schoolchildren helping to clear firebreaks in the city. Sixty years later, he recalled the horror:

The skin on my friends' faces was melting off like wax on a burning candle. I saw people whose eyes had come out, people holding in their internal organs as they walked. From the rubble, people screamed, 'Help me, please!' All I could do was save myself. I scrambled up Hijiyama Hill. The city had vanished, it was an ocean of fire.[73]

The explosive chain reaction of the uranium-235 bathed the centre of Hiroshima with deadly radiation: alpha and beta particles, gamma rays and neutrons. There were significant levels of radiation in the environment for at least three days after the explosion, affecting those who came into the city looking for loved ones. Within an hour of the explosion and until mid-afternoon, a black, sooty rain fell on Hiroshima and its unfortunate inhabitants. The rain came from the towering mushroom cloud hanging over the city like some vengeful god and contained dust that was highly radioactive. For those who survived the initial blast and the searing heat, the one word on their lips was *Mizu!* – water. When it began to rain, they turned their faces skywards looking for relief. But in this radioactive environment, the rain too was poisoned; it brought only temporary relief and at the price of a painful death a few days later.

More than four square miles of Hiroshima were scorched reddish-brown by the intense heat of 'Little Boy', the grotesquely inoffensive name of the first atomic bomb to be dropped on a city. It was as though a giant welder's torch had been held against the earth. Nine-tenths of the city's buildings were destroyed. The infrastructure and essential services were wiped out at one blow. Survivors, often with appalling injuries, found few people able to care for them. Those doctors who were still alive had no idea what kind of weapon had been used. Even when it was announced that an atomic bomb had been dropped, they had no idea how it would damage the human body, or what symptoms to expect. It was a revolution in science and in warfare. 'We were, in effect, the first guinea pigs in such experimentation,' said Father Arrupe, one of the Jesuits who helped to treat the victims.[74]

Of the 350,000 people in the city that day in August, more than 100,000 were killed immediately. Five years later people were still dying. The final death toll is thought to be in excess of 200,000. To this figure must be added the cancers and birth defects caused by the radiation that the survivors of the atomic bomb, the *hibakusha*, would suffer for the rest of their lives. Even today the atomic bomb is still killing people. From the moment the atomic bomb exploded, it released radiation which began attacking the human body at its most fundamental level – the cell. On the day of the bombing, the symptoms of radiation sickness included bloody vomiting and loss of appetite. In the days that followed, victims would become increasingly ill, suffering diarrhoea, purpura (discoloured patches caused by bleeding in the skin), hair loss, bleeding from the nose and fever.

Wilfred Burchett, the first independent journalist to describe what had happened on the ground, described their mysterious sickness as 'an atomic plague'. He arrived in Hiroshima thirty days after the bomb was dropped, having skilfully slipped away from the chaperoned foreign press corps and made his own way to the bombed city. Burchett described how apparently uninjured people were now dying:

They lost appetite. Their hair fell out. Bluish spots appeared on their bodies. And then bleeding began from the ears, nose and mouth. At first, the doctors told me, they thought these were the symptoms of general debility. They gave their patients Vitamin A injections. The results were horrible. The flesh started rotting away from the hole caused by the injection of the needle. And in every case the victim died.[75]

His report for the *Daily Express* was headlined WARNING TO THE WORLD. It appalled readers around the globe. Officials from the American occupying forces called a specially convened press conference to deny that atomic radiation had caused the symptoms described by Burchett. In Hiroshima, rumours spread that everyone would soon die, poisoned by the unknown forces unleashed by the superbomb. The rumours also said that nothing would ever grow in the city again. It would become a radioactive wasteland like the one in Africa that H. G. Wells had described in *Tono-Bungay*.

Three days after Hiroshima was bombed, it was Nagasaki's turn. Nagasaki was chosen as the target only because cloud obscured the first choice, Kokura. This time a plutonium bomb was used, code-named 'Fat Man'. The Hiroshima bomb had exploded with a force equivalent to 12.5 kilotons. The Nagasaki bomb was much bigger, equivalent to 22 kilotons.

The implosion method was far more efficient than the uranium-235 bomb. Although it only contained 13 lb of plutonium, 20 per cent of its mass was converted to energy. According to Farrell this was 'a new type of cosmic weapon, more destructive and easier to make than the first one dropped on Hiroshima'.[76] But due to the lie of the land, fewer people died at Nagasaki on 9 August – at least 70,000. However, the figures do not include the thousands of Korean slave labourers who worked in Japanese factories. The real figure, including subsequent deaths from cancers and other long-term effects of the bomb, is twice as high.[77]

As at Hiroshima, up to 3,000 feet from the hypocentre it was as if the sun had touched the surface of the earth. Every living thing within that radius was instantly carbonized, from people walking on the street to birds in mid-flight. Cast-iron roofs warped and melted into impossible shapes; stone was crushed and shattered by the fantastic forces released as mass was transmuted into energy. Solid granite melted. As far as 6,500 feet from the hypocentre, roof tiles bubbled.

Farther from the explosion, the radiant heat burned exposed skin, and even 10,000 feet away combustible substances burst into flame. White fabric reflected the energy away, while darker materials absorbed it, burning strange patterns into people's skin for the rest of their lives. One and a half miles from the hypocentre a piece of Japanese paper had the characters, which were written in black ink, burned out as neatly as if they had been cut by a laser.[78] The official US Government report on the bombings noted dispassionately that people suffered flash burns to their skin 'out to the remarkable distance of 13,800 feet'.[79] Trees on the hillsides around Nagasaki were scorched by the flash of heat. Afterwards, their browned leaves made it seem as though autumn had come early to Japan.

About 4,000 feet from the hypocentre, reinforced concrete smoke-stacks with eight-inch walls designed to withstand a major earthquake were overturned. The British Mission to Japan estimated that if such a bomb were exploded over a British city it would have seriously damaged every building within two and a half miles of the hypo-centre.[80] Such a bomb dropped on London's Trafalgar Square would have devastated an area extending northwards, past Russell Square to Camden Town. To the south, it would have laid waste to West-minster, the Houses of Parliament and beyond. Buckingham Palace to the west and the Bank of England to the East would have been well within the range of its destructive power. In an instant, one bomb would have obliterated the human and historic heart of the city.

Flying in a B-29 accompanying the Nagasaki bomber, William Laurence had no sympathy for the inhabitants of the Japanese city about to be bombed: 'Does one feel any pity or compassion for the poor devils about to die? Not when one thinks of Pearl Harbor and of the Death March on Bataan.'[81] A correspondent who flew over Nagasaki after the bombing described what he saw:

Great tongues of red and orange flame leaped toward the sky, reaching up and grabbing at what appeared to be a large white cloud of smoke that hung like a mushroom over the region. We ran along the coast over a ridge of hills. The blaze now seemed to stretch over the whole eastern sky, covering an area of at least 10 square miles. The effect of the fire reaching over the hills was that of a volcano, the top of which had been blown clear off and which now was seething lava from its base.[82]

The White House press release following the Hiroshima bombing was triumphant in hailing the new superweapon that its scientists had created:

It is an atomic bomb. It is a harnessing of the basic power of the universe. The force from which the sun draws its power has been loosed against those who brought war to the Far East . . . The battle of the laboratories held fateful risks for us as well as the battles of the air, land, and sea, and we have now won the battle of the laboratories as we have won the other battles . . . We have spent two billion dollars on the greatest scientific gamble in history – we won.[83]

Three months later, the British scientist Jacob Bronowski, who would later work with Leo Szilard, drove through Nagasaki at dusk. It was, he said, a 'desolate landscape' in which 'the skeletons of the Mitsubishi factory buildings, pushed backwards and sideways as if by a giant hand' stood in a 'bare waste of ashes'.[84] Many people looked at the atomic wastelands of Hiroshima and Nagasaki and saw in their ruins the future of their own cities. The dream of a new world order arising like a phoenix from these radioactive ashes now seemed very hollow indeed.

The secret US Government report on the bombings, prepared for the Manhattan Project, declared the work of the scientists to be a resounding success:

In both Hiroshima and Nagasaki the tremendous scale of the disaster largely destroyed the cities as entities. Even the worst of all other previous bombing attacks on Germany and Japan, such as the incendiary raids on Hamburg in 1943 and on Tokyo in 1945, were not comparable to the paralyzing effect of the atomic bombs.

The report also noted that, as well as the terrible damage done to the cities, the bombings provoked 'a panic flight' of people out of the cities. It continued:

On 10 August 1945, the day after the atomic bomb was dropped on Nagasaki, a mother and her son receive a boiled rice ball from an emergency relief party one mile south-east of Ground Zero.

Aside from the physical injury and damage, the most significant effect of the atom bombs was the sheer terror which it struck into the peoples of the bombed cities. This terror, resulting in immediate hysterical activity and flight from the cities, had one especially pronounced effect: persons who had become accustomed to mass air raids had grown to pay little heed to single planes or small groups of planes, but after the atomic bombings the appearance of a single plane caused more terror and disruption of normal life than the appearance of many hundreds of planes had ever been able to cause before. The effect of this terrible fear of the potential danger from even a single enemy plane on the lives of the peoples of the world in the event of any future war can easily be conjectured.[85]

The Manhattan Project scientists had worked their fatal magic, and the war had been won. But the price of peace was that now the inhabitants of every city around the world had to live with the 'sheer terror' that had been visited on the citizens of Hiroshima and Nagasaki.

V

The End of Dreams

From the place of ground zero,
O Lord, deliver us.
From the rain of the cobalt,
O Lord, deliver us.

Walter M. Miller, Jr,
A Canticle for Leibowitz (1959)

17

The Doomsday Decade

Doomsday is near; die all, die merrily.
William Shakespeare, *1 Henry IV*

The American capital is missing in action.

A single enemy atom bomb has destroyed the heart of the city. The rest is rapidly becoming a fire-washed memory. The flames are raging over 18 square miles.

Washington is burning to death. Communications are temporarily disrupted. Help of all kinds is urgently needed from the rest of the country – blood, drugs, bandages, doctors, nurses, food, transportation.

Uncounted thousands are dead. More thousands of injured lie, spread in untended rows, on hospital lawns and parks, or walk unheeded until they fall.

Civil defense has broken down. The few valiant disaster squads are helpless in this homeless flood of agony and misery. Troops are moving in to restore order among maddened masses trying to flee the city.

Fright crowds the rubbled streets and wears the blank face of awe. It couldn't happen here yesterday. It did happen here before dawn today.

The bomb exploded in southwest Washington, midway between the Capitol building and the Jefferson Memorial. It lighted the city as if it were a Roman candle.

For a radius of a mile from the center of the blast the devastation is utter – a huge scorched zero, as if a giant, white-hot hammer had pounded the area into the earth. Blast and fire then reached out in widening waves.[1]

This was how World War III began in 1951, as reported by Associated Press journalist Hal Boyle. His dramatic 'eyewitness account of the

A-bombing of Washington, D.C.' was published in October of that year by *Collier's* magazine, in a special issue devoted to speculation about the next war. The year before, President Truman had authorized the building of the next generation of nuclear weapons, the hydrogen bomb.

Aerial view of the smoking ruins of New York City after an atomic attack in a still from the 1952 film Invasion USA.

The American scientific community was divided as to whether the H-bomb, or Hell Bomb as the press soon dubbed it, was ethical or even possible. In spring 1951 the physicist John Wheeler wrote to Richard Feynman asking him to work on the new bomb. In his letter he estimated that there was 'at least 40 percent chance of war by September'.[2] Feynman declined.

A thousand times more powerful than the bomb that devastated Hiroshima, the H-bomb could literally wipe a city off the map. But its effects were not limited to one city, or even one country. No less a scientist than Albert Einstein had warned the year before that the use of these most appalling of all weapons of mass destruction would result in the 'radioactive poisoning of the atmosphere, and hence annihilation of any life on earth'.[3]

After the atomic bombing of Hiroshima and Nagasaki, many had struggled to come to terms with the new destructive powers at mankind's disposal. The first book on the subject, *The Atomic Age Opens*, was published in August 1945 and described atomic energy as 'a subject for Superman cartoons and wild-eyed fantasy, or at best a project for the 25th century'.[4] After the first use of poison gas as a weapon, in 1915, people found parallels in the scientific romances of Verne and Wells. Now the idea that a lone plane could drop a single bomb and devastate a city seemed straight out of science fiction. The *New York Herald Tribune* said that it was 'as if the gruesome fantasies of the "comic" strips were actually coming true'. The paper speculated that 'self-extinction' was one of the 'strange futures' that humanity now faced.[5]

For advice on this new, science-fictional world, people turned to the experts. The uncrowned king of the science fiction pulps, John W. Campbell, Jr, told *PM* magazine on 7 August 1945: 'Frankly, I am scared. I'm scared because I fear people won't fully realize that, from this day on, war is impractical.' As ever, Campbell was ahead of his fellow commentators. A decade before the dread word 'fallout' became familiar to people, he even alluded to the global implications of nuclear explosions: 'If many of these atomic bombs are used, we can predict magnificent sunsets as the superfine dust drifts all around the world, coloring the sun's rays. Let's hope it isn't sunset for the human race. It could be sunrise – if we're wise.'[6]

For the first time, the people of mainland America felt vulnerable to direct and devastating attack. Having tested their first atomic bomb in autumn 1949, Soviet physicists were well on their way to developing a hydrogen bomb. The British Prime Minister Stanley Baldwin had warned back in 1932 that 'the bomber will always get through'.[7] The idea of even one bomber reaching the American mainland with its deadly atomic cargo struck fear into people's hearts. As a writer in the *New York Times* put it, in the atomic age 'no nation will be invulnerable to attack. No Goliath will be safe. Indeed, a small aggressor nation might have ample resources to destroy a great nation.'[8]

Before the world entered the era of the H-bomb, the civilian body responsible for overseeing atomic energy in America, the Atomic Energy Commission (AEC), had sought to play down the effect of an A-bomb attack on Washington. America would be better prepared than Hiroshima and Nagasaki, said the AEC, implicitly blaming the Japanese themselves for their high death toll:

In Japan the number of casualties was enormous because the attacking planes were not heeded and people were caught in the open or with inadequate cover ... With adequate warning *which was heeded* and adequate shelters *which were occupied*, the casualties could be greatly reduced. Furthermore, doctors with ample medical supplies, hospital facilities, and blood banks would save many of those who were injured by blast or burns.[9]

Similarly, public information films such as *Atomic Alert* (1951) glossed over the true horror of an atomic attack, claiming that 'the chance of your being hurt by an atomic bomb is slight'.[10]

In private, scientists and statesmen were rather more concerned. Within weeks of the first atomic bombs being dropped, the new British prime minister, Clement Atlee, admitted in a personal memorandum that

It is difficult for people to adjust their minds to an entirely new situation ... Even the modern conception of war to which in my lifetime we have become accustomed is now completely out of date ... it would appear that the provision of bomb-proof basements in factories and offices and the retention of ARP [Air Raid Precautions] and Fire Services is just futile waste ... The answer to an atomic bomb on London is an atomic bomb on another great city.[11]

Atlee's foreign secretary, Ernest Bevin, was more outspoken: 'We've got to have this thing over here, whatever it costs. We've got to have the bloody Union Jack on top of it.'[12]

The Royal Air Force received its first atomic bombs in 1953, the year Queen Elizabeth II was crowned amid nationwide celebrations and hopes that a new Elizabethan age was dawning in Britain. Eight years later, the Queen's air forces took delivery of the most terrible weapons on the planet – H-bombs. As Atlee had predicted, deterrence was now accepted as the only defence against atomic attack. According to historian Peter Hennessy, 'the bomb was always put before shelters'.[13]

In the same year that the RAF began carrying atomic bombs, Her Majesty's civil servants calculated the effects of a nuclear attack on the United Kingdom. They assumed that the aerial assault would consist of 132 bombs of the type dropped on Nagasaki, targeted on major cities and facilities. The result, they calculated, would be 1,378,000 of the Queen's loyal subjects dead and 785,000 seriously wounded. London might expect to be struck by as many as thirty-five bombs. Each would produce a crater 140 feet deep and 1,400 feet in diameter – about the size of St James's Park, situated in front of Buckingham Palace. The capital would lose 422,000 of its citizens. During the whole of World War II, Britain had suffered 440,000 military and civilian dead.

In reality, the figures were almost certainly conservative estimates. The Whitehall number crunchers were assuming that nine million civilians, mostly women and children, could be evacuated from the cities before bombing began. This was unlikely. In a surprise attack, the RAF had warned the government that it could expect at best a fifteen-minute warning of attack by bombers operating at high altitude. But if the Soviet bombers came in below 3,000 feet, the warning would be a mere five minutes.

A government memo from 1954 on the subject of evacuation speculated as to whether any people at all would be prepared to remain in 'vulnerable areas' during times of tension. The possibility of mass panic and a breakdown of order had to be faced. 'The standard work on this subject', wrote the memo's author, 'is by Mr H. G. Wells, written, I think, in 1896 – *The War of the Worlds* – which is much better than any piece of Home Office paper that I have yet seen. It is very important to know whether anybody will be willing to stay in London under imminent threat of annihilation . . . .'[14] Even in the 1950s, Wells remained the authority on doomsday.

In America, the trauma of Pearl Harbor remained a fresh wound in the public psyche. After Hiroshima and Nagasaki, the fear of an atomic Pearl Harbor became a national obsession. In 1946, the nightmare of mathematician and science fiction writer Chan Davis was one that many Americans shared: 'A pillar of multicolored smoke rising from the city, erasing the Bronx and Manhattan down to Central Park, shattering windows in Nyack, lighting up the Albany sky. A nightmare, a familiar and very real nightmare, an accepted part of modern life, something you couldn't get away from . . .'[15]

Davis's nightmare is one that has returned to haunt us all in the years following 9/11: an atomic bomb smuggled into a city and detonated without warning. It is not a new threat. Leo Szilard had told James Byrnes in May 1945 that in the atomic age they would face the possibility of bombs being detonated in American cities without warning. In November 1950, a top-secret British Government committee highlighted the danger posed by such clandestine attacks. It also raised the frightening possibility of 'the detonation of an atomic bomb in a "suicide" aircraft flying low over a key point'. The third surprise attack scenario considered by the committee was of atomic bombs concealed on ships and detonated in a harbour, something Szilard and Einstein had warned President Roosevelt about in their 1939 letter. The Whitehall committee concluded, rather bleakly, that 'there are no practicable and efficacious steps that can be taken in peace time to prepare against any of these threats'.[16]

In 1946, no less an atomic authority than Robert Oppenheimer had commented that the most useful tool in the hunt for atomic bombs concealed on ships was not a Geiger counter, but a screwdriver. By 1950, foreign ships were regularly being searched before entering US ports. On 5 August the Polish ship *Batory* was held outside New York harbour for four hours while it was searched. The authorities were notably silent on how their officials would locate any atomic bomb. A customs man in New York admitted that he had no idea what one would look like and it was known that radiation detectors were not able to discover a bomb concealed in a box. The *Batory* was suspected of being a 'Trojan Horse bomb carrier', said the newspapers, but all the search eventually revealed was that 'she carried 832 passengers, a cargo of Polish hams and Czech handicraft work but, apparently, no atomic bombs'.[17] As the British security committee decided that same year, the only defence against such clandestine threats was to maintain 'a confidant assurance that we know all about the problem and can deal with it', in order 'to mystify our enemy and help to dissuade him from taking so fateful a step'.[18] In other words, bluff.

Secret weapons and secret agents became integral parts of cold-war culture. In Robert Aldrich's classic film noir *Kiss Me Deadly* (1955), gumshoe Mike Hammer is hot on the trail of a small chest whose contents are mysterious, and immensely valuable. But others want it too, and will stop at nothing to get their hands on it. 'What is it we are seeking?' one of them asks Mike. 'Diamonds, rubies, gold, perhaps narcotics? How civilized this world used to be. But as the world becomes more primitive, its treasures become more fabulous.' When Mike begins to open the lid, blinding light and searing heat burst from the box. Noticing the burn on his wrist, an FBI man will only offer five words in explanation: 'Manhattan Project, Los Alamos, Trinity'. The 'treasures' of the modern world are radioactive metals – priceless, but lethal. It is a woman who finally opens the fatal box: 'you should have been called Pandora'. The terrible energy contained within it burns her alive. The film ends with the house she is in exploding.[19]

American novelist and civil defence campaigner Philip Wylie turned the post-war fears about a clandestine attack into fiction. His thriller *The Smuggled Atom Bomb* (1948) tells how a physics graduate student discovers a plot to import uranium cores into Florida and conceal them in American cities for later assembly and detonation. But it was Wylie's best-selling novel *Tomorrow!* (1954) that graphically portrayed what Americans dreaded most: a devastating atomic Pearl Harbor.

Tomorrow! was dedicated 'to the gallant men and women of the Federal Civil Defense Administration' and to the other 'true patriots', the volunteers.[20] Wylie's account of the attack and its aftermath is detailed and horrific. When it was first serialized, editors insisted that some scenes be cut. But Wylie clearly wanted to frighten Americans in order to demonstrate the importance of civil defence. 'The truth was that after a number of years,' says his narrator, 'almost nobody believed there was any danger.'[21] Wylie's novel contrasts the fortunes of two 'prairie cities' in the Missouri Basin – Green Prairie and River City – before and after an attack. Predictably, the one that prides itself on its well-organized civil defence suffers least.

The atomic Pearl Harbor happens when America's guard is down: on Christmas Eve. Many choose to disbelieve the warnings on the radio – 'Just like that Martian gag!' says one listener. Philip Wylie

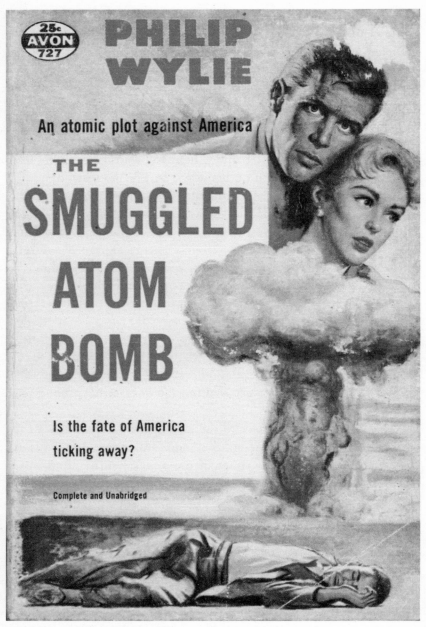

'Is the fate of America ticking away?' This the question posed on the cover of the 1951 Avon edition of Philip Wylie's The Smuggled Atom Bomb. In the atomic age, Americans felt threatened as never before.

creates a chillingly convincing account of those terrible moments after the sirens have sounded, as people rush to escape from skyscrapers and the city centre: the crush of people fleeing down narrow and increasingly congested concrete stairwells; sidewalks packed with desperate people who have been turned away from the few shelters; and cars jammed, bumper to bumper, trapped in the glass and steel canyons of the metropolis. And above the scenes of panic, as the wail of the sirens ebbs momentarily, rise the terrified screams of people who know there is nowhere to hide from the blinding, burning flash of atomic energy that is just minutes away. Wylie gives a graphic and powerful description of an atomic bomb exploding above an American city:

The great region, built so slowly, at such cost, by men, for a second liquefied and stood suspended above the ground: it could fall only sixteen feet in that time. Then, in the ensuing portion of a second, the liquid state was terminated. The white in the sky bellied down, growing big and globular, a thousand feet across and more. The liquids gasified: stone and cement, steel and plaster, brick and bronze and aluminum. In the street – if anyone could have seen at all, as no man could in the blind solar whiteness – there were no howling people at all. None.

On the sidewalks, for a part of a second, on sidewalks boiling like forgotten tea, were dark stains that had been people, tens of thousands of people. The Light went over the whole great area, like a thing switched on, and people miles away, hundreds of people looking at it, lost their sight. The air, of a sudden, for a long way became hotter than boiling water, hotter than melted lead, hotter than steel coming white from electric furnaces.

Clothing caught fire, the beggar's rags, the dowager's sables, the baby's diapers, the minister's robe. Paper in the gutter burst into flame. Trees. Clapboards. Outdoor advertising signs. Pastry behind the bakery windows. In that second it burned . . .

The plutonium fist followed:

It hammered across Front Street, Madison, Adams, Jefferson and Washington, along Central Avenue and rushed forward. The blast extinguished a billion sudden flames and started a million in the debris it stacked in its wake.

Under the intense globe of light, meantime, for a mile in every direction the city disappeared. In the mile beyond, every building was bashed and

347

buffeted. Homes fell by thousands on their inhabitants. Great institutions collapsed.[22]

In the time in which 'a pensive man might draw a breath, hold it reflectively and exhale', there have been three hundred thousand casualties. But for those who have survived, the terror has only just begun. The atomic blast ignites a ferocious firestorm that rages through the city. Then the Soviets follow up their atomic strike with nerve gas and biological weapons ('it's disease war!'). Finally, there comes what 1950s America feared almost as much as atom bombs – the breakdown of social order, when the carefully constructed edifice of civilized life shatters and mob law takes over: 'Here was gigantic panic, uncontrolled and hideous . . . Here was the infectious break-down of the "average mind", the total collapse of man in the presence of that which he had not been willing to face.'[23]

This dreaded breakdown of society – which in Wylie's novel is, of course, more total in the city with no civil defence – was exploited by many writers and film-makers keen to pander to their (male) audience's fantasies of pillage and rape. The *Mad Max* films (1979–85), which portray a barbaric road culture in the aftermath of a nuclear holocaust, have proved the most popular in this genre. In America, the idea of returning to a frontier existence was deeply appealing to some, guaranteeing the commercial success of violent survivalist fantasies such as Dean Owen's *End of the World* (1962) and William W. Johnstone's *Ashes* series (1983–2003). It even led to a bizarre subgenre of atomic fiction – post-nuclear porn, including novels such as George H. Smith's *The Coming of the Rats* (1961) and Jane Gallion's *Biker* (1969).

More thoughtful explorations of the survivalist theme, such as Ward Moore's 'Lot' (1953), reveal that, rather than offering a way to survive the nuclear age, such fantasies were deeply rooted in the very attitudes that fuelled cold-war tensions and brought doomsday closer. As early as August 1945, at the dawn of the atomic age, an American radio commentator pointed to the dangers of such gung-ho attitudes in the new era. Astutely, he predicted an 'armament race such as this world has never seen' in which nations would view 'each other over rocket trajectories, like frontiersmen with their hands on the grips of their six-shooters, knowing that at the first sign of trouble, survival depends upon beating their opponents to the draw'.[24] But in a world poised on the brink of atomic Armageddon, neither side could afford to have trigger-happy cowboys calling the shots.

The breakdown of order for which the survivalists longed was, in fact, the objective of nuclear strategists on all sides. As Hennessy says, ' "breakdown" is a word that lives in many a text of the Cold War secret state'.[25] In the UK between 1958 and 1964, the Joint Inter-services Group for the Study of All-out Warfare (JIGSAW) met to think the unthinkable. Its deliberations included calculating how many A-bombs and H-bombs would be needed to bring about 'breakdown' in any society. JIGSAW estimated that the destruction of three hundred cities in Russia and just twenty in Britain would achieve this goal.

During the cold war, at least $45 billion was spent by the US Government on facilities to protect its officials and key civilians in an attempt to avert a total breakdown of society in the event of war.[26] Government departments held regular rehearsals for atomic dooms-day. Even the Internal Revenue Service conducted exercises to perfect its techniques of tax collecting after a nuclear holocaust. Around the country, over 75 facilities were constructed deep underground to help ensure 'Continuity of Government'. They included 'Site R', aka the Alternate Joint Communications Center, beneath Raven Rock Moun-tain, a few miles north of the presidential retreat at Camp David. Operational from 1953, this facility offered over 700,000 square feet of floor space as well as its own reservoir. Should the Pentagon have been knocked out, Site R, with its three thousand personnel, would have been responsible for unleashing the American dogs of war.

The enemies of America have never managed to launch a significant attacked on the mainland of the United States. At least not until 11 September 2001. After al-Qaeda's suicide planes plunged into the World Trade Center and the Pentagon, procedures and protocols devised for an atomic Pearl Harbor swung into action, from the pro-tection of key government officials to the grounding of civilian air traffic. Vice President Dick Cheney reportedly bunkered down in Site R for several days. The President himself was taken to Offut Air Force Base, near Omaha, Nebraska, until the all-clear was given. In the cold war, Offut's underground facilities (known as The Hole) formed the nerve centre of the Strategic Air Command. From October 1948, this was led by General Curtis LeMay. His task was to ensure the delivery of America's nuclear weapons.

In 1958, US Government officials received what must have been the most terrifying document they had ever seen. *The Emergency Plans Book* (EPB) is a description of what would happen during an actual nuclear attack on the United States of America. Such is the sensitivity of this document that it remained top secret until 1998, when it suddenly turned up in the National Archive at College Park, Maryland. A year later it was reclassified top secret on the orders of an Air Force colonel. Fortunately, historian Doug Keeney had already copied the document, which he subsequently published.

The EPB was prepared by the Office of Emergency Planning (now known as FEMA) just six months after Sputnik had demonstrated that even America was now within the range of Soviet missiles. It reveals that America expected to receive a twenty-five-minute warning of approaching Russian bombers, but for submarine-launched missiles they would have just thirteen minutes. The EPB also anticipated that 'weapons emplaced by clandestine means', such as smuggled atom bombs, would be detonated in cities during a Soviet attack.

This chilling account of America's atomic doomsday shows that an all-out attack would have resulted in carnage and devastation beyond any disaster in human history. America expected to be pounded by the full arsenal of Soviet nuclear weapons – A-bombs and H-bombs. The former would be air bursts, the latter surface blasts producing heavy fallout. Written in the present tense, the EPB gives a real-time account of how the atomic devastation of America unfolds:

Blast and thermal radiation damage extends from 5 miles to as much as 15 miles from ground zeros. Severe fire storms have occurred in heavily built-up cities and many rural fires were started involving growing crops and forests. The surface bursts have resulted in wide-spread radioactive fallout of such intensity that over substantial parts of the United States the taking of shelter for considerable periods of time is the only means of survival.[27]

The nuclear war planners who wrote the EPB estimated that almost one in five Americans would die. That's 25 million people. The same number would be injured, some seriously. But US officials tried to look on the bright side: 'More than 100 million people and tremendous material resources remain. Restoration of the economy and our society will be possible and necessary.'[28] With cities across the length and breadth of America pulverized by nuclear explosions and fallout swathing the Land of the Free, government planners concluded that the situation was desperate, but not yet serious.

Continuity of Government, however, has taken a battering:

Washington was so severely damaged that no operations there are possible . . . Because of heavy fallout, none of the personnel at a few of the relocation sites survived. At several additional relocation sites almost all personnel are sick and many are dying . . . In many areas, including several of the largest cities, where surviving injured outnumber the surviving uninjured active adults, the social fabric has ceased to exist in the pre-attack pattern. Confusion is widespread in these areas and customary control and direction are non-existent.[29]

After a multi-megaton attack, the United States of America teeters on the brink of total breakdown. As Doug Keeney points out, 'this is not science fiction. This is how America might have ended.'[30] The scale of such a disaster is unimaginable. In his popular study *Thermonuclear Warfare* (1963), science fiction writer Poul Anderson observed that it 'would be like nothing ever seen before in history. The Lisbon earthquake and tidal wave of 1755, which made Voltaire stop believing in the goodness of God, killed fewer than 40,000.'[31] The catastrophic tsunami of Christmas 2004 shocked the whole world, yet it killed fewer than half a million people. What Anderson terms the 'technology of hell', but which is really the lethal creation of ordinary men and women, far exceeds the destructive power of nature.[32] Whether any nation on earth could endure such an onslaught is extremely doubtful.

It was left to Leo Szilard to say what no government official dared to: that after such a colossal assault, the Soviet Union might overwhelm the United States. In his short story 'My Trial as a War Criminal', written in 1947 but not published until two years later, Szilard describes how a surprise attack with biological weapons forces America to surrender. As a result, Szilard, together with his fellow

Manhattan Project scientists and politicians such as Truman and Byrnes, are put on trial for war crimes committed during World War II, in particular the atomic bombings of Japan. Szilard's story exposes both the hypocrisy of governments as well as the general atrophy of ethics that accompanies the quest for weapons of mass destruction.

The Soviet bomb designers were attentive readers of the *Bulletin of the Atomic Scientists*, to which Leo Szilard was a regular contributor. 'We thought Szilard was a leading conscience of humanity,' said one.[33] Andrei Sakharov – the father of the Soviet hydrogen bomb – read 'My Trial' in 1961 and was greatly moved by it. He encouraged his fellow nuclear scientists to read the story. One of his colleagues recalled that 'the moral aspect of it would not let [Sakharov] and some of us live in peace'. This story made Sakharov and his fellow bomb designers look anew at their work on weapons of mass destruction. Szilard succeeded, says Richard Rhodes, in delivering 'a note in a bottle to a secret Soviet laboratory that contributed to Andrei Sakharov's courageous work of protest that helped bring the US–Soviet nuclear arms race to an end.'[34]

Of course, Leo Szilard was well aware of the power of the imagination. After all, he had been deeply impressed by H. G. Wells's fictional account of the discovery of atomic energy. Indeed, in that very novel Wells had predicted that 1956 would be the year of the Last War. In the atomic age – which he had helped to found – Szilard began to use the power of his imagination to communicate his fears for the future to colleagues and the general public.

In the 1950 *Chicago Round Table* discussion, Szilard created an imaginary but feasible superweapon, a world-destroying cobalt bomb. In order to explain the logic that led to this doomsday device, he highlighted the escalation of terror in war and the concomitant erosion of ethics that had taken place within a generation. Before World War II, said Szilard, the public thought that it was 'morally wrong and reprehensible to bomb cities and kill women and children'. But as the war progressed, 'almost imperceptibly, we started to use jellied gasoline bombs against Japan, killing millions of women and children; finally we used the A-bomb'.[35]

Statistics confirm Szilard's view. In World War I, 90 per cent of casualties were military. World War II became the most destructive war in history, killing 55 million people. Half of the dead in Europe were civilian casualties. America – whose homeland was untouched by war – lost a hundred thousand personnel in the Asian theatre, fewer than the number killed by one atomic bomb at Hiroshima. Three million Japanese died in the war. However, China lost 20 million people during more than a decade of conflict with Japan, a war which saw Japan use its own weapons of mass destruction – General Ishii's bioweapons.

Within a month of two Japanese cities being obliterated by atomic bombs, the American military had drawn up a war plan for a pre-emptive attack on Russia using the new superweapon. For the first time the United States abandoned its traditional defensive posture in favour of a first-strike strategy. According to the war plan, sixty-six cities were to be attacked and 466 atomic bombs dropped. President Truman was also told by his advisers that 'the United States must be prepared to wage atomic and biological warfare'. The next war, they said, would be a truly 'total' war.[36] Within two years, the new commander of the Strategic Air Command, General LeMay, proposed to his Air Force superiors that America's war plan should have as its objective 'killing a nation'. His proposal was accepted.[37]

From Fritz Haber's clouds of poison gas used on the Ypres killing fields in 1915 to General Ishii's biological weapons and the superbombs of the atomic age, the dream of the ultimate weapon of mass destruction led to a rapidly escalating potential for devastation. The imaginary superweapons of popular writers such as Jack London had finally become reality. As the American and British war plans of the 1950s showed, a world war fought with nuclear weapons would dwarf all previous conflicts. There would be carnage on an unprecedented scale.

The classic science fiction film *The Day the Earth Stood Still* (1951) voiced the anxiety of many in the atomic age. The alien spaceman Klaatu, sent to reason with the warring humans, sums up the dilemma facing planet earth: 'your choice is simple: join us and live in peace or pursue your present course and face obliteration'.[38] But instead of making peace, the countries of the world merely accelerated their arms race. To quote one science fiction story of the period, the doomsday decade became the era of the 'alphabet-bombs': after A-bombs came H-bombs, and then, perhaps, the scientists' ultimate gift of destruction – C-bombs.[39] By summer 1949, President Truman had given up on post-war attempts to secure international control of atomic energy. Instead, he said, 'we must be strongest in atomic weapons'.[40] Until 6 October 1949, the President had not even heard of the hydrogen bomb. But lobbying by scientists such as Edward Teller soon convinced him that this was the winning weapon that America had to have in its arsenal.

At a Chicago Met Lab seminar, Enrico Fermi once discussed the chances of intelligent life existing elsewhere in the universe. According to Fermi, if there were extraterrestrials they would certainly have noticed a planet as 'beautiful' as our earth.

'They should have arrived here by now,' said Fermi, 'so where are they?' He didn't expect an answer to his question, at least not immediately. But he hadn't reckoned on Leo Szilard.

'They are among us,' said Szilard, glancing around knowingly at his colleagues, 'but they call themselves Hungarians.'[41]

Szilard's comment became legendary among the scientists who had worked on the Manhattan Project, in which Hungarian émigrés such as Szilard, John von Neumann, Eugene Wigner and the man who became known as the father of the H-bomb, Edward Teller, played such crucial roles. Soon Szilard and his countrymen became known as the Martians. With their strange language – distinct from any other in Europe – and their other-worldly brilliance, many people thought that the Hungarian scientists might as well have originated on the Red Planet. However, the modest and retiring Wigner was not altogether comfortable with this nickname. 'I think I was the only Hungarian scientist who wished to be a normal American,' he said. 'Szilard, Teller, and von Neumann liked being called "Martians". But I did not.'[42]

After the war, Leo Szilard – who had dedicated his life to promoting the potential of the atom – was barred from working on atomic energy, mainly through the efforts of General Groves. Instead, he retrained and switched disciplines, from physics to biology. But even Groves could not stop him from campaigning vociferously for international control of atomic energy and to raise public awareness of the threat posed by nuclear weapons. Szilard's activism inspired a generation of radicalized scientists who would begin to make their presence felt in the 1960s. But in the cold war, science itself was changing. In the wake of the Manhattan Project came the era of so-called Big Science. Scientists were increasingly working for what President Eisenhower would later bitterly describe as the 'military-industrial complex'. There was now little room for brilliant but eccentric loners like Leo Szilard.

He was also out of sympathy with many former colleagues. In the cold war, the Hungarian Quartet, which had made such a significant contribution to the creation of the atomic bomb, found itself divided politically. While Szilard campaigned for arms control and negotiations with the Soviets, his three fellow countrymen, united by a visceral anti-Communism, committed themselves to facing off the Soviet threat with increasingly powerful weapons of mass destruction. One explanation for this hostility to the Soviet Union may lie in their Hungarian roots. According to John von Neumann, 'Russia was traditionally the enemy. I think you will find, generally speaking, among Hungarians an emotional fear and dislike of Russia.'[43] After May 1949, when Communist one-party rule began in Hungary, this feeling only intensified for Teller, Wigner and von Neumann.

Interviewed in 1973, Eugene Wigner admitted that politically he shared the conservative and anti-Communist views of Edward Teller and John von Neumann. During the 1960s, Wigner was harshly criticized by students at Princeton for being a 'hardliner' on the Vietnam war[44]; by contrast, Leo Szilard was always a 'staunch leftist'.[45] In later life Wigner became fiercely defensive of his 'great friend' Edward Teller. He rejected what he regarded as unfair criticism of Teller's personality ('greediness, ill will, and a rash temper') and his championing of the hydrogen bomb ('Oh, yes, isn't he the one whose hydrogen bomb may blow up the world?'). 'Teller was not a conventional right-winger at all,' said Wigner. 'He hoped deeply that someday all nations might create a world government. But until then, he felt the safety of the West lay in the forceful, unhindered development of nuclear weapons.'[46]

However, even Wigner had to admit that Teller's more extreme atomic views were frankly 'crazy'. These included using nuclear bombs to blast out a harbour in North Alaska, and rejecting the health risks posed by fallout from atmospheric testing as the 'necessary price to pay for military readiness'.[47] Such fallout was, Teller said, no more dangerous than 'being an ounce overweight'.[48] Enrico Fermi once commented that Teller was 'the only monomaniac he knew with a number of manias'.[49] With his thick eyebrows and guttural voice, the brooding Hungarian physicist became one of the most recognizable and controversial scientists of the cold war. Once, in 1970, his Berkeley home on the campus of the University of California had to be cordoned off by riot police to protect Teller from the wrath of radical students.

In fact, Teller seemed to relish his reputation as 'Mr H-Bomb'.[50] But for many, this brilliant scientist became corrupted by his 'obsession for power'.[51] According to colleagues at Los Alamos, he had 'more than his share of the traditional wild Hungarian temperament'.[52] He annoyed neighbours at the weapons lab by seeking inspiration at his beloved piano late into the night. George Gamow, who secured Teller his first academic position in the United States, said he became a different person after working at Los Alamos. According to Emilio Segrè, Teller was 'dominated by irresistible passions' that threatened his 'rational intellect'.[53] Another colleague said simply, 'Teller has a messianic complex.'[54]

As soon as the war ended, Edward Teller began lobbying for both a new Manhattan Project to design the hydrogen bomb and a new weapons laboratory dedicated to building it. Teller's dream of a thermonuclear weapon was originally sparked by a suggestion Fermi made in September 1941. However, Hans Bethe recalled that, perhaps unsurprisingly, it was Szilard, 'the inventor of all things', who had first suggested a self-sustaining thermonuclear reaction, using Urey's newly discovered deuterium, as early as spring 1935.[55]

One of Teller's undeniable talents was his uncanny ability to manipulate his military and government paymasters. His ploy was to exaggerate both the threat posed by Soviet weapons and his scientific ability to meet that threat. In private, President Eisenhower described both Teller and Wernher von Braun as 'super-salesmen', peddling defences against doomsday to scientifically naive politicians.[56] In 1945, Teller announced that he could build an H-bomb in two to five years. It was an outrageously ambitious claim, and no other scientist agreed that it was possible. But he continued to promote his design for the bomb, known as the Super, even though others, including Bethe, doubted it was technically achievable. In particular, Bethe questioned whether it would ever be possible to use a fission device to ignite the deuterium.

Essentially, the Super was 'a pipe of liquid deuterium with an atomic bomb screwed to one end'.[57] Teller worked on this idea both during the war and after, even resisting overtures to apply his undoubted skills to more urgent military problems. The dream of the superbomb obsessed him. After the war, Teller began blaming his Los Alamos boss, Robert Oppenheimer, for blocking development of the hydrogen bomb. This resentment would eventually lead Teller to make fatally wounding statements against Oppenheimer during the infamous AEC security clearance hearings in 1954. According to Herbert York, who became the first director of the Livermore Laboratory (now the Lawrence Livermore National Laboratory), Teller was 'obviously paranoid'.[58] But by July 1948, Oppenheimer's security file was one foot thick and weighed twelve pounds. In the wake of Senator McCarthy's anti-Communist witch-hunts, it didn't take much to turn the authorities against the former boss of Los Alamos.

The explosion of the first Soviet atom bomb in September 1949 meant that doors suddenly opened for Teller in Washington. Ernest Lawrence and Luis Alvarez, both from the University of California in Berkeley, also began lobbying intensively for the hydrogen bomb and for a new weapons lab. David Lilienthal, chair of the AEC, described them as 'bloodthirsty' and 'drooling with the prospect' of building the Super.[59] (Lilienthal's idiosyncratic code name for the Super was 'Campbell's', as in the soup.) Even after President Truman backed the H-bomb, few other scientists supported the project. One Los Alamos physicist noted that it was 'pure fantasy from the design standpoint, as well as a very difficult delivery problem'.[60] Oppenheimer told James Conant bluntly, 'I am not sure the miserable thing will work, nor that it can be gotten to a target except by an ox cart.'[61] As historian Gregg Herken has written, Truman's historic decision was based on an 'imaginary bomb' that existed solely inside Teller's head.[62]

*

Working out how to build an H-bomb is a hugely complex exercise which involves mapping the behaviour of individual subatomic particles at extremes of temperature and pressure. The development of electronic digital computers played a vital role in turning the dream of the H-bomb into reality. In 1945, John von Neumann had become involved in the design of early computers. The ENIAC (Electronic Numerical Integrator and Computer) was one of the first computers to replace gears for doing calculations with vacuum tubes. Its first task, at the end of 1945, was to process calculations for Edward Teller's Super.

The computer took six weeks to do the number crunching that would have taken a hundred Los Alamos staff a year. Initial results were promising, but more calculations were needed. For that, John von Neumann helped to design a new type of computer, one that could store a program in its memory – the direct ancestor of today's PC. With characteristic humour, John von Neumann and its co-designer Nicholas Metropolis named it MANIAC (Mathematical Analyzer, Numerical Integrator and Computer). By 1949 the Polish-born mathematician Stanislaw Ulam had done some calculations on the feasibility of the Super for the new computer. But delays to the new electronic brain (as the media dubbed computers) forced Ulam to fall back on his trusty slide-rule for the complex calculations. The results were bad news for Teller. By the end of 1950, Ulam's calculations and new ones from ENIAC showed conclusively that the Super would never explode. It would merely 'fizzle'.[63]

Edward Teller was furious; others, including Oppenheimer, were delighted. Then, at the beginning of 1951, Ulam came up with the breakthrough that would finally make Teller's thermonuclear dream a reality. It was what Ulam called his 'bomb in a box' idea. Essentially, what he was proposing was that the fission explosion should be contained by a dense material which focuses the energy (rather as the shaped charges had been used to compress plutonium in Fat Man) onto the fusion fuel. On its own this ingenious idea was not enough, but Teller took it a step further by using radiation from the fission bomb to compress the fusion fuel without heating it. He called it 'radiation implosion'.[64]

It was the breakthrough Teller had been waiting for. The crucial insights of both men were described in their top-secret paper, titled 'On Heterocatalytic Detonations I: Hydrodynamic Lenses and Radiation Mirrors'. Hans Bethe, who had predicted that Teller's original Super design would be a dud, described it as 'about as surprising as the discovery of fission had been to physicists in 1939'. It was, he said, a 'miracle'.[65] That year, Bethe reluctantly returned full-time to Los Alamos to work on the H-bomb.

According to Ulam, Teller was 'always intense, visibly ambitious, and harbouring a smouldering passion for achievement in physics'.[66] After they collaborated on the idea that made the H-bomb a reality, the two men scarcely spoke to each other again. Teller conveniently forgot Ulam's role in the hydrogen bomb. In his memoirs, Teller confessed that he had 'developed an allergy to him'. Ulam's contribution to the final design of the H-bomb is entirely elided in Teller's account.[67]

Ulam and Teller's bomb was tested on the Eniwetok Atoll in the Pacific on 1 November 1952, three days before the former US Army Chief of Staff, Dwight Eisenhower, was elected President of the United States. Nicknamed the 'Sausage' by its designers after its distinctive cylindrical shape, the device weighed 82 tons; its housing (known as a shot cab) was the size of a six-storey building. The explosion was code-named 'Mike' – M for megaton, a million tons of high explosive. The blast was far bigger than expected, just over 10 megatons, a thousand times as powerful as the Hiroshima bomb. For one observer on a plane 60 miles away, it was like 'gazing into eternity, or into the gates of hell'.[68]

Having fallen out with the Los Alamos scientists who built the device, Teller had remained in Berkeley, on the University of California campus. In the basement of the geology department he sat hunched over the screen of a seismograph at the time of the explosion. When the compression wave reached California, Teller saw the dot on the screen 'do a little dance'.[69] His ten-year obsessional quest for the hydrogen bomb had succeeded. Triumphantly, he cabled the Los Alamos scientists who had doubted him for so long: 'it's a boy'.[70] And, he implied, I'm the father.

According to many, the Mike test was the 'thermonuclear Trinity'.[71] The outgoing Truman administration concluded that 'a weapon was in the offing which, in sufficient numbers, might have the power to destroy the world'.[72] The new President, who had opposed the use of atomic weapons against Japan, visibly paled when the island of Eluge-lab (part of the Eniwetok Atoll) was described as 'missing' following the explosion.[73]

In 1952, Teller, Lawrence and Alvarez finally got the go-ahead from the AEC to open a laboratory dedicated to thermonuclear weapons – the Livermore Laboratory, located on a former naval air base 50 miles east of San Francisco. 'I have quit the appeasers and joined the fascists,' Teller admitted privately.[74] Bethe and Segrè both turned down Teller's invitation to join him at the new laboratory. After his role in Oppenheimer's downfall in 1954 became known, many of Teller's scientific colleagues refused even to speak to him. Teller himself never regretted developing the H-bomb, saying in true Faustian style: 'I do not want the hydrogen bomb because it would kill more people. I wanted the hydrogen bomb because it was *new*. Because it was something that we did not know, and could know. I am afraid of ignorance.'[75]

The guards at the Livermore soon referred to the scientists as 'Teller's Flying Circus'.[76] In the coming years, Livermore's many lethal creations would include miniature atomic 'back-pack' bombs and atomic grenades, the first megaton-class warhead launchable from a submarine (for the Polaris missile), MIRVs (Multiple Independently targetable Re-entry Vehicles), the N-bomb (neutron bomb) and Teller's brainchild of the 1980s – the third-generation nuclear weapons that formed the basis of the Strategic Defense Initiative, or Star Wars as it became known.

Von Neumann, known to his friends as Jancsi or Johnny, had once successfully cured Richard Feynman of his qualms about being involved in the Manhattan Project. 'You don't have to be responsible for the world you're in,' he told the 26-year-old physicist.[77] Unlike his fellow Hungarian Leo Szilard, who always felt personally responsible for the fate of the world, Johnny von Neumann never doubted the need for the hydrogen bomb. Oppenheimer recalled that when the two of them discussed the question in 1949, von Neumann told him: 'I believe there is no such thing as saturation. I don't think any weapon can be too large. I have always been a believer in this.'[78]

Einstein once criticized Szilard for overemphasizing the role of logic in people's lives. If that was true of Szilard, then it was doubly so for von Neumann. His mind was 'inexorably logical', said Wigner, who knew Jancsi all his life. They had attended the same school in Budapest and worked together at both Berlin and Princeton. At Berlin, Szilard and von Neumann had taught physics courses together. Wigner recalled how Szilard liked to quarrel with the mathematician; 'von Neumann was usually right', he added wryly. He was a genius and he knew it: 'he had been hearing it since he was a 10-year-old boy studying higher mathematics in Budapest'.[79] Johnny had a photographic memory and as a child used to entertain family guests by reciting a page chosen at random from the Budapest phonebook.

With his boyish moon-face and his equally childish sense of humour, von Neumann could be great company. The regular parties he and his wife gave at Princeton were renowned. The centrepiece at one was an ice sculpture of his MANIAC computer. Otto Frisch was greatly impressed by von Neumann's ability to drink sixteen martinis in a row and remain 'quite lucid, though somewhat pessimistic in his utterances'.[80] Johnny had a rich fund of anecdotes about his fellow Hungarians and once quipped that 'it takes a Hungarian . . . to go into a revolving door behind you and come out first'.[81] He loved jokes and limericks. One of his favourites was:

> There was a young man who said: Run!
> The end of the world has begun!
> The one I fear most
> Is that damn' Holy Ghost,
> I can handle the Father and Son.[82]

As well as laying the foundations for the modern computer (based on what is known as 'von Neumann architecture'), he did groundbreaking mathematical work in group theory, mathematical logic and game theory, a pessimistic account of the rules of human behaviour described by one historian as 'the perfect intellectual rationale for the Cold War'.[83] Yet this witty and brilliant man seriously advocated a pre-emptive atomic strike against the Soviet Union. In 1950 he argued that 'if you say why not bomb them tomorrow, I say why not today? If you say today at five o'clock, I say why not one o'clock.'[84] Perhaps unsurprisingly, he also argued that the human race faced doomsday sooner or later, thanks to its misuse of technology. Like Teller, he advocated world government, principally because he believed the world was now too dangerous to let countries govern themselves: 'For the kind of explosiveness that man will be able to contrive by 1980, the globe is dangerously small, its political units dangerously unstable.'[85]

Von Neumann believed that 'total' war with the Soviet Union was unavoidable and for this reason he consistently advocated a 'maximum rate of armament'.[86] The newly elected President Eisenhower appointed von Neumann as an AEC commissioner, a post he took up in 1955 at the same time as Oppenheimer lost his security clearance (and thus his AEC position). Unlike Szilard, who took great pleasure in baiting brass-hats, the hawkish von Neumann had always enjoyed war work and rubbing shoulders with the military. He described himself to the Senate committee as 'violently anti-Communist and a good deal more militaristic than most'.[87]

For scientists like John von Neumann, working on atomic weapons had the thrill and the glamour of a science fiction adventure. He clearly relished being part of what he called 'this Buck Rogers universe'.[88] He had been a consultant on military matters for bodies such as the CIA since 1951. He made his most significant recommendation in 1954, when he advised the government that research should be started immediately into creating a force of intercontinental ballistic missiles (ICBMs) capable of delivering nuclear warheads to the Soviet Union at the touch of a button. The former bomber pilot and later government adviser William Borden had warned in his 1946 book *There Will Be No Time* of a 'rocket Pearl Harbor'.[89] America was determined not to be caught napping again. By the second half of the 1950s, the ICBM would earn itself the distinction of being described as the 'ultimate weapon'.[90]

In the year that he became an AEC commissioner, von Neumann was told that he had bone cancer. Some suggested that he contracted this terminal condition from exposure to fallout during the Operation Crossroads atomic tests at Bikini atoll in May 1946, during which many seamen became contaminated with radiation.[91] Within a year, this painful and debilitating disease had spread to his spine. Despite being confined to a wheelchair he continued to attend AEC meetings,

John von Neumann receives the Medal of Freedom at the White House from President Eisenhower on 16 February 1956 'for exceptionally meritorious service in furtherance of the security of the United States' and for resolving 'some of the most difficult technical problems of national defense'.

ferried back and forth by limousine. This has prompted some people to identify the wheelchair-bound Dr Strangelove in Kubrick's film with the 'militaristic' mathematician.

One of von Neumann's last public appearances was to receive the Medal of Freedom at the White House from President Eisenhower in February 1956. 'I wish I could be around long enough to deserve this honour,' he said poignantly. Even during his final months, he continued to be visited in hospital by the Secretary of Defense and other high-ranking military men. His brother, Michael, sat by his bedside reading aloud from Goethe's *Faust*. When Michael paused to turn a page, Johnny would start reciting from memory the play about the archetypal scientist and his insatiable lust for knowledge.

At the end, as his mind disintegrated, Johnny would awake screaming in the night. Just in case he spilled any military secrets, his orderlies in the hospital were all air force personnel. The other members of the

Hungarian Quartet made the sad journey to his bedside to visit their dying friend. Later, Teller said that Johnny 'suffered more when his mind would no longer function than I have ever seen any human being suffer'.[92] He died aged 53, in the spring of 1957.

The Los Alamos physicist Robert Serber recalled that, during the war, he saw a list on Edward Teller's blackboard that was unusually lethal even by the Hungarian scientist's standards. It was, he said, 'a list of weapons – ideas for weapons – with their abilities and properties displayed. For the last one on the list, the largest, the method of delivery was listed as "Backyard". Since that particular device would probably kill everyone on earth, there was no use carting it else-where.'[93]

In February 1950, Edward Teller proposed building a vast 1,000-megaton H-bomb, which because of its size would have to be transported and detonated on a ship. Such a huge bomb would, he predicted, result in a damage zone of 1,000 square miles, as well as 'very serious' flash burns out to 100 miles. The explosion would be dirty, producing very heavy fallout, with radioactivity blanketing an area 40 miles wide by 400 miles long.

In the same month as his fellow Martian, Leo Szilard, was frightening the world with his prediction of massive bombs rigged with cobalt, Teller was actually designing the gigaton devices that would form the basis of the cobalt bomb. He even described the effect of exploding such a bomb near Washington: 'Let us assume that the winds are blowing north along the Alleghenies, a condition quite frequently encountered. Then Washington, Philadelphia, New York and Boston could all be close to the path of the radioactive cloud and even the farthest point, Boston, would be within reach of the danger.'[94] But it was not until four years later, in 1954, that America and the world realized the true extent of the threat posed by Edward Teller's grandiose Strangelovean fantasies.

18

The Hell Bomb

Ring-a-ring o'neutrons
A pocketful of positrons
A fission! A fission!
We all fall down!
Nursery rhyme, AD 3955, Michael Avallone,
Beneath the Planet of the Apes (1970)

On 1 March 1954, an improved version of the Mike test device was detonated at Bikini Atoll in the Marshall Islands, some 5,000 miles from the west coast of America. This slimmed-down thermonuclear device had been nicknamed 'Shrimp' by the Los Alamos scientists who built it. When fully weaponized it would be small enough to be carried by a B-47 bomber.

But the scientists got their calculations badly wrong. They expected a yield of 5 megatons. Instead it exploded with the power of 15 million tons of TNT, making it the biggest bomb ever tested by the United States. The fireball expanded to four miles wide. Without warning, radioactive fallout began raining down on the nearly ten thousand personnel of the naval task force gathered in the Pacific to observe the test, code-named Bravo.

Among them was theoretical physicist Marshall Rosenbluth. He was exposed to a dose of radioactivity equivalent to about ten chest X-rays. 'I was on a ship that was 30 miles away,' he recalled,

and we had this horrible white stuff raining on us . . . It was pretty frightening. There was a huge fireball with these turbulent rolls going in and out. The thing was glowing. It looked to me like a diseased brain up in the sky. It spread until the edge of it looked as if it was almost directly overhead. It was a much more awesome sight than a puny little atomic bomb. It was a pretty sobering and shattering experience.[1]

Rosenbluth and the other observers were ordered below decks as the naval ships hurriedly retreated another 20 miles from the detonation point. The Shrimp had blasted a crater 250 feet deep and 6,500 feet wide out of the Pacific atoll. The white fallout described by Rosenbluth consisted of radioactive calcium from vaporized coral. Over the next few hours, monitoring stations recorded rising levels of radiation across the Marshall Islands. The next day, a group of American weathermen had to be evacuated from an island 133 miles from the detonation point. But it was not until two days later that the native inhabitants of Rongelap island, 90 miles away from the blast, began to be evacuated.

Snow-like debris had begun settling on their island within four hours of the explosion and continued falling into the evening until it was an inch deep on the ground. Unaware of how dangerous it was, the islanders made no attempt to protect themselves from it. Soon they began to suffer the same symptoms as people at Hiroshima and Nagasaki, including diarrhoea, skin burns and vomiting. In the days to come they began losing their hair and haemorrhaging. It has been calculated that the islanders were exposed to 25 times more radiation during the Bravo thermonuclear test than people are now permitted to receive in a lifetime.

The Bravo test cast a vast radioactive pall over thousands of miles of the Pacific Ocean. But the rest of the world might never have heard about what happened were it not for what occurred two weeks later. A Japanese tuna fishing boat, the *Fukuryu Maru* ('Lucky Dragon'), returned early to its homeport of Yaizu. All twenty-three crew members were suffering from a mysterious illness. It turned out to be radiation sickness. They had been fishing 90 miles east of the Bravo test, several miles outside the exclusion zone. The first the crew knew about the explosion was a blinding flash of light. This was followed three hours later by a 'snowstorm' which left their boat covered in a white, ash-like substance. One of the crew later recalled that the particles were so dense that they made a faint sound as they fell onto the deck. Intrigued by this bizarre phenomenon, some of the fishermen filled bottles with the dust as souvenirs. Then, following good marine practice, they hosed down the deck – an act which probably saved all their lives.

When they arrived back in Japan, none of the crew knew why they had fallen ill. Newsreels showed scientists wearing facemasks scanning the men with Geiger counters. It was like a scene from a science fiction B-movie. In Japan, the incident 'caused something close to panic' as newspapers reported that 'schools of "atomic fish"' might be swimming towards Japan, polluting local fish stocks.[2] Initially, Lewis Strauss, the new chairman of the AEC (who had begun his career as a travelling shoe salesman), falsely accused the fishing boat of having been within the exclusion zone and of being a 'Red spy outfit'.[3]

Less than a month after the return of the Lucky Dragon, further atomic tests were conducted in the Pacific. The Japanese public were appalled and frightened by what was happening in their region. Seafood was part of their daily diet. Fears of radioactive fish prompted the government to begin checking tuna catches, and 135 tons of contaminated fish were destroyed. Six months after the Bravo test, one of the fishermen, Aikichi Kuboyama – who had already been suffering from hepatitis – died, and his colleagues were still in hospital. Japanese unions, politicians and newspapers joined in calling for an immediate end to nuclear tests.

What especially 'alarmed the world' about this 'thermonuclear monster', as the American press labelled the Bravo H-bomb, was the invisible yet lethal fallout from the explosion.[4] In spite of the warnings four years earlier from Albert Einstein and other scientists about radioactive poisoning of the atmosphere, the word 'fallout' had scarcely been mentioned. Now the papers were full of stories describing how the fishermen had been 'burned by fall-out'.[5] The first use of the word 'fallout' in a popular work had been in 1950, in Richard Gerstell's How To Survive an Atomic Bomb. This was also the first civil defence book of the nuclear age. Gerstell's message was that fear was unpatriotic. As Daniel Lang wrote in the New Yorker, Bravo 'was the shot that made the world fallout-conscious'.[6]

After the Bravo test, which contaminated 7,000 square miles of land and sea, the scientific director of the Soviet atomic weapons project, Igor Kurchatov, wrote a secret report concluding that a war fought with H-bombs would 'create conditions under which the existence of life over the whole globe will be impossible'. One hundred such bombs would bring about this situation. He ended by warning his military and political masters that 'mankind faces the enormous threat of an end to all life on earth'.[7] But this dire conclusion did not dissuade the Soviets from exploding their own hydrogen bomb, on 6 November 1955. Edward Teller had also realized before 1947 that a hundred large thermonuclear explosions might raise the world's levels of radioactivity to a 'dangerously high level'.[8]

Despite frequent reassurances from the AEC, the public in America and around the world began to wake up to the threat posed by this new, invisible killer. In its effects – spreading death by air – it seemed to many people little different from chemical or biological weapons. In fact, the H-bomb seemed to combine the worst of all weapons of mass destruction into one hellish device. 'Talk and worry over the H-bomb's radioactive "fallout" is spreading', reported *Time* in November 1954.[9] In the same month one of the most famous atomic movies of the cold war opened in Tokyo: *Gojira*, better known in the West as *Godzilla*.

Right from the start of the atomic age, it seemed to most people that the atomic bomb was straight out of the pages of a science fiction story. In September 1945, one commentator noted: 'The pulp writers could imagine things like the atom bomb; in fact, life is becoming more and more like a Science Fiction story, and the arrival on earth of a few six-legged Martians with Death Rays would hardly make the front page.'[10] Chemical weapons had seemed similarly fantastic when they were first used.

People who had seen the terrible effects of the atomic bombs on Hiroshima and Nagasaki, or observed the test explosions, felt there was something quite literally 'monstrous' about what they had witnessed. When he first saw devastated Hiroshima, Air Force commander General George C. Kenney said that the town 'seemed to have been ground into dust by a giant foot'.[11] William Laurence described the Trinity fireball as 'an elemental force freed from its bonds after being chained for billions of years'.[12] For Laurence, atomic energy

Science fiction had anticipated both the threat and the promise of the atomic age. But as the A-bomb was replaced by the H-bomb and then the C-bomb, reality began to seem ever more like science fiction. Cover by David E. Pattee for Astounding Science Fiction *(November 1950).*

was 'a man-made Titan' who had been bound temporarily by human-kind but was always threatening destruction: 'Left without control for even a few seconds, the giant would run wild.'[13] In 1952, the cartoon film *A is for Atom* described atomic energy as 'the answer to a dream as old as man himself. A giant of limitless power at man's command.' Atomic energy was depicted in the film as a glowing colossus, towering over the earth's horizon.[14]

It was wholly natural, therefore, to translate the widespread horror at the 'thermonuclear monster' of the Bravo test into a real monster. According to Tomoyuki Tanaka, the film's producer, *Gojira* was about 'the terror of the Bomb. Mankind had created the Bomb, and now nature was going to take revenge on mankind'.[15] It was inspired in part by the 1953 American film *The Beast from 20,000 Fathoms*, about a dinosaur thawed from hibernation by nuclear tests which then attacks Manhattan. But *Gojira* was not just another B-movie. It featured distinguished actors and for a Japanese film had quite a large budget.

Gojira begins with a clear reference to the fate of the *Lucky Dragon*: the crew of a ship witnesses a 'blinding flash of light' as the ocean explodes. When a sailor is washed ashore, he talks wildly about a monster. Gojira has been awakened from its Jurassic slumber by the explosion and is now intensely radioactive. The monster's skin is deeply furrowed in a way that resembles the scars of Hiroshima survivors. Gojira wreaks havoc across Japan, trampling people and buildings, or burning them with his fiery, radioactive breath. Scientists armed with Geiger counters discover strontium-90 in the monster's footprints.

Although Gojira is unleashed by a scientific superweapon, ironically it is science that saves the world from the monster. Dr Serizawa – a mad scientist with an eyepatch and dishevelled hair – has invented a doomsday weapon: an oxygen destroyer. 'Used as a weapon, this could be as powerful as a nuclear bomb,' he claims. 'It could totally destroy humankind.' Initially he refuses to use his discovery, as he is afraid of what politicians will do with it: 'Of course, they'll want to use it as a weapon. Bombs versus bombs, missiles versus missiles, and now a new super-weapon to throw upon us all.'[16] But he relents and turns his weapon on Gojira. Determined that no one will misuse his superweapon, this saviour scientist destroys his notes before using it, and while he is underwater he cuts his own air supply – the secret of the doomsday weapon dies with Dr Serizawa.

Gojira was an instant box-office success in Japan. Audiences who knew better than any nation on earth what a superweapon could do, watched in total silence. Many left the cinema in tears. The film's director, Ishirō Honda, wanted to make 'radiation visible'. 'When I returned from the war', he said, 'and passed through Hiroshima there was a heavy atmosphere – a fear the earth was already coming to and end. That became the basis for the film.'[17]

Hollywood responded with a series of films about creatures mutated by radioactivity. The most famous of these is *Them!* (1954), featuring giant ants created by radiation from nuclear tests. 'When man entered the atomic age, he opened a door into a new world,' says a scientist in the film. 'What we eventually find in that new world, nobody can predict.'[18] Popular films such as *Them!* echoed the doubts about science and progress voiced when gas was used as a weapon in World War I.

On his return from the Bravo test site, AEC chairman Lewis Strauss – who pronounced his name 'straws' – boasted to reporters that they could now make an H-bomb 'as large as you wish, as large as the military requirement demands'.[19] Strauss clearly hoped to reassure his fellow Americans that they were winning the arms race. Instead, many asked: But at what price?

By 1954, the hands of the Doomsday Clock on the cover of the *Bulletin of the Atomic Scientists* stood at two minutes to midnight. With the Bravo H-bomb test, the world entered its most dangerous years. Not until 1960 would the hands of the clock move back, and then only by a few minutes.

Within days of the Americans exploding the biggest bomb the world had yet seen, in March 1954, a high-level meeting of civil servants and top scientists took place in London. The man in charge of building the British atomic bomb, mathematician Sir William Penney, briefed them on the hydrogen bomb projects of the Soviet Union and the United States. Joe-4, the West's code name for the most recent Soviet test device, had exploded on 13 August 1953 with a yield of just 400 kilotons. It was not a true hydrogen bomb, as it used high explosives, not radiation, for compression. Only Stanislaw Ulam and Edward Teller's discovery of how to use X-ray radiation from the primary fission explosion to compress the deuterium in the secondary fusion device made possible the megaton yields achieved in the Bravo test. It would be well over a year before the Soviets would make that breakthrough.

Sir William, Britain's atomic knight, described to the assembled Whitehall mandarins what would happen if even a modest 5-megaton bomb were dropped on their city. The blast would create a searing fireball two and a quarter miles in diameter, and leave a crater almost a mile across and 150 feet deep. If such a bomb exploded above Nelson's Column in Trafalgar Square, everything and everyone from the Houses of Parliament and Downing Street in the south (including the room in which they were all sitting) to Soho in the north would be instantly vaporized. Beyond that, buildings would be totally destroyed up to three miles away and badly damaged up to seven miles.

'The world situation has been completely altered' was the assessment of the British Cabinet Committee on Defence Policy that June. The American bomb exploded at Bikini Atoll in March had been 1,500 times more powerful than the 'nominal' atomic bomb. 'There is no theoretical limit to the destructive power which can be achieved with the latest techniques,' they concluded, echoing Strauss's ominous words.[20]

The Prime Minister, Winston Churchill, was appalled. It was, he said, 'the most terrible and destructive engine of mass warfare yet known to man'.[21] But at Cabinet later that year, he still argued that Britain needed to be armed with hydrogen bombs, or risk losing 'influence and standing in world affairs'.[22] As well as deterring an atomic attack from the Soviet Union, Churchill hoped that British H-bombs would deter the United States of America. There was a strong belief in Whitehall that America was quite likely to launch a pre-emptive war against the Soviets. If Britain were armed with thermonuclear weapons, there might be a better chance of preventing what could be the Last War. The RAF had taken delivery of its first British-built atomic bomb, code-named Blue Danube, in November 1953. Churchill's Cabinet gave the go-ahead for the British H-bomb just a year later. It was tested in May 1957 and carried by British bombers from 1961.

The British Government was under no illusions about the appalling effects of a war fought with the new generation of nuclear super-weapons. In the year it authorized the building of the H-bomb, a Whitehall career civil servant, William Strath, was asked to examine whether the United Kingdom could survive a massive assault with hydrogen bombs. The result, known as the Strath Report, was declassified in 2002. It makes grim reading.

Strath estimated that a 'successful night attack' on Britain's major cities with ten hydrogen bombs would kill at least twelve million people and seriously injure four million more – a third of Britain's population. As Strath admitted, 'casualties on such a scale would be intolerable'.[23] A single 10-megaton bomb was sufficient to 'annihilate' any city apart from London. Strath spelled out to his political masters in dry and matter-of-fact language the utter horror that every person in the land might have to face. 'Hydrogen bomb war would be total war in a sense not hitherto conceived. The entire nation would be in the front line.'[24] An attack against the United Kingdom with ten hydrogen bombs, each of 10 megatons, was equivalent to dropping 100 million tons of high explosive. This was '45 times as great as the total tonnage of bombs delivered by the Allies over Germany, Italy, and occupied France throughout the whole of the last war'.

In many of the bombed areas, there would be a total breakdown of civil order. Chaos would reign. 'The household would become the unit of survival,' said Strath. But even those sheltering in their homes would be at risk from radiation and fallout. Up to 50 miles from an explosion, people would receive such heavy doses of radiation that, if they survived, they would be ill for weeks, with the symptoms experienced by the fishermen of the *Lucky Dragon*. For a thousand square miles around each bomb it would be 'suicidal' even to venture outside. 'Morale,' concluded William Strath with breathtaking understatement, 'would be very low.'[25]

A few weeks after the centres of Hiroshima and Nagasaki had been flattened by the first two atomic bombs, John von Neumann was struck by a dark and chilling thought that seemed straight out of science fiction. He told Lewis Strauss what had occurred to him:

[T]he appearance in the heavens of super-novae – those mysterious stars which suddenly are born in great brilliance and, as quickly, become celestial cinders – could be evidence that sentient beings in other planetary systems had reached the point in their scientific knowledge where we now stand, and, having failed to solve the problem of living together, had at least succeeded in achieving togetherness by cosmic suicide.[26]

After the Bravo test in 1954, politicians and public alike began to fear what the conclusion to the arms race might be. The A-bomb had seemed so terrible when it was first dropped that many thought that it had been dreamed up by some science fiction writer. Now scientists had developed the H-bomb, which was many thousands of times as powerful as the A-bomb and a weapon of potentially unlimited destructive power. What would be the next 'alphabet bomb' to emerge from the laboratories? 'It is easy for the scientists to agree that we cannot trust Russia,' said Leo Szilard, 'but they also ask themselves: To what extent can we trust ourselves?'[27] Perhaps, as Szilard had warned just four years earlier, the next type of weapon would be the C-bomb, a cobalt doomsday bomb that would spread its deadly fallout around the entire planet.

A month after the Bravo H-bomb test, a headline in the *New York Times* declared: NOW MOST DREADED WEAPON, COBALT BOMB, CAN BE BUILT. In his article, William Laurence revisited the fears voiced by Leo Szilard in the *Chicago Round Table* discussion on atomic weapons in February 1950. Quoting both Szilard and Einstein, he explained how a thermonuclear bomb with a shell of cobalt around the fission and fusion devices would create a lethal radioactive cloud when it exploded. Such a device would not need to be dropped on a city. It would be in the form of a ship bomb, containing more than a ton of heavy hydrogen. Harrison Brown, who had chaired the *Chicago Round Table* discussion and was now professor of nuclear chemistry at Caltech, told Laurence that if a cobalt ship bomb was set off in the Pacific a thousand miles west of California, 'the radioactive dust would reach California in about a day, and New York in four or five days'.[28] It would kill everything in its path. One bomb could wipe out an entire continent.

This article drew shocked responses from around the world. The

following day, the London *Times* reported Laurence's article promi-
nently. Beneath it was a report on the worsening condition of the
twenty-three Japanese fishermen exposed to radioactive fallout after
the H-bomb test at Bikini on 1 March. In the same issue it was
announced that four Labour MPs, including Tony Benn, were launching a national petition on the hydrogen bomb and calling for disarmament talks.[29] The previous month, a British paper had reported that
the Soviet Union was expected to test a cobalt bomb in late 1955.
It was a 'rigged' hydrogen bomb 'designed to produce widespread
radioactive effects'.[30]

In 1953, suspicions had grown that even Britain intended to develop
such a doomsday device – the ultimate deterrent against any unco-
operative superpower. Assurances had been sought in the Australian
Parliament that in forthcoming British tests at the Woomera rocket
range, a cobalt bomb was not to be exploded.[31] In 1957, Britain did
use cobalt in a 1 kiloton bomb exploded at the Tadje site on the
Maralinga range in Australia, but apparently only as a radiochemical
tracer in order to measure the yield of the device.[32]

In America too, government officials such as Assistant Secretary of
Defense Donald A. Quarles were forced to deny repeatedly to sceptical
reporters that a doomsday weapon was on the bomb-makers' drawing
board. During an appearance on ABC's television programme *At
Issue* in April 1954, Quarles said that although the 'C-bomb' was
possible, it was 'not feasible' as a weapon because 'the radioactive
material it released would kill friend and enemy indiscriminately'. It
was, he said, a 'suicide weapon'.[33] But despite these reassurances,
tension increased around the world when Italian Treasury Guards at
Viggiu intercepted nine tons of pure cobalt carefully concealed in a
truck en route from Italy to Switzerland. Police said they believed it
was bound for the other side of the Iron Curtain.[34] The Soviet Army
newspaper, *Red Star*, retorted that the dangers of the cobalt bomb
had been exaggerated by scaremongering 'imperialists'.[35]

In the weeks following the Bravo test, the *Bulletin of the Atomic
Scientists* noted how newspaper, radio and television were dominated
by talk of 'an annihilating cobalt bomb, or C-bomb, which could
become a world suicide bomb, with winds carrying the lethal dust
around the world'.[36] Across the Atlantic, the letters pages in the daily

papers reflected the widespread concern for the future of humankind. One correspondent summed up the 'universal attitude of mind' among his friends: 'What's the use of bothering, we'll all be blown up soon.' Another expressed the growing sense of global responsibility engendered by the prospect of worldwide fallout: 'There can be few today who do not realize ... that their own welfare is inextricably bound up with the welfare of other people far away.'[37] Such sentiments reveal the origins of today's environmentalism. In 1962, Rachel Carson's *Silent Spring* would confirm the harm that humankind had already inflicted on its planet, and compare the pervasive genetic damage done by artificial chemicals, such as the pesticide DDT, to that caused by radioactivity.

But despite the real fears felt around the world, the British managed to retain their wry sense of humour. 'Sir,' wrote Mr D. H. F. Lay of 51 Cantelupe Road, Bexhill-on-Sea, Sussex:

In the midst of the present public anxiety about atomic warfare readers of *The Times* will doubtless be relieved to know that the British Army remains unruffled. This last weekend I attended Territorial Army training – the morning was passed with lectures on the use and effect of the atomic bomb; in the afternoon we practised sword drill.[38]

As public concern mounted, eminent scientists began to voice their fears about the technologies of destruction. Sir George Thomson, son of the discoverer of the electron and one of the key figures in the British wartime atomic bomb project, spoke out about the hydrogen bomb. It was, he said, 'absolutely crazy as a weapon' and a 'form of world suicide'. 'The fear of an exploding world is unwarranted,' he continued, but 'that of contamination, unfortunately, is not.' Turning directly to address Szilard's doomsday weapon, he delivered this warning:

The so-called cobalt bomb is an imaginative attempt to do the worst. As a weapon, it is absolutely crazy, but how about as a form of suicide? The cobalt bomb is a suicide device because once material from such an explosion is shot into the air, it is at the mercy of the upper winds and can come down anywhere on earth. Certainly it would need a much bigger bomb than has been exploded so far, or a very large number of them to damage the earth.

But it is not completely impossible if the resources of a great nation were set over a period of years to destroy humanity, including themselves.[39]

On the same page that carried Thomson's words, the *New York Times* announced the end of the current series of H-bomb tests in the Pacific. As if to underline Thomson's warning, this article contained Lewis Strauss's remark that atomic scientists could now make an H-bomb 'as large as you wish, as large as the military requirement demands'.[40] The following month – as Godzilla began his cinematic rampage across Japan – Thomson spoke on BBC radio about the cobalt bomb. He compared the effects of such a bomb to that of the volcanic explosion of Krakatoa in 1883, which spread ash around the whole world. He again described the C-bomb as a suicide weapon, adding that 'it was terrible that a sufficiently large group of madmen, if such existed, should have such a possibility open to them'. However, he scotched media rumours of a new alphabet bomb – 'a mysterious thing called the nitrogen bomb'.[41]

Other prominent intellectuals in Britain shared Thomson's concerns. Two days before Christmas, the philosopher and mathematician Bertrand Russell, who had been imprisoned in World War I for his pacifism, gave a radio talk in what *The Times* described as 'the solemn, urgent tones of Cassandra'. 'Is our race so destitute of wisdom, so incapable of impartial love, so blind even to the simplest dictates of self-preservation,' asked Russell, 'that the last proof of its silly cleverness is to be the extermination of all life on our planet?'[42]

As 1955 dawned, the London *Times* attempted to sum up the momentous events of the previous year. In Britain, Roger Bannister had run the first sub-four-minute mile, and the food rationing introduced in World War II finally ended. But one news story had dominated 1954, as the ominous photograph of the atomic mushroom cloud in the middle of the page made plain. The public had not been prepared for either the size of the Bravo test or the subsequent talk of the new cobalt bomb, said *The Times*: 'But when at last the news broke that the nightmare of scientific visionaries had become a reality, that mankind now held the means of its own extermination, few people escaped a feeling of numb horror.' The paper accused political leaders of 'ineffectiveness' and of naively believing that 'the louder the bang the greater the deterrent'. It concluded that 'man was in the predicament of the sorcerer's apprentice, impotent to control the forces he had unleashed'.[43]

In the new year, the cobalt bomb continued to dominate headlines around the world. In West Germany, Otto Hahn, the chemist who first discovered atomic fission in 1938, discussed the cobalt bomb on radio. He too warned that 'man would in the near future be in a position to destroy the world'.[44] In the same month, Val Peterson, head of America's Civil Defense Administration, made what the *New York Times* described as 'one of the frankest statements ever made by a high Government official on the little discussed cobalt bomb'. On NBC's *Meet the Press* TV programme, the civil defence chief was asked whether atomic weapons could destroy the world. 'I think there's only one area in which that were true,' replied Peterson, 'and that was if someone were foolish enough to make a cobalt bomb.' If this were exploded, he said, radioactivity 'would drift around and around the world and kill everybody'. In a somewhat unconvincing attempt to reassure viewers, he added: 'I rather doubt we are going to have suicide.'[45]

Despite such reassurances, people begin to wonder whether the scientists, soldiers and statesmen who had developed such monstrous weapons could be trusted not to destroy the world. *The Times* was certain that the logic of the arms race meant the ultimate weapon of mass destruction – the cobalt bomb – would soon be built. Humankind, *The Times* solemnly declared in its editorial, now stood on the brink of a 'self-made precipice'. Below lay the abyss of nuclear Armageddon.[46]

In 1950, the authorities were quick to condemn Szilard and Einstein as 'prophets of hydrogen doomsday'. Now even official reports admitted that if the Bravo H-bomb was exploded in Washington, 11 million people could die from the blast and fallout.[47] Across America, people would suffer the same fate as the inhabitants of the Marshall Islands or the *Lucky Dragon*.

A new wave of 'hydrogen hysteria' swept America. Nuclear physicist James Arnold, who had corroborated Szilard's idea of a cobalt bomb back in 1950, now revisited the idea. In the four years since then the H-bomb had become reality, and now that cobalt was being used in the production of televisions the metal was more readily available and thus cheaper. 'There is', concluded Arnold, 'correspondingly less doubt that the cobalt bomb could be made. One thing seems clear from recent events – it had better not be tested.'[48]

Some scientists even believed that the cobalt bomb had already been built. Ralph E. Lapp, a physicist with the US Navy's scientific think-tank, the Office of Naval Research, pointed out that 'the official silence of the AEC with respect to the cobalt bomb has led many to assume that the C-bomb is a stockpile item in our nuclear arsenal'. He thought a 'definitive statement' was desirable.[49] In 1956 the Democratic presidential contender Adlai Stevenson challenged President Eisenhower to do just that and reveal the government's plans for the cobalt bomb. Stevenson spoke movingly of 'the millions who tremble on the sidelines of this mad arms race in helpless terror'.[50] Government spokesmen responded by briefing journalists that it was not 'on the drawing boards'.[51]

Despite repeated denials that anyone intended to build a cobalt bomb, many in the military were clearly in favour of its development. Air Force scientists claimed that a 15-megaton cobalt bomb could render 20,000 square miles uninhabitable for a decade. 'Denial of territory' on this scale could be a powerful tool in the military arsenal. (Indeed, this had been one of the perceived military advantages of using mustard gas.) During the Korean War, General MacArthur was so impressed with the idea that he proposed using cobalt-60 to create a radioactive no man's land between Korea and China.

Assurances from eminent atomic scientists, such as Sir John Cockcroft, that only a 'lunatic designer' would dream of building a cobalt bomb did not reassure a public which was growing accustomed to thinking of the scientists responsible for the 'alphabet bombs' as decidedly eccentric if not mad.[52] Freeman Dyson worked on top secret US weapons projects as well as the Project Orion atomic spaceship in the 1950s. According to the British physicist, there was more than a grain of truth in the stereotypical image people now had of scientists, such as himself. 'The mad scientist is not just a figure of speech,' says

Dyson, 'there really are such people, and they love to play around with crazy schemes. Some of them may even be dangerous, so one is not altogether wrong in being scared of such people.'[53]

The idealism of the early years of the twentieth century, when scientists were hailed as saviours of humankind, was long gone. Films were quick to reflect the growing suspicion of scientists. The stock-in-trade character of the mad scientist was as old as cinema itself and had produced such memorable figures as Dr Alexander Thorkel, who uses radium rays to reduce people to the size of garden gnomes in Ernest B. Schoedsack's *Dr Cyclops* (1940). 'What you are doing is mad, it is diabolic,' says his assistant. 'You are tampering with powers reserved to God.'[54]

In the 1950s, more subtly flawed scientists began to appear in the movies. They included scientists like Dr Edward Morbius (Walter Pidgeon) in *The Forbidden Planet* (1956), a classic science fiction film based on Shakespeare's *The Tempest*. Morbius channels his subconscious 'lust for destruction' via an alien super-technology into violence towards his fellow man. The British Oscar-winning movie *Seven Days to Noon* (1950) is a gripping thriller about a scientist, Professor Willingdon, who steals a bomb with the intention of destroying London in the hope that it will 'awaken the rest of mankind to the misuse of powers that might have brought them happiness'. His London landlady, is dismissive of this idea: 'People can be happy alright. We don't ask so much. It's you and your sort. Inventing things. Interfering with nature. That's what's causing all the trouble.'[55]

In the classic science fiction film *The Thing* (1951), based on John W. Campbell's story about alien invasion, the distinctly sinister scientist Dr Carrington is prepared to sacrifice human lives in the cause of science. The military, represented by the clean-cut Captain Patrick Hendry, wants to kill the aliens before it's too late. But it becomes clear that the scientist, a veteran of the Operation Crossroads atomic tests at Bikini, wants to keep the deadly aliens alive to serve a Faustian purpose:

DR CARRINGTON : You're robbing science of the greatest secret that's ever come to it. Knowledge is more important than life, Captain. We've only one excuse for existing: to think, to find out, to learn.

CAPT PATRICK HENDRY : What can we find out from that thing, except a quicker way to die?

DR CARRINGTON : It doesn't matter what happens to us. Nothing counts except our thinking. We've fought our way into nature, we've split the atom.

CAPT PATRICK HENDRY : Yes, and that sure made the world happy, didn't it?[56]

Both *Seven Days to Noon* and *The Thing* accuse science and scientists of undermining people's well-being and peace of mind – quite a reversal compared with the idolization of scientists at the beginning of the century. In *The Thing*, scientists are even shown to value knowledge above human life, the ultimate Faustian betrayal of humanity. Indeed, audiences may well have come away thinking that two alien species were portrayed in this film, both equally hostile to the future of the human race: the extraterrestrials and the scientists. For movie-goers, it was not at all inconceivable that men (and it was always men) like Morbius and Carrington would be capable of constructing a doomsday bomb.

Fiction too looked critically at scientists in the 1950s. Frederic Brown's wonderfully concise story 'The Weapon' (1951) tells how Dr James Graham, a 'key scientist of a very important project', receives an unexpected visitor, a Mr Niemand. Dr Graham tells Niemand that he is designing a new weapon, 'a rather ultimate one', but justifies it in the terms used by Dr Carrington: he is 'advancing science'. Niemand disagrees; his 'scientific work is more likely than that of any other man to end the human race's chance for survival'. He poses the classic question that occurs in most superweapon films and fictions: 'is humanity *ready* for an ultimate weapon?' Before he leaves, Niemand gives a small present to Dr Graham's mentally disabled son. Later, Graham is shocked to find that it is a loaded revolver. Surely, he thinks, 'only a madman' would give a weapon to such a child. The scientist fails to see the irony or to grasp the powerful point Niemand is making, one H. G. Wells had also made in *The World Set Free*.[57]

As had happened in the period after World War I, there were now clear signs in film and fiction of a genuine resentment towards scientists for betraying the high ideals of their profession and, indeed, the best interests of humanity. The French writer and intellectual Albert

Camus did not find it at all surprising that in such a violent world 'science devotes itself to organized mass murder'. The news of Hiroshima's destruction was, he said, evidence that 'technological civilization has just reached its final degree of savagery'. Now the real choice facing humankind was 'between collective suicide and the intelligent use of scientific conquests'. Camus concluded that 'peace is the only battle worth waging'.[58]

In the year after the bombing of Hiroshima and Nagasaki, the historian and critic Lewis Mumford had made a dramatic attack on the insanity of the modern age in an article entitled 'Gentlemen: You are mad!' 'We in America,' he wrote, 'are living among madmen. Madmen govern our affairs in the name of order and security.' The modern superweapon society was, he said, comprised of 'madmen living among madmen', all unable to recognize the looming apocalypse: 'The madmen have taken it upon themselves to lead us by gradual stages to that final act of madness which will corrupt the face of the earth and blot out the nations of men, possibly put an end to all life on the planet itself.'[59] For intellectuals like Mumford, people were sleepwalking towards the abyss. He wanted to shock them out of their stupor. This was precisely what Leo Szilard did in February 1950 with his vision of the cobalt bomb.

More than any other weapon in the twentieth century, Szilard's cobalt bomb came to symbolize the terrible situation faced by humankind. It was the ultimate weapon, a doomsday machine which could contaminate the entire planet with radioactive fallout. In the public mind it was a weapon which combined the worst horrors of both chemical and biological weapons – fallout was an invisible agent which slowly poisoned the body – with the uniquely awesome destructive power of a nuclear explosion.

In the shadow of the cobalt bomb, the dreams of atomic utopia, translated by Wells and other writers into beguiling future worlds, slowly faded and died. Such dreams had inspired scientists like Szilard himself. But in the cold war, these dreams were transformed into nightmares as scientists turned newly discovered physics into ever more lethal technologies.

Governments on all sides have denied developing such a weapon.

This portrait of Leo Szilard in his sixties was used on the cover of the
American journal Saturday Review *that featured a review of his* The Voice
of the Dolphins *(1961). The threat of nuclear war was a central theme of this*
collection of stories. 'If they cannot take it straight, they'll get it in fiction,'
he had said after one of his articles on arms control had been rejected by an
editor.

The truth may not be known for many years. Because of current fears about terrorists armed with dirty bombs, for which cobalt-60 is an ideal and readily available isotope, many documents relating to weapons design and radiological warfare remain classified. But in the 1950s, as far as the general public was concerned the C-bomb was a reality. It became the most tangible symbol of what J. G. Ballard has memorably described as the 'Auschwitz of the soul'. In this 'nightmarish chapter of human history', the cobalt bomb was the ultimate creation of 'Homo hydrogenensis'.[60]

John von Neumann had speculated that supernovae were planets on which atomic energy had been discovered before the maturity to use it safely. This evocative idea echoed the fears expressed by earlier writers and scientists such as Frederick Soddy, with his seminal atomic text *The Interpretation of Radium* (1909), and Pierrepont Noyes, whose novel *The Pallid Giant* (1927) was reissued after the bombing of Japan with a title borrowed from Lewis Mumford – *Gentlemen: You Are Mad.*

The horror of Hiroshima and Nagasaki convinced many people that a decisive point in human history, an apocalyptic moment, had arrived. The *New York Times* commented a few days after Nagasaki that:

Urban civilization might be wholly wiped out, and such as survives at all reduced to the animal level of thousands of years ago. Perhaps the secret of the atomic bomb would thus be lost, and after some thousands of additional years a kind of civilization would be restored. A week ago this kind of speculation would have seemed to most people like something out of a scientific romance. It is not so today.[61]

But the cobalt bomb in its most devastating form promised not just a few devastated cities, or even the annihilation of a whole continent. It meant the end of all life on earth: total extinction. Such a possibility exceeded even the worst fears of H. G. Wells, who – in an age before the dangers of global fallout were known – had dreamed of an atomic utopia being born, like a phoenix, out of the radioactive ashes.

At the end of *Beneath the Planet of the Apes* (1970), the time-travelling astronauts find themselves in St Patrick's Cathedral in what was once New York. But in AD 3955 the object of worship is not

Christ on the cross but a twentieth-century ICBM on which are written two Greek letters: Alpha and Omega. One of the astronauts recognizes the missile as the 'Doomsday Bomb', a nuclear weapon with a 'cobalt casing'. It was 'the last we ever made,' he explains:

Only one. One was enough. The idea was to threaten the enemy by the very fact that it existed. A bomb so powerful it could destroy – not just a city – not just a nation – no, not just every living cell on earth, every insect, every blade of grass – but set nuclear fire to the wind, to the air itself. Scorch the whole planet into a cinder! Like the end of a burnt match. The ultimate bomb—.

As his colleague says, 'not even H. G. Wells at his wildest, not even Jules Verne, had dared conceive of a civilization dedicated to the Bomb'.[62]

At the end of his life, Wells sank into a profound despair about the future he had once portrayed as a shining atomic utopia. 'This world is at the end of its tether,' he wrote. 'The end of everything we call life is close at hand and cannot be evaded.'[63] It was the bleak vision of Wells's final years and not the idealism of the early twentieth century that would now permeate the collective psyche, inspiring the dark worlds of 1950s writers such as William Golding and Samuel Beckett, who were part of a generation that lived with a real threat of nuclear doomsday. For this generation, utopia was a hollow promise and science a compromised ideology.

Other novelists and film-makers quickly grasped the dramatic implications of this fateful moment in human history. Back in 1893, readers of the popular illustrated journal The Idler had enjoyed a chilling story that foretold 'The Doom of London'. Robert Barr described how people and nature colluded to produce 'death so wholesale that no war the earth has ever seen left such slaughter behind it'. A combination of air pollution and unusually calm weather creates a lethal fog which envelops London, suffocating nearly all its inhabitants. The fog became 'one vast smothering mattress pressed down upon a whole metropolis'.[64]

In 1955 a British writer – strangely enough with the same surname – resurrected this theme for the atomic age, describing how a mysterious fog terrifies first America and then the whole world: 'A dark fringe appeared initially over the Pacific horizon, widening rapidly as the black shroud it edged raced towards the land . . .' The fog, a dense wall fifty miles high and full of 'fine dust particles', sweeps in from the Pacific and smothers America for sixteen impenetrable days before continuing on across the Atlantic and around the world.

But the fog in Densil Neve Barr's *The Man with Only One Head* is radioactive, the result of a test conducted in the Pacific of 'a new form of bomb based on the nuclear fission of cobalt'.[65] Barr's description of the atomic fog clearly resembles accounts of World War I poison gas attacks. Thus the horrors of one weapon of mass destruction segue into those of another. In the month after the Bravo test, Harrison Brown had told the *New York Times* of the threat posed to America by huge ship bombs of the kind dreamt up by Edward Teller. Indeed, the idea had also been raised in the original *Chicago Round Table* discussion. Detonated in the Pacific, ship bombs would cause clouds of fallout to be blown inland. Barr was clearly influenced by these reports.

In the novel, newspapers immediately blamed the fog on 'the war-mongers of Wall Street' and 'their mad search for new weapons of mass destruction'. The 'Society for the Banning of the C Bomb' is formed by anxious citizens.[66] Soon insects are dying, and fears grow for the future of humankind. Fortunately (and rather unbelievably) people are unharmed. More realistically, the US Government secretly asks newspapers to play down the story. But the real effect of the C-bomb is too big to conceal: all the men in the world have been made sterile. In Barr's frankly farcical novel, only one man, a million-aire called Vince Adams, remains fertile because he was hiding in his 'funkhole', an underground nuclear shelter in the Arizona desert. When he emerges, the appropriately named Adams finds himself in an unique situation – and with a hundred thousand proposals of marriage.

The Man with Only One Head takes an ultimately lighthearted view of the serious issues of fallout and the cobalt bomb. Other writers were less inclined to see any silver lining in this ominous cloud looming over civilization. Philip Wylie's atomic Pearl Harbor novel *Tomorrow!*, published in the year of the Bravo test, ends with the American President authorizing the use of a secretly built cobalt bomb against the Soviet Union. The huge bomb has been built into America's first atomic submarine, the USS *Nautilus*. According to the President, the *Nautilus* contains 'the largest hydrogen bomb ever assembled, and around it in her sides, replacing armor, and in her keel, for ballast, is the element cobalt with other readily radioactivated elements'.

The *Nautilus* is effectively the largest dirty bomb ever built. She and her crew are sent on a suicide mission to save America. The President admits that exploding this 'greater-than-super-weapon' is not without dangers for America itself: 'Its effect is not known and cannot be calculated.' Scientists have rejected the possibility of a 'planetary chain reaction'. But as well as wiping out the Russian population, the wind-blown fallout may well bring a 'train of death and sickness, sterility, misery, and additional fear' to the United States.[67] Faced with defeat, this is a risk America is willing to take.

Lying at the bottom of the Gulf of Finland, the crew of the USS *Nautilus* detonate the cobalt bomb in an enormous explosion that 'vaporized' Finland and the Baltic States. The blast even reaches Moscow. The fallout is still more deadly:

on the wind currents it came forward, forward across the north-sloping plains, a thick dust that widened to a hundred miles, and then five hundred, moving, spreading, descending, blanketing the land . . . Men swallowed, ate, breathed, sickened, and perished in a day, a week, two weeks – men and women and children, all of them, dogs and cats and cattle and sheep, all of them. Wherever they took refuge, men still perished. On the high Urals in the terrible cold. In the deepest mines, the steam-spitting darkness. There was no refuge from the death; it took them all, the birds of arctic winter, the persistent insects which had survived geological ages, the bacteria – all.[68]

The Russians are wiped off the face of the earth by the cobalt bomb. Wylie's account of their annihilation by the invisible killer is reminiscent of Jack London's story about the genocide of the Chinese by American biological weapons. Such stories typically suggest that, once the enemy is liquidated, all the world's problems will have been resolved and utopia can begin. *Tomorrow!* still clings – somewhat anachronistically – to this deadly utopian dream: 'The last war was finished. The last great obstacles to freedom had been removed from the human path.' The reference to Wells's *The World Set Free* ('last war') is unmistakable, with its implication of a better world beyond the atomic fires. In the future, Wylie's characters naively believe, 'the Bomb would be no catastrophe at all, but pure benefit'.[69] But as people increasingly realized, in the age of H- and C-bombs such thinking led not to a shining utopia but to a nuclear doomsday.

The fact that even a popular crime writer such as Agatha Christie – not known for her scientific themes – features a cobalt bomb in one of her novels, testifies to the cultural impact of Szilard's doomsday device. Christie's 1954 thriller *Destination Unknown* is about a missing nuclear scientist, Thomas Betterton, the discoverer of 'ZE Fission' and 'one of the splitters in chief'.[70] In the novel, Miss Hetherington, who 'could not have been mistaken for anything but travelling English', and an American, Mrs Calvin Baker, are sitting in their hotel knitting and discussing (as one does) the latest weapons of mass destruction.

'I do think all these atom bombs are very wrong. And Cobalt – such a lovely colour in one's paint-box and I used it a lot as a child; the worst of all, I understand *nobody* can survive. We weren't meant to do these experiments. Somebody told me the other day that her cousin, who is a very shrewd man, said the whole world might go *radio-active*.'

'My, my,' said Mrs Calvin Baker.[71]

The cobalt bomb continued to feature as the ultimate symbol of human destructiveness throughout the doomsday decade. In William Tenn's story 'The Sickness' (1955), people have no doubt about their future in a world where many nations possessed C-bombs: 'Everyone waited for extinction.'[72] At the end of the decade, nuclear holocaust entered the best-seller lists with influential novels such as Pat Frank's chilling but ultimately unconvincing tale of nuclear survival *Alas, Babylon* (1959), and Walter M. Miller's *A Canticle for Leibowitz* (1959), the most famous fictional exploration of history as a cyclical process destined always to end in global nuclear destruction. The bleakest of these hugely popular novels both feature cobalt bomb doomsdays: Nevil Shute's *On the Beach* (1957) and Mordecai Roshwald's *Level 7* (1959).

Nevil Shute, an aeronautical engineer who had worked with

bouncing-bomb designer Barnes Wallis, wrote the most famous novel about a war fought with cobalt bombs. By the 1980s it had sold more than four million copies, an astonishing total and more than any other novel about nuclear issues. The war itself is not described, just the lethal after-effects. What Shute depicts is a world dying a slow and creeping death caused by fallout.

The novel centres on the only part of the globe not yet affected by radioactivity, Melbourne in the far south of Australia. Set in 1963, after the Last War, Shute examines how people behave when faced with the inescapable reality that within nine months – when the cobalt-60 fallout finally reaches them – they will all be dead. 'It's just too big a matter for mankind to tackle,' says one character. Indeed, Shute depicts people reacting fatalistically to what lies ahead: 'It's not the end of the world at all. It's only the end of us. The world will go on just the same, only we shan't be in it. I dare say it will get along all right without us.'[73]

As a powerful portrait of a culture in denial about its fate, *On the Beach* has a continuing significance in our own era of global warming. But for Shute and for many readers, the stoicism of his characters and their attempt to continue a normal life, right up to the very end, was deeply poignant. It captured the mood of powerlessness that many felt in the 1950s, facing the awesome possibility of a global nuclear holocaust that might well bring about the end of life on earth. The film version of 1959, starring Gregory Peck, Ava Gardner and Anthony Perkins, became one of the most popular nuclear movies of all time and left audiences around the world 'stunned or weeping'.[74]

When asked who started the war, Julian Osborne (Fred Astaire) replies, only half-seriously, 'Albert Einstein'. But Julian is himself a 'long-hair', one of the British atomic scientists responsible for building the bombs that are slowly killing the world. As well as his own profession, he blames humanity as a whole: 'the war started when people accepted the idiotic principle that peace could be maintained by arranging to defend themselves with weapons they couldn't possibly use without committing suicide'. The film concludes with a lingering shot of a banner flying in a deserted Melbourne street: 'There is still time . . . brother.'[75]

In Shute's novel, an American submarine commander, Dwight

Towers, travels beneath the safety of the oceans from Australia to the United States, where he finds a continent utterly devoid of life. Back in the southern hemisphere, he concludes that a species capable of such destruction deserves to die. Looking at the still populated streets of Melbourne, he sheds no tears for what will happen:

Very soon, perhaps in a month's time, there would be no one here, no living creatures but the cats and dogs that had been granted a short reprieve. Soon they too would be gone; summers and winters would pass by and these houses and streets would know them. Presently, as time passed, the radio-activity would pass also; with a cobalt half-life of about five years these streets and houses would be habitable again in twenty years at the latest, and probably much sooner than that. The human race was to be wiped out and the world made clean again for wiser occupants without undue delay. Well, probably that made sense.[76]

Humankind, in fact, is so barbaric for inventing weapons such as the cobalt bomb that it deserves to die. If the scientists had, as Oppen-heimer put it, known sin by inventing atomic weapons, then the price of that sin – to be paid by all humanity – was extinction. As Shute's character says, the world needed to be 'made clean again'.

More recently, in the age of global warming, this theme has re-emerged. Now humankind deserves extinction for polluting the natu-ral world. At the end of the blockbuster movie *The Day After Tomorrow* (2004), after the northern hemisphere has been cata-strophically changed by a new ice age provoked by global warming, astronauts on the International Space Station gaze down on their transformed planet:

Yuri said, 'Look at that.'
  Parker didn't fully understand. 'What?'
  'Have you ever seen the air so clear?'
  Earth lay like a jewel in the great sky, not only bruised by the storm but also purified, hanging there in space as black as the darkest memory, amid stars as bright as the brightest hope.[77]

Interestingly, the novelization from which this is taken is by Whitley Strieber, who is also the author of the nuclear holocaust best-seller, *War Day* (1984). Just as nuclear war would rid the world of humans and make it clean again, so here earth has been 'purified' of its most polluting species. Indeed, human beings are now often portrayed as little more than a malign virus – as Agent Smith (Hugo Weaving) memorably says in *The Matrix* (1999) – an infection in the otherwise pristine bloodstream of Gaia.

Shute's novel and the subsequent film made a huge impression on audiences around the world. In September 1957, *On the Beach* even became a talking point during a party at Lord Beaverbrook's home in the South of France. Winston Churchill was heard to say that he intended to send a copy to the Soviet premier, Khrushchev. 'I think the earth will soon be destroyed by a cobalt bomb,' declared the former Prime Minister. 'I think if I were the Almighty I would not recreate it . . .', he added, with characteristic dark humour.[78]

Edward Teller, now firmly established in Washington's corridors of power as an influential advisor on nuclear issues, was so concerned by the pessimistic message of *On the Beach* that he wrote a book to 'help the general public better assess the nature of radioactivity and the risks connected with it'.[79] *Our Nuclear Future* (1958), which he co-authored with Albert Latter, discussed the cobalt bomb in detail. Although he admitted that a 'cobalt bomb would indeed be a most unpleasant object', Teller nevertheless argued that 'radiological warfare could be used in a humane manner'.[80] It was a position justified by truly Strangelovean logic. However, he later admitted that this book 'had little or no effect on public opinion'. In contrast, he grudgingly acknowledged that Shute's novel 'had immense and far-reaching effects'.[81]

Like Szilard, Teller was nothing if not persistent. After the film of *On the Beach* was released, he co-authored another book, *The Legacy of Hiroshima* (1962), devoting an entire chapter to a critique of Shute's work. While granting that *On the Beach* had made a deep impression on public opinion, America's leading weapons designer criticized Shute's use of the cobalt bomb, a device Teller had himself justified just four years earlier:

These bombs do not exist. They would have no military usefulness. They would do their greatest damage not on the spot of a target, but around the globe; not immediately, but after the passage of years . . . The cobalt bomb is not the invention of an evil warmonger. It is the product of the imagination of high-minded people who want to use this spectre to frighten us into the heaven of peace.

This final broadside of Teller's was presumably aimed in part at his friend Leo Szilard.

For perhaps the only time in his life, Edward Teller found himself agreeing with the Russian newspaper *Pravda* whose reviewer had condemned Shute for what he saw as the novelist's fatalism. It was an attitude Teller found in 'the overwhelming majority of our people', and he hated it. He was shocked when a young colleague admitted in a discussion about careers that 'The world is coming to an end. There's no sense in planning for the future.' For Teller, the cobalt bomb and *On the Beach* were symptoms of a general malaise: 'we are obsessed by the idea of an impending day of doom'. Fatalism was equated with defeatism, and in the cold war this was tantamount to treachery. The father of the H-bomb refused to tolerate such attitudes. He backed what was the official line in Washington, London and Moscow: 'The biggest nuclear conflict would be a catastrophe beyond imagination. But it will not be the end.'[82]

Mordecai Roshwald disagreed. His 1959 novel *Level 7*, published first in Britain by Heinemann (which had also published *On The Beach*), described the end of the world as the result of a war fought with cobalt bombs. *Level 7* is the diary of the man who pushed the button to launch the doomsday missiles. J. B. Priestley called it 'the best statement there has been so far on the ghastly imbecility of nuclear armaments'.[83] Bertrand Russell also praised it. Roshwald said that he wanted 'to write a book that would frighten people into sanity', an aim with which Lewis Mumford and Leo Szilard would have greatly sympathized.[84] It has since sold over 400,000 copies around the world.

Roshwald's push-button warrior X-127 is deep underground, on Level 7, the lowest level of a command bunker. As X-127 points out, the world has changed for the military and civilians since World War I:

the armed forces now find themselves in the safest place in the world, not in the front lines. Quite a change from the days when a soldier had to advance into a machine-gun volley and a pilot was forever expecting something to blast him out of the sky. Today we, the soldiers of our country, are shielded by an earth crust 3,000 or 4,400 feet thick. No warrior's armour-plating ever compared with that. For once let the civilians tremble while the soldiers feel secure.[85]

As in the film of *On the Beach*, where the war is blamed on a fault in a 'handful of vacuum tubes and transistors', the war itself is caused by a technical accident.[86] Retaliation is ordered automatically by a computerized defence system. It was, says X-127, 'the battle of the gadgets'.[87] The machines destroy themselves along with all life on the surface of the planet. As we shall see, Roshwald's doomsday machine clearly anticipates the one built by the Soviets in Stanley Kubrick's film *Dr Strangelove*. Indeed, it is the classic tragedy of the techno-scientific age, Dr Frankenstein's tragedy: to become the victim of one's own ingenuity. The important difference is that in the atomic age, Dr Frankenstein and Dr Strangelove don't die alone – they take the rest of the world with them. At the end of *Level 7* even the narrator on the deepest level of his underground bunker dies of radiation sickness. 'I am dying, and the world is dying with me. I am the last man on earth, the sole surviving specimen of homo sapiens. *Sapiens* indeed!'[88]

There came a point in the 1950s when people realized that human-kind could, for the first time, create weapons which might end life on earth. Those same scientists who had been praised for curtailing World War II with the atomic bomb now held the fate of the world in their hands. Their undoubted inventiveness and insight into the laws of physics had been transformed into instruments of mass destruction. To many people, the saviour scientists had become mad scientists. Leo Szilard's vision of the cobalt bomb was a key ingredient in this radical change. Bertolt Brecht summed up the dilemma facing cold-war science and society in his great play *Life of Galileo* (1955). In the future, predicts the father of modern physics, the scientists' euphoric shouts of *Eureka!* will be greeted by 'a universal cry of horror' because people will have learnt that, rather than improving the lot of humanity, science now leads to ever more terrible weapons of mass destruction.[89]

From novels such as *Level 7* to blockbuster films such as *Beneath the Planet of the Apes*, Leo Szilard's cobalt bomb became the ultimate symbol of the threat posed to life on earth by science and power politics. The cobalt bomb made real the fear of a doomsday of our

Journalists and military personnel witness the Charlie nuclear test, part of the Operation Tumbler series, on 22 April 1952. This 31 kiloton explosion was the first to be broadcast live on national television.

own devising that had intrigued writers of speculative fiction since World War I. As a concrete symbol of planet earth placed in jeopardy by humankind, the cobalt bomb also gave powerful impetus to the nascent ecological movement.

394

The fear of the cobalt bomb lived on long after the 1950s. For many writers who grew up surrounded by the doomsday anxieties of this period, the cobalt bomb became a defining experience, the ultimate symbol of man's inhumanity to man. Even the work of travel writer Bruce Chatwin reveals its powerful influence. Chatwin's autobiographical book *In Patagonia* (1977) describes how his interest in Patagonia began during the cold war. He was looking for 'somewhere to live when the rest of the world blew up', a land out of reach of the fallout from the cobalt bombs.

At school, Chatwin had watched 'the civil defence lecturer ring the cities of Europe to show the zones of total and partial destruction. We saw the zones bump one against the other leaving no space in between . . . we saw it was hopeless. The war was coming and there was nothing we could do.' Chatwin continues:

Next, we read about the cobalt bomb, which was worse than the hydrogen bomb and could smother the planet in an endless chain reaction.

I know the colour cobalt from my great-aunt's paintbox . . . She did lots of St Sebastians, always against a cobalt-blue background . . .

So I pictured the cobalt bomb as a dense blue cloudbank, spitting tongues of flame at the edges. And I saw myself, out alone on a green headland, scanning the horizon for the advance of the cloud.[90]

19

Khrushchev's Monsters

A child of the nineteenth century would quickly go mad with fear, I think, in the world of today . . . What has become of us?　　　　　Pat Frank, *Alas, Babylon* (1959)

The Air Force Captain took the escalator to the lowest level of the Pentagon. He continued down some grey concrete steps and then strode briskly through the labyrinth of featureless corridors. He stopped abruptly outside a green door identified as Room BD 927 and jabbed his finger on the buzzer. As he spoke his name into the microphone beside the door, the officer stared impassively into a two-way mirror and waited for the door to be unlocked. He went through this routine every working day, but today it had a new significance. Today, as he passed through the door to the War Room of the United States Air Force, the officer wondered if he would ever see his wife and kids again.[1]

At the beginning of the week, President John F. Kennedy had addressed the American people on radio and television in what the *New York Times* justifiably described as a 'speech of extraordinary gravity'. President Kennedy's eighteen-minute address was 'of a grimness unparalleled in recent times', said the newspaper.[2] It was not just America that was listening to his every word, but the whole world. The strain of the last few days was etched into the President's boyish face.

On 14 October 1962, an American U-2 spy plane had photographed what was clearly a missile launch site under construction on the island of Cuba. Nearby, a Soviet medium-range ballistic missile was pictured waiting to be lowered into its firing position. Photographs taken five days later showed four sites where missiles were ready to fire at a moment's notice. From the Caribbean they could hit Washington in under twenty minutes.

In his address to the nation on Monday 22 October, President Kennedy accused Soviet premier Nikita Khrushchev of a 'clandestine, reckless, and provocative threat to world peace'. Until the missiles were removed, he said, the world would stand before 'the abyss of destruction'. In the meantime, he announced that a naval blockade had been set up around Cuba to prevent any more missiles from reaching the island.

The President had resisted calls from the military for immediate air strikes on the missile sites, an action that we now know would have provoked an immediate and devastating response. Even so, imposing the blockade (suggested by Secretary of Defense Robert McNamara) was not a risk-free operation, and Kennedy did not hide the real dangers from his people: 'No one can foresee precisely what course it will take or what costs or casualties will be incurred,' he told them.[3]

In the Pentagon's War Room, presided over by the Chief of Staff of the Air Force, General Curtis E. LeMay, five screens constantly displayed the nation's state of combat readiness. The screen for DEFCON 2 – Defense Condition 2 – was illuminated that week in October 1962. The next step was DEFCON 1: war. On the balcony of the War Room were eighteen upholstered chairs reserved for the generals. From there they could watch the fate of the world in comfort:

Panoramic screens scanned US outposts around the globe, bulb-clustered boxes showed troop movements, lighted maps flashed with blobs of color, each indicating a nuclear warplane or missile aimed and 'cocked' at millions of human beings who lived on in ignorance of their peril. The target: the Soviet Union. Detonation: hours away.[4]

A radar early warning system would keep track of any Russian missiles that were fired and would estimate the likely scale of casualties. In the jargon of the day, casualties were measured in megadeaths – not thousands, but millions of people killed. A map of the United States displayed information from a nationwide network of sensors, and could immediately show the location of nuclear detonations.

It was here in the Pentagon's War Room that the presidential order to go to DEFCON 1 would be received. When the signal arrived, a procedure would be set in motion in which each movement was as precisely choreographed as a dance of death. Observed from above by the top brass on the balcony, two officers would remove keys that were kept on chains around their necks. Then they would 'unlock separate padlocks on a red box, two feet by six inches, take out five-inch-square plastic bags, tear them open, and pull out the same typewritten message to all Strategic Air Commands from Alaska to Guam, Spain to England. The coded message: go to war.'[5]

While this happened, two officers stood by armed with .38-calibre pistols, the only weapons allowed in the War Room. But their snub-nosed, bone-handled weapons were not for use against invaders. They were to be used against any member of the War Room staff who panicked or tried to start World War III prematurely.

At the end of October 1962, it seemed to many people that the presidential order to go to DEFCON 1 was just hours away. Over the Atlantic, up to a hundred B-52 bombers were kept permanently in the air, waiting for the coded signal to proceed to prearranged targets. Each bomber carried up to four bombs of between 1 and 24 megatons. Some five hundred more B-52s waited on the ground, armed and ready to fly. From submarines under the cold grey waters of the North Atlantic and from launch sites across the United States, hundreds of nuclear armed missiles were trained on targets in the Soviet Union. In the words of Robert Oppenheimer, Russia and America were like two scorpions in a bottle. Now the world held its breath as these two armoured warriors prepared for their final battle.

President Kennedy's television address to the nation was the most grave and disturbing statement any president has had to make to the American people. As Leo Szilard watched on that Monday evening, his face went pale. Szilard and his wife Trude were living in Washington's newest hotel, the Dupont Plaza, in what was then one of the city's most cosmopolitan areas, just five minutes by cab from the White House. All Szilard's instincts cried out to him that Kennedy was making a terrible mistake by confronting Khrushchev. 'A blockade is an act of war,' exclaimed Szilard when the President had finished speaking to the nation. 'An act of war.'[6]

Szilard was deeply shocked. The 64-year-old was living on borrowed time. In 1959 he had been diagnosed with bladder cancer. 'I don't expect to live,' he had told a reporter, 'but I hope to be active for a few months and perhaps a year.' But Szilard was never one to give up hope. He designed his own radiation therapy: 'I'm the chief consultant on my own case,' he told a friend.[7] By the spring of that year his doctors declared him free of cancer. 'I feel fine,' he told *Time*, which reported that for most sufferers of this cancer only 5 per cent could expect a long-term cure. In medicine too, it seemed, Szilard's insights worked wonders.[8]

Even from his hospital bed, Szilard had continued his campaign for arms control and peace. But his battle with cancer had left him physically drained. He was thinner now, and his shock of brown hair had turned platinum grey. According to one reporter with a vivid turn of phrase, 'his demeanor was that of a volatile owl'.[9]

President Kennedy's grim words that October evening prompted a group of students to visit Szilard in the hope that he could allay their fears. But Szilard had no comforting words for them. This time, he saw the situation as hopeless. In a moment of deep despair, he admitted that all his efforts to avert nuclear war had been in vain. He had tried and failed to institute controls on the power of the atomic energy he had helped to unleash. Within days, he predicted, this power would be used to kill millions in a holocaust of destruction unparalleled in human history. It might even mean the end of life itself.

That night Szilard tossed and turned in his bed, his mind racing. By the next morning he had reached a decision. He told his wife that they should pack everything and leave for Geneva. For some years now his 'Big Bomb Suitcase', full of essential documents such as his patents, had been packed in readiness for a quick getaway.

Old habits die hard. In 1933, as Hitler's thugs terrorized the streets of Berlin, Szilard had lived with his bags packed and ready to go. Then it had paid off: when Hitler came to power, Szilard had grabbed his bags and jumped on a train bound for Vienna. He was just one step ahead of the secret police who soon began arresting Jews fleeing Germany. Now, in 1960s America, Szilard phoned his friends and advised them to leave as soon as possible. For the third time in his life, war was coming.

The next day, Wednesday 24 October, as the Soviet ships headed for Cuba, Harrison Brown boarded a plane from Los Angeles to Washington. Brown had chaired the *Chicago Round Table* back in 1950. Now he had been asked to write an editorial for the *Bulletin of the Atomic Scientists*. The Chicago journal, with its distinctive doomsday clock still on the front cover, was planning a special edition to mark the twentieth anniversary of the first controlled release of atomic energy, on that cold December afternoon beneath Stagg Field football stadium. Brown wrote his editorial on the plane:

This morning, the governments of the United States and Soviet Union were moving relentlessly toward armed conflict in the Caribbean. By tomorrow ... the great all-out nuclear war, which we have discussed and feared for twenty years, may be triggered. Never in history have people and nations been so close to death and destruction on such a vast scale. Midnight is upon us.[10]

The next morning, Szilard and Trude boarded a flight to Europe. After diversion and delay caused by fog, they arrived in Geneva on what Robert Kennedy christened 'Black Saturday' – the peak of the crisis.[11] Szilard headed straight for CERN, the European laboratory for particle research, where his old friend Victor Weisskopf was director. Although Szilard did have something of a reputation among his scientific colleagues for appearing when least expected, Victor was astonished when Szilard knocked on his office door in Switzerland. 'I'm the first refugee from America,' explained Szilard solemnly. 'There'll be nuclear war in a few days.'[12]

Back in Washington, groups of demonstrators had gathered outside the White House. Pacifists, Cuban refugee groups and even a contingent from the American Nazi Party shouted conflicting advice to President Kennedy and his administration.[13] That evening, as the crisis reached its peak, Robert McNamara took a break from the tense atmosphere of the White House situation room. 'It was a beautiful fall evening,' he recalled, 'and I went up into the open air to look and to smell it, because I thought it was the last Saturday I would ever see.'[14]

Kennedy and Khrushchev faced each other across the 'abyss of destruction', and then both stepped back from the brink. According to a White House insider, 'we were eyeball to eyeball, and the other fellow just blinked'.[15] In the end, both leaders opted for compromise rather than conflict, ignoring the hawkish advice of their military advisors. The Soviets agreed to remove their missiles from Cuba, provided America removed its Jupiter missiles from Turkey. Robert Kennedy secretly visited the Russian embassy to agree the deal.

The American military were furious. General LeMay effectively accused his President of cowardice. 'It's the greatest defeat in our history,' thundered the Air Force commander. 'We should invade today.'[16] The biggest invasion force since World War II was poised in Florida, and its commanders were just itching for an excuse to attack Castro's Cuba. What the American generals didn't realize, however, was that the Soviet forces in Cuba had tactical nuclear weapons and they were under the control of local commanders. Any invasion would have triggered the world's first nuclear conflict.

President Kennedy clearly didn't trust his military commanders. At one point he even asked an aide to ensure that the Joint Chiefs of Staff did not start a war without his authorization. 'I don't want these nuclear weapons firing without our knowing it,' he said, with shocking candour. 'I don't think we ought to accept the Chiefs' word on that one.'[17]

Trust was in short supply during the cold war. Conducted beneath a cloak of secrecy, the arms race bred a culture of fear and suspicion. In novels and movies, the anxieties of the age were expressed through two shadowy professions: the spy and the atomic scientist. The first James Bond film, *Dr No*, featured a sexy mix of spies and scientists that would prove an enduring hit at the box office. It opened in the month of the Cuban Missile Crisis. With its story-line of a secret base on a Caribbean island, powered by a nuclear reactor, and an evil scientist bent on sabotaging America's missile programme, it was eerily prescient. Ian Fleming was a personal friend of Kennedy's, and, according to *Time* magazine, Bond was the 'President's favorite fictional hero'.[18]

As it had in the 1950s, the cobalt doomsday bomb symbolized people's concerns about what further technological horrors the secret alliance between science and power politics might create. In the early 1960s, many feared that one of the superpowers, or even a newcomer to the nuclear game such as China, might develop such a weapon. Now, as weapon systems became increasingly automated and response times ever shorter, Szilard's cobalt bomb was reinvented for the computer age as the doomsday machine.

Throughout the story of weapons of mass destruction, we have seen how popular culture played an important role in inspiring the dream of the superweapon. Similarly, the doomsday machine has its origins in fiction and film – in Peter George's best-selling thriller *Red Alert* (1958) and Stanley Kubrick's cold-war classic (based on George's novel) *Dr Strangelove or: How I Learned to Stop Worrying and Love the Bomb* (1964). By removing human agency and making even the push-button warriors redundant, the doomsday machine took Szilard's cobalt bomb to a new level of inhumanity. But it also posed an irresistible scientific and technological challenge to Strangeloves on either side of the Iron Curtain.

On 5 October 1961, a year before the Cuban Missile Crisis took the world to the brink of nuclear war, Stanley Kubrick called at the offices of the Institute for Strategic Studies, housed in a Georgian building in central London near the Strand Palace Hotel, where 27 years before Szilard had written his patent on the atomic chain reaction.

Kubrick was a 'slightly ageing wunderkind from a middle-class Bronx family who, with his ill-fitting clothes, shaggy hair, and wonder-filled eyes, gives the impression that it still wouldn't be too late for him to enrol in a school for gifted children'.[19] Although he had failed English at school and couldn't get a place at college, the 33-year-old Kubrick had just finished filming one of the twentieth century's literary classics – *Lolita*, by Vladimir Nabokov. He had been working in England on the film at Shepperton Studios in west London for over a year now. For the director of *Paths of Glory* (1957) and *Spartacus* (1960) it had been his first attempt at black comedy, a genre ideal for expressing the anxieties of the doomsday decade.

Kubrick explored the possibilities of film with as much subtlety and brilliance as Nabokov did the written word. It could have been Nabokov speaking when Kubrick talked passionately about the power of film at this time. 'A really great picture has a delirious quality in which you're constantly searching for meanings,' Kubrick told a journalist. 'It's all very elusive and very rich. There's nothing like trying to create it. It gives you a sense of omnipotence – it's one of the most exciting things you can find without being under the influence of drugs.'[20]

Lolita, starring James Mason as Humbert Humbert and the fourteen-year-old Sue Lyon as his nymphet muse, had finally been passed by the censors in September. It was released in England the following year with an X certificate. Kubrick's next project was to be a film about a nuclear war that started by accident. He had been fascinated by the idea since at least 1958 and had read widely on the subject. According to his biographer, Vincent LoBrutto, 'the idea of an impending nuclear holocaust often crept into his already dark and pessimistic vision of the world'.[21]

When Kubrick visited the Institute for Strategic Studies in autumn 1961 in search of inspiration, Alastair Buchan, the institute's head, was not at all sympathetic towards his proposed film. Buchan told Kubrick bluntly to drop the idea. According to Buchan, it would be impossible to show 'precisely what precautions the United States or other nuclear powers take to guard against the danger of accident or false command'. No matter how 'amusing or skilful' the film was, he feared that it would 'mislead anxious people all over the world'.

Kubrick was not to be put off so easily. When he was researching a film, Kubrick's interest in a subject would grow and mature slowly until it attained a critical mass. After that point it would become an all-consuming obsession. *Dr Strangelove* was on the verge of going critical. Kubrick's visit to the research institute was by no means wasted, though. As he was about to leave, Buchan handed him a paperback novel – Peter George's *Red Alert*. It came with a health warning: 'parts of it are quite implausible', said Buchan disapprovingly.[22]

Red Alert, which the British writer had published under his pen name, Peter Bryant, had already sold 250,000 copies in its American Ace paperback edition. In Britain it was published in 1958 as *Two Hours to Doom*. George's crime and mystery novels, with titles such as *The Big H* and *Hong Kong Kill*, had sold millions of copies around the world. He once said that 'if you learn how to construct a mystery, you learn how to write'.[23] Peter George had joined the RAF at the

Is FAIL-SAFE foolproof?

red alert

by Peter Bryant is the original novel about an unauthorized H-bomb attack on the USSR by American B-52s despite our Fail-Safe system. Can our President prevent Russian retaliation?

The 1958 thriller Red Alert *by Peter Bryant (aka Peter George). This undated Ace edition was published at about the time that Stanley Kubrick began filming* Dr Strangelove.

age of 18 and had served in Malta and Italy. Rumour had it that he also worked for British intelligence. He was 34 when *Red Alert* was published. Like Kubrick, George had developed a dark obsession with the subject of nuclear war, and became an active member of CND.

George shared President Kennedy's distrust of America's military commanders, an opinion he formed while he was in the RAF. He once described American generals as 'war hungry psychopaths of the lunatic fringe'.[24] In his best-selling thriller *Red Alert*, George describes how World War III might be started by a maverick military commander. Terminally ill and suffering from depression, General Quinten (the psychotic General Jack D. Ripper in Kubrick's film) orders his B-52 bombers to attack the Soviet Union. He is able to do this because it is sanctioned in an emergency war plan designed to be used if the President and his chiefs of staff were killed in a sneak attack.

But it was Leo Szilard's notion of a cobalt doomsday bomb that symbolized the precarious cold-war balance of terror in both *Red Alert* and, later, *Dr Strangelove*. As Ambassador DeSadeski explains in the film, 'If you take, say, fifty H-bombs in the hundred megaton range and jacket them with cobalt thorium G, when they are exploded they will produce a doomsday shroud. A lethal cloud of radioactivity which will encircle the earth for ninety-three years!'[25]

In an allusion to President Kennedy's campaign slogan about a supposed missile gap, the Ambassador cites fears of a 'doomsday gap' as the reason for building a doomsday device. Reports in the *New York Times* convinced the Soviets that the Americans already had one. Thanks to the articles by its journalist William Laurence, the *New York Times* had indeed led media speculation on the development of Szilard's idea.

In Peter George's novel, the Soviet Union has secretly constructed a doomsday machine beneath the Urals – at least twenty massive hydrogen bombs jacketed with cobalt. The American President in *Red Alert* collaborates with the Russians in tracking down the rogue bombers until just one remains. In Kubrick's film, the bald-headed President Merkin Muffley (described by one reviewer as 'a meek, worried leader of men'[26]) is strongly reminiscent of Adlai Stevenson. In the novel he even agrees that if a Russian city is destroyed, Soviet bombers will be allowed to destroy Atlantic City, New Jersey. This tit-for-tat exchange of cities is remarkably similar to a plan Szilard first proposed in 1957 to the first Pugwash Conference (a forum for discussing how to reduce armed conflict) as a way of preventing an uncontrolled nuclear war. He later published it as a story called 'The Mined Cities'.[27]

George's tense and convincing thriller takes the reader to the edge of the abyss, as the final B-52 manages to evade the Soviet air defences. The fate of the world depends on shooting this plane out of the sky before its bombs cause the Russians to set off their doomsday machine. In the end, apocalypse is postponed when the badly damaged B-52 crashes in open countryside. One of its H-bombs partially detonates – but for now at least, Atlantic City and the world are safe.

In Kubrick's more pessimistic film, the world doesn't get off so lightly. Major T. J. 'King' Kong, the Texan commander of the B-52 played by Slim Pickens, heroically rides his bronco of an H-bomb down onto its Soviet target. This is a superbly comic moment, and also one of the darkest in the film. At this instant the cold-war shibboleths of patriotism and progress appear at their most vulnerable. In the great American novel of the 1950s, J. D. Salinger's *The Catcher in the Rye*, Holden Caulfield calls himself a 'pacifist'. If he is forced to join the army, Holden says, he intends 'to sit right the hell on top of' the atomic bomb. Major Kong, the all-American hero, does just this. But instead of saving the American way of life (as he hopes) by riding the bomb to its target, his action destroys the world.[28] The discoverer of deuterium, Harold Urey, told *Time* magazine in 1950 that although he was unhappy that the H-bomb was to be built, 'I value my liberties more than I do my life.'[29] The crazy logic of the cold war provided Kubrick with the inspiration for his film's dark, doomsday humour.

Dr Strangelove ends with an awesome display of mushroom clouds erupting across the face of the earth, as the cobalt bombs of the Soviet doomsday machine explode. News footage of H-bomb tests is accompanied by British forces' favourite Vera Lynn singing 'We'll Meet Again'. The brutal reality – fully understood by the film's audience in 1964 – was that there would be no reunions after World War III. The age of saviour scientists and winning weapons was dead. Nuclear war could have only one outcome: mutual annihilation. It was the same point Leo Szilard had made back in the doomsday decade, when he first conjured up the spectre of the cobalt bomb.

Stanley Kubrick visited the Institute for Strategic Studies at a time when the war of words between the superpowers had escalated to a new and dangerous level. In the previous month, the Soviet Union had shocked the world by resuming its programme of atomic tests, which both countries had suspended in 1958 because of concerns about the dangers of fallout, particularly strontium-90. For most observers, the Soviet resumption of testing meant one thing – that nuclear war had come a big step closer. *Newsweek* voiced the despair felt by many as the Soviets detonated their latest nuclear device:

Suddenly a light brighter than the sun obliterated every shadow, the ground shook, a hot breath blew across the landscape, and the familiar nuclear fireball burst over the Kirghiz Steppe of central Siberia. After two years and 301 days of respite, after 338 tedious meetings in Geneva to keep it bottled up forever, the atomic genie had once more been let loose by the Soviet Union. In one searing moment, the thin hope that the nuclear arms race could somehow be stopped vanished.[30]

Moscow blamed 'the threatening attitude of the United States and its allies in the Berlin dispute'.[31] That year the notorious Berlin Wall had been built, dividing the city like 'a monstrous guillotine'.[32] Privately the Russians were afraid that the Americans were outstripping them in the arms race. There was indeed a missile gap, but it was the Soviet Union, not the United States, that was lagging behind. Thanks to John von Neumann's advice to the government to develop ICBMs, American magazines now regularly carried full-page advertisements from companies boasting of their role in building missiles such as the Titan or the Minuteman. Beneath a full-page picture of a Minuteman missile blasting into the sky, one company proudly claimed: 'Through Thiokol engineered reliability, the nation's power to deter war is moving up while anticipated costs come down.'[33]

In the first week of September 1961, Khrushchev's rugged features confronted readers from the racks of every news-stand. *Time* showed him in tyrant mode, angrily jabbing his finger out of its cover, while behind him billowed a fearsome atomic fireball. On the same news-stands that week, *Life* contained a three-page profile of Leo Szilard under the headline I'M LOOKING FOR A MARKET FOR WISDOM. He had just published a collection of short stories satirizing the inability of politicians to meet the challenge of the atomic age. Szilard was now a familiar figure to the American public. In the article he was pictured lobbying opinion-formers in Washington with his plans for arms control. Unfortunately, there was scant interest in Szilard's brand of moderate wisdom in the corridors of power on either side of the Iron Curtain. The voices of hawks such as Edward Teller and Wernher von Braun, ever keen to promote their latest projects, carried far more weight.

World opinion had been shocked not just by the resumption of atomic tests, but by Khrushchev's claim that warheads ranging from 20 megatons to an enormous 100 megatons would be detonated. Headlines proclaimed the creation of a 'superbomb'. The largest American test had been 15 megatons, back in 1954. The biggest bomb carried by B-52s was 24 megatons. Generally, missiles had smaller warheads than this, and by the late 1950s American scientists had decided that missiles were the weapons of the future.

President Kennedy immediately condemned Khrushchev's 'atomic blackmail', and journalists were briefed that there was no military value in a 100-megaton bomb. *Time* magazine put it bluntly: 'there is no major city in the world that cannot be wiped out with one well-directed 20-megaton bomb'. But *Time* also printed a picture of Major Yuri Gagarin's six-ton space capsule, in which he had become the first to orbit the earth in April of that year. The caption asked, 'would 100 megatons fit inside?' The answer was yes. Moscow announced that the bomb could be delivered onto its enemies by the same mighty rockets that had carried its cosmonauts into space. Once again it seemed that a giant leap forward for science also meant a step backwards for mankind.[34]

On 30 October at 08.30 GMT, scientists in Europe detected what was described as 'the biggest man-made explosion on record'. At Kew Observatory in the south-western suburbs of London, where the Victorians had created a botanical garden to rival Eden, officials said: 'This was the big one all right.' The air pressure wave hit Kew at 11.51 a.m. Instruments continued to register the force of the huge explosion for a quarter of an hour. 'It is the largest such recording I have ever known,' the observatory's spokesman told *The Times*.[35]

On the same day, Khrushchev wrote a chilling letter to the British Labour Party warning that in any future war the United Kingdom 'may be among the first to experience the destructive power of nuclear blows'.[36] The presence of American nuclear-armed bombers and Britain's own H-bombs (supplied to the RAF this year) made this green and pleasant land a certain target for Soviet weapons, including the new 100-megaton bomb.

Newsweek described the superbomb as 'Khrushchev's monster'.[37] On an aerial photo of Manhattan Island, the magazine mapped the extent of its awesome destructive power. The bomb had a yield of at least 50 megatons. It would leave a crater at least a mile wide and would raze to the ground buildings up to ten miles from ground zero. New York with its proud skyscrapers would – as Szilard had feared back in 1931 – be reduced to a radioactive wasteland. Later, Hans Bethe announced that the Russians had modified the bomb for the test; if it was ever used in war it would have exploded with a force of 100 megatons.

The Soviets nicknamed their superweapon the *Tsar Bomba*, 'King of Bombs'. Andrei Sakharov, who designed it under direct orders from Khrushchev, called it simply the Big Bomb. There could be no more dramatic conclusion to the series of twenty-six nuclear tests conducted by the Soviet Union in the autumn of 1961. Kubrick now had no doubts that his next film would be about nuclear war. It was the subject on everyone's lips. Newspapers were full of stories about the threat of nuclear Armageddon: 'Almost everybody in this country, it seems, is thinking or talking about what to do in case war starts and nuclear bombs fall on the US,' reported one.[38] A Manhattan boutique sold out of 'bright, warm, comfortable things' for women to wear in the public fallout shelters that were now marked in American cities by yellow signs. Strongly recommended were 'gay slacks and a dress with a cape that could double as an extra blanket.'[39]

In America, government agencies reported that public enquiries about fallout shelters increased from 3,000 in May to 100,000 by that October. The Nobel prizewinning chemist and former AEC commissioner Willard F. Libby told a reporter, 'You'd better tell your

In 1994 Edward Teller visited Chelyabinsk, home of one of Russia's two nuclear weapons laboratories. He is pictured here next to a model of the Tsar Bomba, *the biggest ever hydrogen bomb, developed by his Soviet counterpart Andrei Sakharov.*

readers to build bomb shelters now.'[40] During the Cuban missile crisis, Szilard was greatly amused when he read that Libby's own shelter had been left unusable by a mere brush fire.

Groucho Marx was one who took Libby's advice seriously and invested in a personal shelter. But few could afford the cost, of at least $1,000. According to the usually bullish *US News and World Report*, despite what scientists such as Libby and Teller were saying about the survivability of nuclear war, most people were pessimistic about their chances. Few thought that shelters were worth the money. Most were of the opinion that it was better to die quickly above ground, than slowly in a shelter.[41]

A British film, *The Day the Earth Caught Fire*, which was made during the Soviet superbomb tests, captured the mood of public anxiety. In the film, two simultaneous American and Soviet nuclear tests ('anything you can split, I can split better', quips one character[42]) shift the earth on its axis by 11°, pitching it into an orbit which takes it ever closer to the sun. In an earlier and more optimistic age, Pax, the saviour scientist in *The Man Who Rocked the Earth* by Arthur Train and Robert Williams Wood, had threatened to do this unless war was abolished. In 1956, Adlai Stevenson had challenged Eisenhower to 'state whether he proposed to develop the cobalt bomb or some more terrible weapon that might thrust the earth off its axis'.[43] It was the words of Stevenson, now Ambassador to the United Nations, that had inspired writer-director Val Guest.

Filmed partly in the Fleet Street offices of the London *Daily Express* (the paper's former editor, Arthur Christiansen, plays himself), Val Guest's film captures the edginess of the age with its cliffhanger ending. When the film finishes, two different front pages are made up ready for the presses, headlined WORLD SAVED and WORLD DOOMED. But as anarchy – the dreaded social breakdown – and the sun's atomic furnace threaten the future of humanity, the film leaves its audience uncertain whether the attempt to correct the earth's orbit using further atomic explosions has been successful. As A. H. Weiler wrote in the *New York Times*, 'atomic Pooh-Bahs' could question the science in the film, 'but its pleas make sense in a world awesomely aware of possible destruction'.[44]

Stanley Kubrick read Peter George's thriller in October 1961, as Soviet scientists prepared to test their superbomb. He was impressed, and wrote to the author of *Red Alert* as soon as he returned to New York the following month. Having read the American paperback edition, Kubrick had expected George to be an American. He had hoped to meet George on home ground, but now their meeting would have to wait. Addressing him as 'Mr Bryant', even though he knew full well it was a pen name, Kubrick said that he had enjoyed his novel 'immensely'. He told the ex-RAF officer, 'I found your book to be the only nuclear fiction I'd come across that smacked of knowledge.'[45]

Kubrick and George had one thing in common – an obsession with nuclear war. Kubrick reeled off a list of books he'd been reading, including heavyweight studies by war strategists Bernard Brodie, Henry Kissinger and Herman Kahn. He also took out subscriptions to specialist journals such as *War/Peace Report* and *Missiles and Rockets*. Interviewed in *Glamour* magazine, the film's designer Ken Adam said: 'Stanley's so steeped in his material that when we first met to discuss it, his conversation was full of fail-safe points, megadeaths, gyro-headings, strobe markings, and CRM-114s. I didn't know what he was talking about.'[46] Kubrick had been bowled over by Adam's design of Dr No's control room and nuclear reactor in the Bond film and was keen to work with him.

Kubrick couldn't have chosen a better cinematographic designer. From the interior of the B-52 to the War Room, the information needed to create the sets for *Dr Strangelove* was classified top secret. Ken's final designs were based on gleanings from military journals pieced together using informed guesswork. The accuracy of his designs made some military specialists extremely uncomfortable. The dramatic set for the War Room in the White House, with its huge round table – all 380 square feet of it – became an unforgettable symbol of cold-war power politics. When Ronald Reagan took office in 1981 and was given a tour of the White House, the first thing he asked to see was the War Room. Unfortunately, it only existed in the imaginations of Ken Adam and Stanley Kubrick.

In November 1961, the month that Kubrick and George first made contact and started discussing the script of *Dr Strangelove*, Leo Szilard began an American lecture tour entitled 'Are we on the road to war?'. He left his listeners in no doubt about the answer to that question: 'Our chances of getting through the next ten years without war are slim,' he told them.[47] The future looked so bleak that Szilard's friend, James R. Newman – described by *Newsweek* as the 'brilliant 54-year-old mathematician, lawyer, and editor of the *World of Mathematics*' – suggested that all American children should be shipped off to the southern hemisphere to protect them from the coming war. His 'bitter, ironic expression of protest and horror' to the *Washington Post* created quite a stir in the capital.[48]

In the same month, an article on nuclear weapons appeared in one of the specialist journals Stanley Kubrick now subscribed to, the

Bulletin of the Atomic Scientists. The author, W. H. Clark, raised timely fears about nuclear proliferation in countries just joining the nuclear club, such as China. Large, 'dirty' nuclear bombs were much cheaper, easier to build and would kill more people, said Clark, than guided missiles with low-yield warheads. Monster bombs which maximized fallout – the kind Edward Teller had been designing in 1950 – might be used to blackmail the superpowers. It was a far-sighted warning. Four years later, North Korea set up a nuclear research reactor to produce fissile material for nuclear weapons.

Doomsday devices, especially Leo Szilard's 'famous cobalt bomb', were top of Clark's list of future threats. Such devices were now easily within the reach of 'amateurs'. According to Clark, 'any nuclear power can easily destroy the US' using fallout from a cobalt bomb – although, he added, 'the extermination of the human race is a much more difficult task'. For anyone planning doomsday, at least fifty huge bombs (or 'mines') would be needed – the same number as the Russian ambassador DeSadeski quotes in *Dr Strangelove*.[49]

The *Bulletin*'s respected editor, Eugene Rabinowitch, added a timely and chilling note to the article. The 'first steps toward the Doomsday machine', he wrote, 'are the 50 and 100 megaton bombs that premier Khrushchev has described'.[50] To many it seemed that the Soviet Union's latest thermonuclear test showed that they were on their way to building just such a machine.

Also included in the article was an entry from the RAND Corporation's *Glossary of Terms on National Security*, which defined a doomsday machine as 'a reliable and securely protected device that is capable of destroying almost all human life and that would be automatically triggered if an enemy committed any one of a designated class of violations'.[51] For Stanley Kubrick, back in New York with *Red Alert* fresh in his mind, it was clear that the time was ripe for a film about the doomsday machine. It was just a matter of time before fiction became reality, and someone constructed the ultimate weapon.

According to the Russians, the RAND Corporation was 'an American Academy of Death and Destruction'.[52] RAND was the world's first think tank, or as it was known then, a 'think factory'. Its name came from Research *and* Development. For writer and physicist Jeremy

Bernstein (a friend of Kubrick's), it was 'like a malignant university'.[53] Set up after the war by the US Air Force and initially placed under the control of General Curtis LeMay, RAND prided itself on applying science to the art of warfare.

The scientists and engineers at RAND had played a leading role in the development of the US missile force. Its analysts had also come up with the idea of the failsafe procedure in which bombers are kept airborne but proceed to their target only when ordered to do so. (In *Dr Strangelove*, the CRM-114 device is part of this secret procedure. Ken Adam designed it from articles he had read in the military journal *Jane's*.) RAND also devised the nationwide system of detectors that flash warnings of nuclear explosions on American soil to the Pentagon's War Room. By 1963, full-page civil defence advertisements in British newspapers boasted that no citizen was ever more than five to ten miles from a bunker that was constantly monitoring for nuclear explosions.

It was a strategic analyst at RAND, Bernard Brodie, who defined the cold-war theory of deterrence. According to the Prussian war theorist Carl von Clausewitz, war was nothing more than the continuation of politics by other means. But after Hiroshima and Nagasaki, Brodie could see that the costs of nuclear war for both sides would cancel out any political gains. Faced with the appalling aftermath of a war fought with nuclear weapons, it was obvious that there could be no winners. Writers such as H. G. Wells had fully realized, even before World War I, that this would be the effect of creating the atomic bomb, and now so did the organization that advised the US armed forces. 'Thus far the chief purpose of our military establishment has been to win wars,' wrote Brodie in 1946. 'From now on its chief purpose must be to prevent them. It can have almost no other useful purpose.'[54] The idea of deterrence through strength governed nuclear thinking up to the mid-1950s, when it began to be challenged by civilian theorists such as Henry Kissinger and Herman Kahn.

The physicist Herman Kahn had a Falstaffian girth and a vitality to match. He had worked with Hans Bethe, John von Neumann and Edward Teller on the H-bomb project in the early 1950s. Like Kubrick, he grew up in the Bronx (although he moved to Los Angeles at the age of 10 with his mother and sister). After studying nuclear physics at UCLA and CalTech, he worked for the RAND Corporation at Santa Monica, in southern California, from 1948.

Although Kahn started out by using the new computers to solve the complex mathematics of nuclear reactions in H-bombs, he soon established himself as the most influential figure in military strategy and nuclear planning since World War II. His self-declared mission in life was to make people think the unthinkable. 'In our times,' he wrote, 'thermonuclear war may seem unthinkable, immoral, insane, hideous, or highly unlikely, but it is not impossible. To act intelligently, we must learn as much as we can.'[55] Kahn argued that, instead of hoping that nuclear war would never happen, the government and military should regard nuclear war not just as survivable, but as winnable. To this end he campaigned for an extensive programme of shelter building. He also encouraged military chiefs to think of war in terms of 'rungs of escalation', or stages of conflict, rather than just all-out war. In a lecture delivered to senior Strategic Air Command officers, Kahn derided their outdated strategies for total war, telling them, 'Gentlemen, you don't have a war plan, you have a war orgasm.'[56]

By the early 1960s, Herman Kahn was fast becoming the favourite 'prophet of the hard-hats'.[57] Later he also became an influential futurologist, with the vision – if not the politics – of H. G. Wells. According to Thomas Bell, who was President of the Hudson Institute (which Kahn co-founded in 1961), he had given briefings to every president from Harry S Truman onwards.[58] Speaking in May 2003, Secretary of Defense Donald Rumsfeld had glowing words for his friend, who died in July 1981: 'I did value my relationship with Herman, a remarkable man with brilliant ideas on so many subjects – war, peace, trade, energy, transportation and, of course, the future.'[59]

Kubrick read Kahn's controversial study, *On Thermonuclear War* (1960). It contains such intentionally provocative statements as: 'War is a terrible thing, but so is peace. The difference seems in some respects to be a quantitative one of degree and standards.'[60] For many people, including Szilard's friend James Newman, Kahn's 668-page book deserved to be called 'evil' as it seemed to be trying to persuade military leaders that they could fight a nuclear war and win. Writing in *Scientific American*, Newman memorably described Kahn's book as 'a moral tract on mass murder: how to plan it, how to commit it, how to get away with it, how to justify it'.[61]

Kubrick met the 39-year-old Kahn several times as the script for *Dr Strangelove* gradually took shape during 1962. Herman Kahn was a larger than life figure. With a cigar in his hand and a wisecrack never far from his lips, the rotund physicist could pass for the owner of a New York deli. A natural-born iconoclast with an IQ as impressive as his substantial girth, Kahn was allergic to fashionable thinking and liked nothing better than to attack the liberal consensus.

Kahn was familiar with Peter George's *Red Alert* before he met Kubrick. He had referred to it in *On Thermonuclear War* and praised 'the clever way the general negates the elaborate system set up to prevent unauthorized behavior'.[62] He had also used the novel at RAND in training courses for military commanders. In these courses, fictional scenarios (a word RAND reinvented for the cold war) were used in nuclear war games. As a *New York Times* reporter put it, novels like *Red Alert* helped 'stimulate reason and imagination to cope with history before it happens'.[63] At least, that was the theory. Clearly, fiction had lessons to teach the military, as well as the scientists.

Analysts like Kahn wanted to be 'future historians', a category of creative thinker identical to that which H. G. Wells had created for himself at the start of the century.[64] Since RAND was formed, American governments have paid millions of dollars to be advised by Kahn and his successors on the shape of things to come. Kubrick also had strong views about what the future had in store for us. *Dr Strangelove* – which won the Hugo Award for best science fiction film of the year – would be the first of a series of future visions, such as *2001: A Space Odyssey* and *A Clockwork Orange*. But unlike Kahn, Stanley Kubrick showed people a future which their leaders said couldn't happen: a bleak land where science, rather than ushering in utopia, creates machines that turn on their masters.

Herman Kahn had also been intrigued by Szilard's idea of a doomsday bomb, as described in *Red Alert*. He included it in *On Thermonuclear War*, and the idea attracted much media interest. In an article for a popular magazine in 1961, he described the 'doomsday machine' as 'without question the most menacing and the most characteristic of the era'. He told the magazine:

I can build a device – I think I know how to do it today, I doubt that it would take me 10 years to do and I doubt that it would cost me 10 billion dollars – and this is a device which I could bury, say, 2,000 feet underground and, if detonated, it would destroy everybody in the world – at least all unprotected life. It can be done, I believe. In fact, I know it can be done.[65]

On Thermonuclear War explains how such a device would be

connected to a computer which is in turn connected, by a reliable communication system, to hundreds of sensory devices all over the United States. The computer would then be programmed so that if, say, five nuclear bombs exploded over the United States, the device would be triggered and the earth destroyed.[66]

In this vision of a complex computer network which has the power of life and death over its human makers, it is easy to see the prototype of Hal, the computer in Kubrick and Arthur C. Clarke's film *2001*. Kubrick had a profound distrust of machines, eventually shunning planes and becoming reluctant to travel by car (drivers were told to restrict their speed to below 35 mph). According to one of his biographers, 'his films, always preoccupied with systems that fail and plans that don't succeed, increasingly dealt with the same problems but on a global or cosmic scale, as if even the universal order could no longer be relied on'.[67]

Kahn describes the doomsday machine as the ultimate deterrent – invulnerable, automatic and frighteningly persuasive: 'Even an idiot should be able to understand their capabilities.' He makes it clear that he thinks it unlikely that either Russia or America intend to construct such a machine in the near future. But he does raise the possibility that less 'cautious' nations, which are becoming technologically advanced and 'yet desperate or ambitious enough to gamble all' might create the ultimate destructive device. He notes that Hitler 'probably would have been delighted to procure a Doomsday Machine'.[68]

Although the US military rejected the doomsday machine ('it just does not look professional'), Kubrick would no doubt have been struck by Kahn's claim that 'more than a few scientists and engineers do seem attracted to the idea'. In his conclusion, Kahn states that 'a central problem of arms control – perhaps *the* central problem – is to delay the day when Doomsday Machines or near equivalents become practical'.[69]

Herman Kahn's influence on *Dr Strangelove* is clear. The phrase 'doomsday machine', which is used in the film, is from Kahn. In *Red Alert*, Peter George had talked of 'world-killing devices', and the Soviet cobalt bombs are not triggered automatically, but set off by the country's leader.[70] It is also significant that in the film, Dr Strangelove has commissioned a feasibility study of the doomsday machine from the 'Bland Corporation', a transparent allusion to Kahn's former employer.

Some have seen Kahn's irreverent wit and iconoclastic style as the source of the film's unique doomsday humour, prompting one reviewer to describe it as 'the most shattering sick joke I've ever come across'.[71] But of course, Kubrick had already explored this darkly comic approach in *Lolita*. More importantly, Herman Kahn – the man who thought the unthinkable and rationalized the risks of nuclear war – has been identified as one of the models for the film's most memorable character, Dr Strangelove.

20

Strangeloves

Gentlemen, you can't fight in here. This is the War Room!
Dr Strangelove (1964)

On 2 December 1962, the University of Chicago celebrated the twentieth anniversary of the first controlled release of atomic energy. By now, the imposing Gothic battlements of Stagg Field stadium had been pulled down. In its place, a bronze plaque marked the spot where Chicago Pile Number One had been built. Enrico Fermi, the 'Italian navigator' who had led the journey into the nuclear future, had died in 1955, but his name lived on. Across the street now stood the Enrico Fermi Institute for Nuclear Studies, and the following day President Kennedy would present the Enrico Fermi Award to Edward Teller. Apart from four physicists who had died since 1942 and Albert Wattenberg, who led a simultaneous event at Rome University, nearly all the original scientists attended the anniversary at Chicago. Leo Szilard was notable for his absence.

Later that month, a somewhat sheepish Szilard flew back from Geneva. On arrival, he faced criticism from some of his closest colleagues for his flight from America. Many people had placed their trust in Szilard in the search for peace, and now they felt that he had deserted them in their hour of need. Szilard didn't see it that way at all. For him it had been the only rational plan of action. 'If I were to stay in Washington until the bombs begin to fall and were to perish in the disorders that would ensue,' he said, 'I would consider myself on my deathbed, not a hero but a fool.'[1]

The Chicago-based *Bulletin of the Atomic Scientists* marked the 'birth of the atomic age' with a special issue to which even the President contributed.[2] It began with Harrison Brown's dramatic editorial, penned in the middle of the Cuban Missile Crisis as the Doomsday Clock was about to strike midnight. The *Bulletin*'s editor, Eugene Rabinowitch, looking back at those tense days in October, said 'in 1962, mankind came as close as never before to the abyss of nuclear war'.[3]

But other contributors to the *Bulletin*, among them the discoverer of plutonium and now AEC Chairman, Glenn Seaborg, remained doggedly upbeat about the achievements of the atomic age. Thanks to the Chicago experiment, wrote Seaborg, 'we have witnessed . . . the real beginning of a society based on science'.[4] In an interview with William Laurence, he even predicted that within twenty years nuclear rockets would be taking astronauts to Venus and Mars, and the energy of the atom would allow the earth's polar regions to be colonized.[5] Seaborg preferred to direct the public's gaze towards a rosy future rather than linger over the mistakes of the past. Eugene Wigner, with whom Szilard had shared the $75,000 Atoms for Peace Award in 1959 for their contribution to the development of atomic reactors, was less sanguine.

Writing in the *New York Times*, Wigner admitted that the scientists' biggest 'failure of insight' was not in physics but in understanding politics and human nature. Like fictional saviour scientists, they had naively expected 'atomic weaponry to do away with international conflict'. Wigner and his fellow scientists were naturally 'eager to enshrine reason', but they made the mistake of assuming that nations would behave rationally if 'the survival of humanity' was at stake. Many scientists were convinced that the terrible reality of atomic superweapons would force nations to resolve their disputes and work for world peace. As Wigner put it, 'any other outcome seemed utterly irrational.' Today, such faith in humanity's rationality seems naive. An older and wiser Wigner acknowledged that 'the role of reason is real enough, but it does not determine our goals; it merely teaches us how to attain these, and at what cost'.[6]

It was a hard lesson to learn, especially for Wigner and others who had such high hopes for atomic energy. By contrast, Szilard remained an optimist, convinced that the same rational mind that had split the atom would also solve all problems of the human spirit and bring about a utopia of peace and plenty. His old friend Albert Einstein had smiled ruefully at such wishful thinking and gently criticized him for over-estimating the role of rationality in human life. In Leo Szilard, the spirit of the saviour scientist lived on. But its days were numbered.

In a personal message to readers of the *Bulletin* that December, President Kennedy said that the power of the atom, first unleashed in that cold, grey squash court, 'has come to connote not only the unprecedented application of science to man's use; but also the problem mankind faces in whether these uses contribute to welfare or to conflict'. A new scientific era had begun, but the old problem of the proper uses of knowledge had returned to haunt humankind.[7]

As Leo Szilard stepped off the plane and set foot in a country he had thought would by now be a radioactive wasteland, Stanley Kubrick was announcing the title of his next film to the press: *Dr Strangelove or: How I Learned to Stop Worrying and Love the Bomb*. In the same interview, Kubrick also disclosed that the film would star Peter Sellers and that it would be a satire about a 'nuclear Wise Man', co-written by Peter George.[8] Later, Kubrick would bring in Terry Southern to work on the film. Southern, author of the erotic satire *Candy*, brought his uniquely anarchic and subversive humour to the storyline. One version even had the movie climaxing in a riotous custard pie fight in the War Room. The scene was filmed using crates of custard pies ordered from Fortnum & Mason – suppliers to the upper crust of English society – but was wisely cut from the final version.[9]

Initially, Kubrick had been 'fascinated' by *Red Alert* as a 'serious suspense novel about what happens when one of the great powers pushes the wrong button'.[10] But the more he worked on the script, the more he was 'intrigued by the comic aspects – the facade of conventional reality being pierced.' Peter George recalled that they were in a taxi one day, en route to the Bronx, when Kubrick 'suddenly slapped my leg and said, "You're going to hate me for this, but can't you see this thing as a comedy?"'[11]

Although the plot and the characters in *Dr Strangelove* are the same as in Peter George's novel, one character is entirely original to the film – Strangelove himself. The sinister scientist transformed what was a convincing and chilling thriller into a work of symbolic power. Brilliantly portrayed by Peter Sellers, who had played Dr Zempf and Clare Quilty in *Lolita*, Dr Strangelove is an ex-Nazi scientist who has become the director of US weapons research and development. Thanks to the power of this character, Kubrick's film coined a new adjective: Strangelovean, describing a person who has a potentially fatal fascination with the idea of nuclear war. Dr Strangelove came to embody the anxieties of a generation about scientists creating ever more lethal technologies of mass destruction. If the cobalt bomb symbolized the doomsday generation's fears of man-made apocalypse, Dr Strangelove personified the Doomsday Man himself.

Dr Strangelove is a surprisingly complex figure, and the evolution of his character is a fascinating story in itself. He made his first appearance in a draft of the script dated August 1962, called simply at that time 'von Klutz'. From the start he was essentially a comic character. The Bond film *Dr No* was released in autumn 1962, at the same time as the Cuban Missile Crisis. Dr No is a nuclear physicist in league with the criminal underworld and the subversive spying organization SPECTRE. 'My work has given me a unique knowledge of radioactivity,' says Dr No, showing James Bond his black artificial hands, 'but not without its costs, as you can see.'[12]

Like all subsequent Bond baddies, the half-Chinese, half-German Dr No is obsessed with dreams of world domination. He is a classic mad scientist, whose genealogy can be traced from Drs Moreau and Griffin, to Thorkel in *Dr Cyclops*. The secret nuclear reactor Dr No has constructed on Jamaica is used to power a radio jamming system that threatens both US space rockets and ICBMs. He eventually suffers a horrible death at Bond's hands – drowned in the radioactive pond of his own overheating reactor. James Bond's actions cause the reactor to explode. Today, in the post-Chernobyl era, it seems remarkable that the usually well-informed 007 was unconcerned about the consequences of a reactor meltdown, a disaster which would have spread fallout across the Caribbean and America.

Although Stanley Kubrick never admitted that the Bond villain was a prime source for his character, the similarities are clear. With his German origins and artificial hands, Dr No bears a striking resemblance to Dr Strangelove, who is also German (his name was Merkwürdigliebe, literally 'strange-love') and has a black prosthetic hand. However, Dr Strangelove's hand has a life of its own, constantly struggling to rise up in the Hitler salute when he talks to the President. This black-gloved hand can also be traced back to Fritz Lang's sorcerer-scientist, Rotwang, in *Metropolis* (1926). As a scientific archetype, Dr Strangelove has an impressive pedigree stretching back through twentieth-century cultural history.

As well as *Dr No*, the best-selling nuclear thriller *Fail-Safe* (1962), by two political science professors, Eugene Burdick and Harvey Wheeler, almost certainly provided Kubrick with the first seed of an idea that would eventually grow into Strangelove. *Fail-Safe* was strikingly similar to Peter George's novel, so similar in fact that in February 1963, as *Dr Strangelove* went into production at Shepperton Studios, George sued for plagiarism in New York. Both parties eventually settled out of court, but it was a victory for Kubrick and George. The film rights to *Fail-Safe*, which had sold 280,000 copies in its first year, had been bought for $500,000 (Kubrick's company had paid a paltry $3,500 for *Red Alert*). But the lawyers agreed that the distribution of the film of *Fail-Safe* would be delayed until after *Dr Strangelove* opened.

Like Roshwald's *Level 7*, Burdick and Wheeler's novel was about a nuclear war started by a technical fault. A malfunction occurs in the fail-safe system that allowed bombers to be scrambled on warning and then to receive a coded signal while in the air, telling them whether to proceed or return. As in *Dr Strangelove*, there are frantic hotline discussions between the Kremlin and the White House, as B-52 bombers head towards the Soviet Union after the signal to attack is given by mistake. When Moscow is destroyed, the President agrees to bomb New York to avert a global thermonuclear holocaust. Although originally included in *Dr Strangelove*, this like-for-like destruction of cities was eventually dropped from Kubrick's film.

There were many similarities between the two novels, but whatever the rights and wrongs of the plagiarism case, it was Kubrick's film that gained most from the other storyline. In *Fail-Safe* a mathematician called Professor Walter Groteschele (Walter Matthau in the 1964 film) advises the chiefs of staff on nuclear strategy. George's *Red Alert* featured no mad scientist character. But in Kubrick's film, Dr

Strangelove – a key government adviser, like Groteschele – becomes the most memorable figure. This, coupled with Kubrick's decision to address the subject through black comedy, paid off both critically and at the box office. Although it was successful as a thriller, *Fail-Safe* made little lasting impression on the culture of the cold war. Today it is not Professor Groteschele, but Dr Strangelove who is remembered.

Dr Strangelove plays no part in Kubrick's film until near the end. Peter George's novelization of the film introduces the character earlier on and is more revealing about his origins. In the first reference to Dr Strangelove, he is shown to be unmistakably modelled on the German rocket pioneer Wernher von Braun, now working for the American military:

Though he was known personally to few people in this room, he had long exerted an influence on United States defense policy. He was a recluse and perhaps had been made so by the effects of the British bombing of Peenemünde, where he was working on the German V-2 rocket. His black-gloved right hand was a memento of this. He was not sure whether he disliked the British more than the Russians.[13]

A few pages later we are introduced to another important dimension of Dr Strangelove's character: his role in the preparation for nuclear war. 'He was of course familiar with the jargon of the nuclear strategists,' says the narrator. 'Indeed, he himself had created a great deal of it.' Many of Dr Strangelove's later words on the doomsday machine, as well as his final master plan 'to preserve a nucleus of human specimens' in mineshafts, are virtually identical to passages in Herman Kahn's *On Thermonuclear War*.[14] In a discussion of civil defence, Kahn had recommended spending $5 billion fitting out mines to provide people with fallout shelters.

Herman Kahn was not German, however, and although he may have been a neoconservative, he was certainly no ex-Nazi. Neither Kahn nor von Braun is an exact match for the elusive Dr Strangelove, any more than Professor Groteschele or Dr No is. Other possible candidates for the real-life Dr Strangelove are Edward Teller, John von Neumann and even Henry Kissinger, then a Harvard academic who wrote on nuclear strategy. Kubrick himself told Alexander Walker he thought 'Strangelove's accent was probably inspired by the physicist Edward Teller', although he admitted that Sellers didn't sound much like the Hungarian father of the H-bomb.[15]

Dr Strangelove's wheelchair has been seen as an allusion to computer pioneer John von Neumann. As we have seen, the hawkish mathematician was a frequent visitor to the White House in his wheelchair before his death in 1957. Like the other Strangeloves, von Neumann was fiercely patriotic and jingoistic in his advice to President Eisenhower. But it is also possible that the wheelchair was introduced

Wernher von Braun, pictured in about 1947. The 1960 American biopic about him, I Aim at the Stars, *contained no reference to concentration camps or the destruction caused by the V-2. The film was not popular in Britain. One review was titled 'I Aim at the Stars, But Sometimes I Hit London.'*

for more mundane reasons. In *Dr Strangelove*, Peter Sellers upstaged his own performance in *Lolita* by playing three characters – President Merkin Muffley, Group Captain Lionel Mandrake, DSO, DFC, RAF, and Dr Strangelove himself. He had originally intended to play a fourth character, Major Kong, but surrendered the role when he injured his ankle clambering through the B-52's fuselage.

Dr Strangelove is so memorable a character because Sellers succeeds wonderfully in fusing together the traits of the real-life, and indeed fictional, figures on which he is based. Through the alchemy of film-making, Kubrick and Sellers created cinematic gold in the figure of Dr Strangelove. Teller, von Braun and von Neumann were all key players in the sciences of destruction. The references to Peenemünde and the concentration camps in the film's novelization make it abundantly clear that Wernher von Braun was Peter George's main model for Dr Strangelove. However, his words are those of the man who had worked with and admired both Teller and von Neumann: Herman Kahn, the personification of the military intellectual – detached and coldly rational. Like the four riders of the apocalypse, these figures come together in the unforgettable character of Dr Strangelove, the ultimate Doomsday Man.

For Lewis Mumford, responding to the *New York Times*' panning of the film, Kubrick's masterstroke was to make Dr Strangelove 'the central symbol of this scientifically organized nightmare of mass extermination'. For Mumford, the tragedy of the age they were living in was eloquently expressed by the manic figure of this fanatical rationalist: 'This nightmare eventuality that we have concocted for our children is nothing but a crazy fantasy, by nature as horribly crippled and dehumanized as Dr Strangelove himself.' He concluded by hailing Kubrick's film as 'the first break in the catatonic cold-war trance that has so long held our country in its rigid grip'.[16]

Mumford was right to describe Kubrick's film as a crucial moment in the culture of the cold war. For people all over the world, Dr Strangelove soon came to personify the sinister alliance of science and power politics that made it possible to annihilate millions at the touch of a button. Dr Strangelove's logic could transform acts of inhumanity into practical solutions, his rhetoric clothed barbarity in sweet words of reason, and his think tanks – such as the 'Bland Corporation' –

Peter Sellers taking the title role in Stanley Kubrick's Dr Strangelove or: How I Learned to Stop Worrying and Love the Bomb *(1964).*

used computers to transform lives into numbers. For numbers, as Herman Kahn had said, are something you can think the unthinkable about.

In the 1960s, a new generation began to reject a life reduced to numbers and to look for answers beyond science and rationality. This generation no longer felt comfortable with the easy post-war certainties that their parents had accepted without question. For those who grew up in an age haunted by the Strangelovean cobalt bomb, the old ways of looking at the world seemed to lead to a dead end – to doomsday.

The press screening of *Dr Strangelove* was due to take place on 22 November 1963, a day forever etched into the American psyche. When news broke of President Kennedy's assassination in Dallas, the screening was cancelled and the release of the movie, scheduled for the end of 1963, delayed. In Peter George's novelization of the script, which had already been published, General Ripper's recall code for the B-52s is 'JFK'. In the final cut of the film this became POE, for 'Peace on Earth', or alternatively Ripper's more paranoid 'Purity of Essence'.

Although it was panned as a 'shattering sick joke' by the *New York Times*' reviewer when it was finally released in January 1964, Kubrick and George's film was well received.[17] *Sight and Sound* said that it demonstrated how 'power politics have become a Frankenstein monster which one little error can send out of control'. Their critic praised it as 'the most hilariously funny and the most nightmarish film of the year'.[18] For the *New Statesman* it was a 'mesmeric' film that set out 'to create its own category or genre'.[19] Despite Peregrine Worsthorne in the *Sunday Telegraph* likening Kubrick's portrayal of Americans to Soviet propaganda, the film was hugely popular with moviegoers who 'ringed the block' at the Columbia cinema in London.[20] The cinema even had to put on special late screenings at 11 p.m. each night. Ticket sales were 25 per cent higher than for any other film the Columbia had shown, and *The Times* reported that 'all house records have been broken'.[21]

Stanley Kubrick took a keen interest in how his film was marketed. Columbia's publicists focused on a topical aspect to sell the film. It was advertised as 'the wild hot-line suspense comedy', and each character was pictured speaking on the telephone. Both in the book and the film, the hotline between the Kremlin and the White House is a crucial narrative device, connecting the two leaders as they try to pull back from nuclear apocalypse. Originally, the film had been planned as a real-time thriller, reflecting the 'two hours to doom' of George's novel, a device exploited most recently in 24, the cult TV series about terrorists armed with weapons of mass destruction.

Peter George's description of the hotline and its role in averting disaster (in his 1958 novel, at least) made an important contribution to superpower relations. After reading *Red Alert*, Harvard academic Thomas Schelling suggested the idea of a hotline to the Eisenhower administration. Leo Szilard also discussed it with Khrushchev in a personal meeting in New York in 1960. The response was positive. In fact, Khrushchev was so impressed by his meeting with Szilard (who had left his hospital bed, where he was recovering from cancer, to meet the Russian leader) that he sent the scientist a hamper of Russian delicacies, including caviar and smoked fish.

If the idea of the hotline had been accepted in time by both sides, the Cuban Missile Crisis might have been defused far sooner. As it was, the first hotline was not introduced until a year later, on 31 August 1963. But even then it was not the telephone link depicted in book and film, but a pair of teletype machines. Although these were introduced to clear up misunderstandings, communication difficulties still dogged superpower relations. Replying to Washington's first message, Moscow asked, 'Please explain what is meant by a quick brown fox jumping over a lazy dog?'[22]

After the release of *Dr Strangelove*, Peter George continued to be preoccupied by the horrifying prospect of nuclear conflict. It was a fascination that would prove fatal. The aftermath of a devastating war formed the subject of his next two books. The first, *Commander One*, he dedicated to Kubrick, but the second, *Nuclear Survivors*, was never completed. The 41-year-old writer was found dead from a self-inflicted shotgun wound at his home in St Leonards, near Hastings, Sussex, on 1 June 1966.

His friend, the science fiction writer Brian Aldiss, has told how George suffered 'fear and pain about the threat of nuclear war'. He was also an alcoholic. According to Aldiss, he 'would start with a sip of whisky and wake up a fortnight later in a Glaswegian gutter, poor guy'. After *Dr Strangelove* appeared, George began to feel uncomfortable with Kubrick's transformation of his realistic thriller into a black comedy. Aldiss agrees that he was 'sorry' about the way the film turned out.[23] George even wrote to Thomas Schelling, who had been an advisor on the screenplay, apologizing for its tone.[24] Ironically, it is Kubrick's film rather than George's novel that has stood the test of time. Only George's novelization of the script is available today in bookshops. Sadly, his other books have long since gone out of print, including *Red Alert*.

In the month that *Dr Strangelove* was released, Leo Szilard and his wife Trude moved to the town of La Jolla, on the sunny Californian coast. For the last three years since his recovery from cancer, he had been a one-man peace movement in Washington, looking in vain for a market for his unique brand of wisdom. Now he told a friend that he wanted to move to La Jolla because it offered 'a foretaste of paradise'.[25]

At the age of 66, Szilard had accepted his first research position in over a decade. The discoverer of the polio vaccine, Jonas Salk, had offered him a fellowship at his new Institute for Biological Studies in the West Coast town. The Institute was itself a product of Szilard's extraordinarily fertile mind. He had first suggested the idea in 1957, as a place where the biological and social sciences could come together under the same roof. The area he intended to work on was typically at the cutting-edge of science: the chemical and biological basis of memory.

In the spring of 1964, he could not have missed the advertisements for Kubrick's film in almost every newspaper and magazine. Prominent in these advertisements was the question, 'What did President Muffley do about the Doomsday Machine?' As usual, scarcely a month passed without these same journals mentioning one of Szilard's proposals for peace. In February, *Holiday* magazine published a profile of Szilard in which historian Alice K. Smith was quoted as saying that alongside Lincoln, Gandhi, Churchill and Hitler, Szilard was one of the five men who had done most to 'change our times'. Discussing his return to scientific research, Szilard explained why he had switched fields: 'The mysteries of biology are no less deep than the mysteries of physics were one or two generations ago, and the tools are available to solve them provided only that we believe they can be solved.'[26]

Szilard also noted that 'the creative scientist has much in common with the artist and the poet'. As well as 'logical thinking and an analytical ability', the 'subconscious' plays a vital role in truly creative science.[27] A review of his 1961 collection of stories, *The Voice of the Dolphins*, had described Szilard as a 'scientist who also happens to be an artist'. These political satires, which provide an extraordinary insight into the cold war as well as keeping alive the voice of one of its unsung heroes, are most notable for what the reviewer called a 'quality that is half farce and half nightmare'.[28] As Stanley Kubrick later realized, a dark sense of humour was essential for those who had to live with the Bomb.

Unfortunately, Leo Szilard's Indian summer of scientific research was all too brief. He died in his sleep of a heart attack at his La Jolla apartment on 30 May 1964. Never again would his fellow scientists be astonished or infuriated by his unconventional insights. The obituary writers made much of his role in the opening of the atomic Pandora's box which had created the precarious balance of terror in the cold war. But the papers were most impressed by his tireless dedication during the past twenty years 'to the task of closing that box, of seeing to it that no human community ever again suffers the fate that destroyed Hiroshima and Nagasaki'.[29]

If Szilard had been a character in one of his own stories or in a Wellsian scientific romance, science would have allowed him to cheat death, perhaps living on, like Wells's 'sleeper', until progress had caught up with the frailties of the body and allowed him to be cured. If this had happened he would have been pleased to read the *New York Times* the day after he died. The newspaper's editorial stated that Leo Szilard would be most remembered for 'the example he personally set of the responsible scientist deeply concerned that the fruits of research be used to benefit, not harm, mankind'.[30]

Writing about his friend later that year, Edward Teller compared Szilard to a famous sixteenth-century alchemist: 'I cannot but think of that legendary, restless figure, Dr Faust, who in Goethe's tragedy dies at the very moment when at last he declares he is content.'[31] For both the designer of the H-bomb and the man who contributed so much to the development of the atomic bomb, Faust's pact with the devil remains a powerful symbol of the temptations of absolute knowledge and power. For Leo Szilard, who had been impressed at an early age by a Hungarian poem inspired by Goethe's *Faust*, it was an appropriate comparison; although, unlike Faust – and, one might argue, Teller – Szilard never lost sight of the true humanistic purpose of science which was, as he put it, to save the world.

In the year that Leo Szilard died and the doomsday machine hit the big screen in *Dr Strangelove*, the war of words between the superpowers continued unabated. In March 1964 the United States conducted an investigation into shipments of cobalt from Morocco to China as fears were raised about the construction of a cobalt bomb by the nascent nuclear power in the Far East. Later, the US Government itself had to deny that it used cobalt in nuclear weapons, after it was reported that General MacArthur had wanted to seal the border between Korea and China with a radioactive no man's land of cobalt.

Also that year, another American general, the commander of the Air Force, Curtis LeMay, who later threatened to bomb North Vietnam 'back to the Stone Age',[32] called for the United States to develop a 100-megaton bomb like the Soviet one. The suggestion was politely but firmly rejected by government defence advisors. As Einstein had pointed out after Hiroshima and Nagasaki, advances in science and technology were still not being matched by progress in thinking.

Then, in September, a Japanese delegation visiting Moscow brought back an ominous story from behind the Iron Curtain. Khrushchev had spoken of a new and terrible weapon developed by the Soviet Union. He reportedly told them that 'It is a means of the destruction and extermination of humanity – the most powerful and strongest of existing weapons. It is power without limit.'[33]

For two days the world's media speculated feverishly about what the Soviet premier had meant. Was this Leo Szilard's cobalt doomsday bomb, which everyone had feared for so long? Were the fictions of Peter George and Stanley Kubrick finally about to become reality? Stung by accusations that he was threatening the world, Khrushchev eventually tried to clarify his comment. 'I said the scientists showed me a terrible weapon,' explained the Soviet leader, testily. 'It is not nuclear . . . All I said was that I saw a terrible weapon which shows what mankind can do.'[34]

Precisely what apocalyptic weapon Khrushchev had been shown remains unclear. Perhaps it was a biological weapon that could wipe out whole continents with deadly viruses, the dream of General Ishii. Rumours swept through the Western media, but all that was certain was that another shot had been fired in the continuing cold war.

Twenty years after the release of *Dr Strangelove*, on 13 November 1984, a Soviet missile was launched from Kapustin Yar, east of Stalingrad. About forty minutes later an R-36M intercontinental ballistic missile blasted off from an underground silo in Kazakhstan. Familiar to Western intelligence experts as the SS-18 Satan missile, it was capable of carrying either a single 24-megaton warhead or eight independently targeted 600-kiloton warheads (known as MIRVs, for 'Multiple Independently targetable Re-entry Vehicles').

To the West's spy satellites it was an unexceptional moment in the history of the arms race, and it was soon forgotten. Only after the Berlin Wall had been breached, and the ice of the cold war had begun to thaw, did military analysts realize the significance of these otherwise unexceptional rocket launches. They were the first operational test of what newspapers described as 'Russia's doomsday machine'.[35]

The details of the top-secret Soviet system were first revealed in 1993 by Bruce G. Blair, a former launch control officer for Minuteman ICBMs and now one of America's foremost Russian arms experts. He told how, in the 1970s, the Soviet leadership had been disturbed by the possibility of a sneak attack by American submarine-launched missiles. Fired from the North Atlantic, such missiles could strike the Kremlin in thirteen minutes, wiping out the Soviet leadership.

Thirteen minutes gave the Soviet commanders little time to verify whether reports of missile launches were genuine, increasing the likelihood of an accidental war caused by nervous military chiefs. This dangerous situation was not unlike that faced by President Kennedy when missiles began to be sited on Cuba. To deal with this threat, the Soviet leadership authorized the construction of an automated system, nicknamed by its commanders 'The Dead Hand'. Essentially it was a sophisticated system of sensors, communication networks and command bunkers, reinforced to withstand nuclear strikes. At its heart was a computer. As soon as the Soviet leadership detected possible incoming missiles, it activated the system, known by its code name 'Perimetr'. Part of the secret codes needed to launch a Soviet nuclear strike were released and the computerized process set in motion. Then, like a spider at the centre of its web, the computer would watch and wait.

In the 1960s, Dr Strangelove had described how a fictional Russian doomsday machine might function. In Peter George's book of the film, Dr Strangelove explains that the cobalt bombs were

connected to a gigantic complex of computers. A specific and clearly defined set of circumstances, under which the bombs are to be exploded, is programmed into tape memory banks ... In order for the memory banks to decide when such a triggering circumstance has occurred, they are linked to a vast interlocking network of data-input sensors which are stationed throughout the country and orbited in satellites. These sensors monitor heat, ground shock, sound, atmospheric pressure and radioactivity.[36]

The Perimetr system, developed by the Soviet Union in the 1970s, works in a very similar way. Its sensors monitor whether there have been nuclear detonations across Russian territory. The computer also checks whether communication channels with the Kremlin are cut. If the answer to both questions is yes, then the computer concludes that the country is under attack, and the Soviet nuclear arsenal is activated. All that is then needed is the final human approval from a command post buried deep underground. It would be a brave Soviet officer who, having been cut off from his superiors in the Kremlin, could ignore the advice of such a supposedly foolproof system. Once the duty officer releases the final sequence of the authorization code, the system becomes totally automatic. Bruce Blair describes what would happen next:

In a real nuclear crisis, communications rockets, launched automatically by radio command, would relay fire orders to nuclear combat missiles in Russia, Belarus, Kazakhstan and Ukraine. The doomsday machine provides for a massive salvo of these forces without any participation by local crews. Weapons commanders in the field may be completely bypassed. Even the mobile missiles on trucks would fire automatically, triggered by commands from the communications rockets.[37]

The 1984 test firing was successful. The first missile fired by the Perimetr system broadcast a radio signal that launched the SS-18 independently of its commanders. If it ever had to be used in a real emergency, it would be not just one missile launched by remote control, but thousands. It would be the beginning of the end for life on earth.

The Perimetr system went fully operational in January 1985. It was eight years before anyone in the West knew that the system existed. Kubrick's film described precisely the kind of sneak attack the Kremlin leaders feared most. Dr Strangelove is incredulous that the Russians have activated their doomsday machine without notifying the United States: 'Yes, but the . . . whole point of the doomsday machine . . . is lost . . . if you keep it a secret! Why didn't you tell the world, eh?' Perhaps no one in the Kremlin had seen Stanley Kubrick's film.

Bruce Blair has described Perimetr as 'an amazing feat of creative engineering' and has speculated that President Bush's December 2001 proposal for a new generation of weapons, the robust nuclear earth penetrator, or bunker buster, might be intended to knock out the Russian underground command posts that control the system.[38] After facing fierce opposition, the Bush administration withdrew its request for funding at the end of 2005. However, some military analysts believe that research is continuing into these weapons.

If the Soviet Union were ever attacked, the launch of its estimated 2,000 strategic nuclear warheads, with a total destructive power as much as 50,000 times greater than the bomb that destroyed Hiroshima, would be decided by a computer system designed and built in the late 1970s. The possibility of a malfunction making the system think that it is under attack is truly frightening. Such a malfunction occurred in another Soviet defence system on 26 September 1983, when the Soviet Oko early-warning satellite mistakenly reported that a massive salvo of ICBMs had been fired at the Soviet Union from America. The Russian officer on duty that day decided to ignore the repeated warnings, and disaster was narrowly averted.[39] Although, since the collapse of the Soviet Union, nuclear stockpiles have been reduced, as far as Western analysts are aware, the Perimetr system remains 'combat alert' today.

Despite reductions, there are still some 30,000 nuclear weapons in existence, and ever more nations are keen to join the nuclear club. We now know that a large-scale nuclear exchange, like that envisaged by the designers of the Perimetr system, would result in severe damage to the earth's ecosystem, perhaps causing a life-destroying nuclear winter. Leo Szilard saw that the real challenge for scientists, as for all humankind, was to create a world which has no need for weapons of mass destruction. Until we succeed in this goal, the spectre of a doomsday device will remain with us as a warning of where the dream of the superweapon may lead.

Epilogue

'The Tragedy of Mankind'

Since war begins in the minds of men, it is in the minds of men
that the defences of peace must be constructed.

UNESCO Constitution, 1945

On 9 April 2004, a sunny spring day, I joined others in Trafalgar Square in central London to hear the voices of those opposed to nuclear weapons in the twenty-first century. Fifty miles away, at the Atomic Weapons Research Establishment in Aldermaston, Britain was secretly preparing to design a new generation of nuclear warheads. This year the Aldermaston Peace March had been revived to draw attention to the fact that at the beginning of a new century we were about to repeat the mistakes of the last.

At Easter 1958, before the first peace marchers left Trafalgar Square for their four-day trek to the military laboratory, 10,000 people had thronged the square. The year before, Britain had joined the thermonuclear club by exploding its first H-bomb in the Pacific. Now, forty-six years later, barely a thousand turned up, and only four hundred of those took part in the march. 'It makes me angry to see the number of people who have come to support the march today,' said Damon Albarn, lead singer of Blur. 'It's not even raining.'[1]

Clearly, the world had changed. In 2004 a lone Japanese woman held up a placard in Trafalgar Square, but she was not calling on people to remember the fate of Hiroshima and Nagasaki. Instead she was reminding us of the plight of Japanese hostages being held in Iraq. As I looked around at the people who were applauding well-known speakers such as Susannah York, Corin Redgrave and Tony Benn, I couldn't help noticing that many were grey-haired. The event felt rather like a reunion of old school friends.

437

At the end of the doomsday decade, the threat from nuclear weapons was apparent to everyone. Today that threat seems less urgent to many people. After all, the cold war is over – the Russian bear has padded back to its cave, and Uncle Sam has taken his cruise missiles back home. In the end, H. G. Wells got it wrong. The Last War did not start in 1956. Those apocalyptic stories and films of the 1950s – many inspired by Leo Szilard's vision of a cobalt doomsday bomb – convinced leaders around the world that the price of war was too high. In a sense then, the fear of superweapons did prevent another global war. For forty years, the world teetered on the brink of dooms-day, but then drew back, frightened by what it saw in the abyss below.

The nuclear weapons are still there, of course, in their bomb bays and silos. They could yet start falling, this year or next. For now, at least, there are no global wars, but the sciences of mass destruction continue to spread around the world. As is clear from the last century, knowledge knows no borders. The confrontation between India and Pakistan in 2002 brought the world closer to atomic war than at any time since the Cuban Missile Crisis. In the Middle East, Israel already has nuclear weapons and Iraq began developing them in the 1990s. In Iraq, the United States and Britain have waged war on weapons of mass destruction, a unique and, as it turned out, misguided under-taking. It will probably not be the last war against superweapons. Iran is now taking its first steps on the road to atomic power, despite the fact that it is one of the most oil-rich nations in the world. In the Far East, North Korea claims to be developing nuclear warheads for the missiles it has already built.

Terrorists too are said to be actively seeking weapons of mass destruction. Even before the atomic bomb was dropped on Hiroshima, Szilard had raised the possibility that atomic bombs might one day become so small that they could be smuggled into a city and exploded without warning. Commuters travelling on the Tokyo underground have already fallen victim to the nerve gas sarin, released by a dooms-day cult whose members also tried to develop bioweapons and buy nuclear bombs. Today, no one is safe from the sons and daughters of Fritz Haber, Shiro Ishii and Robert Oppenheimer.

The year before he died, Leo Szilard disagreed that it is 'the tragedy of the scientist' to bring about great advances in our knowledge which are then used for 'purposes of destruction'. This is not the tragedy of the scientist, he said, 'it is the tragedy of mankind'.[2] We cannot blame scientists alone for weapons of mass destruction. As we have seen, the dream of the superweapon is a fantasy which goes to the heart of our culture. In a real sense Szilard was right – we are all doomsday men.

In December 1961, Bertrand Russell's Committee of 100 organized demonstrations across Britain, including one at the USAF Wethersfield airbase in Essex, where they believed H-bombs were stored. There and at other NATO bases, what was called 'mass civil disobedience demonstrations' were planned.[3] The authorities deployed nearly 6,000 military and civilian police at Wethersfield alone to meet the 'threat'. On the day, 300 cold and damp protestors sat in the fog outside the gates of the base for about four hours. 'I wish they would get violent,' muttered a bored and 'hulky' London policeman.[4] There were seventy-three arrests for obstructing the Queen's highway. Among them was Pat Arrowsmith, who in 2004, now aged 75, addressed the Aldermaston marchers assembled in Trafalgar Square.

In 1961, Lord Russell praised the nearly 6,000 non-violent protestors across the country who had stood (or rather sat) 'for the survival of Britain and western Europe and for the prevention of an unparalleled disaster to the whole world'.[5] My father, Bernard Smith, joined the day of action at Wethersfield, four days before his 36th birthday. It was not the first time that he had made a stand for peace. He had been 14 when World War II was declared. The following year he left school with no qualifications. In 1943 he stood up in court before a judge and denounced warfare: 'I believe war to be morally wrong and a crime against humanity. Whatever may be the result of a war, war itself can never be reconciled to any worth-while moral code nor the destruction of human life be justified.'[6]

Bernard was registered as a Conscientious Objector at the age of 18. At the same age, in 1906, his father had joined the Grenadier Guards. Company Sergeant Major Albert Edward Smith went to France in 1915 and served there throughout World War I. He first saw action at Loos, where British forces used the new superweapon, poison gas, for the first time, yet still suffered an appalling toll of 50,000 casualties. Albert was himself wounded in 1917, but returned

Company Sergeant Major Albert Edward Smith, around 1915.

to the front and was mentioned in despatches. He was eventually awarded the Distinguished Conduct Medal.

What Albert Smith saw and experienced in World War I can only be imagined. He never talked about it with his three sons. I can still remember as a boy being shown the Luger pistol he brought back from the trenches as a war trophy. It was the first time I had held a real gun in my hands. It was as heavy as a lump of lead, and an ugly thing by any standards. Perhaps it was the same type of pistol that Clara Haber had used to shoot herself through the heart.

There's a snapshot of my father aged about six with his chest thrust out like a sergeant major, saluting with one hand and holding a Union Jack in the other. That was the nearest he came to following in his own father's footsteps. Albert didn't live to see his son hauled away from the road outside the American airbase by a burly London copper. By then, Bernard had a child of his own, a nine-month-old baby daughter. In one of his first letters to my mother in 1959, before they were married, he had mentioned seeing the film of Nevil Shute's *On the Beach*. He had been struck by the scene near the end of the film, 'with the man and wife huddled in each other's arms'.[7] No family was safe in the nuclear age. In December 1961 the Soviet Union had just resumed its programme of atmospheric nuclear tests, and the dangers of fallout were no doubt in his mind. At the end of October the Soviets had detonated the biggest ever H-bomb.

And so my father sat down in an Essex road on a cold winter's afternoon in 1961. It was a small protest. Did it stop the arms race? Of course it didn't. But to me – now that the cold war has ended and Bernard has himself died of the same cancer that killed John von Neumann – it makes a difference. As the protest of a man whose father experienced the horrors of the war to end wars, it is important. As the protest of a father afraid of invisible fallout polluting the very air that his new-born daughter was breathing, it is important. And as a protest against the infernal ingenuity of doomsday men everywhere, it is important.

That is my history. It's a different kind of history from the story I have told in this book. But it is a reminder that the story of super-weapons is of interest not only to historians. It has touched the lives of everyone during the last century. Your parents and grandparents will have fought in wars, cowered in air-raid shelters clutching their gas masks, and protested against superweapons. Although there turned out to be none in Iraq, the weapons of mass destruction have not gone away. Today, cold-war tensions may have faded from the public mind and the media may be preoccupied with global warming, but the weapons are still out there, and the doomsday men are still at work developing new ones. And as the memories of Ypres, Harbin and Hiroshima fade, the temptation to use those weapons may grow.

Bernard Smith saluting the flag in about 1931.

Notes

Abbreviations

For brevity, the following abbreviations are used in the notes and bibliography:

BAS   *Bulletin of the Atomic Scientists*
CP   Einstein's collected papers (see the Bibliography)
CW   Szilard's collected works (see the Bibliography)
NYT   *New York Times*

Prologue

1. Hans Bethe, Harrison Brown, Frederick Seitz and Leo Szilard, 'The Facts about the Hydrogen Bomb', text of 26 Feb. broadcast on NBC network, *BAS*, 6 (Apr. 1950), 107.

2. Frederick Soddy, *The Interpretation of Radium: Being the Substance of Six Free Popular Experimental Lectures Delivered at the University of Glasgow* (London: John Murray, 1912; 1st edn 1909), 251.

3. Leo Szilard, 'Answers to Questions', dictated, 9 May 1963; in CW2, 229.

4. Edwin M. McMillan to Wilfred Mann, 3 Jan. 1952; quoted in J. L. Heilbron, *Lawrence and his Laboratory: A History of the Lawrence Berkeley Laboratory* (Berkeley: University of California Press, 1989), 199.

5. Eugene Wigner and Andrew Szanton, *The Recollections of Eugene P. Wigner* (New York: Plenum, 1992), 121.

6. Oppenheimer recalling John von Neumann's words in 1954; quoted in Richard Rhodes, *Dark Sun: The Making of the Hydrogen Bomb* (New York: Touchstone, 1996), 389.

7. Press reports; quoted in Peter Goodchild, *Edward Teller: The Real Dr Strangelove* (London: Weidenfeld & Nicolson, 2004), 131.

8. Fritz Leiber, 'Coming Attraction' (1950); in James Gunn, ed., *The Road*

to Science Fiction, vol. 3: *From Heinlein to Here* (New York: Mentor, 1979), 173.

Chapter 1

1. William Lanouette with Bela Silard, *Genius in the Shadows: A Biography of Leo Szilard, The Man Behind the Bomb* (University of Chicago Press, 1994; 1st edn 1992), 243.
2. François Jacob, *The Statue Within* (New York: Basic Books, 1988), 293; quoted in Lanouette, 382.
3. Szilard, taped interview, May 1960; in *CW*2, 54.
4. Enrico Fermi, 'Physics at Columbia University', *Physics Today*, 8 (Nov. 1955), 12–16.
5. 'The First Pile', *BAS*, 18 (Dec. 1962), 23.
6. ibid., 23.
7. Herbert Anderson, 'Assisting Fermi', in Jane Wilson, ed., *All in Our Time: The Reminiscences of Twelve Nuclear Pioneers* (Chicago: Bulletin of the Atomic Scientists, 1975), 95.
8. 'The First Pile', 24.
9. Laura Fermi, *Atoms in the Family: My Life with Enrico Fermi* (University of Chicago Press, 1961; 1st edn 1954), 196.
10. 'The First Pile', 24.
11. Eugene Wigner, 'Twentieth Birthday of the Atomic Age', *NYT* (2 Dec. 1962), VI, 126.
12. 'The First Pile', 24.
13. Leo Szilard, 'What Is Wrong with Us?' (21 Sep. 1942); in *CW*2, 154.
14. Szilard, from an interview with Mike Wallace, WNTA-TV, 27 Feb. 1961; in *CW*2, 146.

Chapter 2

1. William L. Laurence, 'First Atomic Fire Ignited Decade Ago', *NYT* (1 Dec. 1952), 12. See also further coverage of the anniversary in *NYT*: 'Atomic Decennial', 2 Dec., p. 30; 'Uranium Supplies Held Rich as Oil', 3 Dec., p. 36.
2. Laurence, 'First Atomic Fire Ignited Decade Ago', 12.
3. Eugene Wigner, 'Twentieth Birthday of the Atomic Age', *NYT* (2 Dec. 1962), VI, 126.
4. 'White House and Hydrogen Bomb', *New Statesman*, 39 (28 Jan. 1950), 85.
5. James B. Conant's annex to the report of the General Advisory Committee

to the United States Atomic Energy Commission on the hydrogen bomb, 30 Oct. 1949, and further annex by Enrico Fermi and I. Rabi: GAC reports 29–30 Oct. 1949, reprinted in Glenn T. Seaborg, *Journal of Glenn T. Seaborg, 1946–1958*, vol. 3 (Berkeley: Lawrence Berkeley Laboratory, 1990), pp. 317A ff. These statements were secret until 1974: see Freeman Dyson, 'Weapons and Hope: II – Tools', *New Yorker* (13 Feb. 1984), 67.

6. Gregg Herken, *The Winning Weapon: The Atomic Bomb in the Cold War, 1945–1950* (New York: Knopf, 1980), 320.

7. Editorial in Louisville *Courier-Journal*, quoted in 'The Urge to Do Something', *Time* (13 Feb. 1950), 15–16.

8. e.g. 'Longer Legs for a Guardian of the Peace', *Time* (9 Jan. 1950), 1.

9. 'The Loaded Question', *Time* (30 Jan. 1950), 16.

10. Edward Shils, 'Leo Szilard: A Memoir', *Encounter*, 23 (Dec. 1964), 41.

11. *Washington Post*, quoted in 'The Choice', *Time* (16 Jan. 1950), 19–20.

12. Laurie Johnston, 'Einstein Sees Bid to "Annihilation" in Hydrogen Bomb', *NYT* (13 Feb. 1950), 1.

13. Einstein to Schrödinger, 27 Jan. 1947; quoted in P. D. Smith, *Einstein* (London: Haus Publishing, 2003), 125.

14. 'Einstein Sees Bid to "Annihilation" in Hydrogen Bomb', *NYT* (13 Feb. 1950), 1.

15. ibid., *NYT*, 13 Feb. 1950, 3.

16. William Faulkner, Stockholm, 10 Dec. 1950; in William Faulkner, *Essays, Speeches and Public Letters*, ed. James B. Meriwether (New York: Modern Library, 2004), 119.

17. 'A Touch of Sun', *Time* (13 Feb. 1950), 48–9.

18. William L. Laurence, '12 Physicists Ask US Not to Be First to Use Super Bomb', *NYT* (5 Feb. 1950), 1.

19. 'What Goes on Here?', *Time* (6 Feb. 1950), 11.

20. *Aurore*; mentioned in Harold Callender, 'Paris Fears Race for Super-weapon', *NYT* (15 Feb. 1950).

21. 'The Logic of the H-bomb', *New Statesman*, 39 (4 Feb. 1950), 117.

22. John and Roy Boulting, dir., *Seven Days to Noon* (London Films, 1950).

23. New York *Daily News*, cited in 'What Goes on Here?', *Time* (6 Feb. 1950), 11.

24. Hans Bethe, Harrison Brown, Frederick Seitz and Leo Szilard, 'The Facts about the Hydrogen Bomb', text of 26 Feb. broadcast on NBC network, in *BAS*, 6 (Apr. 1950), 106–9, 126–7. All quotations from the programme are taken from this source.

25. Laura Fermi, *Illustrious Immigrants: The Intellectual Migration from Europe, 1930–1941* (Chicago: University of Chicago Press, 1968), 178.

26. Edward Shils, 'Leo Szilard: A Memoir', *Encounter*, 23 (Dec. 1964), 35.

27. 'Suicide of World with Bomb Feared', *NYT* (20 Mar. 1950), 4.

28. William L. Laurence, 'Ending of All Life by Hydrogen Bomb Held a Possibility', *NYT* (27 Feb. 1950), 1, 7.

29. 'Hydrogen Hysteria', *Time* (6 Mar. 1950), 88.

30. 'Cult of Doom', *Time* (13 Mar. 1950), 71; see also reports in *NYT* (7 Mar. 1950), 15; Bethe et al., 'The Facts about the Hydrogen Bomb', 109, 126-7.

31. Harold Callender, 'Paris Fears Race for Super-Weapon', *NYT* (15 Feb. 1950).

32. 'Cost of Suicide', *Newsweek* (30 Oct. 1950), 37.

33. James R. Arnold, 'The Hydrogen-Cobalt Bomb', *BAS*, 6 (Oct. 1950), 290-92.

34. 'Cost of Suicide', 37.

35. Shils, 'Leo Szilard: A Memoir', 41.

36. ibid.

37. ibid., 36, 41.

38. Sylvia Plath, 'Doomsday', *Harper's Magazine*, 208 (May 1954), 29.

39. Leo Szilard, 'Answers to Questions', dictated, 9 May 1963; in CW2, 229.

Chapter 3

1. Quotations from the following newspaper reports: 'Jailed in a Theft of Plutonium, Scientist Says He Took "Souvenir"', *NYT* (23 Aug. 1950), 1, 15; 'Plutonium Theft Easy', *NYT* (24 Aug. 1950), 20; 'Bailed in Atomic Theft', *NYT* (28 Aug. 1950), 17; 'US jails Scientist on Atom "Souvenirs"', *NYT* (23 Nov. 1950), 41; 'Bull by the Tail', *Time* (4 Sep. 1950), 14; 'Plutonium Collector', *Newsweek* (4 Sep. 1950), 20.

2. Glenn Seaborg, in *The Swedish Americans of the Year* (Karlstad: Press Forlag, 1982); from <http://seaborg.nmu.edu/gts/auto.html> (accessed 27 Oct. 2004).

3. Quoted in Lennard Bickel, *The Deadly Element: The Story of Uranium* (London: Macmillan, 1980), 208.

4. Seaborg to Ernest Lawrence, May 1941; quoted in Bickel, 193.

5. Bickel, 264-6; see also <http://members.tripod.com/~Arnold_Dion/Daghlian/bio.html>.

6. Quoted in Bickel, 220.

7. Catherine Caufield, *Multiple Exposures: Chronicles of the Radiation Age* (London: Penguin, 1990), 53.

8. Paul Rincon, 'Plutonium Traced in British Soil', BBC News, 6 Sep. 2004,

<http://news.bbc.co.uk/1/hi/sci/tech/3630284.stm>; see, generally, 'Pluto-nium', Nuclear Issues Briefing Paper 18, June 2002, Uranium Information Centre, <http://www.uic.com.au/nip18.htm>.

9. Bickel, 246.

10. Szilard, *CW1*, 178–89.

11. Szilard, 'Answers to Questions', dictated, 9 May 1963; in *CW2*, 229.

12. Susan Quinn, *Marie Curie: A Life* (London: Heinemann, 1995), 183.

13. Bickel, 34–8.

14. 'The Photography of the Invisible', *Quarterly Review*, 183, no. 366 (Apr. 1896), 499.

15. Thomas Commerford Martin et al., 'Photographing the Unseen', *Century Illustrated*, 52, ns 30 (1896), 124.

16. London *Daily Chronicle* (6 Jan. 1896); quoted in Alan Ralph Bleich, *The Story of X-Rays from Röntgen to Isotopes* (New York: Dover, 1960), 4.

17. 'The Photography of the Invisible', 496.

18. ibid.

19. Richard F. Mould, *A History of X-Rays and Radium with a Chapter on Radiation Units: 1895–1937* (Sutton: IPC Business Press, 1980), 40.

20. Martin et al., 124–5. For examples of contemporary X-ray images, see this article and 'The Photography of the Invisible' (both 1896).

21. 'Professor Röntgen Interviewed', *American Monthly Review of Reviews*, 13 (Jan.–June 1896), 437.

22. Bleich, 6.

23. Caufield, 5.

24. Thomas P. Hughes, *American Genesis: A Century of Invention and Tech-nological Enthusiasm, 1870–1970* (University of Chicago Press, 2004; 1st edn 1989), 27.

25. Mould, 40.

26. ibid., 34.

27. 'The Photography of the Invisible', 501.

28. Herbert C. Fyfe, 'The Röntgen Rays in Warfare', *Strand Magazine* (1899), 778.

29. Thomas Mann, *The Magic Mountain*, trans. H. T. Lowe-Porter (London: Penguin, 1960; 1st edn 1924), 214–16.

30. ibid., 215–19.

31. Mould, 4.

32. Caufield, 8.

33. ibid., 13.

34. Mould, 40; on Dally, see Caufield, 13.

35. C. H. T. Crosthwaite, 'Röntgen's Curse', *Longman's Magazine*, 28 (Sep. 1896), 469–70.
36. Crosthwaite, 470.
37. H. G. Wells, *The Invisible Man* (Glasgow: Fontana, 1978; 1st edn 1897), 143.
38. Crosthwaite, 475.
39. ibid., 476–8.
40. ibid., 479.
41. ibid., 484.

Chapter 4

1. Ernest Merritt, 'The New Element Radium', *Century Illustrated*, 67 (1904), 454–5.
2. Frederick Dolman, 'Science in the New Century: What Will Be Its Greatest Achievements?', *Strand Magazine*, 21 (1901), 55.
3. Mr Herbert Paul in the *Contemporary*; quoted in 'Science and Literature', *The Dial*, 42 (1 May 1907), 274–5.
4. W. J. Wintle, 'Life in Our New Century', *Harmsworth Magazine*, 5, no. 30 (1900/1901), 538.
5. ibid., 537, 534–6.
6. ibid., 537.
7. Dolman, 62.
8. Henry Adams; quoted in Richard Rhodes, ed., *Visions of Technology: A Century of Vital Debate about Machines, Systems and the Human World* (New York: Simon & Schuster, 1999), 37.
9. Edward Bulwer-Lytton, *The Coming Race* (London: George Routledge, 1888; 1st edn 1871), 138, 65, 197.
10. ibid., 65–6, 136.
11. A. Hornblow, 'Did Bulwer-Lytton Foretell the Discovery of Radium?', *Critic*, 44 (Mar. 1904), 214–16.
12. Dolman, 63.
13. Ray Stannard Baker, 'Liquid Air', *Strand*, 17 (1899), 459.
14. Baker, 459–60.
15. Dolman, 61.
16. Umberto Eco, *The Name of the Rose* (London: Picador, 1984), 23.
17. Frederick Soddy, 'Some Recent Advances in Radioactivity', *Contemporary Review*, 83 (May 1903), 719.
18. Lennard Bickel, *The Deadly Element: The Story of Uranium* (London: Macmillan, 1980), 25.

19. ibid., 27.

20. Merritt, 457.

21. ibid., 454–5.

22. ibid., 457.

23. ibid.

24. ibid., 458.

25. ibid.

26. Quoted in Susan Quinn, *Marie Curie: A Life* (London: Heinemann, 1995), 155.

27. ibid.

28. ibid., 172.

29. Merritt, 458.

30. ibid., 453.

31. 'The Revelations of Radium', *Edinburgh Review*, 198 (Oct. 1903), 387.

32. Thomson, quoted in Richard Rhodes, *The Making of the Atomic Bomb* (London: Penguin, 1988), 40.

33. Thomson, speaking in 1934; in the film *Atomic Physics* (J. Arthur Rank, 1948); <http://www.aip.org/history/electron/jjsound.htm>.

34. Brian Cathcart, *The Fly in the Cathedral: How a Small Group of Cambridge Scientists Won the Race to Split the Atom* (London: Viking, 2004), 20.

35. N. de Bruyne, *My Life* (Cambridge: Midsummer, 1996), 58; quoted in Cathcart, 95.

36. Soddy, quoted in Muriel Howorth, *Atomic Transmutation: The Greatest Discovery Ever Made. From Memoirs of Professor Frederick Soddy* (London: New World, 1953), 56–7.

37. Soddy, 'Chemical Evidence of the Indivisibility of the Atom', paper presented on 28 Mar. 1901; quoted in David Wilson, *Rutherford: Simple Genius* (London: Hodder, 1983), 150.

38. Michael Meyer, *Strindberg: A Biography* (London: Secker & Warburg, 1985), 281.

39. Howorth, 48.

40. Wilson, 153.

41. Bickel, 32–3.

42. '*The Interpretation of Radium*. By Frederick Soddy. Illustrated. (John Murray)', review in *Athenaeum*, no. 4,254 (8 May 1909), 562.

43. Howorth, 54.

44. ibid., 63–4.

45. ibid., 56–7.

46. ibid., 54.

47. 'The Mystery of Radium', *Times* (25 Mar. 1903), 10; referring to Pierre Curie and A. Laborde, 'Sur la chaleur degage spontanément par les sels de radium', *Comptes rendus*, (16 Mar. 1903).

48. Quinn, 204.

49. 'The Mystery of Radium', 10.

50. ibid.

51. 'The Revelations of Radium', 397.

52. E. Rutherford and F. Soddy, 'Radioactive Change', *Philosophical Magazine*, 5 (1903), 576–91; quoted in ibid., 396.

53. Soddy, 'Some Recent Advances in Radioactivity', 718, 720.

54. Soddy to Rutherford, 19 Feb. 1903; quoted in Spencer R. Weart, *Nuclear Fear: A History of Images* (Cambridge, Mass.: Harvard University Press, 1988), 25; Crookes' comments were reported in New York *Press* (8 Feb. 1903).

55. Weart, 25.

56. Gustave Le Bon, New York *World* (30 Aug. 1903); quoted in Weart, 18.

57. W. C. D. Whetham, 'Matter and Electricity', *Quarterly Review*, 199, no. 397 (Jan. 1904), 126.

58. Soddy on 14 Jan. 1904, lecture published as Paper VIII, *Professional Papers of the Royal Engineers*, 29 (1904); quoted in Howorth, 95.

59. Pierre Curie, 'Radioactive Substances, Especially Radium', Nobel Lecture, 6 June 1905.

60. Cleveland Moffett, 'The Mysterious Card', *The Black Cat* (Feb. 1896); see Mike Ashley, *The Time Machines: The Story of the Science-Fiction Pulp Magazines from the Beginning to 1950* (Liverpool: Liverpool University Press, 2000), 23.

61. Moffett, 'M. Curie, the Discoverer of Radium', *Strand Magazine*, 27 (Jan. 1904), 66.

62. ibid., 65–66.

63. ibid., 66.

64. ibid.

65. ibid., 69.

66. ibid., 65–66.

67. ibid., 67.

68. ibid., 67–8.

69. ibid., 70.

70. Homer's *Hymn to Apollo*, lines 440–42. Crookes refers to this in his lecture to the Congress of Applied Chemistry, Berlin, 5 June 1903, published as William Crookes, 'Modern Views on Matter: The Realization of a Dream', *Science*, 17, no. 443 (26 June 1903), 1002.

71. C. W. Saleeby, 'Radium the Revealer', *Harper's Monthly Magazine*, 109 (June 1904), 85.
72. Oliver Sacks, *Uncle Tungsten: Memories of a Chemical Boyhood* (London: Picador, 2002), 287.
73. Moffett, 'M. Curie, the Discoverer of Radium', 70.
74. ibid., 71.
75. Caufield, 28.
76. Moffett, 72.
77. ibid., 73 (emphasis in original).
78. Walter Pagel, *Paracelsus: An Introduction to Philosophical Medicine in the Era of the Renaissance* (Basel: Karger, 1958), 56.
79. Roy Porter, *The Greatest Benefit to Mankind: A Medical History of Humanity from Antiquity to the Present* (London: HarperCollins, 1997), 204.
80. Moffett, 72–3.
81. ibid., 73.
82. 'The Revelations of Radium', 398.
83. Crookes, 'Modern Views on Matter', 1003.
84. 'The Revelations of Radium', 399.
85. Wells, *The Time Machine* (1895); in *The Science Fiction*, vol. 1 (London: Phoenix, 1998), 64.
86. Alfred North Whitehead, *Science and the Modern World* (Cambridge University Press, 1927), 12–13.
87. 'The Revelations of Radium', 399.
88. Wells, *Tono-Bungay* (London: Everyman, 1999; 1st edn 1909), 111, 128.
89. ibid., 279.
90. ibid., 200.
91. ibid., 297.
92. ibid., 297–8.
93. ibid., 298, 201.
94. 'The Revelations of Radium', 399.
95. Saleeby, 87.
96. Kandinsky, speaking in 1911; quoted in Peter Conrad, *Modern Times, Modern Places* (London: Thames & Hudson, 1998), 83.
97. Joseph Conrad, 9 Sep. 1898; quoted in Edward Garnett, ed., *Letters from Joseph Conrad, 1895–1924* (Indianapolis: Bobbs-Merrill, 1962), 143.
98. Joseph Conrad and Ford M. Hueffer, *The Inheritors: An Extravagant Story* (London: Heinemann, 1901), 16–17.

Chapter 5

1. 'Unser erster weiblicher Doktor', *Breslauer Zeitung* (22 Dec. 1900, evening edn); quoted in Gerit von Leitner, *Der Fall Clara Immerwahr: Leben für eine humane Wissenschaft* (Munich: Beck, 1994), 67; all translations from this are my own.

2. L. F. Haber, *The Poisonous Cloud: Chemical Warfare in the First World War* (Oxford: Clarendon Press, 1986), 26; see also Margit Szöllösi-Janze, *Fritz Haber, 1868–1934: Eine Biographie* (Munich: Beck, 1998), 272–3.

3. Paul Krassa to Johannes Jaenicka, 2 Nov. 1957; quoted in Szöllösi-Janze, 396; all translations from this are my own.

4. James Franck, quoted in Leitner, 224; my trans.

5. Leitner, 9.

6. ibid., 10.

7. Hermann Lütge to Jaenicka, 1958; quoted in Szöllösi-Janze, 396. Hermann Haber took his own life in New York in 1946. Clara's own sister, Lotte, would also commit suicide on the eve of being transported to Auschwitz. See Leitner, 10.

8. Charlotte Haber, *Mein Leben mit Fritz Haber* (Düsseldorf: Econ, 1970); quoted in Szöllösi-Janze, 398.

9. Fritz Haber to Carl Engler, 12 June 1915; quoted in Leitner, 12; my trans.

10. Fritz Haber to Carl Engler, 12 June 1915; quoted in Szöllösi-Janze, 399; my trans.

11. André Malraux, *The Walnut Trees of Altenburg*, trans. A. W. Fielding (University of Chicago Press, 1992; 1st edn 1948 as *Les Noyers de l'Altenburg*), 133.

12. Max Wild, *Mes aventures dans le service secret, 1914–1918* (Lausanne: Payot, 1932).

13. Malraux, 132.

14. ibid., 131–2.

15. ibid., 129.

16. ibid., 135.

17. Haber speaking in 1923; quoted in Robert Harris and Jeremy Paxman, *A Higher Form of Killing: The Secret History of Chemical and Biological Warfare* (London: Arrow, 2002), p. xv.

18. Malraux, 134.

19. ibid., 153.

20. ibid., 155.

21. ibid., 156.

22. ibid., 185.

23. ibid., 165.

24. ibid., 175.

25. ibid.

26. ibid., 176.

27. ibid., 185.

28. ibid., 177.

29. Szöllösi-Janze, 318.

30. Malraux, 180.

31. Szöllösi-Janze, 463; see also Dietrich Stoltzenberg, *Fritz Haber: Chemist, Nobel Laureate, German, Jew* (Philadelphia: Chemical Heritage, 2004), 234-5.

32. Malraux, 130.

33. Otto Hahn, *My Life*, trans. Ernst Kaiser and Eithne Wilkins (London: Macdonald, 1970), 120. On this attack, see Haber, 37.

34. Hahn, 117.

35. Karl Marx and Friedrich Engels, *Correspondence. A Selection, 1846–1895* (London: Martin Lawrence, 1934), 456–7; quoted in Daniel Pick, *War Machine: The Rationalisation of Slaughter in the Modern Age* (New Haven: Yale University Press, 1996), 55–6.

36. In the words of the military historian Basil Liddell Hart, quoted in Richard A. Preston and Sydney F. Wise, *Men in Arms: A History of Warfare and its Interrelationships with Western Society* (New York: Holt, Rinehart & Winston, 1979), 239.

37. Conversation between Hahn and J. Jaenicke, Jan. 1955; quoted in Stoltzenberg, 137.

38. Hague Peace Conference, 1907, Article XXIIIa; quoted in Haber, 18–19.

39. Hahn, 118.

40. Meitner to Hahn, Mar. 1915; quoted in Leitner, 205; my trans.

41. Max Born, *My Life: Recollections of a Nobel Laureate* (London: Taylor & Francis, 1978; 1st edn 1975), 188.

42. Haber, 292.

43. Szöllösi-Janze, 329.

44. S. J. M. Auld, *Gas and Flame in Modern Warfare* (New York: George H. Doran, 1918), 11–12; quoted in Hugh R. Slotten, 'Humane Chemistry or Scientific Barbarism? American Responses to World War I Poison Gas, 1915–1930', *Journal of American History*, 77 (Sep. 1990), 476.

45. 'Asphyxiating Gas in the Trenches', *American Review of Reviews*, 56 (July 1917), 94; see also Wyndham D. Miles, 'The Idea of Chemical Warfare in Modern Times', *Journal of the History of Ideas*, 31, no. 2 (1970), 297–304.

46. Haber, 79.

47. Owen, '*Dulce et Decorum est*', in Brian Gardner, ed., *Up the Line to Death: The War Poets 1914–1918* (London: Methuen, 1986), 141–2.

48. Haber, 29–34.

49. Leitner, 211.

50. Arthur Conan Doyle, *The British Campaign in France and Flanders*, vol. 3 (London: Hodder & Stoughton, 1917), 48–9; quoted in Haber, 231.

51. Letter from V. M. Ferguson, 5 May 1915; quoted in Modris Eksteins, *Rites of Spring: The Great War and the Modern Age* (London: Bantam, 1989), 162.

52. Haber, 39. Haber suggests that there may have been as many as half a million casualties from chemical warfare on the Western Front in World War I, of which 20,000 were fatalities (p. 242).

53. Harris and Paxman, 36.

54. G. W. G. Hughes; quoted in Eksteins, 162.

55. 'Full Story of Ypres: The New German Weapon', *Times* (30 Apr. 1915), 9.

56. Harris and Paxman, 9; see also Haber, *Poisonous Cloud*, 22–3.

57. Bernard Brodie, 'Defense and Technology', *Technology Review*, 43 (1941), 109.

58. General von Deimling; quoted in Edmund Russell, *War and Nature: Fighting Humans and Insects with Chemicals from World War I to* Silent Spring (Cambridge University Press, 2001), 27.

59. Charles Delvert, 27 Jan. 1916, in *Carnets d'un fantassin* (Paris 1935), 138–9; cited in Eksteins, 152–3.

60. Ernst Jünger, *In Stahlgewittern* [*In Storms of Steel*] (private publication, 1920); quoted in Eksteins, 144.

61. Szöllösi-Janze, 319.

Chapter 6

1. Ernest Volkman, *Science Goes to War: The Search for the Ultimate Weapon, from Greek Fire to Star Wars* (New York: Wiley, 2002), 51–2.

2. Both comments are recorded in Bertha von Suttner's *Memoiren* (Deutsche Verlags Anstalt, 1909), the first from 1876 (p. 134), the second from 1892 (p. 271); quoted in R. W. Reid, *Tongues of Conscience: War and the Scientist's Dilemma* (London: Constable, 1969), 17–19.

3. W. W. Knollys, 'War in the Future', *Fortnightly Review*, 54, ns 48 (1890), 274–81.

4. John Bourne, 'Total War I: The Great war', in Charles Townshend, ed., *The Oxford History of Modern War* (Oxford University Press, 2000), 131.

5. Archibald Forbes, 'The New Mechanism of War', *Nineteenth Century*, 29 (1891), 782–95.

6. Bourne, 133–4.

7. 'Revisiting the Enemy', *Times* (12 June 1915), 5.

8. Sir William Crookes, 'Address', *Report of the British Association for the Advancement of Science*, 68 (1898), 17–18; cited in Fritz Stern, *Einstein's German World* (London: Allen Lane, 2000), 81.

9. Tony Harrison, *Square Rounds* (London: Faber, 1992), 27.

10. ibid., 28.

11. ibid., 49.

12. Soddy, 16 Oct. 1914; quoted in Muriel Howorth, *Pioneer Research on the Atom: The Life Story of Frederick Soddy* (St Leonards on Sea, Sussex: King Bros, 1958), 194.

13. Soddy, speaking on 14 Jan. 1904; lecture published as Paper VIII, *Professional Papers of the Royal Engineers*, 29 (1904); quoted in Howorth, *Atomic Transmutation: The Greatest Discovery Ever Made. From Memoirs of Professor Frederick Soddy* (London: New World, 1953), 95.

14. Edward Thomas, *In Memoriam (Easter 1915)*; in John Silkin, ed., *The Penguin Book of First World War Poetry* (London: Penguin, 1996), 93.

15. *Transactions of the Royal Scottish Society of Arts*, 4 (1854), Appendix O, 198; quoted in West, 'The History of Poison Gases', *Science*, 49, no. 1270 (2 May 1919), 415–16.

16. Richard A. Preston and Sydney F. Wise, *Men in Arms: A History of Warfare and its Interrelationships with Western Society* (New York: Holt, Rinehart & Winston, 1979), 56.

17. Charles Nicholl, *Leonardo da Vinci* (London: Allen Lane, 2004), 143.

18. 'Developments in Gas Warfare', *American Review of Reviews*, 57 (Apr. 1918), 425–6. In 1932, the name of the German deserter who tried to warn the Allies was revealed. He was arrested by the Germans and imprisoned for ten years.

19. 'Respirators for the Troops', *Times* (29 Apr. 1915), 10.

20. André Malraux, *The Walnut Trees of Altenburg*, trans. A. W. Fielding (University of Chicago Press 1992; 1st edn 1948 as *Les Noyers de l'Altenburg*), 126.

21. ibid., 146–9.

22. J. B. S. Haldane, *Callinicus: A Defence of Chemical Warfare* (London: Kegan Paul, 1925), 31, 71.

23. 'Gases in 17in. Shells', *Times* (29 Apr. 1915), 10.

24. Harrison, 40.

25. B. W. Richardson, 'Greek Fire', *Popular Science Review*, 3 (1864), 176.

26. Dietrich Stoltzenberg, *Fritz Haber: Chemist, Nobel Laureate, German, Jew* (Philadelphia: Chemical Heritage, 2004), 161. On Haber's post-war involvement in chemical weapons, see 162ff.

27. Soddy, *The Interpretation of Radium: Being the Substance of Six Free Popular Experimental Lectures Delivered at the University of Glasgow* (London: John Murray, 1912; 1st edn 1909), 251.

28. L. F. Haber, *The Poisonous Cloud: Chemical Warfare in the First World War* (Oxford: Clarendon Press, 1986), 18.

29. William le Queux, *The Invasion of 1910* (1906), p. ix; quoted in Daniel Pick, *War Machine: The Rationalisation of Slaughter in the Modern Age* (New Haven: Yale University Press, 1996), 127.

30. The book was: Ivan S. Bloch, *The Future of War in its Technical, Economic and Political Relations*, 6 vols. (St Petersburg, 1897–8; trans. Boston, 1902). See Preston and Wise, 259.

31. Albert Robida, *La Guerre au vingtième siècle* (1887); trans. *War in the Twentieth Century*, in I. F. Clarke, ed., *The Tale of the Next Great War, 1871–1914: Fictions of Future Warfare and of Battles Still-to-Come* (Liverpool University Press, 1995), 99–103.

32. Chas Baskerville, ' "Gas" in this War: The Vast Development of a New Military Weapon', *American Review of Reviews*, 58 (Sep. 1918), 274, 278, 280.

33. See also his article on the tank and its invention in *Strand*: Col. E. D. Swinton, 'The "Tanks" ', *Strand Magazine*, 54 (1917), 270–77.

34. Frank R. Stockton, *The Great War Syndicate* (New York: Dodd, Mead & Co., 1889), 17, 15.

35. ibid., 17.

36. ibid., 24–5, 60, 64.

37. Haber, 34.

38. Bourne, 135.

39. Stockton, 87.

40. ibid., 51–3.

41. ibid., 66; Stockton does in fact use the word 'awe' here.

42. ibid., 184.

43. ibid., 187.

44. American propaganda described Japanese soldiers during World War II as 'Louseous Japanicas'; see Edmund Russell, *War and Nature: Fighting Humans and Insects with Chemicals from World War I to* Silent Spring (Cambridge University Press, 2001), 132.

45. M. P. Shiel, *The Yellow Danger* (London: Grant Richards, 1898), 313.

46. ibid., 338.

47. ibid., 343.

48. Wells, *The War of the Worlds* (1898); in Wells, *The Science Fiction*, vol. 1 (London: Phoenix, 1998), 186.

49. H. G. Wells, *The Last War [The World Set Free]* (Lincoln: University of Nebraska Press, 2001; 1st edn 1914), 29.

50. Simon Newcomb, *His Wisdom The Defender* (New York: Arno Press, 1975; 1st edn 1900), 163, 59.

51. Created by illustrator Harry Lampert for DC Comics: see Margalit Fox's obituary, 'Harry Lampert Dies at 88; Helped Create the Flash', *NYT* (16 Nov. 2004), A, 25.

52. Roy Norton, *The Vanishing Fleets* (New York: Appleton, 1908); quoted in H. Bruce Franklin, *War Stars: The Superweapon and the American Imagination* (New York: Oxford University Press, 1988), 41–2.

53. Norton, 237; quoted in Martha A. Bartter, *The Way to Ground Zero: The Atomic Bomb in American Science Fiction* (New York: Greenwood, 1988), 26.

54. Norton, 243; quoted in Franklin, 42.

55. Hollis Godfrey, *The Man Who Ended War* (Boston: Little, Brown, & Co., 1908), 154, 183.

56. ibid., 47, 158, 246.

57. ibid., 94, 301.

58. Franklin, 20.

59. Peyton C. March, *The Nation at War* (New York: Doubleday, Doran & Co., 1932), 333; quoted in Russell, 40.

60. 'Fog Bombs for London', *Times* (17 May 1915), 7.

61. 'J. H. Lartigue: Photographs 1901–1986', exhibition, Hayward Gallery London, 24 June–5 Sep. 2004.

62. 'Airship Raid on London' and 'The Zeppelin Raiders', *Times* (2 June 1915), 6.

63. Edmund Russell makes this case convincingly in *War and Nature*. He argues that 350,000 people died in World War II as a result of chemical weapons, by which he means principally incendiaries: see Russell, 3, 10ff.

64. Col. H. L. Gilchrist, *A Comparative Study of World War Casualties from Gas and Other Weapons* (Chemical Warfare School, Edgewood Arsenal, 1928); quoted in Gilbert F. Whittemore Jr, 'World War I, Poison Gas Research, and the Ideals of American Chemists', *Social Studies of Science*, 5, no. 2 (May 1975), 149.

65. Baskerville, 278.

66. W. Lee Lewis, 'Is Prohibition of Gas Warfare Feasible?', *Atlantic Monthly*, 129 (June 1922), 840; quoted in Whittemore, 158.

67. Haber, 205.

68. Lord Derby, Secretary of State for War, 26 Dec. 1917, UK Public Record Office, CAB/23–4, War Cabinet 306; quoted in Haber (1986), 206.

69. Walker, quoted in Russell, 45.

70. Will Irwin, *The Next War* (New York: E. P. Dutton & Co., 1921), 37–8; quoted in Whittemore, 154.

71. Editorial, *Nature* (17 June 1915); quoted in Guy Hartcup, *The Effect of Science on the Second World War* (Basingstoke: Palgrave, 2000), 2.

72. Fisher quoted in Linda Merricks, *The World Made New: Frederick Soddy, Science, Politics, and Environment* (Oxford University Press, 1996), 73.

73. 'Christian Conscience and Poison-Gas', *Literary Digest* (8 Jan. 1921), 38; quoted in Hugh R. Slotten, 'Humane Chemistry or Scientific Barbarism? American Responses to World War I Poison Gas, 1915–1930', *Journal of American History*, 77 (Sep. 1990), 486.

74. Professor D. Fraser Harris, 'The Man of Science After the War', *Scientific Monthly*, 7, no. 4 (Oct. 1918), 320.

75. Salomon Reinach, 'Precarious or Lasting Peace?', *Nation* (15 June 1916), 642–3; quoted in Slotten, 481.

76. 'Herbert Kaufman's Weekly Page', *Boston Sunday Herald* (1916); quoted in a letter to the editor, by F. Lyman Wells, 'Science and War', *Science*, 44 (25 Aug. 1916), 275.

Chapter 7

1. H. G. Wells, 'The Mobilization of Invention', letter to *Times* (11 June 1915), 9.

2. Edison, *NYT* (3 Jan. 1915); quoted in H. Bruce Franklin, *War Stars: The Superweapon and the American Imagination* (New York: Oxford University Press, 1988), 69.

3. Edison, *NYT* (16 Oct. 1915); quoted in Franklin, 72.

4. David Wilson, *Rutherford: Simple Genius* (London: Hodder, 1983), 346.

5. A. Wilkinson, Jr, 'When the Earth Melted', *Top-Notch* (15 June 1918), 4, 2, 5, 6.

6. Martin Swayne, 'The Sleep-Beam', *Strand Magazine*, 55 (Mar. 1918), 191, 193.

7. Christian Hülsmeyer tested his *Telemobiloskop* on a stretch of the Rhine near Cologne on 10 May 1904. On reports of the German death ray, see Wilson, 474. On Churchill, see Martin Gilbert, *Churchill: A Life* (London: Heinemann, 1972), 463–4.

8. Gernsback, quoted in Mike Ashley, *Time Machines: The Story of the*

Science-Fiction Pulp Magazines from the Beginning to 1950 (Liverpool University Press, 2000), 28.

9. L. Shaw, Jr, 'What the Housewife Should Know about Electricity', *The Electrical Experimenter* (Nov. 1915), 317.

10. This and the following quotes are from 'Warfare of the Future: The Radium Destroyer', *The Electrical Experimenter* (Nov. 1915), 315.

11. Arthur Train and Robert Williams Wood, *The Man Who Rocked the Earth* (New York: Doubleday, 1915), 4.

12. Train and Wood, 58.

13. Robert Jungk, *Brighter Than a Thousand Suns: A Personal History of the Atomic Scientists* (San Diego: Harcourt, 1986; 1st edn 195), 201.

14. Train and Wood, 68.

15. ibid., 172.

16. ibid., 226.

17. ibid., 110, 100–101.

18. ibid., 108–9.

19. Einstein to Heinrich Zangger, 10 Apr. 1915; in *CP8*, trans. vol., 87.

20. Einstein to Zangger, 6 Dec. 1917; in *CP8*, doc. 403; quoted in Thomas Levenson, *Einstein in Berlin* (New York: Bantam, 2004), 84.

21. Einstein, 'Meine Meinung über den Krieg' [My Opinion of the War] (Oct. 1915), in *Das Land Goethes 1914–1916: Ein vaterländisches Gedenkbuch* (Berlin, 1916); in *CP6*, trans. vol., 96.

22. Otto Friedrich, *Before the Deluge: A Portrait of Berlin in the 1920s* (New York: Harper & Row, 1972), 142.

23. Einstein to Conrad Habicht, 18 or 25 May 1905; in *CP5*, trans. vol., 20.

24. Einstein to Habicht, between 30 June and 22 Sep. 1905; in *CP5*, trans. vol., 20.

25. Einstein to Habicht, between 30 June and 22 Sep. 1905; in *CP5*, trans. vol., 20–21.

26. Einstein, 'Ist die Trägheit eines Körpers von seinem Energieinhalt abhängig?' [Does the Inertia of a Body Depend on its Energy Content?], *Annalen der Physik*, 18 (1905), 639–41; in John Stachel, ed., *Einstein's Miraculous Year: Five Papers That Changed the Face of Physics* (Princeton University Press, 1998), 164.

27. On references to the idea of matter as latent energy before 1905, see Muriel Howorth, *Atomic Transmutation: The Greatest Discovery Ever Made. From Memoirs of Professor Frederick Soddy* (London: New World, 1953), 135–6. According to Soddy, British scientists such as Rutherford were very reluctant to accept the idea.

28. Einstein to A. Schnauder, spring 1907; in *CP5*, 28, my trans.

29. Einstein, *Relativity: The Special and the General Theory. A Popular Exposition*, trans. Robert W. Lawson (London: Methuen, 1920), 75.

30. Max Born, quoted in Denis Brian, *Einstein: A Life* (New York: Wiley 1996), 91.

31. Einstein to Paul Ehrenfest, 17 Jan. 1916; in *CP8*, trans. vol., 179.

32. Einstein to Max Born, 8 Dec. 1919; in *CP9*, doc. 198 (trans. vol.).

33. Dietrich Stoltzenberg, *Fritz Haber: Chemist, Nobel Laureate, German, Jew* (Philadelphia: Chemical Heritage, 2004), 47.

34. Levenson, 197.

35. Einstein, in *CP7*, 90.

36. Arnold Sommerfeld to Einstein, 3 Dec. 1918; in *CP8*, doc. 662 (trans. vol.).

37. Einstein to Sommerfeld, 6 Dec. 1918, *CP8*, doc. 665 (trans. vol.).

38. Haber's daughter, Eva Lewis, interviewed for the documentary 'Science at War', in the series *The Laboratory of War* (BBC2, 12 Nov. 1998).

39. Hitler, *Mein Kampf*; quoted in Friedrich, 31.

40. 'Report on the Committee on Chemical Warfare Organisation' (1919); quoted in Modris Eksteins, *Rites of Spring: The Great War and the Modern Age* (London: Bantam, 1989), 164.

41. Max Born, *My Life: Recollections of a Nobel Laureate* (London: Taylor & Francis, 1978; 1st edn 1975), 177.

42. ibid., 184.

43. Levenson, 198; see also Born, 184-5.

44. F. Lyman Wells, 'Science and War', *Science*, 44, no. 1,130 (25 Aug. 1916), 275.

45. Alfred Döblin, *Berge Meere und Giganten* [*Mountains, Oceans and Giants*] (Olten: Walter-Verlag, 1977; 1st edn 1924), 508 (my trans.).

46. All quotes are from Perley Poore Sheehan and Robert H. Davis, 'Blood and Iron: A Play in One Act', *Strand Magazine*, 54 (1917), 359-65.

47. 'Notes', *Observatory*, 42 (1919), 389-98.

48. 'Revolution in Science', *Times* (7 Nov. 1919), 12.

49. Einstein, *Autobiographical Notes: A Centennial Edition*, ed. and trans. Paul Arthur Schilpp (La Salle, , Ill.: Open Court, 1979), 31.

50. Charles Lane Poor, a Columbia astronomer, described Einstein's science as the product of a Bolshevist age: *NYT* (16 Nov. 1919). See also Einstein's letter to Zangger, Dec. 1919; in *CP9*, doc. 217, p. 306.

51. Arthur Stanley Eddington to Einstein, 1 Dec. 1919; in *CP9*, doc. 186, p. 262.

52. A. Vibert Douglas, *The Life of Arthur Stanley Eddington* (London: Nelson, 1956), 93-4.

53. *Berliner Illustrirte Zeitung* (14 Dec. 1919); reproduced in Smith (2003), 100. The photographer was Suse Byk.

54. Einstein to Zangger, Dec. 1919, *CP9*, doc. 217, trans. vol., 186.

55. Einstein to Mileva Marić, in Peter Michelmore, *Einstein: Profile of the Man* (London, 1963), 82.

56. Einstein to Zangger, 24 Dec. 1919; in *CP9*, doc. 233, p. 326; my trans.

57. Alexander Moszkowski, *Conversations with Einstein*, trans. Henry L. Brose (London: Sidgwick & Jackson, 1972; 1st edn 1921), 24.

58. Rutherford, 'Collision of a Particle with Light Atoms: IV. An Anomalous Effect in Nitrogen', *Philosophical Magazine*, 37 (1919), 581–7; cited in Emilio Segrè, *From X-Rays to Quarks: Modern Physicists and Their Discoveries* (San Francisco: W. H. Freeman, 1980), 110.

59. Brian Cathcart, *The Fly in the Cathedral: How a Small Group of Cambridge Scientists Won the Race to Split the Atom* (London: Viking, 2004), 28.

60. Ruth Lewin Sime, *Lise Meitner: A Life in Physics* (Berkeley: University of California Press,1996), 111.

61. Moszkowski, 36.

62. Einstein, in 'Die Urteile der deutschen Gelehrten', *Berliner Tageblatt* (25 July 1920), 4; from *CP7*, doc 43, p. 339; my trans.

63. Moszkowski, 37.

64. J. J. Connington, *Nordenholt's Million* (London: Penguin, 1946; 1st edn 1923), 126, 127–8.

65. Moszkowski, 37.

Chapter 8

1. William Lanouette with Bela Silard, *Genius in the Shadows: A Biography of Leo Szilard, The Man Behind the Bomb* (University of Chicago Press, 1994; 1st edn 1992), 49.

2. ibid.

3. Recounted by George Klein to Lanouette; ibid., 50.

4. Edward Shils, 'Leo Szilard: A Memoir', *Encounter*, 23 (Dec. 1964), 35.

5. Szilard, *CW2*, 14.

6. Lanouette, 458.

7. Otto Friedrich, *Before the Deluge: A Portrait of Berlin in the 1920s* (New York: Harper & Row, 1972), 13.

8. Alexandra Richie, *Faust's Metropolis: A History of Berlin* (London: HarperCollins, 1999), 326.

9. On Döblin's *Berlin Alexanderplatz* and Berlin in this period, see P. D.

Smith, 'Science and the City: Alfred Döblin's *Berlin Alexanderplatz*', *London Magazine*, 39 (Apr./May 2000), 27–36.

10. Stefan Zweig, *The World of Yesterday* (London: Cassell, 1943), 238.

11. Victor Weisskopf, *The Joy of Insight: Passions of a Physicist* (New York: Basic, 1991), 46.

12. Friedrich, 5.

13. ibid., 6.

14. Einstein to Adolf Hurwitz, 4 May 1914; in *CP8*, doc. 6 (trans. vol.).

15. Otto Hahn, *My Life*, trans. Ernst Kaiser and Eithne Wilkins (London: Macdonald, 1970), 133–4.

16. Max Born, *My Life: Recollections of a Nobel Laureate* (London: Taylor & Francis, 1978; 1st edn 1975), 194.

17. Szilard, taped interview, May 1960; in *CW2*, 8.

18. M. Polanyi to Szilard, 18 May 1961; in Leo Szilard Papers, Mandeville Special Collections Library, Geisel Library, University of California, San Diego, box 15, folder 18; quoted in David A. Grandy, *Leo Szilard: Science as a Mode of Being* (Lanham, Md: University Press of America, 1996), 19. Polanyi already knew Szilard, as they were members of the Galilei Circle in Budapest.

19. Szilard, taped interview, May 1960; in *CW2*, 8.

20. Philipp Frank, *Einstein: His Life and Times*, trans. George Rosen (New York: Knopf, 1947), 241.

21. ibid., 112.

22. William O. McCagg, Jr, *Jewish Nobles and Geniuses in Modern Hungary* (Boulder, Colo.: Columbia University Press, 1986), 221.

23. Eugene P. Wigner and Andrew Szanton, *The Recollections of Eugene P. Wigner* (New York: Plenum, 1992), 71.

24. Frank, 112.

25. Wigner and Szanton, 71.

26. ibid., 17.

27. Friedrich, 11.

28. Wigner and Szanton, 70.

29. ibid., 97.

30. Einstein to Paul Ehrenfest, before 10 Sep 1920; in *CP7*, 107.

31. Wigner and Szanton, 71.

32. Frank, 110.

33. ibid., 118.

34. ibid., 113.

35. Wigner and Szanton, 95.

36. Rabinowitch, in Arnulf K. Esterer and Louise A. Esterer, *Prophet of the Atomic Age: Leo Szilard* (New York: Julian Messner, 1972), 27.

37. Shils, 37.

38. Lanouette, 83.

39. Wigner and Szanton, 96.

40. ibid., 121.

41. Szilard, taped interview, 1963; in *CW*2, 9.

42. Wigner and Szanton, 98.

43. Lanouette, 59.

44. Szilard, taped interview, 1963; in *CW*2, 9.

45. ibid.

46. ibid., 9–11.

47. ibid., 11.

48. ibid. See also Szilard, 'On the Decrease of Entropy in a Thermodynamic System by the Intervention of Intelligent Beings' (1929); in *CW1*, 103–19, 120–29. See too the discussion of this in Charles H. Bennett, 'Demons, Engines and the Second Law', *Scientific American*, 257 (Nov. 1987), 88–96.

49. Quoted in J. Bronowski, *The Ascent of Man* (London: Book Club Associates, 1979; 1st edn 1973), 254.

50. 'Warfare of the Future: The Radium Destroyer', *The Electrical Experimenter* (Nov. 1915), 315.

Chapter 9

1. Eugene Rabinowitch, '[James Franck] 1882–1964; [Leo Szilard] 1898–1964', *BAS*, 20 (1964), 18. (The title of this joint obituary has pictures of Franck and Szilard in place of their names.)

2. Rabi; quoted in William Lanouette with Bela Silard, *Genius in the Shadows: A Biography of Leo Szilard, The Man Behind the Bomb* (University of Chicago Press, 1994; 1st edn 1992), 176.

3. George Marx, *The Voice of the Martians* (Budapest: Akadémiai Kiadó, 1997), 166–7.

4. Dennis Gabor, 'Leo Szilard', *BAS*, 29 (Sep. 1973), 52.

5. ibid.

6. Alice Kimball Smith, 'The Elusive Dr Szilard', *Harper's Magazine*, 221 (July 1960), 77.

7. N[orman] C[ousins], 'The Many Facets of Leo Szilard', *Saturday Review* (29 Apr. 1961), 15.

8. Edwin M. McMillan to Wilfred Mann, 3 Jan. 1952; quoted in J. L.

Heilbron, *Lawrence and His Laboratory: A History of the Lawrence Berkeley Laboratory* (Berkeley: University of California Press, 1989), 199.

9. Marx, 162.

10. Eugene P. Wigner and Andrew Szanton, *The Recollections of Eugene P. Wigner* (New York: Plenum, 1992), 93, 94.

11. ibid., 98.

12. Lanouette, 54.

13. ibid., 55.

14. Wigner and Szanton, 121.

15. Szilard, interview, New York 1960; in *CW2*, 3.

16. Lanouette, 25. Lanouette's biography is an invaluable source on this early period of Szilard's life.

17. 'Anent Warlike Inventions', *The Electrical Experimenter* (Nov. 1915), 315.

18. Rabinowitch, 20.

19. Lanouette, 30.

20. Austin Hall, 'The Man Who Saved the Earth', *Amazing Stories*, 1 (Apr. 1926); in Groff Conklin, ed., *The Golden Age of Science Fiction* (New York: Bonanza, 1980; 1st edn 1946), 668–703, here p. 682. Hall's story first appeared in *All-Story Weekly* in 1919.

21. Szilard, taped interview (1963); in *CW1*, 527.

22. Gene Dannen, 'Leo Szilard the Inventor', lecture, Leo Szilard Centenary, Eötvös University, Budapest, Hungary, 9 Feb. 1998; see <http://www.dannen.com/budatalk.html>. Dannen's website is an excellent resource on Szilard.

23. Leo to Bela, Oct. 1926; quoted in Gene Dannen, 'The Einstein–Szilard Refrigerators', *Scientific American* (Jan. 1997), 75.

24. For example, the Nov. 1915 issue of Gernsback's *Electrical Experimenter* carried an illustrated article on 'The Electro-Magnetic Gun and its Possibilities', pp. 309–11.

25. Dannen, 78; see also Marx, 167–8.

26. Shelley Nickels, ' "Preserving women": Refrigerator Design as Social Process in the 1930s', *Technology and Culture*, 43 (Oct. 2002), 696, n5.

27. B. Feld and Leo Szilard, 'A Magnetic Pump for Liquid Bismuth', Report CE-279 (14 July 1942); in *CW1*, 351–58. The report was declassified on 27 Feb. 1951.

28. Szilard, 'Short Memorandum on Bismuth Cooled Power Unit', Report CP-360 (23 Nov. 1942); in *CW1*, 361.

29. S. L. Sanger, *Working on the Bomb: An Oral History of WWII Hanford* (Portland, Oreg.: Continuing Education Press, 1995), 162, 48–9.

30. Szilard, 'Liquid Metal Cooled Fast Neutron Breeder', Report MUC-LS-60 (6 Mar. 1945); in *CW1*, 371.

31. 'The Breeder Reactor', *Scientific American*, 186–7 (Dec. 1952), 58–60.

32. NanoCoolers, 'Liquid-Metal Cooling Technology for CPU Cooling', <http://www.nanocoolers.com/technology_liquid_new.php>.

33. James Busse, 'Silent Sea Engine for Nuclear Subs', *Popular Science* (Jan. 1966), 113–15; 'Magnetic Propulsion May Be Ready for Small Subs', *Product Engineering* (24 Feb. 1969).

34. Ruth Lewin Sime, *Lise Meitner: A Life in Physics* (Berkeley: University of California Press, 1996), 103.

35. Otto Friedrich, *Before the Deluge: A Portrait of Berlin in the 1920s* (New York: Harper & Row, 1972), 189.

Chapter 10

1. Leo Szilard, *Brandeis University Bulletin* (Feb. 1954), 6–7; quoted in William Lanouette with Bela Silard, *Genius in the Shadows: A Biography of Leo Szilard, The Man Behind the Bomb* (University of Chicago Press, 1994; 1st edn 1992), 104.

2. Szilard, 'Answers to Questions', dictated 9 May 1963; in *CW2*, 229.

3. George Gamow, *Thirty Years That Shook Physics* (New York: Dover, 1985; 1st edn 1966), 51.

4. Paul Dirac, 'Recollections of an Exciting Era', in C. Weiner, ed., *History of Twentieth Century Physics: Proceedings of the International School of Physics 'Enrico Fermi'*, vol. 57 (New York: Academic Press, 1977), 134; quoted in Emilio Segrè, *From X-Rays to Quarks: Modern Physicists and Their Discoveries* (San Francisco: W. H. Freeman, 1980), 130.

5. Quoted in Richard P. Feynman, *Don't You Have Time to Think?* (London: Penguin, 2005), p. xii.

6. Einstein to Bohr, 2 May 1920; in Niels Bohr, *Collected Works*, vol. 3, *The Correspondence Principle (1918–1923)*, ed. J. Rud Nielsen (Amsterdam: North-Holland, 1976), 634.

7. Einstein to Conrad Habicht, 18 or 25 May 1905; in *CP5*, trans. vol., 20.

8. Einstein to Born, 4 Dec. 1926; in Max Born, *The Born–Einstein Letters 1916–1955: Friendship, Politics and Physics in Uncertain Times*, trans. Irene Born (London: Macmillan, 2005; 1st edn 1971), 88.

9. Einstein to Born, 29 Apr. 1924; in Born, 80.

10. Gamow, 167.

11. John Canaday, *The Nuclear Muse: Literature, Physics and the First Atomic Bombs* (Madison: University of Wisconsin Press, 2000), 268, n.

12. Goethe, *Faust: A Tragedy*, trans. Walter Arndt (New York: Norton, 1976), lines 382–3. On the role of science in the play, see P. D. Smith, 'Scientific Themes in Goethe's *Faust*', in Paul Bishop, ed., *A Companion to Goethe's Faust* (Rochester, NY: Camden House, 2001), 194–220.

13. The *Blegdamsvej Faust* is on microfilm 66 of the Archive for the History of Quantum Physics (American Philosophical Society). An English version, together with the illustrations, is in Gamow. This quotation from it is in Canaday, 87.

14. Canaday, 80.

15. Bohr, quoted in Robert Ehrlich, *Eight Preposterous Propositions* (Princeton University Press, 2005), 5.

16. Gamow, 207.

17. Canaday, 100.

18. James Whale, dir., *The Invisible Man* (Universal, 1933).

19. Gamow, 213.

20. Rutherford, quoted in Ruth Lewin Sime, *Lise Meitner: A Life in Physics* (Berkeley: University of California Press, 1996), 111.

21. See Chadwick's Nobel acceptance speech, 'The Neutron and its Properties', 12 Dec. 1935: <http://nobelprize.org/physics/laureates/1935/chadwicklecture.pdf>.

22. See Brian Cathcart, *The Fly in the Cathedral: How a Small Group of Cambridge Scientists Won the Race to Split the Atom* (London: Viking, 2004), 209–13.

23. C. P. Snow, *The Physicists* (London: Macmillan, 1981), 85.

24. Rutherford, quoted in Jungk, *Brighter Than a Thousand Suns: A Personal History of the Atomic Scientists* (San Diego: Harcourt, 1986; 1st edn 1956), 59.

25. Langevin, quoted in Jungk, 50–51.

26. Hitler, quoted in John Cornwell, *Hitler's Scientists: Science, War and the Devil's Pact* (London: Allen Lane, 2003), 27.

27. Von Braun, quoted in Otto Friedrich, *Before the Deluge: A Portrait of Berlin in the 1920s* (New York: Harper & Row, 1972), 238.

28. Von Braun, quoted in NASA, 'The Robotic Exploration of Space', Sect. 1, 'Taking Off', <http://solarsystem.nasa.gov/history/timeline.cfm?Section=1>.

29. Imre Madách, *The Tragedy of Man*, trans. Iain MacLeod (Edinburgh: Canongate, 1993; 1st edn 1861), scene XIV, 149.

30. *New York Post* (24 Nov. 1945); in CW2, 3.

31. Szilard to Niels Bohr, 7 Nov. 1950; quoted in Barton J. Bernstein, 'Introduction', in Leo Szilard, *The Voice of the Dolphins and Other Stories* (Stanford University Press, 1992), 6.

32. Striker, quoted in S. Lessard, 'The Present Moment', *New Yorker*, 63 (13 Apr. 1987), 40.

33. Spender, in 1930; quoted in Friedrich, 306.

34. Striker, quoted in Lessard, 40.

35. ibid.

36. Leo Szilard to Einstein, 27 Sep. 1930; in Gene Dannen, 'The Einstein–Szilard Refrigerators', *Scientific American* (Jan. 1997), 78.

37. Szilard, *C W*2, 22.

38. Szilard, 'Draft Proposal for *Der Bund*', about 1930; *C W*2, 25.

39. ibid., *C W*2, 24.

40. Waldemar Kaempffert, *Science, Today and Tomorrow* (New York: Viking, 1945), 266.

41. Szilard, 'Draft Proposal for *Der Bund*', about 1930; *C W*2, 27.

42. ibid., 28.

43. H. G. Wells, *The Open Conspiracy, and Other Writings* (London: n. pub., 1933), 16, 11.

44. ibid., 93.

45. Szilard to H. G. Wells, 20 Feb. 1929; in David A. Grandy, *Leo Szilard: Science as a Mode of Being* (Lanham, Md: University Press of America, 1996), 137, n25.

46. German original, *unsere Aktion*: Szilard to Einstein, 2 Apr. 1929; quoted in Grandy, 24.

47. Szilard to Wells, 1 Apr. 1929; quoted in Grandy, 138, n35.

48. H. N. Brailsford to Einstein, 31 Mar. 1930; quoted in Lanouette, 99.

49. Einstein to Brailsford, 24 Apr. 1930; in *C W*2, 22.

50. Szilard to Wigner, 9 Oct. 1932; in Leo Szilard Papers, Mandeville Special Collections Library, Geisel Library, University of California, San Diego, box 21 folder 4; whole letter quoted in Lanouette, 108.

51. Wigner to M. Polanyi, 18 Oct. 1932; quoted in Lanouette, 109.

52. Szilard, taped interview, May 1960; in *C W*2, 16–17.

53. Szilard, 'Memoirs', 1960; in Leo Szilard Papers, box 40, folder 10, pp. 2–4; quoted in Grandy, 27.

54. Szilard, in 1956, the year of Wells's 'last war'; in Leo Szilard Papers, box 42, folder 25; quoted in Grandy, 139, n43.

55. W. Warren Wagar, *Terminal Visions: The Literature of Last Things* (Bloomington: Indiana University Press, 1982), 110.

56. 'W.L.R.', 'The World-Republic', *Academy*, 86 (16 May 1914), 616.

57. Wells's *The World Set Free: A Story of Mankind* (1914) has been inexplicably retitled *The Last War* for its publication in the otherwise excellent Bison

Frontiers of Imagination series. All quotations are from this edition (Lincoln: University of Nebraska Press, 2001), 55–8.

58. Stanley Baldwin, 10 Nov. 1932; in *Parliamentary Debates*, 5th series, vol. 270, House of Commons (London: His Majesty's Stationery Office, 1932), 631.

59. *New York Herald* (30 July 1921); quoted in H. Bruce Franklin, *War Stars: The Superweapon and the American Imagination* (New York: Oxford University Press, 1988), 95.

60. W. Mitchell, 'Are We Ready for War with Japan?', *Liberty* (30 Jan. 1932), 12; quoted in Franklin, 98.

61. Wells, *The Last War*, 59.

62. R. Ellis Roberts, 'Mr Wells Let Loose', *Bookman*, 46 (June 1914), 131–2.

63. Wells, *The Last War*, 118.

64. 'W.L.R.', 616.

65. Quoted in John Huntington, 'The Science Fiction of H. G. Wells', in Patrick Parrinder, ed., *Science Fiction: A Critical Guide* (London: Longman, 1979), 47.

66. Jonathan Schell also explores this idea, in *The Unconquerable World: Power, Nonviolence, and the Will of the People* (London: Allen Lane, 2004).

67. Wells, *The Last War*, 61.

68. On infected suicidal terrorists today, see Josh Schollmeyer, 'Blood Feuds', *BAS*, 61 (Nov./Dec. 2005), 8–9.

69. 'The Cosmic Muse', *New Statesman* (30 May 1914), 248–9.

70. Wells, *The Last War*, 149.

71. Yevgeny Zamyatin, *We* (London: Penguin, 1984; 1st 1924), 37.

72. Peter George, *Dr Strangelove: or How I Learned to Stop Worrying and Love the Bomb* (London: Souvenir, 1999; 1st edn 1963), 161.

73. Wells, *The Last War*, 150.

74. Roslynn D. Haynes, *H. G. Wells: Discoverer of the Future. The Influence of Science on his Thought* (London: Macmillan, 1980), 80.

75. Rutherford, 'The Constitution of Matter and the Evolution of the Elements', 1914 Hale Lecture, National Academy of Sciences, in *The Smithsonian Report for 1915* (Washington: Smithsonian Institution, Washington 1916); quoted in David Wilson, *Rutherford: Simple Genius* (London: Hodder, 1983), 388.

76. Brian Aldiss, in Warren Wagar, 'H. G. Wells and the scientific imagination', *Virginia Quarterly Review*, 65 (1989), 390.

77. Brian Easlea, *Fathering the Unthinkable: Masculinity, Scientists and the Nuclear Arms Race* (London: Pluto Press, 1983); cited in Linda Merricks,

The World Made New: Frederick Soddy, Science, Politics, and Environment (Oxford University Press 1996), 7.

78. Soddy, *The Interpretation of Radium: Being the Substance of Six Free Popular Experimental Lectures Delivered at the University of Glasgow* (London: John Murray, 1912; 1st edn 1909), 251.

79. ibid., 236.

80. Wells, *The Last War*, 14–15.

81. ibid., 15.

82. ibid., 163.

83. William Cameron Menzies, dir., *Things to Come* (United Artists, 1936); the producer was Alexander Korda, another Hungarian émigré.

84. Soddy, *The Interpretation of Radium*, 252.

85. Wagar, 'H. G. Wells and the Scientific Imagination', 399.

86. Ingo Cornils, 'The Martians are Coming! War, Peace, Love and Scientific Progress in H. G. Wells's *The War of the Worlds* and Kurd Lasswitz's *Auf zwei Planeten*', *Comparative Literature*, 55 (2003), 24–5.

87. Wernher von Braun, epigraph in Kurd Lasswitz, *Two Planets*, trans. Hans H. Rudnick (Carbondale: Southern Illinois University Press, 1971), 7; quoted in Robert Markley, *Dying Planet: Mars in Science and the Imagination* (Durham, NC: Duke University Press, 2005), 127–8.

Chapter 11

1. Szilard, CW2, 13.

2. ibid.

3. Interview with Rose Scheiber; quoted in William Lanouette with Bela Silard, *Genius in the Shadows: A Biography of Leo Szilard, The Man Behind the Bomb* (University of Chicago Press, 1994; 1st edn 1992), 112.

4. See Szilard, CW2, 14.

5. Meitner to Hahn, 21 Mar. 1933; quoted in Ruth Lewin Sime, *Lise Meitner: A Life in Physics* (Berkeley: University of California Press (1996), 136.

6. Szilard, CW2, 14.

7. P. D. Smith, *Metaphor and Materiality: German Literature and the World-View of Science 1780–1955* (Oxford: European Humanities Research Centre, 2000), 267; and Sime, 139.

8. Max Born, *My Life: Recollections of a Nobel Laureate* (London: Taylor & Francis, 1978; 1st edn 1975), 251.

9. *Toronto Star Weekly*, 8 Apr. 1933; quoted in Sime, 142.

10. Fritz Stern, *Einstein's German World* (London: Allen Lane, 2000), 157.

11. Einstein to Haber, 9 Aug. 1933; quoted in Margit Szöllösi-Janze, *Fritz Haber, 1868–1934: Eine Biographie* (Munich: Beck, 1998), 684.

12. Christopher Frayling, *Mad, Bad and Dangerous? The Scientist and the Cinema* (London: Reaktion, 2005), 70, 83.

13. Interview with Alice Danos; quoted in Lanouette, 70.

14. Francis Simon to Szilard, 23 Aug. 1938; quoted in Lanouette, 171.

15. Szilard to Francis Simon, 9 Sep. 1938; quoted in Lanouette, 171.

16. Szilard, *CW*2, 15.

17. Advertisements in *The Times* on 14 Mar., 10 May and 14 Nov. 1933. Unfortunately the ornate Imperial has been replaced by a utilitarian concrete structure. The Hotel Russell (or the Russell Hotel as it is now called) remains, in all its late Victorian splendour.

18. Szilard, taped interview, May 1960; in *CW*2, 19.

19. Ehrenfest to Donnan, 22 Aug. 1933; quoted in Lanouette, 125.

20. Born, 261.

21. Szöllösi-Janze, 680–89.

22. Edward Teller with Judith Shoolery, *Memoirs: A Twentieth-Century Journey in Science and Politics* (Cambridge, Mass.: Perseus, 2001), 90.

23. Teller, quoted in Peter Goodchild, *Edward Teller: The Real Dr Strangelove* (London: Weidenfeld & Nicolson, 2004), 33.

24. Szilard writing to an unknown addressee from the Imperial Hotel, 11 Aug. 1933; in *CW*2, 35.

25. Rutherford, quoted in 'Splitting the Atom', *Times* (21 Nov. 1932), 19.

26. Quoted in 'The British Association: Breaking Down the Atom', *Times* (12 Sep. 1933), 7.

27. David Wilson, *Rutherford: Simple Genius* (London: Hodder, 1983), 95.

28. Rutherford, quoted in 'The British Association', *Times* (12 Sep. 1933), 7.

29. Szilard, taped interview, May 1960; in *CW*2, 17.

30. ibid.; and Szilard, 'Rough Draft, Outline for Book', June 1960, in *CW*2, 17. In Szilard's *Collected Works*, autobiographical statements from more than one source have here been woven into a narrative.

31. Quoted in 'The British Association', *Times* (12 Sep. 1933), 7.

32. 'Bombardment of the Atom', *Times* (12 Oct. 1933), 7.

33. J. Bronowski, *The Ascent of Man* (London: Book Club Associates, 1979; 1st edn 1973), 369.

34. Szilard to Sir Hugo Hirst, from 6 Halliwick Rd, London, 17 Mar. 1934; in *CW*2, 38.

35. H. G. Wells, *The Last War* [*The World Set Free: A Story of Mankind*] (Lincoln: University of Nebraska Press, 2001; 1st edn 1914), 18.

36. ibid., 13.

37. Goethe, *Faust: A Tragedy*, trans. Walter Arndt (New York: Norton, 1976), lines 382–3.

38. Wells, *The Last War*, 18.

39. ibid., 20.

40. ibid., 21.

41. Goethe, lines 1110–17.

42. Wells, *The Last War*, 23.

43. Glenn Seaborg, 'Nuclear Fission and Transuranium Elements Fifty Years Ago', *Journal of Chemical Education*, 66 (May 1989), 380.

44. Wells, *The Last War*, 21.

45. ibid., 23.

Chapter 12

1. Szilard, writing to an unknown addressee from the Imperial Hotel, 11 Aug. 1933; in CW2, 35.

2. H. G. Wells, *The Shape of Things to Come: The Ultimate Revolution* (London: Hutchinson, 1933), book 2, ch. 9, 214–15.

3. E. M. Forster, *Spectator* (17 Mar. 1933), 368–9; quoted in Martin Ceadel, 'Popular Fiction and the Next War, 1918–39', in Frank Gloversmith, ed., *Class, Culture and Social Change: A New View of the 1930s* (Brighton: Harvester, 1980), 169.

4. Ladbroke Black, *The Poison War* (London: Stanley Paul & Co.,1933), 252; in Ceadel, 161.

5. 'Major von Helders' [Robert Knauss], *Luftkrieg-1936: Die Zertrümmerung von Paris* (Berlin: Verlag Tradition Wilhelm Kolk, 1932); promptly published in English as *The War in the Air, 1936*, trans. Claud W. Sykes (John Hamilton: London, 1932); see I. F. Clarke, *Voices Prophesying War: Future Wars 1763–3749* (Oxford University Press, 1992), 155.

6. 'Miles' [Stephen Southwold], *The Gas War of 1940* (London: Scholartis Press, 1931); quoted in Clarke, 159.

7. Ewald Banse, *Wehrwissenschaft* (Leipzig: Armanen, 1933); quoted in 'German War Science: Nazi Manual for Schools', *Times* (6 Sep. 1933), 9.

8. Harold Nicolson, *Public Faces* (London: Constable, 1932), 18.

9. ibid., 97.

10. Aldous Huxley, *Brave New World* (London: Penguin, 1963; 1st edn 1932), 179.

11. Huxley, 'Foreword', *Brave New World*, 9.

12. 'Archbishop's Appeal', *Times* (28 Dec. 1937), 9.

13. Winston S. Churchill, Departmental minute, War Office, Churchill papers: 16/16, 12 May 1919; quoted in Martin Gilbert, *Winston S. Churchill, Companion volume 4, Part 1: January 1917–June 1919* (London: Heinemann, 1977), 649.

14. Nichols and Browne, *Wings over Europe* (1928), in Montrose J. Moses, ed., *Dramas of Modernism and their Forerunners* (Boston: Little, Brown, & Co., 1931), 518.

15. ibid., 519.

16. ibid., 511.

17. ibid., 544–5.

18. Frédéric Joliot, 'Chemical Evidence of the Transmutation of Elements', Nobel Lecture, 12 Dec. 1935: see <http://nobelprize.org/chemistry/laureates/1935/joliot-lecture.html>.

19. Szilard, taped interview, May 1960; in CW2, 19.

20. Szilard, CW2, 19–20.

21. CW2, 18.

22. CW1, 529, 615.

23. Isaac R. Nathanson, 'The World Aflame', *Amazing Stories* (Jan. 1935), 45–6.

24. ibid., 47.

25. ibid., 48.

26. Quoted in A. S. Eve, *Rutherford* (Cambridge University Press, 1939), 102.

27. Nathanson, 52.

28. ibid., 44.

29. ibid., 76.

30. ibid., 75.

31. This response (recalled by Szilard in 1949) was made in 1938; quoted in Lewis L. Strauss, *Men and Decisions* (London: Macmillan, 1963), 165.

32. William Lanouette with Bela Silard, *Genius in the Shadows: A Biography of Leo Szilard, The Man Behind the Bomb* (University of Chicago Press, 1994; 1st edn 1992), 142.

33. Quoted in Eric Lax, *The Mould in Dr Florey's Coat* (London: Little, Brown & Co., 2004), 207.

34. Lanouette, 143.

35. George Marx, *The Voice of the Martians* (Budapest: Akadémiai Kiadó, 1997), 28.

36. Szilard, taped interview, May 1960; in CW2, 20.

37. Bohr to Szilard, 4 Feb. 1936; in Leo Szilard Papers, Mandeville Special

Collections Library, Geisel Library, University of California, San Diego, box 4, folder 34; quoted in Lanouette, 157.

38. James Whale, dir., *The Invisible Man* (Universal, 1933).

39. This is the view of the editors of Szilard's collected works: *CW2*, 19, n.

40. Szilard, *CW1*, 186.

41. Szilard, 'Draft of Memorandum on the Sino-Japanese War', 24 Apr. 1934; in *CW2*, 37–8.

Chapter 13

1. Jack London, 'The Unparalleled Invasion', written in 1906, 1st published in *McClure's* in 1910; in *The Short Stories of Jack London* (New York: Macmillan, 1990), 278.

2. Jack London, 'The Yellow Peril', *San Francisco Examiner* (25 Sep. 1904); see H. Bruce Franklin, *War Stars: The Superweapon and the American Imagination* (New York: Oxford University Press, 1988), 37.

3. London, 'The Unparalleled Invasion', 272, 275–6, 274.

4. ibid., 277.

5. ibid., 279.

6. ibid., 281.

7. United States Chemical Corps, *Summary of Major Events and Problems, Fiscal Year 1959* (Edgewood, Md: Army Chemical Center, 1960); quoted in Robert Harris and Jeremy Paxman, *A Higher Form of Killing: The Secret History of Chemical and Biological Warfare* (London: Arrow, 2002), 169–70.

8. Wendy Barnaby, *The Plague Makers: The Secret World of Biological Warfare* (New York: Continuum, 2000), 9–11.

9. Truman to Elizabeth Virginia (Bess) Wallace, 10 Jan. 1911; quoted in Robert H. Ferrell, ed., *Dear Bess: The Letters from Harry to Bess Truman, 1910–1959* (New York: Norton, 1983), 19.

10. Truman to Wallace, 26 May 1913; quoted in Ferrell, 126.

11. Truman to Wallace, 26 Jan. 1911; quoted in Ferrell, 21.

12. Truman to Wallace, 22 June 1911; quoted in Ferrell, 39.

13. Tennyson, *Locksley Hall*, 1842, lines 119–30 (see e.g. <http://rpo.library.utoronto.ca/poem/2161.html>).

14. Simon Newcomb, *His Wisdom The Defender* (New York: Arno Press, 1975; 1st edn 1900), 199.

15. Sheldon H. Harris, *Factories of Death: Japanese Biological Warfare, 1932–45, and the American Cover-up* (London: Routledge, 1997), 5.

16. ibid., 14.

17. In the words of Major General Matsumura Chisho: ibid., 32.

18. ibid., 35.

19. Edison, quoted in *NYT* (16 Oct. 1915); cited in Franklin, 72.

20. Harris, 44.

21. ibid., 42.

22. Brian Holmsten and Alex Lubertozzi, eds., *The Complete War of the Worlds* (Napierville, Ill.: Sourcebooks, 2001), 47.

23. Robert Markley, *Dying Planet: Mars in Science and the Imagination* (Durham, NC: Duke University Press, 2005), 204.

24. 'Radio Play Upsets Americans – "Martian Invasion" of United States Taken Seriously', *Manchester Guardian* (1 Nov. 1938): see <http://books.guardian.co.uk/departments/classics/story/0,,109739,00.html>.

25. 'Mr Wells "Deeply Concerned": "Unwarranted" Rewriting of his Novel', *Manchester Guardian*, 1 Nov. 1938: see <http://books.guardian.co.uk/departments/classics/story/0,,109739,00.html>.

26. Markley, 204.

27. ibid., 205.

28. F. N. Maude, 'Can Science Abolish War?', *Contemporary Review*, 93 (Apr. 1908), 471.

29. *McClure's* (1909), quoted in I. F. Clarke, *Voices Prophesying War: Future Wars 1763–3749* (Oxford University Press, 1992), 134.

30. Orville Wright, quoted in Roger Bilstein, *Flight in America 1900–1983: From the Wrights to the Astronauts* (Baltimore: Johns Hopkins University Press, 1984), 39.

31. Theodore M. Knappen, 'Chemical Warfare and Disarmament', *Independent*, 107 (22 Oct. 1921), 73; quoted in Gilbert F. Whittemore, Jr, 'World War I, Poison Gas Research, and the Ideals of American Chemists', *Social Studies of Science*, 5, no. 2 (May 1975), 158.

32. Will Irwin, *'The Next War': An Appeal to Common Sense* (New York: E. P Dutton & Co., 1921), 44; quoted in Hugh R. Slotten, 'Humane Chemistry or Scientific Barbarism? American Responses to World War I Poison Gas, 1915–1930', *Journal of American History*, 77 (Sep. 1990), 488.

33. J. B. Priestley, *The Doomsday Men: An Adventure* (London: Heinemann, 1938), 302.

34. Damian Thompson, *The End of Time: Faith and Fear in the Shadow of the Millennium* (London: Sinclair-Stevenson, 1996), 252.

35. Priestley, 239.

36. ibid., 32–3.

37. ibid., 33, 280.

38. ibid., 289.

39. ibid., 262.

40. Szilard, CW2, 18.

41. Victor Weisskopf, quoted in Charles Weiner, ed., *Exploring the History of Nuclear Physics* (New York: American Institute of Physics, 1972), 188; cited in Richard Rhodes, *The Making of the Atomic Bomb* (London: Penguin, 1988), 206.

42. Segrè, quoted in Robert Jungk, *Brighter Than a Thousand Suns: A Personal History of the Atomic Scientists* (San Diego: Harcourt, 1986; 1st edn 1956), 52.

43. Otto R. Frisch, *What Little I Remember* (Cambridge University Press, 1979), 114.

44. Frisch, 115.

45. Hahn to Meitner, 19 Dec. 1938; quoted in Otto Hahn, *My Life*, trans. Ernst Kaiser and Eithne Wilkins (London: Macdonald, 1970), 151.

46. Frisch, 115.

47. ibid., 116.

48. Frisch and Meitner realized this before their chemist colleagues in Berlin. It is suggested in their joint paper, 'Disintegration of Uranium by Neutrons: A New Type of Nuclear Reaction', *Nature*, 143 (11 Feb. 1939), 239–40, written in the first two weeks of January.

49. Frisch, 116.

50. ibid.

51. Meitner to Hahn, 3 Jan. 1939; in Ruth Lewin Sime, *Lise Meitner: A Life in Physics* (Berkeley: University of California Press, 1996), 242.

52. Einstein, quoted in William L. Laurence, *Dawn over Zero: The Story of Atomic Bomb* (London: Museum, 1947), 32.

53. Laura Fermi, *Atoms in the Family: My Life with Enrico Fermi* (University of Chicago Press, 1961; 1st edn 1954), 154.

54. Eugene P. Wigner and Andrew Szanton, *The Recollections of Eugene P. Wigner* (New York: Plenum, 1992), 193.

55. Szilard interview, May 1960; in CW2, 53.

56. Wigner and Szanton, 193–4.

57. Szilard to Strauss, 25 Jan. 1939; in CW2, 62.

58. Szilard to Director of Navy Contracts, 26 Jan. 1939; in CW2, 60. Szilard wrote to explain the situation on 2 Feb. 1939: CW2, 61.

59. Headlines quoted in William Lanouette with Bela Silard, *Genius in the Shadows: A Biography of Leo Szilard, The Man Behind the Bomb* (University of Chicago Press, 1994; 1st edn 1992), 180; and Lennard Bickel, *The Deadly Element: The Story of Uranium* (London: Macmillan, 1980), 103.

60. 'Is World on Brink of Releasing Atomic Power?', *Science Service* (30 Jan. 1939); quoted in Lanouette, 184.

61. *An Early Time – Edward Teller*, Los Alamos Laboratory film (n.d.); quoted in Lanouette, 181.

62. Quoted in Bickel, 105.

63. Joseph Rotblat, 'Leaving the Bomb Project', *BAS*, 41 (Aug. 1985), 17.

64. Szilard, in *CW*2, 54.

65. Lew Kowarski, interview in Bickel, 110.

66. ibid., 111.

67. Quoted in Lewis L. Strauss, *Men and Decisions* (London: Macmillan 1963), 165.

68. Szilard, memo to A. H. Compton, 12 Nov. 1942; in *CW*2, 55. It is interesting to note that this was written before even the Chicago pile had been built.

69. Paul Harteck to War Office, 24 Apr. 1939; quoted in Peter Wyden, *Day One: Before Hiroshima and After* (New York: Simon & Schuster, 1984), 32.

70. *NYT* (30 Apr. 1939), 35; quoted in Rhodes, 297.

71. Wigner to Szilard, 17 Apr. 1939; in *CW*2, 87.

72. Wigner and Szanton, 198.

73. ibid., 199.

74. Quoted in P. D. Smith, *Einstein* (London: Haus Publishing, 2003), 121.

75. Quoted in Wigner and Szanton, 200.

76. Szilard, 'Memorandum about the Einstein Letter', 18 Apr. 1955; in *CW*2, 83.

77. Szilard, taped interview, May 1960; in *CW*2, 84.

78. ibid.

79. Janet Coatesworth, interview in Lanouette, 202.

80. Einstein to Roosevelt, 2 Aug. 1939; in *CW*2, 95. A facsimile of the letter is downloadable from <http://www.lanl.gov/history/road/birthofmodern physics.shtml>.

Chapter 14

1. Pierrepont B. Noyes, *The Pallid Giant: A Tale of Yesterday and Tomorrow* (New York: Revell, 1927), 21.

2. ibid., 24.

3. ibid., 23.

4. ibid., 197–8.

5. ibid., 259.

6. William L. Laurence, *Dawn over Zero: The Story of the Atomic Bomb* (London: Museum, 1947), 97.

7. ibid., pp. xvii, 180.

8. ibid., 152.

9. 'Leo Szilard Dies; A-Bomb Physicist', *NYT* (31 May 1964), 77.

10. Edward Teller with Judith Shoolery, *Memoirs: A Twentieth-Century Journey in Science and Politics* (Cambridge, Mass.: Perseus, 2001), 148.

11. Szilard, taped interview, May 1960; in CW2, 85.

12. Eugene P. Wigner and Andrew Szanton, *The Recollections of Eugene P. Wigner* (New York: Plenum, 1992), 203.

13. Szilard, taped interview, May 1960; in CW2, 85.

14. Wigner and Szanton, 203.

15. Teller, 149.

16. On this crucial failure, see especially Paul Lawrence Rose, *Heisenberg and the Nazi Atomic Bomb Project: A Study in German Culture* (Berkeley: University of California Press, 1998), 134–5.

17. Interview with Bethe, in William Lanouette with Bela Silard, *Genius in the Shadows: A Biography of Leo Szilard, The Man Behind the Bomb* (University of Chicago Press, 1994; 1st edn 1992), 222.

18. Interview with Elizabeth Silard, in Lanouette, 224.

19. Otto R. Frisch, *What Little I Remember* (Cambridge University Press, 1979), 126.

20. O. R. Frisch and R. Peierls, 'On the Construction of a "Super-bomb", Based on a Nuclear Chain Reaction in Uranium', memo, Mar. 1940; in Ferenc Morton Szasz, *British Scientists and the Manhattan Project: The Los Alamos Years* (Basingstoke: Macmillan, 1992), 143.

21. ibid., 144, 145.

22. ibid., 144–5, 146.

23. Winston S. Churchill, *The Grand Alliance* (Boston: Houghton Mifflin, 1950), 814–15.

24. Oliphant interview; in Lennard Bickel, *The Deadly Element: The Story of Uranium* (London: Macmillan, 1980), 164.

25. Mark Oliphant, 'The Beginning: Chadwick and the Neutron', *BAS*, 38 (Dec. 1982), 17.

26. Lawrence, quoted in Bickel, 165.

27. Conant, quoted in James G. Hershberg, *James B. Conant: Harvard to Hiroshima and the Making of the Nuclear Age* (Stanford University Press, 1993), 153.

28. Szilard, interviewed in 1956; in CW2, 144.

29. Szilard to Compton, 12 Nov. 1942; in CW2, 146.

30. Richard Rhodes, *The Making of the Atomic Bomb* (London: Penguin, 1988), 378–9.

31. Szilard to Bush, 26 May 1942; in CW2, 152.

32. Quoted in Alice Kimball Smith, 'The Elusive Dr Szilard', *Harper's Magazine*, 221 (July 1960), 80.

33. Compton to Bush, 1 June 1942; in Lanouette, 233.

34. Teller, 149.

35. Szilard, 'What Is Wrong with Us?', 21 Sep. 1942; in CW2, 156.

36. Szilard to A. H. Compton, 25 Nov. 1942; in CW2, 160.

37. Szilard, 'What Is Wrong with Us?', 21 Sep. 1942; in CW2, 154.

38. ibid., CW2, 153, 154.

39. Arthur Train and Robert Williams Wood, *The Man Who Rocked the Earth* (New York: Doubleday, 1915), 142.

40. Szilard to A. H. Compton, 25 Nov. 1942; in CW2, 160.

41. Lt Col. Kenneth D. Nichols, quoted in Rhodes, 426.

42. Stephanie Groueff, *Manhattan Project: The Untold Story of the Making of the Atomic Bomb* (New York: Bantam, 1968), 35–6.

43. Samuel K. Allison, interview with A. K. Smith; quoted in Lanouette, 238.

44. Groves, quoted in Carol S. Gruber, 'Manhattan Project Maverick: The Case of Leo Szilard', *Prologue*, 15, no. 2 (summer 1983), 86; cited in Lanouette, 240.

45. Confidential report, June 1943; in CW3, p. xxxiii.

46. Henry D. Smyth, 'The Stockpiling and Rationing of Scientific Manpower', *BAS*, 7 (Feb. 1951), 38.

Chapter 15

1. Bethe, quoted in Jeremy Bernstein, *Hans Bethe: Prophet of Energy* (New York: Basic, 1980), 71.

2. Arthur Holly Compton, *Atomic Quest: A Personal Narrative* (London: Oxford University Press, 1956), 127–8.

3. Heisenberg (in 1946), recalling von Weizsäcker's idea of an '*Atomsprengstoff*'; quoted in Paul Lawrence Rose, *Heisenberg and the Nazi Atomic Bomb Project: A Study in German Culture* (Berkeley: University of California Press, 1998), 14.

4. Heisenberg, 'The Work on Uranium Problems', June 1942; this lecture has only recently been rediscovered: see Rainer Karlsch and Mark Walker, 'New Light on Hitler's Bomb', *Physics World* (June 2005), <http://physicsweb.org/articles/world/18/6/3/1#Pwnew2_06-05>.

5. Albert Speer, *Inside the Third Reich* (London: Macmillan, 1970), 227.

6. Hitler, Aug. 1941; quoted in Michael J. Neufeld, 'The Guided Missile and the Third Reich: Peenemünde and the Forging of a Technological Revolution',

in Monika Renneberg and Mark Walker, eds., *Science, Technology and National Socialism* (Cambridge University Press, 1994), 62.

7. Neufeld, 51.

8. Tom Lehrer, 'Wernher von Braun', on *That Was the Year That Was* (Reprise R/RS 6179, 1965), lyrics as reproduced in Tom Lehrer, *Too Many Songs by Tom Lehrer* (New York: Pantheon, 1981), 125.

9. Carl Sagan, letter to Frederick I. Ordway, III, 30 Nov. 1989; in Ernst Stuhlinger and Frederick I. Ordway, III, *Wernher von Braun: Crusader for Space* (Malabar: Krieger, 1996), 251.

10. Aldous Huxley, *Brave New World Revisited* (New York: Harper & Row, 1989; 1st edn 1958), 94.

11. Jeremy Bernstein, *Oppenheimer: Portrait of an Enigma* (London: Duckworth, 2004), 76.

12. Groves, quoted in John Canaday, *The Nuclear Muse: Literature, Physics and the First Atomic Bombs* (Madison: University of Wisconsin Press, 2000), 143.

13. Groves interview, 8 Mar. 1946; quoted in Richard Rhodes, *The Making of the Atomic Bomb* (London: Penguin, 1988), 448–9.

14. William L. Laurence, *Dawn over Zero: The Story of the Atomic Bomb* (London: Museum 1947), 149.

15. Szilard, quoted in Nuel Pharr Davis, *Lawrence and Oppenheimer* (New York: Simon & Schuster, 1968), 163.

16. Edward Teller with Judith Shoolery, *Memoirs: A Twentieth-Century Journey in Science and Politics* (Cambridge, Mass.: Perseus, 2001), 165.

17. Colgate, quoted in Teller, 166.

18. C. P. Snow, 'A New Means of Destruction?', *Discovery*, ns 2, no. 18 (Sep. 1939), 443.

19. ibid., 444.

20. Douglas W. F. Mayer, 'Energy from Matter', *Discovery*, ns 2, no. 18 (Sep. 1939), 460.

21. 'Civilian', 'The New Weapon', *Times* (28 Sep. 1939), 9.

22. Douglas W. F. Mayer, 'Energy from Matter: Some Recent Developments', *Discovery*, 2, no. 20 (Nov. 1939), 573.

23. Laurence, p. xiii.

24. ibid., p. xv.

25. William L. Laurence, 'Vast Power Source in Atomic Energy Opened by Science', *NYT* (5 May 1940), 1, 51.

26. Laurence, *Dawn Over Zero*, p. xv.

27. ibid.

28. 'V-3?', *Time* (27 Nov. 1944), 88.

29. ibid. On recent discoveries of documents which suggest that German scientists may have attempted to use high explosives to create implosion devices, see Karlsch and Walker, 'New Light on Hitler's Bomb', <http://physicsweb.org/articles/world/18/6/3/1#Pwnew2_06–05>.

30. Louis N. Ridenour, 'Nuclear Fission in Lay Language', *Saturday Review*, 30 (28 June 1947), 15.

31. Robert A. Heinlein, 'Blowups Happen', *Astounding Science Fiction* (Sep. 1940); in Groff Conklin, ed., *The Golden Age of Science Fiction* (New York: Bonanza, 1980; 1st edn 1946), 103, 105, 114, 105.

32. For example, the novels *Command the Morning* (London: Methuen, 1959) by Pearl S. Buck and most recently *Oh Pure and Radiant Heart* (London: Heinemann, 2006) by Lydia Millet. Szilard also makes an appearance (in the bath) in Roland Joffé's film *Shadow Makers* (Paramount, 1989).

33. Don A. Stuart, 'Atomic Power', *Astounding Science Fiction* (Dec. 1934); in Conklin, 140–51. A. E. van Vogt, 'The Great Engine', *Astounding Science Fiction* (July 1943); in van Vogt, *Away and Beyond* (New York: Berkley, 1959; 1st edn 1952), 5–34. Theodore Sturgeon, 'Artnan Process', *Astounding Science Fiction* (June 1941); in Sturgeon, *Starshine* (London: Gollancz, 1969), 45–70.

34. Clifford D. Simak, 'Lobby', *Astounding Science Fiction* (Apr. 1944); in Conklin, 95–6, 90, 93.

35. ibid., 95–6.

36. Cleve Cartmill, 'Deadline', *Astounding Science Fiction* (Mar. 1944); in Conklin, 77, 78.

37. ibid., 82–3.

38. Heinlein, 'Introduction: Pandora's Box' (first published as 'Where To?', 1952), in *The Worlds of Robert Heinlein* (London: New English Library, 1970), 9.

39. Anson MacDonald, 'Solution Unsatisfactory', *Astounding Science Fiction* (May 1941); in Conklin, 4.

40. ibid., 6.

41. ibid., 6, 7, 8, 10.

42. ibid., 12.

43. ibid., 13, 16.

44. ibid., 16, 13, 18.

45. ibid., 21.

46. On censorship, see Greg Mitchell, 'Hiroshima Cover-up Exposed', *E & P Online* (1 Aug. 2005), available at <http://www.wagingpeace.org/articles/2005/08/01_mitchell_hiroshima-cover-up-exposed.htm>.

47. MacDonald, 21.

48. ibid., 26, 27.
49. ibid., 32, 33, 35.
50. John W. Campbell, 'Concerning Science Fiction' (1946), in Conklin, p. xi.
51. National Academy of Sciences report, 17 May 1941; quoted in Rhodes, 365.
52. *PIC* (22 July 1941), 6–8; quoted in William Lanouette with Bela Silard, *Genius in the Shadows: A Biography of Leo Szilard, The Man Behind the Bomb* (University of Chicago Press, 1994; 1st edn 1992), 226.
53. Henry D. Smyth, *Atomic Energy for Military Purposes: The Official Report on the Development of the Atomic Bomb* (Princeton: United States Government Printing Office, 1945); quoted in Conklin, 3.
54. Davis, 182.
55. Oppenheimer to Fermi, 25 May 1943; quoted in Joseph Rotblat, 'Leaving the Bomb Project', *BAS*, 41 (Aug. 1985), 18.
56. ibid.
57. 'General MacArthur Complained of British Perfidy', *Times* (9 Apr. 1964), 11.
58. Quoted in Spencer R. Weart, *Scientists in Power* (Cambridge, Mass.: Harvard University Press, 1988), 96.
59. Robert Wilson to H. D. Smyth, 27 Nov. 1943; quoted in Canaday, 206.
60. Sturgeon, quoted in Mike Ashley, *The Time Machines: The Story of the Science-Fiction Pulp Magazines from the Beginning to 1950* (Liverpool University Press, 2000), 168–9.
61. Campbell, 'Atomic Age', *Astounding Science Fiction*, 36, no. 3 (Nov. 1945), 4–6.

Chapter 16

1. Otto R. Frisch, *What Little I Remember* (Cambridge University Press, 1979), 121.
2. Wells, *The Shape of Things to Come: The Ultimate Revolution* (London: Hutchinson, 1933), book 2, ch. 4, 169.
3. Edward Teller with Allen Brown, *The Legacy of Hiroshima* (New York: Doubleday, 1962), 211.
4. Quoted in George Marx, *The Voice of the Martians* (Budapest: Akadémiai Kiadó, 1997), 59.
5. Laura Fermi, *Atoms in the Family: My Life with Enrico Fermi* (University of Chicago Press, 1961; 1st edn 1954), 206.
6. Quoted in Steven Shapin, 'Don't Let That Crybaby in Here Again', *London Review of Books* (7 Sep. 2000), 16.

7. Ruth Marshak, 'Secret City', in Jane Wilson and Charlotte Serber, eds., *Standing By and Making Do* (Los Alamos Historical Society, 1988), 2.

8. Serber, quoted in Edward U. Condon, 'The Los Alamos Primer', Los Alamos Scientific Laboratory, 1; quoted in Richard Rhodes, *The Making of the Atomic Bomb* (London: Penguin, 1988), 460.

9. Quoted in Rhodes, 464.

10. Leslie R. Groves, *Now It Can Be Told* (New York: Harper & Row, 1962), 296.

11. William L. Laurence, *Dawn over Zero: The Story of the Atomic Bomb* (London: Museum 1947), 3.

12. ibid., 6.

13. Isidor I. Rabi, *Science: The Center of Culture* (New York: World Publishing, 1970), 138.

14. Emilio Segrè, *Enrico Fermi: Physicist* (University of Chicago Press, 1970), 147.

15. Morrison, quoted in Rhodes, 673.

16. Fermi, 239.

17. Laurence, 9.

18. ibid., 10–11.

19. Kistiakowsky, quoted in ibid., 9.

20. Farrell, quoted in ibid., 161–2.

21. Farrell, quoted in Peter Wyden, *Day One: Before Hiroshima and After* (New York: Simon & Schuster, 1984), 212.

22. Conant, quoted in James G. Hershberg, *James B Conant: Harvard to Hiroshima and the Making of the Nuclear Age* (Stanford University Press, 1993), 232.

23. Ferenc Morton Szasz, *The Day the Sun Rose Twice* (Albuquerque: University of New Mexico Press, 1984), 85.

24. McMillan's statement is online: 'Impressions of Trinity Test', 19 July 1945 <http://www.dannen.com/decision/mcmillan.html>.

25. Anderson, quoted in Laurence, 163.

26. V. Weisskopf, Inter-office memorandum to Lt Taylor, 24 July 1945: <http://www.dannen.com/decision/weisskopf.html>.

27. Victor Weisskopf, *The Joy of Insight: Passions of a Physicist* (New York: Basic, 1991), 152.

28. Bhagavad Gita, ch. 11, verse 32.

29. Oppenheimer, 'The Atom Bomb and College Education' (1946); quoted in Rhodes, 676.

30. Oppenheimer to Groves, 20 Oct. 1962; quoted in Rhodes, 571–2.

31. Frederick Soddy, *The Interpretation of Radium: Being the Substance of*

Six Free Popular Experimental Lectures Delivered at the University of Glasgow (London: John Murray, 1912; 1st edn 1909), 251.

32. John Hersey, 'Profiles: Mr. President', *New Yorker* (7 Apr. 1951), 50.

33. Tennyson, *Locksley Hall*, lines 123, 128.

34. Baldwin, quoted in *Bomber Command Continues: The Air Ministry Account of the Rising Offensive Against Germany July 1941–June 1942* (London: His Majesty's Stationery Office, 1942), 49–50.

35. Frederick W. Lanchester, *Aircraft in Warfare: The Dawn of the Fourth Arm* (London: Constable, 1916), 191f; quoted in Sven Lindqvist, *A History of Bombing*, trans. Linda Haverty Rugg (London: Granta, 2002), para. 93.

36. Freeman Dyson, *Weapons and Hope* (New York: Harper & Row, 1984); quoted in Lindqvist, para. 205.

37. 'Now Terror, Truly', *Newsweek* (26 Feb. 1945), 34, 37.

38. Vonnegut, quoted in Rhodes, 593.

39. Kurt Vonnegut, *Slaughterhouse 5* (London: Vintage, 2000), 130.

40. Vonnegut, quoted in Rhodes, 593.

41. Vonnegut, TV interview by James Naughtie, *Culture Show* (BBC2, 10 Feb. 2005).

42. Winston Churchill, memo to Gen Ismay, 28 Mar. 1945, UK Public Record Office, CAB 121/3; quoted in Frederick Taylor, *Dresden: Tuesday 13 February 1945* (London: Bloomsbury, 2004), 430.

43. Curtis E. LeMay with McKinlay Kantor, *Mission with LeMay: My Story* (New York: Doubleday, 1965), 352; quoted in Rhodes, 596.

44. US Strategic Bombing Survey #96; quoted in Rhodes, 599.

45. Max Born, *My Life: Recollections of a Nobel Laureate* (London: Taylor & Francis, 1978; 1st edn 1975), 261.

46. Protocol III of the 'Convention on Certain Conventional Weapons', agreed in 1980, covers 'Prohibitions or Restrictions on Use of Incendiary Weapons'.

47. R. Peierls, review of Rhodes, *The Making of the Atomic Bomb*, *New York Review of Books* (5 Nov. 1987), 48.

48. Churchill, quoted in Ferenc Morton Szasz, *British Scientists and the Manhattan Project: The Los Alamos Years* (Basingstoke: Macmillan, 1992), 30.

49. Joseph Rotblat, 'Leaving the Bomb Project', *BAS*, 41 (Aug. 1985), 18.

50. Rhodes, 459.

51. Rotblat, 18–19.

52. L. R. Groves, 'Memorandum to the Secretary of War', 23 Apr. 1945; quoted in Arjun Makhijani, '"Always" the target?', *BAS*, 51, no. 3 (1995), 23.

53. Rotblat in ibid., 24.

54. Memorandum by Groves, Military Policy Committee, 5 May 1943; quoted in Makhijani, 24. Bush and Conant were present at the meeting of the Military Policy Committee.

55. James F. Byrnes, 'Memorandum for the President', 3 Mar. 1945; quoted in Makhijani, 26.

56. David Robertson, *Sly and Able: A Political Biography of James F. Byrnes* (New York: Norton, 1994), 410.

57. Szasz, *British Scientists and the Manhattan Project*, 30.

58. Szilard, 'Atomic Bombs and the Postwar Position of the United States in the World', Spring 1945; 1st published in *BAS*, 5 (Dec. 1947), 351–3; in *CW*2, 196 (emphasis in original).

59. ibid., *CW*2, 197–8.

60. Szilard, document prepared for President Roosevelt but subsequently given to Byrnes (Mar. 1945); in *CW*2, 206.

61. Szilard, taped interview, May 1960; in *CW*2, 184–5.

62. ibid., 186.

63. Szilard, transcript of magnetic recordings made May 1956; *CW*2, 186.

64. 'avoid mass slaughter': Szilard, 'The Story of a Petition' (28 July 1946); 'what we did not discuss': interview in *US News and World Report* (15 Aug. 1960), 68; both in *CW*2, 186.

65. Szilard, taped interview, May 1960; in *CW*2, 187.

66. Szilard to Teller, dated 4 July 1945, but according to Teller the letter arrived in late June; its full text is in Edward Teller with Judith Shoolery, *Memoirs: A Twentieth-Century Journey in Science and Politics* (Cambridge, Mass.: Perseus, 2001), 204–5.

67. Teller to Szilard, 2 July 1945; in *CW*2, 208–9.

68. Szilard to Ed Creutz, 10 July 1945; in *CW*2, 212–13.

69. Szilard, 'A Petition to the President of the United States', 17 July 1945; in *CW*2, 211.

70. The Hiroshima bomb, 'Little Boy', contained about 130 lb of uranium-235 altogether. See Richard L. Garwin and Georges Charpak, *Megawatts and Megatons: The Future of Nuclear Power and Nuclear Weapons* (University of Chicago Press, 2002), 34–5, 59.

71. The Committee for the Compilation of Materials on Damage Caused by the Atomic Bombs in Hiroshima and Nagasaki, *The Impact of the A-bomb: Hiroshima and Nagasaki, 1945–85* (Tokyo: Iwanami Shoten, 1985); quoted in James N. Yamazaki and Louis B. Fleming, *Children of the Atomic Bomb: An American Physician's Memoir of Nagasaki, Hiroshima, and the Marshall Islands* (Durham, NC: Duke University Press, 1995), 73.

72. The Committee for the Compilation of Materials on Damage . . . ; quoted in Rachelle Linner, *City of Silence: Listening to Hiroshima* (New York: Orbis, 1995), 18.

73. Seiko Ikeda interviewed by Miyko Yamada, 'The A-Bomb Survivors', *Independent* (2 July 2005).

74. Kevin Burke, ed., *Pedro Arrupe: Essential Writings* (Maryknoll, NY: Orbis, 2004), 50.

75. Wilfred Burchett, 'Warning to the World', *Daily Express* (5 Sep. 1945); in Wilfred Burchett, *Shadows of Hiroshima* (London: Verso, 1983), 35.

76. Brig. Gen. T. F. Farrell as reported in 'The Greatest Weapon: Conquest by Atom', *Newsweek*, 26 (20 Aug. 1945), 22.

77. For casualty figures in both cities, see Committee for the Compilation of Materials on Damage Caused by the Atomic Bombs in Hiroshima and Nagasaki, *Hiroshima and Nagasaki: The Physical, Medical, and Social Effects of the Atomic Bombings* (New York: Basic Books, 1981), 113, 367–9.

78. Manhattan Engineer District, 'The Atomic Bombings of Hiroshima and Nagasaki', 29 June 1946: <http://www.atomicarchive.com/Docs/MED/index.shtml>.

79. ibid.

80. ibid.

81. Laurence, 196.

82. Robert Shaplen, 'Boiling Nagasaki Inferno', *Newsweek*, 26 (20 Aug. 1945), 23.

83. 'White House Press Release on Hiroshima: Statement by the President of the United States', 6 Aug. 1945. The full text can be seen at <http://www.atomic archive.com/Docs/PRHiroshima.shtml>.

84. Jacob Bronowski, *Science and Human Values* (London: Hutchinson, 1961), 13.

85. Manhattan Engineer District.

Chapter 17

1. Hal Boyle, 'Washington Under the Bomb', *Collier's* (27 Oct. 1951); quoted in Lewis H. Lapham, ed., *The End of the World* (New York: Thomas Dunne, 2000), 257–8.

2. Wheeler to Feynman, 29 Mar. 1951; Michelle Feynman, ed., *Richard P. Feynman: Don't You Have Time to Think?* (London: Allen Lane, 2005), 83–4.

3. Quoted in Laurie Johnston, 'Einstein Sees Bid to "Annihilation" in Hydrogen Bomb', *NYT* (13 Feb. 1950), 1.

4. Donald Porter Geddes, ed., *The Atomic Age Opens* (New York: Pocket Books, 1945), 40.

5. *New York Herald Tribune*; in Geddes, 41–2.

6. John W. Campbell, interviewed in *PM* (7 Aug. 1945); in Geddes, 159–61.

7. Stanley Baldwin, 10 Nov. 1932; in *Parliamentary Debates*, 5th series, vol. 270, House of Commons (London: His Majesty's Stationery Office, 1932), 631.

8. Brig. Gen. David Sarnoff writing in the *NYT* (10 Aug. 1945); in Geddes, 163.

9. Atomic Energy Commission, 'What Would Happen to Washington Under Atomic Attack?', in *The H Bomb* (New York: Didier, 1950), 34–40, here 36 (emphasis in original).

10. *Atomic Alert* (Encyclopaedia Britannica Films, 1951).

11. Clement Atlee, 'Memorandum by the Prime Minister', 28 Aug. 1945; UK Public Record Office, CAB 130/3; quoted in Peter Hennessy, *The Secret State: Whitehall and the Cold War* (London: Penguin, 2003), 46.

12. Ernest Bevin's comment was made during discussions in the Cabinet Committee on Atomic Energy (GEN 75) on 25 Oct. 1946, as recalled by Sir Michael Perrin on *Timewatch*, BBC 2, 29 Sep. 1982; quoted in Hennessy, 48.

13. Hennessy, 125.

14. R. W. B. Clarke to Sir Alexander Johnston, 10 Sep. 1954; UK Public Record Office, T 227/1129.

15. Chan Davis, 'The Nightmare' (1946), in Gregory Benford and Martin Harry Greenberg, eds., *Nuclear War* (New York: Ace Books, 1988), 15.

16. 'Ministry of Defence Imports Research Committee', 29 Nov. 1950; UK Public Record Office, IR(50)7; in Hennessy, p. xix.

17. 'Search of Batory Yields No Bomb; Ship is Detained Four Hours in Bay', *NYT* (6 Aug. 1950), 1.

18. 'Ministry of Defence Imports Research Committee'; in Hennessy, p. xix.

19. Robert Aldrich, dir., *Kiss Me Deadly* (1955, United Artists).

20. Philip Wylie, *Tomorrow!* (New York: Popular Library, 1963; 1st edn 1954), 6.

21. ibid., 40.

22. ibid., 209–10.

23. ibid., 211, 229, 264.

24. Dr Zorbaugh, 'The Atom Bomb – The End or Rebirth of Civilization?' *WNEW* (New York) (10 Aug. 1945); in Geddes, 174.

25. Hennessy, 151.

26. Stephen I. Schwartz, Foreword to Douglas L. Keeney, *The Doomsday Scenario: The Official Doomsday Scenario Written by the United States*

Government During the Cold War (St Paul, Minn.: MBI Publishing, 2002), 9.

27. Keeney, 62.

28. ibid., 66.

29. ibid., 76.

30. ibid., 33.

31. Poul Anderson, *Thermonuclear Warfare* (Derby, Conn.: Monarch, 1963), 33.

32. Anderson, 11.

33. Victor Adamsky, interviewed in Richard Rhodes, *Dark Sun: The Making of the Hydrogen Bomb* (New York: Touchstone, 1996), 514.

34. Adamsky, interviewed in Rhodes, 582.

35. Szilard, in Hans Bethe, Harrison Brown, Frederick Seitz, Leo Szilard, 'The facts about the hydrogen bomb' *BAS*, 6 (Apr. 1950), 109.

36. Report by Clark Clifford and George Elsey, Sep. 1946; in Arthur Krock, *Memoirs* (New York: Funk & Wagnall's, 1968), 477–8; quoted in Rhodes, 281.

37. LeMay, quoted in David Alan Rosenberg, 'Toward Armageddon: The Foundations of United States Nuclear Strategy, 1945-1961', PhD thesis, University of Chicago, 95, n2; cited in Rhodes, 347.

38. Robert Wise, dir., *The Day the Earth Stood Still* (20th Century Fox, 1951).

39. Fritz Leiber, 'Coming Attraction', *Galaxy* (1950); in James Gunn, ed., *The Road to Science Fiction*, vol. 3: *From Heinlein to Here* (New York: Mentor, 1979), 173.

40. Truman speaking at Blair House in July 1949; quoted in Rhodes, 363.

41. Conversation quoted in Francis Crick, *Life Itself, Its Origin and Nature* (New York: Simon & Schuster, 1981), 13–14. There are many versions of this story: Otto Frisch (*What Little I Remember* (Cambridge University Press, 1979), 174) credits the theory of the Hungarians' Martian origins to Fritz Houtermans, whereas Edward Teller says that a fellow Martian, Theodore von Kármán, first spread the story (Teller with Judith Shoolery, *Memoirs: A Twentieth-Century Journey in Science and Politics* (Cambridge, Mass.: Perseus, 2001), 415).

42. Eugene P. Wigner and Andrew Szanton, *The Recollections of Eugene P. Wigner* (New York: Plenum, 1992), 221.

43. Von Neumann, quoted in Rhodes, 356.

44. John Walsh, 'A Conversation with Eugene Wigner', *Science*, 181 (10 Aug. 1973), 530.

45. Wigner and Szanton, 226.

46. ibid., 262–3.

47. ibid., 263.

48. Teller, 1958; quoted in Peter Goodchild, *Edward Teller: The Real Dr Strangelove* (London: Weidenfeld & Nicolson, 2004), 275.

49. Fermi, quoted in Goodchild, 131.

50. Press reports; in ibid., 249.

51. George Cowan, Los Alamos radiochemist, interview in ibid., 322.

52. Raemer Schreiber, 'Reminiscences' (unpublished MS, 1991); quoted in Rhodes, 478.

53. Emilio Segrè, *A Mind Always in Motion* (Berkeley: University of California Press, 1993), 238; quoted in Rhodes, 416.

54. Los Alamos physicist Charles Critchfield; interview in Rhodes, 462.

55. Bethe's recollection is recorded in William Lanouette with Bela Silard, *Genius in the Shadows: A Biography of Leo Szilard, The Man Behind the Bomb* (University of Chicago Press, 1994; 1st edn 1992), 152; 'the inventor of all things': Edwin M. McMillan to Wilfred Mann, 3 Jan. 1952; quoted in J. L. Heilbron, *Lawrence and his Laboratory: A History of the Lawrence Berkeley Laboratory* (Berkeley: University of California Press, 1989), 199.

56. Conversation between Eisenhower and Herbert York; quoted in Goodchild, 283. President Jimmy Carter was the first and only American head of state to have a qualification in nuclear physics, which he studied in the early 1950s while serving in the US Navy's nuclear submarine programme.

57. Rhodes, 304.

58. Herbert York; interview in Goodchild, 202.

59. David E. Lilienthal, *The Journals of David E. Lilienthal*: vol. 2, *The Atomic Energy Years, 1945–1950* (New York: Harper & Row, 1964), 582.

60. Gregg Herken, *Brotherhood of the Bomb: The Tangled Lives and Loyalties of Robert Oppenheimer, Ernest Lawrence, and Edward Teller* (New York: Henry Holt, 2002), 222.

61. Oppenheimer to Conant, 20 Oct. 1949; quoted in Rhodes, 391.

62. Herken, 223.

63. Rhodes, 423–4, 462.

64. Teller, quoted in Herken, 236.

65. Hans A. Bethe, 'Comments on the History of the H-bomb', *Los Alamos Science* (Fall 1982), 49.

66. S. M. Ulam, *Adventures of a Mathematician* (Berkeley: University of California Press, 1991; 1st edn 1976), 151.

67. Teller, *Memoirs*, 299; Ulam's contribution: see ibid., 312–13.

68. Thomas E. Murray, *Nuclear Policy for War and Peace* (New York: World, 1960), 20–21.

69. Edward Teller, *Energy from Heaven and Earth* (San Francisco: W. H. Freeman, 1979), 150.

70. Herbert York, interview; quoted in Rhodes, 511.

71. William Borden's phrase; quoted in Herken, 257.

72. Senior members of the administration reached this conclusion on 30 Dec. 1952 while discussing the report 'Armaments and American Policy'; *Foreign Relations of the United States*, vol. II, pt 2, 1049; quoted in Goodchild, 210.

73. Herken, 262; on the Mike device, see Rhodes, 482–510.

74. Teller to Stephen White; quoted in Herken, 256. Teller subsequently denied making this comment.

75. Teller, interviewed in Mary Palevsky, *Atomic Fragments: A Daughter's Questions* (Berkeley: University of California Press, 2000), 53.

76. Herken, 260.

77. Richard P. Feynman, *'Surely You're Joking, Mr Feynman!': Adventures of a Curious Character* (New York: Norton, 1997), 132.

78. Oppenheimer in 1954; quoted in Rhodes, 389.

79. Wigner and Szanton, 174, 226, 220.

80. Frisch, 173.

81. Quoted in Lewis L. Strauss, *Men and Decisions* (London: Macmillan, 1963), 235.

82. William Poundstone, *Prisoner's Dilemma* (New York: Anchor, 1992), 22.

83. Fred M. Kaplan, *The Wizards of Armageddon* (New York: Simon & Schuster, 1983), 66.

84. Quoted in Clay Blair, Jr, 'Passing of a Great Mind', *Life* (25 Feb. 1957), 89ff.

85. John von Neumann, 'Can We Survive Technology?', *Fortune* (June 1955), 106ff; quoted in Poundstone, 182.

86. Von Neumann to Lewis Strauss, 21 Nov. 1951; quoted in Kaplan, 63.

87. Von Neumann, 10 Jan. 1955; quoted in Poundstone, 184.

88. Von Neumann in 1954; quoted in Rhodes, 362.

89. William Liscum Borden, *There Will Be No Time: The Revolution in Strategy* (New York: Macmillan, 1946), 225.

90. *NYT* (4 Mar. 1956), 3.

91. See Poundstone, 189; and Norman Macrae, *John von Neumann* (New York: Pantheon, 1992), 331. On the Crossroads tests and incidence of disease, see Catherine Caufield, *Multiple Exposures: Chronicles of the Radiation Age* (London: Penguin, 1990), 99.

92. Poundstone, 193.

93. Robert Serber, *Los Alamos Primer: The First Lectures on How to Build an Atomic Bomb*, ed. Richard Rhodes (Berkeley: University of California Press, 1992), 4, n2.

94. Edward Teller, Los Alamos report from Feb. 1950, 'On the Development of Thermonuclear Bombs', LA-643, 16.ii.50; quoted in Rhodes, 419.

Chapter 18

1. Marshall Rosenbluth; interview in Richard Rhodes, *Dark Sun: The Making of the Hydrogen Bomb* (New York: Touchstone, 1996), 541–2.

2. Lindesay Parrott, 'Japan to Survey Radioactivity of Sea Around the Bikini Tests', *NYT* (17 Apr. 1954).

3. Strauss, quoted in Catherine Caufield, *Multiple Exposures: Chronicles of the Radiation Age* (London: Penguin, 1990), 115.

4. Hanson W. Baldwin, 'H-bomb Fall-out Poses New Defense Problems', *NYT* (20 Feb. 1955), IV, 10.

5. Parrott.

6. Columns Lang wrote for the *New Yorker* were collected in *From Hiroshima to the Moon: Chronicles of Life in the Atomic Age* (New York: Simon & Schuster, 1959); this is from his column for June 1955 (p. 369).

7. Igor Kurchatov, Report on 'The Danger of Atomic War' (1954), <http://www.pbs.org/wgbh/amex/bomb/filmmore/reference/primary/igoratomic.html>.

8. Quoted in David Hawkins et al., eds., *Project Y: The Los Alamos Story* (Los Angeles: Tomash, 1983; 1st edn 1947), 187.

9. *Time* (Nov. 1954); quoted in Caufield, 115.

10. Dwight Macdonald, 'The Decline to Barbarism', *Policy* (Sep. 1945); quoted in Kai Bird and Lawrence Lifschultz, *Hiroshima's Shadow: Writings on the Denial of History and the Smithsonian Controversy* (Stony Creek, Conn.: Pamphleteer's Press, 1998), 266.

11. Kenney, quoted in Donald Porter Geddes, ed., *The Atomic Age Opens* (New York: Pocket Books, 1945), 33.

12. William L. Laurence, *Dawn over Zero: The Story of the Atomic Bomb* (London: Museum, 1947), 9.

13. ibid., 136.

14. Carl Urbano, dir., *A is for Atom* (General Electric Co, 1952); downloadable from <http://www.archive.org/details/isforAto1953>.

15. Tomoyuki Tanaka, quoted in William Tsutsui, *Godzilla on My Mind: Fifty Years of the King of Monsters* (New York: Palgrave Macmillan, 2004), 18.

16. ibid., 29, 30.

17. ibid., 32.

18. Gordon Douglas, dir., *Them!* (Warner Bros, 1954).

19. 'straws': Jeremy Bernstein, *Oppenheimer: Portrait of an Enigma* (London: Duckworth, 2004), 105; 'as large as you wish': 'H-Bomb Tests End; Called a Success', *NYT* (14 May 1954), 5.

20. Cabinet Committee on Defence Policy, 1 June 1954; UK Public Record Office, CAB 134/808.

21. Macmillan Diary, 26 Jan. 1955; quoted in Peter Hennessy, *The Secret State: Whitehall and the Cold War* (London: Penguin, 2003), 52.

22. Winston Churchill, 8 July 1954; UK Public Record Office, CAB 128/27; quoted in Hennessy, 58.

23. Strath Report, Mar. 1955; UK Public Record Office, CAB 134/940; quoted in Hennessy, 140.

24. Strath Report, Mar. 1955; UK Public Record Office, CAB 134/940, 10.

25. ibid., 11.

26. Von Neumann, quoted in Lewis L. Strauss, *Men and Decisions* (London: Macmillan, 1963), 350.

27. Hans Bethe, Harrison Brown, Frederick Seitz, Leo Szilard, 'The Facts About the Hydrogen Bomb', *BAS*, 6 (Apr. 1950), 109 (Szilard speaking).

28. William L. Laurence, 'Now Most Dreaded Weapon, Cobalt Bomb, Can Be Built', *NYT* (7 Apr. 1954), 4.

29. 'Potentialities of Cobalt Bomb', and 'Japanese Affected by Hydrogen Bomb', *Times* (8 Apr. 1954), 9; 'National Petition on Hydrogen Bomb', *Times* (8 Apr. 1954), 6.

30. Mary M. Simpson, 'News and Notes', *BAS*, 10 (Mar. 1954), 107.

31. '"Cobalt Bomb" Fears', *Times* (9 Sep. 1953), 7.

32. This explosion, on 14 Sep. 1957, was the first of three tests in the Antler series. On this and other UK tests, see 'British Nuclear Testing', <http://nuclearweaponarchive.org/Uk/UKTesting.html>.

33. 'Cobalt Bomb Use in War Scouted', *NYT* (12 Apr. 1954), 20.

34. 'Italy Seizes 9 Tons of Cobalt', *NYT* (18 Apr. 1954), 10.

35. Reported in *NYT* (14 May 1954), 5; and 'Experts Analyse Effects of Atomic Explosions', *Times* (22 June 1954), 6.

36. Eugene J. Sleevi, 'Civil Defense News', *BAS*, 10 (May 1954), 172.

37. 'The Hydrogen Bomb', *Times* (12 Apr. 1954), 9.

38. 'The Hydrogen Bomb', *Times* (10 Apr. 1954), 7.

39. Quoted in John MacCormac, 'Scientist Labels H-Bomb as "Crazy"', *NYT* (14 May 1954), 5.

40. Strauss, quoted in 'H-Bomb Tests End; Called a Success', *NYT* (14 May 1954), 5.

41. Thomson, quoted in 'Cobalt Bomb "Absurd as Weapon"', *Times* (10 June 1954), 3.

42. Russell, quoted in '1954 – Portrait of the Year', *Times* (1 Jan. 1955), 11.

43. ibid.

44. Hahn, quoted in 'German Scientist's Broadcast', *Times* (16 Feb. 1955), 8.

45. 'End of World Seen with a Cobalt Bomb', *NYT* (21 Feb. 1955), 12.

46. 'The Moral Crisis', editorial, *Times* (14 Mar. 1955), 9.

47. 'Hydrogen Bomb Devastation', *Times* (16 Feb. 1955), 8.

48. James Arnold, 'Fall-out Hazard', *BAS*, 11 (Feb. 1955), 52.

49. Ralph E. Lapp, 'Global Fallout', *BAS*, 11 (Nov. 1955), 339–43.

50. Harrison E. Salisbury, 'Stevenson Asks Eisenhower Policy on Cobalt Bomb', *NYT* (27 Oct. 1956), 14.

51. Allen Drury, 'Butler and Hall Predict Victory', *NYT* (29 Oct. 1956), 24.

52. 'Atom Radiation Level "Low"', *Times* (21 Apr. 1955), 6.

53. Dyson, in 'Project Orion' (BBC4 TV, 2002).

54. Ernest B. Schoedsack, dir., *Dr Cyclops* (Paramount, 1940).

55. John and Roy Boulting, dirs., *Seven Days to Noon* (London Films, 1950).

56. Christian Nyby, dir., *The Thing from Another World* (RKO, 1951). This film is often referred to as just *The Thing*.

57. Frederic Brown, 'The Weapon' (1951); in Gregory Benford and Martin Harry Greenberg, eds., *Nuclear War* (New York: Ace Books, 1988), 49–52.

58. Albert Camus, 'After Hiroshima: Between Hell and Reason', *Combat* (8 Aug. 1945); trans. by Ronald E. Santoni published in *Philosophy Today* (Spring 1988); quoted in Bird and Lifschultz, 260–61.

59. Lewis Mumford, 'Gentlemen: You Are Mad!', *Saturday Review of Literature* (2 Mar. 1946); quoted in Bird and Lifschultz, 284–7.

60. J. G. Ballard, 'The Terminal Beach' (*New Worlds*, Mar. 1964); in James Gunn, ed., *The Road to Science Fiction*, vol. 3: *From Heinlein to Here* (New York: Mentor, 1979), here 345, 357.

61. Editorial, *NYT* (12 Aug. 1945); in Geddes, 162.

62. Michael Avallone, *Beneath the Planet of the Apes* (New York: Bantam, 1970), 109, 76.

63. H. G. Wells, *Mind at the End of Its Tether* (London: Heinemann, 1945); quoted in Michael Coren, *The Invisible Man: The Life and Liberties of H. G. Wells* (London: Bloomsbury, 1993), 222.

64. Robert Barr, 'The Doom of London', *The Idler*, 2 (1893), 399, 400.

65. Densil Neve Barr, *The Man with Only One Head* (London: Digit Books, 1962; 1st edn 1955), 5, 30, 48.
66. ibid., 43.
67. Philip Wylie, *Tomorrow!* (New York: Popular Library, 1963; 1st edn 1954), 272.
68. ibid., 273–4.
69. ibid., 274, 286.
70. Agatha Christie, *Destination Unknown* (Glasgow: Fontana, 1975; 1st edn 1954), 9. Many thanks to Rebecca Hurst for bringing this novel to my attention.
71. ibid., 49, 55.
72. William Tenn, 'The Sickness', *Infinity Science Fiction* (Nov. 1955); in William Tenn, *Time in Advance* (London: Panther, 1966), 96.
73. Nevil Shute, *On the Beach* (London: Heinemann, 1957), 40, 89.
74. Spencer R. Weart, *Nuclear Fear: A History of Images* (Cambridge, Mass.: Harvard University Press, 1988), 218.
75. Stanley Kramer, dir., *On the Beach* (MGM, 1959).
76. Shute, 268–9.
77. Whitley Strieber, *The Day After Tomorrow* (London: Gollancz, 2004), 249.
78. Martin Gilbert, *Churchill: A Life* (London: Heinemann, 1991), 952.
79. Edward Teller with Judith Shoolery, *Memoirs: A Twentieth-Century Journey in Science and Politics* (Cambridge, Mass.: Perseus, 2001), 445.
80. Edward Teller with Albert L. Latter, *Our Nuclear Future: Facts, Dangers and Opportunities* (New York: Criterion, 1958), 134–6.
81. Teller, *Memoirs*, 445.
82. Edward Teller with Allen Brown, *The Legacy of Hiroshima* (New York: Doubleday, 1962), 239–43.
83. J. B. Priestley, quoted in David Seed, 'Introduction', Mordecai Roshwald, *Level 7* (University of Wisconsin Press, 2004), p. xviii.
84. Mordecai Roshwald, 'Looking Back in Wonder', ibid., p. xxx.
85. Roshwald, *Level 7*, 102.
86. Stanley Kramer, dir., *On the Beach* (MGM, 1959).
87. Roshwald, *Level 7*, 127.
88. ibid., 182.
89. Bertolt Brecht, *Leben des Galilei* (Frankfurt a. M.: Suhrkamp, 1972), scene 14, 126; my trans. On Brecht and physics, see P. D. Smith, 'German Literature and the Scientific World-View in the Nineteenth and Twentieth Centuries', *Journal of European Studies*, 27 (1997), 389–415; and P. D. Smith, *Metaphor and Materiality: German Literature and the World-View of*

Science 1780–1955 (Oxford: European Humanities Research Centre, 2000), 265–318.

90. Bruce Chatwin, *In Patagonia* (London: Vintage, 1998), 3. Thanks to Susan Ng for drawing this passage to my attention.

Chapter 19

1. 'October, 1962 – The Cuba Crisis: Nuclear War Was Hours Away', *Newsweek* (28 Oct. 1963), 18.

2. Anthony Lewis, 'President Grave', *NYT* (23 Oct. 1962), 1, 18.

3. ibid.

4. 'October, 1962 – The Cuba Crisis', 18.

5. ibid., 19.

6. Szilard, quoted in William Lanouette with Bela Silard, *Genius in the Shadows: A Biography of Leo Szilard, The Man Behind the Bomb* (University of Chicago Press, 1994; 1st edn 1992), 456.

7. Quoted in N[orman] C[ousins], 'Many Facets of Leo Szilard', *Saturday Review* (29 Apr. 1961), 15.

8. 'Recovery from Cancer', *Time* (23 Mar. 1962), 40, 42.

9. 'Leo Szilard Dies; A-Bomb Physicist', *NYT* (31 May 1964), 77.

10. Harrison Brown, 'The 20th Year', guest editorial, *BAS*, 18 (Dec. 1962), 2.

11. Kennedy, quoted in Martin Walker, *The Cold War and the Making of the Modern World* (London: Vintage, 1994), 171.

12. Szilard, quoted in Lanouette, 458.

13. Cabell Phillips, 'Pickets Parade at White House', *NYT* (28 Oct. 1962), 1.

14. McNamara, quoted in Walker, 171.

15. Secretary of State Dean Rusk; quoted in Walker, 178.

16. LeMay, quoted in Walker, 179.

17. Kennedy, quoted in Tim Weiner, 'Word for Word: The Cuban Missile Crisis', *NYT* (5 Oct. 1997), IV, 1.

18. *Time* (Oct. 1962). According to *Life* (Mar. 1961), *From Russia with Love* was one of Kennedy's favourite books; see also J. Hoberman, 'When Dr No Met Dr Strangelove', *Sight and Sound*, 12 (Dec. 1993), 16, 18.

19. Lyn Tornabene, 'Contradicting the Hollywood Image', *Saturday Review*, 46 (28 Dec. 1963), 19–21.

20. Quoted in Eugene Archer, 'How to Learn to Love World Destruction', *NYT* (26 Jan. 1964), II, 13.

21. Vincent LoBrutto, *Stanley Kubrick: A Biography* (London: Faber, 1998), 226.

22. Alastair Buchan, 'Basis of a Film' (letter), *Times* (31 Jan. 1964), 13.

23. Quoted in 'Peter George, 41, British Novelist', *NYT* (3 June 1966).

24. 'Mr Peter George' (obit.), *Times* (3 June 1966), 14.

25. Stanley Kubrick, dir., *Dr Strangelove or: How I Learned to Stop Worrying and Love the Bomb* (Columbia Pictures, 1964), dialogue from continuity transcript (see <http://www.visual-memory.co.uk/amk/doc/0055.html>).

26. John Coleman, 'Dr Strangelove', *New Statesman* (31 Jan. 1964), 178.

27. 'The Mined Cities', *BAS*, 17 (Dec. 1961); in Szilard, *The Voice of the Dolphins and Other Stories* (Stanford University Press, 1992; 1st edn 1961).

28. J. D. Salinger, *The Catcher in the Rye* (London: Penguin, 1994; 1st edn 1951), 40, 127. Stephen J. Whitfield draws attention to the link between Holden Caulfield and Major Kong in his excellent essay 'Cherished and Cursed: Toward a Social History of *The Catcher in the Rye*', *New England Quarterly*, 70 (1997), 593.

29. Urey, quoted in 'What Goes on Here?', *Time* (6 Feb. 1950), 11.

30. 'Two Days that Shook the World', *Newsweek* (11 Sep. 1961), 15.

31. Seymour Topping, 'Moscow Cites Berlin Tensions – Boasts of Superbomb Project', *NYT* (31 Aug. 1961), 1.

32. 'Berlin', *Time* (8 Sep. 1961), 26.

33. See e.g. *Scientific American* (Mar. 1961); see also Bell Telephone Co. advert in *Harper's* (Sep. 1960), 1: 'How the Air Force puts Titan *on target!*'

34. 'The Cold War', and 'Russia', *Time* (8 Sep. 1961), 16, 24.

35. 'Russian Bomb Put at over 50 Megatons', *Times* (31 Oct. 1961), 10.

36. James Feron, 'Britain is Atomic-War Target, Khrushchev Warns Laborites', *NYT* (31 Oct. 1961), 14.

37. 'Superbomb', *Newsweek* (30 Oct. 1961), 44–5.

38. 'If Bombs Do Fall on US – What People Look for', *US News and World Report* (25 Sep. 1961), 51.

39. 'Survival: Are Shelters the Answer?', *Newsweek* (6 Nov. 1961), 11.

40. Libby, quoted in 'The Cold War', *Time* (8 Sep. 1961), 16.

41. 'Almost Nobody Building Shelters – Here is Why', *US News and World Report* (25 Sep. 1961), 52–3.

42. Val Guest, dir., *The Day the Earth Caught Fire*, co-written with Wolf Mankowitz (British Lion/Paramount, 1961).

43. Harrison E. Salisbury, 'Stevenson Asks Eisenhower Policy on Cobalt Bomb', *NYT* (27 Oct. 1956), 1.

44. A. H. Weiler, '*The Day the Earth Caught Fire* Opens', *NYT* (16 Mar. 1962), 25.

45. Kubrick to Peter George, Nov. 1961; quoted in W. Russell, *Glasgow Herald* (13 July 2000), 6.

46. Adam, quoted in LoBrutto, 231.

47. Szilard, in *CW3*, 427.

48. 'Let Our Children Go . . .', *Newsweek* (9 Oct. 1961), 26.

49. W. H. Clark, 'Chemical and Thermonuclear Explosives', *BAS*, 17 (Nov. 1961), 356–60.

50. Eugene Rabinowitch, 'Editor's Note', *BAS*, 17 (Nov. 1961), 359.

51. S. M. Genensky and Olaf Helmer, *Glossary of Terms on National Security* (RAND Corporation, 1961); quoted in Clark, 'Chemical and Thermonuclear Explosives', 360.

52. Joseph Kraft, 'RAND: Arsenal for Ideas', *Harper's* (July 1960), 69.

53. Jeremy Bernstein, speaking in the programme 'Project Orion' (BBC4 TV, 2002).

54. Bernard Brodie, 'Implications for Military Policy', in Brodie, ed., *The Absolute Weapon: Atomic Power and World Order* (New York: Harcourt, Brace & Co., 1946), 76.

55. Herman Kahn, *Thinking about the Unthinkable* (New York: Horizon Press, 1962), review: Jack Raymond, 'A Grim Game for Us All', *NYT* (17 June 1962), VII, 10.

56. Quoted in Fred M. Kaplan, *The Wizards of Armageddon* (New York: Simon & Schuster, 1983), 223.

57. Kenneth E. Boulding, '*World Economic Development: 1979 and Beyond* by Herman Kahn', *Economic Development and Cultural Change*, 29 (1981), 645.

58. Thomas Bell, quoted in 'Herman Kahn, a Leading Thinker On War and the Future, Dies at 61', *NYT* (8 July 1983), II, 7.

59. Donald Rumsfeld, after receiving the Hudson Institute's James H. Doolittle Award on 14 May 2003; see <http://www.whitehouse.gov/news/releases/2003/05/20030513-9.html>.

60. Herman Kahn, *On Thermonuclear War* (Princeton University Press, 1961; 1st edn 1960), 45–6.

61. James R. Newman, 'Two Discussions of Thermonuclear War', *Scientific American* (Mar. 1961), 200, 197.

62. Kahn, *On Thermonuclear War*, 228.

63. Arthur Herzog, 'Report on a "Think Factory"', *NYT* (10 Nov. 1963), VI, 42.

64. ibid.

65. Herman Kahn, 'A "Doomsday Machine" – Last Word in the Arms Race?', *US News and World Report* (1 May 1961), 61, 64.

66. Herman Kahn, *On Thermonuclear War*, 145.

67. John Baxter, *Stanley Kubrick: A Biography* (London: HarperCollins, 1997), 167.

68. Kahn, *On Thermonuclear War*, 145–51.

69. ibid., 145–51, 524.

70. Peter Bryant, *Red Alert* (New York: Ace Books, 1958), 138; published in the UK as *Two Hours to Doom* (London: Boardman, 1958). The cobalt bombs are described on p. 79.

71. Bosley Crowther, 'Dr Strangelove, a Shattering Sick Joke', *NYT* (30 Jan. 1964), 24.

Chapter 20

1. Szilard to R. A. Spitz, 29 Mar. 1963; quoted in William Lanouette with Bela Silard, *Genius in the Shadows: A Biography of Leo Szilard, The Man Behind the Bomb* (University of Chicago Press, 1994; 1st edn 1992), 461.

2. William L. Laurence, 'Atomic Forecast', *NYT* (2 Dec. 1962), IV, 7.

3. Eugene Rabinowitch, 'New Year's Thoughts 1963', *BAS*, 19 (Jan. 1963), 2.

4. Glenn T. Seaborg, *BAS*, 19 (Jan. 1963), 2.

5. Seaborg, interview in Laurence, 'Atomic Forecast'.

6. Eugene P. Wigner, 'Twentieth Birthday of the Atomic Age', *NYT* (2 Dec. 1962), VI, 34, 126.

7. 'Message from President John F. Kennedy to the *Bulletin of the Atomic Scientists*', *BAS*, 18 (Dec. 1962), 2.

8. Kubrick, interviewed by A. H. Weiler, *NYT* (31 Dec. 1962).

9. Letter from Alan Earney, Peter George's English publisher, 'Kubrick's Pies', *Independent* (11 Mar. 1999), 2.

10. Kubrick, quoted in Eugene Archer, 'How to Learn to Love World Destruction', *NYT* (26 Jan. 1964), II, 13.

11. 'Peter George, 41, British Novelist', *NYT* (3 June 1966).

12. Terence Young, dir., *Dr No* (Eon, 1962).

13. Peter George, *Dr Strangelove* (London: Souvenir, 1999; 1st edn 1963), 36. This is a novelization based on the screenplay.

14. ibid., 54, 156.

15. Kubrick, in conversation with Alexander Walker, in Walker, *Peter Sellers: The Authorized Biography*; quoted in Vincent LoBrutto, *Stanley Kubrick: A Biography* (London: Faber, 1998), 239.

16. Lewis Mumford, letter, '"Strangelove" Reactions', *NYT* (1 Mar. 1964), II, 8; Mumford was responding to Bosley Crowther's reviews: 'Dr

Strangelove, a Shattering Sick Joke', *NYT* (30 Jan. 1964), 24, and 'Is Nothing Sacred?', *NYT* (2 Feb. 1964), II, 1.

17. Crowther, '*Dr Strangelove*, a Shattering Sick Joke'.

18. Tom Milne, 'Dr Strangelove', *Sight and Sound* 33 (Winter 1963/4), 37–8.

19. John Coleman, 'Dr Strangelove', *New Statesman* (31 Jan. 1964), 178.

20. 'Debate over *Strangelove* Film Echoes Happily at the Box Office', *NYT* (10 Feb. 1964).

21. 'Late-Night Showings at Columbia Cinema', *Times* (6 Feb. 1964), 6.

22. Geoffrey Perrett, *A Dream of Greatness: The American People 1945–1963* (New York: Coward, McCann, & Geoghegan, 1979), 726.

23. Brian Aldiss, 'The Real Kubrick', *Observer* (14 Mar. 1999).

24. Sharon Ghamari-Tabrizi, 'Dr Strangelove', note 11, <http://www.visual-memory.co.uk/amk/doc/0097.html>.

25. Szilard, quoted in Lanouette, 466.

26. Quoted in Tristram Coffin, 'Leo Szilard: The Conscience of a Scientist', *Holiday* (Feb. 1964), 64–7, 92–9.

27. ibid.

28. James Yaffe, 'Of Fission and Fish', *Saturday Review*, 44 (29 Apr. 1961), 16.

29. 'Leo Szilard Dies; A-Bomb Scientist', *NYT* (31 May 1964), 1, 77.

30. 'Leo Szilard' (editorial), *NYT* (1 June 1964), 28.

31. Teller, writing in *Disarmament and Arms Control* (Autumn 1964), 453; quoted in Lanouette, 479.

32. Quoted in Martin Walker, *The Cold War and the Making of the Modern World* (London: Vintage, 1994), 179.

33. 'A Weapon to Kill Everybody . . . or Just Cold-War Bluster?', *US News and World Report* (28 Sep 1964), 8.

34. ibid.

35. Bruce G. Blair, 'Russia's Doomsday Machine', *NYT* (8 Oct. 1993), A, 35. The story was not long in reaching Britain: see Steve Doughty, 'Doomsday at Mercy of a Faulty Switch', *Daily Mail* (9 Oct. 1993), 12.

36. George, 109.

37. Blair, 35; for further information see Steven J. Zaloga, *The Kremlin's Nuclear Sword: The Rise and Fall of Russia's Strategic Nuclear Forces, 1945–2000* (Washington: Smithsonian Institution, 2002).

38. Bruce Blair, 'We Keep Building Nukes For All the Wrong Reasons', *Washington Post* (25 May 2003), also at <http://www.cdi.org/blair/new-nukes.cfm>.

39. Zaloga, 199–201.

Epilogue

1. Damon Albarn, quoted in 'Marchers Revive Nuclear Protest', 9 April 2004, <http://news.bbc.co.uk/1/hi/uk/3613393.stm>.
2. Leo Szilard, 'Answers to Questions', dictated 9 May 1963; in CW2, 229.
3. 'Government Say Keep Away from Bases', Times (8 Dec. 1961), 14.
4. 'Minister Sums up Invasion of Wethersfield – A Flop', Times (11 Dec. 1961), 6.
5. 'Shabby "Success", Says Lord Russell', Times (11 Dec. 1961), 6.
6. Bernard Charles Cyril Smith, 'Application to Local Tribunal by a Person Provisionally Registered in the Register of Conscientious Objectors' (Form N.S. 14), 7 Oct. 1943; the court hearing before His Honour Judge G. P. Hargreaves was on 4 Nov. 1943, as recorded on 'Form N.S. 14 (continuation)'; copies in the author's possession.
7. Bernard Smith to Avril Haas, Dec.? 1959.

Bibliography

This bibliography includes the major works of fiction, non-fiction and the cinema that are referenced in the notes, as well as other books, articles, stories and films of interest. However, it does not list references to sources such as newspaper articles, archives and websites which are included in the notes.

Fiction

Anderson, Poul, 'Tomorrow's Children' (1947). In Miller and Greenberg, eds., *Beyond Armageddon*.

Asimov, Isaac, ed., *Before the Golden Age: A Science Fiction Anthology of the 1930s* (New York: Doubleday, 1974).

—— and Greenberg, Martin Harry, eds., *The Golden Years of Science Fiction*, 2nd series (New York: Bonanza, 1983).

Austin, Frederick Britten, ' "Planes!" ' (1913). In Clarke, ed., *The Tale of the Next Great War*.

Avallone, Michael, *Beneath the Planet of the Apes* (New York: Bantam, 1970).

Ballard, J. G., 'The Terminal Beach' (1964). In Gunn, ed., *The Road to Science Fiction*.

Barr, Densil Neve, *The Man with Only One Head* (London: Digit Books, 1962; 1st edn 1955).

Barr, Robert, 'The Doom of London', *The Idler*, 2 (Aug. 1892–Jan. 1893), 397–409.

Bell, Neil, *The Lord of Life* (London: Collins, 1933).

Benet, Stephen Vincent, 'By the Waters of Babylon' (1937). In Miller and Greenberg, eds., *Beyond Armageddon*.

Benford, Gregory and Greenberg, Martin Harry, eds., *Nuclear War* (New York: Ace Books, 1988).

Bester, Alfred, 'Adam and No Eve' (1941). In Asimov and Greenberg, eds., *The Golden Years of Science Fiction*, 2nd series.

—— 'Disappearing Act' (1953). In Malzberg and Pronzini, eds., *The End of Summer*.

Bone, J. F., 'Triggerman' (1958). In Benford and Greenberg, eds., *Nuclear War*.

Boulle, Pierre, '$E = mc^2$' (1966), in *Time Out of Mind* (New York: Signet Books, 1969; 1st edn 1966).

Brackett, Leigh, *The Long Tomorrow* (New York: Ace, 1955).

Bradbury, Ray, 'The Million-Year Picnic' (1946). In Gunn, ed., *The Road to Science Fiction*.

—— 'There Will Come Soft Rains' (1950). In Miller and Greenberg, eds., *Beyond Armageddon*.

Brecht, Bertolt, *Leben des Galilei* (Berlin: Suhrkamp, 1972; 1st edn 1955).

Brown, Frederic, 'The Weapon' (1951). In Benford and Greenberg, eds., *Nuclear War*.

Bryant, Peter, *Red Alert* (New York: Ace Books, 1958).

Buck, Pearl S., *Command the Morning* (London: Methuen, 1959).

Bulmer, Kenneth, *The Doomsday Men* (New York: Curtis Books, 1968; 1st edn 1965).

Bulwer-Lytton, Edward, *The Coming Race* (London: George Routledge, 1888; 1st edn 1871).

Burdick, Eugene and Wheeler, Harvey, *Fail-Safe* (London: Hutchinson, 1963; 1st edn 1962).

Campbell, John W. Jr, 'Atomic Power' (1934). In Conklin, ed., *The Golden Age of Science Fiction*.

Čapek, Karel, *Krakatit*, trans. L. Hyde (London: Geoffrey Bles, 1925; 1st edn 1924).

—— *The Absolute at Large* (Westport, Conn.: Hyperion, 1988; 1st edn 1922).

Cartmill, Cleve, 'Deadline' (1944). In Conklin, ed., *The Golden Age of Science Fiction*.

Casewit, Curtis W., *The Peacemakers* (New York: Macfadden Books, 1968; 1st edn 1960).

Chesney, Gen. Sir George T., *The Battle of Dorking* (1871). In Clarke, ed., *The Tale of the Next Great War*.

Christie, Agatha, *Destination Unknown* (Glasgow: Fontana, 1975; 1st edn 1954).

Christopher, John, *The Death of Grass* (London: Penguin, 1958; 1st edn 1956).

Clarke, I. F., ed., *The Tale of the Next Great War, 1871–1914: Fictions of Future Warfare and of Battles Still-to-Come* (Liverpool University Press, 1995).

—— ed., *British Future Fiction*, Vols 1–8 (London: Pickering & Chatto, 2001).

Conklin, Groff, ed., *The Golden Age of Science Fiction* (New York: Bonanza, 1980; 1st edn 1946).

—— ed., *Great Science Fiction by Scientists* (New York: Collier Books, 1966; 1st edn 1962).

Connington, J. J., *Nordenholt's Million* (London: Penguin, 1946; 1st edn 1923).

Conrad, Joseph and Hueffer, Ford M., *The Inheritors: An Extravagant Story* (London: Heinemann, 1901).

Cooney, Michael, *Doomsday England* (London: Corgi, 1968; 1st edn 1967).

Cooper, Ralph S., 'The Neutrino Bomb' (1961). In Franklin, ed., *Countdown to Midnight*.

Crosthwaite, C. H. T., 'Röntgen's Curse', *Longman's*, 28 (Sep. 1896), 469–84.

Dann, Jack and Dozois, Gardner, eds., *Armageddons* (New York: Ace Books, 1999).

Davis, Chandler, 'The Nightmare' (1946). In Benford and Greenberg, eds., *Nuclear War*.

—— 'To Still the Drums' (1946). In Franklin, ed., *Countdown to Midnight*.

Dee, Roger, *An Earth Gone Mad* (New York: Ace, 1954; 1st edn 1952).

del Rey, Lester, *Nerves* (New York: Ballantine Books, 1966; 1st edn 1942).

—— ed., *The Best of John W. Campbell* (New York: Doubleday, 1976).

Disch, Thomas M, ed., *The Ruins of Earth* (London: Arrow Books, 1975; 1st edn 1973).

Döblin, Alfred, *Berge Meere und Giganten* (Olten: Walter-Verlag, 1977; 1st edn 1924).

Eco, Umberto, *The Name of the Rose* (London: Picador, 1984).

Ellison, Harlan, 'A Boy and His Dog' (1969). In Miller and Greenberg, eds., *Beyond Armageddon*.

Engel, Leonard and Piller, Emanuel, *World Aflame: The Russian–American War of 1950* (New York: Dial Press, 1947).

Evans, Hilary and Evans, Dik, *Beyond the Gaslight: Science in Popular Fiction 1895–1905* (London: Muller, 1976).

France, Anatole, *Penguin Island*, trans. A. W. Evans (London: Watts & Co., 1935; 1st edn 1908).

Frank, Pat, *Alas, Babylon* (New York: HarperCollins, 1999; 1st edn 1959).

Franklin, H. Bruce, ed., *Countdown to Midnight* (New York: Daw Books, 1984).

George, Peter, *Dr Strangelove: or How I Learned to Stop Worrying and Love the Bomb* (London: Souvenir, 1999; 1st edn 1963).

—— *Commander-1* (London: Pan Books, 1966; 1st edn 1965).

Godfrey, Hollis, *The Man Who Ended War* (Boston: Little, Brown, & Co., 1908).

Goethe, Johann Wolfgang von, *Faust: A Tragedy*, trans. Walter Arndt (New York: Norton, 1976).

Gold, Herbert, 'The Day They Got Boston' (1961). In Benford and Greenberg, eds., *Nuclear War*.

Golding, William, *Lord of the Flies* (London: Faber & Faber, 1971; 1st edn 1954).

Gratzer, Walter, ed., *The Longman Literary Companion to Science* (Harlow: Longman, 1989).

Griffith, George, 'The Raid of *Le Vengeur*' (1901). In Clarke, ed., *The Tale of the Next Great War*.

Gunn, James, ed., *The Road to Science Fiction*, vol. 3: *From Heinlein to Here* (New York: Mentor, 1979).

Hall, Austin, 'The Man Who Saved the Earth' (1919). In Conklin, ed., *The Golden Age of Science Fiction*.

Hamilton, Edmond, 'In the World's Dusk' (1936). In Wollheim, ed., *The End of the World*.

Harrison, Tony, *Square Rounds* (London: Faber, 1992).

Heinlein, Robert A., 'Blowups Happen' (1940). In Conklin, ed., *The Golden Age of Science Fiction*.

—— 'Solution Unsatisfactory' (as Anson MacDonald; 1941). In Conklin, ed., *The Golden Age of Science Fiction*.

—— 'The Year of the Jackpot' (1952). In Pohl, ed., *Nightmare Age*.

Hoban, Russell, *Riddley Walker* (London: Picador, 1982; 1st edn 1980).

Hodgson, William H., *The House on the Borderland* (New York: Manor Books, 1977; 1st edn 1908).

Huxley, Aldous, *Brave New World* (London: Penguin, 1963; 1st edn 1932).

—— *Ape and Essence* (London: Chatto & Windus, 1947).

Ibuse, Masuji, *Black Rain*, trans. John Bester (Tokyo: Kodansha International, 1979; 1st edn 1969).

Janson, Gustaf, 'A Vision of the Future' (1912). In Clarke, ed., *The Tale of the Next Great War*.

Johnstone, William W., *Out of the Ashes* (New York: Windsor, 1996; 1st edn 1983).

Kaiser, Georg, *Gas* (Frankfurt: Ullstein, 1978; 1st edn 1918–20).

Knight, Damon, ed., *Science Fiction of the Thirties* (New York: Avon Books, 1977).

Kornbluth, C. M., 'The Luckiest Man in Denv' (1952). In Pohl, ed., *Nightmare Age*.

Leiber, Fritz, 'Coming Attraction' (1950). In Gunn, ed., *The Road to Science Fiction*.

—— 'A Bad Day for Sales' (1953). In Pohl, ed., *Nightmare Age*.

Leinster, Murray, 'The Wabbler' (1942). In Schmidt, ed., *War and Peace*.

London, Jack, 'The Unparalleled Invasion' (1910), in *The Short Stories of Jack London* (New York: Macmillan, 1990).

Long, Amelia Reynolds, 'Omega' (1932). In Wollheim, ed., *The End of the World*.

Macbeth, George and Bingham, J.S., *The Doomsday Show: A Cabaret*, in *New English Dramatists 14* (London: Penguin, 1970; 1st edn 1964).

Madách, Imre, *The Tragedy of Man*, trans. Iain MacLeod (Edinburgh: Canongate, 1993; 1st edn 1861).

Malraux, André, *The Walnut Trees of Altenburg*, trans. A. W. Fielding (University of Chicago Press, 1992; 1st edn 1948).

Malzberg, Barry N. and Pronzini, Bill, eds., *The End of Summer: Science Fiction Stories* (New York: Ace Books, 1979).

Mann, Thomas, *The Magic Mountain*, trans. H. T. Lowe-Porter (London: Penguin, 1960; 1st edn 1924).

Masters, Dexter, *The Accident* (London: Faber & Faber, 1987; 1st edn 1955).

Merle, Robert, *Malevil*, trans. Derek Coltman (New York: Warner, 1975; 1st edn 1972).

Merril, Judith, 'That Only a Mother' (1948). In Franklin, ed., *Countdown to Midnight*.

—— *Shadow on the Hearth* (New York: Doubleday, 1950).

Miller, Walter M., Jr, *A Canticle for Leibowitz* (London: Orbit, 2002; 1st edn 1959).

—— and Greenberg, Martin H., eds., *Beyond Armageddon: Twenty-One Sermons to the Dead* (New York: Donald I. Fine, Inc., 1985).

Moore, Ward, 'Lot' (1953). In Franklin, ed., *Countdown to Midnight*.

Nathanson, Isaac R., 'The World Aflame', *Amazing Stories* (Jan. 1935), 44–87.

Newcomb, Simon, *His Wisdom The Defender* (New York: Arno Press, 1975; 1st edn 1900).

Nichols, Robert and Browne, Maurice, *Wings Over Europe* (1928), in Montrose J. Moses, ed., *Dramas of Modernism and their Forerunners* (Boston: Little, Brown, & Co., 1931).

Nicolson, Harold, *Public Faces* (London: Constable, 1932).

Nowlan, Philip Francis, *Armageddon 2419 ad* (New York: Ace, 1962; 1st edn 1928).

Noyes, Alfred, *No Other Man* (New York: Frederick A. Stokes, 1940).

Noyes, Pierrepont B., *The Pallid Giant: A Tale of Yesterday and Tomorrow* (New York: Revell, 1927).

Owen, Dean, *End of the World* (New York: Ace Books, 1962).

Padgett, Lewis, 'The Piper's Son' (1945). In Conklin, ed., *The Golden Age of Science Fiction*.

Plath, Sylvia, 'Doomsday', *Harper's Magazine*, 208 (May 1954), 29.

Pohl, Frederik, ed., *Nightmare Age* (New York: Ballantine, 1971).

Pournelle, J. E., ed., *There Will Be War* (New York: Tor Books, 1984).

Priestley, J. B., *The Doomsday Men: An Adventure* (London: Heinemann, 1938).

Prochnau, William, *Trinity's Child* (New York: G. P. Putnam's Sons, 1983).

Rayer, F. G., *Tomorrow Sometimes Comes* (London: Icon Books, 1962; 1st edn 1951).

Ridenour, Louis N., 'Pilot Lights of the Apocalypse' (1946). In Conklin, ed., *Great Science Fiction by Scientists*.

Robida, Albert, *La Guerre au vingtième siècle* (1887). In Clarke, ed., *The Tale of the Next Great War*.

Rose, Horace F., *The Maniac's Dream* (London: Duckworth, 1946).

Roshwald, Mordecai, *Level 7* (University of Wisconsin Press, 2004; 1st edn 1959).

Schmidt, Stanley, ed., *War and Peace: Possible Futures from 'Analog'* (New York: Davis, 1983).

Sheckley, Robert, 'The Last Weapon' (1953), in Frederik Pohl, ed., *STAR Science Fiction Stories* (New York: Ballatine, 1961).

—— 'The Store of the Worlds' (1959). In Miller and Greenberg, eds., *Beyond Armageddon*.

Sheehan, Perley Poore and Davis, Robt. H., 'Blood and Iron: A Play in One Act', *Strand Magazine*, 54 (1917), 359–65.

Shiel, M. P., *Yellow Danger* (London: Grant Richards, 1898).

Shute, Nevil, *On the Beach* (London: Heinemann, 1957).

Simak, Clifford D., 'Lobby' (1944). In Conklin, ed., *The Golden Age of Science Fiction*.

Sinclair, Upton, *The Millennium* (New York: Quality Paperback Book Club, 2000; 1st edn 1907).

Smale, Fred C., 'The Abduction of Alexandra Seine' (1900). In Evans and Evans, eds., *Beyond the Gaslight*.

Smith, Evelyn E., 'The Most Sentimental Man' (1957), in Isaac Asimov, Martin Harry Greenberg and Charles G. Waugh, eds., *The Last Man on Earth* (New York: Ballantine, 1984; 1st edn 1982).

Smith, George H., *The Coming of the Rats* (London: Digit Books, 1964; 1st edn 1961).

—— *Doomsday Wing* (Derby, Conn.: Monarch Books, 1963).

Snow, C. P., *The New Men* (Thirsk, North Yorkshire: House of Stratus, 2001; 1st edn 1954).

Spinrad, Norman, 'The Big Flash' (1969). In Benford and Greenberg, eds., *Nuclear War*.

Stewart, George R., *Earth Abides* (London: Gollancz, 2003; 1st edn 1949).

Stockton, Frank R., *The Great War Syndicate* (New York: Dodd, Mead & Co., 1889).

Strieber, Whitley, *The Day After Tomorrow* (London: Gollancz, 2004).

Stuart, Don A. [John W. Campbell, Jr], 'Atomic Power' (1934), In Conklin, ed., *The Golden Age of Science Fiction*.

Sturgeon, Theodore, 'Artnan Process' (1941). In Sturgeon, *Starshine*.

—— 'Killdozer!' (1944). In Conklin, ed., *The Golden Age of Science Fiction*.

—— 'Memorial' (1946), in Isaac Asimov and Martin Harry Greenberg, eds., *The Golden Years of Science Fiction*, 4th Series (New York: Bonanza, 1984; 1st edn 1982).

—— 'Thunder and roses' (1947). In Franklin, ed., *Countdown to Midnight*.

—— *Starshine* (London: Gollancz, 1969).

Swayne, Martin, 'The Sleep-Beam', *Strand Magazine*, 55 (Mar. 1918), 186–93.

Szilard, Leo, 'My Trial as a War Criminal' (1949). In Szilard, *The Voice of the Dolphins*.

—— 'The Diary of Dr Davis', *BAS*, 6 (1950), 51–7.

—— *The Voice of the Dolphins and Other Stories* (Stanford University Press, 1992; 1st edn 1961).

Tenn, William, 'The Sickness' (1955), in William Tenn, *Time in Advance* (London: Panther, 1966).

Train, Arthur and Wood, Robert Williams, *The Man Who Rocked the Earth* (New York: Doubleday, 1915).

Tucker, Wilson, *The Long Loud Silence* (London: Coronet, 1980; 1st edn 1952).

Vickers, Capt. C. E., 'The Trenches' (1908). In Clarke, ed., *The Tale of the Next Great War*.

Vogt, A. E. Van, 'Secret Unattainable' (1942). In Vogt, *Away and Beyond*.

—— 'The Weapon Shop' (1942). In Asimov and Greenberg, eds., *The Golden Years of Science Fiction*, 2nd series.

—— 'The Great Engine' (1943). In Vogt, *Away and Beyond*.

—— *Away and Beyond* (New York: Berkley, 1959; 1st edn 1952).

Vonnegut, Kurt, Jr, *Cat's Cradle* (London: Penguin, n.d.; 1st edn 1963).

Wallis, George C., 'The Last Days of Earth' (1901). In Evans and Evans, eds., *Beyond the Gaslight*.

Wells, H. G., 'The Lord of the Dynamos' (1894). In Wells, *The Complete Short Stories*.

—— 'The Stolen Bacillus' (1895). In Wells, *The Complete Short Stories*.

—— *The Time Machine* (1895). In Wells, *The Science Fiction*.

—— *The Island of Doctor Moreau* (1896). In Wells, *The Science Fiction*.

—— *The Invisible Man* (Glasgow: Fontana, 1978; 1st edn 1897).

—— 'The Land Ironclads' (1903). In Wells, *The Complete Short Stories*.

—— *The War in the Air* (Thirsk: North Yorkshire: House of Stratus, 2002; 1st edn 1908).

—— *Tono-Bungay* (London: Everyman, 1999; 1st edn 1909).

—— *The Last War* [*The World Set Free: A Story of Mankind*] (Lincoln: University of Nebraska Press, 2001; 1st edn 1914).

—— *The Shape of Things to Come: The Ultimate Revolution* (London: Hutchinson, 1933).

—— *The Complete Short Stories of H. G. Wells*, ed. John Hammond (London: Dent, 1998).

—— *The Science Fiction*, vol. 1 (London: Phoenix, 1998).

Wilkinson, A., Jr, 'When the Earth Melted', *Top-Notch* (15 June 1918), 1–6.

Williams, Robert Moore, *Doomsday Eve* (New York: Ace Books, 1957).

—— *The Day They H-Bombed Los Angeles* (New York: Ace Books, 1961).

Wollheim, Donald A., ed., *The End of the World* (New York: Ace Books, 1956).

Wylie, Philip, *The Smuggled Atom Bomb* (New York: Avon Books, 1951; 1st edn 1948).

—— *Tomorrow!* (New York: Popular Library, 1963; 1st edn 1954).

—— *Triumph* (New York: Crest Book, 1964; 1st edn 1962).

—— *The End of the Dream* (New York: Daw Books, 1973; 1st edn 1972).

Zamyatin, Yevgeny, *We* (London: Penguin, 1984; 1st edn 1924).

Non-fiction

Abrash, Merritt, 'Through Logic to Apocalypse: Science-Fiction Scenarios of Nuclear Deterrence Breakdown', *Science Fiction Studies*, 13 (1986), 129–38.

Alkon, Paul K., *Science Fiction Before 1900: Imagination Discovers Technology* (New York: Routledge, 2002).

Anderson, Poul, *Thermonuclear Warfare* (Derby, Conn.: Monarch, 1963).

Anon., *Bomber Command Continues: The Air Ministry Account of the Rising Offensive Against Germany July 1941–June 1942* (London: His Majesty's Stationery Office, 1942).

Anon., 'The Breeder Reactor', *Scientific American*, 186–7 (Dec. 1952), 58–60.

Anon., 'Developments in Gas Warfare', *American Review of Reviews*, 57 (Apr. 1918), 425–6.

Anon., 'The First Pile', *BAS*, 18 (Dec. 1962), 19–24.

Anon., *The H Bomb* (New York: Didier, 1950).

Anon., 'If Bombs Do Fall on US – What People Look for', *US News and World Report* (25 Sep. 1961), 51–5.

Anon., 'The Interpretation of Radium', *Athenaeum*, no. 4,254 (8 May 1909), 562–63.

Anon., 'Mobilized Science in France', *American Review of Reviews*, 56 (Nov. 1917), 545–7.

Anon., 'A Modern Utopia', *Edinburgh Review*, 202 (July 1905), 56–78.

Anon., 'The New Photographic Marvel: The Röntgen Rays', *American Monthly Review of Reviews*, 13 (Apr. 1896), 175–6.

Anon., 'October, 1962 – The Cuba Crisis: Nuclear War Was Hours Away', *Newsweek* (28 Oct. 1963), 18–20.

Anon., 'The Photography of the Invisible', *Quarterly Review*, 183, no. 366 (Apr. 1896), 496–507.

Anon., 'Professor Röntgen Interviewed', *American Monthly Review of Reviews*, 13 (Jan.–June 1896), 437.

Anon., 'Push-Button War', *Newsweek*, 26 (27 Aug. 1945), 25.

Anon., 'Radioactivity', *Athenaeum*, no. 3,995 (21 May 1904), 657–8.

Anon., 'The Revelations of Radium', *Edinburgh Review*, 198 (Oct. 1903), 374–99.

Anon., 'Science and Literature', *The Dial*, 42 (1 May 1907), 274–5.

Anon., 'Science on the War Path', *Science*, 43, no. 1,106 (10 Mar. 1916), 350–52.

Anon., 'Superbomb', *Newsweek* (30 Oct. 1961), 44–5.

Anon., 'The "Think Factories"', *New Republic* (15 Jan. 1962), 33–40.

Anon., 'The Use of Asphyxiating Gas', *The Scientific Monthly*, 7, no. 4 (Oct. 1918), 381–3.

Anon., 'Warfare of the Future: The Radium Destroyer', *The Electrical Experimenter* (Nov. 1915), 315.

Anon., 'A Weapon to Kill Everybody . . . Or Just Cold-War Bluster?', *US News and World Report* (28 Sep. 1964), 8.

Anon., 'The World Set Free', *New Statesman* (5 Feb. 1916), 415–16.

Arnold, James R., 'The Hydrogen–Cobalt Bomb', *BAS*, 6 (Oct. 1950), 290–92.

Arns, Robert G., 'The High-Vacuum X-Ray Tube: Technological Change in Social Context', *Technology and Culture*, 38 (1997), 852–90.

Ashley, Mike, *The Time Machines: The Story of the Science-Fiction Pulp Magazines from the Beginning to 1950* (Liverpool University Press, 2000).

—— *Transformations: The Story of the Science-Fiction Magazines from 1950 to 1970* (Liverpool University Press, 2005).

Badash, Lawrence, *Radioactivity in America: Growth and Decay of a Science* (Baltimore: Johns Hopkins University Press, 1979).

Baker, Ray Stannard, 'Liquid Air', *Strand Magazine*, 17 (1899), 459–68.

Balmer, Brian, 'How Does an Accident Become an Experiment?', *Science as Culture*, 13 (2 June 2004), 197–228.

Barnaby, Frank, *How to Build a Nuclear Bomb and Other Weapons of Mass Destruction* (London: Granta, 2003).

Barnaby, Wendy, *The Plague Makers: The Secret World of Biological Warfare* (New York: Continuum, 2000).

Bartter, Martha A., *The Way to Ground Zero: The Atomic Bomb in American Science Fiction* (New York: Greenwood, 1988).

Baskerville, Chas, '"Gas" in this War: The Vast Development of a New Military Weapon', *American Review of Reviews*, 58 (Sep. 1918), 273–80.

Battersby, H. F. Prevost, 'The New Mechanism of War', *Edinburgh Review*, 221 (Apr. 1915), 385–403.

Baxter, John, *Stanley Kubrick: A Biography* (London: HarperCollins, 1997).

Benn, Tony, *Out of the Wilderness: Diaries 1963–67* (London: Hutchinson, 1987).

—— *Years of Hope: Diaries, Letters and Papers 1940–1962*, ed. Ruth Winstone (London: Hutchinson, 1994).

Bennett, Charles H., 'Demons, Engines and the Second Law', *Scientific American*, 257 (Nov. 1987), 88–96.

Berman, Marshall, *All That Is Solid Melts into Air: The Experience of Modernity* (London: Verso, 1995).

Bernstein, Barton J., 'Why We Didn't Use Poison Gas in World War II', *American Heritage*, 36 (1985), 40–45.

—— 'Introduction', in Leo Szilard, *The Voice of the Dolphins and Other Stories* (Stanford University Press, 1992), 3–43.

—— 'Truman and the A-bomb: Targeting Noncombatants, Using the Bomb, and his Defending the "Decision"', *Journal of Military History*, 62 (1998), 547–70.

Bernstein, Jeremy, *Hans Bethe: Prophet of Energy* (New York: Basic, 1980).

—— *Oppenheimer: Portrait of an Enigma* (London: Duckworth, 2004).

Bess, Michael, *Realism, Utopia, and the Mushroom Cloud: Four Activist Intellectuals and their Strategies for Peace, 1945–1989* (University of Chicago Press, 1993).

Bethe, Hans, Brown, Harrison, Seitz, Frederick and Szilard, Leo, 'The Facts about the Hydrogen Bomb', *BAS*, 6 (Apr. 1950), 106–9, 126–7.

Bickel, Lennard, *The Deadly Element: The Story of Uranium* (London: Macmillan, 1980).

Bilstein, Roger, *Flight in America 1900–1983: From the Wrights to the Astronauts* (Baltimore: Johns Hopkins University Press, 1984).

Bird, Kai and Lifschultz, Lawrence, *Hiroshima's Shadow: Writings on the Denial of History and the Smithsonian Controversy* (Stony Creek, Conn.: Pamphleteer's Press, 1998).

Black, Jeremy, *War: Past, Present & Future* (New York: St Martin's, 2000).

Bleich, Alan Ralph, *The Story of X-Rays from Röntgen to Isotopes* (New York: Dover, 1960).

Born, G. V. R., 'The Wide-Ranging Family History of Max Born', *Notes & Records of the Royal Society*, 56, no. 2 (May 2002), 219–62.

Born, Max, *My Life: Recollections of a Nobel Laureate* (London: Taylor & Francis, 1978; 1st edn 1975).

—— *The Born–Einstein Letters 1916–1955: Friendship, Politics and Physics in Uncertain Times*, trans. Irene Born (London: Macmillan, 2005; 1st edn 1971).

Bourgin, Simon, 'Those Irresistible Hungarians', *Harper's*, 221 (Nov. 1960), 69–74.

Boyer, Paul, *By the Bomb's Early Light: American Thought and Culture at the Dawn of the Atomic Age* (Chapel Hill, NC: University of North Carolina Press, 1994).

Brian, Denis, *Einstein: A Life* (New York: Wiley, 1996).

Brians, Paul, *Nuclear Holocausts: Atomic War in Fiction 1895–1984* (Kent State University Press, 1987).

Brokoff, Jürgen, *Die Apokalypse in der Weimarer Republik* (Munich: Wilhelm Fink, 2001).

Broks, Peter, *Media Science Before the Great War* (Basingstoke: Macmillan, 1996).

Bronowski, J., *The Ascent of Man* (London: Book Club Associates, 1979; 1st edn 1973).

Brosnan, John, *Future Tense: The Cinema of Science Fiction* (New York: St Martin's, 1978).

Brown, Harrison, 'The 20th Year', *BAS*, 18 (Dec. 1962), 2–3.

Bundy, McGeorge, 'The Missed Chance to Stop the H-Bomb', *New York Review of Books*, 29 (13 May 1982), 13–21.

Burchett, Wilfred, *Shadows of Hiroshima* (London: Verso, 1983).

Burgess, George K., 'Applications of Science to Warfare in France', *The Scientific Monthly*, 5, no. 4 (Oct. 1917), 289–97.

Canaday, John, *The Nuclear Muse: Literature, Physics and the First Atomic Bombs* (Madison: University of Wisconsin Press, 2000).

Caputi, Jane, 'Nuclear Visions', *American Quarterly*, 47 (Mar. 1995), 165–75.

Carpenter, Charles A., *Dramatists and the Bomb: American and British Playwrights Confront the Nuclear Age, 1945–1964* (Westport, Conn.: Greenwood, 1999).

Carson, Rachel, *Silent Spring* (London: Hamish Hamilton, 1963).

Carter, G. B., *Porton Down: 75 Years of Chemical and Biological Research* (London: HMSO, 1992).

Cathcart, Brian, *The Fly in the Cathedral: How a Small Group of Cambridge Scientists Won the Race to Split the Atom* (London: Viking, 2004).

Caufield, Catherine, *Multiple Exposures: Chronicles of the Radiation Age* (London: Penguin, 1990).

Ceadel, Martin, 'Popular Fiction and the Next War, 1918–39', in Frank Gloversmith, ed., *Class, Culture and Social Change: A New View of the 1930s* (Brighton: Harvester, 1980), 161–84.

Chinnock, Frank W., *Nagasaki: The Forgotten Bomb* (London: George Allen & Unwin, 1970).

Clareson, Thomas D., *Some Kind of Paradise: The Emergence of American Science Fiction* (Westport, Conn.: Greenwood, 1985).

Clark, W. H., 'Chemical and Thermonuclear Explosives', *BAS*, 17 (Nov. 1961), 356–60.

Clarke, I.F., 'Forecasts of Warfare in Fiction 1803–1914', *Comparative Studies in Society and History*, 10 (Oct. 1967), 1–25.

—— *Voices Prophesying War: Future Wars 1763–3749* (Oxford University Press, 1992).

—— 'Before and After *The Battle of Dorking*', *Science Fiction Studies*, 24 (Mar. 1997).

—— 'Future-War Fiction: The First Main Phase, 1871–1900', *Science Fiction Studies*, 24 (Nov. 1997).

Clary, David A., *Rocket Man: Robert H. Goddard and the Birth of the Space Age* (New York: Hyperion, 2003).

Clute, John and Nicholls, Peter, eds., *The Encyclopedia of Science Fiction* (New York: St Martin's, 1993).

Coleman, Kim, *A History of Chemical Warfare* (Basingstoke: Palgrave, 2005).

Committee for the Compilation of Materials on Damage Caused by the Atomic Bombs in Hiroshima and Nagasaki, *Hiroshima and Nagasaki: The Physical, Medical, and Social Effects of the Atomic Bombings* (New York: Basic Books, 1981).

Compton, Arthur Holly, *Atomic Quest: A Personal Narrative* (London: Oxford University Press, 1956).

Conrad, Peter, *Modern Times, Modern Places* (London: Thames & Hudson, 1998).

Coren, Michael, *The Invisible Man: The Life and Liberties of H. G. Wells* (London: Bloomsbury, 1993).

Cornils, Ingo, 'The Martians Are Coming! War, Peace, Love and Scientific Progress in H. G. Wells's *The War of the Worlds* and Kurd Lasswitz's *Auf zwei Planeten*', *Comparative Literature*, 55 (2003), 24–41.

Cornwell, John, *Hitler's Scientists: Science, War and the Devil's Pact* (London: Allen Lane, 2003).

Cousins, Norman, 'Modern Man is Obsolete', *Saturday Review of Literature*, 28 (18 Aug. 1945), 5–9.

—— 'The Many Facets of Leo Szilard', *Saturday Review* (29 Apr. 1961), 15.

Crookes, William, 'Radium', *Science*, 17, no. 434 (24 Apr. 1903), 675–6.

—— 'Modern Views on Matter: The Realization of a Dream', *Science* 17, no. 443 (26 June 1903), 993–1003.

Cruickshank, A. D., 'Soddy at Oxford', *British Journal for the History of Science*, 12, no. 42 (1979), 277–88.

Curie, Mme Sklodowska, 'Radium and Radioactivity', *Century Illustrated*, 67 (Jan. 1904), 461–6.

Cushing, H. G. and Morris, A. V., eds., *Nineteenth Century Readers' Guide to Periodical Literature, 1890–1899*, 2 vols (New York: H. W. Wilson, 1944).

Dannen, Gene, 'The Einstein–Szilard Refrigerators', *Scientific American* (Jan. 1997), 74–9.

del Rey, Lester, *The World of Science Fiction: The History of a Subculture* (New York: Garland, 1980).

Disch, Thomas M., *The Dreams Our Stuff Is Made Of: How Science Fiction Conquered the World* (New York: Free Press, 1998).

Dolman, Frederick, 'Science in the New Century: What Will Be Its Greatest Achievements?', *Strand Magazine*, 21 (1901), 55–65.

Dowling, David H., 'The Atomic Scientist: Machine or Moralist?', *Science Fiction Studies*, 13 (1986), 139–47.

—— *Fictions of Nuclear Disaster* (Basingstoke: Macmillan, 1987).

Duncan, Robert Kennedy, 'Radio-activity: A New Property of Matter', *Harper's Monthly*, 105 (Sep. 1902), 356–66.

Dyson, Freeman, 'Weapons and Hope: I – Questions', *New Yorker*, 59 (6 Feb. 1984), 52–73.

—— 'Weapons and Hope: II – Tools', *New Yorker*, 59 (13 Feb. 1984), 67–117.

Dyson, George, *Project Orion: The Atomic Spaceship 1957–1965* (London: Allen Lane, 2002).

Einstein, Albert, 'Arms Can Bring No Security', *BAS*, 6 (Mar. 1950), 71.

—— *The Collected Papers of Albert Einstein* (Princeton University Press, 1987–); for each volume there is a separate English 'translation volume'.

Vol 5: Martin J. Klein, A. J. Kox and Robert Schulmann, eds., *The Swiss Years: Correspondence, 1902–1914* (1993) [cited in the Notes as *CP5*]. Trans. vol. by Anna Beck.

Vol 6: A. J. Kox, Martin J. Klein and Robert Schulmann, eds., *The Berlin Years: Writings, 1914–1917* (1996) [*CP6*]. Trans. vol. by Alfred Engel.

Vol 7: Michel Janssen, Robert Schulmann, József Illy, Christoph Lehner and Diana Kormos Buchwald, eds., *The Berlin Years: Writings, 1918–1921* (2002) [*CP7*]. Trans. vol. by Alfred Engel.

Vol 8: Robert Schulmann, A. J. Kox, Michel Janssen and József Illy, eds., *The Berlin Years: Correspondence, 1914–1918* (1998) [*CP8*]. Trans. vol. by Ann M. Hentschel.

Vol 9: Diana Kormos Buchwald, Robert Schulmann, József Illy, Daniel J. Kennefick and Tilman Sauer, eds., *The Berlin Years: Correspondence, January 1919–April 1920* (2004) [*CP9*]. Trans. vol. by Ann M. Hentschel.

Eksteins, Modris, *Rites of Spring: The Great War and the Modern Age* (London: Bantam, 1989).

Ellis, John, *The Social History of the Machine Gun* (London: Pimlico, 1993).

Engelhardt, Tom, 'Fifty Years Under a cloud', *Harper's Magazine*, 292 (Jan. 1996), 71–6.

Ermenc, Joseph J., ed., *Atomic Bomb Scientists. Memoirs, 1939–45* (Westport, Conn.: Meckler, 1989).

Esterer, Arnulf K. and Esterer, Louise A., *Prophet of the Atomic Age: Leo Szilard* (New York: Julian Messner, 1972).

Everett, Susanne, *Lost Berlin* (London: Hamlyn, 1979).

Farlow, W. G., 'The Popular Conception of the Scientific Man at the Present Day', *Science*, 23, no. 575 (5 Jan. 1906), 1–14.

Feld, Bernard, 'Leo Szilard, Scientist for All Seasons', *Social Research*, 51 (Autumn 1984), 675–90.

Fermi, Laura, *Atoms in the Family: My Life with Enrico Fermi* (University of Chicago Press, 1961; 1st edn 1954).

—— *Illustrious Immigrants: The Intellectual Migration from Europe, 1930–1941* (University of Chicago Press, 1968).

Ferrell, Robert H., ed., *Dear Bess: The Letters from Harry to Bess Truman, 1910–1959* (New York: Norton, 1983).

Feynman, Michelle, ed., *Richard P. Feynman: Don't You Have Time to Think?* (London: Allen Lane, 2005).

Feynman, Richard P., *'Surely You're Joking, Mr Feynman!': Adventures of a Curious Character* (New York: Norton, 1997).

Fisher, Peter S., *Fantasy and Politics: Visions of the Future in the Weimar Republic* (University of Wisconsin Press, 1991).

Fleming, Donald and Bailyn, Bernard, eds., *The Intellectual Migration: Europe and America 1930–1960* (Cambridge, Mass.: Belknap/Harvard University Press, 1969).

Fletcher, W. and Poole, M., eds., *Poole's Index to Periodical Literature, 1897–1902; 1903–1907* (London: Kegan Paul, 1903–).

Foot, Michael, *The History of Mr Wells* (London: Doubleday, 1995).

Forbes, Archibald, 'The New Mechanism of War', *Nineteenth Century*, 29 (May 1891), 782–95.

Fort, Adrian, *Prof: The Life of Frederick Lindemann* (London: Pimlico, 2004).

Foulkes, Maj. Gen. C. H., *'Gas!': The Story of the Special Brigade* (Uckfield, East Sussex: Naval & Military Press, 2001; 1st edn 1934).

Frank, Sir Charles, *Operation Epsilon: The Farm Hall Transcripts* (Bristol: Institute of Physics, 1993).

Frank, Philipp, *Einstein: His Life and Times*, trans. George Rosen (New York: Knopf, 1947).

Franklin, H. Bruce, 'Strange Scenarios: Science Fiction, the Theory of Alienation, and the Nuclear Gods', *Science Fiction Studies*, 13 (1986), 117–28.

—— *War Stars: The Superweapon and the American Imagination* (New York: Oxford University Press, 1988).

Frayling, Christopher, *Mad, Bad and Dangerous? The Scientist and the Cinema* (London: Reaktion, 2005).

Freedman, Michael I., 'Frederick Soddy and the Practical Significance of Radioactive Matter', *British Journal for the History of Science*, 12, no. 42 (1979), 257–60.

Frewin, Anthony, ed., *Are We Alone? The Stanley Kubrick Extraterrestrial-Intelligence Interviews* (London: Elliott & Thompson, 2005).

Friedrich, Otto, *Before the Deluge: A Portrait of Berlin in the 1920s* (New York: Harper & Row, 1972).

Friedrich, Thomas, *Berlin: A Photographic Portrait of the Weimar Years 1918–1933* (London: Tauris Parke, 1991).

Frisch, Otto R., *What Little I Remember* (Cambridge University Press, 1979).

Fyfe, Herbert C., 'The Röntgen Rays in Warfare', *Strand Magazine*, 17 (1899), 777–83.

Gabor, Dennis, 'Leo Szilard', *BAS*, 29 (Sep. 1973), 51–2.

Gamow, George, *Thirty Years That Shook Physics: The Story of Quantum Theory* (New York: Dover, 1985; 1st edn 1966).

Garwin, Richard L. and Charpak, Georges, *Megawatts and Megatons: The Future of Nuclear Power and Nuclear Weapons* (University of Chicago Press, 2002).

Gavroglu, Kostas, *Fritz London: A Scientific Biography* (Cambridge University Press, 1995).

Geddes, Donald Porter, ed., *The Atomic Age Opens* (New York: Pocket Books, 1945).

Gery, John, *Ways of Nothingness: Nuclear Annihilation and Contemporary American Poetry* (Gainesville, Fla: University Press of Florida, 1996).

Gilbert, Martin, *Churchill: A Life* (London: Heinemann, 1991).

Glass, Bentley, 'The Scientist in Contemporary Fiction', *Scientific Monthly*, 85 (Dec. 1957), 288–93.

Goodchild, Peter, *Edward Teller: The Real Dr Strangelove* (London: Weidenfeld & Nicolson, 2004).

Graetzer, Hans and Anderson, David, eds., *The Discovery of Nuclear Fission: A Documentary History* (New York: Van Nostrand Reinhold, 1971).

Grandy, David A., *Leo Szilard: Science as a Mode of Being* (Lanham, Md: University Press of America, 1996).

Grove, Allen W., 'Röntgen's Ghosts: Photography, X-rays, and the Victorian Imagination', *Literature and Medicine*, 16 (1997), 141–73.

Gunn, James, ed., *The New Encyclopedia of Science Fiction* (New York: Viking, 1988).

Gunn, Sidney, 'Science and Literature', *Science*, 34, no. 878 (27 Oct. 1911), 550–56.

Guthrie, Anna L., ed., *Readers' Guide to Periodical Literature*: vol. 1, *1900–1904*; vol. 2, *1905–1910*; vol. 3, *1910–1914*; vol. 4, *1915–1918* (Minneapolis: Wilson Company, 1905–).

Haber, L. F., *The Poisonous Cloud: Chemical Warfare in the First World War* (Oxford: Clarendon Press, 1986).

Hachiya, Michihiko, *Hiroshima Diary: The Journal of a Japanese Physician August 6–September 30, 1945* (Chapel Hill, NC: University of North Carolina Press, 1995; 1st edn 1955).

Hahn, Otto, *My Life*, trans. Ernst Kaiser and Eithne Wilkins (London: Macdonald, 1970).

Haldane, J. B. S., *Callinicus: A Defence of Chemical Warfare* (London: Kegan Paul, 1925).

Hales, Peter Bacon, *Atomic Spaces: Living on the Manhattan Project* (Urbana, Ill.: University of Illinois Press, 1997).

Hall, H. W., ed., *Science Fiction and Fantasy Reference Index 1878–1985. An International Author and Subject Index to History and Criticism*: vol. 1, *Author Entries*; vol. 2, *Subject Entries* (Detroit: Gale Research, 1987).

Hamilton, Cosmo, 'War of the Future', *The New Republic*, 6 (8 Apr. 1916), 261–3.

Hardy, Phil, ed., *The Overlook Film Encyclopedia: Science Fiction* (New York: Overlook, 1995).

Harris, D. Fraser, 'The Man of Science After the War', *The Scientific Monthly*, 7, no. 4 (Oct. 1918), 320–25.

Harris, Robert and Paxman, Jeremy, *A Higher Form of Killing: The Secret History of Chemical and Biological Warfare* (London: Arrow, 2002).

Harris, Sheldon H., *Factories of Death: Japanese Biological Warfare, 1932–45, and the American Cover-up* (London: Routledge, 1997).

Hartcup, Guy, *The War of Invention: Scientific Developments, 1914–18* (London: Brassey's Defence Publishers, 1988).

—— *The Effect of Science on the Second World War* (Basingstoke: Palgrave Macmillan, 2003).

Haynes, Roslynn D., *H. G. Wells: Discoverer of the Future. The Influence of Science on his Thought* (London: Macmillan, 1980).

—— *From Faust to Strangelove: Representations of the Scientist in Western Literature* (Baltimore: Johns Hopkins University Press, 1994).

Heilbron, J. L., *Lawrence and His Laboratory: A History of the Lawrence Berkeley Laboratory* (Berkeley: University of California Press, 1989).

Heims, Steve J., *John von Neumann and Norbert Wiener: From Mathematics to the Technologies of Life and Death* (Cambridge, Mass.: MIT Press, 1980).

Hendershot, Cyndy, 'The Atomic Scientist, Science Fiction Films, and Paranoia: *The Day the Earth Stood Still, This Island Earth*, and *Killers from Outer Space*', *Journal of American Culture*, 20 (Spring 1997), 31–41.

Hennessy, Peter, *The Secret State: Whitehall and the Cold War* (London: Penguin, 2003).

Henriksen, Margot A., *Dr Strangelove's America: Society and Culture in the Atomic Age* (Berkeley: University of California Press, 1997).

Herf, Jeffrey, *Reactionary Modernism: Technology, Culture, and Politics in Weimar and the Third Reich* (Cambridge University Press, 1984).

Herken, Gregg, *The Winning Weapon: The Atomic Bomb in the Cold War, 1945–1950* (New York: Knopf, 1980).

—— *Brotherhood of the Bomb: The Tangled Lives and Loyalties of Robert Oppenheimer, Ernest Lawrence, and Edward Teller* (New York: Henry Holt, 2002).

Hermann, Armin, ed., *Hedwig Born, Max Born: Der Luxus des Gewissens* (Munich: Nymphenburger, 1969).

Hersey, John, *Hiroshima* (London: Penguin, 2001; 1st edn 1946).

Hershberg, James G., *James B Conant: Harvard to Hiroshima and the Making of the Nuclear Age* (Stanford University Press, 1993).

Hiebert, Erwin N., 'The Transformation of Physics', in Mikuláš Teich and Roy Porter, eds., *Fin de Siècle and its Legacy* (Cambridge University Press, 1990), 235–53.

Hirsch, Walter, 'The Image of the Scientist in Science Fiction: A Content Analysis', *American Journal of Sociology*, 63 (Mar. 1958), 506–12.

Hoberman, J., 'When Dr No Met Dr Strangelove', *Sight and Sound*, 12 (Dec. 1993), 16–21.

Hoffmann, Klaus, *Otto Hahn: Achievement and Responsibility* (New York: Springer, 2001).

Hogg, Ian V., *German Secret Weapons of the Second World War* (London: Greenhill, 2002).

Holmsten, Brian and Lubertozzi, Alex, eds., *The Complete War of the Worlds* (Napierville, Ill.: Sourcebooks, 2001).

Houghton, Walter E., ed., *The Wellesley Index to Victorian Periodicals, 1824–1900* (University of Toronto Press, 1966–79).

Howes, Ruth H. and Herzenberg, Caroline L., *Their Day in the Sun: Women of the Manhattan Project* (Philadelphia: Temple University Press, 1999).

Howorth, Muriel, *Atomic Transmutation: The Greatest Discovery Ever*

Made. From Memoirs of Professor Frederick Soddy (London: New World, 1953).

—— *Pioneer Research on the Atom: The Life Story of Frederick Soddy* (St Leonards on Sea, Sussex: King Bros, 1958).

Hughes, J., 'Deconstructing the Bomb: Recent Perspectives on Nuclear History', *British Journal for the History of Science*, 37 (Dec. 2004), 455–64.

Hughes, Thomas P., 'Einstein, Inventors, and Invention', in Mara Beller, Robert S. Cohen and Jürgen Renn, eds., *Einstein in Context*, special issue of *Science in Context* (Cambridge University Press, 1993), 25–42.

—— *American Genesis: A Century of Invention and Technological Enthusiasm, 1870–1970* (University of Chicago Press, 2004; 1st edn 1989).

Hutchins, Robert M., 'Szilard and the Dolphins', *BAS*, 17 (Sep. 1961), 290.

Huxley, Aldous, *Brave New World Revisited* (New York: Harper & Row, 1989; 1st edn 1958).

Hyde, William J., 'The Socialism of H. G. Wells in the Early Twentieth Century', *Journal of the History of Ideas*, 17 (Apr. 1956), 217–34.

James, Edward and Mendlesohn, Farah, eds., *The Cambridge Companion to Science Fiction* (Cambridge University Press, 2003).

Jamison, Andrew and Eyerman, Ron, *Seeds of the Sixties* (Berkeley: University of California Press, 1994).

Jenkins, Dominick, *The Final Frontier: America, Science, and Terror* (London: Verso, 2002).

Jones, Howard Mumford, *The Age of Energy: Varieties of American Experience 1865–1915* (New York: Viking, 1971).

Jungk, Robert, *Brighter Than a Thousand Suns: A Personal History of the Atomic Scientists* (San Diego: Harcourt, 1986; 1st edn 1956).

Kaempffert, Waldemar, 'War and Technology', *American Journal of Sociology*, 46, no. 4 (Jan. 1941), 431–44.

Kahn, Herman, *On Thermonuclear War* (Princeton University Press, 1961; 1st edn 1960).

Kaplan, Fred M., *The Wizards of Armageddon* (New York: Simon & Schuster, 1983).

Keegan, John, *The Face of Battle* (New York: Viking, 1976).

Keeney, Douglas L., *The Doomsday Scenario: The Official Doomsday Scenario Written by the United States Government during the Cold War* (St Paul, Minn.: MBI Publishing, 2002).

Kelly, Jack, *Gunpowder: A History of the Explosive That Changed the World* (London: Atlantic Books, 2005).

Kirsten, Christa and Treder, Hans-Jürgen, eds., *Albert Einstein in Berlin: 1913–1933* (Berlin: Akademie-Verlag, 1979).

Kleiner, Elaine L., 'H. G. Wells, Joseph Conrad and the Scientific Romance', *Cahiers Victoriens et Edouardiens*, 46 (Oct. 1997), 159–66.

Knell, Hermann, *To Destroy a City: Strategic Bombing and its Human Consequences in World War II* (Cambridge, Mass.: Da Capo, 2003).

Knollys, W. W., 'War in the Future', *Fortnightly Review*, 54, ns 48 (Aug. 1890), 274–81.

Lang, Daniel, *From Hiroshima to the Moon: Chronicles of Life in the Atomic Age* (New York: Simon & Schuster, 1959).

Lanouette, William with Silard, Bela, *Genius in the Shadows: A Biography of Leo Szilard, The Man Behind the Bomb* (University of Chicago Press, 1994; 1st edn 1992).

Lapham, Lewis H., ed., *The End of the World* (New York: Thomas Dunne, 2000).

Lapp, Ralph E., 'The Strategy of Overkill', *BAS*, 19 (Apr. 1963), 4.

Laurence, William L., *Dawn over Zero: The Story of the Atomic Bomb* (London: Museum, 1947).

Leitner, Gerit von, *Der Fall Clara Immerwahr: Leben für eine humane Wissenschaft* (Munich: Beck, 1994).

Lessard, S., 'The Present Moment', *New Yorker*, 63 (13 Apr. 1987), 36–59.

Levenson, Thomas, *Einstein in Berlin* (New York: Bantam, 2004).

Lilienthal, David E., *The Journals of David E. Lilienthal*: vol. 2, *The Atomic Energy Years, 1945–1950* (New York: Harper & Row, 1964).

Lindqvist, Sven, *A History of Bombing*, trans. Linda Haverty Rugg (London: Granta, 2002).

Linner, Rachelle, *City of Silence: Listening to Hiroshima* (New York: Orbis, 1995).

LoBrutto, Vincent, *Stanley Kubrick: A Biography* (London: Faber, 1998).

Lodge, Sir Oliver, 'Scientific Developments Probable and Possible', *Strand Magazine*, 54 (1917), 607–12.

Lyons, Gene, 'Invisible Wars', *Harper's Magazine*, 263 (Dec. 1981), 37–52.

McCagg, William O., Jr, *Jewish Nobles and Geniuses in Modern Hungary* (Boulder, Colo.: Columbia University Press, 1986).

McConnell, Frank, *The Science Fiction of H. G. Wells* (Oxford University Press, 1981).

MacKenzie, Norman and MacKenzie, Jeanne, *The Life of H. G. Wells: The Time Traveller* (London: Hogarth, 1987).

Macrae, Norman, *John von Neumann* (New York: Pantheon, 1992).

Madle, Robert A. and Moskowitz, Sam, 'Did Science Fiction Predict Atomic Energy?', *Science Fiction Quarterly* (Nov. 1952), 81–8.

Makhijani, Arjun, ' "Always" the Target?', *BAS*, 51, no. 3 (1995), 23–7.

—— 'Nuclear Targeting: The First 60 Years.' *BAS*, 59, no. 3 (2003), 60–65.

Malik, John, 'The Yields of the Hiroshima and Nagasaki Nuclear Explosions', Los Alamos National Laboratory, report LA-8819/UC-34 (Sep. 1985).

Mangold, Tom and Goldberg, Jeff, *Plague Wars: A True Story of Biological Warfare* (London: Pan, 2000).

Markley, Robert, *Dying Planet: Mars in Science and the Imagination* (Durham, NC: Duke University Press, 2005).

Marseille, Walter W., 'On Thermonuclear War', *BAS*, 17 (Apr. 1961), 157–9, 166.

Martin, Thomas Commerford, Wood, R.W., Thomson, Elihu, Thompson, Silvanus P., McLennan, J.C. and Edison, Thomas A., 'Photographing the Unseen', *Century Illustrated*, 52, ns 30 (May–Oct. 1896), 120–31.

Marx, George, *The Voice of the Martians* (Budapest: Akadémiai Kiadó, 1997).

Maude, F. N., 'Can Science Abolish War?', *Contemporary Review*, 93 (Apr. 1908), 470–77.

Mayer, Douglas W. F., 'Energy from Matter', *Discovery*, 2, no. 18 (Sep. 1939), 459–60.

—— 'Energy from Matter: Some Recent Developments', *Discovery*, 2, no. 20 (Nov. 1939), 573.

Mendelssohn, K., *The World of Walther Nernst: The Rise and Fall of German Science* (London: Macmillan, 1973).

Merricks, Linda, *The World Made New: Frederick Soddy, Science, Politics, and Environment* (Oxford University Press, 1996).

Merritt, Ernest, 'The New Element Radium', *Century Illustrated*, 67 (Jan. 1904), 451–60.

Michaelis, Anthony R., 'How Nuclear Energy Was Foretold', *New Scientist*, no. 276 (1 Mar. 1962), 507–9.

Miles, Wyndham D., 'The Idea of Chemical Warfare in Modern Times', *Journal of the History of Ideas*, 31, no. 2 (1970), 297–304.

Millhauser, Milton, 'Dr Newton and Mr Hyde: Scientists in Fiction from Swift to Stevenson', *Nineteenth-Century Fiction*, 28 (Dec. 1973), 287–304.

Milne, Tom, 'Dr Strangelove', *Sight and Sound*, 33 (1963/4), 37–8.

Moffett, Cleveland, 'M Curie, the Discoverer of Radium', *Strand Magazine*, 27 (Jan. 1904), 65–73.

Moszkowski, Alexander, *Conversations with Einstein*, trans. Henry L. Brose (London: Sidgwick & Jackson, 1972; 1st edn 1921).

Mould, Richard F., *A History of X-Rays and Radium with a Chapter on Radiation Units: 1895–1937* (Sutton: IPC Business Press, 1980).

Muirhead, Prof. James F., 'The Use of Poison Gas', *Nation*, 17 (3 July 1915), 450.

Newman, James R., 'Let Our Children Go . . .', *Newsweek* (9 Oct. 1961), 26.

—— 'Two Discussions of Thermonuclear War', *Scientific American* (Mar. 1961), 197–204.

Norris, John and Fowler, Will, *NBC: Nuclear, Biological and Chemical Warfare on the Modern Battlefield* (London: Brassey's Defence Publishers, 1997).

O'Brien, Daniel, *SF:UK: How British Science Fiction Changed the World* (London: Reynolds & Hearn, 2000).

Oliphant, Mark, 'The Beginning: Chadwick and the Neutron', *BAS*, 38 (Dec. 1982), 14–18.

Palevsky, Mary, *Atomic Fragments: A Daughter's Questions* (Berkeley: University of California Press, 2000).

Parrinder, Patrick, ed., *H. G. Wells: The Critical Heritage* (London: Routledge, 1972).

—— ed., *Science Fiction: A Critical Guide* (London: Longman, 1979).

—— *Shadows of the Future: H. G. Wells, Science Fiction, and Prophecy* (Syracuse University Press, 1995).

Patai, Raphael, *The Jews of Hungary: History, Culture, Psychology* (Detroit: Wayne State University Press, 1996).

Peierls, Rudolf E., *Atomic Histories* (New York: American Institute of Physics, 1997).

Perrett, Geoffrey, *A Dream of Greatness: The American People, 1945–1963* (New York: Coward, McCann & Geoghegan, 1979).

Perrine, Toni A., *Film and the Nuclear Age: Representing Cultural Anxiety* (New York: Garland, 1998).

Pick, Daniel, *War Machine: The Rationalisation of Slaughter in the Modern Age* (New Haven: Yale University Press, 1996).

Porro, Jeffrey D., 'The Policy War: Brodie vs Kahn', *BAS*, 38 (1982), 16–19.

Poundstone, William, *Prisoner's Dilemma* (New York: Anchor, 1992).

Preston, Richard A. and Wise, Sydney F., *Men in Arms: A History of Warfare and its Interrelationships with Western Society* (New York: Holt, Rinehart & Winston, 1979).

Price, Richard M., 'A Genealogy of the Chemical Weapons Taboo', *International Organization*, 49, no. 1 (1995), 73–103.

—— *The Chemical Weapons Taboo* (Ithaca, NY: Cornell University Press, 1997).

Pupin, M. I., 'Röntgen Rays', *Science*, 3, no. 59 (14 Feb. 1896), 231–5.

Quinn, Susan, *Marie Curie: A Life* (London: Heinemann, 1995).

Rabinowitch, Eugene, 'New Year's Thoughts 1963', *BAS*, 19 (Jan. 1963), 2.

—— '[James Franck], 1882–1964; [Leo Szilard], 1898–1964', *BAS*, 20 (1964), 16–20 [the title of this joint obituary has pictures of Franck and Szilard in place of their names].

Rabkin, Eric S., Greenberg, Martin Harry and Olander, Joseph D., eds., *The End of the World* (Carbondale, Ill.: Southern Illinois University Press, 1983).

Ramsay, William, 'The Becquerel Rays', *Contemporary Review*, 81 (Jan.–June 1902), 730–40.

Reid, R. W., *Tongues of Conscience: War and the Scientist's Dilemma* (London: Constable, 1969).

Renn, Jürgen, ed., *Albert Einstein: Chief Engineer of the Universe. One Hundred Authors for Einstein* (Weinheim: Wiley-VCH, 2005).

Renneberg, Monika and Walker, Mark, eds., *Science, Technology and National Socialism* (Cambridge University Press, 1994).

Rhodes, Richard, *The Making of the Atomic Bomb* (London: Penguin, 1988).

—— *Dark Sun: The Making of the Hydrogen Bomb* (New York: Touchstone, 1996).

—— ed., *Visions of Technology: A Century of Vital Debate about Machines, Systems and the Human World* (New York: Simon & Schuster, 1999).

Richie, Alexandra, *Faust's Metropolis: A History of Berlin* (London: Harper-Collins, 1999).

Ridenour, Louis N., 'Nuclear Fission in Lay Language', *Saturday Review*, 30 (28 June 1947), 14–15.

Riley, James F., 'The Sole Meeting of Pierre Curie and Ernest Rutherford', *The Lancet*, 296 (21 Nov. 1970), 1076–7.

Roberts, Adam, *Science Fiction* (London: Routledge, 2000).

Roberts, R. Ellis, 'Mr Wells Let Loose', *Bookman*, 46 (June 1914), 131–2.

Roland, Alex, 'Technology and War: The Historiographical Revolution of the 1980s', *Technology and Culture*, 34, no. 1 (Jan. 1993), 117–34.

—— 'Science, Technology, and War', *Technology and Culture*, 36, no. 2, supplement (Apr. 1995), 83–100.

Röntgen, W. C., 'On a New Kind of Rays', *Science*, 3, no. 59 (14 Feb. 1896), 227–31.

Rose, Paul Lawrence, *Heisenberg and the Nazi Atomic Bomb Project: A Study in German Culture* (Berkeley: University of California Press, 1998).

Rotblat, Joseph, 'Leaving the Bomb Project', *BAS*, 41 (Aug. 1985), 16–19.

Rottensteiner, Franz, *The Science Fiction Book: An Illustrated History* (London: Thames & Hudson, 1975).

Rubinsky, Yuri and Wiseman, Ian, *A History of the End of the World* (New York: Morrow, 1982).

Ruddick, Nicholas, *British Science Fiction: A Chronology, 1478–1990* (New York: Greenwood, 1992).

Russell, A. S., 'The Atom', *Quarterly Review*, 241, no. 479 (Apr. 1924), 311–28.

Russell, Edmund, *War and Nature: Fighting Humans and Insects with Chemicals from World War I to* Silent Spring (Cambridge University Press, 2001).

'S.D.', 'A New Type of Atom-Splitting', *Discovery*, 2, no. 13 (Apr. 1939), 181–2.

—— 'The Splitting of Uranium', *Discovery*, 2, no. 14 (May 1939), 239–40.

Saleeby, C. W., 'Radium the Revealer', *Harper's Monthly Magazine*, 109 (June 1904), 85–8.

—— 'Radium and Life', *Harper's Monthly Magazine*, 113 (June–Nov. 1906), 226–30.

Sandels, Robert, 'UFOs, Science Fiction and the Postwar Utopia', *Journal of Popular Culture*, 20 (1986/7), 141–51.

Sanger, S. L., *Working on the Bomb: An Oral History of WWII Hanford* (Portland, Oreg.: Continuing Education Press, 1995).

Schell, Jonathan, *The Unconquerable World: Power, Nonviolence, and the Will of the People* (London: Allen Lane, 2004).

Schulz, Hans-Joachim, *Science Fiction* (Stuttgart: Metzler, 1986).

Schwartz, Joseph, *The Creative Moment: How Science Made Itself Alien to Modern Culture* (London: Cape, 1992).

Sclove, Richard E., 'From Alchemy to Atomic War: Frederick Soddy's "Technology Assessment" of Atomic Energy 1900–15', *Science, Technology and Human Values*, 14, no. 2 (1989), 163–94.

Sebald, W. G., *On the Natural History of Destruction* (London: Penguin, 2003).

Seed, David, ed., *Imagining Apocalypse: Studies in Cultural Crisis* (Basingstoke: Macmillan, 2000).

—— 'H. G. Wells and the Liberating Atom', *Science Fiction Studies*, 30 (Mar. 2003), 33–48.

Segrè, Emilio, *Enrico Fermi: Physicist* (University of Chicago Press, 1970).

—— *From X-Rays to Quarks: Modern Physicists and their Discoveries* (San Francisco: W. H. Freeman, 1980).

Serber, Robert, *Los Alamos Primer: The First Lectures on How to Build an Atomic Bomb*, ed. Richard Rhodes (Berkeley: University of California Press, 1992).

Shapin, Steven, 'Don't Let That Crybaby in Here Again', *London Review of Books* (7 Sep. 2000), 15–16.

Shapiro, Jerome F., *Atomic Bomb Cinema: The Apocalyptic Imagination on Film* (New York: Routledge, 2002).

Shea, William R, ed., *Otto Hahn and the Rise of Nuclear Physics* (Dordrecht: Reidel, 1983).

Shenstone, W. A., 'Radium', *Cornhill*, 14, no. 84 (1903), 752–64.

Sherwin, Martin J., 'Hiroshima and Modern Memory', *Nation*, 233 (10 Oct. 1981), 349–53.

Shils, Edward, 'Leo Szilard: A Memoir', *Encounter*, 23 (Dec. 1964), 35–41.

Sime, Ruth Lewin, *Lise Meitner: A Life in Physics* (Berkeley: University of California Press, 1996).

Singer, Max, 'The Big Picture of Herman Kahn', *Futures*, 28 (1996), 783–5.

Slotten, Hugh R., 'Humane Chemistry or Scientific Barbarism? American Responses to World War I Poison Gas, 1915–1930', *Journal of American History*, 77 (Sep. 1990), 476–98.

Smith, Alice Kimball, 'The Elusive Dr Szilard', *Harper's Magazine*, 221 (July 1960), 77–86.

Smith, David C., *H. G. Wells: Desperately Mortal* (New Haven: Yale University Press, 1986).

—— 'H. G. Wells and his Contemporary Critics: A Developing Reputation', *Cahiers Victoriens et Edouardiens*, 46 (Oct. 1997), 213–44.

Smith, P. D., 'German Literature and the Scientific World-View in the Nineteenth and Twentieth Centuries', *Journal of European Studies*, 27 (1997), 389–415.

—— 'Science and the City: Alfred Döblin's *Berlin Alexanderplatz*', *London Magazine*, 39 (Apr./May 2000), 27–36.

—— *Metaphor and Materiality: German Literature and the World-View of Science 1780–1955* (Oxford: European Humanities Research Centre, 2000).

—— 'Scientific Themes in Goethe's *Faust*', in Paul Bishop, ed., *A Companion to Goethe's Faust* (Rochester, NY: Camden House, 2001), 194–220.

—— 'Elective Affinity? A Tale of Two Cultures', *Prometheus*, 4 (2001), 46–65.

—— *Einstein* (London: Haus Publishing, 2003).

Smyth, Henry DeWolf, 'The Stockpiling and Rationing of Scientific Manpower', *BAS*, 7 (Feb. 1951), 38–42.

Snow, C. P., 'A New Means of Destruction?', *Discovery*, ns 2, no. 18 (Sep. 1939), 443–4.

—— *The Physicists* (London: Macmillan, 1981).

Soddy, Frederick, 'Some Recent Advances in Radioactivity', *Contemporary Review*, 83 (May 1903), 708–20.

—— 'The Energy of Radium', *Harper's Magazine*, 120 (Dec. 1909), 52–9.

—— *The Interpretation of Radium: Being the Substance of Six Free Popular Experimental Lectures Delivered at the University of Glasgow* (London: John Murray, 1912; 1st edn 1909).

Sontag, Susan, 'The Imagination of Disaster', in *Against Interpretation and Other Essays* (New York: Anchor, 1990; 1st edn 1965), 209–25.

Spiers, Edward M., *Chemical Warfare* (London: Macmillan, 1986).

Stableford, Brian, *Scientific Romance in Britain 1890–1950* (New York: St Martin's, 1985).

Stachel, John, ed., *Einstein's Miraculous Year: Five Papers That Changed the Face of Physics* (Princeton University Press, 1998).

Stein, Jonathan B., *From H-Bomb to Star Wars: The Politics of Strategic Decision Making* (Lexington, Mass.: Lexington Books, 1984).

Stern, Fritz, *Einstein's German World* (London: Allen Lane, 2000).

Stoltzenberg, Dietrich, *Fritz Haber: Chemist, Nobel Laureate, German, Jew* (Philadelphia: Chemical Heritage, 2004).

Stone, Albert E., *Literary Aftershocks: American Writers, Readers, and the Bomb* (New York: Twayne, 1994).

Strauss, Lewis L., *Men and Decisions* (London: Macmillan, 1963).

Strutt, R. J., 'Radium: Its Properties and Possibilities', *National Review*, 44 (1904/5), 68–77.

Stuewer, Roger H., ed., *Nuclear Physics in Retrospect: Proceedings of a Symposium on the 1930s* (Minneapolis: University of Minnesota Press, 1979).

Stuhlinger, Ernst and Ordway, Frederick I., III, *Wernher von Braun: Crusader for Space* (Malabar: Krieger, 1996).

Swinton, Col. E. D., 'The "Tanks"', *Strand Magazine* 54 (1917), 270–77.

Szasz, Ferenc Morton, *British Scientists and the Manhattan Project: The Los Alamos Years* (Basingstoke: Macmillan, 1992).

Szilard, Leo, 'We Turned the Switch', *Nation*, 161 (22 Dec. 1945), 718–19.

—— 'The Physicist Invades Politics', *Saturday Review of Literature*, 30 (3 May 1947), 7–8, 31–4.

—— 'Can We Have International Control of Atomic Energy?', *BAS*, 6 (Jan. 1950), 9–12, 16.

—— Collected works in 3 vols (Cambridge, Mass.: MIT Press):

Vol 1: Bernard T. Feld and Gertrude Weiss Szilard, eds., *The Collected Works of Leo Szilard: Scientific Papers* (1972) [cited in the Notes as *CW1*].

Vol 2: Spencer R. Weart and Gertrud Weiss Szilard, eds., *Leo Szilard: His*

Version of the Facts – Selected Recollections and Correspondence (1978) [CW2].

Vol 3: Helen S. Hawkins, G. Allen Greb and Gertrud Weiss Szilard, eds., *Toward a Livable World: Leo Szilard and the Crusade for Nuclear Arms Control* (1987) [CW3].

Szöllösi-Janze, Margit, *Fritz Haber, 1868–1934: Eine Biographie* (Munich: Beck, 1998).

Taylor, Frederick, *Dresden: Tuesday 13 February 1945* (London: Bloomsbury, 2004).

Telegdi, Valentine L., 'Szilard as Inventor: Accelerators and More', *Physics Today*, 53 (Oct. 2000), 25–8.

Teller, Edward, 'Back to the Laboratories', *BAS*, 6 (Mar. 1950), 71–2.

—— *Energy from Heaven and Earth* (San Francisco: W. H. Freeman, 1979).

—— with Brown, Allen, *The Legacy of Hiroshima* (New York: Doubleday, 1962).

—— and Latter, Albert L., *Our Nuclear Future: Facts, Dangers and Opportunities* (New York: Criterion, 1958).

—— with Shoolery, Judith, *Memoirs: A Twentieth-Century Journey in Science and Politics* (Cambridge, Mass.: Perseus, 2001).

Thomas, G. Holt, 'When Shall We Travel by Flying Trains?', *Strand Magazine*, 55, no. 325 (Jan. 1918), 50–58.

Thomas, Gordon and Morgan-Witts, Max, *Ruin from the Air: The Atomic Mission to Hiroshima* (London: Sphere, 1982).

Thompson, Damian, *The End of Time: Faith and Fear in the Shadow of the Millennium* (London: Sinclair-Stevenson, 1996).

Tornabene, Lyn, 'Contradicting the Hollywood Image', *Saturday Review*, 46 (28 Dec. 1963), 19–21.

Toumey, Christopher P., 'The Moral Character of Mad Scientists: A Cultural Critique of Science', *Science, Technology and Human Values*, 17, no. 4 (1992), 411–37.

Townshend, Charles, ed., *The Oxford History of Modern War* (Oxford University Press, 2000).

Traschen, Isadore, 'Modern Literature and Science', *College English*, 25 (Jan. 1964), 248–55.

Travers, T. H. E., 'Future Warfare: H. G. Wells and British Military Theory 1895–1916', in Louis A. Knafla, Martin S. Staum and T. H. E. Travers, eds., *Science, Technology, and Culture in Historical Perspective* (University of Calgary Press, 1976), 144–72.

Trenn, Thaddeus J., 'The Central Role of Energy in Soddy's Holistic and Critical Approach to Nuclear Science, Economics, and Social Responsibility', *British Journal for the History of Science*, 12, no. 42 (1979), 261–76.

Trowbridge, John, 'What are X-rays?', *Century Illustrated*, 56, ns 34 (May 1898), 128–32.

Trumpener, Ulrich, 'The Road to Ypres: The Beginnings of Gas Warfare in World War I', *Journal of Modern History*, 47 (Sep. 1975), 460–80.

Tsutsui, William, *Godzilla on My Mind: Fifty Years of the King of Monsters* (New York: Palgrave Macmillan, 2004).

Turney, Jon, *Frankenstein's Footsteps: Science, Genetics and Popular Culture* (New Haven: Yale University Press, 1998).

Ulam, S. M., *Adventures of a Mathematician* (Berkeley: University of California Press, 1991; 1st edn 1976).

Vogt, Erich, 'Eugene Paul Wigner: a towering figure of modern physics', *Physics Today* 48, no 12 (Dec. 1995).

Volkman, Ernest, *Science Goes to War: The Search for the Ultimate Weapon, from Greek Fire to Star Wars* (New York: Wiley, 2002).

'W.L.R.', 'The World-Republic', *Academy*, 86 (16 May 1914), 616–17.

Wagar, W. Warren, *Terminal Visions: The Literature of Last Things* (Bloomington: Indiana University Press, 1982).

—— 'H. G. Wells and the Scientific Imagination', *Virginia Quarterly Review*, 65 (1989), 390–400.

—— 'Truth and Fiction, Equally Strange: Writing about the bomb', *American Literary History*, 1 (1989), 448–57.

—— 'Herman Kahn: Teacher', *Futures*, 28 (1996), 791–2.

Waitt, Col. Alden H., 'Poison Gas in this War', *The New Republic*, 106 (27 Apr. 1942), 563–5.

Walker, J. Bernard, 'The Tank and its Work on the Battlefield', *American Review of Reviews*, 58 (Oct. 1918), 381–6.

Walker, Martin, *The Cold War and the Making of the Modern World* (London: Vintage, 1994).

Walsh, John, 'A Conversation with Eugene Wigner', *Science*, 181 (10 Aug. 1973), 527–33.

Ward, Robert, 'Before and After the Bomb: Some Literary Speculations on the Use of the Atomic Bomb', *Ambix*, 44 (1997), 85–95.

Weart, Spencer R., *Scientists in Power* (Cambridge, Mass.: Harvard University Press, 1979).

—— *Nuclear Fear: A History of Images* (Cambridge, Mass.: Harvard University Press, 1988).

Weber, Eugen, *Apocalypses: Prophecies, Cults and Millennial Beliefs Through the Ages* (London: Hutchinson, 1999).

Weisskopf, Victor, *The Joy of Insight: Passions of a Physicist* (New York: Basic, 1991).

Wells, F. Lyman, 'Science and War', *Science*, 44, no. 1,130 (25 Aug. 1916), 275–6.

Wells, H. G., *A Modern Utopia* (London: Collins, 1905).

—— *The Open Conspiracy, and Other Writings* (London: n. pub., 1933).

West, Anthony, *H. G. Wells: Aspects of a Life* (London: Hutchinson, 1984).

West, Clarence J., 'The History of Poison Gases', *Science*, 49, no. 1,270 (2 May 1919), 412–17.

Whetham, W. C. D., 'Matter and Electricity', *Quarterly Review*, 199, no. 397 (Jan. 1904), 100–126.

Whitehead, Alfred North, *Science and the Modern World* (Cambridge University Press, 1927).

Whittemore, Gilbert F., Jr, 'World War I, Poison Gas Research, and the Ideals of American Chemists', *Social Studies of Science*, 5, no. 2 (May 1975), 135–63.

Wigner, Eugene P. and Szanton, Andrew, *The Recollections of Eugene P. Wigner* (New York: Plenum, 1992).

Williams, Henry Smith, 'Some Unsolved Scientific Problems', *Harper's New Monthly Magazine*, 100 (Apr. 1900), 774–83.

Williams, Peter and Wallace, David, *Unit 731: The Japanese Army's Secrets of Secrets* (London: Hodder & Stoughton, 1989).

Willis, Kirk, 'The Origins of British Nuclear Culture, 1895–1939', *Journal of British Studies*, 34 (Jan. 1995), 59–89.

Wilson, David, *Rutherford: Simple Genius* (London: Hodder, 1983).

Winkler, Allan M., 'The "Atom" and American Life', *The History Teacher*, 26 (May 1993), 317–37.

—— *Life Under a Cloud: American Anxiety about the Atom* (New York: Oxford University Press, 1993).

Winter, Jay, *Sites of Memory, Sites of Mourning: The Great War in European Cultural History* (Cambridge University Press, 1995).

Wintle, W. J., 'Life in Our New Century', *Harmsworth Magazine*, 5, no. 30 (1900/01), 531–8.

Withrow, James R., 'The American Chemist and the War's Problems', *Science*, 43, no. 1,120 (16 June 1916), 835–42.

Wittner, Lawrence S., *Resisting the Bomb: A History of the World Nuclear Disarmament Movement 1954–1970* (Stanford University Press, 1997).

Wolfe, Gary K., '*Dr Strangelove, Red Alert* and Patterns of Paranoia in the 1950s', *Journal of Popular Film*, 5, no. 1 (1976), 57–67.

BIBLIOGRAPHY

Wyden, Peter, *Day One: Before Hiroshima and After* (New York: Simon & Schuster, 1984).

Yaffe, James, 'Of Fission and Fish', *Saturday Review*, 44 (29 Apr. 1961), 14, 16.

Yamazaki, James N. and Fleming, Louis B., *Children of the Atomic Bomb: An American Physician's Memoir of Nagasaki, Hiroshima, and the Marshall Islands* (Durham, NC: Duke University Press, 1995).

Zaloga, Steven J., *The Kremlin's Nuclear Sword: The Rise and Fall of Russia's Strategic Nuclear Forces, 1945–2000* (Washington: Smithsonian Institution, 2002).

Zimbaro, Valerie P., *Encyclopedia of Apocalyptic Literature* (Santa Barbara, Cal.: ABC-CLIO, 1996).

Zimmern, Antonia, 'Invisible Radiations', *Nineteenth Century*, 56 (July 1904), 88–96.

Ziolkowski, Theordore, *The Sin of Knowledge: Ancient Themes and Modern Variations* (Princeton University Press, 2000).

Zweig, Stefan, *The World of Yesterday* (London: Cassell, 1943).

Films

A is for Atom, Carl Urbano, John Sutherland/General Electric Co, 1952.
Atomic Alert, Encyclopaedia Britannica Films, 1951.
Beneath the Planet of the Apes, Ted Post, Twentieth Century Fox, 1970.
The Day After, Nicholas Meyer, ABC, 1983.
The Day After Tomorrow, Roland Emmerich, Twentieth Century Fox, 2004.
The Day the Earth Caught Fire, Val Guest, British Lion/Paramount, 1961.
The Day the Earth Stood Still, Robert Wise, Tewntieth Century Fox, 1951.
Dr Cyclops, Ernest B. Schoedsack, Paramount, 1940.
Dr No, Terence Young, Eon, 1962.
Dr Strangelove or: How I Learned to Stop Worrying and Love the Bomb, Stanley Kubrick, Hawk Films, 1964.
Forbidden Planet, Fred M. Wilcox, MGM, 1956.
Frankenstein, James Whale, Universal, 1931.
Gojira [Godzilla], Ishirō Honda, Toho Co., 1954.
Invasion USA, Alfred E. Green, American Pictures Corp., 1952.
The Invisible Man, James Whale, Universal, 1933.
Kiss Me Deadly, Robert Aldrich, MGM, 1955.
Mad Max, George Miller, Mad Mad Pty, 1979.
Metropolis, Fritz Lang, UFA, 1926.
Omega Man, Boris Sagal, Walter Seltzer Productions, 1971.

On the Beach, Stanley Kramer, Lomitas, 1959.

The Satan Bug, John Sturges, Mirisch/Kappa, 1965.

Seven Days to Noon, Boulting Bros., London Films, 1950.

Shadow Makers, Roland Joffé, Paramount, 1989.

Strategic Air Command, Anthony Mann, Paramount, 1955.

The Terminator, James Cameron, Cinema 84/Pacific Western Productions, 1984.

The Thing from Another World, Christian Nyby, Winchester Pictures/RKO, 1951.

Them!, Gordon Douglas, Warner Brothers, 1954.

Things to Come, William Cameron Menzies, London, 1936.

20 Million Miles to Earth, Nathan Juran, Columbia, 1957.

2001 – A Space Odyssey, Stanley Kubrick, MGM, 1968.

War Games, John Badham, MGM/United Artists/Sherwood Productions, 1983.

War of the Worlds, Byron Haskins, George Pal Productions/Paramount, 1953.

The Whip Hand, William Cameron Menzies, RKO, 1951.

Index

Page numbers in *italic* refer to illustrations

atomic bomb – *cont.*
 Hiroshima 6, 19, 34, 134, 270,
  298, 307–8, 316, 328–32, 334,
  368, 382, 384, 435
 Nagasaki 34, 35, 222, 266, 291,
  298, 308, 332–6, *335*, 358,
  384
 origin of name 115, 197
 press stories about 256, 287–91,
  376, 384
 scepticism about 256–7, 269
 Soviet Union 341, 357
 subcommittee to assess feasibility
  (UK) 270
 United Kingdom 269–72, 342–3,
  372–3
 views of Manhattan Project
  scientists on the use of 321–2
 see also Manhattan Project *and*
  Advisory Committee on
  Uranium
atomic energy 143–4, 202–3, 216,
 234, 265, 276
 in fiction and film 127, 130, 145,
  202–4, 231, 291–4, 293, 300,
  302, 345, 422
Atomic Energy Commission (AEC)
 342, 357, 362, 367, 379, 409
atomic science, history of 36–51,
 58–79
atomic structure, theories 37, 62–3,
 76–7, 186
Atomic Weapons Research
 Establishment (UK) 437
atoms 37, 62–3, 76–7, 132
 splitting 143–6, 251, 254, 381,
  388, 411
Atoms for Peace Award 420
Attlee, Clement 342
Auden, W. H. 152
Auld, Samuel 94, 102

Aum Shinrikyo 249, 438
Auschwitz 92, 245, 384

Back to the Future films 43
Bacon, Francis 98
Baker, Josephine 153
Baldwin, Stanley 198, 341
Ball, Hugo 131
Ballard, J. G. 384
balloons 116
Balzac, Honoré de, *Quest for the
 Absolute* 51
Bannister, Roger 377
Barr, Densil Neve, *The Man with
 Only One Head* 385–6
Barr, Robert, 'The Doom of
 London' 385
BASF 100
Baskerville, Chas 106
Batory 344
Beast from 20,000 Fathoms, The
 370
Becker, Herbert 186, 187
Beckett, Samuel 385
Beckmann, Max 152
Becquerel, Henri 58–9, 68, 70
Becquerel rays *see* radioactivity
Bell, Thomas 415
Beneath the Planet of the Apes 365,
 384–5, 393
Benn, Tony 375, 437
Berlin 151–4, 177, 191–2, 208, 407
Berlin Wall 407
Bernstein, Jeremy 413–14
Berthelot, Marcelin 56
beryllium 186, 187, 231–4, 235,
 296
beta radiation 63
Bethe, Hans 15, 16, *18*, 180, 322,
 356, 409
 and CP-1 280–81